Y0-BUB-616

WITHDRAWN
UTSA LIBRARIES

CHRISTIANITY IN A REVOLUTIONARY AGE

*A History of Christianity in the Nineteenth and
Twentieth Centuries*

VOLUME V

THE TWENTIETH CENTURY
OUTSIDE EUROPE:

*The Americas, the Pacific, Asia, and Africa:
the Emerging World Christian Community*

CHRISTIANITY IN A REVOLUTIONARY AGE

A History of Christianity in the Nineteenth and Twentieth Centuries

VOLUME V

THE TWENTIETH CENTURY OUTSIDE EUROPE

The Americas, The Pacific, Asia, and Africa:
the Emerging World Christian Community

By KENNETH SCOTT LATOURETTE

Sterling Professor of Missions and Oriental History,
and Fellow of Berkeley College, Emeritus, in Yale University

GREENWOOD PRESS, PUBLISHERS
WESTPORT, CONNECTICUT

The Library of Congress has catalogued this publication as follows:

Library of Congress Cataloging in Publication Data

Latourette, Kenneth Scott, 1884-1968.
   The twentieth century outside Europe.

   (His Christianity in a revolutionary age, v. 5)
   Bibliography: p.
   1. Church history--20th century.   I.   Title.
II.   Series.
BR475.L33 vol. 5 [BR479]   270.8s [270.8'2]   72-11980
ISBN 0-8371-5705-6

To all, both past and present,
who as his secretaries have aided the author,
these volumes are gratefully
and affectionately dedicated.

Originally published in 1962
by Harper & Row, New York

Reprinted with the permission
of Harper & Row, Publishers, Inc.

First Greenwood Reprinting 1973

Library of Congress Catalogue Card Number 77-138141

ISBN 0-8371-5700-5 (Set)
ISBN 0-8371-5705-6 (Vol. V)

Printed in the United States of America

CONTENTS

Chapter I

Contents

CHRISTIANITY IN A REVOLUTIONARY AGE

*A History of Christianity in the Nineteenth and
Twentieth Centuries*

VOLUME V

THE TWENTIETH CENTURY
OUTSIDE EUROPE:

*The Americas, the Pacific, Asia, and Africa:
the Emerging World Christian Community*

AUTHOR'S ACKNOWLEDGEMENTS

To those named in Volume I should be added, as having later been of assistance, Edward W. Poitras, P. Lawrence Minear, James W. Trowbridge, and Richard H. Davis.

CHAPTER I

Introduction

As we move from Europe, the heart of what had once been called Christendom, to the rest of the world, we are faced with another of the contrasts that characterized the story which we have endeavoured to recount. On the one hand, the impact of forces issuing from the erstwhile Christendom continued to be felt, with increasing revolutionary effects. The effects varied from country to country and from region to region. They were more striking in some than in others and in general were more marked in Asia and Africa than in the geographic extension of the Occident in the Americas and Australasia. In the Americas and Australasia, for example, few such sweeping political upheavals occurred as in Europe or as in most areas in Asia and Africa. In addition, what was described accurately but more mildly than the facts warranted as rapid social change was drastically altering the entire pattern of life of the large majority of the peoples of Asia and Africa. Yet even in the Americas and Australasia under the influence of the forces emanating from the centre of the former Christendom and some of them springing from these regions were social, economic, intellectual, and political transformations which would have been considered drastic had it not been that the revolutions in Europe, Asia, and Africa were even more breath-taking.

On the other hand, in contrast with Europe, where in the post-1914 decades de-Christianization was proceeding apace, in the world outside Europe Christianity was continuing to advance. In the Americas and Australasia—the newer "Christendom" and of greater area than the mother "Christendom"—the forces making for de-Christianization were potent, but in the main the de-Christianization of peoples of Christian ancestry which had been prominent in the nineteenth century was countered by gains which in some respects more than offset them. Thus, in the United States of America, the most populous and richest of the nations of what might be called the larger Christendom, the proportion of church membership to the total population continued the rise which, with the exception of the decade 1860–1869 that included the Civil War, had been one of the features of the record of Christianity in that country throughout the nineteenth century. New movements were continuing to emerge in the Christianity of the United States, and the share of that Christianity in the world-wide life and spread of the faith was mounting, both numerically and in proportion to the efforts of the churches of Europe. In several ways Canadian Christianity was more vigorous in 1962 than in 1914. Latin America presented a varied picture. In some areas and among large numbers the de-Christianization continued which had been a major aspect of the nineteenth-century record. Yet, although it was still the faith of minorities, Protestantism displayed a remarkable growth, and by the 1950's awakenings were taking place among Roman Catholic minorities. In both Australia and New Zealand, in the former against especially heavy odds, by the 1960's Christianity gave indications of greater vigour than in 1914.

In Asia and Africa with their fringing islands the record was mixed, but on the whole the advance of the faith since 1914 was phenomenal. Owing chiefly to the vicissitudes of the wars of the period, Western Asia witnessed a numerical decline of the churches. But South Asia saw a marked advance both in the numerical strength of the churches and in the indigenous leadership which emerged from them. The same was true of Indonesia. On the mainland of East Asia the record was spotty. In the fore part of the period numerical advances and the growth of indigenous leadership were little short of amazing, but beginning in the 1940's and in some large sections in the 1930's political disturbances checked the growth and in Vietnam and China brought grave reverses. In storm-tossed Korea after 1945 growth was resumed in the southern portion of the country. Christianity in Japan remained the faith of a small minority and suffered from the domestic stresses of the 1930's and 1940's and the exhaustion and destruction which accompanied participation in World War II. Yet it came to the 1960's vigorous and making a marked impress upon the life of the nation. Even after its post-1914 growth, in most of Asia and its fringing islands in the early 1960's Christianity remained the religion of small minorities. Some observers believed the churches to be in danger of becoming encysted ghetto communities, purely on the defensive. However, as we shall see, several of them were reaching out to their neighbours not only in their own countries but also in other lands. Moreover, they were increasingly a part of the world-wide Christian community. The Roman Catholics of Asia and Africa had their fellowship through Rome with others of their branch of the faith and increasingly were staffed by bishops and clergy from their ranks. The majority of the Protestants were being drawn into the Ecumenical Movement with close ties with their brethren in Europe, the Americas, Australasia, and Africa, with a mounting indigenous leadership, and with participation as equals in that movement. Most of the areas in Africa south of the Sahara were experiencing what was tantamount to a mass conversion in which both the Roman

Catholic Church and Protestantism shared. It had many facets, but common to most of them was a rapid rise of indigenous African leadership.

So striking was the growth of Christianity in the world outside Europe after 1914 that we must devote to the record a larger proportion of our space than we did to the nineteenth-century story. To the latter, it will be recalled, two volumes were assigned to Europe and one to the world outside Europe. For the twentieth century, to be true to the facts, we must divide our account equally between Europe and the portion of mankind outside it. We must not ignore the fact that in the mid-twentieth century Christianity was still the professed faith of only a minority of mankind, that in Asia, where dwelt the large majority of the human race and where the population was mounting so rapidly that the increase was likened to an explosion, Christians were very small minorities, and that in Africa south of the Sahara, although rapidly increasing, they were also a minority. Europe was by far the smallest of the continents—with less area even than Australia. The prominence of Western Europe, where the forces which created the revolutionary age first appeared, was very recent—dating from no earlier than the close of the fifteenth century, a mere fraction of the total history of mankind. It was in connexion with the prominence of Western Europe and the global expansion of its peoples and its civilization that most of the nineteenth- and twentieth-century geographic expansion of Christianity was achieved. What the future would hold for that prominence and that expansion the historian as historian would not venture to predict. Yet he could note that in the first half of the twentieth century Christianity was spanning the globe as no other faith had ever done and that Christians were being knit the world around into two inclusive fellowships— the Roman Catholic Church and the Ecumenical Movement, the latter embracing the large majority of the Protestants and a mounting proportion of the Eastern Churches. If the historian was a Christian he would recall the dream expressed in the closing verses of *The Gospel according to Matthew,* that all mankind would be won to discipleship, baptized, and taught to obey all that Jesus had commanded the little inner group of his followers, and also the vision recorded in another of the Gospels, that all Christians would become one in a fellowship of self-giving, reciprocal love. As a Christian, the historian might share that hope, but the record, while encouraging, would not assure its realization.

CHAPTER II

The Complex, Multiform Record of Christianity in the United States of America

W E BEGIN the survey of the record of Christianity outside Europe in the twentieth century, as we did that of the nineteenth century, with an account of the response of Christianity in the United States of America to that stage of the revolutionary age. To it we are devoting more space than to any other single country either in Europe or elsewhere, because of the size of the country in area, population, and wealth, because of its role in world affairs, and, especially, because of the part which its churches played in Christianity on the global scale. In each of these respects the United States loomed larger than in the nineteenth century. Even more than in our story of Christianity in Europe, we must seek to stress the response of Christianity to the challenges of the revolutionary age rather than attempt a well-rounded account of all aspects of the history of Christianity in the United States in the half-century which began in 1914. To undertake the latter would extend this chapter to a long volume, so numerous and many-sided were the developments of those decades. Yet we can at least hint at what such an account would entail and here and there offer generalizations and interpretations.

THE MULTIFORM SETTING

Although inhabited predominantly by peoples of European birth or ancestry and profoundly affected by the currents which had their rise in Western Europe and made the age revolutionary, to these currents the United States made distinctive contributions. The effects both resembled and differed from those which we have found in Europe. Whether like or unlike what was transpiring east of the Atlantic, the setting must be viewed if we are to understand the response of Christianity here.

The resemblances of the impact of the revolutionary age on the United States to that in Europe were numerous and fairly obvious. In both regions industrialization proceeded swiftly. In both the cities grew by leaps and bounds and the rural population declined relatively and in absolute numbers. The urbanization was particularly spectacular in the United States late in the 1940's and in the 1950's. It was facilitated by the automobile, the use of which by private owners and public transportation exceeded that in any other part of the world. In several areas a combination of suburbs, with their specially constructed shopping centres offering food, clothing, and other physical facilities without the necessity of seeking the main inner-city centres, and factories built on less expensive land, once agricultural, led to sprawling cities and to a kind of social *milieu* described collectively as suburbia. Thus the region on the Atlantic coast from Washington to Boston was becoming one vast city. Much the same thing was happening in and around Chicago, in Southern California with Los Angeles as the hub, around San Francisco Bay, and to a less extent in several other cities. In the main cities huge apartment houses were constructed. They seldom developed any sense of community, and those who lived in them represented an atomized society. Rural districts were progressively depopulated. Agriculture became a business entailing expensive fertilizers and investments in machinery which cut down the need for labour. The competition was progressively eliminated of those with small tracts who did not have the capital required for large-scale operations. People forced out of farming moved to the towns and cities, and the kind of rural life to which the churches had become adjusted declined.

The growth of cities made for a mobile population. For example, between March, 1957, and March, 1958, one out of every five Americans changed homes. Two-thirds of them moved to another home in the same county and about a sixth moved to another state.[1] The lack of stable residence added to the difficulty of the churches in creating congregations with a continuing constituency.

The United States was a belligerent in World War I and World War II. In both it was late in being drawn into the struggle, and in neither was its soil invaded—except in the Philippines, which by the time of the Japanese attack had become a self-governing dominion and was on the way to complete independence, and a few remote islands in the Pacific. Nor were its cities bombed. Both wars entailed vast expenditure of treasure and the participation of millions of men and heavy casualties. In the ensuing "cold war" with Russia and its satellites the United States bore the heaviest load. It had the major share in the war waged by the United Nations to rescue the Republic of Korea from a Communist invasion.

Upon the United States also played the intellectual currents which challenged Christianity. Some came from Europe, for Americans were increasingly familiar with what was being thought and written there. Others arose in the United States. For example, John Dewey (1859–1952), whose thought dominated much

[1] *The New York Times*, October 14, 1958.

of the educational method of the country in the decades immediately preceding and following World War I, although not openly antagonistic was frankly not a Christian and his philosophy undercut the Christian faith.[2] Behaviouristic psychology, first formulated about 1913 with John B. Watson (1878–1958) as its chief exponent and related to the contemporary German *Gestalt* psychology, had a wide vogue for about a quarter of a century and taught a materialistic kind of determinism which was hostile to Christianity. Much of the popular fiction of the period played up the seamy side of human nature and the tragedy of life and either ignored the Christian faith or poked fun at its representatives.

Contributions to the revolutionary age which were peculiar to the United States affected the life of that country and some had repercussions on the rest of the world. From the standpoint of economic and physical power, by the mid-twentieth century the U.S.A. shared with the U.S.S.R. the hazardous distinction of being the mightiest nation on the planet. It began to emerge in this position during World War I. World War II brought it clearly to the fore, and in the aftermath of that struggle it became the champion of the "free world" against Communist domination. It maintained armed bases in many parts of the world, gave substantial aid to nation after nation for military defense and for aid in the improvement of living conditions, took the initiative in creating alliances against the advance of Communism, and became the home of the headquarters of the United Nations. Here was a challenge to the churches to bring Christian principles to bear upon the foreign policies of the nation. Following World War I the United States greatly curtailed immigration. During that war immigration had all but halted, and with the coming of peace, legislation was enacted which, closing the open door to the overflow from Europe, strictly regulated it and favoured applicants from among peoples akin to the older white stock of the country. As a result, the churches did not need to be as absorbed as formerly in retaining the traditional allegiance of the immigrant flood. The major exception was the Puerto Ricans; being under the American flag, they were unaffected by the immigration laws and came by the thousands from their overcrowded island. Immigration laws were not easily enforced against the influx of Mexicans across the long land border and these poured into the South-west, many as ostensibly transient labourers, but also many who became permanent residents. The westward movement of population continued, particularly to California, Oregon, and Washington, and the churches were challenged to keep pace with it. But the drift of the population frontier-ward was not as prominent as it had been during most of the nineteenth century.

The years which followed 1914 were by no means uniform in their challenge to Christianity. The quadrennium of World War I was distinctive. Even before becoming a belligerent the United States was emotionally deeply involved. The

[2] See John Dewey, *A Common Faith* (New Haven, Yale University Press, 1934, pp. 87).

majority of Americans were against the Central Powers and sympathetic with Britain and its allies. Spurred by Woodrow Wilson, idealism ran high. Millions of dollars were given voluntarily to aid in the relief of the sufferers from the war. During the eighteen months of belligerency idealism was further enlisted in "the war to end war," and additional millions were contributed to humanitarian causes associated with the war. Many of the clergy, chiefly among the Protestants, vigorously advocated the Allied cause while a few, also mostly Protestant, were outspoken pacifists.[4] Some of the clergy stood out against the hysteria of anti-German hate with its persecution of fellow Americans of German birth and ancestry which swept across the country. Hundreds of chaplains, Protestant and Roman Catholic, served with the armed forces. The National Catholic War Council, formed in 1917, coördinated Roman Catholic participation in the war effort.[5] John R. Mott, of the Young Men's Christian Association, was early raising funds for service to prisoners of war. When the United States entered the conflict, he took the lead in forming the War Work Council of the YMCA's of the United States. Under the War Work Council hundreds of men and women were recruited to serve the Allied forces. John R. Mott supervised the raising of the millions of dollars required and in 1918 at the request of President Wilson headed the campaign which brought over $200,000,000 to the seven voluntary organizations then engaged in work connected with the war.[6]

Following World War I something of a reaction was seen against the idealism evoked by that struggle. The Senate failed to give the necessary two-thirds vote for the ratification of the Versailles peace treaty with its appended Covenant of the League of Nations, in spite of the fact that President Wilson was the chief architect of the League of Nations and partly because he insisted on the adoption of the Covenant without reservations. Although a large minority held to the idealism of the war days, the majority welcomed the call of Wilson's successor to return to "normalcy," with as much withdrawal as possible from international entanglements. Protestants formulated an ambitious programme, the Interchurch World Movement, to capitalize on the spirit of giving during the war greatly to expand their efforts at home and abroad. They counted on the gifts of the "friendly citizens" who had contributed to the war work, but the response was so slight that the coöperating denominations were saddled

[3] Sweet, *The Story of Religion in America*, pp. 400–402; Fosdick, *The Living of These Days*, pp. 120–132; Abrams, *Preachers Present Arms*, pp. 51–122.

[4] Sweet, *op. cit.*, p. 403; Abrams, *op. cit.*, pp. 193–207; John Haynes Holmes, *I Speak for Myself*, pp. 160–186.

[5] Ellis, *American Catholicism*, pp. 138, 139; Daniel J. Ryan, *American Catholic World War Records* (Washington, The Catholic University of America Press, 1941, pp. 473), *passim*.

[6] Mathews, *John R. Mott, World Citizen*, pp. 270–281; Hopkins, *History of the Y.M.C.A. in North America*, pp. 485–504; Frederick Harris, editor, *Service with Fighting Men. An Account of the Work of the American Young Men's Christian Associations in the World War* (New York, Association Press, 2 vols., 1922, 1924).

with huge debts which they had incurred to promote the project—and which they loyally paid.[7] Several denominations also undertook to raise substantial sums to enlarge their undertakings in various parts of the world. They obtained pledges for much of what they asked, but with the waning of idealism only a part of the promises were honoured, and the mounting inflation wiped out much of the gains effected.[8]

Yet the immediate post-war years brought some advances. In 1919, growing out of the National Catholic War Council, the National Catholic Welfare Council was inaugurated by the American hierarchy as a continuing peace-time coördinating agency for Roman Catholic action. A minority of the bishops objected, pleading that the proposed council would trespass on their jurisdiction in their dioceses and carried their opposition to Rome. There Benedict XV withdrew his tentative approval on the ground that the council might lead to a national church in the United States. Pius XI at first confirmed the prohibition, but a protest from the administrative committee of the Council led to a reversal, and in 1922 a decree was obtained giving the Papal blessing to the project but substituting for the National Catholic Welfare Council the designation "the National Catholic Welfare Conference"—emphasizing the limitation of the powers of the body to purely advisory functions and thus safeguarding the bishops from encroachment on their prerogatives. The National Catholic Welfare Conference was a gathering of the bishops and under it were eight major departments embracing almost every important area of Roman Catholic interest and policy and akin to the Federal Council of Churches of Christ in America.[9] The new structure did not lead to a strong national church as its critics had feared. The administration of the Roman Catholic Church in the United States still centred in the dioceses and the parishes and was controlled by the Holy See.

A prominent achievement of the Interchurch World Movement was a report on a strike in the steel industry in 1919. It was prepared by a committee headed by Francis J. McConnell, a bishop of the Methodist Episcopal Church, with the assistance of experts. Calling attention to labour conditions, including low wages, a twelve-hour day, a seven-day week, and a twenty-four-hour shift which entailed injustices to the workers, it was given wide publicity and brought criticism from the owners of the mills. Many citizens, however, hailed it as evidence of a social conscience in the churches.[10] It also called forth a

[7] Sweet, *op. cit.*, p. 404; McConnell, *By the Way*, p. 219.

[8] Sweet, *op. cit.*, p. 404; Torbet, *Venture of Faith*, pp. 405, 406.

[9] Ellis, *op. cit.*, pp. 139–141.

[10] McConnell, *op. cit.*, pp. 214–222; *Report on the Steel Strike of 1919 by the Commission of Inquiry, the Interchurch World Movement* (New York, Harcourt, Brace and Co., 1920, pp. viii, 277), *passim*; *Public Opinion and the Steel Strike. Supplementary Reports of the Investigators to the Commission of Inquiry, the Interchurch World Movement* (New York, Harcourt, Brace and Co., 1921, pp. x, 346).

carefully documented animadversion on its accuracy.[11]

A phase of the post-war reaction was disillusionment. Many Christians who had supported the war believed that they had been misled by propaganda and emotion and came to the conclusion that they would either not endorse another war or be more wary of the hysteria and more reluctant to join in condemnation of the enemy.[12]

In the main the 1920's represented a reaction of a large proportion of the population against the idealism displayed in World War I. Criticism of Christianity and the churches was vocal and derisive. Joseph Wood Krutch, H. L. Mencken, and Sinclair Lewis were only the more prominent of the writers who were read with avidity. Moral standards deteriorated. A vivid illustration was the widespread flouting of the Volstead Act, which sought to enforce the Eighteenth Amendment to the Constitution prohibiting the manufacture, sale, or transportation of intoxicating liquors. The amendment had been ratified in 1918-1919 as a result of prolonged agitation by the Anti-Saloon League and other organizations which were supported by Protestants, and its final adoption was due in large part to the desire to safeguard the armed forces and war industries. The later 1920's were marked by a false prosperity which boded ill for Christian living. For Protestantism, as we are to see, the decade witnessed a climax in the fundamentalist controversy and a general recession in fervour. The offering of both lives and money for home and foreign missions declined. Some observers held that the United States had ceased to be Protestant in its cultural and moral traditions and that the Roman Catholic Church, now organized through the National Catholic Welfare Conference, was effectively challenging Protestantism.[13]

The 1920's also saw the enlarged activity of the Ku Klux Klan. Founded in 1915 as a revival of a movement in the years immediately following the Civil War, the Klan was associated with the fundamentalist mentality and was anti-Roman Catholic and anti-Semitic, and favored white supremacy in the South. Some Protestant ministers abandoned their pulpits to be organizers of the Klan. The Klan contributed to the failure of Alfred E. Smith to obtain the Democratic nomination for the presidency in 1924 and to Smith's defeat as the Democratic candidate for that office in 1928.[14]

[11] Marshall Olds, *Analysis of the Interchurch World Movement Report on the Steel Strike* (New York, G. P. Putnam's Sons, 1923, pp. xxiv, 475), *passim*.

[12] Abrams, *op. cit.*, pp. 229–239; Fosdick, *op. cit.*, pp. 292–294.

[13] R. T. Handy in *Church History*, Vol. XXIX, pp. 3–16 (March, 1960). For a picture of the situation in the 1920's, in a representative, small, predominantly Protestant city in the Middle West, see Robert S. Lynd and Helen Merrell Lynd, *Middletown, a Study in Contemporary American Culture* (New York, Harcourt, Brace and Co., 1929, pp. x, 550), *passim*.

[14] Sweet, *op. cit.*, pp. 406, 407; Ellis, *op. cit.*, pp. 150, 151. A form of the "Klan Kreed" circulated during the revival of the movement late in the 1950's—partly stimulated by the Supreme Court's decision in 1954 requiring the integration of whites and Negroes in the state schools—was: "We believe in God; ineffable; infinite; eternal; Creator and Sole Ruler of the universe; and in

Yet in the fevered 1920's many church buildings, both Roman Catholic and Protestant, were erected. The amounts annually invested in such structures more than quadrupled in the decade—much but not all of the money being borrowed.[15]

Then came the crash in Wall Street in the autumn of 1929 and the great depression which stretched into the 1930's. The depression sobered the minds of many. It also brought severe financial problems to Christian as to other institutions. Debts incurred by the churches in the expansion in the 1920's proved burdensome. Mission boards found giving by their supporters sharply reduced, and at least two, in spite of drastic economies, acquired staggering debts. Entire denominations were in a similar plight.[16] The depression years witnessed the repeal of the Eighteenth Amendment to the Constitution and the beginning of the rise in the use of alcoholic beverages which, stimulated by skilful and lavish advertising by the manufacturers, sent their consumption to ever higher levels. Indeed, in the course of the following decades the incidence of alcoholism was so heavy that by 1948 the United States was reported to have nearly four alcoholics to every hundred of the population, a much higher proportion than in any other Occidental country.[17]

The depression had only barely lifted when the country began to be entangled in World War II. The first rumbles of that conflict were the Japanese seizure of Mukden in 1931 and the creation of Manchukuo a few months later, and in a fashion which revealed the weakness of the League of Nations. The civil war in Spain and the Italian adventure in Ethiopia followed in the second half of the decade. Then, in September, 1939, came the German invasion of Poland and the precipitation of the global conflict. The United States was slowly

---

Jesus Christ, His Son, our Saviour, Who is the Divine Word made manifest in flesh and demonstrated in life.

"We recognize our relation to the Government of the United States of America, the supremacy of its constitution, the union of states thereunder, and the constitutional laws thereof, and we shall ever be devoted to the sublime principles of pure Americanism and valiant in the defense of its ideals and institutions.

"We believe that God created races and nations, committing to each a special destiny and service; that the United States through its white Protestant citizens holds a Divine commission for the furtherance of free government, the maintenance of white supremacy, and the protection of religious freedom; that its constitution and laws are expressive of this Divine purpose.

"We believe that it is the duty of men of kindred thought to unite fraternally for the fulfillment of these Divine purposes; that by so doing they increase the fellowship of men and more effectively carry out the will of God; that the Knights of the Ku Klux Klan is an order in all ways conforming to these great principles." (From a flier broadcast in 1960 by U.S. Klans, Inc., Knights of the Ku Klux Klan, P.O. Box No. 3073, Macon, Ga.)

[15] Sweet, *op. cit.*, p. 413.

[16] As examples see Latourette, *World Service*, pp. 86–88; Brown, *One Hundred Years*, pp. 79, 80; Maddry, *An Autobiography*, pp. 71–75; Torbet, *op. cit.*, pp. 417, 418; Barnes, *The Southern Baptist Convention, 1845–1953*, pp. 231, 232. The per capita contributions of fourteen religious bodies fell from $3.47 in 1929 to $2.79 in 1931 and $1.75 in 1934. Not until 1944 did they reach the 1929 level.—*Information Service*, October 2, 1954.

[17] *Information Service*, January 9, 1954.

sucked into the maelstrom, but not until the Japanese attack on Pearl Harbour in December, 1941, did the nation become a belligerent. Participation lasted longer than in World War I, and military and naval operations were much more widely extended and were followed by continuing commitments in Europe, Africa, and Asia on a larger scale than could have been anticipated ten years earlier. Voluntary American philanthropy in connexion with the struggle was not as spectacular as in World War I, but it was extensive. As we are to see later, the Protestant forces were active in supporting the creation of the United Nations and in shaping some of its policies.

The sixteen years which followed World War II and which because of the date when these lines are penned must be the limit of our narrative, were marked by the continuation of American armed forces overseas, mounting investments of American private capital abroad, increasing American commerce across much of the world, and a vast outpouring of government aid to the armaments and the economic development of countries in Europe, Asia, Africa, and Latin America. In spite of what were euphemistically called recessions, the tide of prosperity rose. The 1950's saw an even greater expenditure of funds for the erection of churches and other ecclesiastical structures and institutions than the 1920's had seen. In 1957 what was termed the greatest church building boom in history was in progress. In that year it was said that 8 per cent. of all residential building was of churches as against 2 per cent. in 1946 and that nearly a third of all church expenditure went into buildings. Between 1953 and 1957 $2,567,000,000 was reported to have been spent on erecting churches and of this more than half was said to have been by Roman Catholics.[18] Yet this program could scarcely keep pace with what was approaching a population explosion. In 1916 the population of the continental United States was 101,966,000, in 1926 it was 117,399,000, in 1940 it was 132,122,000, in 1950 it was 151,677,000, and in 1960 it was 179,323,000.

THE DISTINCTIVE CHARACTERISTICS OF THE CHRISTIANITY OF THE UNITED STATES OF AMERICA

As we saw in an earlier volume,[19] the Christianity of the United States of America, while clearly in the historic stream of the faith, differed from that of any other country and had distinctive characteristics. One feature was the separation of Church and state and the absence of an established religion. The world over, the trend was in that direction, but the principle had been longer accepted in the United States than elsewhere in the erstwhile Christendom.

As heretofore, the separation of Church and state was not accompanied by

[18] *The Christian Century*, Vol. LXXIV, pp. 381–383 (March 27, 1957).
[19] Volume III, Chapter II.

anti-clericalism. Indeed, the association of the government with the churches was even closer than in the nineteenth century. Chaplains—Protestant, Roman Catholic, and Jewish—were officers in the armed forces, all the presidents of the first half of the twentieth century were church members, and in the post-1914 years to the pledge of allegiance to the flag the words "under God" were added so that the previous phrase "one nation, indivisible" was altered to "one nation, under God, indivisible."

The change was partly due to antagonism to atheistic Communism and to the U.S.S.R. It was evidence of a widespread superficial religiosity which was popularly identified with "the American way of life" as contrasted with Communism and which had little of intellectual depth or of the kind of conviction that could be called Christian. Nor did it mean that among many the Christian faith was not subject to erosion by the intellectual, social, and economic currents of the revolutionary age. Yet it showed a more general formal acceptance of Christianity than had been seen in the nineteenth century. Here was a kind of folk religion.[20]

The proportion of church members to the total population markedly and fairly steadily increased. In 1910 it was 40 per cent., in 1926 it was 45 per cent., in 1949 it was 53 per cent.,[21] in 1950 it was 57 per cent., in 1955 it was 61 per cent.,[22] and in 1959 it rose to 63.4 per cent.[23] This, it will be remembered, was an advance which had continued from the inception of the republic.

The published figures did not give a fully accurate picture of the extent of the church connexions of the population. For some denominations membership figures included only adults and took no account of children baptized and as yet not full members. Roman Catholics, Orthodox, and Protestant Episcopalians counted all who had been baptized, while few other bodies included children below the teen age. Moreover, many Protestant congregations from time to time removed from their rolls names of those who had become inactive. This meant that the percentage of the population who were related to the churches was much larger than the published statistics showed. In 1956 one estimate placed the total Protestant constituency at about 84,000,000—as compared with a Protestant membership of 58,000,000.[24]

What these figures meant in the quality of Christian faith and living would be impossible accurately to determine. Still less could it be ascertained whether

---

[20] For a stimulating description of the 1950's see Eckardt, *The Surge of Piety in America*, *passim*.

[21] Schneider, *Religion in 20th Century America*, p. 92.

[22] *Yearbook of American Churches, 1957*, pp. 278, 279. Slightly different figures give the proportion in 1850 as 16 per cent., in 1870 as 18 per cent., in 1890 as 22 per cent., in 1910 as 43 per cent., in 1930 as 47 per cent., in 1950 as 57 per cent., and in 1956 as 62 per cent.—Eckardt, *op. cit.*, p. 22.

[23] *Ecumenical Press Service*, October 14, 1959.

[24] *The New York Times*, November 6, 1956.

the quality had improved or deteriorated across the years. Some figures, not necessarily typical, shed a little light on the question. In 1941 the Methodist Church was said to have 625,000 inactive members; in 1951 the total in that category was reported to have risen to 1,735,000. In the 1950's a survey of one Protestant denomination in Ohio appeared to show that of its members a fifth never prayed, a fourth never read the Bible, 30 per cent. never attended church, two-fifths did not contribute to the financial support of their church, only 5 per cent. tithed, nine-tenths did not have family worship, and 95 per cent. had never sought to win another to the Christian faith.[25] In the 1950's the complaint was heard that in the increasingly standardized society the accepted signs of the difference between Christians and non-Christians were disappearing and that in an age of growing sophistication independence of thought was declining.[26] The criticism was also voiced that in the United States a kind of folk religion was developing which was seeking to promote individual and group "welfare"; its objective was personal happiness, adjustment, and success, and it regarded God as Helpmate, Guide, and Friend, Whose function it was to conserve and implement human values. This charge was leveled against Roman Catholicism, Protestantism, and Judaism. It was said that God, especially God as Christians regarded Him, was being made into an ally of the United States against Communism and of "free enterprise."[27]

So far as they could be obtained, statistics appeared to show that church attendance was substantially higher than in countries in Europe for which figures were obtainable and that the 1950's had seen a sharp increase—evidence of what was called "the surge of piety" in that decade. Figures gathered by the American Institute of Public Opinion (the so-called Gallup poll) indicated that in 1940 on an average Sunday over 37 per cent. of the adult population attended church, that in 1950 the proportion had risen to 39 per cent., and that in 1955 it was 49 per cent. The attendance did not vary much with the season of the year. As was to be expected, because of the requirement that each of the faithful assist weekly in the mass, in 1955 the proportion for Roman Catholics was 74 per cent. of their membership as against 42 per cent. for Protestants and 27 per cent. for Jews. For women in 1955 it was 54 per cent. and for men 43 per cent.—also as could have been anticipated. In 1955 the percentage of college graduates who attended church was said to be 53, of those whose education was limited to a high school 49, and of those with only a grade-school education 47. The latter figures seemed to show that the labouring classes were less well reached than those with more education and higher incomes—correspond-

---

[25] *Theology Today*, Vol. X, pp. 252, 253 (July, 1953).
[26] Osborn, *The Spirit of American Christianity*, pp. 206, 207.
[27] Eckardt, *op. cit.*, pp. 42–44, 49, 57, 126–129; Marty, *The New Shape of American Religion*, pp. 31–44.

ing in part to the European pattern.[28] The Gallup poll figures for 1958 showed a still further increase. During an average week in that year over 50,000,000 adults went to church—nearly 1,000,000 more than in 1955. In the Midwest this meant 54 per cent. of the population, in the East 52 per cent., in the South 51 per cent., and in the Far West 35 per cent. Of Roman Catholics 74 per cent. attended and of Protestants 44 per cent. In Britain, on the other hand,— nearly 80 per cent. Protestant—only 14 per cent. of adults said they had attended church on the Sunday preceding the survey.[29]

Another continuing feature was variety. The absence of an established church furthered it. As in the nineteenth century, through immigration nearly all the historic kinds of Christianity existing anywhere in the contemporary world were represented and to them were added several kinds of indigenous origin. Never had any country in any age of the faith exhibited religiously such a Joseph's coat of many colours. After 1914 the varieties increased rather than declined. The proportions between the main branches differed from those main- tained in the Old World, and within some of the branches distinctive develop- ments were seen to which we are later to call attention.

The variety differed from section to section. In the South, to which little of the nineteenth-century immigration had gone, except in Louisiana with its Roman Catholic elements of French and Spanish background Protestants were in the large majority. In the South, too, the major denominations were those which had been recruited from the economically underprivileged of the pre- nineteenth-century stock, whether white or Negro. The Baptists were by far the most numerous, especially among the Negroes, the Methodists were next, the Disciples of Christ and their offshoot the Churches of Christ were third, and the Episcopalians and Presbyterians were small but important minorities. In the North-east and Middle West Roman Catholics, the fruit of the nine- teenth- and twentieth-century immigration, were prominent, and in addition to the denominations of the pre-nineteenth-century stock several kinds of Lutheranism, mainly from the nineteenth-century influx from Germany, Scan- dinavia, and Finland, were strong. On the Pacific coast denominations of recent American origin loomed larger than in the South and the North-east. Among them were the Four-Square Gospel, the Pentecostals, the Churches of God, and the Nazarenes. In the Rocky Mountain area and on the west coast the Mormons were prominent.

The variety seemed greater than it actually was. In 1955, for example, at least 246 Protestant bodies were known to exist. To them were added the Roman Catholic Church and 19 different Eastern Churches.[30] On closer examination,

[28] *Ecumenical Press Service*, February 7, 1956.
[29] *Time*, January 12, 1959.
[30] *Yearbook of American Churches, 1957*, p. 271.

however, it was seen that in 1948, 97 per cent. of the Protestants were in the 50 larger denominations and approximately 80 per cent. were in 8 denominational families: (in the order of their size) Baptist, Methodist, Lutheran, Presbyterian and Reformed, Disciples, Episcopal, Congregational, and United Evangelical Brethren.[31] Yet within each of these families marked differences existed, some organizational and others theological. The absence of a central authority to compel conformity to a single pattern prompted diversity. However, the large majority of Protestants and some of the Eastern Churches and a number of other bodies coöperated through the Federal Council of the Churches of Christ in America, and latterly through its successor, the National Council of the Churches of Christ in the U.S.A. On the state and urban levels councils of churches and ministerial associations also made for fellowship and joint action.

The variety presented by the churches promoted the active affiliation of a larger proportion of the population than might have been obtained by a greater uniformity. The presence of the several churches of the Old World facilitated the recruiting of adherents from their ethnic backgrounds. As in the nineteenth century, immigrants found others of their nationality in churches which they had known in their ancestral homes and for social reasons frequented them. Fully as important was the fact that the churches reflected in part the social stratification of the nation. The vast majority of the Negroes were in purely Negro churches, and in the character of their services the Negro churches tended to reflect the educational and economic levels of their constituencies. Some denominations attracted chiefly the better-educated and upper-income elements of the population; the less highly educated and economically underprivileged did not feel at home in them. Other denominations in their worship and preaching proved congenial to those of middle income and educational attainments. Still others ministered predominantly to the scantily educated and those of the lowest income brackets.[32]

The variety contributed to a changing conception of the Church. No longer, as in Europe with its state and former state churches, could a sharp distinction be drawn between Church and sect. Here in the multiplicity of ecclesiastical bodies, none established by law, the several churches were described as denominations. Even the largest, the Roman Catholic Church, was generally regarded as one denomination among many.

An important aspect of the variety presented by the Christianity of the United States, to which we have called attention in an earlier volume,[33] was the fashion in which the proportionate distribution of membership among the

[31] *Ibid., 1948,* p. vi.

[32] For an understanding analysis see Helmut Richard Niebuhr, *The Social Sources of American Denominationalism* (New York, Henry Holt and Co., 1929, pp. viii, 304), *passim.*

[33] Volume III, pp. 10, 11.

denominational families differed from that in the former Christendom east of the Atlantic. Although it was the largest of the churches, in 1956 enrolling about 35.3 per cent. of the reported membership of the country,[34] the Roman Catholic Church was proportionately smaller than in Western Europe. Since most of its constituency were sprung from the immigration of the nineteenth and twentieth centuries, were in a land which by tradition was predominantly Protestant, and had long been regarded by Protestants as undesirable and even dangerous aliens, they had what might be called a persecution complex. Coming to America, as the large majority of that immigration did, poverty-stricken and with slight or no education, even at the mid-twentieth century their descendants were still painfully aware that in intellectual attainments they were below the average level of the population and did not have as large a share in the cultural and political leadership of the country as their numerical strength would have led the neutral observer to expect.[35]

In proportion to the entire population Protestants increased more rapidly than did Roman Catholics. In 1926 they constituted 27 per cent. of the population of the country and in 1955, 35.5 per cent. In 1926 and 1955 the corresponding figures for the Roman Catholic Church were 16 per cent. and 20.3 per cent. How much the differential growth was due to immigration, relative birth rates, and conversion could not be accurately ascertained. The Roman Catholic Church published the number of its converts, most of them from Protestantism. In 1945, 84,908 were reported.[36] The total for 1957 was said to be 141,525 and for the decade 1948–1957 it was given as 1,252,854.[37] The Roman Catholic authorities frankly recognized that five-sixths of the membership of their church was in the cities and that many city families were not replacing themselves.[38]

---

[34] *Yearbook of American Churches, 1957*, p. 250. Some Roman Catholic estimates declare that this figure is too low. In contrast with the figure of 33,574,017 officially reported in 1956, one estimate said that in that year the total of Roman Catholics may have been nearer to 40,000,000.— Ellis, *op. cit.*, p. 123. Yet because of the tides of secularism many Roman Catholics were lost not only to their mother church but also to any church. They ceased to go to confession because they were using birth control in marriage, were guilty of unholy love, or had fallen victim to alcoholism.—Sugrue, *A Catholic Speaks His Mind*, p. 56.

[35] Ellis, *op. cit.*, pp. 112–115, 146–150.

[36] *The National Catholic Almanac, 1946*, p. 167.

[37] *Ibid., 1958*, p. 421. For parish-by-parish statistics for Chicago in 1950 see Houtart, *Aspects Sociologiques du Catholicisme Américain*, pp. 266–270, 275–283. For some post-1914 converts see Katherine Burton, *In No Strange Land* (New York, Longmans, Green and Co., 1942, pp. xvii, 254), pp. 215–251; John Moody, *Fast by the Road* (New York, The Macmillan Co., 1942, pp. xvii, 308), *passim;* Herbert Elswortlh Cory, *The Emancipation of a Freethinker* (Milwaukee, The Bruce Publishing Co., 1940, pp. xx, 313), *passim.* For the story of one reared a Roman Catholic who became a Communist and later returned to the Roman Catholic Church bringing with him his wife, a former Unitarian, and his three daughters, see Louis Budenz, *This Is My Story* (New York, McGraw-Hill Book Co., 1947, pp. 379). See also the autobiography of one who, reared in slight contact with Protestantism, later a social radical, became a convert, in Dorothy Day, *The Long Loneliness* (New York, Harper & Brothers, 1952, pp. 288), *passim.*

[38] *The National Catholic Almanac, 1946*, p. 172. See also Ellis, *op. cit.*, pp. 123–126. A study in 1959 showed the Roman Catholic Church to be much stronger than Protestantism in metro-

The Protestants had no accurate comprehensive figures of conversions from the Roman Catholic Church. In the 1950's, however, spot samples of shifts from the Roman Catholic Church to Protestantism and vice versa seemed to show that from four to five times as many Roman Catholics became Protestants as moved from Protestantism to the Roman Catholic Church. Since the latter body was only about three-fifths the size of the total Protestant membership, the proportionate loss of the former was even greater than the actual numbers would indicate.[39] Late in the 1950's what appears to have been a careful study reported that in the past six years four times as many Roman Catholics were converted to the United Lutheran Church as left that church for the Roman Catholic.[40]

The Eastern Churches appear to have grown proportionately more rapidly in membership than the Roman Catholic or the Protestant groups. Presumably the increase came chiefly from immigration. Yet in the 1950's they were not as prominent percentage-wise as in Europe. In 1906 the Eastern Orthodox Churches were reported to have 129,606 members. In 1916 the total was 250,340.[41] In 1933 it had risen to 866,000.[42] In 1947 it was said to be 735,000,[43] in 1955 it was reported as 2,024,219, and in 1960 the figure had mounted to 2,807,612 communicants.[44]

As was true at the end of the nineteenth century, at the mid-twentieth-century mark the Protestant churches which had sprung from immigrants once members of established or formerly established churches of Europe—Lutheran, Anglican, Reformed, and Presbyterian—together enrolled only a minority, although a substantial minority, of the Protestants of the country. In contrast, east of the Atlantic they included the overwhelming majority of the Protestants. Of the 58,448,567 Protestants reported in 1956, only a little more than 14,750,000 or approximately a fourth were in these four denominational families. The

---

politan areas, and Protestantism much stronger than the Roman Catholic Church in non-metropolitan areas.—*Information Service*, March 28, 1959.

[39] From a high Protestant source which must remain confidential, October, 1957. As supporting data, in Holyoke, Mass., in the years 1942–1946 Protestant churches, with only about one-fifth of the membership of the Roman Catholic Church, had almost as many converts from the latter as did the latter from Protestantism.—Underwood, *Protestant and Catholic*, p. 48. In New York City, Christ's Mission, an undenominational Protestant enterprise made up of former Roman Catholic priests, assisted Roman Catholics, especially priests, who wished to leave the Roman Catholic Church. For figures of conversions to and from that church see its periodical, *The Converted Catholic*, May, 1953. The figures given in that statement for conversions from the Roman Catholic Church show a fairly steady increase from 36,376 in 1929 to 116,839 in 1952. The number of Roman Catholics received into the Protestant Episcopal Church is recorded as mounting from 2,213 in 1940 to 4,007 in 1949. For the autobiography of a Franciscan who left the Roman Catholic Church see Emmett McLoughlin, *People's Padre* (Boston, Beacon Press, 1954, pp. 228), *passim*.

[40] *The New York Times*, February 13, 1960.

[41] *Year Book of the Churches, 1918*, p. 179.

[42] *Ibid.*, p. 7.

[43] *Ibid.*, *1948*, p. 156.

[44] *The New York Times*, October 16, 1960.

largest was the Lutheran, with about half of the total membership of the four. By far the largest of the Protestant families was that of the Baptists, with approximately 19,000,000 members in 1956, or more than the total of all four of the families which had arisen from the Protestant established churches of Europe. Akin in many ways to the Baptists were the Disciples of Christ and the rapidly growing Churches of Christ, which together counted about 3,500,000 members. Next to the Baptist family of churches came the Methodists, who in 1956 had in their various branches about 11,800,000 members. If to that total was added that of the Evangelical United Brethren Church with a kindred polity and origin and a membership of about 737,000 in 1955, the Methodist total would be in excess of 12,500,000.[45] Other smaller denominational families, like Baptists and Methodists owing their growth to warm Evangelicalism and the revivalism which had flourished chiefly among the pre-nineteenth-century stock, white and black, added to the total and gave a distinctive character to the Christianity, especially the Protestantism, of the United States. In the United States the "folk churches" of Europe became denominations, while the "dissenting" minorities of Europe became "folk churches."

Significant, too, was the rate of growth of the several religious bodies. In the eight years between 1947 and 1955 the Roman Catholics increased by slightly less than a third, but several Protestant bodies exceeded that percentage increase. The Southern Baptist Convention reported a growth of 35.5 per cent., the African Methodist Episcopal Church 33 per cent., the African Methodist Episcopal Zion Church 46 per cent., the Missouri Synod 38 per cent., the Evangelical Lutheran Church 37 per cent., and the Church of Jesus Christ of Latter Day Saints 35 per cent.[46] If a longer reach of time is taken—from the close of World War I to 1955—the picture is slightly altered. In the thirty-six years between 1919 and 1955 Roman Catholics increased by about 90 per cent. In that same stretch of time the following bodies of Protestant origin exceeded that rate of growth: The Southern Baptist Convention multiplied slightly over four-fold; the Protestant Episcopal Church gained 159 per cent.; the African Methodist Episcopal Church had a percentage growth of 112.5 (the African Methodist Episcopal Zion Church showed an increase of 68 per cent., not as striking as that of the eight years after 1947); the two Negro National Baptist Conventions together grew 127 per cent.; The Missouri Synod more than doubled; the United Lutheran Church's gain was 175 per cent.; the Evangelical Lutheran Church mounted by 124.4 per cent.; the Augustana Synod grew by 173 per cent.; the Seventh Day Adventists increased 220 per cent.; the Church of Jesus Christ of Latter Day Saints expanded by 205 per cent.; the Churches of Christ multiplied by 468 per cent.; and the Assemblies of God displayed

[45] *Year Book of American Churches, 1957*, pp. 252–256.
[46] *Ibid., 1949*, pp. 155, 156; *Ibid., 1957*, pp. 155–161.

the startling growth of 436 per cent. While in 1955 the largest Protestant ecclesiastical body was the Methodist Church (a union of the Methodist Episcopal Church, the Methodist Episcopal Church South, and the Methodist Protestant Church), between 1919 and 1955 its growth, even when all three constituent bodies were taken together, was only 43 per cent.[47]

The most striking growth of a Protestant ecclesiastical body between the close of World War I and 1962 was that of the Southern Baptist Convention, made up of white members. So phenomenal was it that the constituency of the Convention was becoming in effect the folk church of the South, far outnumbering any other ecclesiastical body in that region. By the 1960's it was expanding into other parts of the country. The gains of the Protestant Episcopal Church were in part due to the influx of converts, many of them attracted either by its social prestige, its order, or the dignity of its ritual, the latter in contrast with the informality or bareness of the public worship of some of the denominations which enrolled larger numbers. The growth of the Lutheran bodies seems to have been mainly through the natural increase by births of their traditional constituencies. Much the same was true of the Mormons. The phenomenal expansion of the Seventh Day Adventists came before 1947 and slowed down after that year. The even more spectacular growth of the Churches of Christ was chiefly in the South but in later years extended to other parts of the country, notably the Far West. Springing from the movement out of which came the Disciples of Christ, they were far more rural than urban, stressed the autonomy of the local congregation, were much less closely knit in a national body than the Disciples of Christ, had no instruments of music, and were more conservative theologically.[48]

The Assemblies of God, which also enjoyed a major expansion, made up the largest of the Pentecostal bodies. In general the Pentecostals, whom we have already met in Europe and are to note later as becoming outstanding in Latin America, had in common a belief in a repetition of the experience of the Day of Pentecost with its outpouring of the Holy Spirit demonstrated by speaking with tongues and by healings and transformation of character. Most of them had their origin after 1900, many of them after 1914.[49]

Jehovah's Witnesses, of American origin, multiplied rapidly and spectacularly after World War I and especially after World War II. In 1955 they were said to have 187,120 members, but they attracted more attention than these numbers would warrant.[50] Believing that the end of the world was at hand, a conviction

[47] *Ibid.*, *1919*, pp. 197–202; *1957*, pp. 251–254. In the years 1908–1955 Roman Catholics are said to have grown 134.6 per cent.—*World Dominion*, Fall, 1957, p. 98.

[48] U.S. Bureau of the Census, *Religious Bodies, 1936* (Washington, U.S. Government Printing Office, 2 vols., 1941), Vol. II, pp. 462–470.

[49] Du Plessis, *A Brief History of the Pentecostal Assemblies, passim.* For a brief account of European beginnings see *World Dominion*, Vol. XXXV, pp. 51–54 (January, 1957).

[50] *Yearbook of American Churches, 1956*, p. 254.

nourished by the two world wars and the atom and hydrogen bombs, and possessing a tight, autocratically directed international organization, they sought indefatigably to propagate what they believed to be the witness committed to them by Jehovah. After their founder, Charles Taze Russell (1852–1916), died, Joseph Frank Rutherford (1869–1942), called "Judge" by his followers, became the head of the movement. After his death the movement continued under its new president, Nathan Homer Knorr (1905——), with similar dominating direction. Jehovah's Witnesses held that Armageddon was soon to reduce the world's population to a few millions, that then the millennial reign of Christ was to begin and prevail without division, confusion, or wars, that Christ's preliminary reign had already commenced "amid its enemies," and that they were commissioned to draw together a "great crowd" from all races and tongues from out of the world's tribulation.[51] The Church of Christ, Scientist, published no statistics, but that it continued to grow was obvious from the buildings it erected in various cities and the numbers of its organized churches. In 1931 the latter showed a gain of about a fourth since 1922 and nearly 100 per cent. since 1911. Between 1931 and 1941 the increase was a little less than 10 per cent. and between 1941 and 1958 it was about 3.41 per cent. In other words, it was slowing.[52]

A characteristic of the Christianity of the United States which also marked it off from that of Europe with the latter's folk churches and their traditions of state control, and which rapidly mounted in the twentieth century, was the fluid character of denominational lines. It was an accompaniment of the mobility of the population to which we have called attention and arose partly from the multiplicity of denominational families. No accurate statistics for it were available. Because of the rapid shifts in the residence of a large proportion of the population, denominational affiliations were for thousands determined more by geography than by theological conviction. In moving from one locality to another, many changed their denominational affiliations, partly because of the geographical propinquity of their new home to a church different from that of their former affiliation, but sometimes, too, because of the friendliness of the congregation, or the character of the pastor, or the form of public worship.

Late in the nineteenth century what were called community churches began

---

[51] W. J. Schnell, *Thirty Years a Watch Tower Slave. The Confessions of a Converted Jehovah's Witness* (Grand Rapids, Mich., Baker House, 1956, pp. 207), *passim;* Herbert Hewitt Stroup, *Jehovah's Witnesses* (New York, Columbia University Press, 1945, pp. vii, 180), *passim*, a very careful objective study; Marley Cote, *Jehovah's Witnesses. The New World Society* (New York, Vantage Press, 1955, pp. 229), *passim*, also careful and objective.

[52] Contrary pictures of it are in Charles S. Braden, *Christian Science Today, Power, Policy, Practice*, especially pp. 267–285 (Dallas, Southern Methodist University Press, 1958, pp. xvi, 432; factual and critical, based on careful research); and R. Peel, *Christian Science. Its Encounter with American Culture*, especially pp. 137–204 (Henry Holt and Co., 1958, pp. xiv, 239; favourable, and also based on research).

to emerge. They multiplied rapidly after World War I. For the most part they were efforts at a Protestant approach to an entire community. At least one began as the only church in a college community. In other cases the community church was the only Protestant church in a village or a rural district. Many of these churches were in suburbs of great cities and sought to bring together all men and women of good will. They attracted members whose previous connexions had been with two or more denominations, and some enrolled members from twenty or more denominations, including Roman Catholics. Numbers of the community churches kept a tie with an existing denomination, partly to have an outreach broader than their own immediate environment. Increasingly a city, county, or state council of churches in planning to reach the burgeoning suburbs and to avoid duplication assigned a particular area to a specific denomination. The denomination would send a clergyman to organize a church. He might find few or no residents of his denomination and in developing a congregation would attract families of diverse or no ecclesiastical background but would see that the congregation kept its tie with his denomination and contributed to its foreign and home missions and its other collective enterprises. Other community churches had no denominational association but if they gave to projects outside their immediate neighbourhood would choose them from more than one or from no denomination. Here was a practical way of achieving unity in the midst of a highly plural denominational particularism and of preventing the multiplication of weak churches in small towns and villages and even in large cities. For the most part community churches had a minimal creedal basis and sought to embody a faith to which all Christians could subscribe.[53] The trend was towards a general religiosity with an historically Christian background. Such a pattern would have been impossible in Europe with its dominant folk churches and was infrequent in other regions where the variety of churches was not so marked.

Still another characteristic of the Christianity of the United States was the propensity in many heretofore non-liturgical churches to conform to the historic Christian year and to practices in public worship adopted or adapted from the liturgical churches. The trend was by no means universal and was largely in congregations of middle or upper income and educational levels. It constituted a reaction from the extreme Protestantism of the Reformed, Puritan, and free church traditions. It was seen in the observance of Advent, Lent, Holy Week,

---

[53] A general survey is in Albert Clay Zumbrunnen, *The Community Church. A Probable Method of Approach to and Basis for Denominational Unity* (University of Chicago Press, 1922, pp. v, 169). For a particular congregation with no denominational ties and associated with other similar congregations see Roy A. Burkhart, *"I Am the First Community Church"* (Columbus, Ohio, Community Books, no date, ca. 1947, pp. 30). For another approach see Henry E. Jackson, *A Community Church. The Story of a Minister's Experience which Led Him from the Church Militant to the Church Democratic* (Boston, Houghton Mifflin Co., 1919, pp. xxxiii, 390). See also Marty, *op. cit.*, pp. 35–37.

Good Friday, Easter, and Pentecost, in pulpit gowns and vested choirs, and architecturally in divided chancels and altars with crosses.[54]

A further characteristic was the persistence, from an earlier period, of activism, whether in the Roman Catholic Church or in Protestantism. The challenge of the advancing frontier and of the vast influx of immigrants and the absence of state aid made imperative the concentration of energy on the development of ecclesiastical machinery and the erection of churches and educational institutions. Here was an expression of the national spirit—the building of a new nation in a relatively unoccupied vast domain.

In the Roman Catholic Church activism was seen in the absence of the canonization of native-born citizens. Down to 1960 the only person from the United States accorded the official recognition of sainthood was a nun of Italian birth and rearing. By 1960 a convert, Elizabeth Bayley Seton, foundress of the first native community of women, was being investigated as a candidate for beatification and ultimate canonization. But in Rome the general attitude was: "An American saint? Impossible!" The Roman Catholic Church in the United States was regarded as having skill in organization, in publicity, and in the raising of money, but not as the source of the quality of Christian character adjudged by that church to be worthy of emulation by all Christians. It was also significant that the Liturgical Movement originated in Europe and only slowly made headway in the United States. American Roman Catholicism tended to be conventional and conservative and not given to creative spiritual life.

Similarly Protestants to the east of the Atlantic regarded activism with its hope, to them naïve, of building the Kingdom of God within history as so typical of the United States that they labelled it Americanism—or *Americanismus*—and looked to American Protestants to supply the money needed for the geographic expansion of the faith and the Ecumenical Movement, but not for profound intellectual undergirding of the faith in the face of the revolutionary age.

With all the variety which in Protestantism appeared to many to issue in a watered-down Christian faith and a shallow religiosity and which drew many Roman Catholics from their ancestral moorings, and in spite of and in part because of its activism, in the post-1914 decades the Christianity of the United States displayed a continuation of the marked vigour characteristic of it in the nineteenth century. From it, and particularly from Protestantism, additional movements emerged. Some were without parallel in Europe. Increasing efforts were made to transcend the variety presented by Christianity and to achieve an inclusive unity. Because of the diversity with which they had to contend the efforts at unity were less successful than in Western Europe. But they

[54] *Religion in Life*, Vol. XXV, pp. 409–420 (Summer, 1956).

brought together in one form or another more kinds of Christians than came into inclusive fellowship east of the Atlantic. Christians of the United States took an increasing part in the world-wide propagation of the faith. This was especially true of Protestants, but to some extent it was also seen among Roman Catholics. Protestants had a mounting share in the Ecumenical Movement, and Protestant scholarship in theology and in Biblical and historical studies had increasing repercussions in Europe. In the United States was a vital Christianity which in some respects differed from all that had gone before it but yet had fellowship with it and which was deepening its impress upon the Christianity of the rest of the world. Of this we are to hear more in subsequent pages.

FACING THE DE-CHRISTIANIZING CHALLENGE OF THE REVOLUTIONARY AGE

In the United States Christianity faced the forces which were making for the de-Christianizing of the revolutionary age. Their challenge was much the same as in the former Christendom, but the situation was both like and unlike that in Europe.

The same or similar were the intellectual currents which appeared to be eroding the foundations of the Christian faith. Here, too, was the threat of Communism—although while infiltrating some organizations it was not as potent as in several countries in Europe and was met by more intense emotional resistance than in some other lands where the internal danger was greater. Here, as in Europe, among thousands who had been baptized, was an undercurrent of religious uncertainty and scepticism and an absorption in obtaining the material goods of life. Involvement in the world wars and some of the regional conflicts made for a deterioration in morals. As in the Old World, the growth of great cities and the industrialization of society brought a weakening of the hold of Christianity upon many thousands.

Significantly different, however, was the shift in denominational affiliations in the cities. For example, in 1958 a survey of the twenty-two counties in the metropolitan area embraced by New York City and adjacent sections of Connecticut and New Jersey showed that 29.5 per cent. of the population were Roman Catholic, 18 per cent. Jewish, 15.9 per cent. Protestant, 2.2 per cent. "other," and 34.4 per cent. unaffiliated. The unaffiliated were a slightly smaller percentage than in the country as a whole. The figures were evidence of the predominantly urban character of the Roman Catholic Church—a result of the nineteenth- and twentieth-century immigration, coming as that did from the underprivileged in Europe and at first making its livelihood through unskilled labour in the factories and in building railways. Significantly, 55 per cent. of the Protestants in the New York urban area were said to be non-white, 45.8

per cent. being Negroes and 9.2 per cent. Puerto Ricans.[55] These changes were in a region which formerly had been predominantly Protestant and white.

Unlike the other side of the Atlantic, the United States continued to see the westward flow of population, with the tendency of the newcomers to drop whatever church affiliation they may have had in their old homes. For example, in Oregon, where between 1900 and 1950 the population grew by 267.9 per cent. as against a national growth of 99.6 per cent., in 1926 the proportion of the population having a church membership was 22.7 per cent. as against about 45 per cent. in the country at large and in 1952 had risen to only 23.2 per cent. in contrast with the approximately 58 per cent. in the entire country. The proportion was higher in towns of from 2,500 to 5,000 population, but was only 11.2 per cent. in the heart of Portland, the largest city, and in the rural areas was 8.5 per cent. In Oregon the largest denomination, the Roman Catholic, had 23.7 per cent. of the church membership, considerably less than that in the country as a whole, Methodists were second, with 12.4 per cent., and Baptists third with 9.3 per cent. The proportionate increase from 1926 through 1952 was highest for the Lutherans, with the Seventh Day Adventists second, the Protestant Episcopalians third, the Church of Jesus Christ of Latter Day Saints fourth, and the Roman Catholics fifth.[56]

In 1956 Oregon had a smaller proportion of church members than any other state, but the situation was typical of what was happening in the westward movement of population. The highest percentage of church membership was in the North-east, followed closely by the South. The North Central region was a little behind but had a larger Protestant element than the North-east. The Rocky Mountain area was much in the rear of the North Central states and the Pacific coast was the lowest of all, with only 42.4 per cent. of the population in churches in 1956.[57]

Also differing from the situation in Western Europe and parts of Eastern Europe, where the large majority of the people were baptized and therefore were claimed by one or another of the folk churches, was the fact, as we have suggested, that as recently as 1920 only a minority of the population (in that year 43 per cent.) were church members and that even in 1955 only 60.9 per cent. were in that category.[58] Yet, in parallel with the European picture, large numbers of the baptized had only a nominal connexion with a church and many could be described as de-Christianized.

[55] *Time,* January 12, 1959.
[56] Oregon Council of Churches, *Church Membership and Population in Oregon, 1926–1952,* p. 19.
[57] *National Council Outlook,* December, 1956, pp. 8, 9.
[58] *Yearbook of American Churches, 1957,* p. 279.

COUNTERING DE-CHRISTIANIZATION: HOME MISSION SOCIETIES

In general, the Protestant agencies and methods which had developed in the nineteenth century to halt de-Christianization and to draw into church membership those without that connexion were continued in the twentieth century. A major exception was the camp-meeting, which had disappeared with the passing of frontier conditions. In its place, as we shall note in a moment, were summer assemblies with more or less permanent physical equipment in congenial rural or mountain settings. However, they were employed not so much for reaching those without Christian commitment as to nourish the faith of youth and church members and to recruit and train leadership for the churches.

Interdenominational and undenominational organizations, of which the American Bible Society was an outstanding representative, persisted, some of them on an expanding scale. Most of the Protestant denominations had home mission societies, the majority founded before 1914. They modified their programmes to meet the changing scene. As heretofore, they sought to serve the Indians and the Negroes and aided missions and social service agencies in the underprivileged portions of the great cities. They concerned themselves with the altered patterns of rural life. They sent missionaries to the remaining remnants of the frontier and assisted churches there. They had schools and missions in the mountains of the South, cut off by poor roads as the inhabitants were from most of the currents of modern life. They helped immigrants to make their adjustment to the American environment. They sought to improve the conditions of the seasonal migrant workers in harvesting fruits, grain, vegetables, and other farm products by providing wholesome recreation and opportunity for religious services and education. Organized efforts were also made to care for the thousands of men in military installations.[59] In several older states rural churches had multiplied before the advent of good roads. As roads improved and automobiles increased, many of these churches became anachronisms. Here and there to meet the changing conditions efforts were made to reach an entire county or a section of the county by a group ministry which would so far as possible use existing buildings and organizations but would serve the area as a single parish.[60]

[59] For popular surveys of these efforts see Coe Hayne, *For a New America* (New York, Council of Women for Home Missions and Missionary Education Movement of the United States and Canada, 1923, pp. xviii, 174), *passim;* William P. Shriver, *What Next in Home Missions?* (New York, Council of Women for Home Missions and Missionary Education Movement, 1928, pp. vii, 232), *passim;* Robert T. Handy, *We Witness Together. A History of Coöperative Home Missions* (New York, Friendship Press, 1956, pp. xiii, 270), *passim.*

[60] On the situation in one such state see Jesse Marvin Ormond, *The Country Church of North Carolina. A Study of the Country Churches of North Carolina in Relation to the Material Progress of the State* (Durham, N.C., Duke University Press, 1931, pp. xv, 369), *passim.* On one effort at a comprehensive approach to the rural problem see *The Rural Church Today and Tomorrow. A*

In other ways individual congregations attempted to meet the shifting conditions. Thus, as the constituencies of downtown churches moved to the suburbs, many of their former churches dwindled in membership and disappeared. But in some instances the buildings were utilized for wholesome recreation or other activities to attract youth and to fight juvenile delinquency, which became a mounting problem. Efforts were made to serve the aged—a growing proportion of the population with the improvement of medical science.[61]

COUNTERING DE-CHRISTIANIZATION: EVANGELISM

A method which persisted from the nineteenth century was the use of itinerant evangelists. In the half-century following 1914 the outstanding representative of this method was William Franklin Graham (1918——), more familiarly known as Billy Graham. Born in North Carolina, he was converted in his youth and attended ultra-conservative colleges which stressed revivalism—Bob Jones University and Wheaton College in Illinois—and then the Florida Bible Seminary, with a similar theological outlook. Ordained as a Baptist minister, he early became an evangelist and rose to national prominence in 1946. Backed by an efficient organization which enlisted the support of congregations of many denominations and trained local leadership to conserve the results through individual contacts with those making decisions in his meetings, seeking to bring his hearers into church membership and to guide them in their spiritual growth, Graham eventually addressed himself to the chief metropolitan areas. The first campaign to bring him wide attention was in Los Angeles in 1950. Especially notable were his meetings in New York City in 1957 and in San Francisco in 1958.

In New York, embodying to a greater extent than any other urban area the composite nature of the revolutionary age with its many nationalities, its obsession with riches, its extreme wealth and extreme poverty, its many denominations, and the efforts of the churches to capture a citadel of the forces of the era, Graham spoke during the summer on night after torrid night. Most of his sermons were in the Madison Square Garden, a well-known hall. In the Yankee Stadium, noted for its baseball games, a crowd of 100,000 heard him and about 20,000 were turned away for lack of room. Thousands flocked to his open-air addresses in some of the most frequented thoroughfares. Several million heard

Report of the National Conference on the Rural Church (New York, Home Missions Council and the Council of Women for Home Missions, 1936, pp. 90), *passim*. See also *What Emphasis for the Church in Town anod Country? A Report of the National Convocation on the Church in Town and Country, Columbus, Ohio, September 1–6, 1943* (New York, Committee on Town and Country, Home Missions Council of North America, and the Federal Council of the Churches of Christ in America, 1943, pp. 103).

61 William P. Shriver, *Missions at the Grass Roots* (New York, Friendship Press, 1949, pp. vi, 70), *passim*.

and saw him on coast-to-coast telecasts. More than 56,000 men, women, and children formally registered their "decisions for Christ." Of that number about 22,000 were under twenty-one years of age and over 2,000 were college students. The High School Evangelism Fellowship sponsoring the High-School Born-Again Clubs sought to keep in touch with the teen-agers.[62]

San Francisco, a city which high-lighted many of the contrasts of the revolutionary age, was in some respects an even greater challenge than New York. Begun as a Franciscan mission in the last century of Spanish rule in the New World, named after the *poverello,* by a strange antithesis it had been captured by the gold rush of the mid-nineteenth century and embodied in many ways the materialistic adventure, the polyglot population, the gambling fever, the search for pleasure, and the disregard for Christian moral standards which characterized that period. Yet many, both Protestants and Roman Catholics, had sought to bear a Christian witness both through a few years of preaching, as did William Taylor in the days of the gold seekers, and through continuing congregations. There as in New York churches of many denominations co-operated with Graham. Great throngs came from the entire urban area, and thousands registered their "decisions for Christ."[63]

Graham's mission became world-wide. We have already met him in the British Isles. He went repeatedly to the continent of Europe and to Australia, to Africa south of the Sahara, and to several countries in Asia. When these lines were penned he was still in his late youth. Any full appraisal would have to wait for subsequent decades.[64]

However, it was not too early to make a characterization of Graham as he was in 1962. He clearly belonged in the tradition of the great evangelists of the nineteenth century, especially Dwight L. Moody. Transparently sincere, not seeking personal recognition or prestige, at the first advent of fame and the flood of invitations to preach feeling appalled and inadequate but trusting in the Holy Spirit for strength and wisdom to meet the challenge, Graham belonged in the Evangelical tradition embodied in the denominations which enrolled the large majority of the Protestants of the country, especially those of the pre-nineteenth-century stock. He did not profit financially from his campaigns but drew a stated salary from his organization and one which was not as large as those of numbers of the clergy.

[62] Curtis Mitchell, *God in the Garden. The Story of the Billy Graham New York Crusade* (Garden City, N.Y., Doubleday and Co., 1957, pp. 195), *passim.*

[63] Sherwood E. Wirt, *Crusade at the Golden Gate* (New York, Harper & Brothers, 1959, pp. 176), *passim.*

[64] For an admiring account by a Protestant journalist see Stanley High, *Billy Graham. The Personal Story of the Man, His Message, and His Mission* (New York, McGraw-Hill Book Co., 1956, pp. 274), *passim.* For a brief biographical sketch see *Who's Who in America,* Vol. XXX, pp. 1079, 1080. For an account of a trip through Asia see George Burnham, *To the Far Corners. With Billy Graham in Asia* (New York, Fleming H. Revell Co., 1956, pp. 160), *passim.*

For the most part the thousands who responded to Graham's message had had earlier contact with the Gospel as he presented it. The majority of the "decisions," as he said, were by those already members of churches. Graham preferred to regard them not as final decisions but as inquiries. He said frankly that the mass method which he employed was not the ideal kind of evangelism, that it had rather narrow limits, and that he discounted statistics, but he was convinced that many lives were basically changed and that many congregations were quickened to renewed vigour. He faced frankly and humbly the criticisms made of him and his methods, and his head was not turned by the adulation of his many admirers.

Graham was quite aware that he was not a scholar, but he took account of the intellectual currents of the day, including those in theology and Biblical scholarship. Yet after doing so he said that his faith was confirmed in the Bible as the Word of God and in the crucifixion and resurrection of Christ. He was certain that God had acted decisively in history through Christ. He also believed in the completion of history and the final triumph of the Kingdom of God in the second coming of Christ, but he refused to set a date for that event or to enter into debate as to precise details. He recognized the contrast between the revival of religion of his day and the increase in the forces of evil —the growth of both the wheat and the tares—but he did not doubt the ultimate victory of Christ. He did not stress social reform, for he held that if men were basically changed they would work for reforms. Yet, at least in recent years, he declined to address public gatherings in which racial segregation was practised, and his view of the social implications of the Gospel was progressively broadened. He felt that he had earlier been too narrow in defining the boundaries of the Church, but said that he had come to place more emphasis on the Church, rejoiced that he had found true Christians in every visible church, and was happy that the coöperation of churches of many denominations in his campaigns had made for Christian unity.[65]

In the fore part of the twentieth century departments of evangelism became a recognized feature of many Protestant denominations. Between 1920 and 1930 two denominations had full-time secretaries of evangelism. By 1951 thirty-two denominations had forty-seven full- or part-time secretaries for that purpose. In 1932 the Department of Evangelism of the Federal Council of Churches had one staff secretary. In 1951 the Department of Evangelism of the National Council of Churches of Christ in the U.S.A. had a staff of seven and its budget had increased almost ten-fold. Specialized coöperative efforts were made to reach prisons, youth, migrants, children, the armed forces, and visitors to the national parks. Consultations of clergy and of college and university faculty members were held. Radio, television, and films were employed. Teachers in

[65] Billy Graham in *The Christian Century*, Vol. LXXVII, pp. 186–189 (February 17, 1960).

the Sunday Schools were encouraged to bring their pupils to Christian commitment.[66] Men were employed full time by the various denominations as evangelists, and revival services were a scheduled feature of congregations of a number of churches, especially Baptist, Methodist, Disciples of Christ, and similar bodies. Laymen were organized to aid by systematic visitation. In some denominations, usually those of liturgical traditions, the name more frequently employed was "mission" and the purpose was primarily the deepening of the Christian life of the members and not public decisions. Thus in 1952 the Evangelical Lutheran Church began what it called the Preaching-Teaching-Reaching Evangelism Mission. It was a continuing effort over several years and was congregation-centred, sought to enlist clergy and laity, used guest pastors as preachers, and had as its goal deepening the spiritual life of believers and winning the "unreached."[67] Much the same was true of the Roman Catholic Church.

By their very designation what were called revivals had as a major purpose the quickening of the life of the congregation and the existing membership. Whether as revivals or as missions, what was called evangelism proposed to rouse the rank and file of the professedly Christian to a more intelligent understanding of the faith and a deeper commitment to it. That became increasingly important as the proportion of church members in the population continued to mount and the danger increased that, as in much of Europe, the church connexion would become purely formal and conformity to a social convention.

Very different from Graham were the evangelists who did not have in their campaigns the wide coöperative backing of churches of many denominations but depended on their own organizations and the support of individuals rather than ecclesiastical bodies. Their name was legion. In the 1940's and 1950's especially they made extensive use of the radio and television. Some had a nation-wide and even an international outreach. Prominent among them was Charles E. Fuller (1877———). Born in Los Angeles, he became a Baptist minister. In 1925 he began radio broadcasting and through it developed the Old-Fashioned Revival Hour, which eventually had a world-wide coverage. He was also the founder (1947) and president of the Board of Trustees of Fuller Theological Seminary, which, undenominational, became known for its scholarly standard of conservative theological and Biblical scholarship.[68]

Here and there were other Protestant movements which had evangelism as their primary aim. Thus the Montana Gospel Crusade, begun in 1936 by staunch conservatives, had the Rocky Mountain region as its field and sought

[66] Jesse Bader, *The Churches of the United States and Evangelism* (1951, pp. 9,) mimeographed, *passim.*
[67] *A Monthly News Letter about Evangelism* (Geneva, World Council of Churches, December, 1958, mimeographed).
[68] *Who's Who in America*, Vol. XXXI, p. 1023.

by radio, children's Know Your Bible Clubs, adult Bible classes, Bible conferences, and a publications department to "hold forth the Word of life" both to win unbelievers and to strengthen the faith of believers.[69] The Navigators, whose founder was killed in an accident in the mid-1950's, were a semi-monastic Protestant group with headquarters near Colorado Springs who in various ways, including efforts to conserve the results of the Billy Graham meetings and the use of the radio, sought to promote evangelism. Their central group numbered only about a score, but they had friends in many regions and kept in touch with them through a carefully maintained system of correspondence.

After World War II increasing efforts were made to reach the inner city slums. Such were the East Harlem Protestant Parish in New York, the Wider City Parish in New Haven, Connecticut, and similar projects elsewhere. In New York City some churches centred on the members of teen-age gangs.[70]

COUNTERING DE-CHRISTIANIZATION: PREACHING

Great preachers emerged, both in Protestantism and in the Roman Catholic Church. Many were pastors of parishes and, while not professional evangelists, were eminent in presenting the Christian faith in a fashion designed to meet the questions and the challenges of the twentieth-century stage of the revolutionary age. Even a bare listing of the names of the more eminent would extend these pages quite beyond their proper proportions.

As widely known as any of the Protestants was Harry Emerson Fosdick (1878——). He was born in Buffalo, New York, and was reared in and near that city. His father and paternal grandfather were teachers. The family were faithful members of Baptist churches and embodied a strain of independent thinking and action. They had been pioneers in Western New York, and Fosdick's paternal grandfather had departed from the Episcopalianism of his immediate forebears to become a Baptist, was a strong advocate of temperance, and maintained a station on the "underground railway" which facilitated the escape of Negro slaves to Canada. From childhood Fosdick was deeply religious, and the radiant faith of a happy, wholesome family helped to offset whatever morbidity may have come from fears of hell. His college was Colgate. Although as an undergraduate he doubted the basic tenets of the Christian faith, he began his senior year determined to enter the ministry. Yet he did so rebelling against orthodoxy and with no interest in any denomination. His first year in a theological seminary was in Colgate and there William Newton

---

[69] *Montana Gospel Crusade* (Billings, Mont., The Montana Gospel Crusade, 1955, a one-page descriptive leaflet).

[70] See one of these described in C. Kilmer Myers, *Light in the Dark Streets* (Greenwich, Conn., The Seabury Press, 1958, pp. 156), *passim*. See also *A Monthly Letter about Evangelism* (Geneva, World Council of Churches, May, 1957, mimeographed).

Clarke made a deep impression on him. Clarke, dissenting from the current orthodoxy, helped him to face the intellectual currents of the day and to place the emphasis upon a vital, transforming Christian experience. Fosdick then went to Union Theological Seminary in New York City. He had not been there many weeks when over-work in a vacation Bible school and in a mission in the slums, combined with the stimulus of the city and of his studies and the lack of physical care of himself, brought on severe nervous prostration with deep despondency and the necessity for complete cessation of all activity. He recovered, but with after effects which it took him years to overcome. Returning to Union, he was graduated with high honours. Out of the months of invalidism came the experience of the reality of God and of prayer and a desire through preaching and the pastorate to help others.

Fosdick's initial pastorate was in Montclair, New Jersey, a suburb of New York City. At first he found preaching difficult. For him it never became easy. He believed it to be a way of helping his hearers solve their problems—spiritual, intellectual, and moral—and in such fashion as to produce in them Christian faith and to realize the power of God to give them victory over trouble and temptation. From the beginning he was not confined by denominational barriers but invited all Christians to share in the Communion. He concerned himself with the relations of capital and labour and sought, in vain as he later confessed, to keep his church from being a class institution. He was deeply influenced by Walter Rauschenbusch and, in his inner life, by the Quaker Rufus Jones. Although he backed the government in World War I and served for a time as a clergyman with the troops in Europe, later he became a pacifist and in World War II did not waver from that conviction. From Montclair he went to the faculty of Union Theological Seminary and remained on it until his retirement because of age.

Fosdick had already become famous when as guest preacher for over five and a half years (1919–1925) in the Old First Presbyterian Church in New York City, while continuing to teach, he became a target of the fundamentalists. To them he was the embodiment of the liberalism they were attacking. The General Assembly of the Presbyterian Church in the U.S.A. was forced to take action. In 1924 it asked Fosdick to enter the Presbyterian Church and thus become one of the regular pastors of the Old First. This he felt he could not do and resigned, but at the insistence of the congregation he continued to preach until March, 1925.

On leaving the Old First's pulpit, Fosdick was asked to become pastor of the Park Avenue Baptist Church in New York City, of which John D. Rockefeller, Jr., was the leading member. He accepted, but on condition that it would eliminate all sectarian restrictions to membership, becoming in effect a community church, and would build a new and larger edifice equipped for that function. His terms were met and the Riverside Church was erected opposite Union Theological Seminary on Morningside Heights. It was a huge and carefully planned structure, later enlarged to provide ampler facilities for religious education. The Riverside Church maintained official relations with the Baptist and the Congregational-Christian national organizations and presumably would have welcomed them with other denominations if the latter's ecclesiastical structure had permitted them. There Fosdick continued to attract large congregations and also carried on his teaching in the Seminary. Characteristically, he insisted that his salary from the church be only $5,000.

Fosdick's influence reached much farther than his classroom and his pulpit. He spoke in many universities. For years, beginning in 1927, he was the preacher of the "National Vespers" on Sunday afternoons over a radio network of the National Broadcasting Company. Through short-wave facilities he was heard in seventeen different countries. He wrote books which were translated into many languages and had sales running into hundreds of thousands of copies. Classed with the Protestant liberals, he remained at heart an Evangelical and declined to be counted with the extreme radicals. While frankly facing the weaknesses of much of liberalism, he did not espouse the neo-orthodoxy which became popular in his later years.[71]

Fosdick owed his wide appeal partly to the courage, intelligence, and honesty with which he faced the many intellectual, social, and political currents of the revolutionary age, partly to his unwavering faith won by hard struggle, partly to his familiarity through personal counselling with the problems of thousands of individuals, partly to never having departed from the main Evangelical tradition, and partly to the way he presented the historic Evangelical convictions and experience. The latter attracted thoughtful men and women who had been reared in Evangelicalism but were unhappy over what seemed to them to be the intellectually untenable dogmatic forms and the sectarian terms in which it was often presented. His effective mission was mainly to a middle- and upper-class constituents with an Evangelical background.

Late in the 1950's, although after Fosdick's retirement, the erection of the towering Interchurch Centre across the street from the two organizations with which Fosdick had longest been connected, Union Theological Seminary and

[71] See especially Harry Emerson Fosdick, *The Living of These Days. An Autobiography* (New York, Harper & Brothers, 1956, pp. ix, 324), *passim*. Among Fosdick's books, which emerged mainly from his sermons and lectures, some of the most widely read were *The Meaning of Faith* (New York, Association Press, 1917, pp. ix, 318); *The Meaning of Prayer* (New York, Association Press, 1915, pp. xii, 196); *The Meaning of Service* (New York, Association Press, 1920, pp. viii, 225); *The Modern Use of the Bible* (New York, The Macmillan Co., 1924, pp. 291); *On Being a Real Person* (New York, Harper & Brothers, 1943, pp. xiv, 295); *The Assurance of Immortality* (New York, The Macmillan Co., 1913, pp. x, 141); *Christianity and Progress* (New York, Fleming H. Revell Co., 1922, pp. 247); *A Great Time to Be Alive. Sermons on Christianity in Wartime* (New York, Harper & Brothers, 1944, pp. vi, 235); *A Guide to Understanding the Bible. The Development of Ideas Within the Old and New Testaments* (New York, Harper & Brothers, 1938, pp. xvi, 348).

the Riverside Church, reinforced the symbol represented by these institutions. Housing, as it did, the headquarters of several denominational agencies, the National Council of Churches of Christ in the U.S.A., and the American offices of the World Council of Churches, in close physical and spiritual proximity to a great community church and a leading undenominational school for the preparation of leadership for the churches, on a commanding site in the largest city of the country, the Interchurch Centre, with them, demonstrated a coöperative approach by the majority of American Protestants of Evangelical origins to the challenges of the revolutionary age. Significantly, denominations of highly liturgical practice and sprung from the state churches of Europe were but slightly represented—although in the same neighbourhood the Russian Orthodox had a theological seminary and the Protestant Episcopalians a great cathedral—and fundamentalists and near-fundamentalists were, by their own choice, not included.

Another preacher in New York City, Norman Vincent Peale (1898——), was the outstanding figure in another strain in American Protestantism which in various expressions was widely popular in the decades that immediately preceded and followed World War II. Son of a Methodist minister, born and reared in Ohio, educated in Methodist universities, and ordained to the Methodist ministry, after serving three Methodist congregations, in 1932 Peale became pastor of the (Reformed) Marble Collegiate Church in the heart of America's metropolis. There, by preaching, the radio, television, a syndicated newspaper column headed "Confident Living," a question-and-answer page in *Look,* a widely circulated periodical, and as editor of *Guideposts* and the author of several books with enormous circulations, he set forth the Gospel as a means to overcoming defeat—in morals, in health, in marital relations, and in occupations and professions—and attaining victory and success.[72]

This brief summary is a quite inadequate although factually accurate account of a very remarkable career. Like Fosdick, through hard personal experience Peale had become convinced of the truth of the Gospel which he preached. Sensitive, knowing periods of deep depression, he had again and again been driven to do what he advised others to do: forget himself and put himself in the hands of God. He had learned, as had Fosdick, that God is love. He made no pretense of being a scholar. His was a simple faith which was centred in God as he saw Him in Christ and which treasured the Bible. He loved people and was keenly sensitive to their needs. He was at his best when he spoke, both to common folk and intellectuals, in language they could understand, using homely illustrations from life as he had met it. He did not dodge sin or water down the demands of Christ and he urged his hearers to face up honestly to themselves. But he also stressed the desire of God to forgive the penitent and the power of God to transform discouraged and defeated lives

---

[72] *Who's Who in America,* Vol. XXXI, pp. 2250, 2251.

and make them "more than conquerors." During his early years in the Marble Collegiate Church attendance and membership increased slowly. Eventually the congregations grew beyond the capacity of the building. Peale gave much time to personal counselling. Before long he worked in close coöperation with psychiatrists who, like him, believed in the power of prayer. Eventually a clinic was developed in connexion with the church; a staff of twenty-four ministers, psychiatrists, psychologists, and social workers dealt with hundreds of cases each year and carried on a training programme in pastoral counselling for young clergymen. Socially and politically, in contrast to Fosdick, Peale was conservative. He opposed Franklin D. Roosevelt and much of the New Deal. Part of his criticism arose from his total abstinence convictions and his unhappiness over Mrs. Roosevelt's advocacy of drinking, although in moderation. Later, finding himself used by extreme political and economic conservatives, he withdrew from political activities. The sale of Peale's books rose into the millions of copies and one, *The Power of Positive Thinking,* for months headed a list of the best-selling non-fiction books.

A storm of criticism arose, not, as in the case of Fosdick, from the fundamentalists, but from intellectuals, many of them prominent in ecclesiastical circles. They maintained that Peale was cheapening and perverting the Gospel and reducing God to an instrument to be used by men for achieving success. They also said that he was too facile in avoiding or minimizing the sin and evil in the world. So severe and widespread were the strictures that Peale at one time wrote his resignation from the Marble Collegiate Church and from the Christian ministry. But he did not make it public and before long tore it up.[73]

Peale was only one of many of the Protestant clergy who sought to bring Christian faith to bear on the healing of disease and the countering of human suffering. In some congregations, usually in the cities, the clergy had the coöperation of physicians, surgeons, and psychiatrists and stressed prayer as an aid in the art of healing. Others, several of them itinerant evangelists who utilized tent meetings, the radio, television, and the press, made of the prayer of faith the sole means towards health.[74]

[73] For an admiring intimate biography based on material provided by Peale and his family, see Arthur Gordon, *Norman Vincent Peale, Minister to Millions* (Englewood Cliffs, N.J., Prentice-Hall, 1958, pp. 311). Among People's books were *The Art of Living* (New York, Abingdon-Cokesbury Press, 1937, pp. 144); *The Power of Positive Thinking* (New York, Prentice-Hall, 1952, pp. ix, 275); *Amazing Results of Positive Thinking* (Englewood Cliffs, N.J., Prentice-Hall, 1950, pp. 247); *Guide to Confident Living* (Englewood Cliffs, N.J., Prentice-Hall, 1948, pp. 248); *Stay Alive All Your Life* (Englewood Cliffs, N.J., Prentice-Hall, 1957, pp. 300); and *You Can Win* (New York, Abingdon-Cokesbury Press, 1938, pp. 176). With his friend and collaborator Smiley Blanton, a psychiatrist, Peale also wrote *Faith Is the Answer. A Psychiatrist and a Pastor Discuss Your Problems* (New York, Abingdon-Cokesbury Press, 1940, pp. 223) and *The Art of Real Happiness* (Englewood Cliffs, N.J., Prentice-Hall, 1950, pp. 247).

[74] Of the large literature see as examples *Religion in Life,* Vol. XXV, pp. 163–204 (Spring,

A figure who came to prominence in the 1920's was Aimee Semple McPherson (1890–1944). Born in Canada, she was briefly a missionary in China with her first husband, Robert Semple, a Pentecostal. On his early death she returned to America and had an unfortunate second marriage to Harold S. McPherson, which ended in divorce. She became an itinerant evangelist, preaching in Canada, the United States, Australia, and England. In 1918 she made her home in Los Angeles and there was so successful that in 1923 she dedicated Angelus Temple, with a seating capacity of over five thousand. A superb platform speaker, radiantly beautiful, with abounding energy, she promulgated what she called the Four-Square Gospel, basing it, she said, upon the Bible. It proclaimed Christ as the Saviour "to a sin-cursed, Satan-deceived world," the Baptizer "with the Holy Ghost and fire to a timid, weak-kneed Church," the Physician "to a sick and dying humanity," and the "coming King of Peace to a world tired of war, strife, greed, hate, and suffering." Many physical healings were reported. She presented this Gospel in spectacular fashion to vast audiences. Then, in May, 1926, she disappeared and her friends believed her drowned. The next month she reappeared, asserting that she had been kidnaped. Doubt was thrown on her story and a sensational trial ensued. The case was eventually dismissed with what her followers acclaimed as a victory for her. Although her name quickly dropped from the national press, Mrs. McPherson's influence continued through the Church of the Four-Square Gospel, which spread to a number of towns and cities, especially on the west coast. The L.I.F.E. Bible College and the Echo Park Evangelistic Association maintained and promulgated her teachings.[75]

Later than Aimee Semple McPherson and with a much wider following was Oral Roberts. The son of a Full Gospel preacher in Oklahoma, in his youth he suffered from tuberculosis and stammered painfully. He believed himself cured through a Pentecostal spiritual healer and felt called to preach the healing power of God. This he did as a minister of the Assemblies of God. In 1947 he suddenly emerged from obscurity through a tent meeting in Tulsa, Oklahoma. In 1949 the Oral Roberts Foundation was inaugurated in that city. It published a magazine devoted to spiritual healing and broadcast Roberts' sermons.

1956); *Religion and Health. To Bridge the Gap Between Religion and Medicine* (Durham, N.C., 1952 ff.), a periodical begun by the Religion and Health Corporation of Gladwater, Texas; A. Graham Ikin, *New Concepts of Healing, Medical, Psychological, and Religious* (New York, Association Press, 1956, pp. xxiii, 262), *passim*. *The Voice of Healing* (Dallas, Tex., 1949 ff.) was a periodical described as "a monthly inter-evangelical publication of the Last-Day Sign Gift Ministries." Its February, 1953, issue listed its evangelists and "healing campaign schedules" in several cities and states, largely in Assembly of God churches, and spoke of the fourth Annual Voice of Healing Convention in Dallas in December, 1952.

[75] See her *The Holy Spirit* (Los Angeles, Challpin Publishing Co., 1931, pp. 287); *The Foursquare Gospel* (no place or publisher given, 1946, pp. 199). An account of her trial, attempting to be factual and objective, is Lately Thomas, *The Vanishing Evangelist (The Aimee Semple McPherson Kidnaping Affair)* (New York, The Viking Press, 1959, pp. xiv, 334).

Through short-wave radio the sermons reached over twelve countries. Television also spread Roberts' message. He held tent meetings in many cities attended by huge crowds. He depended for healing on prayer and the laying on of hands. An ultra-fundamentalist, he was emphatic on personal morals but had no social message. A master of assemblies, fluent in speech, and apt in the dramatic, he claimed thousands of cures. He did not collaborate with the medical profession and no scientific record could be given of the number of authentic healings and of the failures. He maintained that God is a good God, and that if men would but trust Him He would not only cure bodily and mental ills but also bring a happy home life and enable the believer to become the person he had wished to be.[76]

We have given so much space to the twentieth-century developments in American Protestantism in the healing through faith of physical, mental, and spiritual ills because they revealed a widespread hunger in the revolutionary age. We must not forget that at the same time the Roman Catholic Church was using its historic agencies for the same end. Among them were shrines dedicated to the Virgin. Some Roman Catholic preaching was also devoted to that purpose.

We must also note that the emphasis on healing in the Protestantism of the United States was both greater than before 1914 and much more extensive than in European Protestantism at any time. Before 1914 its chief expression in the United States was through Christian Science. While Christian Science continued after 1914, its growth seems to have slowed. Through the other channels we have mentioned, the appeal of healing through faith had a phenomenal response after World War II. Although something akin to that emphasis was seen in English Protestantism, it was not nearly as widespread as in the United States and did not win as large popular response.

In the Roman Catholic Church the preacher who most nearly commanded a nation-wide hearing was Fulton John Sheen (1895———). Born in Illinois, he had received an excellent education which included doctorates from Louvain and Rome. Ordained priest in 1919, he taught for a time in England and from 1926 to 1950 in the Catholic University of America. In 1950 he was made the national director of the Society for the Propagation of the Faith. In 1951 he was consecrated Titular Bishop of Caesariana and Auxiliary Bishop of New York. Competent, he was especially familiar with the history of thought in the West in the modern period, particularly in the revolutionary age. In substantial works he surveyed what he deemed the decay in the major stream of Western thought beginning in the sixteenth century. He held that it had resulted in the abandonment of reason and the descent into irrationalism. He also maintained

---

[76] *The Christian Century*, Vol. LXXIII, pp. 1018, 1019 (September 5, 1956); *Religion in Life*, Vol. XXV, pp. 163–165 (Spring, 1956); Oral Roberts, *God Is a Good God* (Indianapolis, The Bobbs-Merrill Co., 1960).

that the impact of physical science had issued in the approach to religion as the quest of men rather than the action of God. Like Aquinas he employed reason to prove the existence of God. He spoke of God as both transcendent and immanent, and of Divine providence. Much of his writing, as of his speaking, sought to set forth the Christian faith without presenting the distinctive position of the Roman Catholic Church. He dealt with the crucifixion and the seven last words of Christ. He attacked Communism. During World War II he wrote and spoke on the causes of war and the pillars of lasting peace, setting forth the Papal position. In accord with the temper of the time, he was emphatic that life is worth living, dwelt on that topic at length, and presented what he regarded as the way to happiness and inward peace. He suggested thoughts for daily living. He dealt with the life of Christ and with the true meaning of Christmas. From time to time he also described distinctive features of Roman Catholic teaching, including the meaning of the mass. He was a past master at presenting his themes in ways which appealed to the rank and file of the public, and he could write so as to command the respect of the intellectuals. He could also speak with engaging charm and humour in such fashion that the average listener would find him intelligible and convincing.[77]

COUNTERING DE-CHRISTIANIZATION: RELIGIOUS EDUCATION

Another instrument which was employed to counter de-Christianization, to rear children and youth in a knowledge of the Christian faith, and to deepen the knowledge and loyalty of those in mature life was the Sunday School. Often it was called the Church School. The statistics were impressive. In 1919 the number enrolled was reported to be 21,291,987.[78] In 1954 it was said to be 37,623,530, and in 1955 it had risen to 38,921,033, an advance of 3.4 per cent. over the previous year.[79] Proportionately to the population growth this was a decided increase. Whereas between 1919 and 1955 the population had mounted by about 50 per cent., the enrollment in the Sunday Schools had gained about 80 per cent. Because of the differences in the methods employed for instructing youth, the Sunday School was much more a Protestant than a Roman Catholic institution. The Roman Catholics depended more upon the parochial schools than did the Protestants, and for them the Sunday Schools were primarily a

---

[77] *Who's Who in America*, Vol. XXXI, p. 2619. Among Sheen's books were *Philosophy of Religion. The Impact of Modern Knowledge on Religion* (New York, Appleton-Century-Crofts, 1948, pp. xvii, 409); *Religion Without God* (New York, Longmans, Green and Co., 1928, pp. xiv, 368); *Preface to Religion* (New York, P. J. Kenedy and Sons, 1946, pp. 228); *Seven Pillars of Peace* (New York, Charles Scribner's Sons, 1945, pp. 112); *Whence Come Wars?* (New York, Sheed and Ward, 1940, pp. 119); *Life Is Worth Living* (New York, McGraw-Hill Book Co., 5 vols., 1953–1957); *Liberty, Fraternity, and Equality* (New York, The Macmillan Co., 1938, pp. xiii, 187); *Philosophies at War* (New York, Charles Scribner's Sons, 1943, pp. 200).

[78] *Year Book of the Churches, 1920*, p. 197.

[79] *Ibid., 1957*, p. 257.

means of teaching children who were in the public and not in the parochial schools. As a consequence, in 1919 only 1,932,206, slightly less than 10 per cent. of the Sunday School enrollment, were reported by Roman Catholics and in 1955 only 2,277,948, or a little under 6 per cent., of the total were under Roman Catholic direction.[80] Obviously this was very much less than the Roman Catholic proportion of the church membership of the country.

How effective the Sunday Schools were in imparting religious instruction and in winning those enrolled in them to the Christian faith could not be accurately determined. The large majority of their officers and teachers—in 1955 totalling 3,029,386[81]—were laymen and women. Here was an impressive outpouring of lay devotion. Literature was produced in massive quantities—by denominational, undenominational, and inter-denominational agencies for both teachers and pupils and adapted to various age groups. Many congregations had on their salaried staff professionally prepared directors of religious education. Training courses for teachers were held locally and regionally. Yet regularity in attendance of pupils and even of teachers could not be enforced. Nor could much study by the pupils be expected outside the time spent in class. That time was generally an hour or less a week. Under these circumstances, the knowledge imparted could not, on the average, be more than superficial. Yet numbers of the teachers gave themselves unstintedly to the members of their class and set an example of Christian living which had a profound effect on many who came under their influence. Church membership was largely recruited from the Sunday Schools. Although much of the religious illiteracy characteristic of millions who entered into and kept a church connexion could be ascribed to the Sunday Schools, some of the students and many of the teachers were far from falling under that classification.

Coöperative action in furthering the objectives of the Sunday Schools increased. In the nineteenth century several denominations instituted boards and committees on religious education. In 1910 they joined in organizing the Sunday School Council of Evangelical Denominations. Tension developed with the International Sunday School Association but was resolved when in 1922 the two bodies united to form the International School Council of Religious Education, later called the International Council of Religious Education. In 1950 that body became a constituent of the National Council of the Churches of Christ in the U.S.A. as the latter's Commission on Christian Education.[82]

Through what was known as "week-day released time" provision was made in many places for teaching religion to children in the public elementary schools. This could be Roman Catholic, Protestant, or Jewish, as the parents desired.

---

[80] *Ibid., 1920*, p. 201; *ibid., 1957*, p. 264.
[81] *Ibid., 1957*, p. 257.
[82] *National Council Outlook*, April, 1956, p. 21.

It could acquaint youth with the factual tenets of their hereditary faith, but that it would bring commitment of the will was highly doubtful. The record in Europe where in a number of countries instruction in religion was a part of the curriculum in state schools was not encouraging.

As before World War I, daily vacation Bible schools (also known as daily vacation Church Schools) were held in the summer recess for children enrolled in public schools. They were usually in church buildings.

Much attention was given to training directors of religious education and prospective pastors in the principles and methods of religious education. Chairs and departments with that objective were created in many theological seminaries. During the reaction from World War I and the economic depression which began in 1929 demand for such preparation fell off. But it mounted to new heights after World War II. Luther Allan Weigle (1880——) was long outstanding in the field. From 1916 to his retirement in 1949 he held a chair of religious education in Yale and there trained many of the leaders in the movement. For nearly a generation he was chairman of the executive committee of the World's Sunday School Association, later the World Council of Christian Education and Sunday School Association. Through that and other offices he had a major part in shaping the policies of the Sunday Schools and religious education.[83]

Countering De-Christianization: Conference Centres

Still another agency which was increasingly utilized to curb the de-Christianizing forces and to nourish youth in the Christian faith and strengthen the faith in the adult leadership was the conference centre. The use of conference centres by Protestants mounted rapidly. Some had been begun before 1914, notable among them being Chautauqua in New York State and Northfield in Massachusetts. They proliferated as the years passed. For the most part they were away from cities and in quiet suburban or rural settings. Some were kept busy throughout the year. Others were available only in summer. Many were maintained by individual congregations. Others were supported by independent associations. Still others were the property of state, regional, or national denominational organizations. Groups came to them for periods ranging from a few days to several weeks. Their programmes combined worship, study, and recreation. They had parallels in Europe but were many times more numerous than their counterparts east of the Atlantic. In their monasteries and other traditional institutions Roman Catholics had somewhat similar facilities. They were utilized as retreat centres for clergy and laity where under authorized and skilled direction the spiritual life could be nourished.

[83] *Who's Who in America*, Vol. XXXI, p. 3062.

COUNTERING DE-CHRISTIANIZATION: PRIVATE AND PUBLIC WORSHIP: THE BIBLE

Widely employed by Protestants for deepening and enriching the spiritual life were books and periodicals prepared for daily use and in such fashion that no more than a few minutes a day were required. They were very numerous; book sales sometimes ran into the thousands. Many religious journals had special columns to encourage and guide meditation. Several denominations had inexpensive publications containing a Scripture passage, a brief message, and a prayer for each day of the year. Of these the one most widely used was *The Upper Room,* produced by the Methodists, and with an annual issue in the 1950's of more than a million copies.

The circulation of the Bible continued to mount, to a large extent through the American Bible Society. That society, with its many auxiliary state and regional societies, sought to place a copy of the Bible in every home and to encourage the daily reading of the Bible and Bible reading courses. It put Bibles in hospitals and provided them for the armed forces, for migrants, and for foreign-language groups. It reported a circulation of 9,188,978 (more than 1,000,000 being New Testaments) in the United States in 1958.[84] The Gideons endeavoured to equip every hotel room with a Bible and to make the Scriptures available in other ways for travellers and school children. The Revised Standard Version, prepared by Protestants and to be further noted in a moment, by mid-year 1955 had sold over 4,000,000 copies. The emphasis of the Roman Catholic Church on Bible reading and study was seen, among other ways, in the publication by the St. Anthony Guild Press for the Confraternity of Christian Doctrine translations of the Bible prepared under the auspices of the episcopal committee of the Confraternity. The New Testament was issued in 1941, and in its revised and definitive edition in 1947. Beginning in 1948 sections of the Old Testament appeared.[85] Among Roman Catholics non-liturgical devotions continued and spread, including the Forty Hours, the Novena of Our Lady of the Miraculous Medal, and the popularity of favourite saints such as St. Thérèse of Lisieux.[86]

Books of devotion and on prayer not designed for daily use abounded, written by Protestants and Roman Catholics. Merely to name them would require many pages.[87] A list of the best-selling books on religion, the majority of post-

[84] *One Hundred and Forty-Third Annual Report of the American Bible Society* (New York, The American Bible Society, 1959), pp. 62–142.

[85] *Yearbook of American Churches, 1957,* pp. 286, 287.

[86] Ellis, *American Catholicism,* p. 136.

[87] Picked almost at random from the voluminous Protestant literature produced after 1914 are George Arthur Buttrick, *Prayer* (New York, Abingdon-Cokesbury Press, 1942, pp. 333); John L. Castell, *Rediscovering Prayer* (New York, Association Press, 1955, pp. xiii, 242); and Thomas R. Kelly, *A Testament of Devotion* (New York, Harper & Brothers, 1941, pp. iii, 123). Among the Roman Catholics, chosen also almost at random, is Thomas Merton, *Seeds of Contemplation* (Norfolk, Conn., New Directions Books, 1949, pp. xvi, 191).

1914 publication, showed that most of those meeting a popular demand were by Protestants and had chiefly to do with prayer and faith as the way to overcome futility and to attain physical and mental health and wholeness and richness of life.[88]

Public worship was also a means of off-setting trends towards de-Christianization and of strengthening Christian faith and life. Here, too, the movements were multiform. Particularly in Protestantism some tended towards informality and spontaneity and flourished especially in groups frequented by men and women of lower economic and educational levels. As we have suggested, in Protestant congregations of middle and higher incomes and education, the trend was towards formality and liturgy. In some Lutheran churches a liturgical movement was seen, with a fellowship to renew sacramental life, societies to promote the liturgy, and specialized periodicals.[89] In the Roman Catholic Church the Liturgical Movement, which was making marked strides in parts of Europe, by the year 1961 was beginning to be felt. The main centre from which it radiated (beginning in 1925–1926) was the Benedictine St. John's Abbey at Collegeville, Minnesota. It published the periodical *Orate Fratres*. Other Benedictine houses furthered the movement. A Benedictine of St. John's Abbey, Virgil Michel (1890–1938), was outstanding as a pioneer. He began *Orate Fratres* and was zealous in putting the ritual for some of the sacraments into English. In 1940 Benedictines sponsored the first Liturgical Week in the United States. Here and there churches were being erected which architecturally embodied some of the ideals of the Liturgical Movement. The Confraternity of the Precious Blood, with headquarters in Brooklyn, both promoted the reading of the Bible and supported the *Leaflet Missal*, which contained the masses for the entire Church year. The Liturgical Arts Society was founded. Liturgical retreats were offered the clergy, religious communities, seminarians, and lay groups. In 1916 a school for liturgical music was begun in New York.[90]

Related to worship was an attitude widespread among Protestants, especially of non-liturgical traditions, which had a striking similarity, at first sight not apparent, to the Roman Catholic devotion to the Sacred Heart of Jesus. Many Protestants, largely those with little theological training, centred their loyalty on Jesus. Some observers, indeed, declared that they were Unitarians, in prac-

[88] Louis Schneider and Sanford M. Dornbusch, *Popular Religion. Inspirational Books in America* (University of Chicago Press, 1958, pp. xi, 174), *passim.*

[89] Berthold von Schenk, *Liturgie und Lebendige Gemeinde. Ein Bericht aus der liturgischen Bewegung des amerikanischen Luthertums* (Cassel, Johannes Stauda-Verlag, 1951, pp. 40), *passim.*

[90] Ernest Benjamin Koenker, *The Liturgical Renaissance in the Roman Catholic Church* (University of Chicago Press, 1954, pp. xi, 271), pp. 17, 18, 174, 175; Bögler, *Liturgische Erneurerung in aller Welt,* pp. 104–114; Barry, *Worship and Work,* pp. 264–280; Paul B. Marx, *Virgil Michel and the Liturgical Movement* (Collegeville, Minn., The Liturgical Press, 1957, pp. 466), *passim;* Ellis, *op. cit.,* pp. 134, 135; Gerald Ellard, *Men at Work and Worship. America Joins the Liturgical Movement* (New York, Longmans, Green and Co., 1940, pp. xvii, 307), *passim.*

tice identifying God with the Second Person of the Trinity rather than, as with those who were generally called Unitarians, with the First Person of the Trinity. While in theory Trinitarians, actually in their prayers and hymns they so dwelt on Jesus that they all but ignored God the Father and God the Holy Spirit. Although they would have hotly repudiated the charge of Unitarianism and while they and the Roman Catholics were presumably not aware of the parallel, between the two strains of piety a marked likeness existed.

COUNTERING DE-CHRISTIANIZATION: THE STRUGGLE FOR THE CITY

As in Europe, the tides making for de-Christianization ran strong in the cities and in the centres of mining and industry. How well did Christianity meet the challenge? The challenge to the Roman Catholic Church was particularly acute. That church owed its strength primarily to the immigration of the nineteenth and twentieth centuries. The immigrants were drawn chiefly from the poverty-stricken of the Old World and in the New World at the outset found most of their employment as unskilled labour in factories and mines. In the twentieth century their descendants began to share in the mounting prosperity of the country. Even then the Roman Catholic population, as we have seen, was predominantly urban and lived mainly in the inner city areas. The older American stock, prevailingly Protestant by tradition, earlier profited by the rising wealth and, except for the Negroes, tended to move from the hearts of the cities to the suburbs. Protestantism continued to seek to serve the metropolitan areas, both in the centres and in the suburbs, but it was in suburbia that it chiefly flourished, and its strongholds were there, in the small towns, and in the rural districts. It could not, however, escape the challenge. Moreover, in the post-1914 decades as the South became industrialized, much of the labour for the new factories came from the historically Protestant underprivileged white elements of the region.

The question arose as to whether the size of the congregation made possible adequate pastoral care by the clergy. We have seen that in the state churches and former state churches of Europe the parishes were territorial divisions, and in several lands (notably in the cities) the numbers of clergy were quite insufficient to do more than administer the sacraments and preach. They were too few to give much pastoral care. In the United States some denominations, chiefly but not entirely the Roman Catholic Church, organized their constituencies by territorial parishes. In general in Roman Catholic congregations the membership was larger than in Protestant congregations. It was highest in the cities, averaging 3,497 in cities of more than one million population.[91]

---

[91] *Information Service*, March 28, 1959. In Holyoke, Mass., in the 1940's Roman Catholic churches averaged 3,387 and Protestant churches 388 members.—Underwood, *Protestant and Catholic*, p. 46.

Whether staffs were provided in the larger congregations sufficient to deal with the constituency was not clear. Some Protestant congregations were very large, especially in Southern cities, but nowhere was the average as high as that of the Roman Catholics. One Roman Catholic authority in speaking of the losses of his church in the cities said that to no small extent they were due to the impersonal character of the parish and the impossibility of having the limited number of clergy maintain close contact with those who were disposed to neglect their religious duties.[92]

The size of the Roman Catholic urban parish clearly made for a lack of a close community centring in the church. For example, a study of three such parishes in the 1950's disclosed that only 5.7 per cent. received Communion once a week or oftener and belonged to a parish organization. Of that minority the proportion was highest in the age group from ten to nineteen years inclusive, fell sharply for those in their twenties, and rose slowly thereafter. About three-fourths of that minority had had some high school, college, or postgraduate training. In general, the longer a family had been in the city the less likely it was to be in that minority.[93] About two-thirds of the members of an urban parish were described as attending Sunday mass most of the time, as generally observing the Friday abstinence, and as sending their children to the parochial school. Yet while respecting the priests and the nuns they kept aloof from them. They tended to form their social connexions outside the parish, with members of their occupational groups regardless of religious affiliations—business and professional, and skilled and semi-skilled manual labourers.[94] Perhaps a fourth attended mass very irregularly and sent their children to the public rather than the parochial schools. An indeterminate proportion of the parish could be described as "fallen away." They had been baptized, brought their children for baptism, had not joined another denomination, but had ceased to be faithful to their religious duties. Various studies showed that in the 1950's from 34 to 80 per cent. of the Roman Catholics attended mass regularly, that from 18 to 20 per cent. were irregular in attendance, and that from 18 to 48 per cent. never came.[95] These figures, it must be understood, have to do only with those on parish rolls. Presumably many of Roman Catholic heritage had drifted so far from the religion of their fathers that they had been lost sight of by their church. As we shall see in a moment, the degree of the urban leakage from the Roman Catholic Church differed with the national backgrounds of the constituency.

[92] Ellis, *op. cit.*, p. 126. But although in 1950 Chicago had an average of only one priest to every 2,000 Roman Catholics the proportion had fairly steadily improved since 1880 and particularly since 1910.—Houtart, *Aspects Sociologiques du Catholicisme Américain*, pp. 157–159.

[93] Fichter, *Social Relations in the Urban Parish*, pp. 23–29. See more favourable figures in Houtart, *op. cit.*, pp. 95–102.

[94] Fichter, *op. cit.*, pp. 40–55.

[95] Joseph B. Schuyler, *Northern Parish. A Sociological and Pastoral Study* (Chicago, Loyola University Press, 1960, pp. xxi, 360), p. 203. See also Fichter, *op. cit.*, pp. 68–70.

In general, in the cities and especially in the inner cities, Protestantism appeared to be less able to win or to hold to an active church connexion those historically of its constituency than was the Roman Catholic Church. Yet both lost a large proportion of the population who might have been expected to affiliate with some church.[96] The fluidity of population with the frequent changes in residence made for losses. They were striking among the Protestants, where in one city 10 per cent. of the losses of membership during the twenty years 1899–1919 in three major denominations were due to death, 49 per cent. to transfers to other congregations, and 41 per cent. to the vague "unaccounted for."[97]

The trend was for Protestant churches to abandon the inner city and to build in the outskirts to accompany their membership as the latter moved to the suburbs. In contrast, the Roman Catholic Church both retained its structures in the inner city and erected new ones in the suburbs to care for its members as the latter gained in prosperity and changed their residences to more desirable areas. The comprehensive framework of the Roman Catholic Church with its parish system as contrasted with the weaker coöperation among Protestants made for the difference.[98] Many of the inner city Protestant churches, after struggling for years, died, but some, mostly of the standard denominations, survived and even grew.[99] In the South, where many Protestants of low income and education came from rural districts to the cities to work in the factories which multiplied after World War I, fellowship and religious sustenance were found in "store-front" and other churches of humble physical arrangements, where the services were inclined to be highly emotional and a strong Biblicism prevailed.[100]

Countering De-Christianization: Winning and Holding the Immigrant

Although beginning with World War I the immigrant tide subsided, it did not completely dry up. During the war immigration almost ceased, but after the war it again became important. To what extent were the immigrants and

[96] As in H. Paul Douglass, *The Springfield Church Survey. A Study of Organized Religion with Its Social Background* (New York, George H. Doran Co., 1926, pp. 445), pp. 121, 122.

[97] H. Paul Douglass, *The St. Louis Church Survey. A Religious Investigation with a Social Background* (New York, George H. Doran Co., 1924, pp. 327), p. 218.

[98] Samuel C. Kincheloe, *The American City and Its Church* (New York, Friendship Press, 1938, pp. xiv, 177), pp. 92–113. See also Wilbur C. Hallenbeck, *Urban Organization of Protestantism,* (New York, Harper & Brothers, 1934, pp. xii, 285), *passim.*

[99] H. Paul Douglass, *The City's Church* (New York, Friendship Press, 1929, pp. xi, 244), pp. 126–158.

[100] The same was true in a predominantly Protestant city in the Middle West, into which labourers had come from rural sections in the South.—Robert S. Lynd and Helen Merrell Lynd, *Middletown in Transition. A Study in Cultural Conflicts* (New York, Harcourt, Brace and Co., 1937, pp. xviii, 606), pp. 294–318.

their children held to the allegiance which had been theirs by heredity and social convention in their former homes?

Some generalizations seemed valid. As in the nineteenth century immigrants found in the churches they had known in the Old World institutions where they could meet fellow countrymen and could hear and use their ancestral language. They formed what were essentially ghetto communities. This was particularly true of the Roman Catholics, chiefly settled as they were in the cities and in an environment predominantly Protestant and secular. Progressively, especially in the second and third generations, English replaced the Old Country languages in sermons and, except in Roman Catholic congregations where the liturgy was in Latin, in the public services. As assimilation increased, intermarriages across ethnic and denominational lines mounted. The proportionately larger movement from the Roman Catholic Church to Protestantism than from Protestantism to the Roman Catholic Church which we have noted, and which seems to have grown as the years passed, was in some degree a phase of the assimilation to a culture historically Protestant. That on the whole the churches more and more succeeded in winning and holding the formal allegiance of the immigrants is evident from the rising percentage of the population enrolled in them.

These generalizations hold if the record was viewed in a comprehensive fashion. However, in detail much variety was seen. As might have been expected from the many national backgrounds of its hereditary constituency, the picture in the Roman Catholic Church was far from uniform. Some immigrants and their children were more loyal than others. In general, Italians were less loyal than the Irish. That did not mean that the Italians became Protestants: relatively few did. Instead they became secularized, perhaps because of the progress of secularization in Italy, in contrast with the ardent adherence of the Irish to the Roman Catholic Church in the Emerald Isle as a tie and a symbol of nationalism against the English. For instance, in New Jersey and Connecticut the Italian farmers were said to be too engrossed in making a living to interest themselves in religion.[101] In 1939 one estimate suggested that of six million Italian-Americans, two million were fervent Catholics, one million had abandoned the practice of their religion, and three million were doubtful. They were mostly from South Italy, were seldom accompanied by their clergy, and in their mother land did not have the tradition of building and supporting churches on their own initiative.[102]

Although in 1954, 265,879 Poles were enrolled in the Polish National Catholic Church, which had broken from the Roman Catholic Church in the nineteenth century,[103] the majority of the Poles were said to have held to the Roman

[101] Brunner, *Immigrant Farmers and Their Children*, p. 120.
[102] Thomas, *The American Catholic Family*, p. 110.
[103] *Yearbook of American Churches, 1957*, p. 256.

Catholic Church, in spite of the fact that they had moved from a closely knit peasant economy to a highly industrialized urban environment. They maintained not only parishes and parochial schools but also literary, dramatic, singing, social, athletic, and religious organizations and a Polish press.[104] As with the Irish, the Old Country background appears to have made strongly for their loyalty, for in Europe for generations the Poles had been subject to alien rulers and their church had been a centre of community life not controlled by foreign overlords.

One estimate held that from half to two-thirds of the Czechs were fervent Roman Catholics,[105] but that many were indifferent. In one locality a leading citizen declared that his fellow Czechs, while not agnostic, were indifferent religiously and ascribed the attitude to the memory of Hus and others who had been persecuted by the Roman Catholic Church.[106]

The Slovaks were reported to be loyal to the Roman Catholic Church and to have vigorous religious, social, cultural, and athletic associations.[107] They, like others who in Europe were politically subject peoples and who were moved by the ardent nationalism characteristic of the revolutionary age, found in these associations and in the Roman Catholic Church an expression of their group consciousness. In addition to the Irish, the Poles, the Czechs, and the Slovaks, this was reported to be true as well of the Slovenes, the Croatians, and the Lithuanians, although the last named were declared to be very quickly assimilated. The Magyars, from the dominant ethnic element in Hungary, appeared to have few national associations and, while numbers of parishes which embraced them were found, they were rapidly absorbed into the American cultural environment.[108]

French Canadians, predominantly Roman Catholic, came by the hundreds of thousands to the United States. In the 1930's they and their descendants were estimated to number between 2.5 and 3 million. They tended to resist assimilation and long preserved a distinctive group life centring about their churches, parochial schools, and newspapers, in which French was the language. The loss of the French language was asserted to be followed by a loss of faith.[109]

In the 1950's Mexicans were estimated at 3.5 million. The majority were poverty-stricken, many were "wetbacks" who had crossed the border illegally, thousands were contract labourers, and a very large proportion moved frequently in search of employment. Discriminated against, although not as much as were the Negroes, for the most part they had little or no education and felt insecure. Nominally Roman Catholic, except for a relative few they were not

104 Thomas, *op. cit.*, pp. 109, 110; Brunner, *op. cit.*, pp. 119, 219, 220.
105 Thomas, *op. cit.*, p. 111.
106 Brunner, *op. cit.*, p. 119.
107 Thomas, *op. cit.*, p. 111.
108 *Ibid.*, pp. 111, 112, 117.
109 *Ibid.*, pp. 122, 123.

zealous in practising their faith and yet were not quickly assimilated into the Protestantism which was dominant in the region where most of them settled —the South-west.[110]

Puerto Rico had been annexed by the United States as a result of the Spanish-American War (1898), but not until the 1940's did Puerto Ricans begin coming to the mainland in large numbers. By the mid-1950's they numbered about a half-million, of whom approximately four-fifths were in New York City. They were on the lowest rung of the economic ladder. Most of them were Roman Catholics, but their adherence to that branch of the faith was more nominal than deep-seated. Puerto Rico had on the average only one priest to every 5,800 of the population.[111] To care for the Puerto Ricans priests with a knowledge of Spanish were appointed, but the effort was made to integrate the new arrivals into existing parishes rather than to form them into distinct Spanish-speaking churches.[112]

Uniates, largely but not entirely from the Ukraine, multiplied. By the end of 1954 about ten varieties of the Eastern rites were represented. In 1913 the Ukrainian Greek Catholic Diocese (the Byzantine Slavonic Exarchy of Philadelphia) was erected and in 1924 the Greek Rite Diocese of Pittsburgh (the Byzantine Catholic Exarchy of Pittsburgh) was created. In the mid-1950's the former had 123 parishes, 193 priests, 145 women religious, one seminary, and 219,720 adherents, with 5,092 students in elementary parochial schools and a total of 10,116 youths under confessional instruction. The latter had 185 parishes, one mission, six stations, 296 priests, 169 women religious, one seminary with 62 students, with 13,526 youths under Catholic instruction, and 139,178 faithful. Obviously the Pittsburgh exarchy had a higher proportion of clergy and women religious and of youths receiving instruction than the Philadelphia exarchy. In 1956 the latter was divided and the Exarchate of Stamford, Connecticut, was created, with jurisdiction in New York and New England.[113] The Uniates of the Hungarian Byzantine Rite (in the 1950's about 20,000) and of the Croatian Byzantine Rite (in the 1950's about 3,000) were under the Pittsburgh exarchy. In the mid-1950's the Maronites numbered about 125,000, with 47 parishes and 49 priests; the Melkites about 50,000, with 26 parishes, 30 priests, and one seminary; the Rumanians about 5,500, with 18 parishes and 16 priests; the Chaldeans about 1,000, with 2 parishes and 2 priests; the Italo-Greeks about 10,000; the Armenians about 2,500, with 6 parishes and 8 priests supervised by a patriarchal vicar subject to the local bishops; the Russians about 1,000, with 10 priests and

---

[110] *Ibid.*, p. 123; Burma, *Spanish-Speaking Groups in the United States*, pp. 81–84.

[111] Thomas, *op. cit.*, pp. 123, 124; Burma, *op. cit.*, pp. 172, 173; *The New York Times*, March 23, 1959.

[112] Ellis, *American Catholicism*, p. 128; Elena Padilla, *Up from Puerto Rico* (New York, Columbia University Press, 1958, pp. xiii, 317), pp. 272–274.

[113] Ellis, *op. cit.*, p. 128; *The 1958 National Catholic Almanac*, p. 271.

3 quasi-parishes; and the Syrians about 5,000.[114] Most of the Uniates had come either late in the nineteenth or in the twentieth century.

As time passed and the second and third generations of American-born Roman Catholics became more numerous, the distinctive characteristics of their forefathers faded and more uniformity was seen with increasing assimilation to the surrounding environment. One reason was the desire for social acceptance. The former variety in American parishes—the sentimental Spanish attachment to the faith, the Puritanism of the Roman Catholicism of Ireland, the "relaxed and affectionate Catholicism of Italy, the reasonable and sophisticated Catholicism of France," and the spirit peculiar to the faithful in Hungary and Poland—tended to disappear as the generations of American-born came on and were served by American-born clergy.[115]

Significantly, by the mid-1950's the overwhelming majority of the episcopate had been born in the United States and had received their education in Roman Catholic institutions in that country. A few had had part of their education in Europe, mostly in Rome and several in Louvain, but nearly all were products of the American Church. This was additional evidence that the Roman Catholic Church was firmly rooted in the United States and that, while a loyal part of the world-wide Roman communion, it was taking on a distinctive character. In the main it was activistic and was conservative in theology and ritual. Of the foreign-born episcopate the large majority were natives of Ireland. Fully a third of the archbishops, bishops, and auxiliary bishops were of Irish descent and at least a fifth were of German ancestry. Together the Irish and the German stocks provided about two-thirds of the hierarchy,[116] as was to be expected. From Ireland and Germany had come the overwhelming majority of the immigration in the fore part of the nineteenth century, with the Irish leading. The later immigration was beginning to be a source of the hierarchy, but the leadership of the Roman Catholic Church in the United States was still predominantly of Irish and German provenance.

With the gradual erasure of Old Country differences and the indigenization of the hierarchy through birth and education, a growing tendency was seen among Roman Catholics to accept the status of their church as one among many in a religiously pluralistic society. The spokesmen for the trend did not abate the claims of the Roman Catholic Church to be the true body of Christ, but they were disposed to suggest that their church could live in peace with other churches and not aspire to a position in which it could enforce conformity. Two outstanding representatives of this attitude were the Jesuits John Courtney Murray (1904——) and Gustave Weigel (1906——). Their views did

---

[114] *The 1958 National Catholic Almanac*, pp. 271, 272.
[115] Sugrue, *A Catholic Speaks His Mind*, p. 42.
[116] *The 1958 National Catholic Almanac*, pp. 395–417.

not win universal assent among Roman Catholics.[117]

A striking alteration in the religious affiliation of the twentieth-century immigration was the rapidly mounting numerical strength of the Eastern Churches. In 1919 the two largest, the Greek Orthodox and the Russian Orthodox, were reported to have 119,871 and 99,681 members respectively.[118] In 1955 the Greek Archdiocese of North and South America reported 353 churches and a membership of 1,000,000, and the Russian Orthodox Greek Catholic Church of America gave its totals as 350 churches and 750,000 members. Obviously these figures, in round numbers as they were, must have been at best only approximate; if they and the roster of churches approach accuracy the pastoral care of the faithful must have left much to be desired, for the average membership of the parishes was between 2,000 and 3,000.[119] An Orthodox estimate of 1954 declared that the faithful in the United States totalled 6,000,000.[120] Much of the increase was through refugees from the wars, the transfers of territory, and the Communist rule in historic centres of Orthodoxy.

The Orthodox were badly fragmented, partly by national origins and partly for other reasons. In the 1950's the largest group was the Greek Orthodox Church. It, too, was divided. A small minority, with one bishop and an assistant bishop, held to the old calendar and were not in communion with the majority. Another minority were subject to the Patriarch of Alexandria. In 1947 that ecclesiastic appointed an exarch with jurisdiction over several parishes. The large majority were dependent on the Ecumenical Patriarch of Constantinople, who, indeed, in the 1950's and 1960's had been archbishop of the majority wing of the American Church. In 1952 that branch had an archbishop and five bishops. Between the two world wars numbers of former Ukrainian Uniates joined it. It supported the Holy Cross Seminary in Brookline, Massachusetts, for the preparation of its clergy and in 1951 established a chair of Orthodox theology in the Episcopal Theological Seminary in Cambridge, Massachusetts.[121]

In the 1950's the Russian Orthodox were also in three groups. The large majority desired to be autocephalous, entirely independent of the Moscow Patriarchate. They possessed a seminary in St. Tikhon's Monastery in Pennsylvania for the preparation of clergy and St. Vladimir's Orthodox Academy in New York City. They were called the "Metropolitan" jurisdiction. A much smaller group, called the "Exarchate" or "Patriarchal" jurisdiction, was loyal to the Patriarch of Moscow. In 1951 it had an archbishop and two bishops and retained the old Russian cathedral in New York City, but it possessed no monastery or seminary. The third group, in 1950 with an archbishop, seven bishops,

[117] Herberg, *Protestant-Catholic-Jew*, pp. 165–167.
[118] *Yearbook of the Churches, 1920*, pp. 199, 201.
[119] *Yearbook of American Churches, 1957*, p. 253.
[120] *New Missionary Review*, Spring, 1955.
[121] *Ibid.*, Spring, 1952.

and about sixty priests and thirty-two congregations, not only rejected the restored Moscow Patriarchate but also, consisting as it did largely of refugees from the U.S.S.R., instead of desiring to be autocephalous held to the Russian Orthodox in exile in Europe and stood for the restoration of the tsarist regime in Russia. In 1927 it founded Holy Trinity Monastery in Jordanville, New York, and eventually had another monastic house. It also initiated a mission to propagate Orthodoxy among native Americans.[122]

In 1955 sixteen other Eastern Churches were reported to be represented in the United States. Of them the Nestorians, known as the Church of the East or of the Assyrians, had less than 5,000 members. That church was sadly shrunken from its dimensions in Asia a thousand years earlier and even at the dawn of the nineteenth century. Its head found refuge in the United States from the massacres which during World War I had exterminated many of his followers. The American-Carpatho-Russian Orthodox Church, the Armenian Apostolic Church of America, the Syrian Antiochian Orthodox Church, the Ukrainian Orthodox Church of America, the Rumanian Orthodox Episcopate, the Ukrainian Orthodox Church of the U.S.A., and the Serbian Orthodox Church of America each counted between 50,000 and 150,000 members.[123]

The Serbian Orthodox Church grew from a single congregation in 1894 to about 150,000 members in 1958 scattered in eighteen states and Canada. Its head was appointed from Belgrade by the Patriarch and Holy Synod of the mother church. He had his headquarters at St. Sava's Monastery in Libertyville, Illinois, his cathedral was in New York City, and at times he lived in Chicago. His church aided in bringing thousands of refugees from Jugoslavia to the United States and Canada. It had a seminary for training priests in connexion with St. Sava's Monastery.[124]

As did several other of the Eastern Churches in the United States, in their divisions the Rumanian Orthodox reflected conditions in their mother land. In 1945 they were about as numerous as the Serbian Orthodox. In 1939 their bishop returned to Rumania and was not permitted by the authorities there to resume his duties in America but was replaced by a fresh appointee of the Rumanian Patriarch. The majority of the Rumanian Orthodox in the United States refused to accept the new man. They asserted that he was a Communist agent and elected a refugee as acting bishop. However, a minority stood by the Patriarch.[125]

Much the same was true of the Ukrainian Orthodox. Some adhered to the Ukrainian autocephalous church which had been set up in the Ukraine following the Communist revolution.[126] In an attempt to heal the breach the majority

122 *Ibid., Information Service*, December 24, 1955; *Ecumenical Press Service*, June 17, 1960.
123 *Yearbook of American Churches, 1957*, p. 253.
124 *National Council Outlook*, Vol. VIII, No. 3, pp. 8, 9, 22 (March, 1958); *New Missionary Review*, Spring, 1952, p. 9.
125 *New Missionary Review*, Spring, 1952, pp. 9, 10.
126 Volume IV, Chapter XIX.

of the faithful organized themselves into an independent church in communion with the Ecumenical Patriarch, but a minority dissented.[127]

As was to be expected, in varying degrees the Eastern Churches progressively reflected the influence of the American environment. Several introduced Sunday Schools for the religious instruction of their youth. Summer camps were inaugurated. Pews placed in some of the churches permitted sitting during the services, in contrast with the custom of standing which had prevailed in the Old World. In at least one instance the congregation through its officers controlled the parish, to the distress of the priest—a condition reminiscent of the earlier struggle in the Roman Catholic Church with lay trusteeism. As the second and third generations came on, English was increasingly used. By 1958 the Serbian, Greek, and Syrian Antiochian bodies and branches of the Russian, Rumanian, and Ukrainian Orthodox had become members of the predominantly Protestant National Council of Churches.[128] In March, 1960, a meeting was held in New York City of the archbishops, bishops, and metropolitans of eleven Orthodox churches in the Americas as a preliminary to establishing a standing conference of the Orthodox hierarchy in the Western Hemisphere.[129]

More and more of the Orthodox, especially of the American-born, wished to rise above the divisions inherited from the Old World and to create an American Orthodox Church which would bear a united witness to what they believed to be the true faith. Although founded by Russian Orthodox, and only as recently as 1938, St. Vladimir's Orthodox Theological Seminary in 1948 was raised to the status of an academy, the only graduate school of Orthodox theology in the country. In 1958 it had in its student body members of nine different national traditions. With the friendly coöperation of Union Theological Seminary and Columbia University and staffed by a faculty some of whom were trained in Europe and a few of whom had been connected with St. Sergius' Academy in Paris, it quickly acquired high academic status.[130] In 1956 the first Pan-Orthodox conference on religious education in the United States was convened with the assistance of the National Council of Churches.[131]

The Lutheran churches, which owed their numerical strength largely but not entirely to the immigration of the nineteenth and twentieth centuries, had a phenomenal growth in the four decades after 1914. Between 1919 and 1955 they nearly trebled in membership and in the latter year reported about 7,200,000 members. In the same span of time the Roman Catholics, also profiting by immigration, slightly less than doubled.[132] How much the increase was to be

[127] *New Missionary Review,* Spring, 1952, p. 10.
[128] *Ibid., Spring,* 1956; *ibid.,* Fall, 1959; *National Council Outlook,* Vol. VIII, No. 3, pp. 8, 9, 22 March, 1958).
[129] *The New York Times* March 16, 1960; *Ecumenical Press Service,* June 24, 1960; *St. Vladimir's Seminary Quarterly,* March 15, 1960, p. 47.
[130] *St. Vladimir's Seminary Quarterly,* Summer, 1958, pp. 2–10.
[131] *Ibid.,* January, 1957, p. 33.
[132] *Yearbook of the Churches, 1920,* pp. 199, 201; *ibid., 1957,* pp. 254–256. For an extensive

ascribed to immigration, how much to conversions, and how much to the excess of births over deaths could not be accurately determined. The national sources of the large majority were Germany and Scandinavia.

As time passed, like the other denominations which were recruited chiefly from diverse national backgrounds, the Lutheran churches began to show the unifying effect of the environment. English more and more became the language of the services, for the American-born members were decreasingly familiar with their forefathers' tongues. After several years of committee labour, in 1917 the *Common Service Book* was issued, in English, and was adopted by the United Lutheran Church, a body which came into being in 1918 and brought together the General Synod, the United Synod of the South, and the General Council. Significantly, the United Lutheran Church represented the elements which had been longest in the country and were most in need of such a book.[133] With it went a hymnal, also in English and drawing from many sources, non-Lutheran as well as Lutheran. In time the *Common Service Book* with its hymnal spread to other Lutheran bodies and became a tie which helped bind together most of the Lutherans of North America. The United Lutheran Church was still, in 1962, the largest of the Lutheran bodies in the United States, but other unions were achieved which were efforts towards an all-embracing Lutheran witness. In 1917 the three larger bodies of Norwegian Lutherans merged to form the Norwegian Lutheran Church of America, embracing 92 per cent. of the Lutherans of Norwegian ancestry in the country. As English replaced Norwegian in the services and many who were not of Norwegian descent became members, the name was changed (1946) to the Evangelical Lutheran Church.[134] In 1919 the Evangelical Lutheran Joint Synod of Wisconsin and Other States was formed by the union of the Wisconsin Synod, the Michigan Synod, and the Minnesota Synod. The three bodies had in common a German background, at the outset used the German language, and represented a strong Lutheran confessionalism, in part a reflection of the strict Lutheran reaction against the union of Lutherans and Reformed in Germany.[135] After long preparation and many preliminary negotiations, in 1930 the American Lutheran Church came into being through the union of the Joint Synod of Ohio, the Iowa Synod, and the Buffalo Synod.[136] A more inclusive

---

survey of the literature of Lutheranism in the United States, much of it post-1914, see Herbert H. Schmidt in *Religion in Life*, Vol. XXVII, pp. 583–603 (Autumn, 1958).

[133] Luther D. Reed, *The Lutheran Liturgy. A Study of the Common Service of the Lutheran Church in America* (Philadelphia, Muhlenberg Press, 1947, pp. xx, 692), pp. 180–216; *Common Service Book of the Lutheran Church* (Philadelphia, Board of Publication of the United Lutheran Church in America, 1917, pp. 631), *passim*.

[134] Nelson, *The Lutheran Church among Norwegian-Americans*, Vol. II, pp. 183 ff.; Wentz, *A Basic History of Lutheranism in America*, pp. 259 ff.

[135] Wentz, *op. cit.*, pp. 272–278.

[136] *Ibid.*, pp. 297–301; Fred W. Meuser, *The Formation of the American Lutheran Church. A Case Study in Lutheran Unity* (Columbus, Ohio, Wartburg Press, 1958, pp. xiv, 327), *passim*.

merger was accomplished in 1960 by the coming together of the Evangelical Lutheran Church, the American Lutheran Church, and the United Evangelical Lutheran Church (formerly the United Danish Lutheran Church), as The American Lutheran Church—the definite article "The" being the difference in name from the American Lutheran Church.[137]

A further stage in bringing together the Lutherans of the United States and thus shaking off the Old World national divisions and presenting a united approach to the problems of the United States and of the world at large was the formation of the National Lutheran Council. In 1917, out of the same challenge which led to the formation of the National Catholic War Council in that year, at the instance of laymen the National Lutheran Commission was organized to minister to Lutherans in the armed services. In it thirteen Lutheran bodies coöperated. The members of the Synodical Conference did not join. However, the Synodical Conference coördinated its efforts with those of the Commission. Much as the National Catholic War Council led to the National Catholic Welfare Conference, the National Lutheran Commission was followed (1918) by the creation of the National Lutheran Council. Eventually it enlisted about two-thirds of the Lutherans of the United States and Canada. Only the members of the Synodical Conference did not coöperate through it. In the course of the years its functions were enlarged. It endeavoured, with increasing success, to prevent the overlapping of the efforts of its members in home missions, aided in European relief and reconstruction, assisted refugees, saw that chaplains were recruited for the armed forces, assisted foreign missions, and represented American Lutherans in the Lutheran World Federation. The post-World War I relief given through the National Lutheran Council was a major factor in the creation of the world body. The National Lutheran Council also stimulated the formation of other general Lutheran organizations. From 1930 to 1954 what was called the American Lutheran Conference drew together some of the bodies in the upper valley of the Mississippi, but in view of what the National Lutheran Council had accomplished, it appeared to have no reason for continuing and was dissolved.[138]

In a variety of other ways American Lutheranism began to conform to the patterns of the Protestantism of the older American stock. These were seen in organizations for home and foreign missions; in the introduction of woman's suffrage in some synods; in a reaction against American forms of worship which contributed to *The Common Service;* in the passing of religious festivals appropriate only to European history; in the use of the Sunday School for religious instruction; in the acquiescence of some synods in the membership of their communicants in the secret societies which abounded in the United States; in

[137] *The Christian Century*, Vol. LXXVII, p. 534 (May 4, 1960).
[138] Wentz, *op. cit.*, pp. 302–315, 338–344.

the creation of denominational colleges and their adoption of the standards of non-Lutheran accrediting agencies; and in the support of the churches by voluntary contributions and the American-devised methods of raising and administering them.[139]

In seeking to summarize the efforts to hold the post-1914 immigration to their historic faith we have confined ourselves to the Roman Catholic, the Eastern, and the Lutheran Churches. We have said nothing of the majority of the Protestant denominations. That is not because they ignored the problem, but because it did not have so large a place in the challenges which confronted them or so influenced their development. They sought to reach and win the immigrants, both the nominally Christian and the non-Christian Asiatics, but in our necessarily condensed account we must not do more than call attention to the fact that they were active in serving the new Americans.

Countering De-Christianization: Seeking to Win and Hold Industrial Labour

Closely related to the challenge of the city and of immigration was that presented by labourers in the rapidly growing manufacturing plants. As we have repeatedly seen, the problem was acute in Europe and, with some exceptions, had not been solved. It could not fail to be a concern of thoughtful Christians in the United States. Statistics gathered in 1945–1946 appeared to show that of the church members about 19 per cent. were in business or the professions, about 20 per cent. were white-collar workers, approximately 17 per cent. were farmers, and 44 per cent. were urban manual workers. Although they indicated that nearly half the membership fell in the last class, they did not show to what extent these people were being served and held.

Before World War I, efforts were being made to reach members of the urban working class and they increased as the century wore on. The Roman Catholic Church employed its normal parish methods. Since, because of the type of immigrants among whom it had its strength, it was well supplied with churches and clergy in the inner city areas, it had an advantage over Protestantism. Except in the South, for the most part the Protestant constituency in the cities was in the employing, business, professional, and white-collar classes. Here and there Protestants made an effort to solve the problem, partly through the Federal Council of Churches and its successor, the National Council of Churches; but at best these organizations could only call attention to the situation and be a clearing house for information. By 1960, nine factory chaplains had been employed by companies, practically all of them in the South. In 1956, twenty-

[139] Paul W. Spaude, *The Lutheran Church under American Influence. A Historico-philosophical Interpretation of the Church in Its Relation to Various Modifying Forces in the United States* (Burlington, Iowa, The Lutheran Literary Board, 1943, pp. xvi, 435), pp. 45 *f*.

five industrial chaplains were listed, of whom six were no longer active. Here and there a pastor gave part of his time to the factories, and laymen initiated services in them. In 1945 the Presbyterian Church in the U.S.A. began a programme in Chicago to acquaint ministers through intensive seminars with the problems of the industrial worker. Five years later it inaugurated the Ministers-in-Industry plan, through which theological students were employed in some industry during their summer vacations and discussed pertinent subjects in seminars. In the 1950's several other denominations adopted similar programmes, usually confined to particular areas.[140]

COUNTERING DE-CHRISTIANIZATION: THE NEGROES

Earlier we have summarized progress in winning the Negroes to Christianity.[141] We noted that while conversion had begun before emancipation, in the half-century which followed, proportionately to their numbers the membership of Negroes in churches increased even more rapidly than did that of the white churches and that in 1916, 44.2 per cent. of the Negro population were in churches as against 43.4 per cent. of the population as a whole. We also noted that the large majority of the church members were Protestants and either Baptists or Methodists, more the former than the latter. Disfranchised politically as most of the Negroes were in practice and subject to other discrimination, their churches were the chief institutions in which they were masters. In them a distinctive type of Christianity was seen, emotional, with "Negro spirituals" the characteristic musical expression of their faith, and with an eschatology centring on the destiny of the Negroes. Their pastors were leaders, often with no more education than their illiterate or near-illiterate parishioners. Thanks in no small degree to the schools begun by white churches of the North but also to state schools and Negro initiative, the level of education was rising, and a minority were graduates of colleges, universities, and professional schools. Many of that minority were painfully conscious of the barriers raised against their race by social custom in both South and North and were bitterly resentful.

In the twentieth century great changes were seen. A vast city-ward movement, especially to the North, developed and accelerated. Beginning with World War I the decline of immigration from Europe and the demand for cheap labour in the factories of the North stimulated a swelling migration. It was accentuated by the swift decline of cotton-raising in the South, in which the rural Negro population had found major employment, a decline due to the ravages of the boll weevil.[142] The rapid progress of industrialization in the

---

[140] Clair M. Cook in *Religion in Life*, Vol. XXVIII, pp. 281–291 (Spring, 1959).
[141] Volume III, pp. 77–80.
[142] Mays and Nicholson, *The Negro's Church*, pp. 94–96; Johnston, *The Religion of Negro Protestants*, pp. 79, 80; Richardson, *Dark Glory*, pp. 54–60.

South with its demand for labour, the war industries in the North during World War II and their need for unskilled workers, the introduction of cotton-picking machinery and other mechanical improvements in the Southern planta-tions with the reduction of the number of Negro field hands, the substitution of cattle-raising for cotton, the continued industrialization of both South and North, and the racial discrimination in the South gave additional stimulus to the urban trend. Beginning about 1890 the proportion of Negroes to the white population steadily fell in the South and rapidly rose in the North. Between 1940 and 1950 it markedly increased in California. Although culturally and economically the large majority of the Negroes remained below the median level of the white population, improvement was seen in education and a mount-ing number were the recipients of higher education.[143]

As a result of these developments in environment and education Negro Protestantism displayed notable alterations. In many congregations the high emotionalism of earlier days declined, the itinerant evangelist was not as promi-nent, and "spirituals" were less frequently sung. In the preaching decreasing emphasis was placed on the other-worldly aspects of the faith with their promise of heaven as a release from the poverty and suffering of this world, and more was made of practical living and the problems of every day. The patterns of church life approached conformity to those of white Protestant congregations.[144] Yet in many places, especially in the rural churches of the South, the older customs and attitudes persisted. The overwhelming majority of the membership were still in Baptist churches with the traditional appeal of that branch of Protestantism to a low-income constituency of slight formal education, about a fifth as many were Methodists, with a somewhat better economic and educa-tional status, and only small minorities were in the denominations of middle and higher incomes and education.[145] Proportionately to the total population the membership in Negro churches rose fairly steadily, as did that of the churches in relation to the population of the country as a whole.[146] However, the percentage of adult Negro women who were members of churches was higher than that of white women in that category, and of adult Negro men than of white men, although among both Negroes and whites the proportion of men was lower than that of women[147]—a feature common to the churches in Europe and most other parts of the world. Indeed, it was also a characteristic of most non-Christian religions.

In Northern cities with large Negro populations religious movements arose

[143] Richardson, op. cit., p. 54; Niebuhr, Williams, and Gustafson, The Advancement of Theo-logical Education, p. 227; Johnston, op. cit., pp. 79, 80, 146, 147, 172, 173; Johnston, The De-velopment of Negro Religion, p. 154.

[144] Mays and Nicholson, op. cit., pp. 90, 91, 101, 102, 253; Johnston, The Development of Negro Religion, pp. 155, 156; Johnston, The Religion of Negro Protestants, pp. 121-147.

[145] Yearbook of American Churches, 1957, pp. 251, 255; Richardson, op. cit., pp. 52, 53.

[146] Johnston, The Religion of Negro Protestants, pp. 79, 179.

[147] Work, Negro Year Book . . . 1931-1932, p. 264.

which attracted followings from the less educated Negroes. While ostensibly Christian or having elements derived from Christianity, several were rather remote from the historic Christian tradition. They had resemblances to what we are to see in Africa but did not enroll as large a proportion of the Negroes in the United States as did those in Africa. One which came to prominence in the 1930's and 1940's had as its leader "Father Divine." An attempt to trace the history of the movement shows that "Father Divine" was probably born about 1880 on a rice plantation on an island in the Savannah River and was first called George Baker. He was said to have been a gardener in Baltimore in 1899 and assistant preacher in a Baptist church in that city. In 1915, after a short time in Georgia, he arrived in New York with a small group of followers. He established a centre in Sayville, on Long Island, and there attracted increasing numbers from the New York area. In 1932 he was brought to trial on the accusation of the local authorities that he was becoming a public nuisance. The judge before whom the trial was held and who was regarded by the defendant's followers as strongly biased against him suddenly died, and Father Divine hinted that by his power he had killed him. Father Divine then moved to Harlem in New York City. There and in several other places he opened what he called "heavens" and designated some of his followers as "angels." In these "heavens" he served lavish free meals to all who came. That was when the depression of the 1930's had reached its nadir and thousands were unemployed and in deep distress. To them the food and other relief given them appeared miraculous, especially since the sources of the funds which made them possible were not disclosed. Actually they came from the adherents of the movement. Many of the converts believed themselves cured of physical illnesses. Father Divine claimed to be God and was so regarded by his followers. He called his movement the Divine Peace Mission. The majority of his followers were Negroes but a number were whites. They set up various kinds of business enterprises, including restaurants and boarding houses, which were also "heavens" and to which Father Divine gave the collective title of "God, Incorporated." The movement had nation-wide publicity but although its leader lived into the 1960's it faded from general attention as suddenly as it had begun.[148]

Spectacular as were Father Divine and other similar leaders, the vast majority of Negroes were not touched by them. In cities in the North what were called "store-front" churches abounded—much more than in Southern cities. They met in houses, halls, store buildings, or theatres and afforded a sense of fellowship to migrants from familiar and friendly rural neighbourhoods into impersonal urban centres. They were said to be founded by clergy who sought to

[148] Sara Harris, with the assistance of Harriet Crittenden, *Father Divine: Holy Husband* (Garden City, N.Y., Doubleday and Co., 1953, pp. 320), *passim*; John Hoshor, *God in a Rolls Royce. The Rise of Father Divine: Madman, Menace, or Messiah* (New York, Hillman-Curl, 1936, pp. 272), *passim*.

gain a following but lacked funds to construct more formal buildings.[149]

The level of education of Negro ministers was low, and many of the educated Negroes were not attracted to the churches, even those served by clergymen with high education. Although earlier the ministry had been the main professional opportunity open to Negroes, in the twentieth century medicine and the law increasingly proved more attractive. However, the general educational level of the Negro ministry began to rise. Whereas in 1926, 77.8 per cent. of the ministers of three Negro denominations had neither college nor seminary training and only 7.4 per cent. had both, by 1948 the proportion of ministers in the Central Jurisdiction of the Methodist Church, in which the Negro congregations were grouped, who had both college and seminary preparation had risen sharply—from 5.4 per cent. in the age group 58–72 to 30.2 per cent. for those forty-two years old and under. Between 1942 and 1954 the enrollment of Negroes in theological seminaries almost doubled. Yet between 1949–1950 and 1954–1955 the number of Negroes in seminaries accredited by the American Association of Theological Schools fell sharply and in 1955, against the estimated annual need of 1,132 new Negro ministers, only about 100 were being graduated each year with the B.D. degree.[150]

Negro clergymen, especially in metropolitan areas, particularly but not exclusively in the North, as contrasted with those in rural sections and smaller cities, were increasingly active in advancing the interests of their people through practical action.[151] A spectacular instance was seen in the mid-1950's in Montgomery, Alabama, where in 1955–1956 a Negro peaceable boycott of buses in protest against racial segregation was led by a Negro Baptist clergyman, Martin Luther King, Jr. Well educated, King had been influenced by his faith and by the example of Gandhi.[152] He also led "freedom riders" in 1961 in an effort to end discrimination on interstate bus travel.

Roman Catholics put forth vigorous efforts to win the Negroes and with some success. Part of the attraction was the ceremonial. Much was due to the efforts of Roman Catholic clergy. Some of the priests were seculars serving in their respective dioceses. The majority were regulars. About thirty orders and congregations were represented. In the 1940's by far the largest number of the

149 Mays and Nicholson., *op. cit.*, pp. 97–99, 219, 220.

150 Niebuhr, Williams, and Gustafson, *op. cit.*, pp. 231–234; Richardson, *op. cit.*, pp. 123–126. Another set of figures late in the 1950's said that although 1,500 ministers a year were required simply for replacement, scarcely more than 100 a year were graduated from fully accredited seminaries and a similar number from non-accredited Bible schools. Of the denominations enrolling 90 per cent. of all Protestant Negroes 91 per cent. of the ministers had less than a high school education.—W. C. Hart in *The Christian Century*, Vol. LXXVI, p. 470 (April 22, 1959).

151 Johnston, *The Religion of Negro Protestants*, pp. 188–193.

152 Martin Luther King, Jr., *Stride Towards Freedom. The Montgomery Story* (New York, Harper & Brothers, 1958, pp. 230), *passim;* Martin Luther King, Jr., in *The Christian Century*, Vol. LXXVII, pp. 439–441 (April 13, 1960); L. D. Reddick, *Crusader Without Violence: A Biography of Martin Luther King, Jr.* (New York, Harper & Brothers, 1959, pp. 243), *passim.*

regulars were Josephites, with about a third of the total. The Holy Ghost Fathers were second and the Society of the Divine Word third.[153] Between 1927 and 1941 the Roman Catholic mission units devoted specifically to Negroes almost doubled. In addition to priests, an increasing number of sisters were serving. In 1940 they totalled 870 in 72 different congregations or communities.[154] Converts were confessedly difficult to make,[155] but increased. In 1906 the membership in exclusively Negro Roman Catholic churches was reported to be 44,922, in 1916 it had risen to 51,688, in 1926 it was said to be 124,324,[156] and in 1939 it was 189,423. In addition, in 1939, 107,575 Negroes were counted as members of "white" or "mixed" churches.[157] The majority were in cities in the South and very few were in the rural areas, but an increasing number were in Northern cities. As might have been expected because of the early French and Spanish connexion, in 1939 over half the Negro Roman Catholics lived in Louisiana.[158] The Roman Catholic Church was slow in ordaining American Negroes to the priesthood. However, in the twentieth century the number of Negro priests increased.[159]

A chronic challenge confronting American Christianity was a racial discrimination which palpably contradicted the Gospel. It took many forms but was especially prominent and disturbing to the Christian conscience in the relations between Negroes and whites. The churches were often cited as examples of discrimination. The overwhelming majority of Negro Protestants were in denominations purely of their colour. The choice was partly the Negroes', because, as we have hinted, for many years after emancipation their churches were almost the only institutions they controlled, and they resented any attempts of the whites to dominate them. In several prevailingly white denominations Negro congregations existed. For administrative purposes the Methodist Church placed its Negro congregations in the non-geographic Central Jurisdiction—an arrangement which seemed to many to be discriminatory but which in 1960 official action continued. Here and there, but rarely, and mainly because of

[153] John T. Gillard, *The Negro American. A Mission Investigation* (Cincinnati, Catholic Students' Mission Crusade, 1948, pp. 95), pp. 68, 69. For the Jesuit share see Edward O. Reynolds, *Jesuits for the Negro* (New York, The America Press, 1949, pp. 232), *passim.* Yet Negro priests had no easy time in winning acceptance from their white ecclesiastical superiors. In 1954 only twenty-seven of the fifty Negro priests who were deemed old enough to be assigned to responsible pastorates actually held them.—*Information Service*, April 23, 1955, citing *The Pilot*, January 8, 1955, report of an address by a Jesuit, A. S. Foley, at a meeting of the American Catholic Sociological Society. For an account of an Irish-American priest, a Josephite, who served the Negroes, see Edward F. Murphy, *Yankee Priest. An Autobiographical Journey, with Certain Detours, from Salem to New Orleans* (Garden City, N.Y., Doubleday and Co., 1952, pp. 316), *passim.*

[154] Gillard, *Colored Catholics in the United States*, pp. 128, 192, 193.

[155] Gillard, *The Catholic Church and the American Negro*, p. 64.

[156] *Ibid.*, p. 62.

[157] Gillard, *Colored Catholics in the United States*, p. 138.

[158] *Ibid.*, pp. 138–141.

[159] Albert S. Foley, *God's Men of Color. The Colored Catholic Priests of the United States 1854–1954* (New York, Farrar, Straus and Co., 1955, pp. xiv, 322), *passim.*

geography, congregations existed which had both Negro and white members. Many Protestant national and regional gatherings were deliberately inter-racial. In the 1950's in the mounting tide against discrimination an increasing number of white churches admitted Negro members, but the issue was often acute and at times was a subject of bitter controversy.[160]

THE CONTINUING CHALLENGE OF THE AMERICAN INDIAN

In an earlier volume we summarized the efforts to win the American Indians to the Christian faith.[161] We noted that although by the census of 1910, on the eve of World War I, Indians numbered only 291,014 (of whom 25,331 were in Alaska), a very small percentage of the total population of the country, they were distributed widely in relatively small groups and efforts to reach them were necessarily by many different enterprises in many parts of the country. We also remarked that in 1914 about two-fifths of the Indians were said to be Christians—about the same proportion as that of church members in the rest of the population—and that about half of the Christians were Roman Catholics and about half were Protestants. We gave examples of the fashion in which conversion had been brought about and of the way missionaries had helped in education and had sought to protect the Indians from exploitation and injustice by aggressive and selfish white men.

The problem presented by the Indians was not solved in the half-century which followed 1914. From time to time varying policies were adopted by the government, from seeking to draw the Indians into the dominant culture of the white man to endeavouring to revive their ancestral manner of life. Assimilation proved difficult and efforts to restore the ancient cultural patterns were foredoomed by the fact that, even though tribal organization survived and a partial isolation could be preserved on territorial reservations, escape from the engulfing white man's civilization was impossible. In 1945 Indians were said to number 393,622, but about two-thirds were of mixed Indian and white ancestry and many outside the reservations had not been counted. An increasing number were in the latter category, mobility was rising, ancient tribal customs were disappearing, and more and more Indian children were in the usual public schools rather than in mission or other special institutions. English was taking the place of the Indian tongues. The use of alcohol, traditionally especially disastrous to the Indians, markedly increased after World War II.

---

[160] For a careful study of the situation in one Protestant denomination see Dwight W. Culver, *Negro Segregation in the Methodist Church* (New Haven, Yale University Press, 1953, pp. xii, 218), *passim.*
[161] Volume III, pp. 72–77.

Peyote or mescal, a drug, sometimes associated with religious cults with Christian trappings, was also a curse.[162]

Protestants continued to be active in missions among the Indians. In 1950 thirty-six denominations were engaged in them as against twenty-three denominational and six undenominational organizations in 1930. Among those who had entered in the intervening two decades were the Four-Square Gospel and several Pentecostal groups. In 1950 Protestant church membership was reported to be 39,200 and the Protestant constituency was said to approximate 140,000.[163]

Indian leadership was slow in developing among Protestants. A study made in the 1940's appeared to show that the Five Civilized Tribes, as they were called, whose homes were in Oklahoma where they had been moved in the first half of the nineteenth century and among whom Protestant missions had long been active, had a large proportion of the ordained Indian ministers, but that on the whole the ministers were in the upper age groups. Younger men were reluctant to enter the ministry because of the low salaries, the small size of the average church, the wave of materialism, and alcoholism. On the average the Indian ministers were more poorly trained than were the white and even the Negro clergy.[164]

Roman Catholics continued to be active among the Indians. In 1956 they had missions in 24 states and Alaska, staffed by 230 priests and about 726 sisters, scholastics, brothers, and lay assistants. They had 57 day and boarding schools, 2 hospitals, and 12 medical clinics. Roman Catholic Indians were reported in 1956 to number 117,281, an increase of 5 per cent. during the year, of whom 863 were converts. By far the largest number—about a fifth of the total—were in New Mexico; Montana, North Dakota, and Arizona each had about a tenth; and California, Minnesota, and Wisconsin each contained about a twentieth of the whole.[165] In some areas growth slowed in the 1940's, as it did in several of the Protestant missions.[166]

MOVEMENTS CONTINUE TO EMERGE

As we have again and again suggested, one evidence of vitality in Christianity, as in other religions, is the movements which have arisen from it. They have taken many forms—intellectual and educational, in Protestantism new

---

[162] Lindquist, *Indians in Transition*, pp. 13–26.

[163] *Ibid.*, pp. 31, 32.

[164] B. Frank Belvin, *The Status of the Indian Ministry* (Shawnee, Oklahoma Baptist University Press, 1949, pp. xv, 132), *passim*.

[165] *The 1958 National Catholic Almanac*, p. 470.

[166] See as examples Alban Fruth, *A Century of Missionary Work Among the Red Lake Chippewa Indians, 1858–1958* (Redlake, Minn., St. Mary's Mission, 1958, pp. iv, 125), pp. 67 ff.; Mary Claudia Duratschek, *Crusading Along Sioux Trails. A History of Catholic Missions of South Dakota* (Yankton, S.D., Benedictine Convent of the Sacred Heart, 1947, pp. xiii, 334), *passim*.

denominations and other organizations or the revitalization of existing ones, and in the Roman Catholic Church fresh orders and congregations and lay organizations with the revival and strengthening of those already in being. We have recorded the fashion in which in the nineteenth century Christianity in the United States was an abounding source of organizations.[167] In the five decades which began in 1914 both Protestantism and the Roman Catholic Church were still more prolific in giving birth to fresh organizations and movements akin to organizations and were reinforcing existing ones. Even a bare list would unduly prolong our account. All we can rightly attempt is the brief mention of a few of the many and the indication of some trends.

The majority faith and varied in its forms and expressions, Protestantism was especially notable in the perseverance and growth of existing organizations and its fecundity in new ones. By the outbreak of World War I what were numerically the larger denominations in the next half-century were already operative. We have hinted at their proportionate growth in that period and have mentioned some of the new ones—all of them relatively small—which emerged then. The Young Men's and the Young Women's Christian Associations and the Sunday Schools, although of foreign origin, continued to expand and still had their largest dimensions in the United States. The YMCA and the YWCA, predominantly Protestant and primarily lay in their leadership, became increasingly non-denominational in membership and were more and more social service agencies designed to nourish wholesome living and upright character. The YMCA moved into the public schools with Hi-Y clubs in the high schools and Gra-Y clubs in the grammar schools. It had Y's Men's luncheon clubs modeled in part after the popular "service clubs" of which Rotary was an outstanding pioneer.[168] The interdenominational Young People's Society of Christian Endeavour persisted, but, although in the international scene it grew, in the United States it was largely superseded by denominational youth movements.

Of the many new movements of Protestant origin we can select only a few, choosing them almost at random and not attempting to place them in the order of their importance or according to the date of their inception. In the preceding volume we called attention to one which had a wide spread in Europe and repercussions elsewhere. Latterly known as Moral Rearmament (MRA), at one time it was called "a First Century Christian Fellowship" and then was long named the "Groups" or the "Oxford Groups." Its founder and guiding spirit was Frank Nathan Daniel Buchman (1878–1961). Born and reared in Pennsylvania, a Lutheran clergyman, a Pietist by early environment and conviction,

---

[167] Volume III, pp. 112–139.
[168] Hopkins, *History of the Y.M.C.A. in North America, passim.* On the Y's Men's clubs see George W. Keitel, compiler, *A Topical History of Y'sdom, 1920–1953* (Lawrence, Mass., International Association of Y's Men's Clubs, no date, pp. 354), *passim.*

before World War I Buchman was seeking to beget and nourish in those about him a form of Pietist experience. During and after World War I he travelled across the world, by novel and informal methods seeking to win others to conformity to the standards of absolute purity, honesty, unselfishness, and love which he found in the teachings of Jesus. Later, while not abandoning the four-fold standard, he sought through those "changed" by commitment to them to solve social and international conflicts. He firmly believed in "guidance" which came in "quiet times" to those who were willing to listen to God and obey Him. Buchman came out strongly against "materialism," particularly Communism. He and his associates claimed remarkable results in resolving conflicts between individuals and groups, in politics, and between labour and capital. The Oxford Groups and MRA were severely criticized by many Protestant leaders and organizations.[169]

Alcoholics Anonymous at its outset (it dated from 1934) was deeply indebted to the Oxford Groups and had its first headquarters in Calvary Episcopal Church in New York City, whose pastor at that time, Samuel Moor Shoemaker (1893———), was long associated with Buchman. It soon became an independent movement. Alcoholics Anonymous (AA) had as its purpose the rehabilitation of alcoholics. It was undenominational and worked through small groups of former alcoholics who sought to rescue by counsel and fellowship other victims of alcoholism. Those who joined admitted that they were "compulsory drinkers" who could not of themselves overcome the habit which had gripped them, but who acknowledged a "Power higher than themselves" as the source of strength. They met in homes, in Protestant churches, and in Roman Catholic parish halls. They spread widely.[170]

International Christian Leadership, also known as the Breakfast Clubs, is said to have been begun in 1935 in Seattle, Washington, by a Methodist minister, Abraham Vereide, and a layman. It described itself as "an informal association of concerned laymen banded together to find through Christ the better way of everyday living and to demonstrate and promote in home, community, nation, and world a more effective Christian leadership." One of its early achievements was helping to rid Seattle of political corruption, and a member was elected mayor of the city and then governor of the state. Like MRA it was inspired by

---

169 Of the enormous literature see *Who's Who in America,* Vol. XXXI, p. 397; Walter Houston Clark, *The Oxford Group: Its History and Significance* (New York, Bookman Associates, 1951, pp. 268), a doctoral dissertation; Peter Howard, *The World Rebuilt. The True Story of Frank Buchman and the Achievements of Moral Rearmament* (New York, Duell, Sloan and Pearce, 1951, pp. 250), laudatory; Stephen Foot, *Life Began Yesterday* (London, William Heinemann, 1935, pp. 212), also laudatory; V. C. Kitchen, *I Was a Pagan* (New York, Harper & Brothers, 1934, pp. viii, 186), the autobiography of a convert; Jerome Ellison in *The Saturday Evening Post,* March 1, 1952.

170 *Alcoholics Anonymous Comes of Age. By a Co-Founder* (New York, Harper & Brothers, 1957, pp. xix, 335), pp. 1–74; *Alcoholics Anonymous. The Story of How More Than Eight Thousand Men Have Recovered from Alcoholism* (New York, Work Publishing Co., 1939, pp. viii, 398), *passim.*

the principle that to reform Seattle the members must begin by reforming themselves. The movement spread across the country and established head-quarters in Washington with Vereide as executive director. In connexion with it breakfast groups were carried on in both the Senate and the House of Rep-resentatives.[171]

Spiritual Mobilization, with headquarters in Los Angeles, spoke out for "freedom under God," for "Jesus Christ who promoted persuasion in place of coercion as the means for accomplishing positive good," and against "Com-munist, Socialist, Fascist, or other authoritarian government."[172]

The Christian Business Man's Committee was founded in Chicago in 1930 by laymen from 6 denominations and by 1952 had units in 238 cities and 9 countries. Its initiators were convinced that the churches had failed to reach many with the Gospel, especially the business men. They sought to spread the Gospel by personal contact, and visited jails, preached on streeet corners, called on the sick, and maintained service men's recreation centres.[173]

The Christian Freedom Foundation, with its centre in New York City, pub-lished the fortnightly *Christian Economics* in advocacy of "the economic system with the least amount of government and the greatest amount of Chris-tianity."[174]

The Foundation for Religious Action in the Social and Civil Order, an inter-faith movement, endeavoured to unite "all believers in God" to strengthen the moral and religious foundations of democracy in the struggle with Com-munism.[175] Yokefellows and the Disciplined Order of Christ were other move-ments whose name gave an indication of their purpose.[176]

At least four organizations—Young Life (begun in 1940 in Dallas, Texas, by a Presbyterian clergyman, John Rayburn), Word of Life, Youth on the March, and Youth for Christ—which flourished in the 1940's and 1950's sought to win youth, especially but not exclusively those in their teens, to the Gospel much as it was interpreted by Billy Graham and men of his convictions. Billy Graham had been closely connected with Youth for Christ, and Youth for Christ was frankly indebted to the other three movements. All four were au-tonomous and undenominational, were highly organized, stressed personal testimonials, had clubs of high school students, and conducted camping-ranch-ing programmes. They made much of Bible study, used the radio, and pro-moted mass meetings. Youth for Christ branched out into other activities.[177]

171 Ellison, *op. cit.*; Eckardt, *The Surge of Piety in America*, pp. 46, 47, 123, 124.
172 Eckardt, *op. cit.*, pp. 47, 48.
173 Ellison, *op. cit.*
174 Eckardt, *op. cit.*, pp. 48, 124.
175 *Ibid.*, pp. 125, 126.
176 *The Christian Century*, Vol. LXXVI, p. 873 (July 29, 1959).
177 *Information Service*, November 5, 1955; *Time*, January 4, 1960.

Allied Youth, with Protestant sponsorship, began in 1936 and by the 1950's had clubs or "posts" in many parts of the United States and Canada. It sought to enlist teen-age high school youth against the use of alcohol and for alcohol-free recreation.[178]

Several movements sprung from Protestantism with emphasis on prayer as a means of healing and achievement were akin to what we have seen in Norman Vincent Peale, Aimee Semple McPherson, and Oral Roberts. Glenn Clark (1882–1957) was the inspirer of the Camps Farthest Out. Born in Des Moines, Iowa, he went to Grinnell College and for years was athletic coach and taught literature in Macalester College in St. Paul, Minnesota. In his student days he became enamoured of Christ and through the years was active in the College YMCA's and their summer camps. He became increasingly convinced of the power of prayer in healing disease, in strengthening men and women to accomplish the seemingly impossible, and as a way to a radiant life. *The Soul's Sincere Desire,* his first book, had an enormous sale. Later he began the Camp Farthest Out, to which those who wished could come to learn how to pray better than before and the idea spread.[179] Spiritual Frontiers Fellowship sought to bring psychic phenomena into the purview of the churches.[180] A movement called Unity, the Unity School of Christianity, or the United Society of Practical Christianity began late in the nineteenth century but had a phenomenal spread after 1914. Its founders were Charles Fillmore (1854–1948) and his wife, Myrtle Page Fillmore (1845–1931). Reared in or near the frontier in the Middle West, they had had contact with Protestantism. They believed themselves healed by trust in God Who is all goodness and is everywhere—she suddenly and he by stages. They were also in close touch with various movements akin to Christian Science and embraced in the somewhat vague descriptive term "metaphysical." In 1920 they had acquired several hundred acres near Kansas City and there a centre arose for meetings, publications, instruction, and prayer twenty-four hours of the day to reinforce requests which came from far and near. A temple was erected in Kansas City in 1947–1950. Several radio stations were employed. Unity thought of itself as Christian, was based on the Bible and especially the New Testament and the teachings of Jesus, and stressed prayer for physical and spiritual healing and for success in any worthy undertaking. Its literature reached hundreds of thousands in many parts of the world.[181]

From even this incomplete list of the movements which either went from strength to strength after 1914 or emerged for the first time, something of both

[178] *Do You Know About Allied Youth?* (pamphlet, Washington, Allied Youth, no date, pp. 12), *passim*.
[179] *A Man's Reach. The Autobiography of Glenn Clark* (New York, Harper & Brothers, 1949, pp. 314), *passim*.
[180] *The Christian Century*, Vol. LXXV, pp. 309 ff. (March 12, 1958).
[181] James Dillet Freeman, *The Household of Faith. The Story of Unity* (Lee's Summit, Mo., Unity School of Christianity, 1951, pp. 303, ix), *passim*.

the vigour and the variety of Protestantism in the United States can be seen. Obvious, too, is the contrast with the Protestantism of Europe during that period. In the Old World Protestantism did not give birth to nearly as many new or varied movements as in the New World. Yet similarities existed. On both sides of the Atlantic it was the source of new movements. In both regions the laity had a large share in the initiative—although more west than east of that ocean.

Something of the same pattern was seen in the Roman Catholic Church in the United States. Here, too, existing movements were augmented and many new ones came into being. As in Protestantism, numbers of them were predominantly lay. But because of the hierarchical structure of the Roman Catholic Church they were more under the control of the clergy than were most of the Protestant-initiated organizations.

Several orders and congregations represented in the United States before 1914 had a phenomenal growth after World War I. Striking too was the rapid multiplication of houses of contemplative orders subsequent to World War II. It was all the more impressive because it was apparently contrary to the activism which characterized America and American Christianity. The Trappists, Reformed Cistercians, had appeared in the United States early in the nineteenth century but with their austere manner of life and their rule of silence had not attracted many. After World War II, hundreds, numbers of them returning war veterans, applied for admission.[182] The trend was made spectacular by the autobiography of Thomas Merton (1915——) which for months was on the list of the best-selling books. The son of an artist, Merton had been reared in America, France, and England and had been a student in Cambridge University and in Columbia University. Such religious instruction as he had had was in Protestantism. He was converted and became a Trappist,[183] but continued to write, and his books helped to familiarize the public with the Trappist way of life.[184] Not far from 1950 the Carthusians, the strictest of the orders, opened their initial American house.[185]

In 1957 there were eighty-four orders and congregations of priests in the United States,[186] the large majority of European provenance. Of those of American origin, the Paulist Fathers dated from the nineteenth century, but the Missionary Servants of the Most Holy Trinity were begun in 1929 for pastoral

---

[182] Ellis, *American Catholicism*, pp. 131, 132.
[183] Thomas Merton, *The Seven Story Mountain* (New York, Harcourt, Brace and Co., 1948, pp. 429), *passim.*
[184] See, for example, *The Secular Journal of Thomas Merton* (New York, Farrar, Straus and Cudahy, 1959, pp. 270), pp. 183–205; Thomas Merton, *The Sign of Jonas* (New York, Harcourt, Brace and Co., 1953, pp. 362), *passim.*
[185] Ellis, *op. cit.*, p. 133.
[186] *The Official Catholic Directory, 1958*, pp. 808–821.

and missionary work in the South[187] and in 1957 had 107 priests, 46 students in their major seminary, 115 candidates in their minor seminary, 3 houses, 29 parishes, 40 missions, and 3 mission stations.[188] The Glenmary Home Missioners, founded in 1939 with their objective the large non-Roman Catholic areas, especially in the South,[189] in 1957 had 47 priests, 8 students in the novitiate, 17 professed brothers, 22 brother novices and postulants, 13 mission bases, and 2 seminaries.[190]

Of the orders and congregations of European origin, a number were introduced to the United States after 1914. Among them were the Sons of the Holy Family and the Mariannhill Missionaries in 1920; the Order of Our Lady of Mercy in 1921; the Assumptionist, Camillian, and Oratorian Fathers in 1923; the Oblates of St. Joseph in 1929; the Hospitalers of St. John of God in 1941; the White Fathers in 1942;[191] the Recollets of St. Augustine in 1944;[192] the Discalced Carmelite Fathers in 1924 with six provinces before 1958;[193] the Sons of Divine Providence in 1933;[194] the Missionaries of the Company of Mary (the Montfort Fathers) in 1946;[195] the Society of the Catholic Apostolate (the Pallottine Fathers) in 1946;[196] the Order of the Most Holy Trinity in 1950;[197] the Piarist Fathers in 1946;[198] the Congregation of the Priests of the Sacred Heart in 1934;[199] St. Columban's Missionary Society in 1918,[200] the Society of St. Paul (for the apostolate of the press) in 1932;[201] the Congregation of the Immaculate Heart of Mary (of nineteenth-century Belgian origin, with foreign missions as its purpose) in 1949;[202] the Sons of the Sacred Heart (also of nineteenth-century origin with missions to Africa as the initial objective) in 1950;[203] and St. Joseph's Society for Foreign Missions (with its mother house at Mill Hill, near London) in 1951.[204]

Several of the orders and congregations which had begun in Europe and expanded into the United States before 1914, in the five decades after that year greatly enlarged their membership and geographic scope. Thus the Benedictines

[187] Roemer, *The Catholic Church in the United States*, p. 354.
[188] *The Official Catholic Directory, 1958*, p. 817.
[189] Roemer, *op. cit.*, pp. 384, 385.
[190] *The Official Catholic Directory, 1958*, p. 814.
[191] Roemer, *op. cit.*, pp. 354, 384.
[192] *The Official Catholic Directory, 1958*, p. 808.
[193] *Ibid.*, p. 811.
[194] *Ibid.*
[195] *Ibid.*, p. 816.
[196] *Ibid.*, p. 817.
[197] *Ibid.*
[198] *Ibid.*
[199] *Ibid.*, p. 819.
[200] *Ibid.*
[201] *Ibid.*, p. 820.
[202] *Ibid.*
[203] *Ibid.*
[204] *Ibid.*, p. 821.

added nine abbeys, some of them founded as monasteries before 1914 but raised to the rank of abbey after that year.[205] In the 1940's and 1950's the Trappists added nine abbeys to the three which were in existence in 1940.[206] Between 1914 and 1958 the Franciscans did not increase the number of their provinces, but they inaugurated at least three commissariats and in 1944 initiated the Seraphic Society for Vocations, which operated in several hundred schools and institutions and promoted through prayer and literature vocations to the priesthood and especially to the Order of Brothers Minor.[207] The Capuchins added two provinces—in 1926 and 1939—thus doubling the number they had possessed in 1914.[208] In 1957 the Jesuits had ten provinces, twice the number in 1914.[209] The Marist Fathers divided into three the single province which was theirs in 1914 and which had been organized in 1889.[210] Several other orders and congregations displayed growth in the decades immediately following World War I, but none as impressive as the ones we have cited.

In the United States the congregations of lay brothers were not as numerous as the orders and congregations that included priests. In 1957 only fifteen were listed. Five were of American origin, four of them having come into being between 1914 and 1952. At least two had been introduced from Europe between 1914 and 1958, and three of European creation had added provinces to those in which they had been organized before 1914.[211] Their chief occupation was teaching. By far the largest was the Institute of the Brothers of Christian Schools. Founded by Jean Baptiste de La Salle in 1680 and beginning its first school in the United States in Baltimore in 1848, in 1948, at the end of its first century in the country, the Institute counted 1,582 brothers teaching in 90 schools scattered from New York to San Francisco and enrolling about 43,000 students. It conducted elementary, secondary, and higher schools and also welfare work for boys.[212]

Congregations of women totalled about 245 in 1957 and enrolled far more members than did the orders and congregations of men. Of them about 155 had been begun outside the United States—the overwhelming majority and

[205] *Ibid.*, p. 809. For the history of St. John's Abbey in Collegeville, Minnesota, and the wide extension of its operations see Barry, *Worship and Work, passim.*

[206] *The Official Catholic Directory, 1958,* p. 811.

[207] *Ibid.*, pp. 811–813.

[208] *Ibid.*, p. 813.

[209] *Ibid.*, pp. 814, 815. For a popular and reliable account of the Jesuits see John La Farge and Margaret Bourke-White, *A Report on the American Jesuits* (New York, Farrar, Straus and Cudahy, 1956, pp. 236), *passim.* For the autobiography of a distinguished Jesuit scholar and journalist see John La Farge, *The Manner Is Ordinary* (New York, Harcourt, Brace and Co., 1954, pp. viii, 408), *passim.* For a selection from La Farge's writings see Thurston N. Davis and Joseph Small, editors, *A John La Farge Reader* (New York, The America Press, 1956, pp. xiv, 272), *passim.*

[210] *The Official Catholic Directory, 1958,* p. 815.

[211] *Ibid.*, pp. 821–823.

[212] Angelus Gabriel, *The Christian Brothers in the United States, 1848–1948. A Century of Christian Education* (New York, The Declan X. McMullen Co., 1948, pp. xviii, 700), *passim.*

those with the most members in Europe, a very few in Canada, and fewer still in Latin America. Of the ones inaugurated outside the United States about 79, or slightly more than half, were introduced to the United States after 1914, but in 1960 none approached the dimensions of those which had come before that year. Of the approximately 90 originated in the United States not quite a third were founded after 1914. The large majority of the congregations gave themselves primarily to teaching, orphanages, holding retreats, or care of the sick and the poor, but a few were "enclosed" and devoted themselves to prayer, and in many others perpetual adoration of the reserved sacrament was observed.[213] It was said that the United States had more sisters engaged in teaching than any other country. Better to prepare them for that function, in 1953 the Sisters Formation Movement was begun.[214]

Although a majority of the orders and congregations, whether of men or women, had had their inception in Europe and on their introduction to the United States were staffed principally and in many cases entirely from across the Atlantic, eventually most of their American members were recruited in the United States—a testimony to the vitality of the Roman Catholic Church in that country.

In 1952 the superiors and other officials of religious orders and congregations met for four days in what was said to have been the largest gathering of that kind in the entire history of the Church. Although the faithful of the United States were only 8 per cent. of the world membership of their church, they were estimated to have nearly 20 per cent. of the membership of the Roman Catholic religious organizations.[215]

In the United States as in Europe the post-1914 decades were marked by mounting lay participation in the life of the Roman Catholic Church. Some movements were initiated by members of the clergy and for the most part the movements were supervised by the clergy, but they were evidence of the increasing share of the laity in the Roman Catholic Church, a phase of what was often called the apostolate of the laity, the priesthood of the laity, and the century of the laity. We must take the space for only the briefest mention of a few which came into being after 1914.

Youth organizations proliferated. To supervise and coördinate them the Youth Department of the National Catholic Welfare Conference was estab-

---

[213] *The Official Catholic Directory, 1958*, pp. 827–855. For the record of one of the sisterhoods in a particular diocese see Mary Ellen Evans, *The Spirit Is Mercy. The Story of the Sisters of Mercy in the Archdiocese of Cincinnati, 1858–1958* (Westminster, Md., The Newman Press, 1959, pp. xi, 346), *passim.* For the history of another of the congregations see Louis Callan, *The Society of the Sacred Heart in North America* (New York, Longmans, Green and Co., 1937, pp. xv, 809), *passim,* especially pp. 697 ff. See also Mary Eulalia Herron, *The Sisters of Mercy in the United States, 1843–1928* (New York, The Macmillan Co., 1929, pp. xvii, 434), *passim.*

[214] Ward, *Catholic Life, U.S.A.*, pp. 75–90.

[215] *Time*, August 25, 1952.

lished in 1940. It sponsored the National Council of Catholic Youth, which was formed in 1951 to federate and serve the many youth movements in the country without interfering in their local and independent activities.[216] Among those embraced by it were the Catholic Youth Organization, begun in 1930 to meet the spiritual, cultural, social, and physical needs of out-of-school Roman Catholic boys and girls and to assist young people "without regard to race, creed, or colour" (it grew out of the experience of Bernard Sheil, later a bishop, as a prison chaplain serving wayward boys);[217] the Catholic Students' Mission Crusade, inaugurated in 1918 to acquaint students with missions the world around and by 1958 having about a million members in over three thousand educational institutions in fifty dioceses;[218] the Catholic Youth Adoration Society and the Senior Catholic Youth Adoration Society, founded in New York in 1948 and 1954 respectively, to promote a monthly holy hour adapted to the needs of youth; Fighting 69th, initiated in 1949 for unmarried youth of high school age and above to promote purity in word, action, and dress and with a membership of about a half-million the world over;[219] the National Federation of Catholic College Students, begun in 1937;[220] and the National Catholic Camping Association, inaugurated in 1951, with 114 member camps in 31 states in 1957 but not as yet embracing at least 183 other Roman Catholic camps.[221]

Catholic Action multiplied its activity in a wide variety of organizations. It included the Legion of Mary, which, begun in 1921 in Ireland, spread quickly to many lands and was introduced to the United States in 1931. An association of laity, it sought to intensify the faith of its members, to reclaim lapsed Roman Catholics, and to win converts.[222] The Young Christian Workers (Jocists), founded in Belgium in 1912, first appeared in the United States in 1935 and by 1957 numbered about 3,000 in 35 cities.[223]

The Grail Movement, started in Belgium in 1921 to enlist and train young women to seek to win Protestants and non-Christians, was introduced to the United States in 1944 by the founding of Grailville, near Cincinnati. Other centres soon came into being. The role of the women in modern society was discussed and a spirit of service and joy was dominant. The Grail International Student Centre was inaugurated near Columbia University in New York City for foreign students for hospitality and training. Some young women left Grailville to help in community religious work, several to become missionaries

216 *The 1958 National Catholic Almanac*, p. 539.
217 Roger L. Treat, *Bishop Sheil and the CYO* (New York, Julian Messner, 1951, pp. xi, 211), *passim*.
218 Ward, *op. cit.*, p. 175; *The 1958 National Catholic Almanac*, p. 175.
219 *The 1958 National Catholic Almanac*, p. 540.
220 *Ibid.*
221 *Ibid.*, pp. 541–546.
222 *Ibid.*, pp. 554, 555.
223 *Ibid.*, p. 555.

abroad, others to enter convents, and still others to form Christian homes.[224]

The Christian Family Movement sprang up in several cities in the 1940's when groups of married couples began meeting with the purpose of restoring Christian ideals in family life. It spread rapidly and held annual conventions. By the mid-1950's about 11,000 couples were members.[225] The Cana Conference Movement sought to apply in the United States the ideas developed in the 1930's by the Family Renewal Association of France. It was "an effort to help married people and those preparing for marriage to realize in full the graces and the fruits of the graces which come to them in marriage." In many cities half-day or all-day conferences were held annually or semi-annually to help couples to make their married life a success.[226]

The Confraternity of Christian Doctrine endeavoured to give religious education to all Roman Catholics who were not in Roman Catholic schools and to win converts. To this end it sought to form in every parish a society of the laity which under the guidance of the clergy directed by the hierarchy would actively further that purpose. The members of these societies had a programme for religious instruction of pre-school children in the home, of elementary school pupils in classes and vacation schools, of high school and college students and adults in discussion groups, and of those outside the Roman Catholic Church by literature and other means. The Confraternity of Christian Doctrine was not a twentieth-century creation but dated from the sixteenth century. It was given marked impetus by Pope Pius X, and its first unit in the United States seems to have been organized in 1908. Soon after World War I it enjoyed an extensive spread, but its great period of expansion began in 1934 when in connexion with the National Catholic Welfare Conference the bishops set up a committee to promote it and named one of their number to chair it. That chairman, Edwin Vincent O'Hara (1881–1956), who was appointed Bishop of Great Falls, Montana, in 1930, Bishop of Kansas City in 1939, and later was accorded the personal title of archbishop, gave superb leadership. Progress was made before World War II, but during that struggle attention was diverted to activities demanded by the national emergency. With the coming of peace, momentum was gained and the confraternity expanded its operations. In several dioceses it enlisted and trained hundreds of the laity to teach parents how to instruct their children who were attending public schools and in other ways to extend the faith.[227]

Beginning in 1931, summer schools of six days each for Catholic Action were

[224] *Ibid.*, pp. 555, 556; Ward, *op. cit.*, pp. 107–120.
[225] Thomas, *The American Catholic Family*, pp. 428–433; Ward, *op. cit.*, pp. 32–52.
[226] Thomas, *op. cit.*, pp. 420–427; Ward, *op. cit.*, pp. 53–74.
[227] Ward, *op. cit.*, pp. 138–159; Shaw, *Edwin Vincent O'Hara*, pp. 128–131, 138 ff.; *The 1958 National Catholic Almanac*, pp. 535, 536.

held for priests, nuns, and active lay apostles. Between 1931 and 1957 they had enrolled over 170,000.[228]

An incomplete list published in 1958 of Roman Catholic associations, movements, and societies in the United States gave the names of more than two hundred and did not seek to include the societies of lawyers and newspaper men which were organized on a diocesan basis. The overwhelming majority were composed of laity. The dates of organization of more than half of them were after 1914. They had a variety of purposes. Some were for special occupations and professions, such as broadcasters, music teachers, and band masters. Others were for particular nationalities. One was for war veterans and had about two thousand posts throughout the country. Several interracial councils were included, and Friendship Houses were organized to promote interracial justice between Negroes and whites. The Convert Makers of America had members in most of the states who were especially trained by priest-advisers. The Christopher Movement, begun in 1945 by James G. Keller, a priest, endeavoured by syndicated columns in newspapers, by radio and television, and by millions of copies of books and pamphlets to enlist Christians regardless of their denomination to restore Christian principles in education, government, labour relations, and other aspects of life. The Catholic Association for International Peace sought to further the "peace of Christ in the reign of Christ." The Catholic Civics Clubs of America with about three thousand branches had as their object the promotion of better citizenship by practising democratic techniques and conducting civic projects. Some others of the organizations were for devotional purposes.[229] Several of the organizations held annual meetings.[230] In addition, the Association of Catholic Trade Unionists, founded in New York in 1937, operated labour schools, published labour papers, gave counsel on union problems, and provided free legal advice.[231] In 1922 O'Hara, before becoming burdened with the duties of a diocesan bishop and major responsibility for the Confraternity of Christian Doctrine, founded the National Catholic Rural Life Conference, which eventually had a membership of about ten thousand rural pastors, farmers, teachers, sociologists, economists, and agricultural agents. It endeavoured to promote the general welfare of the rural population, to care specifically for Roman Catholics living on the land, and to seek the conversion of non-Roman Catholics.[232]

To coördinate the many lay activities the National Council of Catholic Women and the National Council of Catholic Men were set up as the Lay

[228] *The 1958 National Catholic Almanac*, p. 554.
[229] *Ibid.*, pp. 559–571. On the Christophers see James Keller, *Careers That Change Your World* (Garden City, N.Y., Doubleday and Co., 1951, pp. xiii, 302), *passim*.
[230] *The 1958 National Catholic Almanac*, p. 558.
[231] *Ibid.*, p. 551.
[232] *Ibid.*, p. 538; Shaw, *op. cit.*, pp. 63–97.

Department of the National Catholic Welfare Conference and, like the latter, were of post-1914 origin. The women's council developed more rapidly than the men's. It functioned through diocesan councils and the many societies which were associated or federated with them. By 1959 it had 98 diocesan councils and 11,000 affiliated organizations and was thought to be reaching 11,000,000 women. The men's council was somewhat slower in getting under way, but by 1954 it numbered 48 diocesan councils and over 8,000 affiliated organizations. It employed field agents who organized diocesan federations and set up leadership training institutes for key men in the diocesan councils. It also was responsible for the weekly *Catholic Hour,* the weekly *Christian in Action,* and the bi-weekly *Church of the Air* over national radio systems, and in 1953 it began producing television programmes called *Look Up and Live* and *Lamp unto My Feet.* It sought to represent Roman Catholic men on national and international issues and through its local and diocesan councils to perform other functions, such as compiling a religious census and operating speakers' bureaus.[233] Interestingly, both the national councils were paralleled by similar Protestant organizations, which were related to the National Council of Churches of Christ in the U.S.A.[234]

Even this cursory glance at the multiplicity of organizations must reveal several characteristics of the Roman Catholic Church in the United States in the four decades which followed World War I. One was the growth of full commitment to the religious life as represented by orders and congregations. In no country in Europe—or anywhere else—was it so marked. Another was the multiplication of predominantly lay organizations. Between 1918 and 1958 they more than doubled in numbers and membership. Again the record was not equalled either in Europe as a whole or in any other portion of the globe. A third was the fashion in which the Roman Catholics of the United States were being knit together in a self-conscious fellowship which transcended their ethnic sources and which in a religiously pluralistic society set them off from their fellow citizens. In many Protestant denominations lay organizations multiplied, but in none were they as numerous, and in few did they set the members of their denominations so apart from those of other denominations. Many of the Protestant organizations transcended denominational lines, but only a minority of the Roman Catholic ones did so.

THE PREPARATION AND SUPPORT OF PROFESSIONAL LEADERSHIP

For the Protestant denominations, the Roman Catholic Church, and the Eastern Churches the rapid growth of membership posed the difficult problem

---

[233] *The 1958 National Catholic Almanac,* p. 536; Ward, *op. cit.,* pp. 121–137.
[234] *Yearbook of American Churches, 1957,* p. 7.

of recruiting, training, and supporting professional leadership, chiefly clergy, to give adequate pastoral care to the burgeoning numbers. Part of the problem was the urgent necessity of seeing that the leadership was prepared to meet the challenges of the revolutionary age.

A comprehensive study of the Protestant ministry made early in the 1930's pointed out how the position of the clergyman had changed in two generations. Formerly he had been the best-educated man in his community and often its leading citizen. Now the education of lawyers and doctors and even of many business men was equal or superior to his. At one time the church was central in the life of the community and performed many moral, social, and educational functions. Latterly in these respects it had been largely superseded by other institutions. The complexity of modern life confronted the minister, as it did his church, with problems scarcely known a few decades before. The psychiatrist was supplanting the clergyman as a personal counsellor. A rising scepticism sprung from the advance of factual knowledge threatened with erosion the convictions to which the minister could formerly appeal.[235] By the mid-1950's one effect of the revolutionary age was that American Protestants were losing their traditional conception of the clergy and had not yet clearly defined the place of the ministry in the fluid times in which they lived. Partly because society was becoming more complex and pluralistic the role of the minister appeared to defy precise description. Historically the Protestant clergyman was at once pastor, preacher, and priest. Those three facets of his profession persisted. In general a new function seemed to be emerging. It did not displace the historic mission of the clergyman but it made of him what was called a "pastoral director." He was to oversee a local congregation and enable it through the manifold organizations which characterized a church in the activistic American society to grow into "the stature of the fullness of Christ" as a unit of the "body of Christ." He was the administrator of a community with the purpose of making that community a "minister" as he himself was a "minister" to increase among men the love of God and neighbour.[236]

As in the nineteenth century, in the post-1914 decades the preparation of Protestant ministers took place mainly in denominational seminaries which were not affiliated with universities. However, increasingly the teachers of denominational schools obtained their post-graduate training in theological schools which were units of a university and which were in fact although not always in theory undenominational. That fact and the professional societies for the specialized disciplines of the theological schools—such as Biblical studies, theology, and

235 Brown, *et al.*, *The Education of American Ministers*, Vol. I, pp. 6–14.
236 H. Richard Niebuhr in collaboration with Daniel Day Williams and James M. Gustafson, *The Purpose of the Church and Its Ministry* (New York, Harper & Brothers, 1956, pp. xvi, 134), pp. 48–94.

church history—which brought together the men teaching in these areas contributed to a common pattern of theological education. Moreover, the American Association of Theological Schools, a post-World War I development, by its meetings of administrators and by setting standards for the accreditation which most of the schools prized, made for uniformity.

Theological education was particularly important, for the level of education for the population as a whole rose rapidly during the twentieth century and the proportion of church members who had college or university degrees mounted with the growth of the "affluent society" of the 1940's and 1950's. If the clergy were to be adequately equipped they must have a formal training equal to that of their parishioners. The level of education differed from denomination to denomination. In those where the standards were lower clergy with more advanced formal preparation might not be able to "communicate"—to employ a much-used word of the period—with parishioners lacking that background. Yet the denominations were few which had no local congregations with college or university graduates. In general the communions with a tradition of official establishment by the state in Europe—Protestant Episcopal, Lutheran, Presbyterian, and Reformed—and the Congregational church, until the nineteenth century the established church in much of New England, had higher educational standards for the ministry than did those stemming from the form of evangelism which prevailed in the United States. In the twentieth century the requirements for ordination were raised in some of the latter, especially in the Methodist Church.[237]

We do not have sufficient data to tell whether the preparation of the Protestant ministry in the United States kept pace with the educational level of the population. Although experience showed that in general the best work was done by men who were graduates of both college and seminary, in 1926 only one-third of the ministers in the seventeen largest white Protestant denominations had that training, and for Protestantism as a whole the proportion was much smaller.[238] The percentage of rural ministers without it was higher than of urban ministers.[239] While we do not possess comparable statistics for the 1950's, we know that in the twenty-five years between 1920 and 1955 the theological schools which required college graduation for admission had a remarkable growth. Early in the 1920's only 28 out of 131 Protestant theological seminaries had more than 75 per cent. of college graduates in their student bodies. In 1955, in contrast, 119 reported at least that proportion in their enrollment and another 58 said that 90 per cent. or more had college degrees.[240] In general, the academic preparation of the members of the faculties showed a decided im-

[237] Brown, *op. cit.*, Vol. I, pp. 34–44.
[238] *Ibid.*, pp. 55, 65.
[239] Fry, *The U.S. Looks at Its Churches*, pp. 64, 65.
[240] Niebuhr, Williams, and Gustafson, *The Advancement of Theological Education*, pp. 7–9.

provement between 1929–1930 and 1954–1955, but in spite of an increase in their salaries in dollars, in terms of purchasing power they were more poorly paid in the latter than in the former year. In that same period the student enrollment increased more rapidly than the teachers, so that the number of students per faculty member rose from 14 to 22.7 or, if part-time teachers were included, from 10.5 to 15.7. Presumably the individual student was not being given as much attention as formerly.[241]

These figures do not take account of the Bible schools which were multiplying after World War I in both numbers and enrollments. For them no comprehensive study was available. Their requirements for admission and graduation were not as high as those of the theological seminaries. The men they trained usually served small churches whose members had slight formal education and were of a theologically conservative Evangelical temper which tended to be anti-intellectual and held that education quenched the Spirit.

For the Roman Catholic Church, with its rapidly growing membership, the problem of a sufficient number of clergy was pressing and chronic. In general, with the falling off of immigration after 1914, progress was made in keeping pace with the need. In 1956 the United States had 48,349 priests, or a ratio of one priest to every 696 Roman Catholics. Of this number 29,734 were seculars (the diocesan clergy), whose primary service was in the parishes, and 18,615 were regulars (members of orders and congregations which were chiefly engaged in teaching, preaching missions, and other special assignments), although some had charge of parishes. A total of 8,995 priests, seculars and regulars, were giving full time to teaching. The situation was not as favourable as in Ireland, where the ratio was one priest to every 560 Roman Catholics.[242] Indeed, each year several scores of priests came from Ireland to the United States, for that island produced more than it required, and, since they had English, language was not a barrier and they came to a church in which the Irish tradition was strong.

That the Roman Catholic Church in the United States was catching up with the demand for clergy was seen in the record in the Archdiocese of Chicago. Here, with nearly 2,000,000 members in the mid-1950's, a fairly steady increase was seen in the proportion of priests to the total of the faithful. In 1910, on the eve of World War I, the archdiocese had one priest to an average of 6,448 Roman Catholics. In 1920, with the abrupt halt of immigration the latter figure had shrunk to 5,425. In 1930 it rose again to 5,812, but in 1940 it fell to 4,798 and in 1950 to 4,162. Yet even in 1950 the Chicago archdiocese was said to be badly under-staffed.[243]

[241] *Ibid.*, pp. 16–20, 38, 39.
[242] Ellis, *American Catholicism*, p. 176.
[243] Houtart, *Aspects Sociologiques du Catholicisme Américain*, p. 158.

How far, if at all, did the preparation of the rank and file of the Roman Catholic clergy equip them to meet the problems of the revolutionary age? For ordination the great majority were given a prolonged course which included philosophy, theology, and other subjects immediately germane to their duties. In 1926 only 6.6 per cent. of the priests were reported to be without college or seminary training and 68 per cent. were said to be graduates of both a college and a seminary.[244] But in the 1950's some Roman Catholic intellectuals who were loyal to their church were insisting that the theological seminaries and their students were completely segregated from the educational life of the community as a whole, and that the attitude fostered was one of passive receptivity of accepted authority with a minimum of critical activity and individual initiative. The complaint was heard that with notable exceptions both bishops and religious superiors who were responsible for the education of religious teachers shared in the general absence of an intellectual tradition in the Roman Catholic population of the country.[245] The lack of that tradition was ascribed to the nature of that population. The Roman Catholic constituency in the United States was predominantly from the nineteenth- and twentieth-century immigration, was drawn from the lower income and social strata of Europe, in the United States tended to live in what were in effect urban ghettos, and suffered from the disdain and dislike of the older American stock and from a sense of inferiority. However, the fact that in the 1950's Roman Catholic scholars in good standing were beginning to voice such criticisms was evidence of a growing awareness of the issues and of a determination to face them.[246]

As we saw a few pages back, in the 1950's the growth of the Eastern Churches was so recent that by 1962 only a beginning had been made in the United States in training clergy for them. However, by that year several institutions which we named had been brought into being for that purpose.

THE CHANGING IMPACT OF CHRISTIANITY ON EDUCATION IN THE UNITED STATES

Closely related to the adequacy of the professional leadership to guide the Christians of the United States in meeting constructively the revolutionary age was the question of the effect of Christianity on the education of the nation. Here, as in so much of the world in the nineteenth and twentieth centuries, the record was one of contrasts. On the one hand Christianity appeared to be fading out of the educational structure and from the intellectual currents which were shaping the nation, and on the other hand vigour was evident in facing the challenge in both new and old ways.

[244] Fry, *op. cit.*, p. 64.
[245] O'Dea, *American Catholic Dilemma*, pp. 10, 68, 69.
[246] For some of the criticisms see *ibid.*, pp. xii, xiii, 10; Ellis, *American Catholics and the Intellectual Life, passim.*

We have noted the large part which Protestantism had in fostering education in the nineteenth century.[247] We have seen that it was responsible for the initiation of much of the primary and secondary education, including that conducted by the state, and for shaping educational ideals. We have remarked that most of the higher education of the country in the nineteenth century and earlier was in colleges and universities founded by Protestants. We have also called attention to the very large share that Protestants had in the beginnings of education for Negroes on all levels from the primary grades to universities and professional schools. We saw that towards the end of the nineteenth century the state had assumed responsibility for a mounting share of the educational process, at first chiefly in elementary schools, then in secondary schools, and eventually in colleges, universities, and professional schools. We also commented on the mounting secularization of education in all its stages but noted that in colleges and universities voluntary student Christian movements assisted by members of the faculty were emerging to offset the trend. In the second half of the nineteenth century they took the form of Young Men's and Young Women's Christian Associations, but by 1914 denominational organizations were beginning to appear.

In the four and a half decades which followed the outbreak of World War I striking developments were seen. At first glance it appeared that the de-Christianizing forces were winning. Many teachers, especially on the university level, regarded religion as incompatible with learning, and Christianity as obscurantist or at best irrelevant. Numbers of students took the same attitude.[248] In elementary and secondary education the influence of John Dewey was dominant, and while not expressly anti-Christian it seemed to be ruling Christianity out of the schools as unnecessary. The vast majority of Protestant children had their elementary education in the public schools. But a few Protestant denominations, notably the Missouri Lutheran Church, maintained parochial schools and by 1960 such schools were increasing in some other denominations, especially in the Protestant Episcopal Church. In higher education a few new colleges were created by Protestant churches or undenominational Protestant movements, but numbers of colleges and universities which owed their founding to churches became independent. Some Protestant colleges died of financial starvation. Between 1940 and 1950 the total of Protestant colleges decreased by fourteen.[249] The rise in enrollment in state colleges and universities far outstripped that in the Protestant colleges. In many of the Protestant church-related

---

247 Volume III, Chapter VI.
248 On student attitudes in the 1950's see Philip E. Jacob, *Changing Values in Colleges. An Exploratory Study of the Impact of College Teaching* (New York, Harper & Brothers, 1957, pp. xvi, 174), *passim.*
249 *The Christian Century*, Vol. LXXVI, p. 385 (April 1, 1959). See a list of the Church-related Protestant colleges in 1954 in Snavely, *The Church and the Four-Year College*, pp. 74-136.

colleges secularization appeared to be proceeding apace with only vestigial remnants of their earlier professed faith. Although the large majority of the students in both state and church-related colleges had been baptized, scepticism was rife. That was part of the rebellion of adolescence against what had been received from the elders, but even when formal ties with the Church were retained indifference and unbelief were chronic.

Yet in many ways vigour was displayed by Protestantism in stemming the secularizing tide. In 1954 nearly five hundred junior colleges, colleges, and universities were listed as church-related.[250] The degree of control by ecclesiastical bodies varied. In some institutions it was entirely absent, in others it was slight, but in others it was very marked. Many denominations had boards of education or corresponding agencies for assisting and supervising their colleges and for initiating or aiding pastoral care for their students in state institutions. In 1915 the Council of Church Boards of Education organized the Association of American Colleges.[251] For further coördinating and stimulating these efforts the National Council of the Churches of Christ in the U.S.A. had the Commission on Christian Higher Education. Among the features of the Commission was the Faculty Christian Fellowship. In 1954 the Commission held the first of a series of convocations on the Christian college. It also promoted the discussion of the nature of the Christian college.[252] To help prepare college and university teachers who would be emphatically and intelligently Christian the National Council for Religion in Higher Education was inaugurated in 1922.[253] A larger enterprise with much the same purpose was later undertaken by the Danforth Foundation. It aided prospective college and university teachers in their graduate studies and, although Protestant in its source and leadership, assisted not only Protestants but also Roman Catholics and Jews. In the decades immediately after World War I mounting evidences were seen that the tide of secularism in higher education had turned. Although it was not denied that secularism persisted in college faculties and that by many of their members Christianity was regarded as peripheral or was even attacked or derided, increasingly administrative officers sought to aid the Christian faith as essential in education.[254]

The church-related colleges were reported to be shifting from defensive to more positive measures.[255] In two-thirds of the colleges chapel was maintained, in the 1940's with attendance required in about half of the colleges. More and more chairs and departments of Bible or religion were introduced, many of

[250] *The Christian Scholar*, Vol. XXXVII, pp. 330–341 (June, 1954).
[251] Snavely, *op. cit.*, pp. 176–183.
[252] *The Christian Scholar*, Vol. XXXVII, pp. 12–29 (March, 1954); *ibid.*, No. 3 (September, 1954), *passim*.
[253] *Ibid.*, p. 169 (June, 1954).
[254] Cuninggim, *The College Seeks Religion*, pp. 23 ff.
[255] *Ibid.*, pp. 54–57.

them in colleges and universities—church-related, independent but originally founded by the churches, and state institutions. Chaplains were appointed and supported by an increasing number of colleges and universities. By 1938 more than two hundred men and women were spending three-fourths or more of their time as denominational university pastors.[256] Comprehensive plans were developed for promoting religion in the state teachers colleges in which a large proportion of the staffs of the public schools were trained.[257]

Voluntary student Christian organizations multiplied. The Young Men's and Young Women's Christian Associations continued but were not as prominent on the campuses as before World War I.[258] The scope of the interests of the Student YMCA's and YWCA's rapidly broadened. Bible study, long characteristic of both movements, continued, but waned. The involvement of the United States in world affairs was reflected in growing attention to international relations and programmes for peace. Race relations and the problems of labour and industry loomed large. Foreign missions remained an interest, but less emphasis was placed on them than formerly. In general a liberal theological outlook prevailed. On some campuses the YMCA and the YWCA merged in one Christian Association.[259] Denominational student movements multiplied. The oldest, the Wesley Foundation, was begun in 1913 at the University of Illinois and spread rapidly after World War I.[260] The largest, the Baptist Student Union, an agency of the Southern Baptist Convention, was begun in 1919 in connexion with the University of Texas.[261] The Intervarsity Christian Fellowship, conservative theologically and undenominational, spread by contagion from England and in the 1940's and 1950's its units multiplied on American campuses.

Roman Catholics were not behind Protestants in their efforts not only to stem the de-Christianization of education but also more than to keep pace with the secularizing trends of the age. Building on foundations laid in the nineteenth century, they developed the largest educational structure of any national Roman Catholic group in the world.[262] Their elementary schools enrolled a large proportion of the children of Roman Catholic parents. In 1956, for example, 9,772 elementary schools had 3,709,030 pupils, and 2,385 high schools had 722,763 students. In 1959, 10,278 elementary schools had 5,090,012 children and 2,401 high schools had 827,912 youths. As was to be expected, the schools were concentrated in states and in urban centres where most of the Roman Catholic

256 *Ibid.*, pp. 135 ff.; Shedd, *The Church Follows Its Students*, pp. 88 ff., 218 ff.

257 *Information Service*, March 29, 1952.

258 S. Wirt Wiley, *History of YMCA-Church Relations in the United States* (New York, Association Press, 1944, pp. xii, 227), pp. 89 ff.; Shedd, *Two Centuries of Student Christian Movements*, pp. 375 ff.

259 Shedd, *Two Centuries of Student Christian Movements*, pp. 375 ff.

260 Shedd, *The Church Follows Its Students*, pp. 20, 125.

261 *Ibid.*, pp. 87 ff.

262 O'Dea, *op. cit.*, p. 9.

population was found. The Archdiocese of New York and the Diocese of Brooklyn together had approximately a fifth of the whole. The Archdiocese of Chicago was next with about a twenty-fifth of the number of schools and a fifteenth of the number of students. The Archdiocese of Philadelphia was third, and the Archdiocese of Boston fourth. By 1959, 259 colleges and universities were supported with a total of 250,277 students.[263] The achievement registered in this bare statistical summary is the more impressive when we recall that it was accomplished with little or no aid from public taxation and made possible by communities which for the most part, because of their recent immigrant origin, were in the lower income brackets, and when we remember that at the same time thousands of parish churches and hundreds of monasteries, theological seminaries, orphanages, and hospitals were being erected and maintained.

As the twentieth century progressed the Roman Catholic record in higher education was increasingly remarkable. It was said that 91 colleges had been founded between 1920 and 1959—26 of them after 1940.[264] Roman Catholics had founded colleges early in the nation's history. For years these institutions had no thought of becoming universities with graduate programmes, for that development was slow in beginning elsewhere in the United States. Towards the end of the nineteenth century, led by St. Louis University, a Jesuit institution, they began to conform to the pattern of a four-year course common among the colleges of Protestant origin. Colleges for women appeared, somewhat later than those founded by Protestants.[265] By 1871 a few master of arts degrees were awarded by eleven colleges.[266] The formal opening of the Catholic University of America in 1889 inaugurated a new era and that institution became the capstone of the Roman Catholic educational structure in the United States. At the outset it had hard going, but by 1914 it possessed faculties of theology, philosophy, law, and technology and also was admitting undergraduates. Yet it did not prove attractive to lay students and in the nation at large it did not have as high a reputation for scholarship as had been attained by several state universities and some of the universities of Protestant origin. Other Roman Catholic institutions developed graduate work and by 1930 their quality was said to be high through the master's degree. Yet by the 1950's only nine offered the Ph.D., and that in just a few fields.[267] In the twentieth century professional schools developed, some in connexion with colleges and universities and others as separate institutions. By 1955 three teachers colleges and twenty-one normal

[263] *The 1958 National Catholic Almanac*, pp. 480–483; *The New York Times*, April 16, 1960; Snavely, *op. cit.*, pp. 115–125, 262.

[264] *The Christian Century*, Vol. LXXVI, p. 385 (April 1, 1959).

[265] Power, *A History of Catholic Higher Education in the United States, passim*, especially pp. 84, 184.

[266] *Ibid.*, p. 208.

[267] *Ibid.*, pp. 234, 235, 266.

training schools had been created. In 1956 twelve colleges had schools for such diverse professions as engineering, architecture, nursing, music, journalism, and foreign service.[268] In the 1940's and 1950's books began to multiply on the place and purpose of the Roman Catholic college.[269]

Although the higher education maintained by Roman Catholics made marked advances, in 1962 it had not caught up with that begun by Protestants and supported by them or the state. As some Roman Catholics sadly confessed, their church was far from bearing a proportionate share of the burden of intellectual achievement required of the United States in the revolutionary age.[270]

To coördinate and promote Roman Catholic education the National Catholic Educational Association was formed in 1904. It held annual meetings and in 1958 reported a membership of 10,276 institutions and individuals.[271] Yet as late as 1961 over four hundred Roman Catholic school systems were in existence in the United States, and as yet were correlated only loosely if at all.

Widespread criticism attended the growth of the Roman Catholic educational system. Chiefly from Protestants, it was part of the persistent opposition to the Roman Catholic Church. Giving strength to it was the fear of Roman Catholic domination. The parochial schools especially were denounced as un-American, a threat to the public schools. The public schools were held to be one of the chief bulwarks of American democracy and a major means of assimilating the many diverse immigrant elements which had flooded the country and of inculcating patriotism. Sectarian elementary education, of which the Roman Catholic parochial schools were by far the largest element, was regarded as a principal enemy. Roman Catholics were loud in protesting their loyalty and in demanding financial assistance from the state for the contribution which they made to the education of the nation's youth. They insisted that they were required to pay taxes for the support of the public schools and then for conscience' sake maintained from their own pockets schools to ensure that their children were given what they regarded as a well-rounded education in which religion was an integral part—contrasting, so they said, with the public schools, in which religion was omitted and secularism was promoted. In Oregon in 1922 the opponents of the Roman Catholic schools succeeded in placing on the statute books legislation requiring all children between the ages of eight and sixteen to attend the public schools. However, in 1925 the United States Su-

---

268 *Ibid.*, p. 253.
269 As examples see M. Redempta Prose, *The Liberal Arts Ideal in Catholic Colleges for Women in the United States* (Washington, The Catholic University of America Press, 1943, pp. xiii, 177); Julian Ryan, *The Idea of a Catholic College* (New York, *Sheed and Ward,* 1945, pp. viii, 136); Edward A. Fitzpatrick, *The Catholic College in the World Today* (Milwaukee, The Bruce Publishing Co., 1954, pp. xii, 269).
270 Ellis, *American Catholicism,* pp. 114–116; Ellis, *American Catholics and the Intellectual Life, passim;* O'Dea, *op. cit.,* pp. 4, 10.
271 *The 1958 National Catholic Almanac,* p. 505.

preme Court declared the law unconstitutional, thus sanctioning parochial schools.[272]

Student organizations proliferated to promote the faith both in Roman Catholic institutions and in non-Catholic colleges and universities. Newman Clubs had been in existence since 1893 and in 1958 numbered 442 with a membership of about 50,000. The Pax Romana, with headquarters in Switzerland, constituted the Youth Department of the National Catholic Welfare Conference. In 1937 the National Federation of Catholic College Students was organized. The International Federation of Catholic Alumnae was begun in 1914. We have seen that in 1918 the Catholic Students' Mission Crusade was initiated.[273]

THE RESPONSE TO THE INTELLECTUAL CURRENTS OF THE AGE: BY WAY OF INTRODUCTION

From the impact of Christianity upon education in the United States we naturally turn to the response to the intellectual currents of the age. In earlier volumes we have sought to record that response in the eighteenth and nineteenth centuries.[274] We have noted that in the nineteenth century the main efforts at adjustment to the intellectual revolution were in denominations which drew largely from the better-educated elements of the older stock—especially the Congregationalists and Presbyterians—but that outstanding individuals and movements were seen in some denominations which owed their growth to the methods of evangelism appealing to the less well educated. We also called attention to the vigorous opposition to that adjustment. We noted that the Roman Catholic Church was so engrossed in caring for the immigrant flood that it was only slightly affected by the intellectual conflicts which punctuated its course in Europe.

In the decades following 1914 the response became still more varied. As with so much of our story, to describe it in all its complexity would extend to a large volume what we must attempt to summarize in a few pages. Even more than for the nineteenth century we must limit our account to a brief sketch of some major trends and to a few individuals. As in the nineteenth century, several of the intellectual challenges to Christianity originated on the other side of the Atlantic and others were of American origin. More numerous than in the nineteenth century were the efforts of Protestants to meet the challenges by using the scholarly procedures which had been developed in the revolutionary age and by accepting many of the findings obtained through them. On the other hand, resistance in Protestantism to these procedures and findings be-

[272] Ellis, *Documents of American Catholic History*, pp. 635–638; Shaw, *Edwin Vincent O'Hara*, pp. 98–107.
[273] *The 1958 National Catholic Almanac*, pp. 540, 541.
[274] Volume I, Chapter IV; Volume III, Chapter VII.

came more determined and vocal. As yet the Roman Catholic Church in the United States was not greatly disturbed. Here and there were those who wrestled with the issues, but the level of scholarship remained so low that relatively little serious and intelligent attention was given them.

Response to the Intellectual Currents of the Age: Protestant Attempts at Accommodation

Since most of the forces which played on Protestant theology in Europe were felt, and since the major theologians of the Continent and the British Isles were read, something of the pattern with which we have become familiar east of the Atlantic was also seen in the United States.[275] In general the liberalism which had prevailed in many circles in the latter part of the nineteenth century persisted into the 1920's and 1930's. Owing in part to the disillusionment brought by World War I, the liberal stream with its optimistic view of human nature and the competence of man's mind dwindled and in its place came what was usually termed neo-orthodoxy, with emphasis upon man's depravity, the fallibility of human reason, and God's initiative in revelation and Christ. The ultra-conservative reaction against the dominant intellectual currents was more widespread and vigorous and took different forms than in Europe.

Two philosophers who taught at Harvard gave impetus to the liberal trend. Alfred North Whitehead (1861–1947) was English-born, of Quaker ancestry, the son of a clergyman and the nephew of an Anglican bishop who served in India. A graduate of Cambridge, he taught mathematics in Cambridge and the University of London. He came to Harvard in 1924 as professor of philosophy, and most of his writing on philosophy was done there. In the United States he maintained no connexion with a church. His thought had strong Christian elements, but in some respects it differed from Christianity. Coming to religion as a metaphysician, Whitehead regarded God, not as the Prime Mover as had Aristotle (whom he esteemed as the greatest metaphysician), but as "the Principle of Concretion." He viewed God as the "Ultimate Limitation," and since no reason could be given for "that limitation which it stands in His nature to impose," God is "the Ultimate Irrationality." God, he held, "is not concrete, but He is the ground of concrete reality." He insisted that "no reason can be given for the nature of God, because that nature is the ground of rationality." He held that God is necessary to the world and the world is necessary to God. He believed that God is not complete, has new possibilities, and needs the world to bring them to realization. He maintained that the names given to God by the several religions corresponded to systems of thought de-

---

[275] See Sidney E. Ahlstrom, "Continental Influence on American Christian Thought Since World War I," in *Church History*, Vol. XXVII, pp. 256–272 (September, 1958).

rived from the experiences of those who coined them. He held that although religion was fading from the life of mankind, particularly among the European peoples, there need not be irreconcilable conflict between science and religion, that the two were constantly changing, the latter more rapidly than the former, and that religion was always recurring and with an added richness and purity of content. He felt that the essence of true religion is worship, and that "worship is a surrender to the claim for assimilation, urged with the motive force of mutual love," and that the "worship of God is not a rule of safety" but "an adventure of the spirit, a flight after the unattainable."[276]

William Ernest Hocking (1873——), slightly younger than Whitehead, born in Cleveland, Ohio, and graduated from Harvard, taught in Andover Theological Seminary, the University of California, and Yale, and from 1914 until his retirement in 1943 was professor of philosophy at Harvard. A Congregationalist, he was deeply religious and was actively connected with the Protestant missionary enterprise and with efforts for world peace. Like Whitehead, he was hopeful. He was persuaded that the older philosophies had failed to satisfy, that the newer philosophies had thus far also failed, that Idealism had been unable to work satisfactorily because it was unfinished, and that pragmatism, with its desire for "more valid objectivity, substantiality in the world beyond self," had limited the effectiveness of Idealism in religion. Idealism, he held, had not found its way to worship, to the historical in religion, or to "the authoritative and the wholly super-personal." Yet he believed that pragmatism was also an imperfect guide; all it could do was show that "that which does not work is not true," but to say that "whatever works is true" was invalid. Mysticism, he said, had forms which must be rejected but, by finding "the Absolute in immediate experience," could make valuable and authentic contributions. He held that we could be more certain that God is than what He is. God, he maintained, is immediately and permanently known as the Other Mind, which in creating nature is also creating us, and it is through the knowledge of God that I am able to know men. He thought of worship, or prayer, which institutes communication with God wherein will answers will, as the special sphere of will in religion. He saw religion as contributing to the wealth of human life by creating men and conferring on them power and freedom to create.[277]

[276] Alfred North Whitehead, *Science and the Modern World* (New York, The Macmillan Co., 1926, pp. xii, 304), pp. 249–276. Among the other books by Whitehead see *Process and Reality. An Essay in Cosmology*, the Gifford Lectures (New York, The Macmillan Co., 1929, pp. xii, 647); *Religion in the Making* (New York, The Macmillan Co., 1926, pp. 160); and *Adventures in Ideas* (New York, The Macmillan Co., 1933, pp. xii, 392).
See his autobiography in Paul Arthur Schilpp, editor, *The Philosophy of Alfred North Whitehead* (Evanston and Chicago, Northwestern University, 1941, pp. xviii, 745).
[277] William Ernest Hocking, *The Meaning of God in Human Experience. A Philosophic Study of Religion* (New Haven, Yale University Press, 1912, pp. xxxiv, 586), *passim*.

Even during the holocaust of World War I with its shaking of the foundations of civilization Hocking was hopeful for the remaking of human nature and saw in Christianity a power to that end. He said that if God exists as good will, He must appear in the temporal order and must suffer not alone with us but also for us, and at our hands. Belief in such a God, he maintained, would give history a meaning over and above any visible or experimental significance that it may have. He doubted that reason could affirm this view of history as a fact but held that it could show that, if it was a fact, the human dilemma would be solved and that some features of the world and its history are in accord with that fact. To him the function of religion was not to prove God but to affirm God. He himself came out on the side of the Christian affirmation.[278]

In a further statement, made soon after the beginning of World War II and subsequent to extensive travel in the Middle East and Asia, Hocking was even more emphatic that Christianity could meet the need for a world faith. He noted that, subjected to the forces of the revolutionary age which were eroding old cultures, men everywhere were searching for a unifying basis for what must be a world culture. Humanism, he held, was insufficient and Christianity alone could fill the vacuum. He maintained that through its conviction of the incarnation of the Christ, the human face of God, born into the world as a special deed of God, in a life far transcending time and place, race, and sect, Christianity was slowly making its way as a possession of mankind. Moreover, Christianity was the only religion which had met, and on the whole successfully, the challenges of the intellectual forces of the revolutionary age. He recognized the handicap inherent in the fact that Western civilization, while not Christian, was in a sense a child of Christianity and went with it. He recognized that although in its ideal character Christianity potentially contained all that any religion had possessed, Christians had not yet solved the problem of the application of their faith to war, property, and family, nor had Christianity thus far included all that other religions contained. If it was to fulfil its mission as a world religion its adherents must seek to realize in practice what was inherent in the essence of their faith.[279]

Looking at developments in the more strictly theological approach as distinguished from the primarily philosophical, we note that, in contrast with the nineteenth century, Unitarians were producing few leaders. The impetus which they had once given to the liberal trend in Protestant scholarship had largely spent its force. The most widely known of their clergy, John Haynes Holmes (1879——), declared that as he grew older he became less and less interested

---

[278] William Ernest Hocking, *Human Nature and Its Remaking* (New Haven, Yale University Press, 1918, rev. ed., 1923, pp. xxviii, 496), *passim*, especially pp. 363 ff.

[279] William Ernest Hocking, *Living Religions and a World Faith* (New York, The Macmillan Co., 1940, pp. 291), *passim*, especially pp. 215 ff.

in theology. In 1919 he left the Unitarian denomination and transformed the Church of the Messiah in New York City, of which he was pastor, into the Community Church, with "primary allegiance to the religion of mankind," and stood in its pulpit as "the representative of nothing less than what Channing proudly proclaimed as 'the Universal Church which is the company of all good and holy men.'" In doing so he removed from the covenant of the Church of the Messiah "all Unitarian and even Christian implications."[280]

Since from its early years until well past the first quarter of the twentieth century the University of Chicago was a major centre of daring Protestant theological thought, it was not surprising that some of the extreme liberals were connected with it. Thus Edward Scribner Ames (1870–1958) was long on its faculty. Reared in the Disciples of Christ and remaining in their fellowship, he studied in the Yale Divinity School, had graduate work there and at the University of Chicago in philosophy, and in addition to teaching in the latter institution was a charter member and the long-time pastor of a church of his denomination in that neighbourhood, was dean of the Disciples Divinity House associated with the University, and wrote extensively. Under his guidance the Chicago church accepted into membership persons from any denomination and on confession of faith with or without baptism. Prospective members were not subjected to formal theological tests. Ames, like Holmes, sought an interpretation of religion which would unify all religious people, both those who were in and those who were outside existing churches, and endeavoured to utilize differences in "the coöperative quest for truer ideas and finer attitudes." He wished to go beyond Protestantism. The only parts of the Apostles' Creed to which he could subscribe were its statements of what he believed to be fact and experience—that Jesus Christ suffered under Pontius Pilate, was crucified, dead, and buried. He was convinced that either Christianity must become a religion of this world, arising from the social process and "seeking to fulfil inherent, natural, social values," or it would have no appeal to the revolutionary age. He repudiated original sin and human depravity and believed in "progressive growth in morality and social idealism."[281]

Henry Nelson Wieman (1884——), the son of a Presbyterian minister, reared a Presbyterian, and educated in Presbyterian schools, came to public attention in the 1920's through teaching the philosophy of religion in the University of Chicago. He had previously studied in Germany and Harvard, had for a brief time been a pastor, and then had taught in Occidental College, a Presbyterian institution. He had never been conscious of traumatic religious adjustments to

280 Holmes, *I Speak for Myself,* pp. 117, 118, 222–227.
281 Edward Scribner Ames, in Ferm, *Contemporary American Theology,* Vol. II, pp. 1–29; *Beyond Theology. The Autobiography of Edward Scribner Ames,* edited by Van Meter Ames (University of Chicago Press, 1959, pp. xii, 223); *Religion* (New York, Henry Holt and Co., 1929, pp. vi, 324); *The New Orthodoxy* (University of Chicago Press, 2nd ed., 1925, pp. xxv, 127).

current ideas, had read much of nineteenth-century literature and science with enthusiasm, and in his undergraduate days had determined to teach the philosophy of religion and had consciously prepared himself for that profession. He studied under Eucken, Troeltsch, and Hocking but did not fully accept the thought of any of them. He was impressed by Dewey and thrilled by Whitehead, although he did not entirely agree with either. He sought to promote theocentric rather than anthropocentric religion. He insisted on the scientific method in religion because he wished "to deal with the objective, existential God, and not merely ideas." He frankly rejected Barth because his idea of God was "simply what tradition hands down" and declared that what Barth and his followers accepted as revelation was "mere prejudice." He maintained that the only way to arrive at a knowledge of God was by observation and reason; it could "be shown that God is not a personality." He held that God was more than personality but that He "is that kind of interaction between things which generates and magnifies personality and all its highest values."[282]

Douglas Clyde Macintosh (1877–1948) was a liberal but was much nearer to the historic Christian position than were Ames and Wieman. Born and reared in Canada, a Baptist, in his teens he had a religious experience of commitment and joy of the Evangelical kind which in his later years as well he deemed valid. For a time in his youth he was a pastor and engaged in evangelistic meetings. After graduating at McMaster University he went to Chicago to study philosophy, psychology, and theology with men who made the early years of that university memorable. He became familiar especially with the German philosophers, theologians, and Biblical scholars of the nineteenth century and with the writings of William James and James Royce. He was influenced successively by several of them. He also covered some branches of the natural sciences. In other words, he cultivated an acquaintance with the various facets of the thought of the revolutionary age. This he did with the purpose of being a Christian apologist—and doing so with an open-mindedness which would lead him to follow what he believed to be truth even if, to use a phrase which he was fond of quoting from an early nineteenth-century theologian, it "took him over Niagara." In 1909 he joined the faculty of the Yale Divinity School and continued to serve on it throughout the rest of his teaching career. There he had as students several who were to help shape American Protestant the-

---

[282] Henry Nelson Wieman, in Ferm, *op. cit.,* Vol. I, pp. 339–352. Among Wieman's many books see *Religious Experience and Scientific Method* (New York, The Macmillan Co., 1926, pp. 387); *The Wrestle of Religion with Truth* (New York, The Macmillan Co., 1927, pp. vii, 253); *Methods of Private Religious Living* (New York, The Macmillan Co., 1929, pp. 219); *The Source of Human Good* (University of Chicago Press, 1946, pp. vii, 311); and *Man's Ultimate Commitment* (Carbondale, Southern Illinois University Press, 1958, pp. x, 318). See also, for brief descriptions and insight, Williams, *What Present-Day Theologians Are Thinking,* pp. 58, 59, 110.

ology in the second and third quarters of the twentieth century—including Reinhold and Richard Niebuhr—and his skill as a teacher was seen in the fact that, although they gladly acknowledged their debt to him, several of his outstanding pupils did not agree with him. He could not be said to have given rise to a particular school of theology. He sought by reason tested by experience to verify and re-state the Christian faith in terms of the thought currents of the age. He early familiarized himself with epistemology—the origin and the validity of knowledge—to lay a basis for the testing of the Gospel by rational processes.[283] He wrote many books, and the titles of some of them were evidence of the wide range of his interest, developed as that was from his rational, empirical approach to the Christian faith and his personal practice in applying the faith to individuals and to the collective problems of mankind.[284] Although he knew from personal experience as a chaplain in World War I and in his family the tragic side of life, he held to what he called "moral optimism." He attempted to formulate a "new, untraditional orthodoxy," holding to the essence of historic Christianity but expressing it in new ways. He maintained "that in religious experience at its best there is a revelation (discovery) of a dependable reality, divine in quality and function which promotes good will in man on condition of his maintenance of the right religious adjustment." This, he believed, could be established through reason tested by experience. He held that the Christian moral ideal is valid, apart from the question of how far it was realized or taught by the historic Jesus, and that belief in the historicity of Jesus is not indispensable to what is essentially Christian faith and life. Yet, he said, belief in the historicity of Jesus and a particular Christology, or conviction about the nature and meaning of Jesus, was psychologically essential to the highest well-being of Christianity.[285] Until physical disability laid him aside, he remained an active churchman and a quiet, earnest evangelist who for a time found fellowship with the Oxford Groups.

Rufus Matthew Jones (1863–1948) was a liberal in theology and with a quite distinct history.[286] Born and reared in a rural Maine community in a sturdy,

---

[283] Douglas Clyde Macintosh, *The Problem of Knowledge* (New York, The Macmillan Co., 1915, pp. xviii, 503).

[284] See his *Theology as an Empirical Science* (New York, The Macmillan Co., 1919, pp. xvi, 270); *The Reasonableness of Christianity* (New York, Charles Scribner's Sons, 1925, pp. xviii, 293); *Personal Religion* (New York, Charles Scribner's Sons, 1942, pp. xvi, 407); and *Social Religion* (New York, Charles Scribner's Sons, 1939, pp. xv, 336).

[285] See his autobiography in Ferm, *op. cit.*, Vol. I, pp. 277–319, especially pp. 306, 308, 311, 312.

[286] See his autobiography in four volumes telling of different stages in his life: *A Small-Town Boy* (New York, The Macmillan Co., 1941, pp. ix, 154); *Finding the Trail of Life* (New York, The Macmillan Co., 1926, pp. 148); *The Trail of Life in College* (New York, The Macmillan Co., 1929, pp. 201); *The Trail of Life in the Middle Years* (New York, The Macmillan Co., 1934, pp. 250). A brief autobiography is in Ferm, *op. cit.*, Vol. I, pp. 191–215. Biographies are by David Hinshaw, *Rufus Jones, Master Quaker* (New York, G. P. Putnam's Sons, 1951, pp. xi, 306), and Elizabeth Vining, *Friend of Life. The Biography of Rufus M. Jones* (Philadelphia, J. B. Lippincott and Co., 1958, pp. 347).

wholesome Quaker atmosphere, he remained loyal to that tradition, with its witness to the inner life and its profound conviction of the guidance of Eternal Love. In him, too, was a bubbling humour which had a tang of Yankee wit. His undergraduate years were in Haverford, a Quaker college, and he had graduate work in Harvard, Oxford, and Germany and accepted the methods of contemporary critical Biblical scholarship. Most of his teaching life was in a chair of philosophy at Haverford. In addition he wrote prodigiously. By editing for many years the *Friends Review* and its successor, *The American Friend,* and by visiting many of the Friends' meetings, he sought to acquaint his fellow Quakers with the findings of contemporary philosophy, theology, and Biblical studies and to do it in such a way that the many divisions among the Quakers would be healed. His books dealt chiefly with mysticism, the history and principles of the Quakers, and the practical application of the Christian faith. To the end of his days he held to the incarnation, resurrection, and continuing life of Christ as God's supreme approach to man. A mystic, like many other great mystics he translated his faith into action. He was chiefly responsible for the American Friends Service Committee, which began as an effort to relieve the suffering attendant on World War I and which continued through World War II and later, and was long its chairman. He also was the main creator of the American Friends Service Council and the Wider Quaker Fellowship, which sought to spread the insights of the Friends beyond Quaker circles among all sympathetic souls of whatever denomination or religion.[287]

The major periodical which embodied the liberal Protestant tradition was *The Christian Century: An Undenominational Journal of Religion.* Begun as a publication of the Disciples of Christ under its first and long-time editor, Charles Clayton Morrison (1874—   ), in accord with the early genius of that denomination it stood for Christian unity. Morrison was noted for the forthrightness and courage of his editorials and the precedent was followed by his successors. The news coverage was world-wide, and many of the articles and editorials were consciously provocative. In the five decades which followed 1914 no other periodical was as widely read in thoughtful Protestant circles in the United States. In his later years Morrison wrote books which continued to stimulate discussion.[288]

---

[287] Representative of his many books are *Social Law in the Spiritual World: Studies in Human and Divine Inter-relationship* (London, Swarthmore Press, 1923, pp. 221); *Spiritual Energies in Daily Life* (New York, The Macmillan Co., 1922, pp. xx, 179); *Spiritual Reformers in the Sixteenth and Seventeenth Centuries* (London, Macmillan and Co., 1914, pp. li, 362); *Pathways to the Reality of God* (New York, The Macmillan Co., 1931, pp. xiii, 253); *A Preface to Christian Faith in a New Age* (New York, The Macmillan Co., 1932, pp. xi, 206); *Mysticism. The Friends of God in the Fourteenth Century* (New York, The Macmillan Co., 1939, pp. 270); *The Flowering of Mysticism. New Eyes for Invisibles* (New York, The Macmillan Co., 1943, pp. ix, 185); *The Radiant Life. New Studies in Mystical Religion* (New York, The Macmillan Co., 1927, pp. 205); and *The Luminous Trail* (New York, The Macmillan Co., 1947, pp. ix, 165).

[288] Among Morrison's books were *What Is Christianity?* (Chicago, Willett, Clark and Co., 1940,

The so-called neo-orthodoxy which flourished after World War I and which largely but not entirely supplanted theological liberalism was, like liberalism, multiform—and more a trend than a clearly definable school of thought. In general it had kinship with what we have seen in Protestant circles in Europe and, like the movement on the other side of the Atlantic, was a swing away from the optimism characteristic of much of the Occident in the latter part of the nineteenth century. The reaction was given impetus by World War I and was due to an awareness of the weaknesses in Western civilization. It was in contrast with the outward confidence of the Communist world, displaying much pessimism, but on its constructive side it led to earnest soul-searching and efforts at countering basic and current evils. Neo-orthodoxy accepted many of the methods and findings of liberal Biblical and historical scholarship, but in common with the outstanding figures of the Protestant Reformation it had a vivid awareness of the sinfulness of man and stressed the Divine initiative and the inability of man without the forgiving and transforming grace of God acting through Christ and the Holy Spirit to overcome the corruption of human nature.

Reinhold Niebuhr (1892——) was widely regarded as the outstanding representative of American neo-orthodoxy. The son of a pastor of the Evangelical Synod, he was reared in that denomination before it coalesced with the Reformed Church in the United States to form the Evangelical and Reformed Church. He had a background of Pietism which was largely Lutheran in character and this may have helped to account for his emphasis on sin and justification. Graduating from a college and a theological seminary of his denomination, he took further theological work at Yale where he was under the influence of D. C. Macintosh. He also felt the impact of John Dewey and for a time was attracted by a Utopian hope and was active in the Fellowship of Reconciliation. He was convinced of the truth of the historical-critical approach to the Bible. Ordained to the ministry in the Evangelical Synod, from 1913 to 1928 he was a pastor in Detroit. In that centre of the manufacture of automobiles he came face to face with the challenge of the urban industrial society of the revolutionary age. Although his congregation grew in membership and he was greatly loved as both pastor and preacher, he felt himself frustrated by man's inhumanity to man and came to believe that the Church was not meeting the issues presented by the world in which it was set. Yet he held that the Gospel must be relevant to that world. He read Marx and Engels, but while he interpreted the situation in Detroit as a dialectical conflict and a struggle for power, he did not become a Communist. He was also interested in depth psychology. In 1928 he became a member of the faculty of Union Theological

pp. ix, 324); *Can Protestantism Win America?* (New York, Harper & Brothers, 1948, pp. viii, 225); and *The Unfinished Reformation* (New York, Harper & Brothers, 1953, pp. xvi, 236).

Seminary and remained there until his retirement (1960) because of age. While on that faculty he wrote prodigiously, preached and lectured widely in university and student circles in America and the British Isles, and took an active part in many movements to help keep mankind from going to complete ruin.

Although he was often spoken of as a theologian, Reinhold Niebuhr disclaimed that role. His special concern was social ethics and the relation to it of the Christian faith. In one of his early books, *Moral Man in Immoral Society*,[289] he pointed out that for individuals it was possible within small groups to conform to ordinary decency and morality and, indeed, to lead a noble life, but that these same men did infinite damage to the lives of thousands through the large impersonal institutions in industrial society in which they were involved. This contradicted the educational philosophy of Dewey, the social gospel, and the presuppositions of much of religious education.

Reinhold Niebuhr was impressed by the grandeur and misery of man—the contrast between man's dignity as a free spirit and man's misery as a sinner. He sought to impress on his generation the inevitability of having even the highest aspirations corrupted by egoistic motives. He held that the Christian must not succumb to either despair or complacency but could rely on the justifying grace of God. Insecurity, he maintained, is the inescapable lot of the individual, but the Christian can accept it because of the redeeming love of God. He viewed tragedy as unavoidable and saw the fulfilment of the Christian hope as beyond the cross and history. He knew that the commands of Jesus were never fully obeyed, even by Christians, but he said that they must not be dismissed as unattainable, for that would deny the grace of God. They were, rather, possible impossibilities, and every moral judgement must have as its ultimate reference the law of love as seen in the incarnation and the cross.

Here was an honest, sensitive soul facing frankly the contradictions in the revolutionary age between the high aspirations awakened by the Gospel and the grim events of the contemporary scene and the fears of man's destruction of himself and all civilization. The contradictions, as we have repeatedly pointed out, were most striking and terrifying within the historic Christendom. Because he so vividly set them forth Niebuhr caught the attention of many thoughtful and perplexed souls in the West, both Christian and non-Christian.[290]

---

[289] Reinhold Niebuhr, *Moral Man in Immoral Society, a Study in Ethics and Politics* (New York, Charles Scribner's Sons, 1932, pp. xxv, 284).

[290] Among the many books by Reinhold Niebuhr the following can be selected as representative of his thought at different stages: *Does Civilization Need Religion? A Study in the Social Resources and Limitations of Religion in Modern Life* (New York, The Macmillan Co., 1928, pp. 242); *Leaves from the Notebook of a Tamed Cynic* (Chicago, Willett, Clark and Colby, 1929, pp. xiv, 198); *Reflections on the End of an Era* (New York, Charles Scribner's Sons, 1934, pp. xii, 302); *Beyond Tragedy. Essays on the Christian Interpretation of History* (New York, Charles Scribner's Sons, 1937, pp. xi, 306); *Christianity and Power Politics* (New York, Charles Scribner's Sons,

Helmut Richard Niebuhr (1894———), younger brother of Reinhold, also graduated from a college and seminary of the Evangelical Synod, had additional theological training at Yale, and was ordained in his denomination. In 1931 he came to the faculty of the Yale Divinity School. Like his brother's, his major interest was in Christian ethics and for years his professorship had that designation. Later, and properly, theology was added to the title. Indeed, he was sometimes called the theologians' theologian. He too accepted the methods of the historical criticism of the Scriptures and was familiar with the many currents of the philosophical, theological, and social thought of the age. He did not write as voluminously as did his brother or preach and lecture as widely. However, among the thoughtful his books and articles, his lectures, and his teaching in the classroom and in seminars made a deep impression. The titles of his books give some indication of the range of his interest: *The Social Sources of Denominationalism, The Kingdom of God in America, The Meaning of Revelation,* and *Christ and Culture.*[291] He thought profoundly and perspicuously on the American religious scene and on the bearing of the Christian faith on civilization. He realized the fashion in which religious beliefs, including those of Christians, were shaped by the cultural traditions in which they were found and fearlessly raised the question of whether Christianity was so indebted to the environment in which it had developed that it was simply the product of the effort of man to solve the riddle of his existence and of the universe. Yet although he said that religion was the great self-defense of man against natural and social change, he came out flatly for the revelation of God in Jesus Christ. He was convinced that revelation meant the self-disclosure of God rather than a conviction of truths about God—that it was the conversion of our human religion through Jesus Christ.[292]

Paul Tillich (1886———) had a marked effect on the theological thought of

1940, pp. 226); *The Nature and Destiny of Man* (New York, Charles Scribner's Sons, 2 vols., 1941, 1943), the Gifford Lectures and his largest work; *The Children of Light and the Children of Darkness* (New York, Charles Scribner's Sons, 1944, pp. xiii, 190); and *Faith and History: A Comparison of Christian and Modern Views of History* (New York, Charles Scribner's Sons, 1949, pp. viii, 257). An extensive bibliography is in D. B. Robertson, *Reinhold Niebuhr's Works, A Bibliography* (Berea, Ky., Berea College Press, 1954, pp. 60). See also, autobiographical, Reinhold Niebuhr in *The Christian Century,* Vol. LXXVII, pp. 568–572 (May 11, 1960), and an intellectual autobiography, a reply to interpreters and critics, and a bibliography to 1956, with appraisals by various authors, in Charles William Kegley, editor, *Reinhold Niebuhr: His Religious, Social, and Political Thought* (New York, The Macmillan Co., 1956, pp. xiv, 486), pp. 1–23, 431–451. See a brief treatment in Soper, *Major Voices in American Theology,* pp. 37–70.

291 H. R. Niebuhr, *The Social Sources of Denominationalism* (New York, Henry Holt and Co., 1929, pp. vii, 309); *The Kingdom of God in America* (Chicago, Willett, Clark and Co., 1937, pp. xvii, 215); *The Meaning of Revelation* (New York, The Macmillan Co., 1941, pp. x, 196); and *Christ and Culture* (New York, Harper & Brothers, 1951, pp. x, 259).

292 See a partial spiritual autobiograhpy in H. Richard Niebuhr in *The Christian Century,* Vol. LXXII, pp. 248–251 (March 2, 1960). See also chapters on him by various authors in Robert Paul Ramsey, editor, *Faith and Ethics. The Theology of H. Richard Niebuhr* (New York, Harper & Brothers, 1957, pp. xiv, 306), with a bibliography of his writings. Soper, *op. cit.,* pp. 153–190, has a brief sketch.

American Protestantism in the 1930's, 1940's, and 1950's. Whether he should be classed with the neo-orthodox is not certain. Perhaps he is best described as an existentialist. He combined various contributions from his Lutheran past with the many currents of events and thought which had played on him during the stormy years of his youth and maturity. He was the son of a pastor and official of the Prussian *Landeskirche*. His boyhood was spent in towns where some of the physical survivals of the Middle Ages persisted in city walls and Gothic churches and where life appeared to be secure. His rearing was in a strict Lutheranism. The atmosphere was authoritarian. He was also influenced by Romanticism. He was impressed by nature and by the Lutheran conviction that the finite is capable of the Infinite. In his *Gymnasium* days he was subjected to the conflict between the humanism of Greece and Rome and the Christian faith. He went through a university course in philosophy and theology, was ordained in the Lutheran Church of Brandenburg, and in World War I was chaplain in the German Army. He felt kinship with Otto's *Idea of the Holy* and under the impact of Kierkegaard broke with Hegel and became an existentialist. For Tillich as for many others World War I and its aftermath had a revolutionary effect. The prolongation of the conflict, the sad plight of Germany in the years of alleged peace, an awakening to the alienation of industrial labour from the Church, and acquaintance with the writings of Marx led to affiliation with a religious socialist movement which agreed with Marx in much of his analysis but rejected his atheism. Tillich taught in several universities in Germany, wrote extensively, and in 1933 was dismissed from his professorship because of his opposition to Nazism and came to the United States. There he was on the faculty of Union Theological Seminary in New York City until the age rule led to his retirement. He then went to Harvard to a chair to which the age rule did not apply. He won a wide and respectful hearing in philosophical and theological circles and lectured and wrote extensively.[293]

Tillich was intent on placing theology in the setting of contemporary thought and current events. He endeavoured to draw on the entire Christian tradition —Catholic as well as Protestant—and to bring existentialism and theology together. He sought to fuse disparate elements in theology and modern culture. With Barth he said that theology is based on revelation, but in contrast with Barth he insisted that theology must not be mere *kerygma*—the announcement of revelation. He agreed with the liberals in accepting the historical-critical approach to the Bible, but he differed from them and agreed with Barth in holding Christ to be the criterion by which the Scriptures are to be read and in stressing the estrangement of man from God. He believed that Catholicism

[293] For an incomplete autobiography see Kegley and Bretall, *The Theology of Paul Tillich*, pp. 3–21.

and Protestantism needed each other. He rejected the authoritarianism of Roman Catholicism but had an appreciation of the sacraments as a means of grace. He valued Protestantism for its prophetic voice and Roman Catholicism for its opposition to the individualism of what he regarded as a degenerate Protestantism. He bore the impress of Kant and Schleiermacher but criticized the latter for basing too much of theology upon religious experience. He maintained that experience should be not the source of theology but a medium of theology. In his existentialism he was indebted to both Kierkegaard and Heidegger. He believed that we must always begin with the relation of the self to the object—a self-world correlation—and that this was basic for a knowledge of being. In approaching the fact of salvation he began with the human situation as conditioned by anxiety and drew heavily on depth psychology. He saw anxiety as arising from the threat of non-being to being and from the feeling of guilt. Anxiety sprang, he believed, from separation from true and essential being. The answer to the threat of non-being he found in the courage to be, the affirmation of the self, and participation in true being. He held to a basic identity between God and man, although he saw that as marred by man's estrangement. To him the philosophical Absolute and the religious Absolute coincided. He regarded God as the presupposition of the question of God and looked upon God as not the object but the basis of the question. Yet, so he said, in the history of Roman Catholic theology God was regarded as a stranger and only probable statements could be made about Him. Thus immediate religious certainty was undermined, faith became less than knowledge, will was made to fill the gap which reason could not bridge, and reliance was placed on ecclesiastical authority. This he saw in theology from Augustine through Anselm to Duns Scotus and William of Ockham. Maintaining that theology led to the dissolution of religion, he suggested, as a way to avoid this unhappy climax, that man is immediately aware of the Unconditioned, and that the awareness is not intuition, experience, or knowledge.

Much of Tillich's theology was expressed in his philosophy of history: culture is the form of religion and religion is the substance of culture. He divided cultures into what he called autonomous (where man is his own law and attempts to construct a culture on the basis of reason and independent of any Absolute), heteronomous (in which man, unable to act on the basis of universal reason, is in bondage to an imposed law which is opposed to his being), and theonomous (in which culture is based on God's law, which is at the same time man's law). Cultures passed from their theonomous period (their early and high ages) through a heteronomous period (as in the late Middle Ages and under Protestant and Moslem orthodoxy) to the autonomous period (as in Europe in the nineteenth and twentieth centuries). He was on the side of theonomous culture and was critical of heteronomous cultures as seeking to impose an indigenous religious culture of one time upon a later time as an absolute rather than a provisional theory. This he saw in the effort of the Roman Catholic Church to make Thomism standard in the twentieth century and in the attempt of Protestantism to bind the contemporary scene to its theory of personality and the Word. He believed that theonomy must agree with autonomy in its criticism of heteronomy but must also protest against the autonomy of the Renaissance and the nineteenth century.

Tillich wished to close the gulf between religion and culture and held to the necessity of symbols as a means to that end. He saw such symbols in the Church as the body of Christ and in the myth of the fall of man as a finite means of relating the finite to the Infinite. He made much of *kairos,* a conception of the time when the Eternal breaks into the temporal, the moment when the opportunity for creativity again occurs. In his own day he found this in the opportunity for religious socialism, made imperative by World War I, when God was judging both the other-worldliness and individualism of ecclesiastical piety and the this-worldly complacency and utopianism of socialism. He saw a demonic element in history, the corruption of the creative impulse in life. But he also viewed the self-estrangement of our existence as met in the manifestation of a new being, the new being in the New Being Jesus Christ. He recognized that the human problem is always the same but must be interpreted in terms of the contemporary situation. He saw a dialectic in the Christian message. He believed in the unchangeable *kerygma,* but he held that we cannot have a purely "kerygmatic" theology as Karl Barth believed but must take account of the circumstances in which the *kerygma* has to be expressed. He maintained that everything in nature, spirit, and history can reveal God but becomes demonic if deified. Faith, to him, is not the affirmation of the absurd but grows on the basis of the invisible process of revelation which secretly runs through history and has found its perfect expression through Christ.[294]

These varied attempts in the United States, whether "liberal," "neo-orthodox," or "existential," were paralleled by developments in Europe. They did not exactly reproduce what was taking place on the other side of the Atlantic and were evidence of a growing independence and maturity of theological thought. They both influenced and were influenced by thought in the eastern and other sections of the Atlantic community.

---

[294] See a bibliography to March, 1952, in *ibid.,* pp. 353–362. Some of Tillich's more important books are *The Religious Situation,* translated by H. R. Niebuhr (New York, Henry Holt and Co., 1932, pp. xxv, 182); *The Interpretation of History,* put into English by various translators (New York, Charles Scribner's Sons, 1936, pp. xii, 284); *The Protestant Era,* translated by James Luther Adams (University of Chicago Press, 1948, pp. xxvi, 323); *The Courage to Be* (New Haven, Yale University Press, 1952, pp. ix, 197); *Dynamics of Faith* (New York, Harper & Brothers, 1957, pp. xix, 127); and *Theology and Culture,* edited by Robert C. Kimball (New York, Oxford University Press, 1959, pp. ix, 213). His *Systematic Theology* (University of Chicago Press, 2 vols., 1951, 1957) was uncompleted when these lines were written. See semi-popular treatments in Soper, *op. cit.,* pp. 107 ff., and Williams, *op. cit.,* pp. 53–57.

After 1914, studies in the Bible, like those in theology, were so numerous and had such multiform approaches that we must not venture even to list them. A large proportion of Biblical scholars were aware of what was being written east of the Atlantic. For example, *Formgeschichte* had its exponents as well as its critics. Bultmann was read and, on his visits, listened to with attention although by no means full assent. Two products of Biblical scholarship enjoyed so wide a circulation that they may be considered representative of what, if they had appeared in Germany in the nineteenth century, would have been described as the mediating school—as being aware of recent and contemporary critical scholarship and accepting much of it, and yet as neither extremely radical nor belligerently conservative.

The first example was the Revised Standard Version of the Bible. It was designed to be a revision of the American Standard Version, published in 1901, which in turn was a revision of the King James Version. Since the International Council of Religious Education held the copyright of the American Standard Version to prevent irresponsible variant editions, the Revised Standard Version was made by committees which it appointed. Their chairman was Luther A. Weigle (1880——), Dean of the Yale Divinity School. In 1951 the undertaking was formally authorized by the National Council of the Churches of Christ in the U.S.A. The Revised Standard Version recognized the King James Version as the most widely used English translation and as having taken advantage of earlier translations. The revisers utilized the latest works which sought to determine the original texts. They also endeavoured to preserve as much of the King James Version as possible but to correct what they deemed incorrect or infelicitous renderings and to substitute contemporary terms for words which had become obsolete in the centuries since the earlier version had been made. The New Testament was issued in 1946 and the Old Testament in 1952. The Apocrypha was soon added. The circulation ran into the millions.[295]

The second example was the multi-volume *Interpreter's Bible*. Intended for clergymen and lay people, for each book of the Bible it had a general article by an expert on the authorship, history, and exegesis, followed by an exposition, usually by a preacher.[296] It, too, was widely used, evidence of the fashion in which the methods and results of the historical criticism of the Bible were permeating the rank and file of a large proportion of American Protestants.

By 1962 most of the main centres of advanced graduate work in theology and the Bible and many of the denominational seminaries were staffed by men who to a greater or less degree were "liberals" or "neo-orthodox."

295 *The Holy Bible. Revised Standard Version* (New York, Thomas Nelson and Sons, 1952, pp. xiii, 997; iii, 293), pp. i–x.
296 *The Interpreter's Bible. The Holy Scriptures in the King James and Revised Standard Version with General Articles and Introduction, Exegesis, Exposition for Each Book of the Bible* (New York, Abingdon-Cokesbury Press, 12 vols., 1951–1957).

RESPONSE TO THE INTELLECTUAL CURRENTS OF THE AGE:
RESISTANCE TO ACCOMMODATION

Although the varied efforts of American Protestants to re-think their faith in the light of the intellectual currents of the revolutionary age were mounting and were pervading much of the constituency, resistance to accommodation was also vocal and widespread. It, too, took many forms and was modified as the years passed. Most of it centred on the inerrancy of the Scriptures as the divinely inspired word of God and attacked any questioning of that inerrancy. Much of it, too, held to convictions which were believed to be supported by the Bible. Wide diversity of interpretation existed and was often hotly debated. Here again we must content ourselves with a few outstanding individuals and movements.

Much of the controversy over accommodation to the currents of the age centred around John Gresham Machen (1881–1937). Machen, of Southern ancestry, was reared in Baltimore in a devout and scholarly Presbyterian home and was profoundly influenced by both his parents, especially his mother. He had his undergraduate course and part of his graduate years in the Johns Hopkins University, went to Princeton Theological Seminary, and had further graduate study in the University of Chicago, Princeton University, Marburg, and Göttingen. Thus, while nurtured in Presbyterian orthodoxy, he was exposed to many of the intellectual forces of his day. After severe struggles for faith, he became a convinced advocate of Reformed theology, especially as embodied in the Westminster Confession. With the interruption of a few months for service with the YMCA in France and Belgium during World War I, from 1906 to 1929 he was on the faculty of Princeton Theological Seminary with his assignment the literature and exegesis of the New Testament. These were years in which the "fundamentalist—modernist" dissension was acute. It engaged much of the attention of the Presbyterian Church in the U.S.A. Machen denied being either a fundamentalist or a modernist, but he had come to the conclusion that, much as he admired and respected the religion of some of the teachers whom he had had, among them Wilhelm Herrmann, they were not Christians as he believed that faith had been set forth in the Bible and in what was historically called Calvinism. He proclaimed that faith in a pulpit in Princeton until opposition led to his resignation. For a time the conflict focused on Princeton Theological Seminary and on his position in it. The battle was carried to the General Assembly with the result that in 1926 that body declined to confirm his appointment to a professorship of apologetics. In 1929 it ordered a reorganization of the administration of the Seminary and put the control of the institution in the hands of the foes of his position. Accordingly Machen left and led in the founding of the Westminster Theological Seminary (1929), in which he and his supporters sought to conserve the spirit which they believed had formerly characterized Princeton Theological Seminary. Since Machen and those associated with him were convinced that the Board of Foreign Missions of the Presbyterian Church in the U.S.A. was appointing some missionaries who were not sound in the faith, they formed an independent board of foreign missions which would hold to their principles. In 1936 Machen was condemned by the General Assembly for insubordination and so of violation of his ordination vows. Thereupon he and his group organized (1936) what they called the Presbyterian Church of America. Death soon removed him from the arena and court action led to the new body's being renamed the Orthodox Presbyterian Church.[297]

Princeton Theological Seminary recovered from the blows dealt it by the controversy and on the whole remained conservative. John Alexander Mackay (1889——), who was its president from 1936 to 1959, attempted to bring together in the Seminary students of all schools of thought. Of Scottish birth, reared in the portion of the Free Church of Scotland which had refused to go into the United Free Church, for years he was a missionary in Latin America and for a time was a secretary of the Board of Foreign Missions of the Presbyterian Church in the U.S.A. Irenic in spirit, prominent in the Ecumenical Movement, he led the Seminary through prosperous years.

Carl McIntire (1906——) made difficult the efforts of Mackay and others who sought to close the gap between the ultra-conservatives and the main body of American Protestants, whether the moderate conservatives, the moderate liberals, or the neo-orthodox. A Presbyterian, he was a student in Princeton Theological Seminary when Machen left that institution. Following him to Westminster Theological Seminary, he was graduated there. For a time he supported Machen and was among those deposed from the ministry by the General Assembly in 1936. He broke with Machen on doctrinal issues and founded the Bible Presbyterian Church and the Faith Theological Seminary in Elkins Park, Pennsylvania. Pastor of the Bible Presbyterian Church in Collingwood, New Jersey, near Philadelphia, and editor of the weekly *Christian Beacon,* he became the first president of the American Council of Christian Churches, formed in September, 1941, to combat what it called "soul-destroying modernism." He attacked the National Council of Churches, the World Council

[297] An incomplete autobiography is in Ferm, *Contemporary American Theology*, Vol. I, pp. 245–274. A sympathetic biography is Ned Bernard Stonehouse, *J. Gresham Machen, A Biographical Memoir* (Grand Rapids, Mich., Wm. B. Eerdmans Publishing Co., 1954, pp. 520). Among Machen's books are *What Is Faith?* (New York, The Macmillan Co., 1925, pp. 263); *Christianity and Liberalism* (New York, The Macmillan Co., 1923, pp. 189); *The Origin of Paul's Religion* (New York, The Macmillan Co., 1921, pp. 329); *The Virgin Birth of Christ* (New York, Harper & Brothers, 1930, pp. vii, 415); *The Christian View of Man* (New York, The Macmillan Co., 1931, pp. vi, 302); *The Christian Faith in the Modern World* (New York, The Macmillan Co., 1936, pp. vi, 258).

of Churches, and the International Missionary Council. He extended his activities to other continents and formed the International Council of Christian Churches. In 1951 he set up the Far Eastern Council of Christian Churches. Several ultra-conservative churches became members of McIntire's movements. In the 1950's he claimed for them a membership of 1,500,000, but an opponent held that the true figure was nearer 170,000. McIntire and the American Council of Christian Churches vigorously criticized the Revised Standard Version of the Bible, describing the members of the committees which produced it as "modernist liberal scholars" and accusing their chairman of "red" affiliations.[298]

The conflict within the Presbyterian Church in the U.S.A. was paralleled by similar dissensions within other denominations. We have seen that what came to be called fundamentalism began in the closing years of the nineteenth century. It attempted to defend what some conservatives were convinced was the Gospel against the (to them) seductive infiltration of "modernism."[299] Fundamentalists stressed five bases of the Christian faith as set forth in the Niagara Bible Conference of 1895 in the Five Points of Fundamentalism—the inerrancy of the Scriptures; the deity and virgin birth of Christ; substitutionary atonement through Christ; the physical resurrection of Christ; and the coming bodily return of Christ to the earth.[300] Any teaching of evolution was held to be contrary to the divinely inspired account of the creation as recorded in the first chapters of Genesis. To the fundamentalists the social gospel was also anathema, for it seemed to them to work for a progressive betterment of human society which was not in accord with the persistence of evil until the Second Coming.

The struggle against "modernism" was particularly acute in the Presbyterian Church in the U.S.A., the Northern Baptist Convention, and the International Convention of the Disciples of Christ.

Among the Northern Baptists the fundamentalists found able leaders in William Bell Riley (1861–1947), long pastor of the First Baptist Church in Minneapolis and founder and head of the North Western Bible Training School in that city, and Curtis Lee Laws (1868–1946), editor of the *Watchman-Examiner,* an influential Baptist paper. Other men, some of them also very able, joined with them. Over a series of years the fundamentalists met in connexion with the annual sessions of the Northern Baptist Convention. They also formed the Baptist Bible Union. They accused the educational institutions affiliated with the Convention of being tainted with "modernism," charged the American Baptist Foreign Mission Society with appointing "liberals," and attempted to induce the Convention to adopt the New Hampshire Confession of

---

298 Roy, *Apostles of Discord,* pp. 186–206.
299 Volume III, pp. 192–194.
300 Cole, *The History of Fundamentalism,* p. 34.

Faith. By majority votes the Convention declined to comply and declared that the New Testament was the "all-sufficient ground" for faith and practice. In 1933 about fifty churches withdrew from the Convention and constituted the General Association of Regular Baptists, which set up several theological seminaries and eventually enrolled about four hundred churches. In 1943 the Conservative Baptist Foreign Mission Society was organized by those who were not convinced that the American Baptist Foreign Mission Society was orthodox, and in 1947 the Conservative Baptist Association of America was constituted by churches dissatisfied with the Northern Baptist Convention (in 1950 renamed the American Baptist Convention), set up societies for home missions and publication, and founded seminaries. The large majority of the churches of the American Baptist Convention remained "conservative," but a minority were "liberal" in varying shades.[301]

The Southern Baptist Convention, much larger than the Northern (American) Baptist Convention, with a more cohesive structure and overwhelmingly conservative theologically, was not as greatly disturbed by fundamentalism as was the latter. Numbers of Baptist churches in the South were not affiliated with it, but bitter fights in the annual gatherings in which the attack was led by the stormy and spectacular John Franklyn Norris (1877-1952) did not issue in secessions of many of the member churches.[302]

The original movement bearing the name of Christian or the Disciples of Christ had seen divisions before the fundamentalist agitation, but the convictions expressed in fundamentalism brought added dissension. The earlier controversies, dating from the first half of the nineteenth century, had led to the emergence of the Churches of Christ, "conservatives," and soon after 1900 these churches began to be clearly distinguished from the Disciples of Christ, who were associated in the International Convention of the Disciples of Christ and in various societies that had been formed for coöperation among the churches for missionary and other purposes.[303] Shortly before 1914 the progress of "liberal" beliefs and practices so alarmed conservatives within the International Convention who had not gone with the Churches of Christ that further controversy arose. The issues were partly over the attitude towards the higher criticism of the Bible, evolution, and the practice of some of the churches of admitting members who had not been immersed. The battle was waged in rival denominational periodicals and over the penetration by "liberal" attitudes of some of the denomination's educational institutions, including Transylvania College and the College of the Bible in Lexington, Kentucky. The United

[301] Torbet, *A History of the Baptists*, pp. 445-451; Furniss, *The Fundamentalist Controversy, 1918-1931*, pp. 103-118; Cole, *op. cit.*, pp. 65-97.

[302] Furniss, *op. cit.*, pp. 119-126.

[303] U.S. Department of Commerce, Bureau of the Census, *Religious Bodies, 1936*, Vol. II, Part I, pp. 469, 470, 543, 544.

Christian Missionary Society, organized in 1919 to bring together six existing agencies, became the focus of much of the struggle. Many of the conservatives associated themselves in the Christian Restoration Association and found kinship with fundamentalists in other denominations. Bible schools and colleges were organized to teach the conservative views. In spite of differences in belief and practice and some secessions of the disaffected, "liberals" and the majority of the "conservatives" continued membership in the International Convention of the Disciples of Christ.[304]

Several other denominations were troubled by the controversy over the issues raised by the intellectual currents. Among them were the (Southern) Presbyterian Church in the U.S., smaller and more conservative than the (Northern) Presbyterian Church in the U.S.A.;[305] the Methodist Episcopal Church and the Methodist Episcopal Church, South, where the fundamentalists did not succeed in bringing about major divisions;[306] and the Protestant Episcopal Church.[307]

The conflict cut across denominations. For the most part the elements who had been most exposed in their education to the intellectual temper of the age —the most highly educated by its standards—tended to side with those who were seeking the adjustment of the faith to the trends in scholarly thought, and most of the support of the fundamentalists came from the less well educated. To this generalization, however, many exceptions could be cited. Moreover, financial support for fundamentalism came often from men and women of wealth, partly because they feared the association of "liberal" views in theology and of the Bible with "liberal" economic and social movements. Many conservatives declared men of liberal theological views to be Communists, or, if not out-and-out Communists, at least "fellow travellers."

One of the characteristics of American Protestantism in the decades after 1914 was the proliferation of movements and organizations which were either frankly fundamentalist or sympathetic with fundamentalist convictions. Many were ephemeral but some were long-lived. Among them were the World's Christian Fundamentals Association, the Bible Crusaders of America, the Anti-Evolution League, and the Research Science Bureau (which sought to prove the harmony of true science with the Bible).[308] Bible schools flourished, some of them founded before 1914 and others in later years. One of the best known was the Moody Bible Institute in Chicago. Theological seminaries were begun or continued to further fundamentalist convictions, some of them undenominational, like Fuller and Dallas, and others denominational, such as Eastern

---

304 Furniss, *op. cit.*, pp. 170–176; Cole, *op. cit.*, pp. 133–162.

305 Furniss, *op. cit.*, pp. 142–147.

306 *Ibid.*, pp. 144–161; Cole, *op. cit.*, pp. 163–192. See on a "high church" movement in Methodism, Lillian Turner in *Christianity Today*, November 10, 1958, pp. 15, 16.

307 Furniss, *op. cit.*, pp. 162–169; Cole, *op. cit.*, pp. 193–219.

308 Furniss, *op. cit.*, pp. 49–75; Cole, *op. cit.*, pp. 259–280.

Baptist in Philadelphia and Northern Baptist in Chicago. Colleges committed to fundamentalist tenets were maintained, a few of pre-World War founding and several begun after 1914.[309]

An event which attracted nation-wide—indeed, world-wide—attention was what was known as the Scopes case. In 1925 under fundamentalist pressure a law was enacted in Tennessee which made it a criminal offense to advocate in any school or college any theory that denied the story of the Divine creation of man as contained in the Bible and taught instead that man had ascended from a lower order of animals. John T. Scopes, a biology teacher in a high school in Dayton, Tennessee, was brought to trial on the charge of violating the statute. Lawyers of national eminence, among them the sceptical Clarence Darrow, came to his defense, and William Jennings Bryan, prominent as a former Democratic candidate for the Presidency of the United States and as a former Secretary of State, noted for his staunch fundamentalist convictions and his opposition to the theory of evolution, was one of the attorneys for the prosecution. The jury brought in a verdict of guilty, but on a legal technicality the state supreme court ordered the case remanded and advised the district attorney not to prosecute a second time. The constitutionality of the law was, accordingly, untested, the statute remained on the books, and in 1926 Mississippi enacted a similar law. Comparable measures were taken in Louisiana and Arkansas.[310]

The Revised Standard Version was attacked in some conservative quarters. The chief but not the only issue was its substitution in Isaiah 7:14 of "young woman" for "virgin" where the King James Version read: "Behold, a virgin shall conceive and bear a son and shall call his name Immanuel." Since the passage had been interpreted as foretelling the virgin birth of Christ, the new version was accused of being "modernist." Although Weigle pointed out that the Hebrew meant "young woman" and that in Matthew 1:23 the word "virgin" had been retained because the original Greek could be translated only in that way, the extremists were not satisfied and were vigorous in their denunciations. However, a number of fundamentalists did not join in the hue and cry.[311]

A phase of fundamentalism, and, indeed, of some groups which would not be strictly regarded as in that movement, was dispensationalism. By that was meant an interpretation of history based on the Scriptures which saw the human story as divided into periods, or dispensations. One widely read writer believed the record to fall into seven ages, corresponding to the seven days of creation—the period before the flood, the time after the flood when human

---

[309] Cole, *op. cit.*, pp. 246–258.
[310] Furniss, *op. cit.*, pp. 3–9, 90–95; Robertson, *That Old-Time Religion*, pp. 87–108.
[311] Roy, *op. cit.*, pp. 165, 204–211.

government was established, the call of Abraham and the separation of Israel from the Gentiles, the Christian dispensation, the period of lawlessness, the era when all things would be under the foot of the Second Adam, and the new heavens and the new earth when Christ will reign.[312] Efforts at such a periodization of history were not new. For example, in the thirteenth century Joachim of Flora (1130–1202) had formulated one which had a wide influence and which set forth three ages—of the Father, the Son, and the Holy Spirit. Nor was the dispensationalism with its premillennial teaching confined to the United States or to the fundamentalists, but it flourished under them.[313] Its chief literary expression was in the *Scofield Reference Bible,* the work of Cyrus Ingerson Scofield (1843–1921),[314] which circulated by the hundreds of thousands of copies and whose interpretative notes were considered by many to be unchallengeable. The *Scofield Reference Bible* helped to standardize the views of the dispensationalists. Yet differences existed and continued. Many of the premillennialists only partly separated the Kingdom of God from the Church and said that the two overlapped; but the prevailing view, fostered by Scofield, sharply distinguished between them. The postmillennialists equated the Kingdom of God with the Church. Other varieties of dispensationalism also developed.[315]

By the 1960's many of the conservatives who would once have been classified as fundamentalists disavowed that designation. They preferred to be called Evangelicals—seeking by the emphasis on that term to claim that they held to the Evangelical tradition and implying that denominational bodies of Evangelical origin which to a greater or less degree had adjusted themselves to the intellectual climate of the age had departed from the faith. They believed the latter to be true of the ecclesiastical bodies which had membership in the National Council of Churches and the World Council of Churches. Yet they claimed for their colleges and theological seminaries high academic rank as measured by the standards of institutions which were either purely secular or did not measure up to their doctrinal requirements. Numbers of their faculty held graduate degrees from universities in the United States or Europe which they did not believe to be orthodox and were acquainted with contemporary scholarship in theology and the Bible. Their widely circulated organ was the fortnightly *Christianity Today.*[316]

[312] Arno Clemens Gaebelein, *As It Was—So Shall It Be. Sunset and Sunrise. A Study of the First Age and Our Present Age* (New York, Publication Office, "Our Hope," 1937, pp. 190), *passim.*

[313] See, for example, a brief critical survey in Harris Franklin Rall, *Modern Premillennialism and the Christian Hope* (New York, The Abingdon Press, 1920, pp. 255), pp. 96–148.

[314] *The Scofield Reference Bible. The Holy Bible Containing the Old and New Testaments* (New York, Oxford University Press, new and improved ed., 1909, 1919, pp. vi, 1362).

[315] C. Norman Kraus, *Dispensationalism in America. Its Rise and Development* (Richmond, Va., John Knox Press, 1958, pp. 151), *passim.*

[316] *Christianity Today* (Washington, 1957 ff.).

On the opposite extreme from this intellectual, educated moderate conservatism were popular movements among the poorly educated or illiterate. They held firmly to the inerrancy of the Bible and had extreme interpretations. Some, relying on Mark 17:18, taught that those who believed could handle deadly snakes and not be injured. Others represented a variety of convictions, some Pentecostal, several dating from the eighteenth century, others springing from groups mentioned earlier in this chapter, and still others whom we have not had the space to record.[317]

In general it could be said that in the half-century between 1906 and 1956 the percentage growth of Protestant denominations which were pronouncedly "conservative" was much more rapid than that of denominations in which accommodation to the intellectual currents of the age had made varying degrees of progress. This was true of both the larger and the smaller denominational families. Other factors than theological conservatism, such as immigration, contributed to the difference, but a decided correlation existed between the rate of increase in membership and "conservative" and "liberal" trends. Although in 1956 the membership of the Protestant ecclesiastical bodies which to a greater or less degree were permeated by "liberalism" still outnumbered that of the "conservative" Protestant bodies, the difference was not as marked as in 1906. In 1906, moreover, the larger Protestant bodies were more nearly "conservative" than they were half a century later. Whether for good or for ill, "liberal" churches were not gaining as rapidly as "conservative" bodies. Here were developments which affected profoundly the Protestantism of the United States and its response to the revolutionary age.[318]

The Roman Catholic Response to the Intellectual Currents of the Age

In general in the decades following 1914 the Roman Catholic Church in the United States was more resistant to the intellectual currents of the revolutionary age than was the Protestantism of that country. Theologically it was much more traditional than were active Roman Catholic minorities in France, Germany, and Belgium. The Modernism of the decades which immediately preceded and followed 1900 had affected only a very few. On the whole the Roman Catholics of the United States were too engrossed in absorbing the nineteenth-century immigration to pay much attention to intellectual pursuits. They were still too largely in the brick and mortar stage, constructing churches, schools, and other institutions, and were too much engaged in raising the educational level of a constituency which had been drawn from the underprivileged of Europe and in ensuring their instruction in the basic tenets and practices of

[317] Robertson, *op. cit.*, pp. 115–140, 144–148, 171–181.
[318] Richard C. Wolf in *Christianity Today*, April 27, 1959.

the faith to give much time to advanced scholarship. Some of their number deplored the backwardness of American Roman Catholics in intellectual matters.[319]

By the mid-twentieth century the situation was changing. As we have seen, the educational level was rising. Here and there theologians and Biblical scholars of distinction were appearing and notable contributions were being made to theological and Biblical scholarship. For the most part American Roman Catholic theology remained conservative. In the nineteenth century it had been largely polemic and had been represented by men trained in Europe. In the twentieth century some scholars of the American Church attracted attention in Europe. In accord with the impetus given by Papal authority the Roman Catholic theology of the United States had a strong Thomistic flavour. Because of the activistic character of the American Church and the urgent necessity of building a sound ecclesiastical life and structure in a pluralistic society to hold the faithful, immersed as they were in a secular revolutionary age, and to win those outside the fold, the theology was practical and did not engage in what the conservatives scorned as the "liberal" trends seen in some places in Europe.[320] Joseph Clifford Fenton (1908——), professor of dogmatic theology and dean of the faculty of sacred theology in the Catholic University of America, was a stanch supporter of orthodoxy. In his ecclesiology and his doctrine of salvation he denounced the position that an invisible church as well as the visible Church exists. He emphatically supported the encyclical *Mystici Corporis Christi* (promulgated by Pope Pius XII on June 29, 1943), which in his view made clear that, while an individual might attain to salvation if he had an implicit desire to be in the Church but was not actually in communion with it, such an individual was in a very insecure position and one strikingly inferior to that of an actual member of the Church. To him the encyclical made it plain that the visible Roman Catholic Church is identical with the social unit designated by Christ as His mystical body. He said that all members of the Roman Catholic Church had a duty to work and pray for the conversion to that church of all who had merely an implicit desire to be in it.[321] The Jesuits John Courtney

---

[319] Ellis, *American Catholicism*, pp. 114–116; *American Catholics and the Intellectual Life, passim;* O'Dea, *American Catholic Dilemma,* pp. 4, 10, 82–84.

[320] Joseph Clifford Fenton, *The Concept of Sacred Theology* (Milwaukee, The Bruce Publishing Co., 1941, pp. xi, 276), pp. 258–264.

[321] Joseph Clifford Fenton, *The Catholic Church and Salvation in the Light of Recent Pronouncements by the Holy See* (Westminster, Md., The Newman Press, 1958, pp. xi, 190), pp. 76–99. A controversy arose in Boston and Cambridge in the 1940's which was provoked by a Jesuit, Leonard Feeney, and St. Benedict Centre in Harvard Square. Protesting against what they deemed the "liberalism" in the American Roman Catholic Church, Feeney and his associates insisted that no salvation was possible outside the Roman Catholic Church. This was contrary to the Baltimore Catechism, an official statement of doctrine for the United States, which taught that salvation outside the Catholic Church was possible under certain conditions where persons of good will were acting according to the dictates of their conscience. Feeney and his group believed this exception to be

Murray (1904———) and Gustave Weigel (1906———), members of the faculty of Woodstock College, were also eminent but they and Fenton did not entirely agree.

An outstanding achievement of American Roman Catholic scholarship was the compiling of *The Catholic Encyclopedia.* Although it was issued early in the twentieth century and by 1960 badly needed revision to bring it abreast of current scholarship and the rapid movement of events, *The Catholic Encyclopedia* continued to be useful and in some of its articles remained standard.[322]

Another major accomplishment was a fresh English translation of the Scriptures from the original texts. For several years Roman Catholic scholars had been engaged on a revision of the now antiquated Douai-Rheims English version. They had undertaken it largely at the suggestion of Bishop O'Hara, who deemed it essential to the work of the Confraternity of Christian Doctrine which he was sponsoring. He presided over the first annual gathering (1940) of the Catholic Biblical Association of America. The journal of that organization, the *Catholic Biblical Quarterly,* begun in 1938 at the instance of O'Hara, was said to be the first periodical in the Roman Catholic Church devoted to the Scriptures in the English-speaking world. Then came Pope Pius XII's encyclical *Divino Afflante Spiritu* with its encouragement of Biblical scholarship and what amounted to a directive to make translations from the original languages rather than through reference to the Vulgate. By December of that year O'Hara had official word from the Pontifical Biblical Commission authorizing the American group to proceed with a new translation from the original texts. Genesis was published in 1948, the remaining portions of the Old Testament appeared at intervals, and the New Testament was issued last of all.[323] Here was a major contribution of American Roman Catholics to Biblical scholarship and to making the Scriptures accessible to the laity in dignified and appropriate English. The step was part of the movement which we have found in Europe and which was fostered by the Papacy to encourage the reading and study of the Bible by the faithful.

Another work of scholarship which, if not as notable as that of the translation of the Bible, was also undertaken to help nourish the laity in the faith was the translation into English of the ritual for baptism, marriage, sick calls, and funeral rites. It, too, had O'Hara as its prime mover and was associated

---

false and publicly said so again and again. They were eventually silenced by the ecclesiastical authorities, including Rome itself, and Feeney was dismissed from the Society of Jesus.—Catherine Goddard Clarke, *The Loyolas and the Cabots. The Story of the Boston Heresy Case* (Boston, The Ravengate Press, 1959, pp. xi, 301), *passim.*

[322] *The Catholic Encyclopedia. An International Work of Reference on the Constitution, Doctrine, Discipline, and History of the Catholic Church* (New York, the earlier volumes by Robert Appleton Co. and the later ones by the Encyclopedia Press, 16 vols., 1907–1914; Supplement and Year Book, 1922).

[323] Shaw, *Edwin Vincent O'Hara,* pp. 173–196.

with his leadership in the Confraternity of Christian Doctrine. He saw in it additional means of educating the laity in the doctrines and worship of his church. Encouraged by what had been accomplished in Germany through the Liturgical Movement and by the centre of the Liturgical Movement in the Benedictine St. John's Abbey in Collegeville, Minnesota, he won the consent of his fellow bishops and of Rome. The coöperation of competent scholars was obtained and the new ritual was published in 1954.[324]

THE EFFECT OF CHRISTIANITY ON THE UNITED STATES IN THE TWENTIETH CENTURY: THE PROTESTANT CONTRIBUTION

What effect did Christianity have upon the collective life of the United States in the five and a half decades which followed 1914? We have seen the sharp contrasts in the nineteenth century. On the one hand there was war—especially the Civil War, which shook the nation to its foundations, left the South prostrate for nearly half a century, and, while freeing the nation from the incubus of Negro slavery, was followed by grave problems brought by emancipation and tensions between Negroes and whites which the twentieth century inherited. The country had been troubled by political corruption on the local, state, and national scale, a corruption which flourished in the aftermath of the Civil War. A wave of intemperance and its attendant alcoholism accompanied and followed the Civil War. Again and again the Indians suffered from the ruthless lust of the palefaces for their lands. Rapidly mounting industrialization brought exploitation of labour, much of it supplied by immigration from Europe; bewildered by the change from their European environment and usually poverty-stricken, the new Americans could not defend themselves. Fortunes, some of them huge, were accumulated, often by methods which the Christian conscience could only excoriate. On the other hand, Christian idealism, acting through the Protestantism which was the prevailing form of religion, had a profound influence. It was largely responsible for the American dream—the hopes of the radical Protestant groups that had sought haven in the New World. Although even in colonial days they were minorities, in several of the colonies very small minorities, these groups helped to shape the ethos of the young nation. From them and from the Evangelical awakenings to which they gave birth came movement after movement for reform. To them can be traced, among others, the anti-slavery movement, the temperance and prohibition campaigns, much in the programmes for education both for the rank and file of the population and in advanced studies, several of the attempts to cleanse the Augean political stables, the efforts to achieve lasting peace among the nations and some form of international government, and

[324] *Ibid.*, pp. 197–205.

what was called the social gospel with its determination through multiform channels to create a domestic structure which would afford justice and equal opportunity for all to the good things of life.

What effects would follow the transition punctuated by World War I? Through that war the United States was catapulted into world politics and in spite of strenuous efforts on the part of some leaders and of a large body of public opinion to keep aloof it was more and more embroiled in global issues. International relations became one of the country's inescapable concerns. Industrialization mounted, with the attendant problems to which we have called attention. In what ways and with what results would Christianity meet the challenge? In the twentieth as in the nineteenth century entirely satisfactory answers cannot be given. In a culture inherited from Europe and further shaped in its new habitat, Christianity had been a major force, but to measure its contributions with some degree of accuracy is impossible.

One change was notable. In the nineteenth century, so far as its impact upon the nation as a whole could be ascertained, the chief influence of Christianity had come through forms of Protestantism of British origin and prevailingly of Evangelical temper. In the twentieth century, because of the nineteenth- and twentieth-century immigration, other branches of Christianity were making bigger and bigger contributions. Roman Catholicism and Lutheranism were looming larger, and the Orthodox Churches could no longer be ignored. As we have had occasion to note repeatedly, the Christianity of the United States was still primarily Protestant of the Evangelical tradition, but in the twentieth century that strain was not as predominant as in the nineteenth century.

We must also remark, as we did in appraising the effect of Christianity in the nineteenth century, that in the twentieth century a major—indeed, the primary—effect of Christianity was on the character of individuals. We must again say, as then, that any generalization, including this one, could be challenged. We know statistically that except during the ten years which included World War I, when it remained stationary, the percentage of the population having church membership rose decade by decade.[325] Sample polls also seem to show that except during World War II, when the proportion dropped, between 1939 and 1956 the percentage of the population over twenty-one years of age who attended church services strikingly increased.[326] However, no satisfactory method had been devised to determine whether these increases were paralleled by an advance towards approximation to the Christian standards of character or whether with the wider dissemination of formal connexion with one or another of the churches the average level declined. We know that the distinctive qualities of Christian character continued to appear. Few if any

---

[325] *Yearbook of American Churches, 1957*, p. 279.
[326] *Ibid.*, p. 281.

branches of the Church were without men and women who clearly bore what Paul called "the fruits of the Spirit." Most of them, however, were known only to their families and their near neighbours, the degree of the fruitage was not susceptible to precise measurement, and any attempt at an inclusive generalization for any one period could not but be subject to question.

The accuracy of some generalizations is undebatable. The Eighteenth Amendment to the Constitution of the United States, which prohibited "the manufacture, sale, or transportation of intoxicating liquors," was enacted in 1917, approved by the necessary three-quarters of the states by the end of 1919, in theory became effective in January, 1920, and crowned the efforts of the Anti-Saloon League and the temperance crusade of the nineteenth century—both expressions of the Protestant conscience. But it was widely flouted and was repealed in 1933. Some advocates of prohibition had fought hard to prevent that outcome. James Cannon, Jr. (1864–1944), a bishop of the Methodist Episcopal Church, South, was especially active. As chairman of the National Legislative Committee of the Anti-Saloon League he had been prominent in obtaining the passage of the amendment, and after its enactment he sturdily defended it. In the presidential election of 1928 he led an attack on the Democratic candidate, Alfred E. Smith, on the ground that the latter was against prohibition, and led enough out of the ranks of the heretofore solidly Democratic South to bring about the defeat of Smith and the election of Herbert Hoover.[327] The election of 1932 swept the Democrats into power and sealed the doom of the controversial amendment. Some Protestant bodies continued to advocate total abstinence, but the per capita consumption of alcoholic beverages mounted. On the other hand, the Nineteenth Amendment, which also became effective in 1920, by extending the right to vote to all citizens regardless of sex, thus enfranchising women, was a climax to prolonged agitation which was deeply although by no means exclusively indebted to the Protestant conscience.

The record of what was called the social gospel was ambiguous. As we have seen,[328] the social gospel arose in the latter half of the nineteenth century in an attempt to combat the ills which were associated with industrialization and was akin to much in Protestantism in the British Isles and the continent of Europe and in the Roman Catholic Church—in the latter given forceful expression in the encyclical *Rerum novarum* of Leo XIII. Among American Protestants the attitude varied. Some stressed voluntaristic social reform move-

---

[327] James Cannon, Jr., *Bishop Cannon's Own Story. Life as I Have Seen It,* edited by Richard L. Watson, Jr. (Chapel Hill, University of North Carolina Press, 1955, pp. xxxi, 465), pp. xvi–xviii, 278–447; Virginius Dabney, *Dry Messiah. The Life of Bishop Cannon* (New York, Alfred A. Knopf, 1949, pp. 353, ix), pp. 98–189. The thesis that it was the prohibition issue and not his Roman Catholic faith which defeated Alfred E. Smith in 1928 is set forth by Robert M. Miller in *Church History,* Vol. XXV, pp. 145–159 (June, 1956).

[328] Volume III, pp. 223–233.

ments, to be sparked by converted individuals. The extreme radicals denounced
that method as inadequate and called for a thoroughgoing re-making of institutions such as that advocated by the Socialists. In between were many who did
not anticipate Utopia but wished institutional as well as individual moral
changes.[329] A reaction from the exuberant idealism which supported the participation of the United States in World War I set in. The widespread disillusionment and frustration accompanying and partly causing the repudiation of
membership in the League of Nations issued in a kind of anti-Communist
hysteria which endeavoured to curb the freedom of the press and public speech,
in the refusal of the New York state legislature to seat regularly elected Socialist
members, and in the deportation of immigrants without trial. In the wake of
World War I a surge of rebellion against conventional moral standards gripped
much of the youth of the country. Many Protestant leaders sought to adopt the
methods of American business in promoting their churches through advertising
—"selling"—the Christian faith. In numbers of pulpits complacency and an
uncritical attitude towards American society prevailed.[330] In some places the
churches were bulwarks of the existing economic order. They coöperated with
the factories in furthering industriousness, dependability, and good personal
morality among the labourers and sided with employers against strikers.[331] The
wave of fundamentalism which swept across Protestantism in the 1920's and
1930's attacked the social gospel as an alleged companion of "modernism."
Many laymen, whether in liberal or conservative churches, objected to sermons
by their ministers on social issues. They declared that the pulpit was moving
outside its proper domain and was speaking on questions in which it had no
competence. Much of neo-orthodoxy, especially as interpreted by one of its
most robust spokesmen, Reinhold Niebuhr, appeared to discredit the social
gospel as utopian. The trend was in practice to substitute for

> Rise up oh men of God, the Church for you doth wait, . . .
> Rise up and make her great.

(an expression of the optimism in some Protestant circles on the eve of World
War I) by an attitude which might be summed up as

> Sit down oh men of God, you cannot do a thing.

To be sure, Niebuhr gave himself unsparingly to fighting collective evils, but
some who listened to him felt themselves helpless. In the Ecumenical Movement many Protestant leaders from the Continent of Europe scoffed at the

---

[329] Carter, *The Decline and Revival of the Social Gospel*, pp. 12–14.
[330] *Ibid.*, pp. 17–28; Miller, *American Protestantism and Social Issues, 1919–1939*, pp. 17–30.
[331] See an example in 1929 which in its day had nation-wide notoriety because of the Communist
share in a strike, in Liston Pope, *Millhands & Preachers* (New Haven, Yale University Press, 1942,
pp. xvi, 369), pp. 29, 207 ff.

social gospel as the expression of Americans who did not know either the correct interpretation of their Bibles or the sad state of Western civilization. Their mood was aggravated by the wars and upheavals that were ushered in by the events of the summer of 1914.

On the other hand, a good deal of American Protestantism continued to hold to the ideals of the social gospel, even if that term was in bad odour. The Federal Council of Churches owed its inception in part to the desire for co-operative action in making the social gospel effective. It persisted and grew. In 1920 it had as members thirty-one denominations, including 148,532 local churches with 19,504,102 members. In that year, the commissions, later called departments, under which it performed many of its functions concerned themselves, among other things, with the Church and social service, temperance, and international justice and good will.[332] By 1949 departments on race relations and on the Church and economic life had been added.[333] Several denominations in their central structure had councils, committees, or other bodies charged with social, economic, and international issues. Sometimes they came under fire from critics of the social gospel.

Repeatedly through individuals and ecclesiastical organizations Protestants endeavoured to bring their religion to bear upon the international scene in which the nation was increasingly entangled. Woodrow Wilson's Christian faith inspired and sustained him in formulating the aims which he believed should guide the country and its associated powers in World War I and in his efforts to achieve them. That faith was the chief factor in bringing into being the League of Nations, for he obtained the framing of its covenant and its incorporation in the Treaty of Versailles against the indifference and scepticism of the other key figures in the Paris peace conference.[334]

During World War II the Federal Council of Churches appointed a Commission to Study the Bases of a Just and Durable Peace. It had a large membership representative of several denominations and of pacifist and non-pacifist convictions. Its chairman was John Foster Dulles (1888–1959), later to be Secretary of State. The son of a Presbyterian clergyman, in his student days Dulles had thought seriously of entering the ministry but instead became a lawyer. He retained his Christian faith and, with an interest in international relations dating from his boyhood, gave much time to the Commission. Under his leadership it met frequently, issued statements—largely of his composition—to help shape public opinion, and held large study conferences whose findings were circulated among the churches to promote discussion. Led by Dulles, the Commission placed much emphasis upon the importance of creating the United

[332] *Yearbook of the Churches, 1920*, pp. 237–245.
[333] *Yearbook of American Churches, 1949*, p. 95.
[334] Arthur Woolworth, *Woodrow Wilson* (New York, Longmans, Green and Co., 2 vols., 1958), Vol. I, p. 13; Vol. II, pp. 373, 416, 421, 422.

Nations. Its findings were presented to officials in Washington to acquaint them with the facets of thought for which it could speak. Dulles himself, chiefly in his private capacity and not as chairman, was repeatedly in Washington urging the United Nations on responsible officials, especially senators whose voice would be important in the ratification of the country's membership in the body. He was also influential in the international meeting which framed the charter of the United Nations. As Secretary of State he never wavered from his insistence on coöperation with that venture in international government. Dulles later said that it was his association with the Commission which led him to accept the task of negotiating the treaty of peace with Japan—an assignment which he undertook before becoming Secretary of State—and to make it a document embodying the spirit of forgiveness rather than of hate.[335]

After the coming of peace the Commission was discharged but the Department of International Affairs was a continuing agency of the National Council of Churches and was very active in helping the Protestant churches formulate intelligent opinion on foreign policy. The precedent set by the Commission led to the formation of the Churches' Commission on International Affairs, an organ of the World Council of Churches and the International Missionary Council. That body spoke repeatedly on international issues, and its director, O. Frederick Nolde (1899———), an American Lutheran clergyman, kept closely in touch with the United Nations and had a major part in initiating, framing, and obtaining the adoption of its Declaration on Human Rights.[336]

On some concrete issues pressure from the Protestant churches clearly contributed to the action of the federal government—in the repeal, for example, of the Chinese Exclusion Act in 1943.[337]

Some of the men high in the national government and with influence in both foreign and domestic relations endeavoured to put into practice their Christian faith. Thus Charles Evans Hughes (1862-1948), son of a Baptist clergyman, in his early maturity taught a Sunday School class in a Baptist Church in New York City and was president of the Northern Baptist Convention. As an attorney and then a governor of New York State he was noted for his vigour in fighting corrupt business and politics and in obtaining reform

---

[335] John Foster Dulles, "A Diplomat and His Faith," in *The Christian Century*, Vol. LXIX, pp. 336-338 (March 19, 1952).

[336] The author was a member of the Department of International Justice and Goodwill, the Commission to Study the Bases of a Just and Durable Peace, and the Department of International Affairs and is here drawing on his first-hand knowledge. See *The Message to the Churches of Christ in the U.S.A. Adopted by the Fifth World Order Study Conference, Cleveland, O., Nov. 18-21, 1958* (New York, The Department of International Affairs, . . . , National Council of the Churches of Christ in the U.S.A., 1958, pp. 4). It aroused much controversy because of its recommendation of the recognition of the (Communist) People's Republic of China and the admission of that regime to membership in the United Nations.

[337] See F. W. Riggs, *Pressures on Congress: A Study of the Repeal of Chinese Exclusion* (New York, King's Crown Press, 1950, pp. xii, 260), *passim*.

legislation. As Secretary of State he was the chief figure in the international conference on the limitation of armaments held in Washington in 1921–1922, later served on the Hague Court of Arbitration, and in the Sixth Pan-American Conference (1928) helped to ease the tensions among the American states.[338] Herbert Clark Hoover (1874——), famous for his leadership in relief during and after World War I and President of the United States from 1929 to 1933, was born to Quaker parents. His mother was a Quaker preacher and he was reared in that faith. Franklin Delano Roosevelt (1882–1945), four times President of the United States, a highly controversial and powerful figure in national and international affairs, never talked about religion but had a simple and direct religious faith. He insisted on having a church service on each inauguration day, and when great crises impended his belief in the guidance of God gave him courage in making and carrying through decisions.[339] The parents of Dwight David Eisenhower (1890——) were devout members of the River Brethren, a small movement which sprang from a revival in the eighteenth century. Commander of the Allied armies in World War II and twice President of the United States, in the latter office Eisenhower was regular in his church attendance, and the satellite launched in December, 1958, broadcast to the world his voice in the Christmas message: "Peace on earth, good will to men."

Protestants were active in giving relief to sufferers from war and other disasters in many different parts of the world. Much was done through denominational agencies—too numerous even to be catalogued here. Although begun by the Quakers and continuing under their direction, the American Friends Service Committee obtained much of its financial support from non-Quakers. In later years a chief agency for relief was Church World Service, a department of the National Council of Churches. Comprehensive figures were lacking, but clearly, enormous as was the relief given by Protestant agencies during and immediately following World War I, it was surpassed by that which accompanied World War II and its aftermath.

On the domestic scene the social gospel, whether under that designation or not, had many expressions. We must confine ourselves to a few illustrations culled at random from a wide variety. Between World War I and World War II a Presbyterian pastor organized in a county in Georgia the Carroll Service Council to link together coöperative efforts of farmers, business men, teachers, preachers, and every one interested in the county as a whole. It survived World War II and continued to flourish in an inconspicuous way.[340] In 1916 James

[338] Merlo J. Pusey, *Charles Evans Hughes* (New York, The Macmillan Co., 2 vols., 1951).
[339] Eleanor Roosevelt, *This I Remember* (New York, Harper & Brothers, 1949, pp. x, 387), pp. 67, 69.
[340] Robertson, *That Old-Time Religion*, pp. 230–242.

Gore King McClure (1884–1956), a young, highly educated Presbyterian clergy-man, an invalid, went to the mountains of North Carolina and began farming to regain his health. There in the course of the years he created the Farmers' Federation to organize coöperatively the farmers in that underprivileged region to develop markets and stimulate production. In connexion with it he brought into being the Lord's Acre Movement to aid in the support of the local rural churches. He also headed other institutions to assist the farmers in that area, among them the Farmers' Loan Corporation, the Farmers' Coöperative Council, Appalachian Mutual, and the Treasure Chest Mutual Coöperative.[341]

On the national scale, the Social Creed of the Churches, adopted by the Federal Council of Churches in 1912, had its continued advocates. Among the principles which it expressed were the abolition of child labour, the abatement and prevention of poverty, the right of all men to the opportunity to self-maintenance and protection against enforced unemployment, the right of em-ployees and employers to organize and the provision of means of conciliation and arbitration in industrial disputes, release from employment one day in seven, the reduction of the hours of labour, a living wage, a minimum wage, the equitable division of the products of industry, and provision for old age and for those incapacitated by injury.[342] By 1962 many of these principles had been made a reality by legislation and other measures, but in the 1920's num-bers of the laity denounced them as "socialistic." In the decade after World War I, while not adopting the Social Creed in detail, several of the larger denominations expressed themselves in favour of unselfish coöperation rather than selfish competition in the struggle for daily bread.[343]

Numbers of the Protestant clergy stood out boldly for the Social Creed of the Churches or similar programmes. Several became national figures and a few gave up the pastorate and even the ministry to devote themselves to pro-moting them. Prominent among these were Norman Thomas (1884——), a former Presbyterian minister and perennial candidate of the Socialist Party for President of the United States; Harry Frederick Ward (1873——), once on the national staff of the Methodist Episcopal Church and for many years a teacher in Union Theological Seminary in New York City; Kirby Page (1890–1957), author, lecturer, and fearless proponent of pacifism; and John Nevin Sayre (1884——) and Abraham John Muste (1885——), both officers of the Fellowship of Reconciliation. Throughout the three or four decades which fol-lowed World War I they made their voices heard in no uncertain words.

During the depression years of the 1930's some of the denominations ex-pressed themselves officially as challenging a social and economic order which

---

341 *Who's Who in America*, Vol. XXVI, p. 1798; the author's personal knowledge.
342 Harry F. Ward, *The Social Creed of the Churches* (New York, The Abington Press, 1914, pp. 196), p. 7.
343 Miller, *op. cit.*, pp. 36–38.

did not ward off such catastrophes. The Methodist Episcopal Church was especially emphatic.[344] In general, the Federal Council of Churches, owing its origin as it did largely to the desire for coöperative action on social issues, supported the New Deal of Franklin D. Roosevelt for the alleviation of the depression and the prevention of its recurrence.[345] In the 1920's many Protestant churchmen, especially among the clergy, protested against what they believed to be the unjust conviction and death in the electric chair of Nicola Sacco and Bartolomeo Vanzetti, foreigners, draft dodgers, and philosophical anarchists, who were accused of the murder of a paymaster and his guard in Massachusetts. The animus against them, so their defenders claimed, was aroused by their social radicalism. They were arrested in 1920 and executed in 1927 by what hundreds of Protestant clergy and laity asserted was a miscarriage of justice.[346]

Not all Protestants agreed either with the Federal Council of Churches or with the utterances of their respective denominational bodies. Fundamentalists and theological conservatives were intensely critical, and in most of the larger denominations the majority of the rank and file of the members were either indifferent or in the opposition. The Southern denominations were, in general, conservative socially as well as in their attitude towards the Bible and evolution, but they were not alone; their position was paralleled in many churches in the North. But there were minorities, largely but not entirely of clergy, who stood courageously against the conservative majorities.[347]

The Federal Council of Churches and its successor, the National Council of Churches, were undiscouraged by the opposition. In the 1950's, for instance, the latter sponsored studies which dealt with the changes taking place in the economic and social life of the nation. The studies held that a sustained Christian criticism of business practices was necessary "because of the constant tension between Christian standards of life and the secular rules of the game which reflect human imperfections and perversities." They maintained that on the whole Protestant documents on economic life showed a conviction "that the road to economic and social welfare lies not in dogmatic adherence to some closed system, but rather in evolution toward a mixed system containing elements of private enterprise, coöperative enterprise, and public enterprise."[348]

A major set of racial conflicts was precipitated by decisions of the Supreme Court of the United States in the spring of 1954. The decisions interpreted the

---

[344] *Ibid.*, pp. 65–87, 101–112.

[345] *Ibid.*, pp. 88–90.

[346] *Ibid.*, pp. 169–173.

[347] *Ibid.*, pp. 154–168, 203 ff.

[348] Howard R. Bowen, *Social Responsibilities of the Businessman* (New York, Harper & Brothers, 1953, pp. ii, 276), *passim*, especially pp. 39, 258. Among other volumes in the series of studies, reflecting their attitude in their titles, were John C. Bennett *et al., Christian Values and Economic Life* (New York, Harper & Brothers, 1954, pp. xv, 272), and A. Dudley Ward, *The American Economy—Attitudes and Opinions* (New York, Harper & Brothers, 1955, pp. xx, 199).

Constitution as requiring the integration of white and Negro students in the public schools of the nation. The issue was particularly acute in the South, especially in states where Negroes constituted a large proportion of the population. For several years integration in higher education in that region had been proceeding slowly and for the most part unspectacularly. Nor did integration constitute a major problem in most of the North. But in the South it was counter to long-established custom. Resistance mounted and was given wide publicity through the action of state officials, notably in Little Rock, Arkansas, and in Virginia.[349] In ensuing years the issue was further complicated by Negro protests against discrimination in public transportation, at lunch counters in stores, and in public beaches in Mississippi. In general, church pronouncements opposed segregation.[350] For example, in November, 1958, 309 of the Protestant clergy in Atlanta, Georgia, while doubting the wisdom of massive integration and opposed to the amalgamation of the races, advocated obedience to the decisions of the Supreme Court and stood for orderly legal procedures to obtain an alteration in the decisions rather than openly or tacitly flouting them. They also came out for freedom of speech, the preservation of the public school system, and the maintenance of communication between the responsible leaders of the races.[351]

The Christian faith continued to express itself in voluntary gifts, large and small, to philanthropic projects. Hundreds of foundations were established. Although not all could be traced to a Christian motive and the largest of them, the Ford Foundation, set up by the millions acquired in the manufacture of automobiles, appeared not to have that origin, some were clearly sprung from the Christian faith. John Davison Rockefeller, Jr. (1874–1960), was outstanding. An only son, he was reared in a deeply religious home. There was daily morning worship, and the family were faithful attendants at church services. He himself was conscientious and hard-working, and took seriously the responsibilities of great wealth. He taught the men's Bible class in the Fifth Avenue Baptist Church in New York City which had been relinquished by Charles Evans Hughes because of the pressure of other duties. It was he who in cooperation with Fosdick made possible the Riverside Church—both its physical structure and its community character. Reared a Baptist, he was increasingly non-sectarian. In the business responsibilities which he assumed as his father's son he endeavoured to act as a Christian. As a member of the board of directors of the Colorado Fuel and Iron Company, of which his father was a major stockholder, he became involved in a prolonged strike which broke out in 1913 and through its violence had nation-wide publicity. He came in for much

349 *Information Service*, April 14, 1956.
350 *Ibid.*, January 29, 1955.
351 *The New York Times*, November 23, 1958.

criticism, but after the strike was over, through a friendly visit for personal investigation and with the advice of Mackenzie King, also a devout Christian, a Canadian expert on industrial relations who was soon to rise to prominence in his native country, he obtained the adoption of a plan for employee representation on work councils on matters of common interest to employers and labourers. As much as possible he withdrew from business and gave himself to the philanthropic use of the fortune accumulated by his father. Complete confidence existed between father and son. It was largely at the latter's suggestion that the former initiated the Rockefeller Foundation as one channel for utilizing his wealth for the benefit of mankind. Space must not be taken even to list the many benefactions of the younger Rockefeller. He planned them carefully and called into council experts to obtain the facts on which to base his decisions. His gifts ranged widely from strictly religious movements and institutions to education and art—and always with the good of humanity as their object.[352]

The Effect of Christianity on the United States in the Twentieth Century: The Roman Catholic Contribution

As a minority, although a large minority, and largely from what were at the outset underprivileged strata of society, Roman Catholics did not have as great an impact on American life as did Protestants. Yet as they were longer in the country, gained in wealth, and became more and more integrated among the people of the United States, their influence mounted. As we have seen, it was expressed in education. It was also apparent in the social and economic aspects of the nation's structure, in rapid transition as they were under the stress of the forces of the revolutionary age. For inspiration and guidance the Roman Catholics of the United States, as of other countries, had the social teachings of the Holy See. In 1957, for instance, Bishop John J. Wright of Worcester deplored the failure to rise to the Pope's ideals of international relations and called attention to the small number of American Roman Catholics who were identified with programmes for the study of peace, world order, and international organization and were hesitant to give the United Nations the endorsement accorded it by Pius XII. But he believed that members of the younger generation were more responsive to Papal pronouncements on social, economic, and international issues than were their elders.[353]

During the depression years of the 1930's with their intense physical suffering, especially marked among the Roman Catholics who constituted so large a part of the underprivileged and therefore unemployed portions of the urban

---

[352] Fosdick, *John D. Rockefeller, Jr.: A Portrait, passim.*
[353] *Information Service*, April 19, 1958, quoting an article by Bishop Wright in *The Pilot*, the newspaper of the Boston archdiocese, January 4, 1958.

population, Charles E. Coughlin rose to national prominence as the advocate of radical measures for the relief of distress.[354] Coughlin, a descendant of Irish immigrants, was born in Hamilton, Ontario, in 1891. Educated in Roman Catholic schools, in due time he became a priest at Royal Oak, a suburb of Detroit. Like Reinhold Niebuhr, he was thus early in his ministry brought face to face with the problems of one of the burgeoning industrial centres whose workers were soon to be plunged into the great depression. Here he built a church under the patronage of the recently canonized Saint Thérèse of Lisieux, the "Little Flower,"[355] said to have been the first parish bearing her name. He began broadcasting his sermons over the radio, and by 1932, with the depression deepening, he was heard through twenty stations stretching from Kansas City to Bangor, Maine. Later his voice carried even more widely. He sought to base his addresses on accepted Roman Catholic teaching, including Papal pronouncements, especially the encyclical *Rerum novarum* and, after it appeared, the encyclical *Quadragesimo anno*. He endeavoured to be meticulous in his factual accuracy, for he spoke boldly and aroused controversy. Early in his radio career he attacked birth control, prohibition, and the Treaty of Versailles. As the depression worsened he assailed Hoover and held up to ridicule the latter's hopeful assertion that prosperity was just around the corner. He advocated the seizure of the gold of the country by the government and the devaluation of the dollar. He denounced some of the leading bankers of Detroit for what he claimed were dishonest practices which, so he said, were robbing the people. He poured out the vials of his wrath on Communism and Communists, but he condemned unbridled capitalism, the unequal distribution of wealth, and the unfair payment for labour on the basis of piece work and insisted on his idea of a just and living wage. At the outset he supported President Roosevelt but later was critical of him. Inevitably he created enemies, including the powerful Detroit *Free Press,* and he was accused of falsifying the facts about the banks, misusing funds, and evading the income tax. Cardinal O'Connell, Archbishop of Boston, publicly expressed his disapproval, but he did not have jurisdiction in Detroit. Coughlin was long supported by his bishop. However, in time the ecclesiastical authorities silenced him.

The multitudinous works of charity of the Roman Catholic Church, while less spectacular than Coughlin, had a far more continuing effect on the life of the country. Hospitals, orphanages, old people's homes, and other institutions bore unobtrusive witness to the active concern of that church for the unfortunate and underprivileged. Occasionally they suffered from inefficiency, but from time to time able bishops brought improvement.[356]

---

[354] Louis B. Ward, *Father Charles E. Coughlin, an Authorized Biography* (Detroit, Tower Publications, 1933, pp. xv, 352), *passim*.

[355] Volume I, pp. 361, 362.

[356] As one example see William Cardinal O'Connell, *Recollections of Seventy Years* (Boston, Houghton Mifflin Co., 1934, pp. ix, 395), pp. 270–299.

An undertaking which was also less spectacular than Coughlin and which endeavoured to give relief to the great masses of unemployed during the depression of the 1930's was the Catholic Worker Movement. It was begun in 1933 by Dorothy Day (1898——), a convert who had been a member of the Socialist Party, of the Industrial Workers of the World, and of several Communist affiliates and who now, through the Roman Catholic Church, attempted to remedy the ills to which she had sought a cure in the years before she had made the change. A journalist, she began publishing a paper, the *Catholic Worker*. Out of it came the Catholic Worker Movement, with Houses of Hospitality, farming communes, discussion groups, study clubs, hundreds of "Christ Rooms" in private homes where temporary shelter was given to the unfortunate, and publications to disseminate the social teachings of the Roman Catholic Church. The Catholic Worker Movement gave a fresh start to many victims of the depression and inspired and trained men and women who reinforced the Association of Catholic Trade Unionists and the Catholic youth movements.[357]

Among the Roman Catholic clergy many could be numbered who were working for better social conditions. Thus Edwin Vincent O'Hara, whom we have had occasion to mention as active in other good causes, while a priest in the Archdiocese of Portland, Oregon, championed such legislation as workingmen's compensation for accidents, a maximum hours law, and a minimum wage law. He was chairman of the state commission of Oregon to obtain the enforcement of the minimum wage and had the satisfaction of seeing the constitutionality of that measure upheld in the Oregon and United States Supreme Courts.[358] O'Hara was chiefly responsible for the initiation of the Catholic Rural Life Movement, which had as its purpose both better religious instruction of the rural Roman Catholic population and the improvement of other conditions for that element of the population.[359] As Bishop of Kansas City he established the Catholic Community Service, which made its facilities available to all of whatever faith, stood for equality of opportunity for Negroes, and championed Japanese residents during the wave of hysteria against them which swept the country soon after the Pearl Harbour incident.[360] John Augustus Ryan (1869–1945) was long an advocate of social justice. He was the director of the Social Action Department of the Catholic Welfare Conference, was professor of moral theology and industrial ethics in the Catholic University of America, drew up a minimum wage law for Minnesota, and was the author or

[357] *The Long Loneliness. The Autobiography of Dorothy Day* (New York, Harper & Brothers, 1952, pp. 288), *passim;* Ellis, *Documents of American Catholic History,* pp. 647–651; *The New York Times,* March 22, 1956.
[358] Shaw, *Edwin Vincent O'Hara,* pp. 38–62.
[359] *Ibid.,* pp. 72–85.
[360] *Ibid.,* pp. 223–236.
[361] John Augustus Ryan, *Social Doctine in Action, a Personal History* (New York, Harper & Brothers, 1941, pp. vii, 297), *passim.*

editor of many books.[361] Peter E. Dietz (died in 1947), born in the under-privileged East Side of New York City and educated by the Society of the Divine Word in Germany, shortly before World War I began trail-blazing years in behalf of the workingman and continued in the decade which followed the peace. He attempted, vainly, to bring into more effective coöperation the Roman Catholic societies which were striving for social reform and founded the American Academy for Christian Democracy for Women to train young Roman Catholics for social work. But he had difficulties with his ecclesiastical superiors and much that he attempted proved abortive.[362] Later, and with a much wider hearing, Fulton J. Sheen by his radio and television appearances and his books popularized the Papal social teachings. He said that the Roman Catholic Church was not opposed to capitalism as private ownership of the production of wealth for profit, but he was adamant against capitalism when it appropriated all the products and profits and critized it when it placed the control of wealth in the hands of a few and sought to regulate credit and to dominate government and economic life.[363]

Friendship Houses were sponsored by some of the clergy to improve racial relations, although the one in New Orleans had to be closed because of the intense animosity which followed the Supreme Court's decisions in 1954 ordering integration in the schools.[364]

In a somewhat different way the Sodalities of Our Lady contributed to social improvement. Lay organizations associated with the Society of Jesus and begun in the sixteenth century in Rome, they had a remarkable extension in the United States in the twentieth century, with a national federation organized in 1957. Through one of their journals, *The Queen's Work*, by blacklisting the objectionable ones, they fought moving pictures which were deemed immoral and, aided by the Legion of Decency, encouraged youth to stay away from those labelled bad and to patronize good ones.[365]

THE SHARE OF CHRISTIANITY IN THE LITERATURE AND MEDIUMS OF MASS COMMUNICATION

A full treatment of the effects of Christianity on the United States in the twentieth century would entail a study of the older and current literature that was read and of such mediums of mass communication as the daily press, the

[362] Mary Harrita Fox, *Peter E. Dietz, Labor Priest* (University of Notre Dame Press, 1953, pp. xiv, 285), *passim* John N. Moody, editor, *Church and Society. Catholic Social and Political Thought, 1789-1950* (New York, Arts, 1953, pp. 914), p. 858.

[363] Fulton J. Sheen, *Liberty, Equality, and Fraternity* (New York, The Macmillan Co., 1938, pp. xiii, 187), *passim.*

[364] J. B. Gremillion, *The Journal of a Southern Pastor* (Chicago, Fides Publishers Association, 1957, pp. vi, 305), pp. 266-268.

[365] *The 1958 National Catholic Almanac*, p. 554; Joseph T. MacGloin, *Backstage Missionary Father Dan Lord, S.J.* (New York, Pageant Press, 1958, pp. 134), pp. 110-113.

weekly and monthly periodicals, the theatre, the "movies," the radio, and tele-vision. But such an attempt, if seriously made, would carry us far beyond all proper dimensions of this volume. Moreover, it would necessitate both detailed and comprehensive investigations such as have not been made. We know enough to be clear that if the study was faithfully and competently carried through it would reveal ambiguities and contradictions, just as have appeared in other aspects of the life not only of the United States but also of the rest of the world, especially in the former "Christendom." It would point to the fact that the Bible remained the "best seller," both in the King James Version and in newer translations, especially the Revised Standard Version. It would note the presence on "best seller" lists of Bruce Barton, *The Man Nobody Knows,* an interpretation of the life of Christ, of Millar Burrows, *The Dead Sea Scrolls,* and of works of fiction dealing sympathetically with Christian heroes and Biblical stories, such as Costain, *The Silver Chalice.* But it would also call attention to popular fiction, plays, moving pictures, and a "tabloid" press in which Christian values were ignored or derided.

CHRISTIANITY AND THE STATE IN A PLURALISTIC SOCIETY

In the mounting variety of religions, relations between Church and state were increasingly complicated. Through most of the nineteenth century, when the ethos of the country, so far as it was religious, was Protestant, some patterns prevailed. The federal Constitution forbade the Congress to enact a law "re-specting the establishment of religion or prohibiting the free exercise thereof." Such remnants of establishment as existed in the states disappeared early in the nineteenth century. Yet neither the national government nor the govern-ment of any of the states was atheistic, the constitutions of several of the states endorsed Christianity, the President took his oath of office on a Bible, both the Senate and the House had chaplains, and in the armed services chaplains ap-pointed and paid by the government had the status of officers. The reading of the Bible was common practice in the opening exercises of the public schools. Christians did not hesitate to bring pressure on the government, whether national, state, or local, to enact measures they deemed in accord with the principles of their faith. Sometimes they did it through their churches and sometimes through organizations, like the Anti-Saloon League, which they supported as individuals rather than through ecclesiastical bodies.

In the twentieth century the scene was more complex. Protestants continued in the majority, but Roman Catholics became more prominent in local and national affairs and the Jews increased in numbers and influence. In that re-ligiously pluralistic setting some problems were acute. As in many other coun-tries and as in the nineteenth century in the United States, the support and control of education gave rise to controversy. Under what auspices was youth to be reared—by the Church or by the state? The majority maintained that if the nation was to survive and flourish it must have primary charge of education, especially in the elementary grades. However, many deplored the absence of religious instruction as an integral part of the public schools. The varieties of religion were so great that no one form could be inculcated without injustice to the others. In 1922 forty-five states had constitutional provisions forbidding sectarian religious instruction in the public schools. Yet fifteen states had laws which forbade the exclusion of the Bible on the charge that it was sectarian and prescribed methods for its use.[366] In 1934 it was said that the majority of the public schools were opened daily by the reading of the Bible without comment and that a substantial minority were opened as well by the singing of a hymn and the Lord's Prayer.[367] The number of states which required the reading of the Bible increased from six in 1922 to twelve in 1946, those that permitted it mounted from six in 1922 to twenty-five in 1946, and those forbidding it declined from ten in the earlier to eight in the latter year.[368] Experiments continued to be made in religious instruction by the several religious groups in "released time"—in separate classes during school hours for those children whose parents requested it. A plan of that kind in operation in New York State in 1939–1940 appeared to be giving satisfaction.[369]

The Roman Catholic Church, with its extensive and growing system of parochial schools maintained with the purpose of making instruction in its tenets part of the curriculum, constituted a major problem. As we have seen, attempts to require the enrollment of all children in the public schools and so to strangle the parochial schools were declared unconstitutional. The parochial schools, therefore, persisted. Tension was further created by the effort of Roman Catholics to obtain financial aid from the state for their schools. In 1949 Cardinal Spellman, Archbishop of New York, said that he was against asking for general public support for denominational schools, but that he favoured such auxiliary aid as the transportation of children to and from school, the purchase of non-religious textbooks, free lunches, and provision for the health of the pupils.[370] In the 1950's it was on the issue of such assistance that the debate largely centred. Yet a demand was expressed, notably in 1961, for much more inclusive assistance, including federal subsidies to the erection of school buildings.[371]

[366] Stokes, *Church and State in the United States,* Vol. II, p. 498.
[367] *Ibid.,* p. 551.
[368] Orville H. Zabel, *God and Caesar in Nebraska. A Study of the Legal Relationship of Church and State, 1854–1954* (Lincoln, University of Nebraska, 1955, pp. xii, 198), p. 105.
[369] Stokes, *op. cit.,* Vol. II, pp. 541 ff.
[370] *Ibid.,* pp. 754, 755.
[371] William E. McManus, in Masse, *The Catholic Mind Through Fifty Years, 1903–1953,* pp. 189 ff.

The dissemination of information on artificial methods of birth control was also controversial. The Roman Catholic Church consistently opposed it and in some states had sufficient power to obtain legislation forbidding it. Yet many Protestants, including several denominational bodies, favoured the use of such methods and tensions developed.

Another issue which was chronically acute arose from the structure of the Roman Catholic Church. Its apex was in the Pope, who not only was the head of a great religious organization but also, as the ruler of Vatican City, a sovereign state, had the status of a temporal monarch. The loyalty given him by all good Roman Catholics, especially the bishops and clergy, was interpreted by some critics as entailing disloyalty to the United States. It was an old and chronic accusation, often made in the nineteenth century and reiterated again and again in the twentieth. A member high in the hierarchy might protest, as did Archbishop Ireland on the eve of World War I, that no contradiction existed between his religious faith and his civil and political faith, between his creed and his country.[372] But many Protestants were not convinced and feared that the growing strength of the Roman Catholic Church would, if allowed to go unchallenged, lead to interference by the Vatican in American life and even domination. The active part of the hierarchy in the politics of some countries where Roman Catholics were in the majority, as in Italy in the nineteenth and twentieth centuries, gave ground for the fear. Although some Roman Catholics rejoiced in the separation of Church and state and held that under it their church had experienced its phenomenal growth in the United States, no unanimity existed among them as to what their attitude should be in case they were ever in the substantial majority—whether they should use that power to restrict the religious liberty of those not of their faith or to permit the kind of liberty which they enjoyed while they were in a minority.

The issue was heightened by the respect paid by the Congress to the memory of Pius XI on the latter's death, by the President's appointment of an official representative at the coronation of Pius XII, and by the erection in Washington of an imposing building as the headquarters of the apostolic delegation.[373] Criticism became especially vocal when, in December, 1939, President Roosevelt announced his purpose to send Myron C. Taylor to the Vatican as his personal representative with the rank of ambassador. Such an appointment did not require the consent of the Senate, so there was no constitutional way of nullifying it. Taylor was received at the Vatican with respect but in a different category from that of ambassadors regularly appointed by their governments.[374] The issue was raised again and in a still more controversial form when in October,

---

[372] Ireland, in Masse, *op. cit.*, p. 146. See also John P. Carroll in *ibid.*, pp. 176–178.

[373] Stokes, *op. cit.*, Vol. II, pp. 96 ff.

[374] *Ibid.*, pp. 96–112; Robert A. Graham, *Vatican Diplomacy. A Study of Church and State on the International Plane* (Princeton University Press, 1959, pp. xii, 442), pp. 326–348.

1951, President Truman nominated Mark W. Clark to be ambassador to Vatican City, a nomination which to be effective would require the approval of the Senate. A storm of protest arose, largely from Protestants, and in January, 1952, Clark asked that his name be withdrawn.[375]

APPROACHING UNITY IN DIVERSITY

Could any degree of unity be achieved in the variety presented by Christianity in the United States in the twentieth century? Christianity was more many faceted there than in any other country or region in which it had ever existed. As we have repeatedly said, to the deep-seated divisions brought from across the Atlantic, others had been added.

We have seen that some attempts toward unity had been made in the nineteenth century.[376] Early in that century, through some societies and coöperative projects, advance appeared to be in progress. However, Schmucker's proposal did not bring the response for which he had longed, and for a time denominational rivalry was intensified. The Evangelical Alliance awakened hopes, the Sunday School movement and the Young Men's and Young Women's Christian Associations brought thousands together across denominational lines, the Young People's Society of Christian Endeavour and the Student Volunteer Movement for Foreign Missions enlisted many regardless of their denominations, in the 1890's the Foreign Missions Conference of North America was constituted, and in 1908 the Federal Council of the Churches of Christ in America was formed. The movement towards Christian unity came to the eve of World War I on a rising tide.

In the decades which followed 1914 further advances were made, but they did not erase the cleavages. Indeed, new ones appeared. In general, however, by 1962 in a number of ways the dream of the unity—although not the union— of all Christians in the United States was appreciably nearer to realization than it had been half a century earlier.

The movement towards unity was seen in the fusion of some existing ecclesiastical bodies. Unlike what we are to find in Canada and in some of the countries of Asia, with one exception, and that only partial, they were not of radically diverse denominations but were branches of the same denominational family. We have already mentioned one—The American Lutheran Church, consummated in 1960. We have hinted at others—the United Lutheran Church, achieved in 1918, and the American Lutheran Church (later a constituent body of The American Lutheran Church of 1960). In 1962 the Augustana Synod, the Finnish Evangelical Lutheran Church, and the American Evangelical

---

[375] *The Catholic Historical Review*, Vol. XLIV, pp. 421–439 (January, 1959).
[376] Volume III, pp. 96–100.

Lutheran Church were in process of merging with the United Lutheran Church.[377] In addition, the Methodist Church was a union of the Methodist Episcopal Church, the Methodist Episcopal Church, South, and the Methodist Protestant Church. It grew out of long negotiations, which began in 1910 and culminated in 1939 in the numerically largest Protestant ecclesiastical body in the United States.[378] In 1934 the Evangelical Synod and the Reformed Church in the United States, both serving constituencies of predominantly German ancestry and having similar doctrines and polity, merged in the Evangelical and Reformed Church.[379] In 1946 a union was achieved of the United Evangelical Church and the United Brethren in Christ. Both bodies resembled the Methodists in polity and in temper and originally served constituencies of German background. The resulting ecclesiastical organization took the name "the Evangelical United Brethren Church."[380] The Congregational Christian Churches came into being in 1931, a union of the Congregationalists and Christians, both with a tradition of congregational autonomy. In 1957–1961, after long negotiations, they joined with the Evangelical and Reformed Church in the United Church of Christ. In polity, theology, and the national ancestry of its members the United Church of Christ was more inclusive than any union heretofore effected in the United States. A minority of Congregational churches vigorously dissented.[381] The year 1958 witnessed the coming together of the Presbyterian Church in the U.S.A. and the United Presbyterian Church in North America to form the United Presbyterian Church in the U.S.A.[382] Earlier, in 1920, the Welsh Calvinistic Methodist Church had joined the Presbyterian Church in the U.S.A.[383] In 1961 the Universalist Church of America and the American Unitarian Association merged into the Unitarian Universalist Association.[384] Between 1911 and 1952 fourteen Pentecostal churches were reduced to five bodies.[385]

Although what was called "organic union"—the integration of different ecclesiastical structures—had not been as marked as in Canada and in several countries in Asia, by the mid-twentieth century coöperation across denominational lines had made striking progress through many organizations—local, state, and national. In the cities ministerial alliances and councils multiplied. The states had councils of churches. On the national scale the Federal Council of the Churches of Christ in America greatly expanded its activities. In 1950

[377] Ecumenical Press Service, June 24, 1960.
[378] Rouse and Neill, A History of the Ecumenical Movement, pp. 451–454.
[379] Information Service, December 27, 1952; Sweet, The Story of Religion in America, p. 425.
[380] Information Service, December 27, 1952.
[381] Britannica Book of the Year, 1958, p. 160. See also Christianity Today, May 25, 1959, pp. 10–14.
[382] Britannica Book of the Year, 1959, pp. 160, 161.
[383] Sweet, op. cit., p. 425.
[384] The New York Times, May 24, 1960.
[385] Information Service, December 27, 1952.

it was succeeded by the National Council of the Churches of Christ in the United States of America, bringing together eight bodies: the Federal Council of the Churches of Christ in America, the Foreign Missions Conference of North America (formed in 1893), the Home Missions Council of North America (begun in 1908), the International Council of Religious Education (with beginnings going back to the first half of the nineteenth century), the Missionary Education Movement in the United States and Canada (inaugurated in 1902), the National Protestant Council on Higher Education (founded in 1911), the United Stewardship Council (dating from 1920), and the United Council of Church Women (begun in 1940, partly to promote a world day of prayer). To it were soon added Church World Service (brought into being in 1946 to further coöperation in meeting the world-wide needs which accompanied and followed World War II), the Interseminary Movement (begun in the 1880's), the Student Volunteer Movement for Foreign Missions (dating from 1886), the Protestant Radio Commission (started in 1949), and the Protestant Film Commission (organized in 1947). Since 1941 a committee chaired by Luther A. Weigle had been in charge of the complicated negotiations which issued in the new body, but talks had begun earlier. Samuel McCrea Cavert (1888——) was the last general secretary of the Federal Council of Churches and the first general secretary of the National Council of Churches. The Canadians were not included, as they had been in several of the constituent bodies, for their interests were better served by the Canadian Council of Churches, of which we are to speak later. At the outset the National Council had twenty-nine denominational bodies as members, and among them were three of the Eastern Churches.[386]

Not all the Protestant denominations came into the National Council. The Southern Baptist Convention, next to the Methodist Church the largest Protestant ecclesiastical body in the country, remained firmly aloof. Many of the fundamentalists did not join. In 1942 the National Association of Evangelicals was formed "to represent all evangelical believers in all denominations and groups." It had as members not only denominations but also several hundred individual congregations, eight conferences of other churches, and nearly one hundred colleges. In 1941 several smaller and more extreme conservative bodies established the American Council of Christian Churches. As we have seen, it had Carl McIntire as its leader.[387] With varying degrees of intensity individuals and organizations not affiliated with the National Council of Churches attacked that body and those associated with it. They charged them with falsifying the Christian faith and being infiltrated by Communism.

[386] *Christian Faith in Action. Commemorative Volume. The Founding of the National Council of the Churches of Christ in the United States of America* (New York, Central Department of Publication and Distribution, National Council of the Churches of Christ in the United States of America, 1951, pp. 273), *passim.*
[387] Roy, *Apostles of Discord*, pp. 183–186.

In the pluralistic religious scene presented by the United States efforts were made towards sympathetic understanding between the several faiths—especially Protestants, Roman Catholics, and Jews. In 1928 the National Conference of Christians and Jews was brought into being, mainly through the leadership of its first president, Everett Ross Clinchy (1896———), a Presbyterian clergyman. Its first national seminar of Protestants, Catholics, and Jews met in Washington in 1932 and before long it had several scores of local committees.[388] It was especially vigorous in the 1930's, but although it enlisted many individuals and in its early days Clinchy was also a secretary of the Federal Council of Churches, only minorities were active and eventually it dwindled, although it did not disappear. It was in part succeeded by World Brotherhood, of which Clinchy was the administrative president.[389]

THE GROWING SHARE OF THE CHRISTIANITY OF THE UNITED STATES IN THE WORLD-WIDE SPREAD OF THE FAITH

One of the most striking features of the Christianity of the United States in the twentieth century was the increasing share of both Protestantism and the Roman Catholic Church in the world-wide spread of the faith.

The course of Protestant missions from the United States was somewhat irregular. In the effort to realize the dreams that had been aroused by the idealism of World War I, the years immediately after the armistice saw extensive plans for advance by several denominations. They paralleled the Inter-church World Movement and, although to a less extent than that ill-starred enterprise, suffered from the reaction which characterized the 1920's.

A phase of the reaction was a widespread questioning of the programme and the effectiveness of foreign missions. It found spectacular expression in what was known as the Laymen's Foreign Missions Inquiry. A group of laymen, mainly centring in New York, all of whom had contributed generously to foreign missions, were concerned for the lack of interest in them among the younger generation, including their own children. Substantially aided by John D. Rockefeller, Jr., they undertook an impartial study of the foreign missions of seven American denominations in India, Burma, Japan, and China. First a large number of "fact-finders" were sent to make careful surveys. They were followed by a Commission of Appraisal of fifteen eminent clergy and laity, with William Ernest Hocking as chairman and all deeply committed to the Christian faith. Their report won some support but aroused a storm of criticism among many of the leaders in foreign missions. Rockefeller heartily

---

[388] *Who's Who in America*, Vol. XXXI, p. 557; Everett R. Clinchy, *All in the Name of God* (New York, The John Day Co., 1934, pp. 179), pp. 140, 141.

[389] For the sympathetic aid of a prominent Roman Catholic bishop see Shaw, *Edwin Vincent O'Hara*, pp. 321, 322.

approved the report; its adverse reception led him and his father to withdraw their support from the missions of their denomination, the Northern Baptists.[390] Yet the missions of the Protestant churches of the United States survived the reaction of the 1920's, the depression years of the 1930's, and World War II. They did not suffer as severely as those of Europe and the British Isles, and before the 1960's more than half of both personnel and funds of Protestant foreign missions were from the United States. In 1911, of the 15,286 Protestant missionaries from all countries, 7,239, or not quite half, were from the United States and Canada. In 1925, out of 29,188 Protestant foreign missionaries, 14,043 were from the United States and Canada, or about the same proportion as in 1911. In 1936, owing chiefly to the depression, the total from all lands had fallen to 27,577, a shrinkage due primarily to the decline of the North American contribution to 11,239. In 1952 North American missionaries (from the United States and Canada) totalled 18,576, or slightly more than half of the 35,533 from all lands. In 1958 missionaries from all countries had risen to 38,606, and of these 25,058, or nearly two-thirds, were from the United States and Canada.[391] Clearly, in view of the greater average cost of maintaining a missionary from North America than from the British Isles and the Continent of Europe, an even larger proportion of the financial burden of the Protestant foreign missionary enterprise was borne by the churches of the United States and Canada. The total received by North American agencies in 1957 was $147,282,881.47, an increase of 11 per cent. over 1955. This was at least six times the giving to Protestant missions in all the rest of the Western world.[392]

A significant shift took place after World War II in the source of the missionaries from the United States. A much larger proportion came from theologically conservative or fundamentalist groups than before that struggle. The Division of Foreign Missions of the National Council of Churches represented denominations which enrolled the majority of the Protestants of the country. In 1958 the agencies affiliated with it supported 41.2 per cent. of the North American foreign missionary force, a decline from 43.5 per cent. in 1956, but contributions to them were 54 per cent. of those of all agencies. At the beginning of 1958 the Evangelical Foreign Missions Association and the Interdenominational Foreign Mission Association, both conservative theologically, had together about as many missionaries as had the Division of Foreign Missions,

---

[390] For selections from the reports of the fact-finders, see Orville A. Petty, editor, *Laymen's Foreign Missions Inquiry. Fact-Finders' Reports* (New York, Harper & Brothers, 7 vols., 1933). For the much discussed report of the Commission of Appraisal see *Re-Thinking Missions. A Layman's Appraisal after One Hundred Years* (New York, Harper & Brothers, 1932, pp. xv, 349), *passim*. For selections from regional reports of the Commission of Appraisal see Orville A. Petty, editor, *Laymen's Foreign Missions Inquiry. Regional Reports of the Committion of Appraisal* (New York, Harper & Brothers, 3 vols., 1933). For Rockefeller's part see Fosdick, *John D. Rockefeller, Jr.*, pp. 214–220.

[391] *Occasional Bulletin from the Missionary Research Library*, December 8, 1958, p. 30.

[392] *Ibid.*, pp. 2, 29.

but the increase since 1956 had been 1,412 as against that of 475 connected with the Division of Foreign Missions. The disparity was due partly but not entirely to the accession of a number of societies to the two conservative bodies in the two-year interval. In addition, on the conservative side were the Associated Mission Agencies of the International Council of Christian Churches and 64 missionary societies which did not belong to any of the four coöperative associations, 28 of them denominational and 36 spanning denominational lines, and most of them conservative theologically.[393] The mounting proportion of theologically conservative missionaries going from North America made for a prospective increase in theological conservatism of the Protestant communities served by these missionaries in Latin America, Asia, and Africa.

The Roman Catholics of the United States shared increasingly in the foreign missions of their church, both in personnel and in finances. Before World War I few missionaries went from the United States. In 1955 a total of 5,126—2,914 men and 2,212 women—were in active service outside the country. They represented 54 religious institutes of men and 80 communities of sisters. More than half of the men were Jesuits, Maryknollers, Redemptorists, or Steylers (the Society of the Divine Word). A third of the women were either Maryknoll Sisters, Marist Sisters, School Sisters of Notre Dame, or Medical Mission Sisters.[394] In 1960, Roman Catholics of the United States had 6,782 missionaries, 2,405 of whom were in Latin America. Of the priests only 42 were seculars.[395]

As yet far fewer Roman Catholic missionaries went from the United States than from several of the countries of Europe. In the 1950's the total was about one-ninth of the entire Roman Catholic foreign missionary force. The only one of the congregations which sent any considerable number and which had its origin in the United States was the Catholic Foreign Mission Society of America, inaugurated in 1911 and with headquarters at Maryknoll, near Ossining, New York.[396] No comprehensive figures for the financial contributions of Roman Catholics to foreign missions were obtainable, for they were made through scores of orders, congregations, and societies in many different parts of the world. However, the Society for the Propagation of the Faith, of French origin and long under French direction but in 1922 placed directly under Papal control with headquarters in Rome, raised more than any other single agency. It sent no missionaries but assisted those of the many organizations whose agents they were. In 1957 about 65 per cent. of its total income came from the United States.[397]

[393] *Ibid.*, pp. 2, 3.
[394] *Worldmission*, Vol. VIII, p. 101 (Fall, 1957). For a detailed statement, see *U.S. Catholic Missionary Personnel Oversees in 1951* (Washington, Mission Secretariat, 1951, pp. 56), *passim.*
[395] *Worldmission*, Vol. XI, pp. 4 ff. (Summer, 1960).
[396] For a description of the Maryknoll Sisters see *Time*, April 11, 1955, pp. 76–84.
[397] *Worldmission*, Vol. VIII, p. 101 (Fall, 1957).

Although they were not contributed primarily to assist the spread of Christianity, many millions of dollars and the tons of clothing, food, and medicines sent to other countries by the churches of the United States and their agencies were part of the impact of the Christianity of the United States upon the rest of the world. They went to many lands and peoples. Both Protestants and Roman Catholics were active. Inclusive statistics could not be obtained. In connexion with World War I and its aftermath what was accomplished was impressive, but the extent and the dimensions of the aid during and after World War II reached unprecedented proportions and were not equalled by the relief given by Christians of any other country or, indeed, by the total from all the rest of the world. Although motives were mixed and included the desire to counter Communism, the outpouring was clearly from predominantly Christian impulses. It was made possible by the great wealth of the country but it was purely voluntary and was in addition to the billions of dollars contributed, also voluntarily, by Christians for religious and philanthropic institutions and agencies in the United States. How far Christianity was responsible for the vast sums given by the Government of the United States to aid in the relief and economic and cultural development of underprivileged peoples across the world could not be determined. That self-interest, particularly in curbing the spread of Communism, was a major factor was indubitable. That the motives were in part of Christian origin, from a national ethos which the faith had done much to shape, was also clear. But the proportion of self-interest and Christian idealism could not be ascertained.

SUMMARY

The preceding pages with their multiplicity of details require a summary, especially because they constitute the longest chapter in our entire five volumes. We have devoted so much space to the United States of America partly because of the size of the nation and partly because of the outstanding role which it played in the twentieth century, but chiefly on account of the influence of the Christianity which developed in that country upon the faith the world around.

Along with the rest of the world, the United States was profoundly affected by the revolutionary age. The forces which played upon mankind flung the American people, reluctant and ill prepared, into mid-stream of the flood which was hurrying this planet toward an unpredictable future. On the domestic scene industrialization was proceeding apace with vast shifts of population, the rapid advance of urbanization, and a mobile and largely atomized society in which, even in a single year in the 1950's, one person out of every five changed his place of residence. The intellectual and ideological currents of the day were challenging the faith in the United States. The breathless rush of events carried the nation and the churches, bewildered, from one stage of the revolution to another. World War I with its idealism precipitated a reaction of disillusionment and the feverish "gay twenties." Then came the depression of the 1930's. The nation was only beginning to emerge from that catastrophe when it was sucked into the maelstrom of World War II. World War II was immediately followed by the "cold war" between the two colossi, of whom the United States was one, with its recurring crises and its mounting atomic armaments. In this kaleidoscopic era the Christianity of the United States was summoned to rise to the occasion fully as sharply as was that of Europe.

The Christianity confronted by the challenges of the day was both like and unlike that of Europe. It was, similarly, the heir of all the past centuries of the faith. But it was much more multiform than the Christianity of Europe had ever been. All the varieties which had developed in Europe and elsewhere were represented in it and in the new environment the vigour inherent in the faith had added fresh varieties. This Christianity not only was more complex than that of the Old World; its constituent elements were differently proportioned. Here was no state church with dissenting sects, as formerly in the several countries of Europe. The Christianity of the United States was prevailingly Protestant, but that branch of the faith was divided into many denominations, large and small. What had been the established Protestant churches of Europe were a minority, and the majority of Protestants were in churches which in Europe were minorities, usually small ones. They owed their strength to an evangelism which in the British Isles would have been called Evangelicalism and on the Continent of Europe Pietism. The Roman Catholic Church grew by the immigration of underprivileged elements in Europe and was in the minority, although an increasingly well-knit and substantial minority. Its members embodied an attitude which on the one hand was that of a defensive, persecuted community and on the other hand was one of confident determination to play a growing and ultimately a dominant role in the nation's life. By the mid-twentieth century the Eastern Churches were being rapidly augmented by immigration but were still not fully integrated into the life of the nation.

In contrast with Europe, where de-Christianization was engulfing the majority and was either erasing connexion with the churches, as with the majority in Russia, or reducing it to formal baptism and perhaps confirmation and where loyal minorities were holding out against the tide, in the United States Christianity was displaying marked vitality. With the exception of the decades which included World War I, every ten years witnessed an increase in the proportion of church members to the population. In the 1940's and 1950's attendance at church services was rising. The percentage growth among Negroes, Indians, and the newer immigration was about equal to that among the whites of colonial stock and the nineteenth-century immigration. Thousands of new church buildings were erected. In both the Protestant churches and the Roman Catholic Church old movements and organizations flourished and many new ones came into being. On the whole, the Roman Catholic Church was dominant in the urban centres, especially in the inner cities, and Protestantism tended to move out of the inner city and was strongest in the suburbs and the smaller cities and towns. It was chiefly the faith of the older American stock, white and Negro, with important additions from the nineteenth-century immigration. The Roman Catholic Church owed its strength to the immigration of the nineteenth and twentieth centuries. The Eastern Churches were recruited chiefly from the immigration of the twentieth century.

Much movement was seen across denominational lines. It was due partly to the physical mobility of the population and to the desire to conform to whatever church was convenient, attractive, and active where a new domicile was found. It was most marked within Protestantism but took place also across the Protestant-Roman Catholic barrier, with Protestantism gaining more than Roman Catholicism.

Looking toward the formation of oncoming generations, the Roman Catholic Church built, with amazing rapidity, an educational structure with major emphasis on parochial schools but, using these as a foundation, inclusive of secondary schools, colleges, and universities. By the mid-twentieth century in its higher levels the Roman Catholic Church had not achieved equality with the best of the institutions begun by Protestants or financed by the state, but it was making progress. In the twentieth century Protestants did not have as marked effect on education as in the eighteenth and nineteenth centuries, when individual Protestants had had much to do with the inauguration of state-supported primary education and Protestant churches had founded numerous secondary schools, colleges, and universities. In the twentieth century Protestants discontinued many of their secondary schools, for the public high schools were supplanting them. They founded relatively few new colleges and lost control of a number which they had inaugurated and had helped financially through their initial struggles. Many Protestant educational institutions were becoming secularized. Yet before the mid-century in a variety of ways Protestants were registering gains against the infiltration of education by secularism. They did this partly through encouraging student Christian organizations, partly through chairs and departments of religion, and partly through the men who gave full time as chaplains.

In preparing professional leadership the churches were not fully keeping pace with the rising level of education. But they were not blind to the challenge. The numbers of Protestant clergy with both college and theological education were increasing. Roman Catholic education for the priesthood was more strictly professional than was that of the higher grades of the Protestant ministry and was less oriented to the general cultural environment, but it entailed more prolonged preparation in philosophy and theology.

Protestants were more responsive to the intellectual currents of the revolutionary age than were Roman Catholics. Much of that response appeared in the effort to re-think the Gospel in terms of the new knowledge and the climate of opinion of the day and to bring to the study of the Bible the methods of contemporary historical scholarship. In the fore part of the century what was called liberalism was prominent. Later a reaction was seen which, while not rejecting the approach of the liberals towards the Scriptures, placed more emphasis upon the formulations of the faith by the great reformers of the sixteenth century. On the other hand, large and varied elements among the Protestants rejected the approach of both liberals and neo-orthodox, held to the inerrancy of the Bible, and stressed what they regarded as the fundamental distinguishing Christian doctrines. The line of cleavage between the two approaches ran through most of the major denominations and sharp controversy followed. On the whole Roman Catholics were more traditional and had fewer distinguished scholars. Yet, while they did not depart from the official faith of their church, some Roman Catholic scholars emerged who were taking full account of what was transpiring in the world about them.[398]

Both Protestants and Roman Catholics attempted to bring the Christian Gospel to bear upon the life of the nation. In general, among the Protestants the social gospel, with its hope of transforming human civilization, shared the fate of theological liberalism. Yet the social evils of the day continued to be fought; the challenges of the industrialized and urbanized society and of the chaotic international order continued to be faced. The League of Nations and the United Nations were deeply indebted to the Protestant conscience. Efforts were made to bring more of justice in the economic life and in race relations. Millions of dollars were given by Protestants and Roman Catholics to philanthropic projects. Many Roman Catholics sought to interpret and apply to the American scene the Papal teachings embodied in *Rerum novarum* and *Quadragesimo anno*.

In the realm of politics conflicts occurred between Protestant and Roman Catholic conceptions of the role of the Church. Both attempted to influence the state. The issues over which the major clashes arose were financial aid to public schools, birth control, and the establishment of diplomatic relations with the Vatican. Neither contestant achieved all that it desired.

Both Roman Catholics and Protestants tried to create a comprehensive national organization. As a result, following World War I the National Catholic Welfare Conference came into being and in succeeding years took on increasing responsibilities. The divisions among Protestants were so deep that no

[398] For a summary see James Collins in *Religion in Life*, Vol. XXIX, pp. 179–188 (Spring, 1960).

comparable inclusive structure was achieved. However, in a number of ways the majority of Protestants coöperated on a national scale, and in 1950 the National Council of the Churches of Christ in the United States of America was inaugurated and brought together several of the national agencies through which Protestants had consulted for joint action. In 1960 that coöperation was given a physical symbol in the Interchurch Centre in New York City. Large minorities of Protestants remained aloof and some of them established fellowship among themselves through smaller organizations.

In the twentieth century both the Protestants and the Roman Catholics of the United States had a mounting share in the world-wide extension of the faith. By 1962 American Protestants were supplying approximately half the personnel and more than half the funds of the foreign missions of their branch of the faith. The share of the American Roman Catholics in the overseas spread of their branch of the faith was not nearly as large. It took the form of financial assistance more than of personnel. Yet both were growing.

Christianity in the United States came to the mid-twentieth century on a rising tide. It had not fully countered the secularizing forces of the revolutionary age. Some observers saw in the growth of church membership a religiosity which was more nationalistic than Christian, more intent on utilizing the faith to preserve "the American way of life" than to rise fully to "the high calling of God in Christ Jesus." For an undetermined proportion of the growing church membership baptism was only a social convention, approximating its status in much of Western Europe. Even church attendance, more general than in Western Europe, was for many a custom which was part of the mores, with slight or no deeply Christian meaning. Millions of nominal Christians regarded the ethical standards of the New Testament as impractical and at best gave them only lip service. There was much religious scepticism. Whether in these respects conditions had deteriorated or improved as against the nineteenth century could not be determined. Yet some facts were unassailable: In 1961 the proportion of church members was higher than in any other year in the nation's history. From Christianity were emerging many new and varied movements. In spite of the variety of denominations Protestants were coming together and were prominent in the Ecumenical Movement. In many ways Christianity was placing its impress on the life of the nation. Both Protestants and Roman Catholics were increasing their participation in the world-wide spread of the faith. Christianity was clearly more vital than in contemporary Europe.[399]

[399] For an inclusive bibliography see Nelson R. Burr, *A Critical Bibliography of Religion in America,* (Princeton University Press, 5 parts in 2 vols., 1961).

CHAPTER III

The Changing Scene in Growing Canada

IMMEDIATELY to the north of the United States of America was a nation which in population and wealth was proportionately growing even more rapidly than its southern neighbour. By 1960 Canada embraced all of British North America, for Newfoundland with Labrador had been added to it in 1949. In land area, therefore, it continued to be larger than the United States. Yet a substantial part of the country was arctic and sub-arctic and as heretofore the majority of the population was in the southern sections. In 1956 the population totalled 16,080,701, a marked increase and between 9 and 10 per cent. of that of the United States, as against about 8 per cent. at the turn of the century.

Like the United States, Canada was feeling the full impact of the revolutionary age. It was a belligerent in both World War I and World War II. Urbanization and industrialization were proceeding apace. The vast natural resources in soil, forests, and minerals made possible striking developments in agriculture, mining, and manufacturing. Since these were stimulated by the demands of the world market, Canada too was affected by the international economic situation. The slump following World War I hit Canada. From 1929 to 1935 the depression which began in the United States brought much unemployment. Recovery began late in the 1930's. World War II and its aftermath had repercussions.

Increasingly conscious of being a nation, Canada exhibited the exuberant nationalism which was a feature of the revolutionary age. Although membership was retained in the Commonwealth, Canada insisted on having its own diplomatic corps independent of that of the United Kingdom and on the right to enter into treaty relations with other governments instead, as formerly, being subject to arrangements entered into on its behalf through Westminster. It also had its own membership in the League of Nations and in the United Nations. Friendly relations were maintained with the United States, but Canadians resented any hint that they were less than equal to their more powerful neighbour and were made unhappy by any attempt at economic or cultural control from south of the border.

The population of Canada continued to be augmented by immigration as well as by an excess of births over deaths. It was still overwhelmingly British and French in its origin. In 1951, for example, about 48 per cent. either were born in the British Isles or traced their ancestry to those islands, and 31 per cent. were of French ancestry. Of the stock labelled "British," slightly more than half was of English origin, and slightly less than a quarter each was from Scotland and Ireland, with the Scottish slightly in excess of the Irish. Of the other ethnic strains, those of German background comprised 4 per cent. of the population, Ukrainians 3 per cent., with the Netherlands, Poland, and Italy coming next, in that order.[1] Much of the immigration came from the United States. Except for France, the Continent of Europe was much less strongly represented than in the United States. In 1951 Indians and Eskimos numbered 165,607,[2] a smaller total but a much larger proportion of the population than in the United States.

Largely because of the difference in the ethnic origins of the population, the denominational complexion of Canadian Christianity differed from that of the Christianity of the United States. It did not display as great variety, the proportionate distribution among the churches was far from being the same, and the overwhelming majority of the population were in three communions—Roman Catholic, Anglican, and the United Church (which, as we are to see, was a merger of Presbyterians, Methodists, and Congregationalists). Under the census taken by the government, almost all Canadians expressed a religious preference. In 1951, 44.7 per cent. were classed as Roman Catholics. This was in contrast with approximately 33 per cent. in 1958 of the Roman Catholic proportion of the church membership in the United States. About 14.7 per cent. reported themselves as Anglicans as against about 3 per cent. of Episcopalians in the church membership in the southern neighbour, and 20.5 per cent. expressed a preference for the United Church. When those with a Presbyterian preference who did not go into the union were included (about 5.5 per cent. of the population), this was a much larger proportion of the population than was the combined Methodist, Presbyterian, and Congregational strength in the United States—in 1958 about 17 per cent. of the church membership. Baptists, who constituted the largest of the Protestant denominational families in the United States, with about a fifth of the church membership in 1958, in Canada in 1951 had only between 3 and 4 per cent. of the population.[3]

THE VIGOROUS ROMAN CATHOLIC CHURCH

As had been true in the nineteenth century, the Roman Catholic Church was vigorous. Percentage-wise it was slightly stronger—being claimed by 44.7 out

[1] *The Statesman's Year Book*, 1959, p. 363.
[2] *Ibid.*
[3] *Ibid.*, pp. 365, 584, 590; *Information Service*, February 14, 1953; Dominic of Saint-Denis, *The Catholic Church in Canada*, p. vi.

of every hundred of the population in 1951 as against 41.7 in 1901.[4] Again, after
1914 by far the strongest element was French; in 1951 it constituted 66.7 per
cent. of the Roman Catholic constituency, 1.1 per cent. less than ten years
earlier. The decline was due to the large post-World War II immigration. In
1951 the proportion of English origin was 5.9 per cent. as against 4.3 per cent.
in 1941, that of Irish provenance was 7.9 per cent., a decrease from 8.1 per cent.
a decade earlier, and that of Italian ancestry was 2.2 per cent., contrasted with
2.1 per cent. in 1941. In 1951 the Poles were 2.6 per cent., compared with 2.7
per cent. in 1941, and the Ukrainians were 3.5 per cent. as contrasted with 3.8
per cent. in 1941. Yet each of the two latter nationalities, in spite of a percentage
decline, showed a large increase in numbers between 1941 and 1951—a decade
which had witnessed a growth of about a quarter in the total number of Roman
Catholics. Lesser numbers and percentages were from several other European
countries. Although, chiefly because of immigration, the French proportion
slightly declined, the French element had grown by about 400,000 in the decade,
or approximately 30 per cent., and was still dominant.[5]

Not only were the French numerically two-thirds of the Roman Catholic
Church in Canada. They also were a distinct segment of that church which
was not assimilated to the Anglo-Saxon culture of the majority. Nor, on the
whole, were the non-French elements absorbed by the French. As a result, no
national Canadian Roman Catholic Church came into being comparable to the
national Roman Catholic Church which emerged south of the border as a
fusion of many ethnic elements. In the United States Rome had been able to
prevent permanent division along lines of national origins. That issue had been
decided in the Cahensly incident in the 1880's, when the Pope had insisted that
the distinctions inherited from Europe, especially as between the Irish and the
Germans, should not be perpetuated.[6] In the United States the problem was
made easier by the fact that the Irish, long the most active element in the Roman Catholic Church, were English-speaking and that, if the prejudice against
the Roman Catholic Church on the ground that it was alien was to be overcome, loyalty to the United States must be stressed. Loyalty included the use
of English in the parochial schools and by the second and third generations of
the immigrant stock. Indeed, if that procedure had not been adopted, the losses
through assimilation to a predominantly Protestant culture, large as they were,
would have been much greater. In Canada, in contrast, the French element had
been well established before the advent of the English. On completion of the
English conquest the new masters, to prevent adhesion to the restless Thirteen
Colonies, interfered as little as possible with French life and institutions. The

---

[4] Dominic of Saint-Denis, *op. cit.*, p. vi.
[5] *Ibid.*, p. viii.
[6] Volume III, pp. 103, 252, 253.

precedent thus established was continued and the French in effect remained a distinct nation. To them their language and the Roman Catholic Church were the symbols of their inheritance and the ties which bound them together.

An example of the identification of the French heritage with the Roman Catholic faith was seen in the revival of Acadian self-consciousness in the twentieth century. Memories of the disaster of the eighteenth century were re-awakened, contacts were made with the descendants of the exiles deported to Louisiana in 1755, the creation (1937) of an archiepiscopal see for the Acadian area was obtained, and use of the French language and education in that tongue were stressed. The movement was part of a general strengthening of French-Canadian nationalism.[7]

Their educational system was a major means employed by the French to preserve their religion, their language, and their culture. The British North America Act of 1867 under which the Dominion of Canada was erected left education to the provinces but specified that in some areas separate schools could not be curtailed by provincial legislatures. Under this provision the relation of the schools to religious instruction varied from province to province.

In Quebec, where the French-speaking were 82 per cent. of the population and 87 per cent. were Roman Catholics, two systems existed, one for Protestants and Jews under Protestant supervision and one for Roman Catholics under Roman Catholic direction. In the Roman Catholic schools French was the language of instruction and up to the seventh year much emphasis was placed on the inculcation of the Roman Catholic faith in preparation of the pupils for their first Communion. One objective was to make rural life attractive to forestall emigration to the cities—for urban life in the revolutionary age was recognized as making for the erosion of faith. From the seventh year through the twelfth, education was vocational in character. Secondary education was in French and prepared for study for the liberal professions in *collèges classiques*. The latter numbered about thirty and their staffs were members of religious communities. In them the French language and literature were emphasized. Normal schools and technical schools were also conducted by members of religious orders and congregations and were subsidized by the state. Laval University and the University of Montreal (a branch of Laval until 1919) sought to maintain the best traditions of French culture. Loyola College and Marianapolis College, the one conducted by the Jesuits and the other by the Congregation of Notre Dame and both affiliated with the University of Montreal, granted degrees in arts to English-speaking men and women.[8]

In the other provinces the French language and instruction in the Roman

---

[7] Antoine Bernard, *La Renaissance Acadienne au XXe Siècle* (Quebec, Le Comité de la Survivance Française, Université Laval, no date, pp. 193), *passim*.

[8] *The Encyclopedia Americana*, Vol. V, pp. 399, 401, 409, 410.

Catholic faith were not as prominant as in Quebec. In Ontario, where in 1951 Roman Catholics were 25.7 per cent. of the population,[9] schools might be either public or private, but in 1949 almost all of the private schools were Roman Catholic and about half of them had French as their language. Religious instruction was supervised by the parish priests. Ontario also had Roman Catholic high schools, and crowning its Roman Catholic education structure was the University of Ottawa, conducted by the Oblates.[10] In Newfoundland all the schools were denominational, financed by government grants and by fees levied by the local school boards. Nova Scotia, New Brunswick, and Prince Edward Island had no denominational elementary schools, but by a kind of gentlemen's agreement Roman Catholic children attended certain schools and Protestant children others, and the school boards employed teachers of the same faith as the children.[11] In Manitoba, where sharp controversy had raged over the issue in the preceding century and separate schools had not been permitted, in a section where the population was mostly Roman Catholic by tacit understanding French and religion were taught in the schools.[12] In Alberta and Saskatchewan separate schools were permitted, but they were not allowed in British Columbia.[13]

Another method employed by the Roman Catholic Church to hold its constituency to the faith was the control which it exerted through the parish. This was especially effective in the French population, notably in Quebec. There all members of the parish conformed and all aspects of life bore the imprint of the dominant religion.[14]

For the third of the Roman Catholics who were not French by descent and language their church made careful provision. In the decades which followed 1914 several new dioceses and vicariates apostolic were erected for them and many of the bishops were of Irish ancestry. The adherents of the Ruthenian rites, totalling 190,831 in 1951, were mostly from the Ukraine but included some of other nationalities, the majority of them Poles. They lived chiefly but not entirely in the West and were under four dioceses or exarchates.[15] Of the Indians in Canada over half were counted as Roman Catholics and in 1951 less than 3 per cent. were said to be non-Christians. The Anglicans enrolled about 23 per cent. and the United Church of Canada about 14 per cent. But the Anglicans had almost three-fourths of the Eskimos, the Roman Catholics

---

[9] Dominic of Saint-Denis, *op. cit.,* p. ix.
[10] *The Encyclopedia Americana,* Vol. V, p. 411.
[11] *Information Service,* October 20, 1951.
[12] *The Encyclopedia Americana,* Vol. V, p. 411.
[13] *Ibid.*
[14] Horace Miner, *St. Denis. A French Canadian Parish* (University of Chicago Press, 1939, pp. xix, 283), pp. 91 ff.
[15] Dominic of Saint-Denis, *op. cit.,* pp. 247–250.

only about 14 per cent.[16] The missions, Roman Catholic and Protestant, responsible for the high percentage of Christians among the Indians and Eskimos had records of heroism and devotion unsurpassed anywhere or at any time. They continued into the twentieth century.

As in other countries, the Roman Catholics of Canada were ministered to by secular and regular clergy and by many communities of women. In the 1950's Canada had about 7,500 seculars, or about one to every 900 of the faithful. This was a slightly higher ratio than in the United States. For their preparation sixteen diocesan seminaries were maintained.[17] In 1951 the secular clergy were supplemented by 66 communities of men and over 140 communities of women.[18] The overwhelming majority of the communities of men were of European origin and a little more than half had been introduced before 1914, some of them during the French period. After 1914 about thirty congregations of priests were established in Canada. Almost all were of French origin, but two, the Society of Foreign Missions of Quebec and the Society of the Scarboro Foreign Missions, were Canadian creations and were evidence of the growing part which Canadian Roman Catholics were having in the world-wide spread of the faith.[19] Between 1914 and 1951 more than seventy congregations of women were introduced from Europe. In addition at least two congregations were founded in Canada during those years. Significant of the emphasis on social service was the fact that one of the latter, the Sisters of Our Lady of Good Counsel of Montreal, begun in 1923, had as its purpose family and parochial betterment.[20]

An outstanding example of the contributions of Roman Catholics to the educational, economic, and social improvement of Canada was the life work of two priests of Irish ancestry, James J. Tompkins (1870–1953) and his cousin, Moses Michael Coady, several years his junior. Of Nova Scotian birth, Tompkins had much of his theological education in Rome in the Urban College maintained by the Propaganda and was ordained priest in the Basilica of St. John Lateran in that city. Returning to Nova Scotia, he taught for many years in St. Xavier's College, later St. Xavier's University, in Antigonish. He obtained funds for the enlargement of that institution and in time became its vice-president. He also dreamed of adult popular education. An ardent advocate of the federation of the higher education of the province, when his bishop decided against that measure, at fifty-two years of age he was transferred (1922)—in a sense exiled—to a parish of poverty-stricken fisher folk on Cape Breton Island. There, with the assistance of others, including the Carnegie Corporation, he

[16] *Ibid.*, p. 250.
[17] *Encyclopedia Canadiana*, Vol. IX, p. 64.
[18] *The Encyclopedia Americana*, Vol. V, p. 423.
[19] *Encyclopedia Canadiana*, Vol. IX, p. 70.
[20] *Ibid.*, pp. 71–82.

helped to improve the lot of his parishioners through adult education and co-operative associations. He was one of the first officers of the American Association of Adult Education and (1924) shared in organizing the Canadian Association for Adult Education. After a few months (1934-1935) as chaplain of the mother house of the Sisters of St. Martha in Antigonish Tompkins was appointed to a parish of miners at a time when recovery from the depression of the 1930's had not yet relieved the hard lot of the population. There he continued in fresh ways—especially through libraries—to further adult education and to help his flock to rise above their poverty. Coady was appointed head of the extension department of St. Xavier's and through it did much to put into effect the dreams of his cousin.[21]

In another direction Canadian Roman Catholics had a notable achievement —in this instance in advanced scholarship. They maintained the Pontifical Institute of Medieval Studies in Toronto, which had an extensive collection of medieval manuscripts, much of it on microfilm, and became a major centre for research in that field. While independent of the University of Toronto, it had an arrangement by which its degrees were granted through that institution.[22]

The Liturgical Movement made itself felt. Cardinal Rodrigo Villeneuve, who for sixteen years (1931-1947) was Archbishop of Quebec and head of the French-Canadian hierarchy, was zealous in advocating it. He wrote much on the Movement and appointed three liturgical commissions to further it. Groups of Catholic Action sponsored it. Gregorian music was studied and promoted. The Movement was more potent in French than in English-speaking Canada but made some progress in the latter.[23]

In proportion to their numerical strength the Roman Catholics of Canada sent far more missionaries to other lands than did the Roman Catholics of the United States. In the mid-1950's they had 2,650 in addition to 1,277 to Indians and Eskimos in Canada itself. The United States had 5,126—although the Roman Catholics of that country were five times as numerous as those of Canada. French-speaking Canadian Roman Catholics did much better than those whose tongue was English. The former had one missionary for every 1,121 of the faithful, while the average for Canada as a whole was one missionary to every 1,616 of the faithful. The Canadian missionaries came from twenty-one orders and societies of priests, eight institutes of brothers, and sixty-one women's congregations. The Oblates supplied about a seventh of the whole but were chiefly engaged in missions to the Indians and Eskimos in Canada. The White Fathers had about a fifteenth and the Sisters of Providence about a twentieth of the total. Others followed with lesser proportions. Canada had thirteen missionary

[21] George Boyle, *Father Tompkins of Nova Scotia* (New York, P. J. Kenedy and Sons, 1953, pp. xi, 234), *passim*.

[22] *Encyclopedia Canadiana*, Vol. X, p. 197.

[23] *Ibid.*, Vol. II, pp. 383, 384; Bögler, *Liturgische Erneuerung in aller Welt*, pp. 115-117.

foundations, of which six were exclusively for missions. More than a third of the Canadian missionaries serving abroad were in Africa south of the Sahara, and the next largest number were in Japan and the West Indies.[24]

This substantial share of the French Canadian Roman Catholics in the Liturgical Movement and the missions of their church was evidence of marked vigour. Presumably their concentration in Quebec and part of Ontario and their partial isolation from the currents of the revolutionary age through their predominantly rural character, their language, and their education contributed to their loyalty. How long they could be thus safeguarded against the corrosive forces of the day remained to be seen.

Some passage was seen of Roman Catholics to Protestantism and of Protestants to the Roman Catholic Church. Protestant agencies sought to win French Roman Catholics, and with partial success. Colporteurs distributed Bibles and told the Gospel as Protestants understood it, and from some Protestant schools which enrolled Roman Catholics conversions were made.[25] Numbers of French Canadians became Anglicized and as a phase of that transition became Protestants. Roman Catholics were late in making organized efforts to win Protestants. In 1949 only Toronto had a centre distinctly for that purpose, but in the 1950's more active steps were forecast.[26]

THE UNITED CHURCH OF CANADA

In the 1950's the largest of the Protestant denominations was the United Church of Canada. As we have said, it came into being as an organic union of the Methodists, the Congregationalists, and the majority of the Presbyterians, consummated in 1925 after more than two decades of negotiations. The Congregationalists were the least numerous of the uniting bodies. For a variety of reasons they had never been more than a small minority. In 1871 they had been only 0.63 per cent. of the population and in 1891 had declined to 0.35 per cent.[27] The Methodists were much more numerous and all but small minorities had come together in 1884. The resulting polity had abandoned the episcopate, adopted a general superintendency, and given a large place to the laity. In that

[24] Delacroix, *Histoire Universelle des Missions Catholiques*, Vol. IV, pp. 102, 103. On the Oblate missions among the Indians and Eskimos in the twentieth century see personal narratives in Gabriel Breynat, *Bishop of the Winds. Fifty Years in the Arctic Regions*, translated from the French by Alan Gordon Smith (New York, P. J. Kenedy and Sons, 1955, pp. viii, 266); Rogers P. Buliard, *Inuk* (New York, Farrar, Straus and Young, 1951, pp. ix, 322); Paul Schulte, *The Flying Priest over the Arctic. A Story of Everlasting Ice and Everlasting Love* (New York, Harper & Brothers, 1940, pp. xiii, 267); William A. Leising, *Arctic Wings* (Garden City, N.Y., Doubleday and Co., 1959, pp. 335).

[25] Paul Villard, *The Story of French Protestantism in Canada* (Toronto, Board of Home Missions of the United Church of Canada, 1928, pp. xvii, 237), *passim*.

[26] Irénée Beaubien, *Towards Christian Unity in Canada. A Catholic Approach* (Montreal, Palm Publisher, 1956, pp. 184), pp. 49–66, 83 ff.

[27] Silcox, *Church Union in Canada*, pp. 41–47.

form Methodism had much kinship with the Presbyterians. It had expanded rapidly and its temper was that of evangelism.[28] In 1875 the great majority of the Presbyterians, previously in several different bodies, partly of Old World and partly of Canadian origin, had been consolidated into the Presbyterian Church in Canada. That church was augmented by immigration from Scotland. Like the Methodist Church, it expanded its efforts in the rapidly developing West.[29]

With the precedent established in the two larger denominations, under the pressure of the opportunity to make a concerted approach to the burgeoning West steps were taken towards a more inclusive union. Negotiations were initiated by the Methodists in 1902. For a time approaches were made to the Baptists and the Anglicans, but the former early decided to maintain their separate existence and the latter, while cordial, believed that they could proceed only on the conditions set forth by the Lambeth Conference—conditions which the others were not prepared to accept.[30] Some opposition developed among the Congregationalists and the Methodists, and in all three denominations there were those who preferred federation or coöperation to union, but the controversy was most acute among the Presbyterians. When, in 1925, union was achieved, a substantial minority among the Presbyterians did not enter it but continued their existing body. The reasons for dissenting were many, but underneath them seem to have been a feeling of superiority among the Scottish elements which constituted most of the Presbyterian membership; a preference for their own form of worship with its solemnity, as against the emotion and informality in much of Methodism; a dislike of the hierarchical structure of Methodism and of the aggressiveness of the Methodists; the belief that the Methodists did not maintain a high standard of morality; and the tradition inherited from Scotland which distrusted sects and remembered that in the home land the Church of Scotland was the church of the nation. But the majority of the Presbyterians and the overwhelming majority of the Congregationalists and Methodists concurred, and the United Church of Canada became a fact.[31]

The United Church of Canada, thus constituted, gradually developed an inner unity of spirit and grew. A generation later a discerning visitor could tell from which tradition—Methodist, Presbyterian, or Congregationalist—any par-

---

[28] *Ibid.*, pp. 47–54.
[29] *Ibid.*, pp. 56–70.
[30] *Ibid.*, pp. 125–133.
[31] *Ibid.*, pp. 165–213; Kenneth H. Cousland, in Thomas Buchanan Kilpatrick, *Our Common Faith* (Toronto, Ryerson Press, 1928, pp. vii, 216), pp. 1–56; George C. Pidgeon, *The United Church of Canada. The Story of the Union* (Toronto, Ryerson Press, 1950, pp. 107), *passim;* John T. McNeill, *The Presbyterian Church in Canada, 1875–1925* (Toronto, General Board, Presbyterian Church in Canada, 1925, pp. xi, 276), pp. 255–261; Gershom W. Mason, *The Legislative Struggle for Church Union* (Toronto, Ryerson Press, 1956, pp. vii, 162), *passim;* R. J. Wilson, *Church Union in Canada after Three Years* (Toronto, Ryerson Press, 1929, pp. 54), *passim.*

ticular congregation had emerged, but as the years passed the sense of being in one ecclesiastical body mounted. The statistics showed a striking growth. In 1926 the membership had totalled 609,729 and those under pastoral care were said to be 1,261,778. In 1957 the corresponding figures were 955,303 and 2,407,846.[32] They indicated an increase which about kept pace with that of the population of Canada as a whole—from a membership of about 6.4 per cent. and those under pastoral care of about 13.2 per cent. of the population in 1926 to a membership which was approximately 6 per cent. and those under pastoral care about 15 per cent. of the population in 1957. The funds raised for all purposes rose from $16,968,243 in 1926 to $47,694,571 in 1957.[33] In other words, they had nearly trebled in thirty-one years as against an increase of a little over 50 per cent. in membership and not quite 100 per cent. in persons under pastoral care. But it is not clear that they kept pace with the mounting inflation of those years.

THE PRESBYTERIAN CHURCH IN CANADA

The Presbyterians who did not enter the United Church of Canada but maintained the Presbyterian Church in Canada also increased. In 1958 they reported 196,096 communicants, an increase of 3,682 over the preceding year, and $11,286,614 raised for all purposes in 1958 as against $10,223,934 in 1957.[34]

THE ANGLICAN CHURCH IN CANADA

The Anglican Church in Canada, the name adopted in 1955 by the body previously known as the Church of England in Canada, was the second largest of the non-Roman Catholic ecclesiastical bodies in the nation. It had achieved a national organization in 1893 through the formation of a General Synod in which four ecclesiastical provinces joined. At that time the metropolitan of each province was given the title of archbishop, the first in the Anglican Communion outside the British Isles to have that designation. The structure of the Anglican Church in Canada showed the influence of the Protestant Episcopal Church south of the border.[35] The proportion of those who expressed a preference for the Church of England in Canada declined from about 16 per cent. in 1931[36] to 14.7 per cent. in 1951.[37] Much of the work of the Anglican Church

---

[32] *The United Church of Canada. Year Book, 1958* (Toronto, The United Church of Canada, 1958, pp. xvi, 685), pp. 260, 261.
[33] *Ibid.*
[34] *The Acts and Proceedings of the Eighty-Fifth General Assembly of the Presbyterian Church in Canada . . . 1959* (Toronto, Thorn Press, 1959, pp. 627), p. 532.
[35] Neill, *Anglicanism*, pp. 300–302; C. W. Vernon, *The Old Church in the New Dominion* (London, Society for Promoting Christian Knowledge, 1929, pp. viii, 215), pp. 169 ff.
[36] *The Statesman's Year Book, 1933*, p. 288.
[37] *Ibid.*, 1959, pp. 363, 365.

in Canada was among the Indians and Eskimos and on the frontiers of white settlement.[38]

In the 1950's negotiations were in process looking towards the merger of the United Church and the Anglican Church. In 1954 the United Church through its General Council gave approval to the plan which had been developed, but in 1961 the two bodies were still separate.[39]

THE SMALLER PROTESTANT DENOMINATIONS

After 1925 the overwhelming majority of the Protestants of Canada were in the United Church and the Anglican Church. The Baptists ranked fourth—after the two largest bodies and the Presbyterian Church. In 1951 those expressing a Baptist preference and actual members of Baptist churches were reported to be 519,585. Slightly less than two-fifths of them were in the Maritime Provinces and a little over two-fifths were in Ontario.[40] A far smaller proportion of the population than in the United States, the Baptists of Canada were badly divided—although not as badly as in the southern neighbour—owing to different origins, geography, and lack of agreement in doctrine. Baptists were much slower in coming together in a nation-wide organization than were Anglicans, Presbyterians, and Methodists. Indeed, even in 1961 not all Canadian Baptists were an inclusive fellowship. As in the United States, the first effort in which the majority coöperated was foreign missions. In 1912 the Canadian Baptist Foreign Mission Board was organized to provide dominion-wide association in the overseas outreach. In 1944 the Baptist Federation of Canada came into being as a means of coördinating the programmes of the three existing conventions which embraced the majority of the Baptists—namely, that in the Maritime Provinces, that in Ontario and Quebec, and the Baptist Union of Western Canada. The Baptists of the Maritimes suffered from the impact of the revolutionary age. Between 1910 and 1935 their numbers actually declined, partly because of dislocations brought by World War I, but chiefly on account of the movement from rural to urban areas.[41]

The Disciples of Christ were much less numerous than the Baptists. In 1951 they were reported as totalling 14,920. They owed their origin partly to the similar movement in the United States and partly to impulses from Scotland

---

[38] As examples, see Richard C. Warder, *Northern Exposure. Tales of the North Country* (New York, Pageant Press, 1957, pp. 179), *passim; One Day at a Time, the Autobiography of Robert John Renison* (Toronto, Kingswood House, 1957, pp. x, 322), pp. 15–149.

[39] *Ecumenical Press Service,* October 20, 1954.

[40] *The Statesman's Year Book, 1960,* p. 365.

[41] Torbet, *A History of the Baptists,* pp. 179–181; C. C. McLaurin, *Pioneering in Western Canada. A Story of the Baptists* (Calgary, published by the author, 1939, pp. 401), pp. 168–240; George Edward Levy, *The Baptists of the Maritime Provinces, 1733–1946* (St. John, N.B., Barnes-Hopkins, 1946, pp. xi, 336), pp. 293–317.

which stemmed from the Haldanes and the Glassites.[42] They began in the first half of the nineteenth century and increased in several provinces, to some extent through immigration from south of the border. In 1922 an All-Canada Convention was instituted for the coöperation of the churches in various common projects such as religious education, publication, and missions. It functioned through an All-Canada Committee.[43]

Two denominational families of Continental European origin, the Lutherans and the Mennonites, were represented by substantial minorities. In 1951 those expressing a Lutheran preference totalled 444,923 and the Mennonites 125,938.[44] Between 1921 and 1930 about 6,000 Mennonites went from Manitoba to South America and approximately 8,000 arrived in the province as refugees from Communist Russia.[45]

The Protestant denominations to which we have thus far called attention ministered for the most part to constituencies with some degree of education and economic security. They embraced the vast majority of those who were regarded as Protestants. In general their clergy had the kind of education which made it difficult for them to speak in the language of the poorly educated or uneducated, and their services of worship seemed to many of the lower income groups to be too formal.

Various religious movements filled the gap. Several were from the United States. Others were of British origin. Still others were indigenous. Some were clearly Protestant. Some others came out of a Protestant environment but were more or less remote from historic Christianity. Numbers had doctrines which were akin to the fundamentalism of the United States or were identified with it. They usually stood for an ascetic morality—against alcohol, tobacco, dancing, card-playing, and attendance at the theatre—and in their local congregations provided for close fellowship of those from the same social background. They flourished especially in the West. Others appealed to "reason" and assured "success"—in the search for health, peace of mind, or material achievement. Among the former were the Evangelical Mission Covenant Church, the Holiness Church of the Nazarene, the Evangelical Free Church, the Plymouth Brethren, the Apostolic Church of Pentecost, and other Pentecostal groups. Among the latter were the Rosicrucians and Unity Truth. The Great I Am, begun in Chicago in 1934 by Guy Ballard, was introduced to Alberta in 1937. Ballard professed to have truths revealed to him and stressed asceticism, vegetarianism, and reincarnation. Jehovah's Witnesses also entered. By 1946 about

---

[42] Volume I, pp. 103, 183, 184.

[43] Reuben Butchart, *The Disciples of Christ in Canada since 1830* (Toronto, Canadian Headquarters' Publications, Churches of Christ [Disciples], 1949, pp. xv, 674), *passim*, especially pp. 175–189.

[44] *The Statesman's Year Book, 1960*, p. 363.

[45] E. K. Francis, *In Search of Utopia. The Mennonites in Manitoba* (Glencoe, Ill., The Free Press, 1955, pp. xv, 294), pp. 187 ff.

fifty of these minority groups and movements were represented. In 1947 the Prairie Bible Institute, fundamentalist in its theology, at Three Hills, Alberta, was said to have the largest daytime enrollment of any theological seminary or Bible school on the American continent. By 1950 it was reported to have prepared about three hundred foreign missionaries. In 1946 about a fifth of the Protestant population of Alberta belonged to religious movements outside the standard denominations. The fundamentalists largely controlled the religious broadcasting of the province.[46]

In the 1930's and 1940's the Social Credit Party, a political movement, was closely identified with one of the minority groups. What was called the Prophetic Baptist movement was founded by William Aberhart. He had a large radio audience and inaugurated the Prophetic Bible Institute. Aberhart advocated his Social Credit programme as a panacea for the economic ills associated with the depression of the 1930's. In 1935 he was elected premier of Alberta. He died in 1943 and his protégé, E. C. Manning, reorganized the Institute and also became premier of the province.[47]

THE PROTESTANT MINISTRY

For the churches which enrolled the large majority of the Protestants of Canada, the standards for preparation for the ministry were fairly high. Most of the schools in which that training was given were aware of the intellectual currents of the revolutionary age and of the adjustment to them of Biblical and theological studies. Although fundamentalism, with its rejection of that adjustment, was not lacking, for the most part it remained in the minority groups.

However, both the numbers of theological students and the degree of academic preparation given them left much to be desired. In 1954-1955 twenty-seven institutions classed as theological seminaries had only about one thousand students, and the total appeared to be no higher than thirty years earlier—in spite of the great growth in population. This was approximately one to every 7,300 of the Protestant church members as against one to every 2,375 in the United States. Moreover, of the forty-five schools in the United States and Canada which reported 100 per cent. of their students as having college graduation before entering, only one was in Canada, and of twenty-seven theological schools in Canada only three reported having 90 per cent. or more of their students as college graduates and eight said that 75 per cent. of their enrollment could be so classified.[48]

[46] Mann, *Sect, Cult, and Church in Alberta*, pp. 4–22.
[47] *Ibid.*, pp. 22 ff.
[48] Niebuhr, Williams, and Gustafson, *The Advancement of Theological Education*, pp. 9, 11. On

Growing Protestant Coöperation

Protestants of Canada moved more rapidly towards inclusive coöperation and unity than did those of the United States. No union of ecclesiastical bodies in the United States embraced such diverse denominations as did the United Church of Canada. The large majority of Canadian Protestants joined in the Federal Council of the Churches of Christ in America. When, in the 1940's, the National Council of the Churches of Christ in the U.S.A. was in process of formation, the Canadians felt that the time was ripe for a similar movement in their country. As a result, in 1944 the Canadian Council of Churches was created. It drew together several existing groups, such as the Joint Committee on Evangelism, the Committee for the World Council of Churches, and the Religious Education Council of Canada. Its members included all the major Protestant bodies—the Anglican Church of Canada, the United Church of Canada, the Presbyterian Church in Canada, and the Baptist Federation of Canada, as well as several of the smaller bodies and the Ukrainian Orthodox Church.[49] The bodies which kept aloof from it did not embrace as large a proportion of Protestants as did those south of the border which refused to join in the National Council of the Churches of Christ in the U.S.A.—such as the Southern Baptist Convention and the Missouri Synod. Yet in the mid-1950's the Canadian Council of Churches was said to have won much less recognition as the mouthpiece of Canadian Protestants than had the corresponding body in the United States.[50]

The World-Wide Outreach of Canadian Protestants

Canadian Protestants' mounting share in the world-wide extension of the faith had begun even when many of their clergy came from the British Isles. Indeed, not until 1921 did the Methodist Church in Canada decide to seek no more recruits from the British Isles for its ministry but to rely solely upon indigenous sources.[51] Long before that year Canadian Methodists had been going as missionaries to other countries. In 1958 Canadian mission boards had in their service 774 missionaries in other lands. Nearly a third were from the United Church of Canada, more than a fifth were Baptists, and a seventh were from the Pentecostal Assemblies. The Anglican Church of Canada did not send a fifth as many as did the United Church of Canada nor as many as the much smaller Presbyterian Church in Canada.[52]

---

the creation of a new theological college after 1925 see John Dow, *Alfred Gandier, Man of Vision and Achievement* (Toronto, The United Church Publishing House, 1951, pp. 138), pp. 112 ff.

[49] Rouse and Neill, *A History of the Ecumenical Movement, 1517–1948*, p. 624.

[50] Walsh, *The Christian Church in Canada*, p. 340.

[51] J. R. Riddell, *Methodism in the Middle West* (Toronto, Ryerson Press, 1946, pp. xii, 371), p. 344.

[52] *Occasional Bulletin from the Missionary Research Library*, Vol. IX, No. 10 (December 8, 1958), p. 11.

In proportion to their numbers Canadian Protestants sent far fewer missionaries abroad than did Roman Catholics. Their total was between a third and a fourth of that of the Roman Catholics, although the latter were less numerous than the Protestants. Moreover, Canadian Protestants supported proportionately far fewer missionaries than did those of the United States. Had they equalled the latter's record, in 1958 they would have had between three and four times as many as did their fellow Protestants south of the border. The difference was partly but not entirely due to different bases for statistics on church affiliation. In Canada the figures used were those reported in the census as showing a church preference, while in the United States they were those having actual church membership. The contrast can also to some degree be ascribed to the fact that Protestantism was younger than in the United States and until recently had been depending on the British Isles for a large percentage of its clergy.

A mission which must be classified as domestic rather than foreign but which continued to be widely heralded was that of Grenfell on the Newfoundland and Labrador coasts. Begun before 1914 and long directed by Wilfred Thomason Grenfell (1865–1940) for the Eskimos and the other residents, mostly fisher folk, it attracted personnel from universities, largely volunteers serving at their own expense, and was continued after the death of its founder. Under Grenfell's energetic example and direction, hospitals were created, some of them headed by able and distinguished physicians and surgeons, coöperatives were organized, and doors of opportunity were opened to many youths. In the epidemic of influenza of 1918 many of the population died, the staff gave heroic service, and the hospitals were full to overflowing. The enterprise had originally been supported by the Royal National Mission to Deep Sea Fishermen, with headquarters in England, but shortly before World War I the International Grenfell Association was incorporated under the laws of Newfoundland and drew its funds mainly from the United States and Canada. In 1926 the Grenfell Association of Great Britain and Ireland was organized. With abounding energy and contagious enthusiasm, Grenfell travelled and lectured widely, raising money for the enterprise. After his death the mission ceased to attract the attention that he had drawn to it during his lifetime.[53]

THE EASTERN CHURCHES

Rising immigration caused the Eastern Churches to increase as part of the Canadian religious scene. By the census of 1951 "Eastern Catholics"—Uniates —totalled 191,061, and "Greek Orthodox" numbered 172,271.[54]

[53] J. Lennox Kerr, *Wilfred Grenfell, His Life and Work* (New York, Dodd, Mead and Co., 1959, pp. xiv, 270), *passim;* Volume III, p. 274.
[54] *The Statesman's Year Book, 1960,* p. 363.

The Dukhobors, whose first contingent arrived in Canada from Russia in 1899, although numbering only a few thousand, were given much notoriety. By the mid-twentieth century their assimilation to Canadian life was making headway.[55]

THE EFFECT OF CHRISTIANITY

As in other countries, no accurate appraisal can be made of the effect of Christianity upon Canada. Because of its predominance in the French elements and its close control of the individual and collective life of their parishes, notably in Quebec, the Roman Catholic Church did much to shape the morals, the religious practices and convictions, the social structure, and the cultural outlook of a large proportion of the population. Except for minorities and individuals, the impact of Protestantism, while pervasive, was not as pronounced.

A few examples will serve to show something of the influence of the faith. Wilfred Laurier (1841–1919), a Roman Catholic, the first of the French Canadians to be premier of the country, was educated chiefly in Roman Catholic schools but for a time in his student days lived with a Presbyterian family. He sought to bridge the gap between Protestants and Roman Catholics and was against the ultramontane elements in his church.[56] William Lyon Mackenzie King (1874–1950) was a deeply devout Presbyterian, a mystic, with a great reverence for his mother. Named for his maternal grandfather, the radical and fiery William Lyon Mackenzie, he long led the Liberal Party, served as premier, was active in the League of Nations and in the formation and early days of the United Nations, and consistently sought to better the lot of the underprivileged and to bridge the gulf between capital and labour.[57] We have already noted the part which William Aberhart and E. C. Manning, leaders of the Prophetic Baptist movement, had in the Social Credit Party in Alberta. The official attitude of some of the Protestant forces was illustrated by the action of the United Church of Canada's Board of Evangelism and Social Service in urging, in 1959, that Canada set an example to the world by disarming immediately and using the money thus saved to help develop a United Nations police force, to promote the peaceful uses of atomic energy, to assist undeveloped countries, and to improve education and social programmes in Canada.[58] However, such pronouncements were said to have no wide influence.[59]

[55] John P. Zubek and Patricia Anne Solberg, *Doukhobors and War* (Toronto, Ryerson Press, pp. ix, 250), pp. 192 ff.; J. F. C. Wright, *Slava Bohu. The Story of the Dukhobors* (New York, Farrar and Rinehart, 1940, pp. x, 438), pp. 267 ff.; Harry B. Hawthorn, editor, *Report of the Doukhobor Research Committee* (Vancouver, The University of British Columbia, 1952, pp. ix, 342), *passim*.
[56] *The Encyclopaedia Britannica*, 1955 printing, Vol. XIII, pp. 770, 771.
[57] *Who Was Who, 1941–1950*, pp. 641, 642; Fosdick, *John D. Rockefeller, Jr.*, pp. 153 ff.
[58] *Ecumenical Press Service*, March 13, 1959.
[59] *Ecumenical Study Documents* June 19, 1953, No. 538/348 (mimeographed).

SUMMARY

At the mid-twentieth century, Canada, still young and rapidly growing in population and wealth, while independent politically, had only recently fully emerged from colonial status. The Roman Catholic Church, solidly based on the French portion of the population and with a large and more recently arrived Irish contingent, was vigorous and was not only holding to the faith the large majority of its hereditary constituency, a symbol and tie of both the French and the Irish nationalism, but was reaching out more actively than were its children in the United States in the world-wide spread of the faith. The census showed that the overwhelming majority of the population professed a religious preference, either for the Roman Catholic Church or for one or another of the Protestant churches. Most of the professed Protestants were connected with either the Anglican Communion, the United Church of Canada (a merger of the Methodists, the Congregationalists, and over half of the Presbyterians, consummated in 1925), or that large portion of the Presbyterian Church in Canada which did not go into the United Church. The Baptists and a number of denominations and movement sprung from Protestantism, many of them growing rapidly after 1914, especially in the West, added variety. Presumably because of their youth and their recent emergence from dependence on the British Isles for their clergy, by the mid-twentieth century, in proportion to their numbers, the Protestants were not as well supplied with native-born pastors as were the Protestant churches of the United States, nor did they have relatively as large a share in the world-wide spread of the faith. But in both respects they were displaying marked vitality. The Eastern Churches were too recent arrivals to play much part in the life of the nation. Christianity was having a marked effect on Canada—individual citizens as well as collective life—but no proof could be offered that the impact was either growing or receding. On the whole, however, by 1962 Christianity was more deeply rooted in Canada than at any earlier time.

CHAPTER IV

Christianity in Greenland, the British, Danish, and Dutch West Indies, and the British and Dutch Enclaves on the Mainland of South and Central America

WHAT developments in Christianity were seen in the islands off the shores of the Americas and in the enclaves on the coasts of the Caribbean which were in the possession of traditionally Protestant powers? They included Greenland, several islands in the Caribbean, the Bahamas, Bermuda, British Honduras, and British and Dutch Guiana. In an earlier volume we sketched rapidly the course in the nineteenth century.[1] Because of the limitations of space we must content ourselves with an even more condensed account of changes in the post-1914 years.

A feature common to almost all the islands and areas covered in this brief chapter was shared as well by much of Asia, Africa, and the islands of the Pacific: the governing colonial powers gave more and more autonomy to the governed. Paralleling this were more indigenous leadership and initiative in the churches.

Both movements were seen in Greenland but were complicated by growing involvement in the international tensions of the age. In 1921, with the consent of the United States, Great Britain, and others of the powers, Danish sovereignty was extended to all the island. Religiously the island was placed under the Bishop of Copenhagen. In 1953, already self-governing, Greenland was made an integral part of the Danish realm and had the same measure of self-government as the rest of the kingdom. With a moderation in the climate, fishing became the chief occupation. In 1955 the population was 27,101, of whom 1,867 were Europeans. Practically all were Lutherans, members of the Church of Denmark. They were moving into the towns, all the settlements had schools, scores of youths were studying in Denmark, a theological seminary had been

[1] Volume III, pp. 277–283.

begun, and such aspects of the revolutionary age were seen as moving pictures, free public health service, and old-age pensions. In April, 1941, after the occupation of Denmark by the Germans, with the consent of the Danish government Greenland was made a temporary protectorate of the United States. In 1951 Denmark and the United States entered into an agreement for the joint defense of the island within the North Atlantic Treaty Organization. These arrangements brought American armed services to Greenland with large installations, notably of the air force.[2]

In 1917, to protect her interests in the Caribbean, the United States purchased the Danish portion of the Virgin Islands. In 1927 the United States gave the islands a civil government with powers of local legislation, in 1938 vested the franchise in resident citizens of the United States who were able to read and write English, and in 1954 dropped the English requirement.

Church membership had fallen during the generation before the annexation. The largest denominational group was Anglican, followed in descending order by Roman Catholics, Moravians, and Lutherans. The tie between the Lutherans and Denmark was severed and one with the Lutherans of the United States was created. Thousands of the islanders, mostly coloured, emigrated and settled in New York City.[3] The British portions of the Virgin Islands were badly isolated, but the large majority of their population were Methodists and were said to maintain a high standard of social and home life.[4]

The Netherlands Antilles, of which Curaçao was the largest, were accorded self-government in 1951. For the most part the Negroes, who constituted the overwhelming majority of the population, were Roman Catholics. The vicariate apostolic which embraced them was under the Netherlands province of the Dominicans. Several other congregations, most of them engaged in teaching, were represented. In 1951 a local congregation was authorized for social work.[5]

In the British West Indies advances towards self-government and federation were made. Jamaica was granted a constitution in 1944, which was amended in 1953, 1957, and 1959. In the Leeward and Windward Islands ministerial government was introduced in 1956. In 1958 the West Indies were made a federation with a legislature. Full independence within the Commonwealth was slated for the 1960's. The population in 1958 was said to be 3,152,000, of which slightly more than half—1,651,463—was in Jamaica. Next to Jamaica in size and population was Trinidad.

[2] *The Encyclopaedia Britannica*, 1955 printing, Vol. X, pp. 859, 860; *The Statesman's Year Book, 1960*, p. 942.
[3] Jens Larsen, *Virgin Islands Story* (Philadelphia, Muhlenberg Press, 1950, pp. xii, 250), pp. 224 ff.
[4] F. Deauville Walker, *The Call of the West Indies. The Romance of Methodist Work and Opportunity in the West Indies and Adjacent Regions* (London, The Cargate Press, no date, pp. 190), pp. 143, 144.
[5] *De Katholieke Encyclopaedie*, Vol. XVIII, p. 559.

By the middle of the century more than half the people of Jamaica were said to have membership in, or at least to have a preference for, some church. The largest denominations were the Church of England, with 255,000, the Baptists, with 252,000, the Roman Catholics, with 100,000, the Methodists, with 84,000, the Church of God, with 65,000, the Moravians, with 40,000, and the Seventh Day Adventists, with 43,000. A Christian Council brought several of the denominations into a coöperative approach to the island. All, or nearly all, the population had some familiarity with Christianity.[6] A major problem was the extreme poverty of large elements of the population—a problem intensified by the increase in numbers, which in Jamaica as in others of the islands complicated a situation produced by earlier overcrowding and the legacy of slavery. Although by the mid-twentieth century the British possessions had been free of slavery for more than a hundred years, the heritage of that system combined with poverty made for instability of family life, widespread illegitimacy, and garbled remnants of African superstitions.[7] As in most of the rest of the world in the revolutionary age, urban population was mounting. The drifting to the towns of thousands, most of them barely subsisting, brought challenges to the churches.[8] Striking contrasts were seen, especially in the towns and cities, between extreme wealth and dire poverty. Three-fourths of the population were Negroes, but the coloured, a mixture of white and Negro blood, were gaining in numbers and influence. Other racial strains were represented.

Jamaican Christianity presented a mixed picture. In the two decades which followed World War I communicant membership and the number of ordained foreign missionaries declined.[9] In addition to the multiplicity of denominations were many movements which appealed to the highly emotional ill-educated or illiterate masses.[10] Most of the children left school before finishing the elementary course. The better-established churches tended to be confined to the more respectable members of society and the poor did not feel at home in them.[11] On the positive side were the facts that the churches sponsored a large proportion of the education, that no racial segregation was seen in them, and that much of the business of the island and of the government administration was in the hands of the coloured.[12] An indigenous body of clergy, although still at mid-century far too small to meet all the needs, was begining to come

---

[6] *The Statesman's Year Book, 1960*, pp. 420, 425, 434; Davis, *The Church in the New Jamaica*, pp. 14–22.

[7] *The International Review of Missions*, Vol. XLI, p. 57; Davis, *op. cit.*, pp. 30–38.

[8] *The International Review of Missions*, Vol. XLV, p. 64.

[9] Ernest A. Payne, *Freedom in Jamaica. Some Chapters in the History of the Baptist Missionary Society* (London, The Carey Press, rev. ed., 1946, pp. 119), p. 116.

[10] Davis, *op. cit.*, pp. 41–47; Frederick Pilkington, *Daybreak in Jamaica* (London, The Epworth Press, 1950, pp. 220), pp. 135–138.

[11] Davis, *op. cit.*, pp. 38, 39.

[12] *Ibid.*, p. 54, 57, 58.

forward, theological schools for their training were maintained,[13] and in 1960 a Jamaican was elected chairman of the World's Student Christian Federation.

The Roman Catholics of Jamaica, who in 1847 were placed under the English province of the Society of Jesus, in 1894 were transferred to the Maryland-New York province of the Jesuits. In 1911 the Jesuits were reinforced by Dominican Nuns of the Perpetual Rosary from the mother house in Hoboken, New Jersey. A minority, the Roman Catholics were served by schools under the direction of their clergy which reached from the parochial to the college level.[14]

Trinidad had a mixed population. In addition to the Negroes, who were in the majority, and the whites, the ruling minority, were large numbers of Hindus and Moslems, Indians who had been brought in to provide needed labour after the abolition of slavery. A degree of self-government was given in 1956 through a constitution (amended in 1959) which provided for a uni-cameral legislature with elected members in the majority. The Negroes were nominally Christians. Roman Catholics were the most numerous. Protestants nearly equalled them in numbers, with the Anglicans by far the largest denomination, but with substantial contingents of Presbyterians, Methodists, and Baptists.[15] Religious sects among the Negroes included the "Shouters" (presumably a branch of the Baptists), whose highly emotional services were proscribed by the state, and various branches of the worshippers of Shango, the god of thunder of the Yorubas of Nigeria. The "Shouters" had transformed the Moody and Sankey hymns to meet their purposes. The Shango cults contained features derived from Roman Catholic beliefs and practices. Divination and magic were also widespread among the Negroes, and Obeah was prevalent. The "Shouters," the Shango cults, divination, magic, and Obeah found their adherents chiefly among the socially, economically, and educationally underprivileged.[16]

Related to the prevalence of these religious movements, either professedly Christian or of pagan African provenance, was the extensive spread of emotional types of Protestantism in the West Indies. In the twentieth century they grew much more rapidly than did the historic denominations, which ministered to the members of social strata of higher educational and economic attainments. Since the underprivilaged elements were often in the majority, these movements had a larger proportionate growth than did the more staid older denominations. Typical was the multiplication of the Pentecostals. In Jamaica they were said to have totalled 75,000 late in the 1950's. They are reported to have

[13] *The International Review of Missions*, Vol. XLIII, pp. 57, 58.

[14] Francis K. Delany, *A History of the Catholic Church in Jamaica, B.W.I., 1494 to 1929* (New York, Jesuit Mission Press, 1930, pp. xi, 292), pp. 114 ff.

[15] *The Statesman's Year Book, 1960*, p. 431.

[16] Melville J. Herskovits and Frances S. Herskovits, *Trinidad Village* (New York, Alfred A. Knopf, 1947, pp. viii, 351, xxv), pp. 167-255, 321-348; J. P. Hickerton, *Caribbean Kallaloo* (London, The Carey Kingsgate Press, 1958, pp. 99), pp. 73-79.

begun on that island in 1907, through the Church of God of Cleveland, to have prospered through a striking movement in 1939, and to have been strengthened by the arrival of the Assemblies of God in 1941. These emotional movements sprung from Protestantism were prominent on several other islands.[17]

In British Guiana the political setting brought problems. A new constitution came into force in 1953 and the government which rose to power proved to be near-Communist. After a few months the constitution was suspended and tensions between the various communities—West Indians, Amerindians, East Indians, Chinese, and Europeans—were heightened.[18] Yet efforts were being made through "cottage meetings" to bring the Gospel to non-Christians.[19] However, of the East Indian population, from which many of the radical political measures came, only about seven out of a hundred were Christian, and resistance to the spread of the faith was marked.[20] In the 1950's a resurgence of Hinduism and Islam was seen—both among the East Indians.[21]

In 1957 the International Missionary Council sponsored a "West Indies Consultation" which met in Puerto Rico.[22] That year too a conference was held to devise a Christian education curriculum for the English-speaking West Indies; the Union Theological Seminary in Jamaica, organized in 1953 and serving much of the Caribbean, could report encouraging growth; and two Anglican theological colleges, one in Jamaica and one in Barbados, reported their largest enrollments.[23]

Here, in these widely separated and diverse areas the contrasts were seen, familiar features of the twentieth-century stage of the revolutionary age, between secular threats to Christianity and mounting vigour in the churches.

---

[17] Du Plessis, *A Brief History of the Pentecostal Assemblies;* H. P. Van Dusen, "Caribbean Holiday," in *The Christian Century,* August 17, 1955.
[18] *The International Review of Missions,* Vol. XLIII, p. 57.
[19] *Ibid.,* Vol. XLII, p. 53.
[20] *Ibid.,* Vol. XLV, p. 65.
[21] *Ibid.,* Vol. XLVIII, p. 68.
[22] *Ibid.,* Vol. XLVII, p. 60.
[23] *Ibid.,* Vol. XLIX, p. 60.

CHAPTER V

Contrasting Developments in Burgeoning
Latin America

THE SETTING

THE FIRST half of the twentieth century witnessed major impacts of the revolutionary age on Latin America. It was in this context that important developments were seen in the Christianity of the region. The setting must be briefly described before we pass to the religious scene. Here we are concerned with movements in the region as a whole. As we go on to a country-by-country survey we will say more, but still with necessarily brief summaries.

Latin America was not drawn as actively into the two world wars of the period as was much of the rest of mankind. During World War I most of the republics remained neutral. Brazil was an exception. In 1917 it declared war on Germany. Some of the countries profited by the demands for their raw materials by the belligerents. During World War II after Pearl Harbour the majority of the republics broke with the Axis powers and in 1945 several formally entered the war. But Mexico and Brazil were the only ones to take an active part in the fighting. However, Latin America could not fail to be profoundly affected by the wars and their aftermath. Its foreign markets were involved, at times favourably, then unfavourably. For example, the reaction from the high prices paid for its nitrates and copper during World War I brought great suffering to Chile's masses, and their misery was intensified by the world-wide depression of the early 1930's. After World War II the price of copper again fell, with accompanying unemployment and hardship for the miners.

Relations with the United States were often tense. By its nationalization of many foreign holdings and by other features of its internal politics, from time to time Mexico faced possible intervention by its northern neighbour. Beginning in 1959 the Castro regime in Cuba took vigorous action against the United States and in the 1960's the latter retaliated. Ostensibly to protect the interests of foreign creditors and to establish stable governments, marines from the United States occupied Haiti from 1915 to 1934, the Dominican Republic from

1916 to 1924, and Nicaragua from 1909 to 1933. Fear, envy, and dislike for the United States were chronic and widespread.

Yet large amounts of capital came from the United States. Much of it was in the form of private investment. Much was through the Export-Import Bank and direct grants from the Washington government to aid in the development of the region's resources with the hope of raising the standard of living of the poverty-stricken masses. More and more students enrolled in the colleges and universities of the United States. Business firms and banks of the United States established branches in Latin America, and, especially after World War II, the number of citizens of that country increased in the urban centres.

Attempts were made by the colossus of the North to maintain and increase the friendly coöperation in the Western Hemisphere which had long been the purpose of many of its statesmen. In 1933 President Franklin D. Roosevelt enunciated what he called the "good neighbour policy," directed particularly to Latin America. It was pursued more or less intermittently by him and his successors. In 1958 Vice-President Nixon visited several countries. In 1960 President Eisenhower went on an official tour of part of the region. In 1961 Adlai Stevenson made a trip as an ambassador of the Kennedy administration.

The International Conferences of American States which began in 1889–1890 were held about once every decade. In 1910 the Pan American Union was formed, with headquarters in Washington. In 1933 at the International Conference of American States the United States accepted the principle of nonintervention. In 1936 at a meeting of the Conference the delegates voted that any threat to the peace of one state was the concern of all. Two years later an agreement was reached to maintain the solidarity of the region against foreign intervention, and in 1945 and 1947 provision was made for joint defense of all states in the event of aggression against any of them. Because the Pan American Union was regarded in Latin America as too much dominated by the United States, in 1948 it was superseded by the Organization of American States, in which the staff was widely representative of Latin American governments as well as of the United States.

Communists became a chronic and increasing problem which varied from country to country. Taking advantage of the poverty of the masses and the nationalistic sentiment, they mixed in the internal politics and stirred up enmity against the United States. They became especially prominent in Mexico, Guatemala, and Cuba. In some countries they were outlawed as an organized party, but often in spite of that prohibition they continued to be a force with which to reckon. In 1954 at the instance of the United States and after stormy debate, the Organization of American States, with Guatemala voting in the negative and Argentina and Mexico abstaining, called for consultation to consider the adoption of appropriate action in case international Communism threatened the sovereignty and political independence of any American state.

Communists were able to take advantage of the increase in population and its accompanying poverty. Poverty was, unfortunately, no novel experience for Latin America. It had characterized the region for centuries. From colonial days the contrast between the wealthy, a minority, often highly cultured and cosmopolitan, and the uneducated masses living on or below the barest subsistence level had been chronic. In the post-1914 years and especially after World War II the problem had been made acute by two factors. One was found in many lands in this period—an increase in population so rapid that it could rightly be called an explosion, and the accompanying failure of production to keep pace with it. Improvements in drugs, vaccinations, and inoculations accounted for the wide disparity between births and deaths. In 1960 the population of Latin America was estimated to be 192,000,000 with an annual rate of growth of 2.7 per cent. But in that year per capita income was less than before World War II. Although a middle class, largely absent before 1914, had expanded impressively, the destitute and the semi-destitute were even more numerous and the social gulf between them and the wealthy was widening.[1]

To the traveller in the 1950's who touched only the main centres the starkness of the poverty was not immediately apparent. He saw cities sprouting at a breath-taking rate with huge, substantial office buildings and apartment houses, hotels to match the best in Western Europe and North America, streets crowded with motor vehicles, decently dressed and apparently well-fed crowds, comfortable middle-class homes, and the palatial residences of the rich. But if his hosts gave him an inclusive view, he was taken to fetid slums which for festering poverty were equalled only in some of the overcrowded cities of Asia. Out of the poverty came a rising tide of unrest which was part of the revolutionary wave in many other parts of the planet. The silent millions were becoming vocal. Agitators, some sincere and some self-seeking, were stirring them to vigorous and often angry and violent protests. Efforts to correct the situation were not confined to Communists. Determined liberals, leftist intellectuals, and dictators catering to popular demand enacted legislation designed to remedy the ills. Collective bargaining by labour, minimum wage standards, unemployment insurance, old-age pensions, and separation allowances for discharged labourers were familiar devices. Financial aid from abroad, largely from the United States Government, helped to allay some of the conditions. Yet mounting inflation and spiralling prices often more than offset the gains. In the 1950's thousands of Communist paid workers were in the slum areas. But the Communist CTAL controlled as yet only about 12 per cent. of organized labour, and scarcely half the labour in industry was organized.[2]

[1] Tad Szulc, *New Trends in Latin America* (New York, Foreign Policy Association, March 20, 1960, pp. 62), p. 14.
[2] Considine, *New Horizons in Latin America*, p. 231.

Outwardly democratic forms of government such as were known in Western Europe, the United States, Canada, Australia, and New Zealand were preserved. For the most part constitutional forms inherited from the nineteenth century were continued, although through frequently changing documentary expressions. But dictators and revolutions, usually followed by other dictators, repeated the experience of that century. In the main, by the 1960's democracy as Western Europe, the United States, and the British Commonwealth understood it seemed to be gaining, but dictators had not completely disappeared and in Cuba a Communist-oriented regime was in power. The military were a powerful element and in several countries made and unmade governments.

Exuberant nationalism was present in Latin America as in many other lands, for it was characteristic of the revolutionary age. Here, as elsewhere, it spurred armaments. Yet the armament race did not assume dimensions comparable to that in North America and Europe, and no intra-Latin American wars as serious as those which had marred the nineteenth century punctuated the first half of the twentieth century.

Hyper-nationalism made for movements towards governmental expropriation of foreign holdings. They were seen in the confiscation of the properties of the foreign oil companies in Mexico and Bolivia in 1938, in the seizure of United States-owned power plants and the purchase of British-owned railways in Argentina, and in the extensive nationalization of the banks, lands, and enterprises of United States citizens in Cuba in 1960.

From the economic standpoint Latin America was still living, as it had since the Spanish and Portuguese conquests, by what might be called the extractive industries—mining and agriculture. It continued to be a source of food and raw materials for the industries and industrialized populations of Western Europe and the United States. Silver-mining was not as important as formerly, but from Latin America came petroleum, nitrates, copper, wheat, meat, wool, sugar, tropical fruits, and coffee. The economy was subject to the changes in prices of these commodities in the international market. Ambitious plans for industrialism were made. Some growth in manufactures was seen, but it was not rapid enough to supply sufficient employment for the burgeoning population.

Contrasting Religious Developments: Progressive De-Christianization

The religious developments in Latin America continued, with modifications, as in the nineteenth century. But the contrasts which we have noted elsewhere in the twentieth century were accentuated. On the one hand the de-Christianization of a nominally Christian population appeared to be mounting. On the other hand a fresh surge of life was seen in the Roman Catholic Church, and Protestantism displayed a phenomenal growth.

Evidences of the progress of de-Christianization were numerous. The conflict between clericalism and anti-clericalism, while present and at times intense, was declining, partly because in the political scene the Roman Catholic Church was weaker than it had been. In more than one country state and Church were separated, with the disestablishment of the Church. The overwhelming majority of the population would, if questioned, protest that they were Catholics. Much of a cultural Roman Catholicism persisted. Thousands who had little other contact with the Church cherished a warm devotion to the Virgin Mary and prized locally popular saints. Yet one Roman Catholic expert declared that in the twentieth century by the most generous estimate only about 10 per cent. of the nominally Roman Catholic were practising their faith.[3] As in the nineteenth century, the clergy were entirely too few to give adequate religious instruction or pastoral care. In the mid-1940's a sympathetic observer declared that for the Roman Catholics of Latin America to have one priest for every two thousand of the population, forty thousand more priests would be needed. He said that although a third of the Roman Catholics of the world were in Latin America, religious life as prescribed by the Church existed in a relatively few thickly settled areas. He reported that two-thirds of the Brazilians were without organized parish life, that over half the people of Peru were practically without clergy, that comparable conditions existed in several other countries, and that only a few regions had a satisfactory number of vocations for the priesthood.[4] Formerly many of the owners of the great landed estates felt an obligation to make provision for religious services for their employees. But latterly, with the increase in absentee ownership, that concern was declining. As a result, in many estates two-thirds of the marriages were without religious rites and a large proportion of the youth were not baptized. In the slums in the great cities the shortage of priests meant that for two generations or more little clerical care had been given and half the people never attended church. Yet in one of the worst of the slums, in Santiago, Chile, three-fourths of the residents believed in God and recognized Christ as true God and true man, and about 85 per cent. of the children had been baptized. In 1959 it was reported that of 20,500,000 children in school in Latin America only 2,500,000 were receiving instruction in Roman Catholic institutions and another 5,000,000 were being given catechetical instruction.[5]

As we have seen,[6] the reasons for the dearth of clergy were to be found in

---

[3] Coleman, *Latin-American Catholicism. A Self-Evaluation*, pp. 20–22; Allen, *A Seminary Survey*, p. 461.

[4] Considine, *Call for Forty Thousand*, pp. 9–11. See a detailed estimate in Allen, *op. cit.*, p. 463, which shows that the range was from 2,660 to a priest in Chile to 10,000 to 12,000 to a priest in Guatemala.

[5] Considine, lecture, December 9, 1959.

[6] Volume III, pp. 285, 298, 299.

part in the colonial period, when the Church was under the domination of the Spanish or Portuguese Crowns, in part in the sceptical forces issuing from the Enlightenment and the French Revolution in the fore part of the nineteenth century, in no small degree in the struggle during the wars of independence between the Spanish Crown and the new governments to control appointments to the episcopate and so to dominate the Church, and then, after independence had been achieved, in the chronic contests between the clericals and the anti-clericals. Anti-clericalism was augmented by nineteenth-century intellectual currents, among them Positivism and Krausism.

In the decades which followed World War I, Positivism was a waning force.[7] But few of the Latin American philosophers who helped to form the intellectuals came out positively for Christianity. To be sure, José Vasconcelos (1882——), rector of the University of Mexico and minister of education in that country, after a period of scepticism came back to the Roman Catholic faith and believed that without the supernatural youth could not be inspired to the highest ideals.[8] However, in trying to synthesize his philosophy with Christian dogma he did violence to the latter. Antonio Caso (1883-1946), also a Mexican who wrote extensively, was a Christian personalist and moralist and repeatedly turned to Jesus to illustrate "existence as charity."[9] The Brazilian Jackson de Figueiredo (1891-1928) in middle life returned to the Roman Catholic faith of his youth.[10] He was swayed to some extent by another Brazilian, Raimundo de Farias Brito (1862-1917), who, not a Roman Catholic but a pantheist, had marked religious fervour.[11] But most of the contemporary thinkers who exerted a wide influence did not come out positively for the faith. Some were Communists and others were affected by one form or another of materialism and a non-Christian humanism.[12] Yet Nicholas Berdaiev was not without admirers.[13] As was to be expected, José Ortega y Gasset made a deep impression and while he was critical of historic Christianity he was not a materialist.[14] Bergson, Husserl, Heidegger, and Sartre were influential.[15] None of the Latin American philosophers who made a deep impression on their

[7] Crawford, *A Century of Latin American Thought*, pp. 141, 221, 267, 276; Leopoldo Zea, *Apogeo y Decadencia del Positivismo en Mexico* (Mexico, El Colegio de Mexico, 1944, pp. 303), *passim*.

[8] Crawford, *op. cit.*, p. 263; Romanell, *The Making of the Mexican Mind*, pp. 95-140; José Sanchez Villaseñor, *El Sistema Filosofico de Vasconcelos. Ensayo de Critica Filosofico* (Mexico, Editorial Polis, S.A., 1939, pp. 207), *passim*; Sánchez Reulet, *Contemporary Latin-American Philosophy*, pp. 189-210.

[9] Crawford, *op. cit.*, pp. 276-292; Romanell, *op. cit.*, pp. 69-94; Sánchez Reulet, *op. cit.*, pp. 211-236.

[10] Sánchez Reulet, *op. cit.*, pp. 237-251.

[11] *Ibid.*, pp. 76-100.

[12] Crawford, *op. cit.*, pp. 188, 212.

[13] *Ibid.*, p. 287.

[14] Romanell, *op. cit.*, pp. 150 ff.; Ramos, *Historia de la Filosofia en Mexico*, pp. 149-151.

[15] F. S. C. Northrop in *Civilizations*, Vol. V, No. 4, pp. 523-539.

fellow intellectuals conformed fully to the Christian faith. Christianity did not really grip the thought life of Latin America.

Such forces as mounting urbanization, the disintegration of the family, and industrialization, common features of the revolutionary age in other parts of the world, posed a threat and made difficult the work of the Roman Catholic Church, already weakened when it entered the twentieth century.[16]

In parts of Latin America, notably in Brazil, Spiritualism was popular. About a third of the population of Brazil were said to have that as their real religion. Most of them were nominal Roman Catholics, but it was Spiritualism in one or another of its expressions which gripped them. The lowest form was chiefly African in its origin and clearly animistic. A slightly more sophisticated variety had a mixture of African beliefs and sacrificed to the Sea Goddess. The better educated were much influenced by Hinduism with its teaching of metempsychosis and *karma:* they valued good works as a means of improving their *karma* and so of advancing their status in subsequent incarnations.[17]

CONTRASTING DEVELOPMENTS: THE REVIVING ROMAN CATHOLIC CHURCH

In contrast with the progress of de-Christianization among a large proportion of the population, fresh movements were seen in the Roman Catholic Church. By 1962 they had deeply affected only minorities and were stronger in some countries than in others, but they were mounting. We must content ourselves with citing a few that were more than local and briefly mention other developments as we take up a country-by-country survey. Eucharistic Congresses were late in appearing, but after World War I they became prominent and among hundreds of thousands kindled devotion to the Church's central rite. In 1934 an international Eucharistic Congress convened in Buenos Aires, the first in Latin America, drawing delegations from most of the Roman Catholic world. Thus the faithful were given a vision of the mankind-embracing Roman Catholic Church, and their horizons were lifted above the grim picture in their own part of the world.[18] Beginning slightly earlier, but for the most part after 1914, national Eucharistic Congresses were held in several countries and repeated as the years passed.[19] We also hear of a Marian congress, a congress of missions, a congress of Catholic youth, and a congress of young Catholic workers. The Company of Saint Paul, sanctioned by a cardinal in 1920 and with the original purpose of combatting atheism and Communism through lay and clerical co-

---

[16] Coleman, *op. cit.,* pp. 36–43.

[17] Information obtained by the author in Brazil in June, 1956; Considine in *Worldmission,* Vol. VIII, No. 4 (Winter, 1957), pp. 83–95; Considine, *New Horizons,* pp. 40–51; Henrique Maurer, Jr., in *The Student World.* Vol. LI, pp. 356–359.

[18] *The Catholic Historical Review,* Vol. XXVI, p. 65.

[19] *Ibid.,* pp. 13, 43, 215–221; Considine, lecture, December 9, 1959.

operation, was introduced to Argentina in 1927 and spread to other countries.[20] The fourth South American Congress of the Young Christian Workers (JOC) met in Lima, Peru, October 21 to November 1, 1959.[21] Here and there missions to the pagan or semi-pagan Indians achieved striking progress.[22] Catholic labour unions were formed to offset the influence of Communism.[23]

Out of the world Eucharistic Congress of 1955, in Rio de Janeiro, came the Latin American Bishops Conference, known by the initials CELAM. It established its headquarters at Bogotá and had as its purpose inter-American coöperation.[24] Part of its programme was the stimulation of Catholic Action and the employment for that purpose of the press, television, the radio, moving pictures, and education in an attempt to reach all Latin America.[25] Even before the 1950's Catholic Action was spreading rapidly.[26] From time to time CELAM brought together the Latin American episcopate. The third of its conferences was held in Rome in November, 1958, and was attended by fifty bishops from twenty-two countries. It resolved to promote an intensive campaign to spur the establishment of the Confraternity of Christian Doctrine in all the 17,000 parishes in Latin America to improve the teaching personnel, materials, and projects for combatting ignorance of the faith among professing Roman Catholics.[27] To ensure the comprehensive achievement of its purpose CELAM had several departments—the propagation and defense of the faith in a systematic struggle against religious ignorance; aid to the clergy and religious institutions; the education of youth; the lay apostolate; and social action, including social and industrial relations, social reform, the struggle against alcoholism, improving the condition of the thirty million tribal Indians, and assistance to approximately four thousand charitable institutions which cared for about a million of the population.[28]

Partly as a result of CELAM, Roman Catholic organizations launched campaigns against pornographic shows and literature, gambling, prostitution, and other moral and social ills. New translations of the Bible into Spanish were made from the original languages and were widely circulated. In many churches the Scripture for the day was read aloud to the congregation in Spanish and after the services was distributed to those present in printed form. Something of a revival was seen in theological thought and was said to be indebted in

[20] *The Catholic Historical Review*, Vol. XXVI, pp. 215–221; Bates, *The Lay Apostolate in Latin America Today*, pp. 27–31.
[21] *Worldmission Fides Service*, October 31, 1959.
[22] *The Catholic Historical Review*, Vol. XXVI, pp. 215–221; Considine, *New Horizons*, pp. 193–201.
[23] Considine, *New Horizons*, pp. 231, 232.
[24] *Ibid.*, p. 233; Bates, *op. cit.*, pp. 8–13.
[25] Considine, *New Horizons*, p. 233.
[26] *The Catholic Historical Review*, Vol. XXVI, p. 65.
[27] *Worldmission Fides Service*, September 26, 1959; Bates, *op. cit.*, pp. 14, 23.
[28] Considine, lecture, December 9, 1959.

part to the circulation of the works of such European scholars as Maritain.[29] In several countries the episcopate was seeking to increase the influence of the Roman Catholic Church with the government.[30]

Here and there indications of the Liturgical Movement were seen. That movement was hindered by the illiteracy of the majority of the Roman Catholics and the nominal character of the faith of most of the population. Yet through it some of the clergy and laity displayed renewed life.[31]

Efforts were not lacking to recruit and train an indigenous clergy. Late in the 1950's Latin America had 216 major seminaries and scholasticates with a combined enrollment of 8,808 students taking courses in philosophy and theology. But this was estimated to be 9 per cent. less than was required to fill the annual vacancies. Moreover, of the major seminary students 82 per cent. were in Mexico, Colombia, Brazil, and Argentina. In Brazil and Argentina the number graduated were insufficient for the needed replacements. In the other countries in Latin America only about half enough were being graduated to make good the attrition brought by death.[32] So serious was the situation that in 1959 the heads of the major seminaries in Latin America met in Rome to study ways and means of increasing the number of vocations.[33] Encouragement was seen in the fact that in 1959, of the forty priests enrolled in the international centre for social service in the Gregorian University in Rome, thirty were from Latin America.[34] Ground for hope lay also in the establishment in 1927 in Colombia of a seminary to train missionaries. In 1957 it had on its rolls over a hundred priests, thirty-five missionary brothers, and more than four hundred candidates. Yet it was the only one of its kind in South America and it seems not to have been sending men to other countries but simply to mission territories in Colombia.[35]

As in the centuries before 1914, so in the five decades which followed that year a large proportion of the priests, lay brothers, and sisters of the Roman Catholic Church in Latin America came from outside the region. That portion of the Church continued to be parasitic: it was kept alive only by transfusions from other sections of the Church. This fact was the more sobering because here were the fruits of the major missionary enterprise of the Roman Catholic Church in the sixteenth, seventeenth, and eighteenth centuries in the vast outpouring of devotion which issued from the Catholic Reformation. Although the anaemia could be explained, it was no less thought-provoking—even ominous. Not only did Latin American Roman Catholicism not produce enough

[29] G. Báez Camargo in *Christianity and Crisis*, Vol. XII, pp. 125–127 (September 29, 1952).
[30] *Ibid.*
[31] Bögler, *Liturgische Erneuerung in aller Welt*, pp. 118–132.
[32] Allen, *A Seminary Survey*, pp. 487–489.
[33] *Worldmission Fides Service*, September 26, 1959.
[34] *Ibid.*, November 28, 1959.
[35] Considine, *New Horizons*, p. 230.

clergy to supply its need for pastoral care, but it had almost no share in the world-wide spread of the faith and displayed but little effort to reach the non-Christian elements of the population. In 1959 seventy of the ecclesiastical divisions of the area were under the Congregation for the Propagation of the Faith[36] and for the most part drew their personnel from Europe and North America.

Efforts continued to be made to supply from other countries the deficiency in personnel. Some of them were new. Thus, in spite of the fact that Belgium had been overrun in the two world wars, in 1954 a college was founded in Louvain to prepare priests for Latin America. By 1959 about forty-two of its former students were serving in that region and about eighty were enrolled. Most of them were Flemings and Walloons, but a minority were from Germany, France, the Netherlands, Luxemburg, Spain, and Italy, with a very few from Latin America.[37] A survey of the Franciscans in South America in the 1940's after World War II showed that the majority of the vicariates apostolic, the missions, and the provincial commissaries in charge of the Brothers Minor were entrusted to European and Canadian provinces. More of these provinces were in Spain than in any other country, but Austria, Italy, Belgium, Hungary, and Czechoslovakia, as well as Canada, were also represented.[38] Other examples could be given. For the most part the reinforcements from Europe were members of orders and congregations. In 1960 Pope John XXIII announced the founding of what were called "Papal Volunteers for Latin America" to enlist personnel from other lands to aid church lay organizations in that area.[39]

A striking development after World War II was the large influx of missionaries from the United States. By 1958 Latin America had become the major mission field of the Roman Catholics of that country: of the 6,120 priests, brothers, sisters, and lay missionaries from the United States who were serving overseas, 2,127, or more than a third, were in South America, Central America, and the West Indies—an increase from 489 in 1940.[40] They were in all the republics and in Puerto Rico, Jamaica, the Leeward Islands, and Trinidad. The largest number, 571, were in Puerto Rico, the next largest, 298, were in Brazil, followed by Bolivia, with 146, Peru, with 135, and Chile, with 122. They were from many orders and congregations and included a few seculars. By far the largest number were Maryknollers—of the Catholic Foreign Mission Society of America—whose organization in its earlier years had had China as its major objective. Next was the total of the various branches of the Franciscans. Redemptorists were also numerous.[41] The number so rapidly increased (in 1960,

---

[36] *Worldmission Fides Service*, September 26, 1959.
[37] *Ibid.*, October 3, 1959.
[38] Arcila Robledo, *La Orden Franciscana en la America Meridional*, pp. 6–12.
[39] *The New York Times*, September 14, 1960.
[40] Considine, *New Horizons*, p. 337.
[41] *Ibid.*, pp. 338–357.

of the 6,782 Roman Catholic missionaries from the United States 2,405, still over a third, were in Latin America) that in that year the hierarchy in the United States made it known that they would give substantial financial backing to their church in Latin America, and the National Catholic Welfare Conference created the Latin American Bureau to coördinate and promote the efforts of the Roman Catholics of the United States among their southern neighbours and placed at its head John J. Considine, a Maryknoller.[42] In 1960 the Grail, an international movement of lay women, announced that it would soon open a training centre in the United States to prepare young women for the lay apostolate in Latin America.[43]

CONTRASTING DEVELOPMENTS: A GENERAL PICTURE: BURGEONING PROTESTANTISM

An important incentive to efforts to revive the Roman Catholic Church in Latin America was the spectacular growth of Protestantism after 1914, some of it by immigration but most of it by conversions of Roman Catholics. In the latter the Roman Catholic authorities saw a major challenge.[44] As we have seen, except through immigration, mostly from Germany, by the time of the outbreak of World War I Protestantism had made very little headway.[45] Statistics were admittedly imperfect, but such figures as were obtainable showed 1,840,762 communicants in 1957 as against 1,193,715 in 1952, an increase of over 50 per cent. in five years, and a total Christian constituency in 1957 of 4,534,000 as against 2,866,000 in 1952, or a still larger percentage of growth. The real totals were undoubtedly greater.[46] Every country showed a marked advance, but the republic having the largest number of Protestants was Brazil, with nearly half the total number of Latin American Protestant communicants. Nor did the Brazilian figures of communicants include those of the Lutherans, descended from German immigrants and with a constituency counted as 514,243 in 1957.[47] Incomplete figures of missionaries for 1957 gave about 2,300 ordained men, about 1,100 laymen, and approximately 2,800 women, or a total of about 6,400 foreigners engaged in furthering Protestantism. That Protestantism was becoming firmly rooted was seen in the number of nationals who were in the service of the Protestant forces. In 1957 they included about 2,400 ordained men, about 7,000 laymen, and approximately 1,400 women, a total of 10,800.[48] The overwhelming majority of the foreign staff were from the United States.

Although Latin American Protestantism was deeply indebted to the Protes-

---

[42] *The New York Times,* September 14, 1960.
[43] *Ibid.*
[44] As samples see Considine, *New Horizons,* pp. 234–274; Coleman, *op. cit.,* pp. 46–50.
[45] Volume III, Chapter XII.
[46] *World Christian Handbook, 1957,* pp. 115–149.
[47] *Ibid.,* p. 120.
[48] *Ibid.,* pp. 115–149.

tantism of the United States, its denominational distribution differed significantly. Because of the German immigration, Lutherans and the Evangelicals (unions of Lutherans and Reformed) were not far from the same proportion as in the United States. The numerically larger Protestant denominational families of the northern republic were widely represented—Methodists, Baptists, Presbyterians, Disciples of Christ, Congregationalists, and Episcopalians. But they constituted a much smaller proportion of the Protestantism of Latin America than of that of the United States. In contrast, the Seventh Day Adventists, who were scarcely one-half of one per cent. of the Protestants of the United States, in the 1950's had about 5 per cent. of the Protestant communicants of Latin America.[49] Even more prominent were Pentecostals. In 1957 they constituted between a third and a half of the Protestants of Brazil and the large majority of the Protestants of Chile. They were found in several other countries, divided into many groups.[50] The initial impetus for some came from Sweden, for others from Italy, but most of them ultimately stemmed from the United States. A striking characteristic was the fashion in which they quickly took root, spread, developed an indigenous leadership, and became independent of financial aid or any direction from abroad.[51] They drew especially from elements on a low economic and educational level. Many other movements, not as numerous as the Pentecostals, but attracting members as did they from underprivileged strata of the population, were found in several countries. All—Pentecostals and others recruited from the same classes—had a profound belief in the inspiration and inerrancy of the Bible, were emotional, stressed conversion, and insisted on a high standard of honesty, frugality, industry, cleanliness, and freedom from sexual irregularities. As we pass to Asia, Africa, and the islands of the Pacific we will find Christianity having its major numerical growth among similar elements of the population—the depressed classes and hill tribes of India, and animistic peoples in Burma, Indonesia, Africa, and various Pacific islands.

Coördination of much of the Protestant effort in Latin America was sought by the Committee on Coöperation in Latin America. It was organized in 1913 as an aftermath of the World Missionary Conference in Edinburgh in 1910. That gathering specifically excluded Latin America from its consideration, for it had limited its purview to non-Christians, and the majority of the population of Latin America were professedly Christian. Robert E. Speer, prominent as a leader in the missionary forces of the United States, was dissatisfied with the omission. Largely at his instance, at a gathering held in New York in 1913 by the Foreign Missions Conference of North America the Committee on Co-

[49] *Ibid.; Information Service*, November 3, 1956.
[50] *World Christian Handbook, 1957*, pp. 120, 121, 126.
[51] David J. Du Plessis in conversation with the author, October 29, 1959.

operation in Latin America was formed, with the purpose not of proselyting Roman Catholics but of bringing the Gospel to those ignorant of it. Its membership being predominantly of Protestant missionary societies of the United States, it established headquarters in New York City. Under it the notable Panama Congress of 1916 was held, followed by similar gatherings in later years.[52]

From this inclusive picture of the Latin American setting and of the contrasts between the forces making for de-Christianization and reviving and strengthening the Christian faith we now turn to a country-by-country survey of post-1914 developments.

Revolutionary Mexico

As in the nineteenth century, so in the first half of the twentieth century the course of Christianity in Mexico was profoundly affected by shifting currents in the political scene. In an earlier volume we have noted the kaleidoscopic introduction of Mexico to the twentieth century.[53] In 1910 the aging José de la Cruz Porfirio Díaz, who had been president continuously since 1877, was forced out of power by a popular revolt led by Madero. Madero faced the opposition of the clerical forces. In 1913 he was displaced by Victoriano Huerta, supported in general by the Church. Huerta publicly declared his conviction that only through belief in God could man have true moral strength. The Roman Catholic Church was beginning to organize coöperative societies, run grocery stores, start banks, and construct theatres—activities that some regarded as hopeful social measures.[54]

But in July, 1914, partly because of pressure from the United States, Huerta was forced to give way to Venustiano Carranza. Carranza came to power through a popular, anti-clerical movement which demanded measures that would give more opportunity to the underprivileged masses, both through land reform and through better conditions for labour. In 1917 a new constitution was adopted affirming the nation's ownership of all lands, waters, and mineral resources such as mines and petroleum and restricting foreign ownership. To the workers it promised the eight-hour day and employers' liability, and it forbade child labour. It confirmed the anti-clerical laws of the 1850's which took from the Church its landed wealth. It also declared temples of worship to be the property of the state, excluded the Church from any share in public educa-

---

[52] Hogg, *Ecumenical Foundations*, pp. 131, 132, 173, 174, 267, 268; Latourette, *A History of the Expansion of Christianity*, Vol. VII, pp. 172, 173.

[53] Volume III, pp. 303–308.

[54] Callcott, *Liberalism in Mexico 1857–1929*, p. 235. See also Cuevas, *Historia de la Iglesia en México*, Vol. V, pp. 423–429; Wilgus, *The Caribbean Area*, pp. 347, 348; Ledit, *Rise of the Downtrodden*, p. 20.

tion, denied priests the franchise and the right to hold public office, gave to the local authorities the power to determine the number of clergy of any denomination to be permitted in their jurisdictions, and forbade the clergy to criticize "the fundamental laws of the country, the authorities in particular, or the government in general."[55]

The bishops publicly denounced the articles in the constitution which they regarded as infringing on religious liberty. Many of the clergy opposed the agrarian policies of the government. Here and there violence broke out against the Church. For example, in Yucatan, where conditions approaching slavery of the masses existed and the landlords and clergy had long presented a common front, a mob sacked the cathedral and burned vestments and sacred images.[56] Yet the supporters of Carranza declared that, although the churches were the property of the state, the government would permit the use of such of them as might be necessary for worship.[57] In December, 1915, Carranza ordered all state governors as well as other officials to cease alienating local church properties.[58] But many priests were deported, others were imprisoned and were subjected to forced loans, and numbers of churches were closed. The Archbishop of Guadalajara issued a pastoral letter in opposition to the constitution, and priests who read it from their pulpits were imprisoned and fined. Some priests went into hiding.[59]

On the other hand, Protestantism was expanding. Carranza showed an interest in Protestant schools. Even though some Protestant institutions were closed for a time, Protestant properties were respected. In contrast with many Roman Catholics in the United States, Protestant spokesmen in the great northern neighbour opposed intervention by their government. Protestant institutions were well filled and many graduates of Protestant schools were in prominent government positions.[60] An opportunist, Carranza allowed the generals and other politicians to loot the national and state treasuries, made himself wealthy, and in 1920 while attempting to flee from the country was killed.

Carranza was followed briefly by Adolfo de la Huerta (not related to Victoriano Huerta) and then by Álvaro Obregón. Although lip service was paid by orators to democracy, free elections were a myth and many generals and others in power plundered the country. Yet a few officials were honest and attempted to make effective the ideals incorporated in the constitution of 1917.

[55] Herring, *A History of Latin America*, pp. 360, 361; Wilgus, *Modern Hispanic America*, p. 244; Felix Navarete, *De Cabarrus a Carranza. La Legislación Anticatólica en Mexico* (México, Editorial Jus, 1957, pp. 150), pp. 104 ff.
[56] Callcott, *op. cit.*, pp. 245, 355; Gruening, *Mexico and Its Heritage*, pp. 216–219.
[57] Callcott, *op. cit.*, pp. 245, 246.
[58] *Ibid.*, p. 253.
[59] *Ibid.*, pp. 252, 253.
[60] *Ibid.*, pp. 251, 252; Wheeler, Day, and Rodgers, *Modern Missions in Mexico*, pp. 202 ff.

From 1920 to 1924 Obregón was dictator under the guise of president. He kept the peace by winning the support of the generals, organized labour, and those who advocated agrarian reform. Under him and with his protection José Vasconcelos carried through a sweeping reorganization of the educational system. Given a large budget, Vasconcelos introduced a new kind of rural school designed to enrich many aspects of the life of the village, not only by reducing illiteracy but also by fostering the arts and recreation and instructing in better methods of sanitation and agriculture. He enlisted and trained teachers to spread his enthusiasm and his methods. He encouraged and subsidized artists to depict Mexico's history in murals on public buildings and launched on his public career the man who became the most famous musician of the country.

Under Obregón radicals carried on vigorous anti-clerical propaganda; in retaliation, some of the most ardent Roman Catholics violently opposed the teachers in the rural schools fostered by Vasconcelos. Moreover, the prohibition of religious orders and of foreign clergy was not respected. In January, 1923, the conflict came to a crisis when the hierarchy, supported by a vast throng and the apostolic delegate, dedicated a monument to "Christ, King of Mexico," set in a commanding position on a hill in Guanajuato. Obregón took it as a challenge and ordered the apostolic delegate out of the country. Many of the Roman Catholics responded by placarding available places with *Viva Cristo Rey*.[61] Roman Catholics were also organizing a number of associations to hold the allegiance of the faithful. Among them were the Catholic Association of Mexican Youth, the National Catholic Parents Association, the National Defense League of Religious Liberty, the Knights of Columbus, and the C.N.C.T. (*Confederación Nacional Católica del Trabajo*), a Catholic labour union. By 1925 the C.N.C.T. reported a membership of about 22,000.[62] The first national Eucharistic Congress was held in 1924, and in connexion with it committees were formed to block efforts to enforce the anti-clerical clauses of the constitution of 1917. In 1922 the government authorized the opening and reconstruction of thirteen Roman Catholic and ten Protestant churches, and the following year similar permission was given for twenty-four Roman Catholic and eleven Protestant churches.[63]

In December, 1924, Obregón was followed by Plutarco Elías Calles. Calles had risen from a humble home of industrious parents and in his youth had been a teacher. In a few months he brought improvement in the government's finances and markedly reduced corruption. Coming out of the revolutionary movement, he strongly supported the powerful C.R.O.M., a labour organization dominated by Luis Morones. He pushed the confiscation of the huge landed

[61] Herring, *op. cit.*, p. 366; Callcott, *op. cit.*, p. 295; Gruening, *op. cit.*, pp. 224, 225; Ledit, *op. cit.*, p. 21; Mecham, *Church and State in Latin America*, p. 475.
[62] *Callcott, op. cit.*, p. 293; Ledit, *op. cit.*, pp. 24, 25.
[63] Callcott, *op. cit.*, pp. 294, 295.

estates and their division among the peasants and sought to aid the latter by tools, fertilizers, seeds, and agricultural credit banks. He also took steps to expropriate the holdings of the British and American oil companies. He sought to improve the roads, the railways, and the telegraph system. He stressed education, especially the rural and secondary schools. He promoted public health, endeavoured to reduce lotteries and the sale of liquor, and encouraged athletics.[64]

Calles had a head-on collision with the Roman Catholic Church. Many of the clergy were inclined to label as socialists, atheists, Bolsheviks, Protestants, or Masons all who did not agree with them and their church. Their critics held that the Roman Catholic organizations, now mounting in numbers, were seeking to influence the elections. Calles himself had Protestant connexions through his wife and contributed to the Young Men's Christian Association. In March, 1925, the government ordered the enforcement of the article in the constitution which forbade clergymen to be active in politics and restricted clerical functions to natives of Mexico. Soon several schools connected with ecclesiastical institutions in contravention of the law were ordered closed. One of the states commanded all priests to marry—ostensibly to legitimize existing children of the clergy. In February, 1926, Pope Pius XI endorsed efforts to bring about the repeal of the anti-clerical articles in the constitution of 1917. In February of the following year the Archbishop of Mexico City, speaking for the bishops, clergy, and faithful laity, declared that they would combat the articles. Within a few days Calles said that the laws would be enforced against ministers of all creeds and nations. Several scores of foreign-born clergymen were deported. Many monasteries were closed. In July, 1926, the archbishops and bishops had issued a pastoral letter ordering the suspension of services requiring the presence of priests. The government, retaliating, decreed that church buildings be taken over by lay committees. The churches were kept open and thousands of the faithful entered to worship before the various images and in services read by lay people. Yet many of the masses felt themselves emancipated from the moral standards of the Church, including the insistence on monogamy. Open rebellion followed. Several of the bishops were expelled for alleged endorsement of the violence and took refuge in the United States, where they sought support for their cause. Some bishops remained in Mexico in hiding. Numbers of priests and lay folk were killed. Famous among those who perished was the young Mexican Jesuit Miguel Pro Juarez. He was shot by a firing squad, with his eyes on a crucifix, pardon on his lips for his enemies, and crying *"Viva Cristo Rey."* Troops tore down the statue of Christ in Guanajuato which had been the occasion for the crisis of 1923.[65]

---

[64] *Ibid.*, pp. 316–350.

[65] For a Roman Catholic account see Parsons, *Mexican Martyrdom*, pp. 14–100. For biographies of Pro see Franchon Royer, *Padre Pro* (New York, P. J. Kenedy and Sons, 1954, pp. viii, 248), Mrs. George Norman, *God's Jester. The Story of the Life and Martyrdom of Father Michael Pro, S.J.* (London, Longmans, Green and Co., 1931, pp. viii, 226), and Antonio Oragon, *Vida Intima*

The episcopate in the United States issued a pastoral letter which, while disclaiming any intervention by their government, denounced the laws of Mexico forbidding the Church to hold property. A flood of books and pamphlets from Roman Catholic pens, especially under the auspices of the Knights of Columbus, sought to arouse public opinion. Extremists demanded intervention. In general the Protestant press opposed such a step and upheld the Calles administration. The issue was complicated by resentment in the United States over the expropriation of the property of many citizens of that country.[66] The agitation spread to other countries.

In Mexico tempers flared. Some Roman Catholics attacked the Protestants and said that liberalism and socialism led to complete slavery. Anti-clericals declared that Roman Catholic education warped the minds of its pupils, and the more violent accused the Church of obscurantism and the clergy of using the confessional to debauch women and girls. When the term of Calles approached its close Obregón was chosen to succeed him. Before he could take office he was assassinated (1928) by a man who frankly declared that his action was a service to God and against the enemies of the Church.[67]

For a short time peace seemed to have been achieved between the state and the Church. Emilio Portes Gil was appointed provisional president for a year's term. Partly through the kindly offices of the tactful ambassador of the United States, Dwight Morrow, an arrangement was made (June, 1934) by which the clergy resumed their functions and the government acknowledged the authority of the Church in spiritual matters and permitted religious instruction within the churches. The Pope gave his approval. But the apostolic delegate still lived in exile in Texas. Portes Gil did not accompany his achievement by a reaction against the social revolution. Instead he furthered it. He continued land reform and gave impetus to athletics. He sought to reduce the consumption of alcoholic liquors and assigned as his reason the deleterious effect of alcohol on economic conditions and public and private health. He had a new labour code adopted which provided for mediation by the courts in labour disputes, a share by labour in the management of industrial plants, workman's insurance, and the safeguarding of the conditions of employment of women in factories. A new criminal code abolished capital punishment.[68]

de Padre Pro, translated from the French (Mexico, Buena Prensa, 1940, pp. xvi, 386). For other accounts of the Church-state struggle see Mecham, *op. cit.*, pp. 478–495; Gruening, *op. cit.*, pp. 275–286; Felipe Morones, *Capitulos Sueltos. Apuntes Sobre la Persecucion Religiosa en Aguascalientes* (México, Impenta Aldina, 1955, pp. 230), *passim;* Cuevas, *op. cit.*, Vol. V, pp. 429–472. See also Ledit, *op. cit.*, pp. 26–43.

[66] As one example of the debate in the United States see *The Catholic Historical Review*, Vol. XLV, pp. 309–326 (October, 1959).

[67] Callcott, *op. cit.*, pp. 353–377.

[68] Callcott, *op. cit.*, pp. 378, 381, 382; Herring, *op. cit.*, p. 373; Parsons, *op. cit.*, pp. 101–108; Mecham, *op. cit.*, pp. 497, 498; Ledit, *op. cit.*, pp. 45–52; MacFarland, *Chaos in Mexico*, pp. 139–151.

The peace in Church-state relations achieved under Portes Gil proved to be only a truce. From 1929 to 1932 Ortiz Rubio occupied the presidential chair. He was a creature of Calles and was followed by another of the puppets of Calles, Abelardo Rodriguez. Under Ortiz Rubio the states limited the number of officially authorized priests and by 1933 only two hundred were permitted in the entire nation.[69] In 1935 the number was still about 230 as against a previous total of about 4,500.[70] Over much of Mexico the Roman Catholic Church almost ceased to function except for the partial use of church buildings by the laity. The bishops continued to protest against what they deemed the rationalistic education given in the public schools, with its mechanistic and humanistic view of life, and excommunicated those who submitted to it. Yet some teachers were far from being anti-Christian.[71] In the 1930's the University of Mexico, with a faculty whose members ranged from Marxist convictions to a devout Roman Catholic faith, broke with the government on the latter's policy of making the educational system a means of socialist propaganda, became autonomous, and was hailed as the last citadel of freedom.[72]

Under Lázaro Cárdenas, who was inaugurated as president in December, 1934, conditions were not improved. Cárdenas had come up from poverty in the revolutionary movement, was honest, lived simply, was incorruptible, early freed himself from the control of Calles and the Calles clique, set himself to carry out the purposes of the revolution, and endeavoured especially to help the underprivileged in the rural areas. Under him the holdings of the foreign oil companies were expropriated. In his ecclesiastical policy he stiffened the teaching of socialism and sought to put an end to the private schools which had been conducted by members of Roman Catholic congregations teaching in lay garb unless they would incorporate socialism in their instruction. Catechetical classes in the churches had already been banned. In some states teachers in the public schools were said to be required to take an oath declaring that they were atheists and enemies of the Roman Catholic Church.[73] To counter these moves clandestine schools sprang up for children of parents who did not wish their offspring exposed to socialist education. They had as instructors former public school teachers or members of religious congregations. Theological education was also carried on secretly, some of it in remote mountain fastnesses. Here and there armed mobs sought to break up the schools which were teaching socialism.[74] In August, 1935, Cárdenas promulgated an edict for the sweeping nationalization of every "building that has been used for the administration,

---

[69] Herring, *op. cit.*, p. 374; Mecham, *op. cit.*, p. 500.
[70] MacFarland, *op. cit.*, pp. 70, 71.
[71] *Ibid.*, pp. 75, 87, 89, 96–102, 132–134.
[72] *Ibid.*, pp. 102–110.
[73] Parsons, *op. cit.*, pp. 229–235.
[74] *Ibid.*, pp. 250 ff.

propagation, or teaching of a religious cult." This applied to Protestants and Jews as well as to Roman Catholics. It was made to include private houses and all property the income on which was "in any way related to religious projects or objects." The bishops petitioned the president asking for the abrogation of the edict and of the anti-religious provisions of earlier decrees. They also circulated messages to keep up the morale of the faithful. From his place of exile in Texas the apostolic delegate sent a letter enjoining the clergy to tell their people to avoid the socialist type of education. In 1935 and 1936 the bishops issued pastoral letters warning parents that they were guilty of mortal sin if they did not remove their children from schools which taught socialism. In the United States the Knights of Columbus urged President Roosevelt to step in, but he refused, on the ground that he would not intervene in the domestic affairs of another country. A number of Chileans asked the ambassadors of their country, Argentina, and Brazil to use their good offices to bring about a cessation of the attacks on the Church.[75]

In 1940 Manuel Ávila Camacho succeeded Cárdenas in the presidency and the acute conflict was over. In his first press interview Ávila Camacho declared, "I am a believer." Under him and his successors through the 1950's the restrictions on the Church, if not formally repealed, were allowed to fall into abeyance. Although the constitution of 1917 remained, in practice its anti-clerical features were relaxed. The Roman Catholic Church opened schools and gave its blessings to *Acción Nacional*. In one of its aspects *Acción Nacional* was a political party made up of practising Roman Catholics. It also had other phases of Catholic Action. In 1945 with impressive public ceremonies which attracted thousands and in the presence of a Canadian cardinal, a new jeweled crown was placed on the head of the statue of the Virgin of Guadalupe, long the patron saint of the country and officially recognized as such by Papal decree.[76]

Although subsequent presidents did not come out as frankly for the faith as did Ávila Camacho, at least they preserved a discreet silence. In 1959 President Adolfo López Mateos publicly declared that religious belief "should prove no obstacle in the march of the Mexican revolution," that there existed in Mexico "absolute freedom of belief," and that "the ample programme of the revolution can encompass all men of good will."[77]

By the end of the 1950's a marked resurgence of religious faith was seen. It was apparent in Protestant circles, but it was especially striking in the Roman

[75] *Ibid.,* pp. 264–276.
[76] Herbert Cerwin, *These Are the Mexicans* (New York, Reynal and Hitchcock, 1947, pp. 384), pp. 295, 296; Ledit, *op. cit.,* pp. 81–86; Richard Pattee, *The Catholic Revival in Mexico. A Report of the Inter-American Committee* (Washington, The Catholic Association for International Peace, 1944, pp. 60), *passim.*
[77] *The New York Times,* December 4, 1959.

Catholic Church. The wives of some leaders in the government publicly went to church. Church attendance in general mounted. Very noticeably it included many men and that was unusual in Latin America. The law forbidding the wearing of religious garb in public was still on the statute books, but it was not uncommon to see priests on the streets in dark suits and with clerical collars and to observe nuns, while not in formal attire, wearing distinguishing uniforms, and monks in their robes. An undetermined number of foreign clergy and other personnel were present. When the news arrived of the death of Pius XII, the president, the president-elect, and a former president sent messages of condolence, and leaders of both the lower and the upper house of congress gave public expression to their sorrow, an action which a decade earlier would have meant political suicide.[78] Rome took cognizance of the more favourable climate. In 1951 it created a new ecclesiastical province headed by the Archbishop of Vera Cruz. That same year it elevated the Archbishop of Mexico City to be the Primate of the Mexican Church.[79] In 1946 the *Asociación Nacional Guadalupana de Trabajadores* was formed, a branch of an earlier movement of Roman Catholic labourers, in an effort to "reconquer the labouring class for Christ," and centring about the Virgin of Guadalupe. It enlisted several scores of thousands in a pilgrimage to Guadalupe. Some Roman Catholics made much of the social teachings of their church, especially of the papal bulls *Rerum novarum* and *Quadragesimo anno*.[80] In 1949, under the guidance of Maryknollers from the United States, the Foreign Mission Society of Our Lady of Guadalupe was begun—said to be the first Latin American organization to prepare missionaries to serve outside the Western Hemisphere and thus to share in the wider aspects of the world mission of the Church. In 1956 it sent a contingent to Japan and in 1959 it had 168 seminarians enrolled in its mother house in Mexico City.[81]

The clergy still lacked sufficient numbers to give adequate pastoral care to the nominally Roman Catholic population. In 1958 there was only one priest to every 4,000 or 5,000 of the population. But this was a higher ratio than in most other Latin American countries.[82] In spite of the efforts of the government in the 1920's and 1930's to close the theological schools, in 1956 twenty-five major seminaries were in operation, one of them interdiocesan in New Mexico under the Jesuits, with 300 students, and the twenty-four others in Mexico itself, with a total enrollment of 2,213 preparing for the secular priesthood. The

[78] *Ibid.*, October 12, 1958.
[79] Jesus Garcia Gutierrez, compiler, *Bulario de la Iglesia Mejicana. Documentos relativos a erecciones, desmembraciones, etc. de Diócesis Mejicanas* (México, Buena Prensa, 1951, pp. 595), pp. 522, 582.
[80] Joaquin Marquez Montiel, *La Doctrina Social de la Iglesia y la Legislacion Obrera Mexicana* (México, Editorial Jus, 2nd ed., 1958, pp. 218), *passim*, especially pp. 57, 58.
[81] *Worldmission Fides Service*, February 21, 1959.
[82] Allen, *A Seminary Survey*, p. 463.

seminary in New Mexico had been opened in 1937 by funds raised in the United States augmented by a donation from the Pope to train seculars for Mexico when this was difficult or impossible in that country. In addition, in 1957 a total of 170 scholastics were affiliated with the various religious orders and congregations. It was said that in 1956 Mexico had 2,383 men studying for the priesthood, a larger number than in any other country in Africa, Asia, or Latin America.[83] In 1950 the priests in Mexico were put at 4,577, or more than in any other Latin American country except Brazil.[84]

Reinforcements to the priesthood and the sisters arrived from abroad, and that in spite of the official prohibition of foreign clergy. Over half from the United States were Maryknollers. For example, in 1943 Maryknollers came to the Mayans of Yucatan, said to have been the first priests in that section for over a century.[85]

In the mid-twentieth century about 97 per cent. of the population were still nominally Roman Catholic. Many of the educated were sceptical and nonpractising. Among the Indians and mestizos, constituting the large majority of the population, the faith was mixed with superstitious beliefs and customs. Much of the paganism of pre-Spanish days persisted under a thin Christian veneer.[86] Spiritualism had its adherents. Yet ostensibly, as in most of Latin America, the majority, if asked, would call themselves Catholics.

In spite of the years of storm, years which posed almost as great obstacles as to the Roman Catholic Church, in the four and a half decades which followed 1914 Protestantism grew in Mexico. One set of figures estimates that in 1957 Protestant communicants numbered 221,873 as against 161,698 five years earlier, and that the total Protestant community in 1957 was 910,951 in contrast with 334,756 in 1952. The government census of 1950 showed 330,111 Protestant church members.[87] This was more than in any other Latin American country except Brazil.

In an earlier volume we have seen the beginnings of Protestantism in Mexico. We noted that in 1914 the number of communicants was about 22,000.[88] Thus in the ensuing forty years, although still only a small minority of the population, they had multiplied about ten-fold. Yet even in 1957 the Protestant community constituted slightly less than 3 per cent. of the population.

Protestants were of many denominations. In 1957 the one with the largest

[83] *Ibid.*, pp. 465–469. But Considine, in *New Horizons in Latin America*, p. 332, puts the number in 1957 at 1,990.

[84] *World Christian Handbook, 1957*, p. 167. Considine, *New Horizons*, p. 332, says that in 1957 the total was 5,885, of whom 4,518 were seculars and 1,367 were regulars.

[85] Considine, *New Horizons*, pp. 295–299, 348.

[86] As examples, see Anita Brenner, *Idols Behind Altars* (New York, Payson and Clarke, 1929, pp. 359), *passim.*

[87] *World Christian Handbook, 1957*, pp. 139, 140; *The Statesman's Year Book, 1960*, p. 1223.

[88] Volume III, pp. 309, 310.

number of communicants was the Presbyterian Church, followed by the Swedish Free Mission, the Methodist Church, the Seventh Day Adventists, and the (Pentecostal) Assemblies of God, in that descending order. But the Baptists claimed by far the largest constituency, followed by the Presbyterians, the Swedish Free Mission, and the Seventh Day Adventists.[89]

The Protestantism of Mexico was characterized by several features. As was to be expected, it owed its origin chiefly to missionaries from the United States. It was strongest in the cities and villages and near the border of the United States and drew its adherents mainly from the mestizos and from the small traders, manual labourers, carpenters, primary school teachers, and students. It had made almost no impression on the rural folk, the overwhelming majority of the population. In spite of the fact that some missions were directed primarily to them, it had reached relatively few of the full-blooded Indians. Nor, on the opposite level of the social scale, had it had much impact on the intellectuals, the professional classes, or those of pure European descent. Only a small percentage of its churches were fully independent of financial help from abroad. It was especially weak on the west coast. In the mobile population a great many of its members drifted away from the churches. Protestants often were snubbed or suffered persecution, either subtle or overt, from the social and political liberals on the one hand and from fanatical Roman Catholics on the other hand.[90]

Efforts were made at coöperation among the Protestant forces, but with less success than in some other countries. In 1917 a meeting was called in Cincinnati, Ohio, in an attempt to divide responsibility for different areas among the several denominations to prevent overlapping. In 1919 a conference in Mexico City ratified the findings of the Cincinnati gathering. Eight denominations shared in it, but some, such as the Baptists, the Seventh Day Adventists, and the Episcopalians, did not participate. For several years a committee on coöperation existed which was a child of the Committee on Coöperation in Latin America. It was eventually merged with the National Council of Evangelical Churches in Mexico.[91] Partial coöperation in training for the ministry was attained through the Union Theological Seminary of Mexico, founded in 1917. It was supported by the Methodists, the Congregationalists, the Disciples of Christ, and the Friends, but most of its students were Methodists.[92]

Tensions between the United States and Mexico in 1914 and later led to the withdrawal of some of the Protestant missionaries who came from the northern

---

[89] *World Christian Handbook, 1957*, pp. 139, 140. For a comprehensive survey of Mexican Protestantism in 1939 see Davis, *The Economic Basis of the Evangelical Church in Mexico, passim.*
[90] Báez Camargo and Grubb, *Religion in the Republic of Mexico*, pp. 89–102; Davis, *op. cit.*, pp. 30, 31, 43, 46, 49, 78–87.
[91] Báez Camargo and Grubb, *op. cit.*, pp. 104–107; Inman, *Christian Coöperation in Latin America*, pp. 43–46.
[92] Allen, *op. cit.*, p. 180.

republic.[93] The actions of the Mexican Government, directed primarily against the Roman Catholic Church, could not but have repercussions upon Protestantism. The laws enacted against foreign clergymen and in the field of education were given a blanket application to all religious bodies. One result was to hasten the movement towards autonomy of the Protestant churches and the turning over of administrative responsibility to Mexican clergy and laity. Thus in 1934 the Episcopal Church consecrated a Mexican, Salinas y Velasco, as bishop in Mexico.[94] Even before 1914 steps had been taken to promote self-government in some of the churches. For example, in 1901 the General Synod of the Presbyterian Church had been inaugurated and in 1903 the National Baptist Convention had been organized. As the laws excluded missionaries from exercising their ministry, Mexicans were given a larger share in the various churches.[95]

In spite of the numerical increase of the Protestants and the growing autonomy of their churches, the situation late in the 1950's was sobering. Although the Presbyterians had the largest body of communicants, they had only seventy-five ordained ministers, and their salary scale was so low that some left the pastorate for more remunerative work to support their families and others took on outside jobs to supplement their income. The academic preparation of most of the clergy left much to be desired.[96] Many of the Protestants were conservative, resistive to the intellectual currents of the day, suspicious of the Ecumenical Movement, and inclined to be uncoöperative across denominational lines.[97]

Yet in the 1940's Methodism was said to be making more solid advances in Mexico than in any other Latin American country except Brazil. Presbyterians were represented in twenty-two states and were organized into nine presbyteries. They also had a large publishing house in Mexico City. The Wycliffe Bible Translators supported a force of several scores at work reducing Indian vernaculars to writing and putting the Bible into them.[98]

The Changing Scene in Central America

As in Mexico, so in the republics of Central America the changes in the political scene affected the course of Christianity.

Guatemala had a chequered political history which centred about a succession of dictators in the guise of presidents. Relations with the United States were mixed. From 1898 to 1920 Manuel Estrada Cabrera was dominant, reëlected

[93] Wheeler, Day, and Rodgers, *Modern Missions in Mexico*, pp. 103–107.
[94] Frank Whittington Creighton, *Mexico. A Handbook on the Missions of the Episcopal Church* (New York, The National Council of the Protestant Episcopal Church, 1936, pp. 111), pp. 71–77.
[95] Báez Camargo and Grubb, *op. cit.*, pp. 109, 110.
[96] Allen, *op. cit.*, pp. 180, 181.
[97] First-hand information to the author from confidential sources.
[98] Considine, *New Horizons*, p. 269.

from time to time as president, always "unanimously." He kept himself in power through an efficient force of informers and secret police. The country seemed to profit from the increase in agricultural exports through German coffee growers and the United Fruit Company and from improved public health through the efforts of the Rockefeller Foundation. Estrada Cabrera was finally ousted by an outraged public and with the moral support of President Woodrow Wilson. He was succeeded by Jorge Ubico, who was in office from 1931 to 1944. Frugal and skilful, Ubico balanced the national budget, restored the country's credit, built roads, furthered sanitation, and on paper abolished the peonage of the Indians. In 1944 revolts led by students and army men—the nearest approach to a middle class—unseated him and his puppets. He was followed by Juan Arévalo from 1945 to 1950 and Jacobo Arbens from 1950 to 1954. In 1945 a constitution was framed with many of the features of the Mexican constitution of 1917, including endorsement of basic rights for labour, free institutions, and land reform. In 1950 Communists began an infiltration of the government and won control of the radio and the press. Under their prodding, measures were taken against the United Fruit Company which in 1952 led to the expropriation of much of its land. In 1954, through pressure from the United States, the Pan American Conference adopted a resolution against Communism and Communist attempts to seize power anywhere in the Western Hemisphere. In that year Russian arms were imported, but opponents of Arbens staged a revolt, removed him and his leading supporters, and placed Carlos Castillo Armas in the presidential chair. A new constitution was adopted (1956). In 1957 the president was assassinated and was succeeded by the vice-president, Luis A. Gonzales Lopez, as provisional president. An election soon placed Miguel Ydígoras Fuentes in the presidency. Ydígoras was a moderate conservative. But unrest was far from quieted.

With its slightly more than three millions, in the 1950's Guatemala had the largest population although not the largest area of any of the republics of Central America. Less than one per cent. was white, about two-thirds had Indian blood, and of the latter about two-thirds were pure-blood descendants of the pre-Spanish stock and about a third were mixed, *mestizo,* or, as they were called in Guatemala, *ladino.* The remainder were Negroes, mostly in the lowlands. It was the *ladino* element which was the most restless, eager to advance in the revolutionary age, and intensely nationalistic. Nominally Roman Catholic, as was most of Latin America, the *ladino* men seldom went to church. The *ladino* women were eager to teach the catechism, but Roman Catholic missionaries from the United States found them with only a sketchy knowledge of the basic doctrines of their faith.[99]

The Roman Catholic Church entered the twentieth century handicapped by

[99] Holleran, *Church and State in Guatemala,* pp. 221–224.

the anti-clerical legislation of the second half of the nineteenth century.[100] The upheavals of the twentieth century further weakened it. In 1922 the archbishop, a Jesuit, was expelled less than a month after his consecration. At the same time all other Jesuits and all who had ever belonged to the Society of Jesus were ousted. Several seculars were compelled to leave the country because of their opposition to the political regime. Not until 1928 and after long negotiations between the Holy See and the government was a new archbishop appointed. A Frenchman from Havana, he held office until his death (1938). Ubico somewhat relaxed the state's measures against the Church. He permitted a few of the religious orders to return and allowed the Maryknollers to enter. Moreover, the constitution of 1956 did away with anti-Catholic laws. Yet most of the clergy were of foreign birth or poorly trained. Sisters of Charity of St. Vincent de Paul, at the outset French, were tolerated and might wear their garb, for they served in one of the hospitals. In theory nuns who taught in schools were excluded, but under Ubico Belgian sisters came, supposedly as lay teachers, to conduct a private secondary school. The Marists and some Spanish clergy also had schools. Friction between anti-clericals and clericals sometimes reached fever heat. In the first half of the twentieth century most of the clergy were Spaniards, with some Germans, Costa Ricans, and Mexicans.[101] The proportion of priests to the population was lower than in any other Latin American country and was said to average only about one to every 30,000. Many of such clergy as existed were concentrated in the capital.[102]

Partly because of the inadequate body of clergy, among the Indians who constituted the majority of the population religion was a mixture of beliefs and customs of pre-Christian pagan origin and Roman Catholic teaching. Fiestas and pilgrimages were popular, the latter especially to the black Christ of Esquipulas.[103]

In spite of the adverse factors, the twentieth century saw some improvement in the Roman Catholic Church in Guatemala. For example, in 1928 the major seminary was reorganized with a capacity for sixty students and in 1957 had an enrollment of thirty-two. Catholic Action was formally instituted in 1957.[104] The Maryknollers reported progress in improving the quality of the faith of the Mayan Indians in areas which had long been without adequate pastoral

[100] Volume III, pp. 311, 312.

[101] Holleran, op. cit., pp. 208–218; Worldmission Fides Service, June 27, 1959.

[102] Holleran, op. cit., pp. 235–237; Allen, op. cit., p. 463.

[103] Holleran, op. cit., pp. 233–239; Considine, New Horizons, pp. 301–308; Grubb, Religion in Central America, p. 39. See also Maud Oakes, The Two Crosses of Todos Santos. Survivals of Mayan Religious Ritual (New York, Bollingen Foundation, pp. xiii, 274), passim; Oliver La Farge, Santa Eulalia. The Religion of a Cuchumatán Indian Town (University of Chicago Press, 1947, pp. xix, 211), passim.

[104] Allen, op. cit., pp. 469, 470; Pattee, El Catolicismo Contemporaneo en Hispanoamérica, pp. 254, 255.

care.[105] The Guatemalan clergy were said to have increased from 75 in 1930 to 250 in 1959. Late in the 1950's many Roman Catholic schools were reported as opened and television and the radio were called into service for the Roman Catholic cause. Between 7,000 and 8,000 members of apostolic associations were reported to be working as catechists in family groups.[106]

Before 1914 Protestantism had barely obtained a foothold. But following that year it made substantial advances. In 1952 it was reported to have 24,566 communicants and a constituency of 75,190. Five years later the corresponding figures were 28,956 and 142,465. Although they constituted a smaller proportion of the population than in Mexico, Protestants were rapidly advancing in numbers. In Quesa Henango, the second city in size, in the 1950's about 13 per cent. of the population were said to have Protestant sympathies. Several denominations were represented, all of them planted by missionaries from the United States. As might have been expected, the ones with the largest constituencies in 1957 were those which had entered before 1914—the *Iglesia Evangelica en Guatemala* (founded by the Central American Mission), the Presbyterians, and the Southern Baptists.[107] Progress was being made in recruiting and training an indigenous ministry. For example, in 1940 the Presbyterians raised their Bible school to theological seminary status and planned to make high school graduation a condition for admission.[108] In 1957 Protestants reported 123 ordained Guatemalans and 52 foreign clergymen, or more ordained men than the Roman Catholics had priests.[109] In addition to winning converts and gathering them into churches, Protestants had schools and at least one hospital, and were translating the Bible into the Indian languages. The Liberal governments tended to favour them.[110]

El Salvador was the smallest in area of the Central American republics, but in the 1950's its census showed a population of a little over two millions. It was the most densely peopled of the Central American states. In their main outlines developments paralleled those in Guatemala. Indians constituted about a fifth of the population but were culturally more advanced than those of Guatemala. *Ladinos* were in the large majority. The country was predominantly agricultural. Coffee constituted the chief crop and the major export. The name of the capital and largest city, San Salvador, together with that of the country testified to the influence of the Christian faith in the colonial period. However, as in many another Latin American country, "Liberal" and "Conservative" regimes took contrasting attitudes towards the Church. In general, power was held by

[105] Considine, *New Horizons*, pp. 299–308.
[106] *Worldmission Fides Service*, June 27, 1959.
[107] Considine, *New Horizons*, p. 265; *World Christian Handbook, 1957*, pp. 134, 135.
[108] Allen, *op. cit.*, p. 181.
[109] *World Christian Handbook, 1957*, p. 135.
[110] Considine, *New Horizons*, p. 265; Holleran, *op. cit.*, pp. 245–249.

great families and competition among them largely determined the dominant elements in the successive regimes. Literacy was higher than in some of the sister republics.

In 1871 a Liberal revolution brought action such as was usually associated with regimes of that temper. Ecclesiastical properties were not nationalized as they had been in Guatemala, but cemeteries were secularized, civil marriage was authorized, monastic orders were abolished, freedom of thought was declared, and priests were excluded from teaching in the public schools. Schools under Church auspices were permitted. In principle this attitude of the government persisted into the twentieth century. In 1928 the country was made an archiepiscopal see, and in the mid-thirties about a fifth of the schools were conducted by the Church.[111]

In the mid-twentieth century the Roman Catholic Church was in slightly better condition than in Guatemala. It was somewhat better supplied with priests. A theological seminary taught by the Jesuits in San Salvador had thirty-six students in 1957—more than the corresponding one in Guatemala City.[112] Yet the country had on the average only one priest to every 8,100 of the population and was worse off in this respect than any other Latin American country on the mainland except Guatemala and Honduras. In its constitution of 1950 El Salvador recognized the juridical personality of the Roman Catholic Church but limited its freedom.[113]

In the 1950's Protestants did not have as large a percentage of the population as in either Mexico or Guatemala, nor were they growing as rapidly. In 1952 they reported 9,199 communicants and 20,189 adherents. In 1957 the corresponding figures were 10,406 and 29,198. The denomination with the largest constituency was the Baptists, followed closely by the (Pentecostal) Assemblies of God, the Seventh Day Adventists, and the Central American Mission.[114] These figures represented a marked advance over 1937, when the Protestant communicants were said to total 4,130 and the Protestant community to be 7,260.[115]

Honduras, next to Nicaragua the largest in area of the Central American republics, but with a population of only about a million and a half in the 1950's, was peopled chiefly by mixtures of white, Indian, and Negro stocks. A minority were pure-blooded Indians. The country was troubled by even more political instability than was customary in Latin America. In the course of its independence it had seen more than ten constitutions adopted and its presidency had usually been filled through revolutions and occupied by dictators. Ostensibly the successive regimes had been either "Conservative" or "Liberal." When

[111] Grubb, *op. cit.*, p. 75.
[112] Allen, *op. cit.*, p. 469.
[113] Considine, *New Horizons*, pp. 263, 329.
[114] *World Christian Handbook, 1957*, pp. 132, 133.
[115] Grubb, *op. cit.*, p. 76.

in power the "Liberals" placed restrictions on the Roman Catholic Church of the kind which were associated with their rule elsewhere in Latin America, such as the free exercise of religion, the secularization of cemeteries, and the legalization of divorce. The constitution of 1936 forbade monasteries and subsidies for churches or religious education. Although the overwhelming majority of the population was professedly Roman Catholic, next to Guatemala the country was more poorly supplied with priests than any other in Latin America. In 1957 the ratio was one to every 9,900 of the population.[116]

In spite of the weakness of the Roman Catholic Church, Protestantism had a slow growth. About 1937 communicants were reported to be 4,181;[117] in 1952, 6,103; and in 1957, 6,724. The numerically largest bodies were the Quakers, affiliated with the California Yearly Meeting of Friends (a mission which was also strongly represented in Guatemala and El Salvador), the Seventh Day Adventists, the Plymouth Brethren, the Central American Mission, and the Moravians.[118]

Nicaragua, slightly larger than Honduras and with a population somewhat over a million in the 1950's, was predominantly *mestizo* in blood with about a sixth of pure white stock and smaller proportions of Indians and Negroes. We have seen[119] the alternating swing from "Conservatives" to "Liberals" in the political control of the country, the separation of Church and state late in the nineteenth century, the coming to power of the Conservatives, and their formulation of the constitution of 1911, which, while declaring that the majority of the population were Roman Catholics and requiring the teaching of their faith in the public schools and the payment of priests for carrying on that instruction, still stood for freedom of religion. The constitution of 1948, which invoked the protection of God, continued the separation of Church and state.[120] Anastasio Somoza became president in 1937 and in the 1950's was still in power. In 1957 Nicaragua was better supplied with priests, with one for an average of every 4,840 of the population, than was any other republic in Central America except the adjacent Costa Rica. To supplement them, missionaries came from the United States—Capuchins, Christian Brothers, and Maryknollers.[121]

Protestantism was widely represented and was growing. In 1937 it had 6,242 communicants and a community of about 20,000. By 1952 these figures had mounted to 11,493 and 29,173 respectively, and by 1957 to 12,598 and 37,666. The largest mission, and one which enrolled more than half of both the Protestant communicants and community, was that of the Moravians. They were

---

[116] Considine, *New Horizons,* p. 329; Grubb, *op. cit.,* p. 83.

[117] Grubb, *op. cit.,* p. 123.

[118] *World Christian Handbook, 1957,* p. 137.

[119] Volume III, p. 313.

[120] Bates, *Religious Liberty,* p. 228; Pattee, *El Catolicismo,* p. 352.

[121] Considine, *New Horizons,* pp. 264, 329, 349.

strongest on the east coast among the Indians and had been there since 1849. By the mid-1930's the entire east coast was reported to have been so influenced that it could be said to be Christianized. To it came Capuchins (1939) and Maryknollers. They spoke well of what had been accomplished by the Moravians. Next to the Moravians in numerical strength were the Baptists—both from the (Northern) American Baptist Convention and from the (Negro) National Baptist Convention—the Assemblies of God, and the Central American Mission.[122]

Costa Rica, predominantly white, was somewhat more stable politically than most of its Central American neighbours and had a high literacy rate. It was largely a country of small landowners, with coffee, bananas, abaca fibre, and cacao as its major export products. Its only large city and capital, San José, had a population of less than 100,000 in the 1950's in a land of about one million people. In 1950 the army was abolished in principle.

Like its neighbours Costa Rica was overwhelmingly Roman Catholic. Although that allegiance was for many only nominal, in 1957 there were more priests in proportion to the population, one to every 4,140, than in any other Central American republic, yet not as many as in several of the South American countries. In 1957 Costa Rica had an archbishop, two bishops, 120 seculars, 108 regulars, 45 seminarians, and 437 sisters. In 1948 slightly more than a third of the priests were foreigners. Missionaries came from the United States: by 1958 there were twenty-five Franciscans from Syracuse, New York, and seven Franciscan School Sisters from Milwaukee, Wisconsin.[123] The major seminary in San José, with more students than other in Central America in 1957, was under the German Lazarists.[124] Something of the religious temper of Costa Rica was seen in the fact that it had national Eucharistic Congresses and that, as the culmination of the second one, in the presence of a great throng the president of the country dedicated the land to the Sacred Heart of Jesus.[125] The social legislation of 1943 took its direct inspiration from Papal encyclicals such as *Rerum novarum, Quadragesimo anno,* and *Divini Redemptoris.*[126]

In the 1950's Protestantism was represented chiefly, as to numbers of adherents, by the Latin American Mission (earlier the Latin American Evangelization Campaign, which had been organized in 1921 with all of Latin America as its objective), the Central American Mission (the pioneer Protestant enterprise), and the Seventh Day Adventists (who had more communicants and a larger community than any of the others). The total of Protestant communi-

[122] *Ibid.,* p. 264; Grubb, *op. cit.,* pp. 91–95; *World Christian Handbook, 1957,* pp. 141, 142.
[123] Considine, *New Horizons,* pp. 329, 332, 346; Pattee, *El Catolicismo,* p. 167.
[124] Allen, *op. cit.,* p. 469.
[125] Considine, *New Horizons,* p. 262.
[126] Pattee, *El Catolicismo,* p. 164.

cants is said to have risen from 3,544 in 1952 to 4,847 in 1957, and of their community from 8,475 in 1952 to 10,992 in 1957.[127]

Panama owed its existence as a separate country to the United States and to the latter's desire for a route for a canal. That canal, opened in 1914, was the chief centre of the life of the country. Panama's population, numbering not quite 900,000 in the 1950's, was chiefly a mixture of white and black, about 10 per cent, white, another 10 per cent. Negro, and perhaps 5 per cent. Indian. In area Panama was larger than Costa Rica and El Salvador combined. About three-fourths of the population were counted as Roman Catholics, who in 1957 had 100 priests, or about one to every 6,780, a ratio higher than that in Guatemala, El Salvador, or Honduras, but lower than that in Mexico, Nicaragua, and Costa Rica. By its constitution of 1941 Panama recognized the Roman Catholic Church and prescribed religious instruction in its schools as requested by parents. To Panama, too, came missionaries from the United States, mostly Lazarists from Philadelphia.[128] Catholic Action was vigorous, especially in providing salaries for teachers in Roman Catholic primary schools.[129]

Protestantism was represented by several churches and missions, all but one, that of British Methodists, from the United States. The largest membership in 1957 was claimed by the Four-Square Gospel. The Seventh Day Adventists were second with only about half the number of the other. In 1952 Protestant communicants were said to total 20,131 and in 1957 to have increased to 23,630. In addition, seven union churches in the Canal Zone, begun in 1914 and in the main successful, served the men and women employed there from the denominationally varied backgrounds in the United States.[130]

HAITI

In the twentieth century the Negro republic of Haiti, with a population in the 1950's of about three and a third millions, had a chequered history politically and was faced with economic and social problems which made difficult the course of Christianity. Occupied by armed forces from the United States from 1915 to 1934 to restore order in its government and finances, when it was given full control of its affairs it was again plagued by internal disorder. The political picture was complicated by the poverty and attendant illiteracy of most of the

[127] Grubb, *op. cit.*, p. 103; *World Christian Handbook, 1957*, p. 129.

[128] Considine, *New Horizons*, pp. 262, 329, 350.

[129] Pattee, *El Catolicismo*, p. 359.

[130] *World Christian Handbook, 1957*, p. 142; Robert H. Rolofson, *Christian Coöperation at the World's Crossroads* (privately printed, The Union Church of the Canal Zone, 1950, pp. 425), *passim*. For an account of a mission to the Indians on the San Blas Islands, off the coast of Panama, ultimately supported by the Southern Baptists of the United States, see *I Married a San Blas Indian. The Story of Marvel Elya Iglesias*, by Christine Hudgins Morgan (New York, The Vantage Press, 1958, pp. 81), *passim*.

population. The population mounted, but agricultural land was limited and its fertility was depleted by floods and over-cultivation.

Religiously Haiti had long been under the influence of the Roman Catholic Church, but animistic cults, either of African origin or arising from an African background, were widely prevalent. One set of figures, from a Roman Catholic source, counted only about two-thirds of the population as affiliated with the Church in 1957. Much of that two-thirds was said to be shot through with the animistic beliefs dominating the other third. The long French connexion had provided some training in France for the Haitian clergy. Until World War I about ten Haitian priests a year had been graduated from a seminary in France maintained for that purpose. During the war only one a year was graduated and after peace came, to replenish the depleted ranks of the clergy in France, the hierarchy limited the number of its products who were permitted to go overseas. The seminary continued to train a few Haitians, but by the 1950's most of its alumni serving in Haiti were French. When Jesuits from Canada opened a seminary in Port-au-Prince, the capital of Haiti, the Haitian Government made it an annual subvention, and in the 1950's it was graduating about five priests a year. In the episcopate of the republic, in 1957 only one, auxiliary to the archbishop, was a Negro.[131] The clergy were mainly French, and in 1959 two of them were expelled by the government for opposing it.[132] In 1957 the priests were said to total 442, of whom 266 were seculars and 176 were regulars, and to average one to every 5,380 of the faithful. Reinforcements came from the United States; in 1957 they were mostly Oblates of Mary Immaculate from Lowell, Massachusetts.[133] In December, 1942, in the presence of a great throng outside the national palace in Port-au-Prince, the bishops consecrated the country to Our Lady of Perpetual Succour.[134] Yet friction with the state was the occasion for the expulsion from the country of two priests in 1959, and of Archbishop François Poirier, a native of France and primate of his church in Haiti, in 1960. In January, 1961, another bishop and four more priests were ordered out of the country. Those having anything to do with these actions were excommunicated by the Vatican.[135]

Numerically, in proportion to the population, Protestantism was stronger in Haiti than in Central America or Mexico. In 1957 it was reported as having 91,330 communicants and a community of 313,279, an increase from 75,451 communicants and a constituency of 259,523 in 1952. The largest number of communicants were Baptists, the result of missions of the Northern Baptists

[131] Allen, *op. cit.*, pp. 471, 472.
[132] *Britannica Book of the Year, 1960*, p. 309; Mecham, *Church and State in Latin America*, p. 348.
[133] Considine, *New Horizons*, pp. 330, 333, 352.
[134] Pattee, *El Catolicismo*, p. 268.
[135] *The New York Times*, November 25, 1960; January 13, 1961.

of the United States. Next in descending numerical strength were those associated with the Protestant Episcopal Church, the Seventh Day Adventists, the Church of God, the Unevangelized Fields Mission, the West Indies Mission, the indigenous Jacmel Baptist Church, and the World Evangelization Service.[136]

THE DOMINICAN REPUBLIC

The Dominican Republic emerged from the troubled nineteenth century only to fall into still more grave internal disorder and a financial morass. Occupation by United States marines from 1916 to 1924 was accompanied by gross abuses and by restlessness among the Dominicans. When the marines were withdrawn the most powerful force was a constabulary which had been trained by them. Backed by the constabulary, in 1930 their head, Rafael Leonidas Trujillo y Molina, made himself master of the country and ruled under ostensibly republican institutions. He retained the real power when, in 1952, his brother, Hector B. Trujillo y Molina, became president. Under the masterful hand of the first Trujillo marked improvements were wrought in the country. Internal order was restored, banditry and lawlessness were eliminated, the foreign and domestic debts of the government were paid, roads and public works were constructed, the capital, Santo Domingo rechristened Ciudad Trujillo, was made into an impressive modern city, industries were fostered, exports, mostly of sugar, coffee, and cacao, mounted, the cities were provided with pure water, hydroelectric plants were built, public health was improved, hospitals were erected, and schools so multiplied that by 1960 over half the population were literate. In 1961 the dictator was assassinated.

The Roman Catholic faith was the state religion. The Roman Catholic Church was subsidized, and although no concordat existed, friendly relations were maintained with the Vatican. The constitution of 1942 recognized Roman Catholicism as the religion of the majority. At the request of parents religious instruction could be given in the public schools. The clergy could teach in them but did not control them. Yet civil marriage was permitted and no restrictions were imposed on other religious bodies.[137]

Yet the population of nearly three millions, nominally Roman Catholic though it was, as late as 1957 was poorly supplied with clergy. The average was then only one priest for every 8,420 of the population, a ratio which was lower than in any other country in Latin America except Guatemala and Honduras. Of the 272 priests 77 were seculars and 195 were regulars. The country was said to have 655 sisters. Foreign priests were partly filling the near vacuum. Thus we hear in the 1950's of a priest of the Scarboro Foreign Missions of

[136] *World Christian Handbook, 1957*, p. 136.
[137] Bates, *Religious Liberty*, pp. 83, 223, 518.

Canada who had fostered a coöperative organization to aid in a rural valley; it had about 150 units and over 15,000 members. Missionaries also came from the United States. In 1957 four orders and congregations of men, mostly Redemptorists from New York City, and one congregation of women, Dominican sisters from Adrian, Michigan, were reported.[138] In 1957 a major seminary in Ciudad Trujillo, conducted by Jesuits, had ninety-nine students—half of the total of major seminarians in the entire Caribbean—and so gave promise of augmenting the clergy.[139] In 1960 the bishops had the courage, on the feast day of Our Lady of Grace, regarded as the protectress of the Dominican Republic, to issue a pastoral letter on behalf of the thousands of citizens imprisoned by the regime as revolutionary plotters. It stood up sturdily for the rights of individuals, which, it declared, took precedence over the rights of the state.[140]

Favoured by the official religious toleration, Protestantism grew, but in proportion to the population its adherents were not as numerous as in Haiti. In 1957 Protestant communicants were said to total 10,091 as against 9,647 in 1952. By far the largest number were Seventh Day Adventists, with Protestant Episcopalians and the Assemblies of God, each with slightly over 1,000 in 1957, the next in size.[141]

CUBA

Politically and in its economy Cuba was caught in the currents of the revolutionary age. Independence from Spain, won in 1898 by a combination of internal revolt and the intervention of the United States, was followed first by the military rule of the army of the United States (1898-1902) and then by the attempt of the northern neighbour under the so-called Platt Amendment to guide what it deemed its ward to efficient, honest, democratic self-government. The experiment was neither happy nor successful and in 1934 the Platt Amendment was abrogated and Cuba was left politically to its own devices. From 1934 to 1959 the island was under virtual dictatorship—although in various guises and always with the outward trappings of republican institutions. The dictator was Fulgencio Batista, who had risen from poverty by his skill in establishing control over the army. The ineptitude of the presidents who seemed to supplant him appeared to many to make him indispensable. He gave the island the best government it had yet known. Public works were pushed through on a large scale, the school system was enlarged, and for a time considerable liberty was

---

[138] Considine, *New Horizons,* pp. 290, 291, 330, 333, 352. On a Jesuit mission see Antonio L. De Santa Anna, *Mision Fronteriza . . . 1936-1957* (Dajabon, no publisher or date, pp. 81), *passim.*
[139] Allen, *op. cit.,* p. 470.
[140] *The New York Times,* February 3, 1960.
[141] *World Christian Handbook, 1957,* p. 131.

granted to the press. But in the later years of Batista's rule the press was muzzled, the university was closed because of the restlessness of its students, and critics either fled the country or were jailed. Revolt broke out, led by Fidel Castro. In 1959 Batista took refuge first in the Dominican Republic and then, with Portugal's permission, in Madeira. Castro increasingly flouted the United States, denouncing it as Cuba's exploiter and major enemy, and sought and obtained help from the U.S.S.R. and Communist China.

In its economy Cuba was more and more dominated by sugar. Its rich soil and its tropical climate favoured the raising of sugar cane, and most of the island's industry centred around the processing of the cane and its products. Tobacco was an important but minor export. Most of Cuba's export and import trade was with the United States. An arrangement with the latter country which gave Cuban sugar a favoured place in its markets and the extensive investment of private capital from the North stimulated the production of sugar and furthered the control of a large proportion of Cuban economy by absentee owners. One result was the progressive impoverishment of a growing section of the island's population. More and more of the land passed out of the hands of small proprietors into great estates. The seasonal nature of employment on the sugar plantations left most workers without wages during the larger part of the year. Society was marked by a sharp contrast between the extreme wealth of a small minority and the grinding misery of the majority, with a small middle class in between. Castro attempted to solve the problem by expropriating the lands and other holdings of citizens of the United States, by a redistribution of the land, by more and better schools, and by an extensive programme of building model housing for the underprivileged.

The population of Cuba, about six millions in the 1950's, was predominantly a mixture of white and Negro blood and had a minority of Negroes and a smaller minority of pure white stock. The Cuban mentality was said to differ not only from that of peoples of the United States but also from that of the rest of Latin America. Both the whites on the one hand, predominantly of Spanish descent, who were proud of their culture, maintained their separate traditions, and seldom intermarried with the Creoles, and the Negroes on the other hand, some of whom rose in education and civil and economic position but who seldom married with the Creole majority, formed distinct enclaves.[142]

The Roman Catholic Church in Cuba suffered from the long association with Spain. Before 1898 most of the clergy were from that country, and few Cubans entered the priesthood. After independence a similar condition persisted. As a result, in 1957 the ratio of priests to the population was one to every 8,145. The disproportion was greater than in any other country in Latin America except the Dominican Republic, Guatemala, and Honduras. Of the 514 priests in

---

[142] Davis, *The Cuban Church in a Sugar Economy*, pp. 35–39.

Cuba in 1946, only 82 were born in the country; 432 were from other countries —Spain, the United States, and Canada among them.[143] Although the overwhelming majority of the population were nominally Roman Catholics, few of the men went to church.[144] Spiritualism flourished in several of its many forms and African cults were popular among the Negroes. Some of the Spiritualists baptized children, had churches (in at least one city outnumbering Roman Catholic and Protestant churches), displayed images of saints on their altars, and believed in faith healing.[145] It was said that in 1942 in the Archdiocese of Havana, with a population of a million, only about 51,000 went to church on Sunday. Another estimate put the number of practising Roman Catholics in Havana in 1960 as 2 per cent. and reported only six churches in the city.[146]

Yet in the 1950's in several ways improvement was seen in the Roman Catholic Church's position. A few examples must serve to give a hint at the general trend. Between 1946 and 1957 the ratio of priests to the total population appears to have increased—from one to every 9,300[147] to one to every 8,145.[148] Preparation for the priesthood continued, although not for large numbers; in 1957 thirty-four students were said to be enrolled in two major seminaries.[149] In 1956 the attendance at church services was held to have improved markedly since 1920.[150] In 1950 the Cuban Congress formally recognized Villanova, the first private university in the island, a frankly Catholic institution under Augustinians from the United States.[151] In 1931 a Jesuit founded the *Agrupación Catolica Universitaria* (Group of Catholic University Students) in the University of Havana. It was both for fellowship and for service in an underprivileged area.[152] In 1957 twelve Augustinians from Villanova, Pennsylvania, and thirty sisters from the United States, most of them Dominicans from Albany, New York, were in Cuba.[153] Although the constitution of 1940 gave full freedom of religion, declared Church and state separated, and did not authorize a financial subvention to any cult, it invoked the favour of God, diplomatic relations were maintained with the Holy See, and in 1916, on petition of veterans of the war of independence, Gregory XV declared the Virgin of Charity

[143] Pattee, *El Catolicismo*, p. 175.

[144] Considine, *New Horizons*, pp. 278, 330.

[145] Davis, *The Cuban Church*, pp. 50, 51; authoritative information given to the author by a Cuban in 1955; Sumrall, *Through Blood and Fire in Latin America*, pp. 94–97.

[146] Pattee, *El Catolicismo*, p. 177; private information given to the author in 1960.

[147] Pattee, *El Catolicismo*, p. 175.

[148] Considine, *New Horizons*, p. 330.

[149] Allen, *op. cit.*, p. 470. But Gibbons, *Basic Ecclesiastical Statistics for Latin America, 1956*, p. 44, gives the number of seminaries in 1956 as forty-four, presumably not discriminating between those in major and minor seminaries.

[150] Considine, *New Horizons*, pp. 278, 279.

[151] *Ibid.*, pp. 312, 313.

[152] *Ibid.*, pp. 310, 311.

[153] *Ibid.*, pp. 351, 352.

of Corbe, whose image had been held in veneration since the seventeenth century, to be the patroness of Cuba.[154]

In 1959, 1960, and 1961 the Roman Catholic Church was in conflict with the Castro regime, especially because of the latter's association with Communism. In November, 1959, the first national Catholic congress, said to have been the greatest demonstration of Roman Catholic faith ever seen in Cuba, held in a stadium in Havana, erupted with cries of "Down with Communism," and the leader of the Catholic Youth Movement told the gathering that Catholic teaching could be summed up in "Totalitarian states, no; social justice, yes." Yet Castro, who had denounced the assembly as counter-revolutionary, sat through the mass in homage to the Virgin of Charity.[155] In August, 1960, the Archbishop of Havana declared that he would close all the churches in Cuba unless guarantees of safety were given for churchgoers to protect them from the gangs of jeering youths. That same month a pastoral letter of the hierarchy was read in the churches warning the faithful against the increasing advance of Communism in the country.[156] Later in the year youthful demonstrators attempted to interrupt a service in the Havana cathedral.[157] In May, 1961, Castro declared that all foreign-born priests must leave the country unless given special permission to remain. Many of the clergy were Spaniards and Castro denounced them as Falangists. Several priests were arrested. Priests and nuns were departing and Church schools were said to be seized and closed by the authorities.[158] Presumably much of the opposition to the Roman Catholic Church came from the fact that a large part of its income was derived from lands which it had acquired in colonial times and from the fees charged by its clergy for the sacraments.[159]

Protestantism in Cuba had gained a slight foothold before 1898, but its major growth came after that year. It owed its existence to missionaries from the United States and in the 1950's continued to derive much of its financial support from the Protestants of that country. In 1942 it was said to have a membership of about 40,000 and a community of about 150,000.[160] In 1952 communicants were reported to be 38,620 and the community to total 165,622. In 1957 the corresponding figures were 47,955 and 215,732. Numerically the leading denomination was Baptist. It had originated among the Northern, Southern, and Free Will Baptists of the United States. Next were the Epis-

[154] Pattee, *El Catolicismo*, pp. 73, 174, 177.

[155] *The New York Times*, November 30, 1959.

[156] *Ibid.*, August 10, 1960. See also an earlier pastoral letter to the same effect, *ibid.*, May 18, 1960.

[157] *Ibid.*, November 14, 1960.

[158] *Ibid.*, May 8, 1961; *Ecumenical Press Service*, May 26, 1961.

[159] Davis, *The Cuban Church*, p. 80.

[160] *Ibid.*, p. 52.

copalians, the Methodists and the Presbyterians, in that order.[161] By a comity arrangement the major denominations made themselves responsible for particular portions of the country but two or more were represented in the main cities. The large majority of the Protestants were in the cities: rural areas were relatively untouched. Since most Protestants were from the lower middle class and from the humbler elements of society, few Protestant congregations were fully self-supporting financially. Protestants increasingly turned over pastoral and other leadership to Cubans. In 1957, for example, of the 381 ordained men only 90 were foreign, and of the lay staff of 430 only 42 were aliens. The missionaries from the United States were largely engaged in teaching and in administration. Protestants placed much emphasis on education and in the 1940's several of the schools with the highest reputation were founded and maintained by them.[162] Some of the Cuban churches had home mission societies which attempted to plant their faith in rural areas. In spite of the numerical growth, a chronic erosion in membership was noted. Many became inactive or drifted away entirely. The reported totals apparently took account of this fact, and the numbers of people once associated with Protestantism and to a greater or less extent influenced by it were much larger than those in the statistical tables.[163] Academically the strongest Protestant theological seminary in Cuba was a union institution at Matanzas supported by Methodists, Episcopalians, and Presbyterians. Founded in 1947, it drew its students from seven Latin American countries and in 1957 was considered the most vigorous of the Protestant theological schools in the Caribbean and Central American areas.[164]

PUERTO RICO

Puerto Rico, annexed by the United States in 1898 as an outcome of the Spanish-American War, presented some of the economic problems of Cuba. It had a rapidly growing population—mounting from 1,869,255 in 1940 to 2,210,703 in 1950 and to an estimated 2,340,000 in 1959. This meant a density of nearly 684 a square mile. Like Cuba, its economy was predominantly agricultural, with its chief product sugar and with coffee as a secondary crop. Exports also included tobacco, pineapples, grapefruit, coconuts, and winter vegetables. The emphasis upon sugar meant, as in Cuba, brief seasonal employment with low wages, extreme poverty, undernourishment, and disease. In contrast with Cuba, however, Puerto Rico had something of a relief to its population pressure in

---

[161] *World Christian Handbook, 1957*, p. 130.
[162] *Ibid.*; Davis, *The Cuban Church*, pp. 52–80.
[163] Davis, *The Cuban Church*, p. 56.
[164] Allen, *op. cit.*, pp. 183, 184; Elwyn A. Smith, *Report to the Seminario Evangelico de Teologia* (Matanzas, March 30, 1960, mimeographed).

unrestricted emigration to the mainland of the United States. Thousands made their way there, mainly to cities on the north-eastern seacoast—New York in particular.

Valiant efforts were put forth by the Government of the United States to improve the situation. The Puerto Rico Reconstruction Administration sought to promote a better way of life. Although most of the more fertile lands were in the hands of a few large companies and estates, after 1934 the number of small cane growers increased. Education was furthered.

The advances were continued under the self-governing Commonwealth. Puerto Rico made a large step towards that status when in 1947 the Congress of the United States authorized it to elect its governor and a legislature. In 1951 Puerto Rico voted for full autonomy and in 1952 a constitution of its own framing was proclaimed. Under that document it remained voluntarily associated with the United States. Progress continued in a number of directions. By 1960, 82 per cent. of the population from six to eighteen years of age were enrolled in public, private, day, and night schools, and higher education was burgeoning—through the state University of Puerto Rico, a Protestant and a Roman Catholic university, and a Roman Catholic college.

A survey made in 1941 estimated that the Roman Catholic Church, inherited from Spanish days, was the professed religion of 94 per cent. of the population, that 4 per cent. were Protestants, and that 2 per cent. were Spiritualists. Church attendance was claimed by 62 per cent. of the Roman Catholics and 81.3 per cent. of the Protestants.[165] Increasingly personnel to staff the Roman Catholic Church came from the mainland of the United States. In 1957 priests and lay brothers from that source totalled 186 and women 385. Yet in the same year there was only one priest to every 5,800 of the allegedly Roman Catholic population, a lower proportion than in any South American country; in the rest of Latin America only the Dominican Republic, Cuba, Guatemala, Honduras, and El Salvador had a lower ratio. Yet, thanks largely to the efforts of the mainlanders, by 1957 a system of parochial schools had been started. In 1948 sisters from the mainland opened the college for women which became the nucleus of a rapidly growing Catholic university. The Legion of Mary, organized in 1949, was noted for the fashion in which its members by house-to-house visitation encouraged more faithful observance of religious duties, including the solemnizing of marriages by the Church. The Association of Catholic Social Action, founded in 1953, was a large organization. So was the group called the Brothers of Joseph, begun in 1898 and receiving official approval in 1927; it sought to deepen the faith in rural districts. A beginning was made in raising up an indigenous clergy. In 1957 seminarians were said to number

[165] Davis, *The Church in Puerto Rico's Dilemma*, p. 9.

thirty-one, but in proportion to the population they were fewer than in Cuba, Haiti, or the Dominican Republic.[166]

In 1960 a clash occurred between the state and the Roman Catholic Church. At that time the governor, Luis Muñoz Marin, was seeking reëlection. Although he was professedly a Roman Catholic, the three bishops in a pastoral letter forbade the faithful to vote for him and his party chiefly on the ground that he was not standing for religious instruction in the public schools, that he was promoting birth control, and that he advocated the legalizing of common-law marriages. In spite of the episcopal opposition and a small Christian Action party organized by the bishops, the governor was retained in office by an overwhelming vote of the electorate.[167]

As was to be expected from the connexion with the United States, Puerto Rico saw a substantial growth of Protestants. In 1941 the total membership was 32,122 and the constituency was estimated at 81,854.[168] In 1952 the communicants were reported to be 44,279 and the Protestant community 137,185. In 1957 the totals had mounted to 48,136 communicants and a constituency of 147,441.[169] This was higher in proportion to the population than in any other Latin American country except Brazil. Some Roman Catholic priests became Protestants and several entered the Protestant ministry.[170] In 1957 the denomination which reported the largest membership was the (Pentecostal) Assemblies of God. Next were the Baptists, then the Disciples of Christ, then the Presbyterians, followed closely by the United Evangelicals and the Methodists.[171] Through an early comity arrangement, respected by all the major denominations except the Seventh Day Adventists and the Pentecostals, responsibility for a particular area was assigned to one of them and only in the large cities was more than one represented. Financial self-support progressed and in 1942 had been attained by about a third of the congregations. That fraction was enlarged by the policy of the Seventh Day Adventists and the Pentecostals, most of whose churches were fully self-sustaining. Six denominations joined in supporting the Union Theological Seminary on the outskirts of San Juan across the street from the University of Puerto Rico. Other institutions and projects were maintained, among them the Polytechnic Institute of Puerto Rico, a farm project connected with a hospital, and a social settlement in a depressed area. The majority of the Protestants were from the lower income brackets of the population and early in the 1940's two-thirds of them were in debt.[172]

[166] Considine, *New Horizons,* pp. 273, 281, 314–318, 330, 333, 354, 355; Bates, *The Lay Apostolate in Latin America Today,* pp. 56–66.
[167] *The New York Times,* October 22, 29, and November 9, 1960.
[168] Davis, *The Church in Puerto Rico's Dilemma,* p. 13.
[169] *World Christian Handbook, 1957,* p. 145.
[170] First-hand confidential information given to the author, December, 1955.
[171] *World Christian Handbook, 1957,* p. 145.
[172] Davis, *The Church in Puerto Rico's Dilemma,* pp. 13, 14, 16, 31, 32, 47–52.

The French Island Possessions

We need only two sentences to summarize the situation in Guadelupe and Martinique, islands which in the twentieth as in the nineteenth century were French possessions.[173] They continued to be served chiefly by French personnel. They were still overwhelmingly Roman Catholic, in 1957 were moderately supplied with priests (on an average one for every 2,570 of the population), had twenty-three seminarians preparatory to an indigenous clergy, and had nearly 5,000 students in 17 schools.[174]

Venezuela

After its stormy course in the nineteenth century,[175] the Roman Catholic Church in Venezuela was not in a good position to face the twentieth-century stage of the revolutionary age. The drastic measures of Guzmán Blanco had greatly weakened it. Although under his successor, Cipriano Castro, a rough soldier who held power from 1899 to 1908, a constitution was adopted (1904) which declared the Roman Catholic religion to be that of the nation, and the state contributed to the support of the Church, the government insisted on the right of patronage.[176] Moreover, Castro, dictatorial, corrupt, and dissolute, was not a man either to tolerate independence in the Church or to encourage its religious mission. He was followed by Juan Vicente Gómez, who dominated the country from 1909 until his death in 1935. Hard-working, sparing in food and drink, the father of many illegitimate children, he imposed internal peace, paid off the national debt, maintained friendly relations with the powers, and saw to it that both he and the country profited from the taxes levied on the foreign companies which were exploiting the enormous oil resources. Coffee also proved a valuable export.

Under Gómez the Roman Catholic Church made some gains. As a partial compensation for its insistence on the right of patronage the state increased its still meagre financial subsidies to the Church. Although it had no concordat with Rome, Venezuela maintained a diplomatic representative at the Vatican and the Papal nuncio was the dean of the diplomatic corps in Caracas. The Roman Catholic Church was not formally established, but in fact it was the state church. In 1923 four new bishoprics were erected and one bishopric was raised to aň archbishopric. All foreign ecclesiastics were required to be naturalized and several who did not comply with the rule were deported, but to make good the deficiency in native-born clergy some were admitted from abroad.

---

[173] Volume III, p. 317.
[174] Considine, *New Horizons*, pp. 330, 336. See slightly different figures in Gibbons, *op. cit.*, p. 47.
[175] Volume III, pp. 318–321.
[176] Mecham, *Church and State in Latin America*, pp. 135, 136.

Church schools continued but enrolled only about one-tenth as many as the public schools. Religious instruction could be given in the latter if the parents of ten children of the same faith requested it.[177]

In the twenty-five years after the death of Gómez the Roman Catholic Church continued to make some advance. The political scene was turbulent. For several years two army officers in succession were all but dictators under the guise of president. Then for a time democracy appeared to be making progress. *Acción Democratica*, a leftist but not Communist party, gained control (1945), and in 1947 what was said to have been the first popular and honest presidential election put its candidate in the presidential chair. But in 1948 a military *junta* seized the upper hand. In 1952 one of its members, Marcos Pérez Jiménez, made himself president. In 1958 he was ousted by a revolt. Late that year Rómulo Betancourt, the candidate of the anti-Communist elements in the *Acción Democratica*, was elected president and took office early in 1959. The income from the vast mineral wealth, petroleum and iron ore, was utilized to erect public buildings and to construct roads. The rich minority became richer and some improvement was made in the living standards of the poverty-stricken masses. Meantime the clergy increased from about 300 secular and 356 regular priests in 1951[178] to 477 seculars and 578 regulars in 1956.[179] The total members of women's congregations appears to have risen from 1,535 in 1951[180] to 2,201 in 1956.[181] In spite of the growth in the number of clergy, in 1957 the ratio was an average of one priest to every 5,396 Roman Catholics,[182] which was less favourable than in any other country in South America except Brazil. But in the 1940's Catholic Action was seeking to awaken the consciences of the masses and to develop intellectual leaders.[183] In 1960 Spanish Capuchins were using airplanes to make contacts with a hitherto inaccessible tribe of Indians.[184]

Under the constitutional provision of religious liberty, Protestantism in Venezuela showed a substantial growth. In 1924 the number of baptized Protestants was given as 1,557.[185] In 1929 communicants numbered 2,310,[186] in 1952 they were said to have been 5,943, and in 1957 the number was given as 8,690. The Protestant community was reported to have risen from 13,775 in 1952 to 17,766

---

[177] *Ibid.*, pp. 134–139; Watters, *A History of the Church in Venezuela, 1810–1930*, pp. 217–219; Pattee, *El Catolicismo*, pp. 459–471.

[178] Pattee, *El Catolicismo*, p. 461.

[179] Gibbons, *op. cit.*, p. 41. But Considine, *New Horizons*, p. 331, gives the number of seculars in 1957 as 405 and of regulars as 542.

[180] Pattee, *El Catolicismo*, p. 461.

[181] Gibbons, *op. cit.*, p. 41.

[182] Considine, *New Horizons*, p. 328.

[183] *The Catholic Historical Review*, Vol. XXV, p. 468 (January, 1941).

[184] *Worldmission Fides Service*, September 4, 1960.

[185] Beach and Fahs, *World Missionary Atlas*, p. 77.

[186] Grubb, *The Northern Republics of South America*, p. 107.

in 1957.[187] The largest numbers and the most striking increase had been of the Canadian Brethren (usually called "Plymouth Brethren" by others), the Evangelical Alliance, and the Seventh Day Adventists.[188] In general, most of the bodies represented had similar theological positions. This, and the fact that several of the bodies had agreed to the allocation of territory to prevent overlapping, contributed to coöperation. Much emphasis was placed on the printed page, including periodicals and the Bible, but fewer schools were maintained than in some other Latin American republics.[189]

<h2 style="text-align:center">COLOMBIA</h2>

Colombia, as we have seen,[190] presented a quite different picture religiously from Venezuela. The conflict between Liberals and Conservatives had often been acute, but from 1880 until after 1914 the Conservatives were in power. Although Church and state were formally separated, a concordat had been entered into (1887) with the Vatican, religious instruction in the schools, colleges, and universities was required and through texts endorsed by the ecclesiastical authorities, and the approval of the latter was necessary for texts in other subjects. Religious orders were permitted. Criticism of the Roman Catholic Church was common among Liberal intellectuals but was not crassly materialistic and sought a spiritualized interpretation of life.[191] In 1930 the Liberals came to power and in 1942 they obtained a modification of the concordat of 1887. The revision ended the clerical control of education and required bishops to be Colombian citizens.[192]

In 1946 the Conservatives once more took over. After a period of tumult Laureano Gómez became not only president but, in effect, dictator as well (1950). The press was throttled, civil disorder was rife, and freedom of worship largely disappeared. In 1953 Gómez was unseated by Gustavo Rojas Pinilla, for a time regional fighting subsided, the freedom of the press was restored, and, thanks in part to high prices for coffee, the major export, and the rising exploitation of the petroleum resources, large public works were undertaken. Yet the lull was only temporary. Internal disturbances again broke out, Rojas Pinilla curbed the press, the nation's foreign credit fell sharply, and the development of transportation and industrialization was slowed. Rojas Pinilla met with strong

---

[187] *World Christian Handbook, 1957*, p. 149.
[188] *Ibid.* On a mission to the Indians on the edge of Venezuela, Brazil, and British Guiana, see Elizabeth Buhler Cott, *Trailing the Davis Indians* (Mountain View, Calif., Pacific Press Publishing Association, 1936, pp. 95), *passim.*
[189] Grubb, *The Northern Republics,* pp. 112, 113; Wheeler and Browning, *Modern Missions on the Spanish Main,* p. 292.
[190] Volume III, pp. 322–324.
[191] Wheeler and Browning, *op. cit.,* pp. 252, 253.
[192] Herring, *A History of Latin America,* p. 490.

opposition, including that of the Roman Catholic Church. In 1957 a group of army officers forced him to leave the country, and a coalition of Liberals and Conservatives formed the National Front and controlled the government. Attempts to unseat the coalition by force were put down. In 1959 the economic situation was improving, labour organizations were favoured, and in the towns and villages the populace was encouraged to improve their community life by providing schools and small-scale public works. Population, estimated to be 13,823,600, was increasing. About a third of the population were white, slightly less than two-thirds were a mixture, about a twentieth were Negro, and a still smaller percentage was Indian.

In spite of the disorder which punctuated much of the first half of the twentieth century the Roman Catholic Church displayed marked vitality. As in much of the rest of Latin America, a vast gulf separated the rich from the poor, but outwardly the country was Catholic, public forms of religion were observed in a way which confirmed that impression, national Eucharistic Congresses were held in 1913 and 1935, the year 1919 saw a Marian congress, and in the 1930's congresses were convened of Catholic youth and young Catholic workers. Catholic Action was organized in 1934, and in 1936 a Catholic university was founded in Medellin, next to Bogotá the largest city in the country and the centre of Roman Catholic conservatism. Missions were carried on among the Indian minority, and by 1940 in a region where fifty years earlier the Indian population was savage and pagan the large majority were said to have become Roman Catholics and to be advancing in civilization.[193]

In the 1940's a priest, José Joaquin Salcedo, inaugurated a plan in a mountain parish which by the end of the 1950's had taken on national dimensions. By means of broadcasting through a radio station and of receivers in the homes he fostered religious devotion and set up schools for teaching the illiterates. To enable the method to reach the many rural communities in the country as a whole the *Acción Cultural Popular* (the Popular Education Movement) was created with headquarters in Bogotá. From there by 1957 about 6,500 radio schools were conducted, mostly in the mountain regions. Each school enrolled ten to twenty under a leader. To participate, a family was required to buy a receiving set; thus the pauperizing of the recipients was discouraged. Instruction came over the air. Its purpose was to fight illiteracy and to give religious instruction. The radio also encouraged and directed athletic sports and furthered education in agriculture, health, and domestic economy.[194] The Roman Catholic Church developed in Colombia the largest educational system under Church auspices in any country in Latin America. It was particularly strong on the

193 *The Catholic Historical Review*, Vol. XXVI, pp. 215–221 (July, 1940). See also Karl Boxler, *Indianer Missionar* (Wartensee Rorschacherberg, Switzerland, Missions-Franzikanerinnen, 1953, pp. 268), *passim*.
194 Considine, *New Horizons*, pp. 219–228.

secondary level and in 1957 embraced about two-thirds of the secondary schools.[195] In 1927 the Yarumel Foreign Mission Seminary was organized, the only one of its kind in South America. Its graduates confined their efforts to Colombia, operating in four mission territories in that country.[196] In 1944 the bishops organized *Coördinación Social,* for a comprehensive approach to the social problems of the country. In connexion with it various movements were carried on, among them the *Federación Agraria Nacional,* to promote the well-being of the agricultural population. Many charitable institutions were maintained, some of them with subventions from the government.[197]

With all this vigour, in 1957 the Roman Catholic Church in Colombia had a ratio of only one priest to every 3,574 of its adherents. Yet that was better than in any other country in South America except Ecuador and Chile. Slightly more than half the priests were seculars.[198] To prepare an indigenous clergy 19 major seminaries were maintained which in 1957 enrolled 1,001 students. In addition 8 scholasticates enrolled 404, who were presumably headed for the regular priesthood.[199]

Protestantism had heavy going in Colombia. In spite of the fact that the constitution of 1887 guaranteed freedom from molestation on account of one's religious beliefs and liberty of worship which was not contrary to Christian morality,[200] and although the revision of the constitution under Liberal influence reaffirmed and strengthened this provision (in theory a parent could obtain the exemption of his children from the instruction in the Roman Catholic faith which was required in the schools), in practice Colombia was admitted by at least one Roman Catholic authority to be the most Catholic and the least tolerant of any of the South American states.[201] In the 1940's and 1950's severe persecution broke out against Protestants. It was partly a phase of the contest between Liberals and Conservatives and of the civil strife which characterized those years. Several Protestant churches were destroyed and numbers of pastors and their congregations were terrorized. Some missionaries sought refuge in Venezuela.[202] Efforts were made by Protestants, including the International Missionary Council and the World Council of Churches, to bring the situation to the attention of the world and to prevent the continuation of the terror.[203] After a seeming lull in the opening months of Rojas Pinilla's regime, violence

---

[195] *Ibid.,* p. 228.
[196] *Ibid.,* p. 230.
[197] Pattee, *El Catolicismo,* p. 148.
[198] Considine, *New Horizons,* pp. 326, 331.
[199] Allen, *A Seminary Survey,* p. 473.
[200] Mecham, *op. cit.,* p. 156.
[201] Bates, *Religious Liberty,* p. 82.
[202] *The International Review of Missions,* Vol. XXXIX, p. 58 (January, 1951); Vol. XLII, p. 51 (January, 1953); William C. Easton, *Colombian Conflict* (London, Christian Literature Crusade, 1954, pp. 85), *passim.*
[203] *The International Review of Missions,* Vol. XLII, p. 51 (January, 1953).

again broke out. Much of it was led by priests. Some Protestant schools were closed, services were interrupted, and Bibles were confiscated. In the eight years 1948–1956 about 46 church buildings were destroyed, 75 individuals were killed because of their faith, and over 200 primary and secondary Protestant schools were closed by the government—and this in the face of the statement of the Colombian National Secretariat of the Roman Catholic bishops that "destructive force" was "never justifiable."[204] In explanation of the persecution, Roman Catholics cited what they charged were offensive acts by tactless Protestant missionaries.

Protestantism grew. In 1924 baptized Protestants were reported to total 2,866 and the Protestant community was said to number 3,567.[205] In 1952 the corresponding figures were 11,325 and 30,186 and in 1957 they were 14,325 and 45,405.[206] Numerically the largest bodies were the Seventh Day Adventists, with more than a third of the communicants, followed first by the Presbyterians, then by the Southern Baptists of the United States, and then by the Christian and Missionary Alliance.[207] Delay was experienced in giving an adequate training to a Colombian ministry. In 1957 it was said that only one Protestant theological school existed in Colombia. It had been opened in 1953 by the Southern Baptists and in 1957 had twenty-five students from Colombia and Ecuador.[208]

ECUADOR

Ecuador, the smallest of the South American republics except Uruguay, had a mounting population. In 1930 an estimate placed the total at 1,785,000.[209] The official census of 1950 gave it as 3,202,757, an estimate of 1955 said 3,675,000, and one of 1959 reported the total as 4,116,451.[210] The population was about a tenth white, about two-fifths Indian, approximately two-fifths mestizo, and about a tenth Negro, mulatto, and other racial strains. The highlands in which the capital, Quito, was situated had the majority of the inhabitants.

Politically, during most of the second half of the nineteenth century, as we saw in the preceding volume, Ecuador was in the hands of the Conservatives.[211] Their great leader, García Moreno, dominant from 1860 to his assassination in 1875, sought to purify the Roman Catholic Church and to make of the country an embodiment of its faith. For twenty years after his death Ecuador was in a state of chronic civil war, brigandage, and economic depression from which

204 *Ibid.*, Vol. XLIX, p. 59 (January, 1960); Allen, *op. cit.*, p. 177.
205 Beach and Fahs, *op. cit.*, p. 77.
206 *World Christian Handbook, 1957*, p. 128.
207 *Ibid.*
208 Allen, *op. cit.*, p. 190.
209 Grubb, *The Northern Republics*, p. 18.
210 *Britannica Book of the Year, 1957*, p. 279; *1960*, p. 216.
211 Volume III, pp. 325–327.

a rapid succession of Conservative dictators sought to rescue it. In 1895 the Liberals seized power and in the constitution promulgated in 1906 effected the partial separation of Church and state, guaranteed liberty of conscience, made primary education obligatory but recognized the right of parents to give their children whatever kind of education they wished, and forbade state aid to schools which were not official. The constitution of 1929 continued the provision for freedom of worship. In 1927 the immigration of foreign clergy or lay religious workers was forbidden. In the mid-1920's about 15 per cent. of the private schools and most of the secondary education were in the hands of the Church.[212] In 1937 a *modus vivendi* was reached between the government and the Vatican which renewed the diplomatic relations that had been broken by the partial separation of Church and state through the constitution of 1906.[213] Beginning in 1944 the state was dominated by José María Velasco Ibarra until he was exiled by the army in 1947. But, with varying vicissitudes, Velasco Ibarra, theoretically a Liberal, returned to power and in 1956 ended a four-year term as president. He was followed by Camilo Ponce Énriguez, a Conservative who found it necessary to govern through a coalition cabinet and could not enact Conservative ecclesiastical measures, even if he had so desired.

Except for about 200,000 pagan Indians, most of them in jungle fastnesses in the eastern part of the country and on the upper reaches of the tributaries of the Amazon, and for the few Protestants, in 1962 the population of Ecuador was professedly Roman Catholic. To care for it, in 1957, 1,184 priests were serving, an average of one priest to every 3,027 Roman Catholics. More than half of the priests were regulars. They were supplemented by 2,429 sisters. A total of 160 seminarians was reported in 1957.[214]

Protestantism was slow in making its way in Ecuador, partly because of the conservative attitude of the people and partly because the terrain made access difficult. In 1929 only 290 communicants and a Protestant community of from 300 to 400 were reported.[215] By the 1950's the numbers had markedly increased —in 1952 to 1,862 and 3,894, and five years later to 2,669 and 4,888. In 1957 the largest staff, both foreign and Ecuadorian, and two-fifths of the communicants were those of the Christian and Missionary Alliance, which had been in the country since at least 1897. Next in its foreign personnel but third in its total of communicants was the Gospel Missionary Union, the first Protestant body to establish itself in Ecuador (it had a representative in Guayaquil in 1896);

---

212 Mecham, *op. cit.*, pp. 190, 191.

213 Juan Ignacio Larrea, *La Iglesia y el Estado en el Ecuador (La Personalidad de la Iglesia en el Modus Vivendi Celebrado entre la Santa Sede y el Ecuador)* (Seville, Escuela de Estudios Hispano-Americanos de Sevilla, 1954, pp. xi, 168), *passim*.

214 Considine, *New Horizons*, pp. 328, 331. Allen, *op. cit.*, pp. 478, 479, says that in 1957 major seminary students, in one seminary in Quito under the direction of Lazarists, numbered 115, and that 10 scholasticates were training 184 men for the regular clergy.

215 Grubb, *The Northern Republics*, p. 34.

second in communicants were the Seventh Day Adventists, who had entered the country in 1904.[216] The Voice of the Andes (*La Voz de los Andes*), a powerful radio station (HCJB) in Quito, in which in the mid-1950's a number of societies coöperated, broadcasted twenty-four hours a day seven days a week in seven languages under a contract with the government (1931). Its programmes included not only daily prayers, Bible lessons, meditations, hymns, and church news, but also sessions of congress, government information, and cultural, educational, and entertainment features.[217] Here, too, the Wycliffe Bible Translators were represented, their purpose being to reduce languages to writing, translate the Bible into them, and by radio and airplane keep in touch with their missionaries in remote fastnesses among non-Christian, primitive Indians.

Attempts to reach the Aucas, an Indian tribe in the jungle near the headwaters of tributaries of the Amazon, led to a disaster which aroused wide interest. Five men representing "faith missions" in the United States attempted by flights over their territory to win the confidence of the Aucas, a people feared by their Indian neighbours because of their fierceness and their hatred of strangers. In January, 1956, all five were killed.[218]

PERU

Peru, the centre of the pre-Columbian Inca empire and of the Spanish viceroyalty which succeeded it, in 1959 had an estimated population of 10,524,000. About half were Indians, about a third mestizos, or *cholos* as the Peruvians called them, and about a tenth whites of Spanish descent. Here, as elsewhere in much of Latin America, the extremes of wealth and poverty were marked. In Lima, for example, with a population of more than one million in 1961, the traveller saw on the one hand palatial hotels, imposing public buildings, and a residential section of homes with every evidence of comfort and wealth and on the other hand a slum scarcely matched elsewhere on the planet for abject

[216] *Ibid.*, pp. 33, 34, 124; *Christian World Handbook, 1957*, p. 132; W. F. Jordan, *Ecuador, A Story of Missionary Achievement* (New York, The Christian Alliance Publishing Co., 1926, pp. 130), *passim.*

[217] Rycroft, *Indians of the High Andes*, pp. 302, 303; Clarence W. Jones, *Radio, the New Missionary* (Chicago, Moody Press, 1946, pp. 147), *passim;* Considine, *New Horizons*, p. 256. For a broadcaster in Spanish, Manuel Garrido Aldama, a Basque and former Roman Catholic priest, see Sumrall, *Through Blood and Fire in Latin America*, pp. 50–57.

[218] Elisabeth Elliot, *Through Gates of Splendour* (New York, Harper & Brothers, 1957, pp. 256), *passim;* Elisabeth Elliot, *Shadow of the Almighty. The Life and Testament of Jim Elliot* (New York, Harper & Brothers, 1958, pp. 256), *passim;* Russell T. Hitt, *Jungle Pilot. The Life and Witness of Nate Saint* (New York, Harper & Brothers, 1959, pp. 303), *passim.* For efforts to renew the mission to the Aucas after that disaster, see Ethel Emily Wallis, *The Dayuma Story. Life under the Auca Spears* (New York, Harper & Brothers, 1960, pp. 288), *passim;* Elisabeth Elliot, *The Savage My Kinsman* (New York, Harper & Brothers, 1961, pp. 159), *passim;* mimeographed letter, Quito, December, 1960, Don and Jeanne Smith of the Wycliffe Bible Translators.

poverty and physical and moral degradation. Here, too, was the chronic contest between Conservatives and Liberals, with dictators under the guise of presidents, and efforts, with a degree of progressive achievement, at honesty and free elections in government and improvement in education and physical well-being for the masses. Augusto B. Leguía, president from 1908 to 1912 and dictator from 1919 to 1930, in a constitution framed in 1920 provided for the direct election of the president and members of congress and gave the right to vote to all males over twenty-one years of age. He also in theory abolished serfdom and made citizens of all who had once been serfs, organized schools, and constructed highways and railroads. But radicals and Liberals denounced him for his tyranny and his favours to the Church. An outspoken radical, Manuel González Prada (1848-1918), believed that Christianity and the professed republic were lies. One of his disciples, Victor Raúl Haya de la Torre, exiled for his views, organized APRA (*Alianza Popular Revolucionaria Americana*), which demanded the nationalization of land and industry, resistance to the "imperialism" of the United States, and the union of labourers and intellectuals. In 1930 Leguía was succeeded by Sánchez Cerro, who was assassinated in 1933. Oscar Benavides, who followed him, outlawed APRA. Manuel Prado y Ugarteche, president from 1939 to 1945, allowed Haya de la Torre to return. José Luis Bustamente, elected in 1945 by the Liberals and adherents of APRA, now renamed *Partido del Pueblo* (People's Party), was ousted by the Conservatives. The latter placed Manuel Odría in power (1948). Odría suppressed the *apristas,* as the members of the former APRA were called, and Haya de la Torre found a haven in the Colombian embassy. Odría sought to promote order and permitted a free election which in 1956 placed Manuel Prado in the president's chair. Prado permitted APRA to resume its legal existence.

During these various changes in the government the Roman Catholic Church remained the church of the nation. Not until the constitution of 1920 was the public exercise of any other religious cult formally permitted. That constitution granted full liberty of conscience and religion.[219] Before 1926 the president and congress insisted on their right to present to the Pope the names of bishops, but in that year the constitution was amended to give the Vatican the right to appoint directly to those posts.[220] The constitution of 1933 declared that although the state was non-confessional it protected the "Catholic Apostolic and Roman religion."[221] The state continued to give subventions to the Roman Catholic Church and permitted it to hold real estate. No serious movement developed to expropriate its vast holdings. Although the Church was granted no authority over state schools, instruction in the Roman Catholic religion was required in

[219] Mecham, *op. cit.,* p. 202.
[220] *Ibid.,* p. 207.
[221] Pattee, *El Catolicismo,* pp. 379, 380.

them. National and diocesan Eucharistic Congresses were held. In spite of much anti-clerical sentiment, religious indifferentism among the men, and lack of respect for the rank and file of the secular clergy, in the mid-twentieth century the Roman Catholic Church was a factor to be reckoned with in politics and was ardently supported by many of the women.[222]

Under these favouring circumstances, some observers declared Peru to be the most Catholic country in Latin America. In the twentieth century Catholic Action was vigorous, instituted by the episcopate in 1935 at the first national Eucharistic Congress, and *Opus Dei* was organized, an almost exclusively lay movement to improve the moral and religious quality of the laity. Social service on the parish level was promoted. Benavides founded a National Social Service School and its directors saw to it that it maintained a distinctly Catholic atmosphere.[223] In 1958 the Archbishop of Lima established the *Mision de Lima,* of fifteen priests, mostly seculars, to promote the welfare of the working classes and to raise the living standards of the poor.[224]

Yet in 1957 the number of Peruvian clergy was palpably insufficient to give adequate pastoral care. In that year the ratio was one priest to every 5,107 Roman Catholics, a paucity which was exceeded in South America only by Brazil, Venezuela, and Paraguay; the ratio was better, however, than in Guatemala, Honduras, Panama, Cuba, the Dominican Republic, Haiti, and Puerto Rico. Less than half the priests in Peru were seculars.[225] The majority of the clergy were foreign and more of them were from Spain than from any other country.[226] In 1957 seventy-seven of the priests were from the United States, more than half of them Maryknollers. Maryknoll Sisters totalled fourteen, and the Sister Servants of the Immaculate Heart of Mary of West Chester, Pennsylvania, numbered thirty-eight.[227] Efforts were being made to remedy the shortage of Peruvian clergy, and in 1957 students in major seminaries totalled 257, two-thirds of them in San Toribio, said to be the oldest seminary in the Western Hemisphere and conducted by the Holy Spirit Fathers of Mexico.[228]

Protestantism met determined opposition in Peru from some Roman Catholics. The long imprisonment of Penzotti (1889–1891) and the successful struggle for his release[229] helped to break down barriers. From time to time priests stirred up their parishioners to mob action, and pastoral letters condemning Protestant activities led to violence by some of the clergy. In 1945 a Supreme

---

[222] Mecham, *op. cit.,* pp. 208–219; Pattee, *El Catolicismo,* pp. 381, 382.

[223] Considine, *New Horizons,* pp. 207–212; Pattee, *El Catolicismo,* p. 401.

[224] *Worldmission Fides Service,* December 17, 1958.

[225] Considine, *New Horizons,* pp. 328–331. See also Pattee, *El Catolicismo,* pp. 395, 396.

[226] Considine, *New Horizons,* p. 209.

[227] *Ibid.,* pp. 343, 344; Maria del Rey, *In and Out the Andes,* pp. 189–203.

[228] Allen, *op. cit.,* p. 479. Considine, *New Horizons,* p. 209, gives the enrollment of San Toribio in 1957 as "some 300," against the 169 given by Allen.

[229] Volume III, p. 329.

Decree forbade non-Catholic propaganda in public places and gave local officials grounds for prohibiting Sunday Schools, Daily Vacation Bible Schools, and even prayer meetings and family worship in private homes.[230]

In spite of opposition, Protestantism grew. Early in the 1920's communicants and baptized non-communicants were said to total 4,568.[231] In 1940 the government census reported Protestants as numbering 54,818 and an independent count by the National Evangelical Council showed 4,322 in full communion and 6,659 others who had made a profession of faith but were not yet admitted to the Communion.[232] In 1952 communicants were said to be 25,151 and the Protestant community was reported to number 68,180. Five years later the corresponding figures were 28,922 and 72,789.[233] In 1957 the Seventh Day Adventists had by far the largest membership, followed at some distance by the indigenous *Iglesia Evangelica Peruana* (Peruvian Evangelical Church), which was Baptist in doctrine and Presbyterian in government. The Assemblies of God had the most places of worship and, next to the Wycliffe Bible Translators, the biggest staff.[234] The Wycliffe Bible Translators, renamed the Summer Institute of Linguistics, in 1945 entered into an agreement with the Government of Peru for the reduction to writing of the languages of tribes across the Andes in the upper reaches of the Amazon tributaries, the translation of the Bible into those tongues, and the provision of primers for bi-lingual schools to promote literacy. In 1957 the Institute was represented in twenty-nine tribes. In that year it had a staff of 180, including experts in linguistics and radio and aviation technicians, the latter to keep in touch with the outposts in the jungles.[235] In 1956 twenty-seven Protestant bodies were represented, of whom sixteen coöperated through the National Evangelical Council of Peru. In 1953 the Government of Peru had signed a contract with Le Tourneau del Peru, Inc., in which the latter, founded by a wealthy and missionary-minded manufacturer of the United States, was granted a concession of 400,000 hectares of forest land to be cleared and used for Christian colonization. In the 1950's the erection of a number of handsome church buildings in Lima, three for foreign residents, helped to give prestige to Protestantism. Most of the Protestants were humble city-dwellers, for members of the upper and middle classes did not wish to suffer the ostracism which attended breaking with the state church, and few

---

230 Herbert Money in *Religion in Life*, Vol. XXVII, pp. 29, 30 (Winter, 1957–1958).

231 Beach and Fahs, *op. cit.*, p. 77. For the situation in 1930 see Browning, Ritchie, and Grubb, *The West Coast Republics of South America*, pp. 86–102.

232 Money, *op. cit.*, Vol. XXVII, pp. 25, 26.

233 *World Christian Handbook*, 1957, p. 144.

234 *Ibid.*

235 Money, *op. cit.*, Vol. XXVII, p. 32. For a readable account of representatitives of the Christian and Missionary Alliance among the Indians across the Andes on one of the tributaries of the Amazon, see Ruth Stull, *Sand and Stars. Missionary Adventure on the Jungle Trail* (New York, Fleming H. Revell Co., 1951, pp. 189), *passim*. For the Evangelical Union of South America and its work among the Indians in the *altiplano* in southern Peru, see Rycroft, *op. cit.*, p. 305.

advances had been made among the poverty-stricken and ignorant rural Indians. In the 1950's some Protestant schools, notably those mantained by the Methodists and by the Free Church of Scotland, were making an impression on cultivated urban circles.[236]

Yet in the main the intellectual life of Peru went on with little or no commitment to the Christian faith. Thus Alejandro O. Deusta (1849–1945) early led in a reaction against Positivism and was profoundly influenced by Krausism.[237]

Bolivia

As we have seen,[238] the latter part of the nineteenth century witnessed the weakening of the tie between the Roman Catholic Church and the Government of Bolivia. In principle freedom of religion was guaranteed, tithes were abolished, and the teaching of religion in the state schools was not required. Yet the state still subsidized the Roman Catholic Church. Moreover, although the majority of pupils enrolled in elementary education were in the public schools, the best secondary education was maintained by the religious orders.

In the half-century which followed 1914 no striking changes were seen in the position of the Roman Catholic Church. The country still had a Papal nuncio, and a concordat with the Holy See was signed in 1957. No serious movement was seen fully to separate Church and state. Bolivia, rich in minerals, but with the majority of the population living on the high interior mountain region, remained to some degree isolated from the main currents of the revolutionary age. Slightly over half the population, which in 1959 was estimated to be 3,416,000, was Indian, about a third was mestizo, and about a seventh was white. In the 1950's the illiteracy rate was said to be more than 85 per cent. To reduce illegitimacy among the Indians, in 1920 the law of 1911 requiring a civil before a canonical marriage ceremony was so amended as to permit the Indians to substitute the religious for the civil ceremony.[239] In the 1930's an unsuccessful war with Paraguay disrupted the national economy. Political unrest with riots and uprisings was chronic. In the 1950's Victor Paz Esterosoro, who while in exile in Buenos Aires had studied the methods of Perón, declared the nationalization of the tin mines, the source of a large proportion of the nation's exports and of the world supply of that metal and controlled chiefly by capital from the United States, Chile, Great Britain, and Switzerland. From time to time violent criticism of the United States broke out, notably in 1959.

---

[236] Money, op. cit., Vol. XXVII, pp. 26–28, 30, 33. For the life of Walter Manuel Montano, a former Dominican who became a Protestant pastor, see Sumrall, op. cit., pp. 33–43. For some other converts to Protestantism see ibid., pp. 123–128, 145–151.

[237] Sánchez Reulet, Contemporary Latin-American Philosophy, pp. 23 ff.

[238] Volume III, pp. 330, 331.

[239] Mecham, op. cit., pp. 228, 229.

As heretofore, the Indians, nominally and fanatically Roman Catholic, had a religion which was a mixture of their pre-Christian paganism with superficial features of the Roman Catholic faith; their drunken fiestas were professedly associated with the Christian calendar. Unfortunately the secular clergy who served as pastors of the Indians were little if any better morally or in intelligence than their parishioners. In the 1930's it was said that a marked decline was seen in the already low quality of the candidates for holy orders.[240] In 1957 an average of one priest to every 4,553 of the Catholic population was reported, a better proportion than in four of the nine other South American countries, but of the total of 678 clergy only 241 were classed as diocesan and 437, or almost twice the number, were regulars, most of them not in charge of parishes. Fifty-three seminarians were listed, a smaller number than in any other South American republic.[241] Between 1900 and 1930 only 45 priests were ordained for the See of La Paz and in 1947 the native-born diocesan priests in the entire country were said to be 227.[242] Much of the labour unrest had Marxist features and was directed against the Church and the priests.[243]

The Roman Catholic Church put forth determined efforts to remedy the situation. In 1956 at the instance of Jesuits in connexion with the commemoration of the fourth centenary of the death of Ignatius Loyola a national mission to Bolivia was undertaken. It was composed of 148 preachers, including 22 of several orders from Spain, contingents from 8 Latin American countries, and some Indian-speaking Bolivian priests. It was divided into teams, each of which spent about fifteen days in the district assigned to it, preaching, hearing confessions, and giving the Communion. At the time much enthusiasm was aroused, and some continuing improvement was reported. A Spanish priest who specialized in social and economic problems gave an impetus to Catholic Action among employers, intellectuals, and university students. At the suggestion of the Papal nuncio a band of Canadian Oblates of Mary Immaculate trained in social action undertook work among the labourers in the tin mines. They were opposed by the leftist minister of mines. In 1926 the Archbishop of La Paz launched a national crusade for better basic education of the Indian masses, but he met bitter opposition from the great landowners, the anti-clericals, and some students and was eventually forced to resign. The Christ Schools of Potosí, begun by the Franciscans in 1907, were dealt blows in the Bolivian-Paraguayan war of the 1930's but were revived and in 1957 numbered over one hundred. At least one became a centre of rural improvement in health, homes, and leisure-time recreation. Many missionaries came from the United States. In 1957 most of them were Maryknoll priests and sisters. Indeed, more Mary-

[240] *Ibid.*, pp. 231, 232.
[241] Considine, *New Horizons*, pp. 328, 331.
[242] Allen, *op. cit.*, pp. 480, 487.
[243] Pattee, *El Catolicismo*, p. 79.

knollers were then serving in Bolivia than in any other country in Latin America. In 1961 they were employing radio to reach Indian villages. Several missionaries were seculars from the Archdiocese of St. Louis, responding to an appeal from their archbishop, who had sensed the need during a visit to Bolivia.[244] In 1925 the first national Eucharistic Congress was held.[245]

More ecclesiastical territorial units were created. In 1917 an additional vicariate apostolic was authorized and was entrusted to the Spanish Franciscans; in 1919 another new one was assigned to the Italian Franciscans and then in 1925 was divided. In 1930 still another was set up and placed in charge of Franciscans from the Tyrol. In 1924 an archdiocese was divided into four parts with two new sees, and two vacant sees were filled.[246] Catholic Action was introduced in 1939 and worked an improvement in the attendance of men at the Mass. The Association of Indigenous Catholicism, founded in 1939 at La Paz, created normal schools to train teachers. Religious instruction in the public schools was reëstablished by a decree in January, 1942.[247]

As elsewhere in most of Latin America, Protestantism had barely gained a foothold in Bolivia by 1914 but made a substantial growth in the next fifty years. In 1924 Protestant communicants were said to total 323 and the Protestant community to be 438.[248] In 1938 the corresponding figures were 3,920 and 15,650,[249] in 1952 they were 6,826 and 16,475, and in 1957 they were 11,240 and 29,373.[250] In 1957 the denomination with the largest number of communicants and affiliated community was the Seventh Day Adventists, who began their mission in 1907. Next in numerical strength were the Canadian Baptists, followed closely by the Friends of two yearly meetings in the United States, the Bolivian Indian Mission, and the Church of the Nazarene. The reported Protestant totals were patently imperfect and below the true sum, for figures were not obtained from several missions.[251] In the 1950's self-support and self-government were increasing and some congregations were undertaking to

244 Considine, New Horizons, pp. 149–186, 338, 339; Maria del Rey, op. cit., pp. 3–119; Worldmission Fides Service, February 11, 1961.
245 The Catholic Historical Review, Vol. XXVI, p. 39 (April, 1940).
246 Ibid., pp. 41–43. See also Arcila Robledo, La Orden Franciscana en la America Meridional, pp. 203, 208, 210, 214, 216, 222, 224.
247 Pattee, El Catolicismo, pp. 80, 81.
248 Beach and Fahs, op. cit., p. 77. For the situation in 1930 see Browning, Ritchie, and Grubb, op. cit., pp. 125–133.
249 The Evangelical Handbook of Latin America, 1939, p. 108. For the situation in 1946 see Rycroft, op. cit., pp. 307–312.
250 World Christian Handbook, 1957, pp. 118, 119.
251 Ibid. On a Seventh Day Adventist missionary from the United States who was first in a station in the Amazon Valley and was then transferred to Lake Titicaca, see From Football Field to Mission Field with Richard Hayden as told by Gwendolen Lampshire Hayden (Washington, Review and Herald Publishing Association, 1951, pp. 318), passim. For a narrative of a representative of the Bolivian Indian Mission see Sally Reese Hawthorne, Cloud Country Sojourn (London, The Bolivian Indian Mission, no date, pp. 128), passim. For a history of the mission of the Canadian Baptists see Dabbs, Dawn Over the Bolivian Hills, passim.

spread into new regions. An indigenous ministry was also emerging. In 1949 the Canadian Baptists inaugurated a radio station. Persecution was encountered, in at least one instance (1959) with several deaths at the hands of Indians who were said to have been incited by a priest.[252]

CHILE

Chile, stretching in a long narrow ribbon along the west coast of South America from the southern tropics close to the southern extreme of the South Temperate Zone, with its contrasts between deserts and dense forests and between seacoast and great mountains, saw important religious developments in the four decades which followed World War I. With its sharp distinction between the wealthy minority and a growing middle class on the one hand and the poverty-stricken majority on the other, Chile resembled its sister countries. Yet its shifts in government, usually accomplished without the violence which characterized several other Latin American states, brought some improvement in legislation to protect the labourers. Population mounted—for example, from the census figure of 5,932,995 in 1952 to an estimated 7,384,403 in 1958—and was paralleled by an even greater proportional growth in the cities. The population was slightly less than a third white, nearly two-thirds mestizo, and a small fraction Indian. By the constitution of 1925 and its accompanying legislation full separation of Church and state was accomplished. This was with the concurrence of the archbishop and not through the strong anti-clericalism which characterized that step in some other countries. The vast ecclesiastical holdings were handed over to the Roman Catholic Church with no restrictions. These properties included not only church buildings, monasteries, schools, and two universities but also great revenue-producing landholdings. Church property used exclusively for religious purposes was exempted from taxation, but other ecclesiastical possessions were subject to the same imposts as were levied on non-Church property. The state no longer controlled appointments to the episcopate, and the clergy were left free to communicate directly with the Vatican. To ease the transition, provision was made for continuing for a time state grants to the Church, but these were eventually terminated. No priest could teach in the public schools, but religious instruction in those schools, while not required, could be voluntarily elected. In the 1930's the Roman Catholics maintained a number of schools and in most of them no tuition was charged. After the separation of Church and state no organized anti-clericalism was seen. The bishops were usually recruited from the aristocratic families which had long

252 *The International Review of Missions*, Vol. XLVII, p. 60 (January, 1958); Vol. XLV, p. 60 (January, 1956). For two Protestant converts and the martyrdom of three Bolivian and one Canadian, see Dabbs, *op. cit.*, pp. 250–268.

ruled the country, attendance at Mass increased, a better quality of young man-hood entered the priesthood, and the Church concerned itself with the social problems inherited from the past or brought by the revolutionary age.[253]

In a number of other ways the post-World War I decades witnessed advances in the Roman Catholic Church in Chile. Catholic Action was introduced by a decree of the episcopate and was organized after a Canadian pattern. In the mid-1940's it had 3,063 centres and 58,078 members. It emphasized the devotional and liturgical life. Partly through its efforts a Eucharistic Congress was held in 1941 and a Marian Congress in 1944. It stimulated literary work and the promotion of Catholic libraries, sought to promote Christian family life, and encouraged social Christianity and Catholic eleëmosynary societies and institutions.[254] In the 1950's a magazine was begun, *Mensaje,* with the watchword *Inquietud,* which aroused youths from the leading families to dissatisfaction with their round of parties and aimless living to a desire to serve God and men. They held retreats and went in groups to fraternize with labourers on the *haciendas* and in remote towns, and had worship marked by sung dialogue Mass.[255] In the 1950's the ASICH was active. It was made up of Catholic leaders of a labour movement which sought to improve the workers' lot, but Church leaders were troubled by the lack of Christian knowledge among the employed in the lower income strata and the spread of Communism among them. Influential conservatives opposed the programme outlined in the Papal encyclicals *Rerum novarum* and *Quadragesimo anno.*[256] In 1938 at the invitation of the Chilean bishops the Abbot of Solesmes founded the Priory of the Holy Trinity near Santiago as a radiating centre for the Liturgical Movement.[257] In general, in the 1950's at least some Protestant missionaries were of the opinion that the Roman Catholic Church had made marked advances in the preceding thirty years—with priests of higher character, with much more preaching, and with an increasing use of the radio.[258]

In spite of these advances, late in the 1950's the situation was far from satisfactory. To be sure, the ratio of priests to the population, which was one to every 2,660 of the Roman Catholics, was better than in any other Latin American republic, and the number of seminarians, 187, was better than in several other Latin American countries, but the diocesan clergy, the seculars, were only 816 as against 1,381 regulars, a proportion which indicated a lack of sufficient pastoral care in the average parish. The clergy tended to be concentrated in the

253 Mecham, *op. cit.,* pp. 269–274.
254 Pattee, *El Catolicismo,* pp. 196–198.
255 Considine, *The Catholic Church in Today's Latin America.*
256 Considine, *New Horizons,* pp. 125–148.
257 Bögler, *Liturgische Erneuerung in aller Welt,* pp. 122, 123.
258 Information given the author in Santiago, July, 1957.

cities, leaving the rural areas only thinly supplied if at all.[259] In 1945 not a single Chilean was ordained in five dioceses which had a total population of over one million Roman Catholics, and in the 1950's a careful survey indicated that in all Chile only 3.5 per cent. of the men and 9.5 per cent. of the women went to mass on a Sunday and those who fulfilled their Easter duty were 14 per cent. About half the dying were said to be without the last sacraments and at least that proportion were married outside the Church.[260] Moreover, much of the personnel of the Roman Catholic Church in Chile was foreign. Indeed, in the 1950's the majority of the priests were said to be Spaniards. Here, as in so much of the rest of Latin America, the Church suffered from an anemia which required transfusions from the faithful in other lands to prevent its demise. A large proportion of the regulars came from abroad. A substantial contribution to the personnel, both men and women, was from the United States; approximately half were Maryknollers, but several other congregations were represented.[261] Belgian Franciscans were among the regulars from Europe.[262]

In the four decades which followed World War I Protestantism had a phenomenal growth. In 1924 the number of baptized was said to be 11,169 and the Protestant community to total 11,551.[263] In 1952 the number of full members was given as 93,315 and of the community as 277,178. Five years later the corresponding totals were put at 133,180 and 370,428.[264] This meant that in 1957 on the average at least five out of every hundred Chileans were Protestants. Indeed, Protestants were almost as numerous as practising Roman Catholics.

The major Protestant numerical growth was that of the Pentecostals. In the 1950's they had more than half of both the Protestant communicants and the Protestant community. They were in more than one body, but the largest two groups had their origin in the labours of W. C. Hoover. In 1902 Hoover, a Methodist missionary from the United States, became pastor of a congregation in Valparaiso. Eventually he had the characteristic Pentecostal experience of speaking with tongues. His faith proved contagious. He reluctantly broke with the Methodist Church because some of his fellow missionaries disapproved of the emotional features of his movement. The movement spread rapidly, and after Hoover's death its leadership was entirely Chilean. It retained certain

[259] Considine, *New Horizons,* pp. 328, 331. Allen, *op. cit.,* p. 485, gave the number of major seminary students as 176 in 1957, and of scholastics as 291.

[260] Allen, *op. cit.,* p. 485.

[261] Considine, *New Horizons,* pp. 341, 342; Maria del Rey, *op. cit.,* pp. 156–188; information given the author while in Latin America in 1956.

[262] Arcila Robledo, *op. cit.,* pp. 252 ff.

[263] Beach and Fahs, *op. cit.,* p. 77. For the situation in 1930 see Browning, Ritchie, and Grubb, *op. cit.,* pp. 32–50.

[264] *World Christian Handbook, 1957,* p. 127.

features derived from Methodism, among them a year's probation before admission to full membership. A third Pentecostal variety was introduced by the Assemblies of God in 1941. The Pentecostals believed in faith healing and tithed for the support of their ministry and various projects. They were drawn chiefly from the humbler ranks of society. They were said, even by Roman Catholics, to be cleaner and more honest and to have a purer family life than the rank and file of their fellow countrymen. The marked decline in drunkenness among the lower classes in Chile in the 1940's and 1950's was said to be due in part to their influence.[265]

Other Protestant denominations were represented. Of the three British organizations the South American Missionary Society, of Anglican origin, had the most numerous constituency. In 1957 four introduced from the United States —the Southern Baptists, the Seventh Day Adventists, the Methodists, and the Christian and Missionary Alliance, beginning with the one with the most numbers—had larger communicant memberships. The Church of the Four-Square Gospel was growing rapidly but in 1957 had not overtaken the others. The German Evangelical Church, serving the German community, in the 1950's had a reported membership of 6,840.[266] In general, Protestants drew from the socially and economically underprivileged, but in the 1950's they were beginning to reach the white-collar elements. Protestant churches, especially the Pentecostals, experienced a large erosion in their membership, but few of those who drifted away returned to the Roman Catholic Church.[267] Soon after World War I in an effort to better the living conditions on the landed estates—the *haciendas*—Methodists from the United States purchased 3,750 acres in the heart of the major agricultural valley of the country and there sought to develop a pilot project, with diversified crops, fruits, dairy products, and an agricultural school, and with improved housing and better share-cropping for the employees.[268]

PARAGUAY

As we saw in an earlier volume,[269] Paraguay entered the twentieth century impoverished by a devastating war brought on by the overweening ambition of one of its dictators and by the civil wars which racked the country for a generation after defeat and occupation by the victors. Through most of the

[265] W. C. Hoover, *Historia del Avivamiento Pentecostal en Chile* (Valparaiso, Imprenta Excelsior, 1948, pp. 128), *passim; Chile Pentecostal* (monthly organ of *La Iglesia Metodista Pentecostal en Chile,* Santiago, 1913 ff.), June, 1956, *passim; Fuego de Pentecostes* (monthly official publication of *La Iglesia Evangélica Pentecostal,* Santiago, 1913 ff.), July, 1956; information given the author while in Santiago, July, 1956; Du Plessis, *A Brief History of the Pentecostal Assemblies.*
[266] *World Christian Handbook, 1957,* pp. 126, 127.
[267] Information given the author by Protestant missionaries in Santiago, July, 1956.
[268] Ralph E. Diffendorfer, *A Voyage of Discovery* (New York, Board of Foreign Missions, Methodist Episcopal Church, 1934, pp. 104), pp. 18–36.
[269] Volume III, pp. 334–336.

nineteenth century the Roman Catholic Church, holding the professed religious allegiance of the nation, had been weakened by the domination of successive political dictators and their insistence on utilizing her for their purposes. Their policies, superimposed upon a church already suffering from the expulsion of the Jesuits in the eighteenth century and the impossible handicaps imposed on their successors, the Franciscans, brought the Church to as parlous a condition as in any Latin American country.

The twentieth century witnessed some improvement in Paraguay's political and economic life. However, in the 1930's an exhausting war with Bolivia over the Chaco, while ending in an ostensible Paraguayan victory, slowed recovery from the nadir reached in the third quarter of the nineteenth century. A rapid succession of dictators under the guise of president gave the country some able and some ruthless leadership. Immigration of a few tens of thousands, mostly from Argentina, Germany, Italy, and Spain, with about 5,000 Mennonites from Europe and North America, partly filled the population gap. The gap was also progressively eliminated by the excess of births over deaths. The population total, estimated at about 800,000 in 1926, rose to 1,408,400 in 1950 and to a conjectured 1,677,000 in 1958. Foreign capital, much of it from Argentina, aided in the exploitation of the country's natural resources. But at mid-twentieth century the overwhelming majority of the population were illiterate and poverty-stricken.[270]

In the first half of the twentieth century the Roman Catholic Church began to recover and made notable progress. It was the state church and received a small subsidy from the government. But religious instruction was not permitted in the public schools as part of the regular curriculum. The state exercised the right of patronage, and Liberals sought to use it to handicap the Church. Yet in 1929, against their opposition, the national congress permitted Rome to increase the number of dioceses from one to three, with an archdiocese. After the war with Bolivia a prefecture apostolic was created for the Chaco.[271] In 1940 Paraguay was given a Papal nuncio after sharing one with Uruguay and Argentina from 1920.[272] The Roman Catholic Church suffered from a dearth of clergy, but that lack was being repaired. As late as 1949, out of 154 parishes 73 were without a priest, but by 1954 the latter number was reduced to 60.[273] In 1957 three seminaries were functioning, the largest in Asunción, and the number of vocations to the priesthood was said to be increasing.[274] Young clergy

270 For a good account of Paraguay in the twentieth century see Philip Raine, *Paraguay* (New Brunswick, N.J., Scarecrow Press, 1956, pp. 443), pp. 195 ff.
271 Mecham, *op. cit.*, pp. 242, 243; Considine, *New Horizons*, pp. 119, 120; Pattee, *El Catolicismo*, p. 369.
272 Pattee, *El Catolicismo*, p. 369.
273 Considine, *New Horizons*, p. 120.
274 Allen, *op. cit.*, p. 482; Pattee, *El Catolicismo*, p. 369.

were sent to Argentina to complete their preparation and returned with a broader outlook. In 1956–1957 a special nation-wide effort was made to augment the number of vocations. In 1957 Paraguay was said to have an average of one priest for every 5,217 Roman Catholics, a poorer showing than in any other South American republic except Brazil, Venezuela, and Bolivia. Slightly less than half of the priests were seculars.[275] Only about 150 of the clergy were giving themselves to the parish ministry—or an average of less than one to every 10,000 of the population. Indeed, in 1944 when Redemptorists from Baltimore were placed in charge of a section in Asunción which included a new parish of about 30,000, only 16 came to the first mass. Yet in 1959 about 7,000 in the district were considered to be practising Catholics.[276]

Catholic Action was introduced, at first recruited from university students, religious instruction was being given to youth by catechists, the "dialogue mass" was begun, and the Young Christian Workers grew in numbers and influence. Organized efforts were made to win back the elements alienated from the Church. In 1957 Pax Romana enrolled about 200 of the 3,000 students in the University of Paraguay, and in the 1940's the Third Order of the Franciscans and several other lay associations and confraternities were growing.[277] Assistance in the form of personnel was coming from Roman Catholics of other countries. Indeed, in 1958 the majority of the clergy were foreign, mostly regulars, and in addition to those from the United States there were German Oblates, Austrians of the Society of the Divine Word, Basque Franciscans, and Spanish Jesuits.[278]

Protestantism grew. In 1924 only ten missionaries were reported and no communicants were mentioned.[279] In 1939 an incomplete report gave the missionary staff as 39, from 8 societies, membership as at least 1,723, and the Protestant community as 5,550.[280] In 1952 the communicants were reported to be 1,985 and the community 10,056. Five years later the corresponding figures were 3,441 and 22,839. In 1952 the Mennonites, an immigrant group, had by far the largest Protestant community. The New Testament Missionary Union, a conservative body with support from various countries and represented in Spain and in several South American countries, displayed the largest increase in communicants. The Baptists, who owed their origin to the Southern Baptists of the United States, were next in numerical gains and had an even more rapid growth, both in communicants and in their non-communicant community. In

---

[275] Considine, *New Horizons*, pp. 328, 331; Bates, *The Lay Apostolate in Latin America*, pp. 48–50.

[276] Bates, *The Lay Apostolate*, p. 49.

[277] Considine, *New Horizons*, pp. 120–122; Pattee, *El Catolicismo*, pp. 370–372.

[278] Considine, *New Horizons*, p. 343; Bates, *The Lay Apostolate*, pp. 49–53.

[279] Beach and Fahs, *op. cit.*, p. 77. On the situation in 1928 see Browning, *The River Plate Republics*, pp. 48 ff.

[280] *The Evangelical Handbook of Latin America, 1939*, p. 117.

1957 the foreign personnel were said to be 113 in 13 organizations, and the Paraguayan personnel were reported to be 57.[281]

ARGENTINA

We have already recounted[282] the slow recovery, by irregular stages, of the Roman Catholic Church in Argentina from the nadir reached in the first half of the nineteenth century. We have noted the large influx of population from Europe, mainly but not entirely from Italy and Spain, the rapid growth of cities, especially Buenos Aires, and the exploitation of the large natural resources of the country, much of it through British capital and the building and operation of railways under British direction. We also noted the beginning of Protestantism.

In the twentieth century Argentina experienced a further rapid development. Population rose—from 7,885,237 in 1914 to 16,052,765 in 1947 and to an estimated 20,438,334 in 1958. The overwhelming majority of the population were white, less than 10 per cent. were mestizos, and less than 2 per cent. were Indians. The European element continued to be greatly strengthened by immigration—chiefly, as heretofore, from Spain. Two-thirds of the population lived in Buenos Aires or in the immediate hinterland. Buenos Aires became the largest city in the Southern Hemisphere, not exceeded even in Brazil, South Africa, Australia, or New Zealand. As in so much else of Latin America, sharp contrasts were seen between a wealthy minority, many of them highly cultured and in contact with the intellectual currents of the revolutionary age, a poverty-stricken majority, and a growing middle class. As had been true in the nineteenth century, the government, ostensibly republican, was usually dominated by a succession of strong men who in fact although not in theory were dictators. Between 1914 and 1961 the ones with the longest tenure were Hipólito Irigoyen, who was in control from 1916 to 1930, with the seeming interlude of the presidency of Marcelo T. de Alvear from 1922 to 1928, put into office at the behest of Irigoyen; Agustin P. Justo, president from 1932 to 1938; and Juan Domingo Perón, who ruled from 1944 until overthrown by a violent uprising in 1955. Irigoyen favoured the underprivileged, had generous social legislation enacted, and aided the labour unions, but when the latters' leaders disobeyed him and called for a general strike he had his army break it by force. Perón, an army officer, posed as the champion of the proletariat. He was assisted by an extremely able woman, María Eva Duarte, popularly known as Evita, first his mistress

281 *World Christian Handbook, 1957*, p. 143. For an account of the beginning of a mission school of the Disciples of Christ see Clement Manly Morton, *Paraguay, The Island Republic* (Cincinnati, Powell and White, 1926, pp. 177), pp. 117-177. For the Mennonites see Sanford Calvin Yoder, *Down South American Way* (Scottdale, Pa., Herald Press, 1943, pp. 148), pp. 98 ff.
282 Volume III, pp. 336-340.

and then his wife. The years which immediately followed Perón's deposition were marked by relative quiet, but, in exile, he continued to be a menace and from time to time his followers made a bid for power.

On the eve of Perón's regime the Roman Catholic Church was established, but with gradually loosening bonds between itself and the state. No concordat existed, but tacit agreement provided for all that such a document might have formalized. Theoretically the Pope reserved the right to name the bishops, but in practice, with some exceptions, he assented to the names presented him by the government. The provinces insisted on the right of patronage to posts within their respective borders. A Papal nuncio resided in Buenos Aires, and Argentina had a representative in the Vatican, in 1927 raised to the rank of ambassador. Papal decrees could not be published in Argentina without the consent of the state. The state made annual, but not large, appropriations to the hierarchy, cathedrals, seminaries, and Indian missions, but not to the parochial clergy or the Church's charitable institutions. Religious instruction could not be given in the public schools during regular hours. However, it might be imparted after school hours to those who remained for it. But Roman Catholics maintained a large number of elementary and especially secondary schools. Civil marriage was compulsory but could be followed by a religious ceremony. Even under Perón the constitution required the president to be a Roman Catholic. Complete freedom of worship was guaranteed to all.[283]

In spite of the privileged position of the Roman Catholic Church, in the first half of the twentieth century Christianity in Argentina was weakened by a number of factors. The great majority of the population, if asked, would have said they were Catholics. But Spiritism had tens of thousands of adherents and was reported to be represented by about 150 centres in Buenos Aires. This did not mean illiteracy, for nine-tenths of the adult population could read.[284] Most of the contemporary Argentinian philosophers who had standing among the intelligentsia could hardly be called Christian. Alejandro Korn (1860–1936), a physician trained in psychiatry, in his later years centred on philosophy as a member of the School of Philosophy and Letters in Buenos Aires. At first a Positivist, he was attracted by Schopenhauer, then explored mysticism, both non-Christian and Christian, and in the end based his philosophy on Kant and was respectful of religion but did not subscribe to it. For a time José Ingenieros (1877–1925) through his writings exercised a wide influence not only in Buenos Aires but also in intellectual circles throughout Latin America. He held that certainty was grounded on experience and denied the existence of a transcendent reality. Francisco Romero (1891——), popular in Latin America in

---

[283] Mecham, *op. cit.*, pp. 300–304; Kennedy, *Catholicism, Nationalism, and Democracy in Argentina*, pp. 11–28.
[284] Considine, *New Horizons*, pp. 99, 100.

the twentieth century, long taught philosophy in Buenos Aires. While stressing the life of the spirit, he was not within the Christian tradition. Alberto Rougès (1880–1945) was an exception. One of the founders of the University of Tucumán and in the last year of his life elected to its rectorship, he was unashamedly and devoutly Catholic. Although a close reader of Hume, through Augustine and Neo-Platonism he found an intellectual basis for his Christian faith.[285]

As in most of the other countries in Latin America, a serious weakness in the Roman Catholic Church in Argentina was the lack of a sufficient body of clergy, especially indigenous clergy, to give suitable pastoral care to those who called themselves Catholics. In 1957 the average was one priest to every 3,795 Roman Catholics. This was a better ratio than in several other Latin American countries, but it still was inadequate, especially since more than half of the priests were regulars and only slightly more than two-fifths were seculars with a parish as their major responsibility.[286] Many of the clergy were from Europe, a large proportion from Spain. The latter were augmented by refugees from the civil war of the 1930's. In 1956 a Spaniard, a former priest then resident in Argentina, said that in his opinion the quality of the clergy was higher in Spain than in Argentina, where, he said, numbers of priests, disillusioned, had left the Church and had given up all religion.[287]

In the social struggles of the time much of organized labour regarded the Roman Catholic Church as allied with the upper classes and so, in effect, repudiated it.[288] In 1953 a Roman Catholic report declared that of the professed Catholics—who constituted 93 per cent. of the population—less than 20 per cent. attended mass on Sundays and only about 5 per cent. belonged to some Catholic organization. It ascribed this situation to the lack of a sufficient number of clergy, faulty family education, and the absence of leadership.[289]

Unsatisfactory though the condition of the Roman Catholic Church was in Argentina, in the twentieth century some advances were seen which made it clear that the faith was far from moribund. Opinions of informed observers were divided: several said that the Church was losing ground and others believed it to have made some gains. Part of the evidence adduced by the latter can be quickly summarized. In not a few parishes pastoral care of excellent quality was given and the level of Catholic living was higher than in the country as a whole.[290] In the 1950's progress was being made in recruiting and training a body of Argentinian clergy. Approximately 710 major seminary students

[285] Sánchez Reulet, *Contemporary Latin-American Philosophy*, pp. 51–75, 148–185, 252–275.
[286] Considine, *New Horizons*, pp. 328, 331. Gibbons, *Basic Ecclesiastical Statistics for Latin America, 1956*, p. 42, gives the proportion of priests to Catholics as one to every 3,565.
[287] Confidential information given the author in Buenos Aires in 1956.
[288] *Ibid.*
[289] Coleman, *Latin-American Catholicism*, p. 26.
[290] Considine, *New Horizons*, p. 99.

were enrolled in 11 institutions, and 13 institutions maintained by 11 religious communities had 402 scholasticates. The Metropolitan Seminary in Buenos Aires was staffed by Jesuits and in 1957 was the largest in the country. Associated with it were a minor seminary with 171 students and the Theological Faculty of the Immaculate Conception canonically erected in 1944 for studies on the graduate level. In 1957 Buenos Aires was said to be the leading centre in Latin America for theological enquiry and discussion.[291] In 1910 a Catholic university had been founded.[292] Most of the Argentinian recruits for the priesthood were from the middle classes and the rural areas. A few were from the upper classes, but for the most part they entered the Society of Jesus.[293]

In the decades following World War I Miguel de Andrea, Titular Bishop of Temnos, was the outstanding spokesman in Argentina for social Catholicism. He led a welfare programme which sought to relieve the poverty of the urban working classes. The *Unión Popular Católica*, in which he was the outstanding clerical figure, came into being as the result of a week of strikes and riots and had as its purpose the alleviation of the conditions that had provoked them. He endeavoured especially to improve the wages and working conditions of women in the needle trades. Through what was called *Democracia Corporative* he strove to bring into policy-making organs of the state representatives of all the economic and social groups.[294]

The strength of the Roman Catholic Church was demonstrated in its part in the overthrow of Perón. Perón and Evita attempted to take over the hundreds of Catholic organizations for social welfare. That and Perón's other efforts to supplant and master the Church contributed to the uprising which expelled him from the country.[295] Catholic Action, organized in Argentina in 1930, helped to reinforce Catholic Congresses and the *Liga Social Argentina*.[296] In 1935 Rome took the occasion of the International Eucharistic Congress in Buenos Aires to create twelve new dioceses for the advancement and better administration of the Roman Catholic Church in the country.[297] After the fall of Perón the state agreed to the establishment of twelve additional dioceses and two new archdioceses.[298] Much of the Roman Catholic literature was excellent. Some of it was in translation from other languages. In 1944 in connexion with a Eucharistic Congress an elaborate edition was issued of a Spanish translation of the Bible.[299] Following World War I the Liturgical Movement was intro-

[291] Allen, *op. cit.*, pp. 483, 484.
[292] Zuretti, *Historia Eclesiastica Argentina*, p. 315.
[293] Information given the author in Buenos Aires, July, 1956.
[294] Kennedy, *op. cit.*, pp. 139–146.
[295] Considine, *New Horizons*, pp. 95, 96; Coleman, *op. cit.*, pp. 26, 27. For a list of Roman Catholic institutions of various kinds see Alameda, *Argentina Católica, passim*.
[296] Pattee, *El Catolicismo*, p. 39.
[297] Zuretti, *op. cit.*, pp. 310–314.
[298] B. F. Stockwell in *Religion in Life*, Vol. XXVII pp. 16, 17 (Winter, 1957–1958).
[299] Information given the author in Buenos Aires in July, 1956.

duced. Among its leaders, as in Europe, were Benedictines, but late in the 1940's the centre was the Salesian Institute in Cordoba. The use of the Gregorian music did not spread as widely as some other phases of the Movement.[300] In October, 1960, the first Inter-American Marian Congress met in Buenos Aires, with clergy and laymen from the United States, Canada, and all the Latin American countries. Its purpose was to draw up plans to counter Communism.[301] That same month a two-year campaign was launched to further the Roman Catholic faith. In it two thousand missioners were engaged with Bishop Fulton J. Sheen, famous in the United States as a preacher over television, in an effort to reach the nation.[302] In a somewhat different direction, in 1958 Carlos Cuccetti, a priest, initiated the *Confraternidad,* modeled after the National Conference of Christians and Jews in the United States and the first organization of its kind in Latin America. Catholic, Protestant, and Jewish leaders endorsed it.[303]

In the twentieth century Protestantism made striking progress in Argentina. In 1924 Protestant communicants were reported as 8,880 and the Protestant community as 11,341.[304] In 1939 the Protestant church membership was said to be 55,162 and the Protestant community to total 135,053.[305] The corresponding figures in 1952 were 84,982 and 257,621, and in 1957 they were 116,557 and 364,369.[306] A substantial proportion of the totals for 1952 and 1957 were immigrants or descendants of immigrants of Protestant stock. In the latter year about a third of the members and nearly half the Protestant community were in that category.[307] Yet the totals were admittedly incomplete and if they could have included all Protestants would have been considerably higher. The churches of Protestant immigrant stock usually maintained their services in the languages of their ancestral homes and had little contact with the Spanish-using Protestant bodies; for example, the Missouri Synod found its constituency largely among Germans from the Ukraine. The Waldensians were an exception. Originating in immigration from Italy, by the mid-twentieth century their churches had become entirely Spanish-speaking. The United Lutherans also were drawn mainly from the Spanish-speaking. Of the churches recruited predominantly from the Spanish-speaking population the largest were the Pentecostals, the Baptists (founded by the Southern Baptists of the United States and increasing in church membership from 578 in 1913 to 10,874 in 1952), and the Seventh Day Adventists. The Methodists were numerous and had important educational

[300] Bögler, *Liturgische Erneuerung in aller Welt,* pp. 124–127.
[301] *The New York Times,* October 9, 1960.
[302] *Time,* October 31, 1960.
[303] *The New York Times,* December 10, 1956.
[304] Beach and Fahs, *op. cit.,* p. 77. For the situation in 1928 see Browning, *op. cit.,* pp. 48 ff.
[305] *Evangelical Handbook of Latin America, 1939,* p. 107.
[306] *World Christian Handbook, 1957,* p. 116.
[307] *Ibid.*

institutions. Pentecostals were of several branches and were the outgrowth of the initiative of missionaries from Chile, Canada, Sweden, and Italy. Several of the denominations coöperated through a federation which included Paraguay, Argentina, and Uruguay.

Protestants were originally drawn from the humbler elements. The Pentecostals especially attracted adherents from the lowest economic level. However, with their emphasis on sobriety, honesty, and diligence, Protestants tended to rise in the economic and social scale. They included many lawyers, teachers, and other intellectuals. Numbers of Protestants, including the laity, were active in propagating their faith. Converts were harder to win than in Brazil but were less inclined to drift from the faith than in the latter country. In the twentieth century the numbers and preparation of Protestant clergy rapidly advanced. In Buenos Aires the Union Theological Seminary (*Facultad Evangélica de Teologia*), a joint enterprise of the Methodists, Presbyterians, Disciples of Christ, and Waldensians, had a growing student body and faculty and was said to be academically the strongest Protestant institution in South America for the education for the ministry. The Southern Baptists maintained a theological seminary in Buenos Aires which trained pastors and women workers from Argentina, Uruguay, Paraguay, and Chile. Lutherans had two seminaries, one supported by the Missouri Synod and the other sponsored by the Lutheran World Federation and drawing students from several Lutheran bodies. Some other denominations conducted training schools or seminaries.[308]

We must note that, in addition to the revival in the Roman Catholic Church and the growth of Protestantism, there were some among the intelligentsia of Argentina who, though they would not be classed with either wing of the faith, thought of themselves as basically Christian. Not primarily philosophers, they still had the ear of many of the educated. Such a one was Ricardo Rojas. Son of a distinguished senator, acclaimed publicly in Argentina, honoured by universities in Latin America and highly regarded in some circles in Europe, he was rector of the University of Buenos Aires. In a moving book, *El Cristo Invisible,* recording a conversation between himself and a Roman Catholic bishop, he spoke of his spiritual pilgrimage, his search among the mystics of several faiths. While neither Roman Catholic nor Protestant, he declared himself a Christian, held the Gospels in high esteem, and valued Christ's Gospel as his law.[309] Julio Navarro Monzó, born and reared in Portugal, a naturalized

[308] *Ibid.;* Stockwell, *op. cit.,* pp. 18–23; information acquired by the author at first hand from authoritative sources, July, 1956. On the Disciples of Christ see J. Dexter Montgomery, *Disciples of Christ in Argentina, 1906–1956* (St. Louis, The Bethany Press, 1956, pp. 180), *passim; Argentine Baptists Move Ahead* (Richmond, Foreign Mission Board of the Southern Baptist Convention, 1954, pp. 86), *passim.* For an account of one missionary in the Argentinian Chaco see Winifred Revill, *Chaco Chapters* (London, Hodder and Stoughton, 1947, pp. 192), *passim.*

[309] Ricardo Rojas, *The Invisible Christ,* translated by W. E. Browning (Cincinnati, Abingdon Press, 1931, pp. 336), *passim.*

citizen of Argentina, had served on the editorial staff of an important news-paper in Buenos Aires and had held important posts in the government. A man of wide reading, great erudition, and profound thought, he was probably spiritually most nearly akin to the Friends. From 1922 to 1934 under the auspices of the Young Men's Christian Association he lectured on religion to audiences in several Latin American lands and directed small groups in unhurried periods of devotion.[310] Presumably both Rojas and Monzó were simply two of many who constituted one of the several complex and often contradictory currents of thought and life of the revolutionary age in Latin America and who were deeply indebted to Christianity.

URUGUAY

Uruguay, the smallest in area and the next to the smallest in population, but with the highest average population per square mile of any of the South Ameri-can republics, entered the post-World War I years with a more secular atmos-phere than any of its South American sisters. As we have seen,[311] its outstanding figure was José Batlle y Ordóñez (1856–1929). The son of a president, of the *Colorado* and hence anti-clerical wing in the political arena, he had himself been president from 1903 to 1907. Then after four years in Europe he returned to Uruguay, was again elected president, and in that office and as editor of his newspaper, *El Dia,* inspired in part by what he had seen in Switzerland, he led the country into the ways of a welfare state. He insisted on freedom of speech and of the press, uninhibited suffrage, university education for women, the right of workers to organize and strike, the eight-hour day, minimum wages, old-age pensions, and compensation for industrial accidents. He had government go into business—including banking, insurance, light and power, the railways, and the packing industry. Although Batlle's programme met with opposition from both the extreme right and the extreme left, in spite of the world-wide depression of the 1930's which reduced the foreign markets for wool, hides, and meat, the country's chief exports, and in the face of Perón's attempts to bring Uruguay under his sway, in the main the Batlle tradition persisted. Uruguay faced continuing problems which were in large part due to a combination of its dependence on world markets, friction among political factions, corruption in the government and various organizations, and the difficulties attendant upon the operation of the Batlle and related measures. In 1958 the *Blancos,* the traditional conservative opponents of the liberal *Colorados,* came to power for the first time in over ninety years.

The population of Uruguay shared in the increase which characterized most

[310] Latourette, *World Service,* p. 210.
[311] Volume III, pp. 341, 342.

of Latin America. It rose from a little over a million in 1908 to an estimated 2,800,000 in 1958. Nearly a third were in Montevideo. Approximately nine-tenths of the population were white. The mestizos, about 8 per cent. of the whole, were mostly in the rural sections, and about 2 per cent. were Negroes.

In the middle of the twentieth century the position of Christianity was ambiguous. On the one hand were a pervading secularism, religious indifference, and pronounced scepticism. For example, *El Dia,* the leading newspaper in Montevideo, printed the name of God without capitalizing it, but used a capital for Jesus as an historical figure. Most of the men influential in politics were either atheists or agnostics. Christmas was officially called Family Day, Epiphany was re-named Children's Day, and Holy Week was known as Tourist Week and Gaucho Week. Under the constitution promulgated in 1919 Church and state were completely separate and full religious toleration was guaranteed. The state did not contribute financially to any cult. Yet the Roman Catholic Church had full title to its property acquired before 1919, held it free from taxation, was not restricted in its acquisition of property, made its ecclesiastical appointments without reference to the state, and enjoyed unrestrained liberty of communication with the Holy See. Although no religious teaching could be given in the public schools, the Church was free to develop a system of schools in which it could give instruction in the faith.[312] Uruguayan philosophic thought tended to depart from the Positivism which had dominated intellectual circles in much of the nineteenth century. That did not mean, however, that it accepted Christianity. Thus José Enrique Rodó (1871-1917) rejected the Christian faith in which he had been reared but combined a religious temperament with philosophic agnosticism. Carlos Vaz Ferreira, educator and philosopher, trained in law and with a high ethical sense, and who from a chair in the university which he obtained in 1898 and from a special lectureship created for him in the university in 1913 was for more than thirty years a kind of intellectual pontiff, was an agnostic in religion. Materialism based upon science had its advocates. Roman Catholic thought had intelligent exponents among whom Aquinas was dominant, and Duns Scotus was represented by a Capuchin Archbishop of Montevideo: yet Roman Catholic intellectual activity was largely confined to ecclesiastical circles.[313]

Under these conditions the Roman Catholic Church had something of a revival, but limited to a minority. Although the large majority of the population were still counted as Catholics, the clergy were quite insufficient in numbers to give them adequate pastoral care.[314] But in Montevideo in the 1950's women

---

[312] Mecham, *op. cit.,* pp. 338, 339; Browning, *op. cit.,* pp. 33, 34. Information acquired by the author in July, 1956; Considine, *New Horizons,* pp. 107, 108.

[313] Aruro Ardao, *La Filosofía en el Uruguay en el sigle XX* (México, Fondo de Cultura Economica, 1956, pp. 193), *passim;* Sánchez Reulet, *op. cit.,* pp. 119-147.

[314] Considine, *New Horizons,* pp. 38, 331, gives the total of priests in 1957 as 662, of whom

were appointed two by two with responsibility for particular blocks to care for the sick and needy, to conduct block prayers, and to organize sports and festivals. In the rural sections which were without priests lay folk and missionary sisters attempted to fill the gap. By the 1950's the number of men attending Mass, formerly negligible and still a small minority, was increasing and some were following the service intelligently through missals. Montevideo had a Catholic daily paper. In the 1950's Roman Catholics maintained 160 private schools.[315] Catholic Action was introduced by a pastoral letter of the bishops in 1934. In the late 1940's the number of vocations for the priesthood was increasing, a Catholic labour union in Montevideo had about 25,000 members, and Catholic coöperatives were to be found in the rural areas.[316] National Eucharistic Congresses were held. The third, in 1938, had an attendance estimated at half a million.[317]

In the prevailingly secular atmosphere Protestants were a small minority but, as elsewhere in Latin America in the twentieth century, were growing. They were made up partly of immigrant stock and foreign residents who were Protestants by heredity and partly of accessions from the traditionally Catholic elements of the population. In 1924 the baptized were said to be 1,321,[318] but the true total was probably above that figure. An estimate of 1928 placed the Protestant community at 15,000.[319] Figures for 1939 put the Protestant membership at 7,071 and the Protestant community at 20,860. Of these totals the Waldensians had 3,625 of the membership and 10,000 of the community.[320] The 1952 figures were 4,262 members and 8,394 for the Protestant community.[321] However, the survey for 1952 did not include the Waldensians: the membership gathered from the historically Roman Catholic section of the population had risen, although not spectacularly. The growth had proportionately been only slightly more than that of the population as a whole. Exclusive of the Waldensians, in the 1950's the Seventh Day Adventists had the largest number of members, followed closely by the Methodists. Not included in the figures which we have quoted were Jehovah's Witnesses and the Mormons. In 1956 the latter had two temples in Montevideo and were active in social work.[322]

---

198 were seculars and 464 were regulars, and says that the ratio was one priest to every 3,636 of the Roman Catholics. But he reports that the average number of Catholics in a parish was 15,732, larger than in any other South American republic and exceeded in Latin America only by El Salvador, Guatemala, Honduras, Cuba, the Dominican Republic, and Puerto Rico. Gibbons, *op. cit.*, p. 41, says that in 1956 Uruguay had only 334 priests, of whom 181 were seculars and 153 were regulars.

315 Considine, *New Horizons*, pp. 104–111.
316 Pattee, *El Catolicismo*, pp. 435–444.
317 *The Catholic Historical Review*, Vol. XXVI, p. 13 (April, 1940).
318 Beach and Fahs, *op. cit.*, p. 77.
319 Browning, *op. cit.*, p. 130.
320 *Evangelical Handbook of Latin America, 1939*, p. 120.
321 *World Christian Handbook, 1957*, p. 148.
322 Information given the author in Montevideo in 1956.

BRAZIL

In the twentieth century huge Brazil, containing nearly half of South America, continued the rapid development which it had experienced in the second half of the nineteenth century. Its population increased from about thirty millions in 1920 to nearly fifty-two millions in 1950 and to an estimated sixty-four millions in 1959. As heretofore, most of the population was concentrated in the South-east, mainly in the coastal states—Minas Geraes, São Paulo, Paraná, Santa Catarina, and Rio Grande do Sul. Much of the growth was by immigration from various parts of the world. A beginning was made in developing the vast and only partially explored natural resources of the country.

From 1930 to 1945 Brazil was under the dictatorship of Getulio Vargas. Between 1946 and 1950 an army man, General Eurico Dutra, a good Catholic, was in the presidential chair. In 1950 Getulio Vargas was returned to power, but he made no progress in solving the economic situation, disaffection spread, and in 1954 he committed suicide. Rapidly shifting administrations followed, but in 1956 Juscelino Kubitschek de Oliveiro was elected president. In 1961 he was succeeded by Jânio Quadros. The Communists, although outlawed as a party, were a factor in politics. Inflation mounted. Exports of coffee, long important, declined, and rural labour poured into the burgeoning cities. Yet the nation's economy expanded and industrialization mounted.

In the decades which followed 1914 Brazil was swept into the revolutionary age with wide-ranging results. The impact was marked in the coastal provinces from Minas Geraes southward, but much of the vast interior was as yet but little affected. Sharp contrasts continued between the extreme wealth of the minority and the poverty of the masses, and there was a small but increasing middle class. In spite of the growth of the cities most of the population was still rural. Social legislation was enacted but left agricultural labour on the great landed estates largely unprotected. In urban industries labour unions, the eight-hour day and forty-eight-hour week, the minimum wage, dismissal and separation allowances, and old-age pensions were standard.

Religiously the census of 1950 enumerated 93 per cent. of the population as Roman Catholic, 1,741,430 as Protestants, 41,156 as Orthodox, 69,957 as Jews, 152,572 as Buddhists (for the most part Japanese), 824,353 as Spiritualists, and 274,236 as avowed atheists.[323] The Spiritualists outnumbered the census figures, for many reported themselves as Catholics who were actually practising the Spiritualist rites. In 1957 the Spiritualists claimed ten million adherents, and some priests were said to be influenced by them. If all those listed as Catholics

---

[323] *The Statesman's Year Book, 1960*, p. 850. On the Spiritualists see Azevedo, *O Catolicismo no Brazil*, pp. 34, 35, 62, 63; *Time*, January 12, 1959; M. R. Shaull, in *Religion in Life*, Vol. XXVII, p. 6 (Winter, 1957–1958); confidential information from a Roman Catholic priest who had been in Brazil.

could rightly be counted as belonging to the Roman Catholic Church, Brazil had more of that faith than any other country in the world.

As we saw in an earlier volume,[324] the Roman Catholic Church was much weaker in the colonial years than in much of Spanish America, and although some progress was made in the latter part of the nineteenth century, a good deal of it was achieved through personnel from Europe. Vast areas had little clerical care.

In the half-century introduced by the outbreak of World War I the record of the Roman Catholic Church, as in much of the rest of Latin America, was one of contrasts. For example, the connexion between Church and state was severed in 1889, restored in 1934 under Getulio Vargas, and again abolished in 1946. Yet in the 1950's Brazil continued to have a diplomatic representative in the Vatican.[325] Intellectual circles included both those who did not hold to Christianity and those who supported it. Thus Raimundo de Farias Brito (1862–1917), said to have been the most original and the greatest of Brazilian philosophers, while marked by religious fervour, was clearly not a Catholic and in his later years tended towards pantheism.[326] José Pereira da Graca Aranha (1868–1931), a founder of the Brazilian Academy of Letters, whose novels helped to give wide circulation to his views, affirmed a kind of dualism in which what might be called original sin with pain and grief was one phase, but it could be transcended by a higher unity marked by infinite joy. Although he seemed to have kinship with some Christian views of human nature, he could not be called a Christian.[327] On the other hand, Jackson de Figueiredo (1891–1928), lawyer, politician, and writer, in adolescence departed from the faith in which he had been reared. Then, in his twenties, partly through Pascal and partly through Farias Brito and a spiritual crisis in a severe illness, he returned to the Church and became its active advocate. With Anselm, he believed in order to understand.[328]

In proportion to the population which was classed as Catholic, Brazil had far fewer priests—in 1957 an average of only one to every 6,112—than any other of the South American republics. About two-fifths of them were seculars and nearly three-fifths were regulars, most of the latter engaged in the work of institutions and not in the parochial care of souls.[329] Priests tended to be more numerous in the cities and the coastal provinces than in the rural sections and the sparsely settled Amazon Valley. In 1960 the complaint was voiced that in Mato Grosso, the second in size of the states, Roman Catholics had declined

---

[324] Volume III, pp. 343–349.
[325] *The Statesman's Year Book, 1960,* p. 850.
[326] Sánchez Reulet, *op. cit.,* pp. 76–100.
[327] *Ibid.,* pp. 101–118.
[328] *Ibid.,* pp. 237–251. O'Neill, *Tristão de Athayde and the Catholic Social Movement in Brazil,* pp. 46–56, 106, 107.
[329] Considine, *New Horizons,* pp. 328, 331.

from 93 per cent. of the population in 1950 to 80 per cent. in 1956. The loss was attributed to the inroads of Spiritism, Communism, Freemasonry, and Protestantism.[330]

The twentieth century witnessed a revival of the Roman Catholic Church in Brazil. By the 1960's only a minority had been markedly influenced, but the influence was growing. Some progress was being made in recruiting and training an indigenous priesthood. In 1957, for example, students in major seminaries were reported to number 1,119, of whom 77 per cent. were in institutions staffed by seculars and the remainder in four seminaries maintained by the Lazarists. If to them were added the students enrolled in scholasticates under various orders and congregations, the total of major seminarians was 2,268. This was larger than in any other South American country but was slightly less than in Mexico—although the latter country had only about half the population of Brazil—and was barely a third larger than in Colombia, and Colombia had no more than a third as many people as Brazil. Students were sent to the Pontifical Latin American College in Rome and in 1929 a Brazilian college was founded in that city. Because of the number of immigrants from the Uniates of the Middle East, services using the rites of these bodies were regularly held and some scholasticates were maintained to prepare clergy for them.[331]

Catholic Action was formally introduced in 1935, but the way for it was prepared late in the nineteenth century and in the fore part of the twentieth century. A forerunner was Júlio Maria. Earlier a lawyer and a Positivist, converted when his second wife died, he became a Redemptorist, stood for democracy against those who believed monarchy and the Catholic faith to be inseparable, became an advocate of the principles of *Rerum novarum,* and sought to arouse the masses to take their professed faith seriously. In 1915 Sebastião Leme, Bishop of Olinda-Recife, later to be Archbishop of Rio de Janeiro, issued a pastoral letter which incorporated many of the ideas of Júlio Maria. He excoriated the Catholics of Brazil for being an inefficient, somnolent majority and urged them to come alive. In 1922 Jackson de Figueiredo founded the Centro Dom Vital in Rio de Janeiro to attract the intelligentsia to the Church and until his death published the review *A Ordem,* with that objective. After his death the work of the Centro Dom Vital was carried forward under the presidency of Tristão de Athayde (Alcu Amoroso Lima). Born in 1893, a journalist who had had part of his education in France, Tristão de Athayde was long an agnostic. He was already noted as a literary critic when in 1928 he was converted through his friendship with Jackson de Figueiredo and the writings of Jacques Maritain. After his conversion he dedicated his life to Catholic Action. He worked out his social and political theories and sought to further Roman Catholic higher education. In 1930 several Roman Catholic lay

[330] Orlando Chaves in *Worldmission,* Vol. XI, p. 36 (Spring, 1960).
[331] Allen, *A Seminary Survey,* pp. 475–479.

organizations were already in existence. Among them were *Acão Universitaria Católico, Federacão Nacional de Operários Católico, Instituto Católico de Estudos Superiores,* and *Associacão de Bibliotecas Católicas.* Under the favouring eye of Getulio Vargas religious instruction was introduced in the public schools. In 1934 Sebastião Leme, now a cardinal, founded the *Liga Eleitoral Católica,* usually known as the LEC and directed by laymen, through which Roman Catholics could bring influence to bear on the political life of the country without forming a Catholic party. The constitution of 1934, with features favouring the Roman Catholic Church, embodied some of the ideals of LEC. When in 1935 Cardinal Leme officially organized Catholic Action, the foundation had been laid for its effectiveness. Thus inaugurated, it concerned itself with social problems, the poor, and rural reform. Helder Camãra, who was a successor of Leme as Archbishop of Rio de Janeiro and cardinal, also stressed Catholic Action.[332]

By 1960 Roman Catholics were addressing themselves in a variety of ways to the problems of Brazil. In 1957 they had eight social centres in the *favelas,* as they were called, the hilltops of Rio de Janeiro on which the poor lived without adequate sewage, water, lighting, or police.[333] Roman Catholics maintained some very good schools for social work, whose graduates went into government service. Aided by grants from the government, the Archbishop of Rio de Janeiro built model apartments for some of the inhabitants of the *favelas.*[334] In 1957 Roman Catholics were operating 2,900 schools with 450,000 students. The 252 Roman Catholic normal schools had trained 65 per cent. of the teachers of the country. There were Catholic universities in São Paulo and Rio de Janeiro. A Catholic Education Association directed and coördinated the system and in 1957 had the able Jesuit Artur Alonso as its head. About 40 per cent. of the secondary school students of the country were in Catholic institutions. In 1957 Rio Grande do Sul could boast the best system of parochial schools in Brazil. Although the law permitted instruction in religion in the public schools to children of the majority faith, the Roman Catholics did not take full advantage of it by providing teachers. Yet they gave as an excuse for not expanding the parochial school system the opportunity which this legislation afforded for teaching their children religion in the state elementary schools. In accordance with its current policy elsewhere, in the twentieth century the Roman Catholic Church encouraged the reading of the Bible.[335] In 1948 JOC, the Young Christian Worker's Movement, was brought to South America and had its first centre in São Paulo. By 1957 it had nine full-time staff leaders in that area, eight in

---

[332] Bates, *The Lay Apostolate in Latin America,* pp. 44–47; Pattee, *El Catolicismo,* pp. 123–128; O'Neill, *op. cit.,* pp. 56–140.
[333] Considine, *New Horizons,* pp. 1–9.
[334] Information acquired by the author in Brazil in 1956.
[335] Considine, *New Horizons,* pp. 14–17. On figures for the 1940's see Pattee, *El Catolicismo,* pp. 116–118. Information obtained by the author in Brazil in 1956.

Rio de Janeiro, and more in other parts of the country. The bishops took the occasion of the International Eucharistic Congress in Rio de Janeiro in 1955 to further a large-scale movement of religious instruction of the laity which used lay people as teachers. Retreats were systematically conducted, some of them in connexion with social work in the large cities. Catholic newspapers were published and a large body of literature in Portuguese was produced.[336]

Extensive help came to the Roman Catholic Church in Brazil from other lands. In 1946 nearly all the secular clergy were Brazilians, but of the regulars about two-thirds were foreign—Germans, Italians, Spaniards, French, Dutch, Poles, Portuguese, and others.[337] It was indicative of the rapid increase of the aid coming from the Roman Catholics of the United States that in 1957 the personnel from that country included 217 men, of whom 91 were Franciscans and 96 were Redemptorists; 79 women, nearly half of them Bernadine Sisters from Villanova, Pennsylvania; and 2 lay missioners from Grailville, Loveland, Ohio.[338] The Liturgical Movement was introduced by German Benedictines and made headway in spite of some opposition. In the 1940's several bishops encouraged it.[339]

Roman Catholics had long been engaged in missions to the Indians in the vast Amazon Valley. In the twentieth century they continued to be active. The personnel was predominantly foreign. They were not wanting in martyrs. For example, in 1934 two Swiss Salesians were killed while attempting to make friendly contacts with the Chavantes. Undiscouraged, other Salesians continued the effort and succeeded in winning the confidence of some of the tribe.[340]

Evidences of the place of the Roman Catholic faith in Brazil and of some of its features were the towering figures of Christ erected in the twentieth century, one crowning a hill back of the harbour of Rio de Janeiro and at least one other in an inland city of moderate size. Of a somewhat different character was a shrine to the Virgin of Apercida, believed to be miraculous, to which many cures were attributed.[341]

---

[336] Considine, *New Horizons*, pp. 18–24.

[337] Azevedo, *op. cit.*, p. 42. On German Franciscans see Cletus Espey, *Festschrift zum Silberjubiläum der Wiedererrichtung der Provinz von der Unbefleckten Empfängnis im Suden Brasiliens 1901–1926* (Werl i.W., Franziskus-Drukerei, 1929, pp. 175), *passim*. On Franciscans from several countries see Arcila Robledo, *La Orden Franciscana en la America Meridional*, pp. 353 ff. For the autobiography of a German Franciscan see Petrus Einzig, *Mönch und Welt. Erinnerungen eines rheinischer Franziskaners in Brasilien*, translated by Maria Kahle (Freiburg im Breisgau, Herder & Co., 1925, pp. ix, 294), *passim*. See also Chrysostomus Strömer, *Von Bahia zum Amazonenstrom. Das Arbeitsfeld der deutschen Franziskaner in Nordbrasilien* (Berlin, Burchverlag Gemania, 1931, pp. 133).

[338] Considine, *New Horizons*, pp. 340, 341.

[339] Böfiler, *Liturgische Erneuerung in Aller Welt*, pp. 120–122.

[340] *Ibid.*, p. 76. A semi-popular autobiographical account of a Portuguese priest who fled from Portugal to escape persecution and who began his mission to Indians of the Amazon in 1915 is Joseph Cacella, *Jungle Call* (no place, publisher, or date, pp. 399), *passim*.

[341] Seen by the author in 1956.

The Roman Catholic Church in Brazil experienced a few schismatic movements led by bishops. The censuses of 1940 and 1950 reported respectively four-tenths of one per cent. and three-tenths of one per cent. of the population as being in such groups.[342]

Protestantism had a very rapid growth in Brazil. In 1960 the country contained more Protestants than all the rest of Latin America. As in other Latin American lands, the statistics were incomplete and imperfect. One set for 1925, but not including the immigrants and their descendants of Protestant ancestry, gave a total of 69,147 communicants and a Protestant community of 101,454.[343] A set of statistics for 1930, again confined to the churches recruited from the nominally Roman Catholic population, said that the communicants totalled 135,390 and that the Protestant community was 406,170. It also reported that the German Evangelical Church, representing the union of the Lutherans and the Reformed imported from Germany, had 60,401 communicants and a community of 215,740, and that the Missouri Synod, also made up of German immigrants and their descendants, had 10,229 communicants and a community of 20,467. According to the 1930 statistics, therefore, the entire Protestant community totalled 702,377.[344] The standard survey of the 1950's gave the total of communicants in 1952 as 550,333 and of the Protestant community in that year as 847,789, and reported that in 1957 the communicants were 809,576 and the community 1,775,927. The figures for both 1952 and 1957 included the Lutherans of German stock.[345] The censuses of 1940 and 1950 said that in the former year Protestants were 1.2 per cent. and in 1950 1.7 per cent. of the population.[346] In 1958 Bishop Barbieri of the Methodist Church, one of the presidents of the World Council of Churches, declared that in 1957 Protestants in Brazil numbered 4,000,000.[347] In 1956 a prominent Brazilian Protestant executive gave it as his opinion that the Protestant Church members in the country totalled 1,083,000, together with their families were about 2,500,000, and proportionately were growing more rapidly than the expanding population.[348] Protestant growth was chiefly in the cities. Here self-support, indigenous clergy, independence of foreign control, and self-propagation by laity and clergy made for rapid advances.

Several of the Protestant churches were of immigrant origin, the largest being the German Lutherans. In 1957 the main body was said to have a community of 514,243.[349] More than half were in Rio Grande do Sul. A quite different

[342] Azevedo, *op. cit.*, p. 66.
[343] Beach and Fahs, *op. cit.*, p. 77.
[344] Braga and Grubb, *The Republic of Brazil*, pp. 140, 141.
[345] *World Christian Handbook, 1957*, pp. 120–122.
[346] Azevedo, *op. cit.*, p. 66.
[347] *Time*, September 15, 1958.
[348] Rodolfo Anders in conversation with the author, June, 1956.
[349] *World Christian Handbook, 1957*, p. 120.

source in 1957 said that those connected with the Evangelical Lutheran Church numbered 700,000.[350] The first large immigration of Germans began early in the nineteenth century. As it mounted, more Roman Catholics than Protestants came. Missions to hold the Protestants to their faith stemmed initially from Basel and Neuendettelsau. From them arose a loyally Lutheran synod which numbered 99,000 in 1954. Others, as we have suggested, were held to the Evangelical union of Lutherans and Reformed. In 1950 they constituted three synods. Until World War II most of the pastors were from Germany. However, as an accompaniment of that struggle, the Brazilian Government forbade the use of German in the worship of the churches. In 1950 four synods, one Lutheran and three Evangelical, came together in an autonomous federation which had severed its ties with the parent bodies in Germany and which in 1954 adopted the designation "the Evangelical Church of the Lutheran Confession in Brazil." All used Luther's catechism and none the Heidelberg catechism. The church became a member of the Lutheran World Federation and of the World Council of Churches. At its centre on the Spiegelberg in São Leopoldo, about twenty miles from Pôrto Alegre, it had a theological seminary for the preparation of clergy. The seminary was formerly in São Paulo and was moved to the Spiegelberg in 1931. In the 1950's its teachers were from Germany. In 1939 a school for training deaconesses was begun on the Spiegelberg. At least two Roman Catholic priests had become pastors, but in general few converts were won from the Roman Catholics and some Lutherans became Roman Catholic through marriage.[351]

In addition to the Evangelical Church of the Lutheran Confession in Brazil, in 1957 the Missouri Lutheran Synod was said to have a membership of 84,000, mostly of German ancestry, but some gathered from the Roman Catholics. It had a seminary in Pôrto Alegre.[352] A number of smaller Protestant immigrant groups were also in Brazil, among them Russian Baptists, Estonian Baptists, Hungarian Baptists, and German Baptists.[353]

In the 1950's the Pentecostals were the most rapidly growing branch of Protestantism in Brazil. They were of various origins, some Italian, some Swedish, some North American. One set of figures said that in 1952 the Assemblies of God, as the chief wing was called, had a membership of 200,000 and a con-

---

[350] Allen, *op. cit.*, p. 195.

[351] Information given the author in São Leopoldo in 1956. *Almanaque do Sinodo Riograndse. Jahrweiser für die evangelischen Gemeindem in Brasilian, 1955 (26, Jahrgang)* (São Leopoldo, Oficinas Graficas Rotermund & Co., 1955, pp. 227), *passim; Bericht über die 1.Kirchenversammlung des Bundes der Synoden, São Leopoldo, 14–16 Mai 1950* (São Leopoldo, Rotermund & Co., 1955, pp. 29), *passim; o 51.⁰ Concilia Geral do Sinodo Riograndense em Lajeado, 7 a 10 de Julho de 1955* (São Leopoldo, Sinodo Riograndense, 1955, pp. 26), *passim.*

[352] Allen, *op. cit.*, pp. 192, 195.

[353] Information obtained by the author in Brazil in 1956. The author visited a Russian Baptist congregation with a large building in São Paulo.

stituency of 220,000 and in 1957 claimed 400,000 members and a constituency of 680,000.[354] The other branch, by 1959 described as fully indigenous, had its initial impulse from an Italian from the United States. The two main branches of the Assemblies of God together were said in 1959 to enroll about 750,000. Other expressions of Pentecostalism were quite independent of the two chief groups.[355] The first Pentecostal missionaries seem to have reached Brazil in 1910. They were from the United States and one, a Swedish immigrant, had been pastor of a Swedish Baptist church in South Bend, Indiana. Early reinforcements were also of Swedish stock and from the United States.[356] The warm emotionalism, with instrumental music, congregational singing, spontaneous prayer, and prayer meetings, made an appeal to the Brazilian temperament. The participation of the men was notable. The preachers were given simple training in the Bible, and evangelism was stressed. The brotherhood in the congregations was welcome to people who knew the bitterness of life and shared a hope for a better social and moral order. With its daily meetings and activities the church became a centre around which the members could organize their lives. They contributed to it financially, participated in its entire programme, and went out to witness to what they had found in it. Through the daily reiteration of what had come to them and the fellowship in meeting the trials and perils of their lives, the largely illiterate or nearly illiterate members who constituted the bulk of the membership were sustained in the faith and given zeal to propagate it. The Pentecostal appeal was mostly to humble folk, and their leaders were near enough to their cultural and educational level to maintain communicable contact with them. The situation was not unlike that of the early days of the Baptists and Methodists in the United States, or of some of the sects of the Middle Ages such as the Waldensians, the Anabaptists of the sixteenth and seventeenth centuries, and the rank and file of the Pietists of the seventeenth, eighteenth, and fore part of the nineteenth century. Church buildings were erected, some of them seating two or three thousand, with funds raised from the membership.[357]

Next to the Pentecostals in numerical strength in the 1900's were the Baptists. They owed their origin to Southern Baptists, immigrants and missionaries, from the United States and in 1914 had been the largest Protestant denomination in Brazil. Although by 1961 the Pentecostals had outstripped them in membership, they continued to grow. They counted 124,710 communicants in 1952 and 135,590 in 1957.[358] They drew from much the same elements of the population

[354] *World Christian Handbook, 1957*, p. 120.
[355] D. J. Du Plessis to the author, October, 1959.
[356] Allen Törnberg, *Från Amazonas till La Plata. Med. Svenska Pingstmissionärer i Sydamerica* (Stockholm, Förlaget Filadelfia, 1956, pp. 136), pp. 42–112.
[357] Davis, *How the Church Grows in Brazil*, pp. 83, 84. The author's observations in 1956.
[358] *World Christian Handbook, 1957*, p. 120.

as did the Pentecostals, but as time passed they tended to rise in the economic and educational scale. Extensive assistance came from the Southern Baptist Convention of the United States, chiefly in the form of missionaries and of aid in theological education. In the mid-twentieth century Brazil was said to absorb more of the effort of the Foreign Mission Board of the Southern Baptist Convention and to have a larger numerical achievement than any other country.[359] In 1950 more than three-fifths of the churches, annual baptisms, and overseas membership connected with the Southern Baptists were in Brazil.

In 1882 the first missionaries to the Brazilians, consisting of two couples and a former Roman Catholic priest, reached Bahia and in that year a Baptist church was organized there.[360] Soon, in spite of persecution, more missionaries arrived, converts increased, and Brazilian clergy were trained. By 1907 there were 84 churches and 26 ordained Brazilian ministers.[361] Centres were established not only in the chief cities and in the better-populated states on the coast but also in the vast Amazon Valley. In 1907 a national convention was organized.[362] A home mission board and a foreign mission board soon followed. The former encouraged Baptist beginnings in hitherto untouched areas, and among the uncivilized Indians (with not much success), and the latter assisted Baptist efforts in Chile and Portugal.[363] Colleges, theological seminaries, training schools for women, and the production, publication, and distribution of literature were begun and augmented. Brazilian pastors and self-supporting churches rapidly increased and membership with them. The churches multiplied in the cities, partly through migration from the rural sections.[364]

Seventh Day Adventists also grew rapidly, from a reported membership of 27,367 and a community of 64,758 in 1952 to a membership of 39,697 and a community of 92,857 in 1957.[365] Most of the growth was among the nominally Christian population, but some came from heroic missions among the non-Christian Indians in the Amazon Valley.[366]

The Presbyterians were strong and in the main drew from a higher educational and economic bracket than did some of the other denominations. They

[359] Crabtree, Baptists in Brazil, p. 10.

[360] Ibid., p. 44.

[361] Ibid., p. 65.

[362] Ibid., pp. 121, 125, 126.

[363] Ibid., pp. 130–137.

[364] Ibid., pp. 153 ff.; for charts see pp. 218–221. See also Arthur B. Deter, Forty Years in the Land of Tomorrow (Nashville, Broadman Press, 1946, pp. 207); L. R. Scarborough, A Blaze of Evangelism Across the Equator (Nashville, Broadman Press, 1937, pp. 137); Loren M. Reno and Alice W. Reno, Reminiscences: Twenty-five Years in Victoria, Brasil (Richmond, Educational Department, Foreign Mission Board, 1930, pp. 170); Everett Gill, Pilgrimage to Brazil (Nashville, Broadman Press, 1954, pp. xiii, 144). On Baptist theological seminaries see Allen, op. cit., pp. 192, 193, 195. On Baptist home missions see Davis, How the Church Grows in Brazil, p. 87, 88.

[365] World Christian Handbook, 1957, p. 121.

[366] Leo B. Halliwell, Light Bearer to the Amazon (Nashville, The Southern Publishing Association, 1945, pp. 160), passim.

owed their origin to the Northern and the Southern Presbyterians of the United States and the foundations had been laid in the nineteenth century.[367] The two branches coöperated and in 1888 the churches connected with them formed an autonomous synod made up of four presbyteries. In 1903, partly because of differences on policy toward Freemasonry and theology and a clash of personalities, some churches withdrew and formed the Independent Presbyterian Church of Brazil.[368] Both bodies continued to grow. In 1952 the parent organization reported 67,695 members and a community of 123,738, and in 1957 it claimed 76,307 members and a community of 137,234. The younger body was said to have a membership of 21,500 in 1952 and of 22,300 in 1957.[369] In association with their brethren in the United States, the Brazilian Presbyterians were spreading the faith in the far interior.[370] The Presbyterians also were active in reaching the intellectuals and cultured classes. As we have noted, most Protestants were from the lower income and less well-educated strata. To be sure, even in the early days of the Protestant churches, some of the oldest and most respected families, notably in São Paulo, were converted and from them came outstanding leadership for the young churches. In the interior, several owners of the large landed estates became Protestants and formed Protestant churches which embraced most of those who worked on the *fazenda*.[371] On the whole, however, Protestantism had no effective appeal for members of the upper classes. In several ways the Presbyterians sought to change that tradition. In São Paulo a pastor of one of their largest churches concentrated on reaching the intelligentsia.[372] Presbyterians stressed college and theological education. In the 1950's the strongest Protestant institution of its kind was Mackenzie College in São Paulo. The theological seminary at Campinas, about sixty miles from São Paulo, was the leading one maintained by Presbyterians in Brazil.[373]

The Methodists, while not as numerous as the Presbyterians, in the 1950's had a larger membership than the Seventh Day Adventists and were growing. They, too, were autonomous and in 1930 were constituted as the Methodist Church of Brazil. Like the Presbyterians, while having many members among the very poor, they also drew from the middle class. They likewise made much

[367] Braga and Grubb, *op. cit.*, pp. 57–61. For the Southern Presbyterians see James Porter Smith, *An Open Door in Brazil. Being a Brief Survey of the Mission Work Carried on in Brazil since 1869 by the Presbyterian Church in the United States* (Richmond, Presbyterian Committee on Publication, preface 1925, pp. 235). For the Northern Presbyterians see Brown, *One Hundred Years*, pp. 794–802.

[368] Brown, *op. cit.*, p. 796; Davis, *How the Church Grows in Brazil*, pp. 103, 104; Allen, *op. cit.*, p. 194.

[369] *World Christian Handbook, 1957*, p. 120.

[370] Davis, *How the Church Grows in Brazil*, pp. 91, 92.

[371] Shaull in *Religion in Life*, Vol. XXVII, pp. 7, 8 (Winter, 1957–1958).

[372] Davis, *How the Church Grows in Brazil*, pp. 93, 94.

[373] *Album Commemorativo dos Cincocentenario Annos de Existencia da Faculdade de Theologia da Igreja Christã Presbyteriana do Brasil* (Campinas, 1938, pp. 40), *passim*.

of education and, among other institutions, had a school in Rio de Janeiro which carried its students through junior college, a theological seminary on the outskirts of São Paulo, a training school, also in that city, for deaconesses and other women church workers, a summer camp, and a social centre serving a *favela* in Rio de Janeiro. Many of their members were recruited in the rural districts by itinerant preachers. They employed the radio to broadcast the Christian message.[374]

Many other Protestant groups were represented. The Congregationalists, having their inception in the second half of the nineteenth century and by the twentieth century with indigenous leadership and support, did not grow rapidly but had some strong churches.[375] The Church of Jesus Christ of Latter Day Saints (Mormons) sent hundreds of missionaries, mostly after World War II, and in 1960 were said to have over 30,000 members.[376] The Episcopal Church, with its chief strength in Pôrto Alegre, reached out into other areas and won over many Japanese immigrants.[377] In the mid-twentieth century the Four-Square Gospel was growing fast, partly through the use of tent-meetings—new in Brazil—and with emphasis upon faith healing.[378] The American Bible Society had a phenomenal record in distributing the Scriptures in several tongues. In this activity it was deeply indebted to Hugh Clarence Tucker, who during much of his long life served as its agent, stimulated campaigns against yellow fever and leprosy, and founded the People's Central Institute in Rio de Janeiro which among its many services provided dental and medical clinics and playgrounds for children. Under the impulse given by the American Bible Society, the British and Foreign Bible Society, and the National Bible Society of Scotland, in much of the twentieth century the sale of the Scriptures exceeded that of any other book except text-books for day schools.[379]

A feature of Protestantism in Brazil was extensive missions to the non-Christian Indians in the Amazon Valley. Several by undenominational faith missions had records of heroism and devotion.[380]

---

[374] Information obtained by the author in Brazil in 1956; Braga and Grubb, *op. cit.*, p. 63.

[375] Davis, *How the Church Grows in Brazil*, pp. 100–102.

[376] *Time*, November 28, 1960.

[377] Davis, *How the Church Grows in Brazil*, p. 92; Powel Mills Dawley, *Brazilian Destiny* (New York, National Council, Protestant Episcopal Church, 1951, pp. 47), *passim*.

[378] *World Christian Handbook, 1957*, p. 121; information acquired by the author in Brazil in 1956.

[379] Basil Mathews, *Forward Through the Ages* (New York, Friendship Press, new ed., 1960, pp. xii, 276), pp. 200, 201; Braga and Grubb, *op. cit.*, pp. 71–75.

[380] On some of these missions see Alex. Rattray Hay, *Saints and Savages, Brazil's Indian Problem* (London, Hodder and Stoughton, no date, pp. viii, 91), *passim;* Rosemary Cunningham, *Under a Thatched Roof in a Brazilian Jungle: A Missionary Story* (Toronto, Evangelical Publishers, 1947, pp. 126), *passim;* Rosemary Cunningham, *Harvest Moon on the Amazon* (Grand Rapids, Mich., Zondervan Publishing House, 1958, pp. 151), *passim;* Martha L. Moennich, *Pioneering for Christ in Kingu Jungles* (Grand Rapids, Mich., Zondervan Publishing House, 1942, pp. 196), *passim;* Erik Jansson, *På Indianstigar i Brasilien* (Örebro, Orebro Missionsforenings Forlag, 1945, pp. 103),

Three comments are needed to round out the picture of Protestantism in Brazil in the mid-twentieth century. First, in spite of rapid numerical growth, difficulty was encountered in holding many of the members, especially the youth of the second and third generations. Some tended to drift away as they moved from the rural sections into the city. Others were excluded from membership because of moral lapses. Others married outside Protestant circles. Numbers were repelled by the prohibitions by several of the churches of dancing, smoking, card-playing, and attendance at the theatre and moving pictures. In the 1940's the loss for various causes was said to be from 30 to 70 per cent. of the youth. Attempts were made to stem the defections by programmes of recreation and summer camping connected with the churches and various methods of education. With the industry, self-discipline, education, and moral integrity nourished by the Protestant churches, many members rose to a middle-class status and their children, acquiring improved social, intellectual, and economic position, at best tended to retain only a nominal connexion with the churches of their parents. Second, difficulty was encountered in recruiting and training a body of clergy who would be willing to make the sacrifices entailed by their vocation and could meet the needs of the rising generation.[381] Associated with this problem was the extreme conservatism of much of Protestantism, which had as one of its expressions distrust of the Ecumenical Movement and unwillingness to join even on a national or a local scale in coöperative interdenominational activities. Thus, although in the Evangelical Confederation of Brazil the Methodists and Presbyterians were members, the Lutherans, Pentecostals, and Baptists, as well as several others, held aloof.[382] And third, the Protestant churches were growing in self-support and self-government. More and more they were independent of financial aid and direction from abroad.

THE EASTERN CHURCHES

A feature of Christianity in Latin America in the twentieth century was the immigration of thousands who by heredity were members of the Eastern Churches. Most of them came to the coastal states of Brazil and to Argentina. Some were Uniates, especially Maronites and Melkites. But the majority were from churches which were not in communion with Rome.[383] The greatest number, estimated in the 1950's as between 300,000 and 500,000, appear to have been

---

passim; K. G. Grubb, *The Lowland Indians of Amazonia. A Survey of the Location and Religious Condition of the Indians of Colombia, Venezuela, the Guianas, Ecuador, Peru, Brazil and Bolivia* (London, World Dominion Press, 1927, pp. 159), pp. 90–123.

[381] Davis, *How the Church Grows in Brazil,* pp. 103, 119–124.

[382] Information given the author in Brazil in 1956.

[383] Alexander Wyse in *Worldmission,* Vol. VIII, pp. 43, 44 (Winter, 1957); J. H. Ryder in *ibid.,* Vol. XI, pp. 96–102 (Spring, 1960).

Orthodox, mainly refugees from the lands captured by Communism after World War I and especially after World War II. The pioneer in providing them pastoral care was Archpriest Constantin Israstzov (1865–1953), who came to Buenos Aires in 1891. Many in Brazil were lost to Orthodoxy. Some became Protestants and Spiritualists. Yet by 1962 progress was being made in holding the Orthodox to their historic faith. In 1934 a diocese was founded for them. A monastery was begun in Villa Alpina in Brazil—but soon moved to Canada.[384] Early in the 1950's a large church was erected in Caracas by a group of 115 of the faithful. Congregations were organized elsewhere in Venezuela and four were gathered in Paraguay, under the Russian Episcopal Synod Abroad.[385] Well-organized parishes were found in Argentina, Chile, Uruguay, and Lima.[386] In 1955 the Greek Orthodox had eight congregations in Brazil, Argentina, Chile, and Uruguay under a bishop who resided in Buenos Aires. For all the Orthodox a great shortage of clergy was noted.[387] In 1953 the Orthodox Patriarchate of Antioch took steps to create two dioceses in Brazil and one in Argentina. In 1954 the Greeks were said to have 40,000 Orthodox in South America.[388]

SUMMARY

Christianity in Latin America entered the twentieth century in what seemed a moribund condition. The heritage of the colonial era was a population which was overwhelmingly Roman Catholic by profession. Only in distant recesses of mountains, thinly peopled plains, and tropical river valleys did frankly pre-Christian cults survive. Yet that Christianity was dependent for its vigour upon continued aid in personnel from Europe. In the nineteenth century the impact of the revolutionary age had startling effects. Political and ecclesiastical ties with Spain and Portugal were severed, with a grave weakening of the ecclesiastical structure. The anti-clerical, anti-Christian currents from Europe gave rise to tension and struggle in each of the successor governments. The quality of the clergy, already low, declined, and priests were quite insufficient in number, even had their character been higher, to give adequate pastoral care. Some help in personnel came from Europe, but in too few numbers to meet the needs of a rapidly mounting population. Although at the outset of the twentieth century a third of the Roman Catholics of the world were in Latin America, they were a dead weight, bearing no part of the burden of giving the faith to

[384] *New Missionary Review*, Autumn, 1952, pp. 11, 12; Spring, 1953, pp. 13, 14; Autumn, 1953, p. 13; Autumn, 1955, p. 11.
[385] *Ibid.*, Spring, 1955, pp. 12, 13.
[386] *Ibid.*, Spring, 1956, p. 12.
[387] *Ibid.*, Autumn, 1955, p. 12.
[388] *Ibid.*, Spring, 1954, pp. 9, 10.

mankind and drawing from their fellow believers in Europe aid which was greatly needed elsewhere. Protestantism had as yet gained only a few footholds and except for some immigrant bodies appeared to be negligible.

The twentieth century witnessed a surge of life in Latin American Christianity. It was perceptible only among minorities, but the minorities grew. The awakening was in the Roman Catholic Church and Protestantism. In both, the impulses came from abroad, but they brought rising vigour which was less and less dependent on foreign contributions.

In the Roman Catholic Church were seen the characteristic forms of the revival which had started in Western Europe but which was having repercussions elsewhere. Catholic Action, with its stress upon lay piety and activity, Eucharistic Congresses, emphasis upon Bible reading, and the Liturgical Movement were among them. When World War II impoverished much of Western Europe, substantial aid in personnel came from the Roman Catholics of Canada and the United States, especially the latter. Into Latin America was poured more of the rising foreign missionary effort of the Roman Catholic Church in the United States than into any other area. In nearly every country responses were seen in indigenous Christian life. In a few countries, notably Mexico, the anti-clerical movements, now augmented by Communism, brought crises, but on the whole the struggle between clericals and anti-clericals was not as general or as acute as in the nineteenth century—partly but not entirely because of the growing separation of Church and state and the sentiment among the majority that the Church was not as powerful and hence as much to be feared as previously.

Protestantism grew by leaps and bounds, chiefly through missionaries from the United States. But the Protestantism which was emerging differed strikingly from that of the United States. Except for the Lutheran immigration from Germany, the proportions among the denominations were in sharp contrast to those in the northern republic. The denominations—Baptist, Methodist, Disciples of Christ, Presbyterian, Reformed, Congregationalist, and Episcopalian —which enrolled the overwhelming majority of the Protestants of the United States, even when taken together had only a minority of the Protestants of Latin America. The most rapidly growing movements were the Pentecostals, the Seventh Day Adventists, and other varieties of Protestantism which appealed to the illiterate or semi-literate masses of the lower income strata constituting more than half of the population. Emotional, with an unquestioning faith in the inspiration and inerrancy of the Bible, and demanding an unequivocal and personal morality, they caught the ear of the dispossessed and offered a door to a richer life. The numerically major denominations of the United States had become largely middle class or upper class. They had but little attraction for Latin American intellectuals, and the middle class, which had become the majority in the United States, was still represented only by minorities in Latin America and regarded Protestantism as alien to the Latin American heritage and temperament. In general, by the mid-twentieth century, Latin American Protestants were only beginning to participate in the Ecumenical Movement. To most of them, if they thought of it at all, it appeared to be unsound in the faith. But Latin American Protestantism was less and less dedendent on assistance from other countries and was spreading through its inner vitality.

By the mid-twentieth century, then, Christianity in Latin America displayed much vigour. Although the majority of those who professed to be Catholics did not comprehend the inner meaning of the faith and were at best lukewarm, a growing minority, both Roman Catholics and Protestants, were committed to the faith. Much of the renewed vitality came through missionaries from Europe and North America, but increasingly, especially in Protestantism, it was finding expression through indigenous leadership. In Protestantism it was taking distinctive forms. If, as was sometimes said, Protestantism so bore the stamp of its development in North-western Europe and in the offshoot of North-western Europe in the United States and Canada that it was alien to the Latin mind, here was emerging a kind of Protestantism on which some elements in the Latin American world were placing their stamp. That those elements were from the underprivileged was no new experience for Christianity. Even now parallels could be pointed out among the peoples of "primitive" and near-"primitive" cultures in Asia, Africa, and the islands of the sea.

Although Christianity was displaying augmented vigour, neither Roman Catholics nor Protestants were having more than a very small part in the propagation of the faith outside Latin America. Both branches of the faith were still largely dependent on assistance from Christians of other regions.

CHAPTER VI

The Record in Changing Australia

IN THE twentieth century special features of the revolutionary age presented Christianity in Australia with distinctive challenges. The continent embraced by the Commonwealth of Australia was smaller by a sixth than the land area of its sister commonwealth, Canada, and its population, estimated in 1959 at 10,008,665, was less than two-thirds that which the census of 1956 gave to Canada —16,080,791. As much of the area of the latter was too far north to be easily or densely habitable, so much of the surface of Australia was too arid to support a large population. Unlike Canada, whose initial peopling was by the French, at the outset inspired in part by a Christian missionary motive later modified by other considerations, and whose nineteenth-century immigration, chiefly from the British Isles, was attracted by the economic opportunities and furthered by the transportation facilities of the revolutionary age, for the first several decades of white settlement Australia was used as a dumping ground for elements undesired in the British Isles, mostly convicts for political or other offenses. Not far from the time when the use of Australia as a penal colony was stopped, a gold rush attracted many on whom Christianity also sat lightly if at all.

For various reasons, largely growing out of the Industrial Revolution and the character of the soil and climate, in the twentieth century Australia's cities were more prominent in proportion to its population than were Canada's. For example, early in the 1960's Canada's two chief cities, Montreal and Toronto, together were only slightly more than half the size of Sydney and Melbourne, the two major cities of Australia. Since conditions for Christianity were usually more unfavourable in urban than in rural areas, Australia offered greater obstacles to the faith than did Canada. Partly because cities, with their industrialization, had a large element of organized labour difficult to reach with the Christian message, Australia evidenced more of a drift towards secularization and de-Christianization of traditionally Christian peoples than did Canada. Moreover, the character of Australian rural life, with a much more thinly scattered population than in most of the rural areas of Canada, hindered the creation of an effective parish life. Then, too, both the Roman Catholic Church and the Protestant churches were younger in Australia than in Canada and by the mid-twentieth century had not had time to strike such deep roots before the revolutionary age reached the peak of its de-Christianizing impact in the post-1914 decades.

Like the rest of the world, Australia was deeply affected by World War I and World War II. An active belligerent in both, in the second it was seriously threatened by the Japanese. In World War I the effort to adopt conscription to the armed forces brought a deep division in public opinion. Conscription was not enacted, but proportionately to its population Australia contributed quite as much in personnel to the Allied cause as did other members of the British Commonwealth. As in several other countries, the population of Australia was modified by the migrations which followed the wars, particularly the second. The government and people of Australia continued to insist on the pre-1914 policy of maintaining a "white Australia" against the population explosion in the islands and the continent on the north. As in the nineteenth, so in the twentieth century the overwhelming majority of the population either were descendants of immigrants from the British Isles or themselves had come from that region. Yet the Continent of Europe was more strongly represented in the twentieth than in the nineteenth century, a change reflected in Australia's religious complexion. In 1947 out of 607,000 European-born residents of at least five years' standing, 507,000 were from the British Isles, 325,000 were from Italy, and 13,500 were from Germany. From 1947 to 1951 inclusive, 480,000 more had come from Europe, and of these the leading non-British groups were from Poland and Eastern Europe. Obviously the additions of the 1940's and 1950's greatly strengthened the Roman Catholic Church.[1]

The altered origin of the population in part accounted for the shifting ratio in the denominational affiliation recorded in the census. In 1954, 855,810, or a little over 8.5 per cent., left unanswered the question of religious preference. The omission could indicate indifference or open scepticism. About 34 per cent. registered as Church of England, 20.6 per cent. as Roman Catholic, 9.77 per cent. as Methodist, 8.7 per cent. as Presbyterian, 7.15 per cent. in smaller Christian bodies, and .54 per cent. as non-Christian.[2] Compared with the 1921 figures, this listing showed a decline in the percentage of the larger Protestant bodies —from 40 per cent. to 34 per cent. in the Church of England, from about 12

---

[1] The Encyclopaedia Britannica, 1955 edition, Vol. II, p. 726. Of the refugees resettled by the World Council of Churches in 1958, more—a total of 3,928—went to Australia than to any other country. They included 1,799 Greeks, 860 Jugoslavs from Italy, 706 Russians, mainly from China, and 446 Hungarians. The Christian Century, Vol. LXXVI, p. 470 (April, 1959).

[2] The Statesman's Year Book, 1960, p. 461.

per cent. to about 8.7 per cent. in the Presbyterian bodies, and from about 12 per cent. to 9.77 per cent. in the Methodist communion.[3] On the other hand, the Roman Catholics showed an increase—from 19.4 per cent. in 1910[4] to 20.6 per cent. in 1954. To put it in another way, between 1947 and 1954 Roman Catholics had increased 29.9 per cent., the Church of England 15.3 per cent., the Presbyterians 16.9 per cent., and the Methodists 12.2 per cent. Of the smaller bodies, in the 1947–1954 interval the Lutheran growth was 73.7 per cent., that of the Seventh Day Adventists was 44.3 per cent., and that of the Baptists was 12.3 per cent.[5]

Although these figures show that the overwhelming majority of the population of Australia counted themselves as Christians, in 1961 the churches were still partly in a colonial status and the Protestants were not making a united approach to the nation. Only about one in ten Australians attended religious services with any degree of regularity. Theological training of an indigenous clergy was making progress but was weak compared with the training in Canada. The various Protestant denominations were slow to achieve comprehensive national organizations. Sharp theological differences among Protestants were marked—between liberals and conservatives, and in the Church of England between Anglo-Catholics and Evangelicals.[6] Industrialization, accelerated by World War II, and the accompanying expansion of the cities had been so rapid and the trend towards secularism so potent that the churches could not keep pace with them; the urban population was becoming de-Christianized—if, indeed, it could ever have been said to be Christian. In some of the rural areas the churches had been able to hold a larger proportion of the population and to make more impression on the community.[7] Yet when in 1959 Billy Graham held meetings in several cities, crowds thronged the largest stadiums and auditoriums.[8]

The largest ecclesiastical body, the Church of England, displayed growth but by the late 1950's had not been fully emancipated from its colonial status. Church buildings, large and small, were erected. Early in the twentieth century three separate ecclesiastical provinces were created for the civil provinces of New South Wales, Victoria, and Queensland, and later one was added for Western Australia. Although a shortage of indigenous clergy was a handicap, theological education was strengthened, and in the 1950's two of the four arch-

[3] Robert Wilson, *Official Year Book of the Commonwealth of Australia*, No. 32, 1939 (Canberra, Commonwealth Government Printer, 1940, pp. xxxi, 992), p. 381.
[4] *The Australian Catholic Directory for 1910*, table after p. 193.
[5] *The Australian Encyclopaedia*, Vol. VII, p. 404.
[6] Information given to the author by Australians in 1958 and 1959.
[7] E. H. Burgmann, (Anglican) Bishop of New South Wales, *The Effect of Recent Events on Religion in Australia* (no date or place, pp. 5, mimeographed), *passim*.
[8] *Britannica Book of the Year, 1960*, p. 75.

bishops were Australians.[9] Provincial synods met every three years and a general synod once in five years, but efforts to achieve a national organization which would make the Church of England in Australia fully autonomous were frustrated. In 1960 it remained a part of the Church of England and the legal title of much of its property was tied to that connexion. As early as 1916 efforts were begun to achieve complete independence, but in 1954 attempts to win approval of a constitution for a body with that status failed. The obstacle was largely a difference in churchmanship between Evangelicals, who were strong in the Archdiocese of New South Wales, and Anglo-Catholics, who were powerful in some other sections.[10] In the 1940's what was called the Red Book Case, centring on the issue of the ritualistic practices of the Bishop of Bathurst to which some Anglicans in New South Wales strongly objected, provoked controversy, was fought out in the civil courts, and resulted in a partial victory for each side.[11]

In individual dioceses progress was being achieved. For example, Western Australia, in 1914 still very much a pioneer region, displayed advances in Christian education in which assistance was given by sisterhoods and brotherhoods first recruited in England.[12] A similar story was told of Gippsland, a rainy, rural section in Victoria, which became a diocese in 1902 and to which after World War I came members of the Brotherhood of St. John the Evangelist and deaconesses from England.[13] The Bush Brotherhood continued, begun in 1897 as a means of serving thinly settled areas in the eastern portions of the country by young men living in community. Several bishops were chosen from them and by 1947 the majority of their members were Australians.[14] From the Church of England in Australia missionaries went to Papua, the adjacent archipelagos (politically connected with Australia and for which Australian Christians naturally felt a responsibility), India, and Tanganyika.[15]

The Presbyterians, largely of Scottish descent, were growing. The national organization which they formed in 1901 through the creation of a General Assembly continued to function. The aftermath of World War II brought to Australia numbers of Dutch and Hungarians who were akin ecclesiastically to the Presbyterians, but a conservative minority from the Netherlands organized themselves into a Dutch Reformed Church. Under the General Assembly

[9] Neill, *Anglicanism*, pp. 310, 311.

[10] *Ibid.; The Australian Encyclopaedia*, Vol. II, pp. 377, 378.

[11] *The Australian Encyclopaedia*, Vol. II, pp. 377, 378.

[12] C. L. M. Hawtry, *The Availing Struggle. A Record of the Planting and Development of the Church of England in Western Australia, 1829–1947* (no place, publisher, or date, pp. 208), pp. 108 ff.

[13] Albert E. Clark, *The Church of Our Fathers. Being the History of the Church of England in Gippsland, 1847–1947* (Melbourne, Rialto Press, 1947, pp. 294), pp. 194 ff.

[14] J. W. S. Tomlin, *The Story of the Bush Brotherhoods* (London, A. R. Mowbray & Co., 1949, pp. 105), pp. 66 ff.

[15] Neill, *op. cit.*, p. 312.

various committees and boards sought effective united action in social service, the naval and military chaplaincy, foreign missions, theological education, other forms of education, work for youth, home missions, church extension, religious education in the state schools (as permitted by law), and organizations for women and laymen.[16] The Presbyterians maintained the Australian Inland Mission. Its purpose was to minister to the thinly peopled 2,000,000 square miles which in 1912 had a population of about 50,000. In that year the first missionary was sent by the General Assembly to what was then known as the Northern Territory and Central Australia. As it developed, the enterprise included itinerant ministers, the "flying doctor service" to the scattered homesteads, and a transmitting and receiving radio network, ideally reaching every home.[17] As in several other countries, Presbyterians were divided on their attitude towards the intellectual currents of the revolutionary age. In the 1930's, for instance, when the controversy between "fundamentalists" and "liberals" was acute in the United States, Samuel Angus (1881–1943), who had been educated in Ireland, the United States, and Germany, and who held the chair of New Testament and historical theology in the University of Sydney, was formally accused of heresy. He had advocated a unitive Christianity and held that the essence of the faith was not confined to any particular creedal formulation. The charge came before the General Assembly and was given much publicity, but that body postponed consideration.[18] As time passed, more of the clergy were recruited and trained in Australia and fewer came from the British Isles, partly because the latter found it increasingly difficult to accommodate themselves to the Australian pattern of life and thought.[19]

Methodism grew. In 1954, to care for its Australian members and its wide mission field, it had 937 white ministers—about one for every thousand who expressed a preference for that denomination—127 home missionaries, 3,457 local preachers, and five institutions for training ministers. In the capital of each state Methodists had what was called a central mission—a centre for reaching the urban population in a variety of ways on a pattern first developed in England.[20] In 1926 an inland mission was begun, covering 1,500,000 square miles. In 1953 a nation-wide campaign, "the Mission to the Nation," was launched with the purpose of encouraging "a return to Christian standards in public and private life." It was hoped to reach the 50 per cent. of the Australians who did not have normal contacts with the churches. Public meetings were held, where possible in non-ecclesiastical buildings, and within three years several thousand

---

16 *The Australian Encyclopaedia*, Vol. VII, p. 271; C. A. White, *The Challenge of the Years. A History of the Presbyterian Church in the State of New South Wales* (Sydney, Angus and Robertson, 1951, pp. xviii, 614), pp. 84 ff.
17 Margaret Ford in *The Student World*, Vol. XLVI, pp. 333–338 (Fourth Quarter 1953).
18 *The Australian Encyclopaedia*, Vol. I, p. 188.
19 Information from an Australian clergyman in 1956.
20 *The Australian Encyclopaedia*, Vol. VI, p. 66.

signed personal commitments "to Jesus Christ in the fellowship of His Church." Wherever Australians gathered—on football fields, in theatres, in railway shunting yards, and in large open-air meetings—speakers presented the Christian message. From sixty-four radio stations a half-hour "drama with challenge" was presented each week. Special literature was prepared and the public press gave extensive coverage. Local congregations were encouraged to approach their respective communities.[21]

The Baptists were a much smaller denomination than the Anglicans, Presbyterians, or Methodists. In the census of 1954 those registering as Baptists were 127,444. Between 1947 and 1954 they had increased 12.3 per cent., not as rapidly as the Presbyterians or the Anglicans but slightly faster than the Methodists. In 1926 the majority of the congregations formed the Baptist Union of Australia, an outgrowth of the Australian Baptist Congress which had met periodically since 1908. The Baptist Union had the boards which were characteristic of such national organizations—for foreign missions, home missions, evangelism, education, and young people's work.[22]

We cannot take the space even to enumerate all the smaller denominations in Australia. We can simply note that the Congregationalists, with their strong emphasis upon their traditional independency, with some outstanding scholars, and with a willingness to enter into conversations looking towards church union, totalled 69,452 in 1954,[23] and that in that year the Churches of Christ were reported to have 31,000 members.[24] We must pause long enough to remark that partly out of their rapid growth (73.7 per cent. between 1947 and 1954), the Lutherans were gathered in several synods, largely by the nations of origin. In 1921 all but two of the synods joined in forming the United Evangelical Lutheran Church of Australia. That body was a member of the Lutheran World Federation and had missions in New Guinea. Its services were mostly in English, but with the post-World War II influx of refugees some were in Latvian, Estonian, Polish, and Hungarian. The theologically more conservative who did not go into the United Evangelical Lutheran Church of Australia formed the Evangelical Lutheran Church in Australia and were affiliated with the Missouri Synod in the United States. The 1954 census listed 116,178 as Lutherans, and of these 42,057 were in South Australia.[25]

To obtain an approach to a well-rounded picture of Australian Protestantism, we must call attention to a development akin to that found in the United States,

[21] *A Monthly Letter about Evangelism* (mimeographed by the World Council of Churches, Geneva, Switzerland), April, 1956.

[22] *The Australian Encyclopaedia*, Vol. I, p. 426; Vol. VII, p. 404.

[23] *Ibid.*, Vol. II, p. 500. See also Edward S. Kiek, *One Hundred Years. The Century Record of the South Australian Congregational Union* (Adelaide, Hankin, Ellis and King, no date, pp. 123), *passim*.

[24] *The Australian Encyclopaedia*, Vol. II, p. 379.

[25] *Ibid.*, Vol. V, p. 386; Vol. VII, p. 404.

Canada, and Latin America: the growth of movements appealing to elements in industrial areas and in some suburbs which the larger denominations did not touch and which were mainly from lower educational and economic levels.[26]

Nor should we omit at least some mention of such a characteristic feature of nineteenth- and twentieth-century Anglo-Saxon Protestantism as the British and Foreign Bible Society with its mounting distribution of the Scriptures through the Evangelization Society, the Salvation Army, the Traveller's Aid Society, home mission societies, seamen's missions, city missions, orphanages, prisons, hospitals, aborigines' missions, bedrooms of hotels, boarding houses, and other channels, and its increasing rootage in Australia through gifts from that country and the formation in 1925 of a commonwealth council.[27] The Salvation Army, also an accepted movement in Anglo-Saxon Protestantism, was prominent.[28] The Young Men's Christian Association was represented in the cities, like the Salvation Army an attempt to meet phases of the challenge presented by the urban aspects of the revolutionary age.[29]

Something of the vigour of Australian Protestantism was seen in its missions. The Protestants of the commonwealth felt an obligation to the peoples of other countries. Through denominational and undenominational agencies, some of the latter branches of societies founded in Europe, they had missions in the islands of the Pacific, in several countries in Asia and Africa, and among the Australian aborigines. To the aborigines not only denominational societies sent representatives, but several undenominational organizations made them their sole objective.[30]

As was to be expected from the trend in other countries and regions, in the twentieth century coöperation among denominations and talks of possible union spread. They did not come as early or attain such dimensions as in the United States, Canada, and some countries in Europe and Asia, but they were more successful than in Latin America and in most of Africa. In 1906 conversations were held in Melbourne on the possibility of the union of Anglicans and Presbyterians. In 1919 a proposal came before the Presbyterian General Assembly in Queensland outlining the considerations to be taken into account in church union.[31]

Other efforts in that direction can be quickly summarized. In 1913 a Congress

---

[26] Information obtained from a well-informed Australian, October, 1959.

[27] A. T. Thompson, *Australia and the Bible. A Brief Outline of the Work of the British and Foreign Bible Society in Australia, 1807–1934* (London, British and Foreign Bible Society, 1935, pp. 206), pp. 142 ff.

[28] Percival Dale, *Salvation Chariot. A Review of the First Seventy-One Years of the Salvation Army in Australia, 1880–1951* (Melbourne, Salvation Army Press, 1952, pp. xv, 175), *passim.*

[29] J. T. Massey, *The Y.M.C.A. of Australia, a History* (Melbourne, F. W. Cheshire, 1950, pp. xii, 609), *passim.*

[30] Parker, *Directory of World Missions*, pp. 1–5.

[31] Richard Bardon, *James Gibson, M.A., D.D.* (Brisbane, W. R. Smith and Paterson, 1955, pp. 119), pp. 104–110.

on Union of Churches met in Melbourne with members from eight denominations. It dealt with such issues as the possibility of a uniform curriculum of studies and, even more, of the amalgamation of theological colleges, some of them weak and in the same area; the elimination of competition in small communities in organizing denominational congregations; and organic union. The discussions were frank and friendly.[32] In 1918, after years of conference and discussion, a joint committee of the Presbyterian, Methodist, and Congregational Churches presented a basis of union as to doctrine and polity on which they had agreed. Votes were taken by the responsible bodies, but union did not follow.[33] In 1920 the United Missionary Council of Australia was organized, and in 1927, after a visit by John R. Mott, chairman of the International Missionary Council, this gave way to the National Missionary Council of Australia.[34] In 1922, as the result of the Lambeth Appeal and an attempt to implement it by the Church of England in Australia's General Synod Reunion Committee, a conference of representatives of the Anglican, Presbyterian, Methodist, and Congregational Churches met in Sydney.[35] In 1937, the question of inter-communion arose, posed by the problems faced in Papua by the moving of Christians of various denominations from one area to another. Leaders among the Anglicans, Methodists, Presbyterians, and Congregationalists met and eventually (1943) formulated what were known as the Australian proposals for intercommunion. They included a plan for the reciprocal recognition of ministries for the administration of the Communion. The Lambeth Conference of 1948 viewed them guardedly but did not discourage further conversations if they could lead to eventual organic union.[36] From the Amsterdam Assembly (1948), at which the World Council of Churches was formally constituted, came the Australian Council for the World Council of Churches. Under its auspices the First National Conference of Australian Churches was held in Melbourne (1959) with 450 lay and clerical leaders in attendance.[37]

In several ways in the first half of the twentieth century the Roman Catholic Church in Australia was approaching maturity, was feeling the impact of the currents within that church which we have found elsewhere in the world, and was making specific emphases in its Australian setting. It was approaching maturity in its leadership. From the earliest days the membership of the Australian Roman Catholic Church had been predominantly Irish. This was still the case in the five decades which followed the outbreak of World War I. Yet through immigration, especially after World War II, other ethnic elements entered and were in process of integration into one national body. For the most

[32] *Congress on Union of Churches* (Melbourne, Brown, Prior and Co., 1913, pp. 124), *passim*.
[33] *Australia and Reunion*, pp. 143, 144.
[34] Rouse and Neill, *A History of the Ecumenical Movement, 1517–1948*, p. 375.
[35] *Australia and Reunion, passim*.
[36] Rouse and Neill, *op. cit.*, pp. 482–484.
[37] *Ecumenical Press Service*, January 29, 1960.

part the members of the hierarchy were Irish-born. For example, Patrick Francis Moran (1830–1911), Archbishop of Sydney from 1884 to his death and the first Australian prelate to be created cardinal (1885), was from Ireland,[38] as was Moran's successor, Michael Kelly (1850–1940). The latter came to Australia from the rectorship of the Irish College in Rome.[39] However, Kelly was followed by N. T. Gilroy, who was elevated to the purple in 1946, the first native of Australia to be accorded that honour.[40] In 1956 the Roman Catholic Church had twenty-five dioceses and four *sui juris* territories and vicariates. Its provinces were made to coincide with the states. Its bishops gave a national complexion to the church by meeting annually and by using episcopal committees, each with a secretary, which dealt with such matters as the lay apostolate, the rural movement, and organizations of men, women, and youth. In 1914 an apostolic delegate was appointed to the country. An extensive system of schools was developed, from the parish level upward, and chiefly by contributions from the faithful. In 1954 seventy hospitals were maintained. Orders and congregations of religious were introduced from abroad, but before 1914 at least two sisterhoods had sprung up in Australia. Increasingly the members of the orders and congregations were recruited in Australia.[41] In 1950 the major seminaries enrolled 422 students, 256 of them in institutions conducted by seculars.[42] Yet in 1956 Australia was still under the supervision of the Congregation for the Propagation of the Faith and had not been given the status achieved in the United States and Canada in 1908.[43] The Liturgical Movement only tardily made itself felt, but by 1950 the Gregorian chant was adopted in most of the Roman Catholic schools and convents and in all the theological seminaries. Here, as elsewhere, the Benedictines were pioneers.[44]

In view of the prominence of cities, industrialization, labour unions, and social legislation, we need not be surprised that the Roman Catholic Church had a large place in the affairs of labour. Its concern was all the more urgent since much of the Roman Catholic population was urban. Thus soon after 1900 Cardinal Moran gave his support to the Labour Party and rejoiced in the social achievements of the country—an eight-hour day, a minimum wage, overtime payments, arbitration, and pensions.[45] In World War I Archbishop Mannix threw his weight against conscription in the emotionally charged debate over the issue.[46] The large majority of the Roman Catholics supported the

[38] Serle, *Dictionary of Australian Biography*, Vol. II, pp. 155–157; Murtagh, *Australia: the Catholic Chapter*, pp. 138, 139.
[39] Serle, *op. cit.*, Vol. II, pp. 486, 487.
[40] *The Australian Encyclopaedia*, Vol. VII, p. 483.
[41] Brother Aloysius, *The De La Salle Brothers in Australia, 1906–1956* (Sydney, Halstead Press, 1956, pp. xvi, 160), *passim*, especially pp. 15, 16, 59.
[42] Allen, *A Seminary Survey*, p. 460.
[43] *The Australian Encyclopaedia*, Vol. VII, pp. 486, 487.
[44] Bögler, *Liturgische Erneuerung in aller Welt*, p. 133.
[45] Murtagh, *op. cit.*, pp. 180, 181.
[46] *Ibid.*, pp. 188, 189.

Labour Party, but that did not mean that they were Socialists.[47] During the years of the world-wide depression, in which the Australian economy was a severe sufferer, Communists made a determined effort to capture the Labour Party. Against them the Roman Catholics were adamant. What was known as the Campion Society, founded in Melbourne in 1931 by a young lawyer as a Catholic adult education movement, led in the attack. It was composed chiefly of lay intellectuals and was influenced by such contemporary English Catholic social thinkers as Hilaire Belloc and G. K. Chesterton. Similar groups under various names arose in several of the state capitals. In 1934 at the National Eucharistic Congress at Melbourne representatives of these bodies met and issued an appeal as a prelude to inaugurating Catholic Action. Contacts were made with such movements as *Jeunesse Ouvrière Chrétienne* and *Action Populaire* in France. In 1936 *The Catholic Worker* was begun in Melbourne by a group which had sprung from the Campion Society. In 1937 the bishops issued a pastoral letter after their Fourth Plenary Council in Sydney which commended *The Catholic Worker* and in that year Pope Pius XI gave the periodical his blessing. The episcopate approved a proposal of the Campion Society that a national secretary be appointed to prepare the way for Catholic Action. The founder of the Society was the first to fill the post. Under him a Young Christian Workers' Movement, a National Catholic Girls' Movement, a Young Catholic Students' Movement, and a National Catholic Welfare Movement were initiated. During the Spanish civil war both bishops and laity made clear their sympathy with Franco.[48] In 1938 Catholic Action extended its programme to further a rural movement and by the mid-1940's it published an organ, *Rural Life*, and had groups and centres in every state. In 1940 the bishops established "Social Justice Sunday" as an annual feature. In the document which inaugurated that observance they came out for the reorganization of society on occupational lines.[49]

As we have suggested, the Roman Catholic constituency in Australia was augmented by the post-World War II immigration. Of the approximately 1,500,000 immigrants between 1945 and 1956 about 47.5 per cent. were reported to be of that faith. In 1951 the bishops said that within a century Australia could become "a great Christian commonwealth"—and by Christian they obviously meant Roman Catholic. Beginning in 1945 the national secretariat for Catholic Action (inaugurated in 1937) had as its director the able and devout lawyer Bartholomew Santamaria. Under him the National Catholic Rural Movement adopted the policy of "back to the land" and, with the plea that half the Roman Catholics who went to the cities were lost to their church,

[47] *Ibid.*, pp. 200, 201.
[48] *Ibid.*, pp. 214–220; *The Australian Encyclopaedia*, Vol. VII, p. 487.
[49] *The Australian Encyclopaedia*, Vol. VII, p. 487.

urged that the faithful be encouraged to become owners of small farms. At the same time the National Catholic Social Movement, later called the National Civic Council, endeavoured to promote Roman Catholic policies in organized labour. Finding that Roman Catholics could not fully control the Labour Party and declaring that under the leadership of Herbert V. Evatt that body was swinging to the left and was in danger of being dominated by the Communists, Santamaria led in the formation of the Catholic Front Labour Party, soon to be called the Democratic Labour Party. It contributed to the defeat of the Labour Party and the coming to power of the Liberal-Country coalition under Robert Gordon Menzies as premier.

Roman Catholic leadership was divided on the political question. Thus in 1960 the Archbishop of Melbourne declared that no Roman Catholic could in good conscience vote for a candidate of the Labour Party, while a spokesman of the Archdiocese of Sydney said that Roman Catholics had every right to vote for that party. Accordingly the Roman Catholic vote was divided, to the profit of Menzies and his government. The lack of political accord did not prevent Roman Catholics from pressing for financial aid for their schools. In 1956 the latter enrolled about a fifth of the school-going population of the country.[50]

Australian Roman Catholics were sharing in the world-wide extension of their faith. For example, in 1956 at least a dozen were serving in the schools maintained by the De La Salle Brothers in Papua, Borneo, and Malaya.[51]

The Orthodox Churches were much augmented by the immigration which followed World War II. Before 1945 Australia had only two Orthodox parishes. By 1952 fifteen new congregations had been formed among refugees from Europe and East Asia. For them the Russian Episcopal Synod Abroad organized a diocese with headquarters in Sydney, and in 1953 a cathedral for a thousand worshippers was completed and dedicated in that city. In the 1950's an archpriest from Florida was named Bishop of Melbourne. In addition to the Russian diocese, by 1954 the country had a Greek Orthodox diocese and several Syrian Orthodox parishes.[52] The Serbs and Bulgarians usually went to Russian churches. In 1960 the Greeks were said to number at least 120,000 and the total number of Orthodox in the country was estimated to be about 200,000.[53]

In retrospect, in 1962 Christianity was seen to have registered some gains in Australia since 1914. In spite of conditions adverse to the faith which had attended the beginnings of the European settlement of the country and in face

[50] *The Christian Century*, Vol. LXXIII, pp. 1406–1408 (November 30, 1956); Vol. LXXVI, p. 979 (Auust 26, 1959); Vol. LXXVII, p. 861 (July 20, 1960); *The New York Times*, November 21, 1958; January 30, 1961; *Time*, April 14, 1960.

[51] Aloysius, *op. cit.*, p. x.

[52] *New Missionary Review*, No. 5 (6), Spring, 1954, p. 14.

[53] *Ibid.*, Nos. 17–18, 18–19, 1960, pp. 22, 23.

of the urban and industrial character of a higher percentage of the population than in some portions of the lands outside Western Europe settled by Europeans, Christianity was achieving advances. These were in part a decreased dependence on the British Isles for clerical personnel and an increasing proportion of native-born clergy. The numbers of the latter were still inadequate and theological education was weak as compared with Canada and the United States. But in that respect the situation was improving. Australian Protestantism was more backward in the trend towards unity which characterized the age than in some other lands, but it was beginning to respond. A slight shift was seen in the relative strength of the great branches of the Church. The land was still predominantly Protestant, but, thanks mainly to the post-World War II immigration, the proportion of Roman Catholics was mounting and the Eastern Churches were becoming important. The growing number who in the census returns failed to indicate a religious preference may have indicated a progressive secularization. Here, as in so much of the nineteenth and especially the twentieth century, the contrast was becoming sharper between the anti-Christian forces and the enhanced vigour in the churches.

CHAPTER VII

The Growing Church in New Zealand

ALTHOUGH a small country, both in area and population, and on the extreme geographical fringe of the Western world, New Zealand felt to the full the impact of the twentieth-century stage of the revolutionary age. It was an active participant in both World War I and World War II and was a member of the League of Nations and its successor, the United Nations. Because of the large part which dairy products, meat, and wool had in its export trade, its economy suffered severely from the world-wide depression of the 1930's. In spite of the prominence of agriculture in its livelihood, New Zealand displayed many of the features of an urban civilization. In the 1950's three-fifths of its population was urban and more than a third of that urban element was concentrated in the two cities of Auckland and Wellington on the North Island. Yet industrialization was slow to develop and in the twentieth century was still chiefly confined to the processing of dairy products and meat and to woolen fabrics. In the half-century which followed 1914 the population more than doubled—from 1,005,585 in 1911 to 2,036,911 in 1956 and to an estimated 2,326,129 in 1959.[1] The increase was due more to a low death rate and the resulting excess of births over deaths than to immigration. The latter was not as notable in the post-World War II years as it was in Australia. The population was still overwhelmingly from the British Isles or of stock which had its origin in those islands. The Maoris, Polynesians who had been in possession when the white man arrived, were much more prominent than were the aborigines in Australia. Although in the 1950's they constituted less than 8 per cent. of the population, proportionately they were increasing more rapidly than the whites and had an accepted part in the political and religious life of the country. In the twentieth century New Zealand continued on the path of the welfare state which it had entered in the nineteenth century.

In its statistical proportions the Christianity of New Zealand did not change as much in the twentieth century as did that of Australia. The percentage of those who in the census returns refused to state a religious preference rose from

---

[1] *The Statesman's Year Book, 1960*, p. 536.

about 3.5 in 1911 to 8.6 in 1956. This may be evidence of progressive seculariza-tion. In 1911 adherents of the Church of England constituted 41.14 per cent. of the population (exclusive of the Maoris), Presbyterians were 23.32 per cent., Methodists were 9.43 per cent., and Roman Catholics were 13.97 per cent.[2] In 1956 the Church of England was reported to have 38.57 per cent. of the popula-tion, Presbyterians 23.5 per cent., Methodists 8 per cent., and Roman Catholics 15 per cent.[3] These figures seemed to indicate losses from the Anglicans and the Methodists and very slight gains for the Presbyterians and the Roman Catholics. Much lesser numbers were counted as constituencies of other de-nominations—in descending order in 1956 beginning with 33,910 Baptists, 22,444 Brethren, 13,133 Mormons, 10,852 in the Salvation Army, and going on to several still smaller bodies. Most of the denominations had their rootage in the British Isles. Indeed, in its Christianity as in other aspects of its life New Zea-land was very British—more so than Canada or Australia.

Progress was registered in acclimatizing Christianity among the Maoris in the form of indigenous leadership. In the 1950's most of the Maoris professed to be Christians. Some belonged to movements of indigenous origin: before 1914 chiefly Hauhau (Primarire) and Ringatu, which combined elements from Christianity with features derived from paganism. In the 1840's, 1850's, and 1860's wars between the Maoris and the whites were accompanied by the re-nunciation of Christianity by many Maoris as the white man's religion, and the white missionaries were forced to leave Maori districts. During the struggles the Maori clergy held true to the faith. In the decades which followed the coming of peace, most of the Maoris returned to the Church. In 1925 one of their number was consecrated bishop for the Maori Anglicans. By 1949 no white missionary was giving full time to the Maoris, and the pastoral care was mostly by Maori clergy. In the census of 1945 all but 8,284 of the Maoris de-clared themselves to have an affiliation with some religious group. Of these a third were connected with the Church of England, not quite a sixth were Roman Catholics, about a twelfth were Methodists, a sixteenth were Mormons, a few thousand were affiliated with the Hauhau and Ringatu movements, a few were Presbyterians or members of some other Protestant denomination, and slightly more than a sixth called themselves followers of Ratana.[4] Ratana rose to prominence in the 1920's. A Maori farmer, through the illness of his child he was led to advocate healing by faith in God. From him sprang a movement whose members zealously studied the Bible and hundreds of whom were freed from alcoholism and were healed physically. At first Ratana co-operated with the churches, but eventually a separate church arose from his

[2] Ibid., 1914, p. 370.
[3] Ibid., 1960, p. 538.
[4] W. G. Williams, editor, The Child Grew. The Story of the Anglican Maori Mission (Welling-ton, A. H. and A. W. Reed, 1949, pp. 76), pp. 48–55, 76.

movement with a temple in his village and with a distinctive ritual. It became an expression of Maori particularism.[5]

The position of Anglicanism and Presbyterianism was due partly to the important role they had played in the early settlement of the country. As we have seen,[6] the Anglicans had led in the settlement of Christchurch, on the South Island, a city which had the advantage of being the natural port of the largest area of flat land and the chief wheat-producing region. The Presbyterians had been responsible for the founding of Dunedin, the main city in the extreme south of the South Island. In the twentieth century Christchurch remained strongly Anglican and Dunedin Presbyterian. Both the Church of England and the Presbyterian Church spread widely, with their initial advantage and their inclusive organizations—the one due to the leadership of the great bishop George Augustus Selwyn, and the other consummated in the comprehensive union achieved in 1901.[7] They were able to establish themselves in both the cities and the rural villages and communities. In the twentieth century both had a larger proportion of their members in the rural districts than in the towns. Interestingly, Anglicans, Presbyterians, and Roman Catholics had a higher percentage of men than of women among their adherents.[8] The extension of the churches, with the erection of buildings, the maintenance of the clergy, and the large share in foreign missions, was brought about predominantly through the free-will offerings of the faithful. Little or no help came from outside. This record was made possible by the high income level of the population and the absence of extremes of wealth and poverty. But it would not have been achieved without widespread religious conviction. At least among the Presbyterians the average giving per member was slightly higher in the rural than in the urban districts.[9]

Although in the 1950's the Church of England and the Presbyterian Church together accounted for two-thirds of the population who expressed a religious preference, and percentage-wise the characteristic free churches of England—Methodist, Baptist, and Congregationalist—were declining, in many places, especially in towns and villages, an unhappy multiplication of small and competing denominations was seen[10] and coöperation was obviously called for. In the first half of the twentieth century distinct progress was made towards collaboration among most of the Protestant denominations. As we have noted,[11] a Bible Class movement with units in several denominations had prepared the

[5] Elder, *The History of the Presbyterian Church of New Zealand, 1840–1940*, pp. 267, 268.
[6] Volume III, pp. 372, 373.
[7] *Ibid.*, pp. 371, 374; Elder, *op. cit.*, pp. 213, 218.
[8] Elder, *op. cit.*, p. 187.
[9] *Ibid.*, p. 193.
[10] *Ibid.*, p. 187.
[11] Volume III, p. 376.

way for more inclusive coöperation, and in 1896 John R. Mott, by organizing a Student Christian Movement as a branch of the World's Student Christian Federation, had brought the more earnestly Christian educated youth into contact with the emerging Ecumenical Movement. In 1926, also as an outcome of a visit by Mott, the National Missionary Council of New Zealand was created and became a member of the International Missionary Council. In February, 1948, the National Missionary Councils of Australia and New Zealand promoted a conference to devise a comprehensive programme for promoting Christianity in the South-West Pacific.[12] In 1921 at the instance of Campbell West-Watson, later Bishop of Christchurch and Archbishop of New Zealand, the Council of Religious Education was formed with six denominations as members. The initiative of West-Watson was also responsible for the organization in 1941 of the National Council of Churches with the purpose of examining "existing differences between the churches in order to bring out the underlying unity" and "to facilitate common action by the churches on all matters where there is agreement or the possibility of agreement." The members of the council were eight denominations which together enrolled 90 per cent. of the non-Roman Catholic church membership of the country. In 1945 delegates from the eight denominations met in Christchurch and dealt with such subjects as evangelism, the future of the Maoris, the country's responsibilities in the South Pacific, education, and Christian principles in the use of land and in industry and commerce. Partly at the suggestion of the National Council of Churches the University of New Zealand undertook to give degrees in divinity. The Council also had a Maori section.[13] In 1958 under the auspices of the Council a conference on theological education was held to promote coöperation among the theological colleges of the various denominations.[14] Steps towards the organic union of the Church of England and the Presbyterian Church of New Zealand were seen. In 1959 the General Assembly of the Presbyterian Church responded favourably to an invitation by the General Synod of the Church (of England) of the Province of New Zealand to enter into "exploratory conversations."[15] In 1960 the Presbyterian, Methodist, and Congregational Churches and the Associated Churches of Christ were studying a proposal for the union of their respective bodies.[16]

The interests and range of activity of the larger denominations were evidence of a purpose to make an impress upon the revolutionary age, not only in New

---

[12] Rouse and Neill, *A History of the Ecumenical Movement, 1517–1948*, p. 375.

[13] *Ibid.*, pp. 626, 627.

[14] *Proceedings of the General Assembly of the Presbyterian Church of New Zealand Held in Hamilton, November, 1958* (Dunedin, Otago Daily News, no date, pp. xxxiv, 74, 411s, 52s), p. 30s.

[15] *Proceedings of the General Assembly of the Presbyterian Church of New Zealand Held in Invergargill, November, 1959* (Dunedin, Otago Daily News, no date, pp. xxxv, 80, 395a, 86s), p. 49.

[16] *Ecumenical Press Service*, December 16, 1960.

Zealand but also throughout the world. For example, the Presbyterian Church maintained old people's homes, hospitals, and children's homes, appointed chaplains to hospitals, and employed deaconesses to watch over unmarried mothers and to care for the sick, the aged, and the lonely. Its General Assembly was concerned with international relations, the population explosion in the world, family planning, the problem of the inner city and of religious ministry to those who dwelt there, the racial situation in Nyasaland, and the threat of war in the atomic age.[17] We also hear, in Anglican circles, of a concern for the increase in juvenile delinquency and the break-down of home life, of an effort to assist sufferers from the economic depression which followed World War I, and of an active desire to remedy the absence of religious instruction in the state schools.[18]

New Zealand Christians continued to be engaged in enterprises for spreading the faith throughout the world. In the post-World War I decades they had missions in several of the islands of the Pacific and in China, India, and Latin America.[19]

In New Zealand, then, was a vigorous Christianity. That Christianity continued to be predominantly Protestant and was represented chiefly by denominations which reflected the background of the British Isles. To it came as well contributions from other sources. For example, there were a few Orthodox, the fruits of twentieth-century immigration. The Christianity of the United States had important repercussions: John R. Mott was repeatedly in the islands and left continuing results in organizations; the Mormons and the Missouri Lutherans were represented; and in 1960 Billy Graham attracted thousands to his meetings.

[17] *Ibid.*, pp. 184a–214a.
[18] John Russell Wilford, *Southern Cross and Evening Star. Reflections and Recollections* (London, Martini Publications, 1949, pp. 248, 7), pp. 198 ff.
[19] Parker, *Directory of World Missions*, pp. 5–7; *World Christian Handbook, 1957*, pp. 226–228.

CHAPTER VIII

The Accelerating Revolution in the World Outside "Christendom"

M ARKED and mounting in the former "Christendom" in the twentieth century as was the revolution which issued therefrom, its course was much more rapid and its effects more basic and sweeping in the lands outside Western "Christendom."

In the preceding volume and a half we have sought to describe the twentieth-century phase of what was happening in the erstwhile "Christendom" and the course of Christianity among the peoples embraced by it. In doing so we have given most of our attention to the heart of this area—Western Europe. We have noted the progressive fading of Christianity from large elements in that region, but also the fresh ways in which the vigour inherent in Christianity was finding expression. We have sketched the even more drastic effects of the revolution on other sections of Europe—Russia, and the lands on the western and southern fringes of that country which World War II and subsequent events brought under its domination. We saw that through Communism, given its first standard formulation in Great Britain by former Protestants, more basic changes were wrought in what became the Union of Soviet Socialist Republics and its satellites than in Western Europe, and that the threat to Christianity was more avowed and open there than in Western Europe. Yet in spite of the threat Christianity survived in Russia and its European appendages. By the mid-twentieth century it was recovering from the blows it had been dealt and in some respects was more vital than on the eve of 1914.

We have devoted the initial half of the present volume to the record of Christianity in the larger "Christendom" in the first half of the twentieth century—in the vast areas where through immigration, chiefly from Western Europe, the peoples and the cultures were overwhelmingly Western European. We have concerned ourselves mainly with the United States of America, for that country embraced more than half the population of the "larger Europe" and in its wealth, its economic and political power, and its impact upon the rest of mankind was rivalled only by the U.S.S.R. We also have devoted space to

British North America, the Caribbean, Latin America, Australia, and New Zealand. We pointed out the vigour of the Christianity of the United States, somewhat ambivalent but more marked than in the nineteenth century; the mounting strength of Christianity in Canada; the revival of the faith in Latin America by the very rapid growth of Protestantism and by fresh currents of life in the Roman Catholic Church but affecting as yet only minorities; and the fashion in which Christianity was becoming less colonial and more deeply rooted in Australia and New Zealand.

Except for a concluding chapter of summary and interpretation we must devote the remainder of this volume to the twentieth-century course of Christianity in those portions of the globe which lay outside what was once called "Christendom." It is well to remember that they embraced the large majority of mankind and included areas of high civilizations in comparison with which Western civilizations seemed youthful. From the standpoint of historical perspective the dominance of Western peoples and their culture was a recent phenomenon, one which began in the sixteenth century and reached its crest in the nineteenth century.

The revolutionary flood in the twentieth century which engulfed the non-Western portions of the human race had several striking characteristics. They did not fall into any logical sequence but together constituted a pattern whose main features were so closely intertwined that they could not be disentangled from one another without doing violence to the whole. Yet an attempt at such a disentanglement may contribute to an understanding of the whole.

First of all is a fact to which we have repeatedly called attention. Historically the revolution had its origin in Western Christendom, mainly in Western Europe and in the Protestant sections thereof. Its impact upon the rest of mankind was often through other channels: Latin Europe, the United States, latterly Russia. But as the currents were traced to their source they and the channels created by them were seen to have had most of their major springs in the Protestant portions of Europe.

Next is the fact that in the first half of the twentieth century the revolution was vastly accelerated. What would happen in the second half of that century the historian, if he stuck to his craft, would not venture to predict. He could simply note that up to the 1960's the record was such that every indication pointed towards an increasing rather than a declining rate of change.

In the same breath it must be said that the revolution embraced all mankind. Revolution was not a new experience for men. Again and again portions of the race had passed through periods of rapid change. But heretofore the changes had been confined to particular areas, some large and others small. Now all the world was involved. From the standpoint of intercommunication the globe had shrunk and continued to shrink. The steamship, the railroad, the automobile, the electric telegraph, the telephone, and more recently the airplane, the radio, and television had all but annihilated distance—and they had originated among Western European and largely Protestant-influenced peoples. What transpired in any one part of the globe, even in an area previously as isolated as Tibet or Antarctica, within a few hours became of world interest.

The rate of change varied from people to people and from region to region. Some tribes in the Upper Amazon continued on their way much as their ancestors had done, but even they could not entirely escape the airplane and the efforts of the white man's governments to extend their control over them and to bring them the white man's forms of education. As recently as the middle of the nineteenth century the vast Chinese Empire, with its ancient civilization and embracing about a fourth of the human race, appeared to be only slightly touched by the incursion of the West; in the third quarter of that century it seemed indeed to be making an adjustment which would preserve the essential features of its heritage. Yet beginning in the 1890's its peoples were experiencing what was called the collapse of a civilization, and by the middle of the twentieth century most of its inherited basic institutions and the philosophy on which its life had been built had been swept aside. The effect of World War II on China's neighbour, Japan, had been to create a yawning gulf between the generation which had come to maturity before that struggle, fought with the weapons of the West, and the generation which was in its infancy or as yet un-born when hostilities began. In the Indian sub-continent, with its fifth of the human race, at the mid-twentieth century the changes were not as catastrophic as in China, but they were breath-taking and were prevented from being more so by a political, economic, and educational structure erected by the British *raj* and by men shaped by a combination of the Indian heritage and British training. At the turn of the century only the coastal fringes of Africa south of the Sahara had been much affected by Western Europe. By the 1960's the entire area was suffering from the disintegration of its traditional ways of life under the irruption of the European and his culture. Great cities with buildings of Western style and with features typical of urbanized "Christendom" were appearing and, in conjunction with mining and industries introduced by the white man, were causing the traditional social patterns to crumble.

Fully as striking as any of these changes was the collapse of the rule of non-Western peoples by Westerners. By the 1960's the colonial era which had had its inception late in the fifteenth century and had reached its climax in the nineteenth was fading so rapidly that only a few fragments remained and they were clearly doomed. From the perspective of the mid-twentieth century the triumph of Western imperialism in the nineteenth century could be seen to have been due to two factors: the possession by Western European peoples of the science and the machines which they had created, and the decline of the three major regimes by which most of the non-European world had been governed—the Ottoman Empire in the Middle East and North Africa, the Mogul Empire in India, and the Manchu Empire in China. What was called "the rising tide of colour" had been apparent before World War I. However, the world wars of the first half of the twentieth century gave it impetus. The first of these conflicts was really an exhausting European civil war. Because of it Western European governments were in a much poorer position than previously to impose their will upon Asia. World War II, although bringing collapse to existing regimes in China and Japan, had its main centres in Europe and added to the palpable weakness of the Western European powers. Under these circumstances, most of the Middle East and of East and South Asia and the fringing islands achieved their independence of Western rule and by 1962 the larger part of Africa had become politically independent of the white man.

A complicating factor in the emancipation from Western European imperialism was the spread of Communism. Communism, of Western origin but with its radiating centre in Russia, both gave zest to the revolt against Western European colonialism and was accompanied by another form of imperialism. In the name of Communism the U.S.S.R. attacked the fading Western colonialism and its attendant capitalism. At the same time it endeavoured to control the Communist regimes which it had set up or fostered in other countries and thus in effect to create a more inclusive empire than the world had yet seen. In the 1960's its hegemony was threatened by Tito in the relatively weak Jugoslavia, by the still more feeble Albania, and by the self-confident and intensely nationalistic Communist government which had captured the mainland of China.

Another striking feature of the revolution in the non-Occidental world was ambition to take full advantage of the science, the industrial and mechanical appliances, and the education which led to them that had been developed in the West, and thus to raise the material standard of living of the population. While rejecting hotly the political and economic domination of the West, non-European peoples avidly sought to avail themselves of what they believed had given Europeans their wealth and power.

Along with the search for the secret of the physical prosperity of the Occident went what we have again and again noted in the former "Christendom"—the growth of secularism and the weakening of the inherited religions. This was especially marked in lands dominated by Communism (notably China) but it was also seen in many other countries. It especially affected the intelligentsia who had been educated after the Western fashion, but it was felt as well by large numbers who, with little or none of that kind of education, were caught in the urban and industrial life which was part of the revolution.

In contrast with the secularizing trend, non-Christian religions revived and fresh religious movements arose. Much of the revival of the older faiths was associated with the surging nationalism which endeavoured to free itself from all vestiges of Western imperialism. The ancestral religions were stressed as distinctive possessions and were cherished in scorn of the West. We may cite the renewed interest in Islam, Hinduism, and Buddhism—the latter in Ceylon and Burma. Some followers of these faiths sought to win converts in the West. Their missionaries were found in great cities in Western Europe and the Americas and attracted adherents. Presumably out of a religious hunger which would not be stifled by secularism, in some places, notably in Japan after World War II, new religious movements sprang into being or old ones revived and won followers. Most of them were syncretistic. Numbers of them, like several forms of contemporary Christianity, claimed to promote faith healing, material success, and a sense of security, and attracted thousands, even millions, who had been uprooted by the revolutionary tides of the day.

A feature of the revolutionary age which issued from the impact of the West was what came to be called a population explosion. It was seen in many countries but was particularly acute in Japan, China, India, and Java. It was largely a consequence of the lowering of the death rate through the treatment of disease by methods developed in the West. By the middle of the twentieth century the application of various forms of birth control, some by the ancient method of abortion and others by devices developed in the Occident, was reducing the increase in Japan. But as yet they had been partially or completely ineffective in several lands in Asia and in Indonesia.

In the mid-twentieth century over both non-Occidental and Occidental peoples hung the Damocles sword of nuclear war. The atomic bomb was first developed in the predominantly Protestant United States, and by 1961 the stock-piling of nuclear weapons was confined to the United States, Russia, Great Britain, and France. Less publicized instruments for waging war were also being created, among them poison gases and lethal germs. All were being produced in either Russia or the West. Here was a sombre feature of the revolutionary age. The product of the science initially arising in "Christendom" but being adopted in other regions, it carried with it the threat of the destruction of the civilization out of which it had sprung. On the other hand, the United Nations, also born of dreamers in "Christendom," mostly Protestants, and ostensibly made up of "peace-loving" governments, endeavoured to reduce friction among the nations and to be an instrument for disarmament. Thus, in heightened form we see the contrast which characterized the revolutionary age and to which we have repeatedly referred: between the accentuation of the chronic ills of mankind and the increased efforts to alleviate and if possible to eliminate them. The contrast was sharpest among the peoples who had been longest under the continuous influence of forms of Christianity which had had the nearest approach to freedom to incorporate the inner genius of the faith.

CHAPTER IX

The Mounting Role of Christianity in the World Outside "Christendom"

WHAT happened to Christianity in the first half of the twentieth century in the world outside "Christendom"? Because of the challenges to Christianity in the erstwhile "Christendom" and the rising tide of "anti-colonialism" and Communism in the rest of the world, the normal expectation would have been that such footholds as Christianity had acquired among non-Occidental peoples would be weakened or lost. The missionary movement through which the faith had been planted in many tribes and nations, especially in the heyday of Western imperialism, the nineteenth century, appeared to be the ecclesiastical phase of that imperialism. It had been inspired by a striking wave of devotion, but it had been maintained by sums of money and staffs which when compared with the wealth of the Occident and the energy and personnel expended in the economic and political expansion of the West were very small. In most areas only minorities had been won. Except among classes and peoples of primitive or near-primitive cultures they were at most less than one per cent. of the population. These minorities were regarded by the majorities from which they had been gathered as having succumbed to the religion of the foreign masters and as being unpatriotic aliens in the lands of their birth. The churches and the associated educational and philanthropic institutions were largely controlled by men and women from the West and for the most part were dependent on financial subsidies from the churches of "Christendom." It was to be expected that as the wave of Western imperialism was pushed back the Christian communities would dwindle. That was the more to be anticipated in view of the surge of secularism and notably of Communism which was part of the twentieth-century stage of the revolutionary age. Moreover, the accentuation of nationalism and the revival of non-Christian religions affiliated with nationalism militated against Christianity.

By a strange contrast, akin to what we have seen elsewhere in the revolutionary age, by the mid-twentieth century Christianity was more potent in the world outside "Christendom" than it had ever been. It was far from being dominant, but it was gaining. This was seen in at least four ways. (1) Christianity was more widespread geographically than it or any other religion had ever been. (2) It was more deeply rooted among more peoples than ever before. (3) Christians were coming together and were closer to presenting a united front in seeking to win the world than in many centuries. (4) Christianity was exerting a wider influence on mankind outside "Christendom" than in any earlier time. These generalizations will be supported by concrete examples as we pursue our narrative, but here we must amplify them a little further.

1. In the first half of the twentieth century Christianity became more widespread geographically than it or any other religion had ever been. That spread was most marked, as in the nineteenth century, among peoples and classes of primitive or near-primitive cultures. Among some of these folk what resembled mass movements to the faith were developing—among the Bataks in Sumatra, the Karens in Burma, and some of the depressed classes and hill tribes of India, Africa south of the Sahara, Madagascar, and several islands of the Pacific. Advance was much slower among peoples of higher cultures, and here and there recessions were seen. On the mainland of China, for example, the political triumph of Communism after 1949 was accompanied by a decline in the number of Christians, a total which had never been as much as one per cent. of the population. In Japan, owing largely to political vicissitudes, growth was uneven, and by the mid-twentieth century Christians were scarcely one in two hundred of the population. In the Middle East, again mainly because of political factors, a sharp decline was seen. But in India as a whole, in spite of a phenomenal increase in population, in the first half of the twentieth century the proportion of Christians rose from about one per cent. to approximately two per cent., mainly from the depressed classes and the animistic hill peoples.

The geographic expansion was facilitated by missionaries from "Christendom," both Roman Catholic and Protestant. By 1961 they were more numerous than at any previous time. Because of Communist regimes they were compelled to leave some regions where they had been active—notably the mainland of China, North Korea, and North Vietnam. The rising tides of nationalism made difficult their reinforcement in several countries, India among them. In other words, missionaries from the Occident were being excluded from a third of the non-Occidental world and were finding difficulty in remaining or gaining entrance in another third. Yet their numbers were increasing and, with or without them, the faith was spreading.

The geographic spread of Christianity had less assistance from governments than at any time since the conversion of Constantine early in the fourth century. Indeed, even suspected association with Western, nominally "Christian" governments was a handicap, for the acceptance of Christianity was interpreted as submission to "cultural imperialism." In spite of that obstacle, in most of the non-Occidental world the numbers of Christians continued to mount.

2. Christianity was more deeply rooted among more peoples than ever before. More and more of the leadership in the churches and their affiliated institutions was passing from Westerners to nationals. For one thing, the pressure of anti-colonialism was strong, and the realization spread that if the Church was to survive and grow it must be through indigenous personnel and initiative. For another, missionaries and those who sent them had long been resolved—to use a cliché coined early in the nineteenth century—to bring into being "self-supporting, self-governing, and self-propagating churches" and for many decades had been keeping that objective before them. Now their purpose was reinforced by the obvious necessities of the situation. Moreover, and most important of all, the goal could not have been attained had the Gospel not had within it a vitality which inspired men and women regardless of their racial or cultural backgrounds. As the most discerning Christians had seen from the beginning, the Gospel was for all men.

3. Christians were coming together and were closer to presenting a united front in seeking to win the world than in many centuries. The trend towards unity was more marked than in "Christendom" and was confined chiefly to Protestantism. It had begun before the twentieth century, but it was accelerated in the half-century which followed 1914. It was a phase of the Ecumenical Movement. Indeed, it contributed to that movement and in notable instances it was in advance of what was being achieved in Europe and the Americas. In several countries it took the form of coöperation among denominations—for example, in the national councils of churches which embraced the majority of the Protestants in particular areas and nations. In the 1950's the East Asia Christian Conference came into being as a joint approach of churches of that area, small minorities that they were, to the peoples there. More striking were the organic unions achieved. As we pursue our country-by-country survey we shall find them in several lands, mainly in East and South Asia. Among them were the Church of Christ in Japan, the Church of Christ in China, the Church of North India, and the Church of South India. The Church of South India was especially notable in bringing together denominations as diverse in their polities as Anglicans, Methodists, Presbyterians, and Congregationalists.

4. Christianity was exerting a wider influence on mankind outside "Christendom" than in any earlier time. Minute minorities though the churches were in many countries, notably in East and South Asia, in these very areas Christianity was making an impression quite out of proportion to its numerical strength. Some of it was achieved through members of the churches, but much was contributed through other channels, such as the elements of Christian origin in Western civilization as the latter impinged on the rest of the world.

We shall have occasion to note examples of this influence as we pass from country to country. Here we can pause to note that after World War II most of the politically independent governments were members of the United Nations, an institution created mainly by Christian faith and idealism, chiefly through Protestantism. The Red Cross, entirely of Protestant origin, had branches not only in the West but also in one nation after another outside the Occident.[1] The Olympic Games were of pre-Christian Greek origin; their revival in the 1890's, although in "Christendom," could only indirectly if at all be ascribed to Christian ideals. Yet in several lands in East and South Asia the initial participation was stimulated and made possible by secretaries of the Young Men's Christian Association.[2] Although its Christian significance was seldom appreciated, Sunday was increasingly adopted as a day of rest and recreation. Similarly Christmas was extensively observed, notably in post-World War I Japan, but little if any of its Christian import was recognized.

THE ROMAN CATHOLIC SHARE

Christianity was spread outside "Christendom" almost entirely by Roman Catholics and Protestants. In the first two of the four ways in which it became more potent—namely, in extension and in rootage—as compared with the Protestants Roman Catholics were in some respects more prominent than they had been in the nineteenth century. In the nineteenth century the gains by Protestants had been proportionately greater than those by Roman Catholics. Now the latter were coming to the fore.

A few figures will make clear the aspects in which Roman Catholics were proportionately increasing their gains in the spread of the faith more rapidly than Protestants. In 1925 the ratio of Roman Catholic to Protestant missionaries in Asia, Africa, and the non-Occidental islands was approximately three to four. In 1956 it was about five to three. There were 5,028 fewer Protestant missionaries from Europe in this period.[3] The decline might be ascribed to the impoverishment of the Protestant churches in Europe wrought by World War II were it not for the fact that during the same period the Roman Catholic missionary force from Europe rose by about 18,000. Indeed, as we shall note in a moment, the differential in proportions was due not to a decline in the Protestant staff, for, taking "Christendom" as a whole, the latter had been augmented, but to a more rapid increase in the Roman Catholic personnel. It must also be remembered that between 1933 and 1953—in other words, shortly before and

[1] Volume II, pp. 216, 217.
[2] Latourette, *World Service*, p. 439.
[3] Allen, *A Seminary Survey*, p. 295. *Time*, April 18, 1960, said that there were then 38,606 Protestant missionaries as compared with 29,188 in 1925, and 51,000 Roman Catholic missionaries as contrasted with 22,477 in 1925.

a few years after World War II—an increase was registered in those going from France (which, as in the nineteenth century, sent more than any other country) and that in Belgium and the Netherlands, the countries of origin of Roman Catholic missionaries which ranked next after France, the totals more than doubled.[4] When we recall that with the possible exception of Germany these three countries suffered fully as much from World War II as did any of the predominantly Protestant lands, it becomes clear that the alteration in the ratio cannot be ascribed entirely to those years of destruction. Significantly, perhaps, in the same years the totals of Roman Catholic missionary priests from Germany fell, and before World War I more Protestant missionaries had gone from Germany than from any other country on the Continent. Between 1933 and 1953 the number of Roman Catholic missionary priests from England more than doubled[5] and the Protestant personnel from that land fell off. Yet in 1958 in proportion to their numerical strength English Protestants still had more missionaries than English Roman Catholics. Moreover, again in proportion to their numerical strength, late in the 1950's French, Belgian, British, and German Protestants were sending more missionaries than were their Roman Catholic fellow countrymen. It must also be said that percentage-wise the increase of missionaries from the Roman Catholics of the United States, while notable, was only slightly greater than that from the Protestants—for the Roman Catholics 152 per cent. between 1940 and 1958[6] as compared with the Protestant 123 per cent. between 1936 and 1958.[7] In actual numbers, relative to their numerical strength, in the United States the Roman Catholic participation in the personnel of foreign missions in 1958 was still far below that of Protestants—6,124 Roman Catholics from the United States[8] as against 25,058 Protestants from the United States and Canada,[9] of whom the overwhelming majority were from the former country. It is true that in the 1950's between 60 and 70 per cent. of the financial support of the Worldmission Aid Society, a Roman Catholic organization for raising funds, which embraced the Society for the Propagation of the Faith, the Society of St. Peter the Apostle for Native Clergy, the Holy Childhood Association, the Missionary Union of the Clergy, and the Catholic Near East Welfare Association, was from the United States, but in 1954 the total subscribed by Roman Catholics in that country to foreign missions through these agencies totalled only $19,567,725,[10] as against about $120,000,000 contributed to Protestant foreign missions from the United States

---

[4] Allen, *op. cit.*, pp. 295, 296.
[5] *Ibid.*, p. 296.
[6] *Ibid.*, p. 297.
[7] *Missionary Research Library, Occasional Bulletin*, December 8, 1958, p. 30.
[8] Allen, *op. cit.*, p. 298.
[9] *Missionary Research Library, Occasional Bulletin*, December 8, 1958, p. 30.
[10] Allen, *op. cit.*, p. 336.

in 1958. About $20,000,000 came to Protestant missions from other countries.[11] No accurate figures were obtainable for the total contributions from all countries to Roman Catholic foreign missions, but competent authorities estimated that about four times the sums raised by the societies we have mentioned came through other channels, chiefly to particular orders and congregations. This meant that in the 1950's the annual gifts to Roman Catholic missions totalled about $100,000,000,[12] which was much less than that supporting Protestant missions.

From the standpoint of relative numerical growth outside "Christendom" statistics were too imperfect to warrant comprehensive generalizations as between Roman Catholics and Protestants. Because in several countries, notably China and India, Roman Catholic missions antedated Protestant missions by two and a half centuries or more, Roman Catholics continued to outnumber Protestants. In most countries the phenomenal Protestant gains of the nineteenth century continued, but it was not clear whether in the twentieth century they were proportionately as great as in the preceding ten decades. In the Belgian Congo and in the adjacent Belgian trusteeship of Ruanda-Urundi Roman Catholics fairly steadily outstripped Protestants, but chiefly because the vigorous Roman Catholic Church of Belgium centred its missionary efforts on these areas and often had the support of friendly Belgian regimes. In South Africa by the mid-twentieth century Roman Catholic adherents among the Bantus, although still a small minority of the Christians, percentage-wise had grown more rapidly than Protestants, but at the beginning of the century they had been almost negligible. Further comparisons will be made as we go from country to country.

In the rootage of the faith among non-European peoples the Roman Catholic Church made striking advances. Whether they were greater than those achieved by Protestants cannot be established, for the differences in polity were too great to permit accurate comparison. The major fashion in which the rootage was achieved was through the creation of an indigenous priesthood and episcopate and the substitution of a hierarchy of bishops and archbishops for vicars apostolic. Here was a recognition of the passing of European colonialism. But it would have been impossible without wise statesmanship in Rome and especially a vigour in the churches which produced men who could be entrusted with the responsibilities entailed in the transition. We shall meet most of the concrete examples in our geographic survey, but here we will mention a few illustrations chosen almost at random.

In China the native-born personnel increased from 721 priests, 86 lay brothers,

---

[11] *Missionary Research Library, Occasional Bulletin,* December 8, 1958, pp. 8-11, 29.
[12] Allen, *op. cit.,* p. 337.

and 1,429 sisters in 1912 to 2,026 priests, 466 lay brothers, and 3,852 sisters in 1939. In the same period the foreign staff mounted, but less rapidly, from 1,365 priests, 247 lay brothers, and 743 sisters in 1912 to 2,979 priests, 585 brothers, and 2,281 sisters in 1939.[13] Percentage-wise in both Chinese and foreign staffs the increase was greater (strikingly so in Chinese personnel) than the growth in the total of Chinese Roman Catholics—from 1,406,659 in 1912 to 3,182,950 in 1939.[14] By 1939 the political situation had become so adverse that later figures were unreliable and the changes reflected the Japanese invasion, the internal disorder, and then, after 1949, the triumph of Communism on the mainland. In 1922 an apostolic delegation was created for China and the first apostolic delegate stressed the creation of a national church within the global fellowship of the Roman Catholic Church. In 1926 six Chinese priests were raised to the episcopate—the first step of that kind since the seventeenth century—in a dramatic ceremony in St. Peter's in Rome in which the Pope, Pius XI, was the consecrator. By 1940, out of 138 vicariates apostolic, prefectures apostolic, and independent missions in China, at least 14 vicariates were under Chinese bishops and at least 5 prefectures were also under Chinese.[15] In 1946 Rome created a hierarchy for China and promoted a Chinese, Thomas Tien, previously vicar apostolic in Shantung, to be Archbishop of Peking and cardinal.[16] As late as 1934 the apostolic delegate to Africa, Archbishop Arthur Hinsley, subsequently Archbishop of Westminster and cardinal, was of the opinion that, while Africans would be ordained to the priesthood, many years must elapse before any of them would be raised to the episcopate.[17] Yet in 1939 Joseph Kiwanuka was consecrated bishop and was assigned to a vicariate in Uganda. Later he was made an archbishop.[18] In 1939 a Malagasy was appointed bishop in Madagascar. In 1950 Kiwanuka was still the only Roman Catholic bishop south of the Sahara but by 1959 twenty-two Africans had that rank.[19] In 1960 Pope John XXIII consecrated six Africans south of the Sahara and two Malagasy as bishops or archbishops.[20] A few weeks earlier he had raised to the cardinalate an African, a Japanese, and a Filipino. In 1923 an Indian was consecrated Bishop of Tuticorn, in India, the first in Asia to be raised to that rank in territories under the Propaganda.[21] The total of indigenous priests in Asia mounted from 919 in 1918 to 5,553 in 1957, and in Africa south of the Sahara between those years

[13] Latourette, *A History of the Expansion of Christianity*, Vol. VII, p. 335.
[14] *Ibid.*, pp. 333, 334.
[15] *Ibid.*, pp. 335–337.
[16] Delacroix, *Histoire Universelle des Missions Catholiques*, Vol. III, p. 275.
[17] Hinsley, in conversation with the author in Rome, April, 1934.
[18] Allen, *op. cit.*, p. 415.
[19] *Worldmission Fides Service*, July 25, 1959.
[20] *Ibid.*, May 14, 1960; *The New York Times*, May 9, 1960.
[21] *Worldmission Fides Service*, July 25, 1959.

from 30 to 1,554. Between 1950 and 1959 the native bishops in Asia increased from 33 to 66.[22]

Part of the reason for this rapid growth was the emphasis placed on the recruiting and training of an indigenous clergy. The Society of St. Peter the Apostle for the Native Clergy had as its purpose the raising of funds to make possible the education of that clergy. In 1957 it collected $2,863,000 and in 1958, $3,472,000. Yet in the latter year plans for theological education called for $7,400,000 and the Society for the Propagation of the Faith contributed enough to make up the difference.[23] In 1956 the students in major seminaries on the mainland of Africa south of the Sahara totalled 1,766.[24] In the same year the major seminaries in India had 1,321 students and the scholasticates had 659 scholastics, in 1950 Malaya had 75 in major seminaries and Vietnam had 378, in 1958 Japan had 366 in major seminaries, and in 1958 Korea counted 243 in that category.[25] Many students were sent to Rome for training, especially in an institution maintained under the Propaganda.

Roman Catholics were encouraging indigenous art which used national traditions to depict Christian themes. That, for example, was one of the emphases of the first apostolic delegate to China, Celse Bénigne Louis Costantini.[26] It was also seen elsewhere, in both Asia and Africa.[27]

Use was made of contemporary means of communicating the Christian message to the masses. One method was a powerful radio station in the Vatican which used the Japanese language for Japan, Chinese for the Chinese, and English, Portuguese, and French for Africa.[28]

Roman Catholics paid increasing attention to the theology and practice of missions. Several scholarly journals were published, some of them begun after World War I. Many books appeared. Conferences on missions were held, including those which met annually in Louvain.[29] In Rome the Congregation for the Propagation of the Faith greatly enlarged its library as a tool for research.

The surge of Roman Catholic missions in the first half of the twentieth

---

[22] *Ibid.*

[23] *Worldmission Fides Service*, May 2, 1959.

[24] Allen, *op. cit.*, pp. 414, 424.

[25] *Ibid.*, pp. 432, 433, 440, 442, 449, 454.

[26] Latourette, *A History of the Expansion of Christianity*, Vol. VII, p. 337.

[27] Fleming, *Each with His Own Brush, passim.*

[28] *Worldmission Fides Service*, February 21, 1959.

[29] For a summary and for extensive bibliographical references see Andrew V. Seumois in Anderson, *The Theology of the Christian Mission*, pp. 122–134. For samples of reports of these conferences, dealing with obviously urgent problems, see *Les Aspirations Indigènes, et les Missions* (Louvain, Éditions du Museum Lessianum, 1925, pp. 200); *Problèmes Sociaux et Missions. Le Rôle des Läics dans les Missions* (Bruges, Desclée de Brouwer, 1953, pp. 374), and *Communisme et Missions* (Brussels, Desclée de Brouwer, 1958, pp. 192). The series began in 1923.

century arose from a number of sources. Some of the Popes were deeply interested. Pius XI especially gave the weight of his high office and his remarkable administrative ability to the promotion of foreign missions. When bishops paid him their required visits he regularly asked them what they were doing for the cause and urged them to make it one of their primary concerns. He also was insistent that the heads of the orders and congregations hold the extension of the faith to be a major objective and was not content with a general exhortation but emphasized it in the audiences which he granted them individually.[30] Again, he stressed the creation of an indigenous body of bishops and clergy. In this he was assisted by Willem van Rossum, who as head of the Propaganda not only agreed with the Pope in these measures but also made concrete suggestions. But while Popes and the Propaganda gave effective leadership, their efforts would have been unavailing had not a swelling tide of life among large elements of the faithful, both clerical and lay, provided funds and personnel.

THE PROTESTANT SHARE

Protestant participation in the spread and planting of Christianity outside "Christendom" also increased in the twentieth century. In missionaries and adherents and in the numbers of countries in which it was represented Protestantism registered gains. It, too, was becoming ever more deeply rooted among peoples outside the Occident. Moreover, in movements bringing Christians together Protestantism made far greater advances than the Roman Catholic Church and, so far as they could be traced to their sources, through it came most of the influence of the faith upon mankind as a whole and outside the organized churches, both within and outside "Christendom."

Although after World War II Roman Catholic missionaries to peoples outside the Occident were more numerous than Protestant missionary personnel in those regions, the totals of the latter had fairly steadily mounted. If the Americas, including Latin America, to which went between a seventh and an eighth of those classed as missionaries be excluded, the Protestant force in the non-Occidental world grew from 17,212 in 1911 to 24,762 in 1925,[31] to about 30,000 in 1952, and to 34,181 in 1958.[32] The next to the last figure compares with 42,689 Roman Catholic foreign missionaries in the same vast region in 1950.[33]

A post-World War II Protestant development was the recruiting, selecting, and training of laymen, their wives and fiancees, who served abroad at their own expense or in private or public employment in various capacities, such as

[30] Confidential information given the author.
[31] Beach and Fahs, *World Missionary Atlas*, p. 76.
[32] *Missionary Research Library, Occasional Bulletin*, December 8, 1958, p. 30.
[33] Allen, *op. cit.*, p. 295.

teachers. The chief initiative was through the British Council of Churches and the Conference of Missionary Societies in Great Britain and Ireland.[34]

We must also note that more and more the world-wide spread of the faith was consciously assumed as the responsibility of all Protestants and not simply of minorities within the churches. At the outset, with a few exceptions, Protestants regarded "foreign missions" as the undertaking of societies within the churches but not supported by them. In the nineteenth century the trend, especially in North America, was to insist that each denomination must regard itself as a missionary society. In the post-World War II decades this conviction grew in North America[35] and, more slowly, in the British Isles and on the Continent of Europe. That development was seen, among other ways, in the inclusion of the Foreign Missions Conference of North America as the Division of Foreign Missions in the National Council of the Churches of Christ in the United States of America and, in 1961, in the integration of the International Missionary Council with the World Council of Churches.

As we have more than once suggested, the increase in Protestant missionaries in the post-World War I half-century was primarily from the United States and Canada. In 1911, of the Protestant foreign personnel, including those sent to Latin America, 7,239 were from North America and 14,068 from all other countries, predominantly Europe. In 1925 the corresponding figures were 14,043 and 15,145. In 1936 they were 11,289 and 16,288 (the decline in the North American figure was attributable to the impact of the economic depression of the 1930's). In 1956 they were 23,432 and 11,260 (the decrease in the contribution from Europe was clearly due to World War II), and in 1958 they were 25,058 and 13,548.[36]

A feature of the missionary personnel from North America was their reflexion of the diversity of the Protestantism of that continent, and particularly of the United States. In 1958 the nearly fifty agencies, most of them denominational, which were associated in the Division of Foreign Missions of the National Council of the Churches of Christ in the United States of America were supporting 10,977 of the missionary personnel, or slightly more than 40 per cent., from North America. In that year the more than fifty organizations in the Evangelical Foreign Missions Association, more numerous but together with a smaller membership than the bodies in the first group, were maintaining 4,688 missionaries. In general they were more conservative theologically than those in the larger organization. At the same time the Inderdenominational Foreign Missions Association, with about forty members, none of them de-

[34] Conference of Missionary Societies in Great Britain and Ireland (in Association with the British Council of Churches), Report for the Year 1959–60 and Minutes of Annual Meeting (no place or date, pp. 80), pp. 31, 32, 35.

[35] For one example see The New York Times, December 14, 1960.

[36] Missionary Research Library, Occasional Bulletin, December 8, 1958, p. 30.

nominational and all depending on gifts from individuals in many denominations, were responsible for 5,902 missionaries. The four with the largest staffs and budgets, in descending order, were the Sudan Interior Mission, the Evangelical Alliance Mission (with a slightly larger income but a staff second to that of the Sudan Interior Mission), the Wycliffe Bible Translators, and the African Inland Mission. Of the others, only the China Inland Mission Overseas Missionary Fellowship had as much as half the personnel and income of any one of the leading four. The much more theologically conservative Associated Missions Agencies of the International Council of Christian Churches, with sixteen members, maintained 851 missionaries, but none of its members supported as many missionaries as the four largest in the preceding group. In addition, one body which coöperated through none of the preceding groups—the Southern Baptist Convention—in 1958 had 1,186 missionaries. In 1958 fifteen Canadian boards, of whom eight were members of the Canadian Council of Churches, were responsible for 774 missionaries. Of all these many agencies the Seventh Day Adventists supported more than any other—about 2,000, but that figure included personnel from other home bases as well as the United States.[37]

By the outbreak of World War I Protestants were to be found in all European colonies and the large majority of the countries which claimed political independence, and in the following half-century Protestant communities, though sometimes very small, arose in each of the others except Outer Mongolia. They were, for example, in the hitherto unpenetrated Nepal and in the almost solidly Moslem Afghanistan.

Whether in the mid-twentieth century Protestantism was more deeply or less deeply rooted among more peoples than was the Roman Catholic Church would be difficult to determine. The ecclesiastical structures of the two branches of the faith were so different that reliable comparisons were impossible. In the Roman Catholic Church, moreover, except for some schismatic bodies such as that fostered by the Communists in China, indigenous movements, evidences of vitality, were kept under the control of the hierarchy. In Protestantism the absence of any acknowledged central administrative authority permitted a large and growing number of movements sprung from the soil, some of which, while professedly Christian, departed far from the historic forms of the faith. Among them were the hundreds of Bantu sects in South Africa and various prophet cults in other parts of Africa. However, numerous indications were seen that in country after country in the non-Occidental world ecclesiastical "imperialism" or "colonialism" was rapidly passing. We will note some of them as we proceed. To mention only a few here, during the Japanese occupation of much of South-east Asia during World War II when foreign missionaries were

[37] *Ibid.,* pp. 3–11.

compelled to leave or were imprisoned, the Batak churches in Sumatra and the Karen churches in Burma continued to grow and after the Japanese were expelled retained their autonomy. In India by 1960 all the Methodist bishops were nationals and the sole Lutheran episcopal see had an Indian bishop. The numerous councils for interdenominational coöperation which sprang up after World War I, notably in Asia, bore the name Christian rather than missionary and in them nationals were increasingly in control. A mounting number of ecclesiastical bodies passed into the hands of nationals and to many of them were transferred the property acquired and the buildings erected through foreign contributions. Administrative offices to which was attached the title of bishop or, more often, some other designation, were increasingly filled by nationals. By 1961 several of the ecumenical bodies had officers from outside Europe and North America. Thus for several years the chairman of the World's Student Christian Federation was D. T. Niles, from Ceylon, and in 1960 its chairmanship and general secretaryship were filled, respectively, by a Jamaican of African descent and a Latin American. By 1960 the chairman of the International Missionary Council was from Ghana and the presidium of the World Council of Churches included an Indian and a Latin American. From modest beginnings in 1954, in 1959 the East Asia Christian Conference came officially into being in a gathering in Kuala Lumpur, within the framework of the International Missionary Council and the World Council of Churches as an "organ of continuing coöperation among the churches and national Christian councils in East Asia," through which the Protestant churches of the area, most of them small minorities, could work together to spread the faith, partly by sending missionaries across national lines.[38]

In accord with these developments, increasingly the attitude of Protestants was that the traditional distinctions between "home" and "foreign" missions and between "Christian" and "non-Christian" nations were anachronisms—if, indeed, they had ever been valid. The name of one of the great boards was changed from "foreign missions" to "ecumenical mission and relations." Western personnel going overseas were often called "fraternal workers" and were placed under the direction of the churches with which they were associated. Christians from Asia and Africa were put on staffs which served the churches in the Occident. The mission of the Church was regarded as being to "frontiers" of every kind, in whatever part of the world they might be.

The recruiting and training of an indigenous clergy presented grave difficulties to Protestantism. The Roman Catholic Church with its celibate priests did not face the problem of financial support for a family such as confronted Protestants. Because of its use of Latin as its language, the Roman Catholic Church employed it as a medium of instruction in its theological seminaries and pos-

38 *The International Review of Missions*, Vol. XLIX, p. 12 (January, 1960).

sessed a vast literature in Latin which made available to seminarians and priests both the ancient and much of the recent thought of that church. By contrast, with their emphasis on preaching in the vernacular, Protestants were handicapped by having a pitifully inadequate body of suitable literature in most of the languages of Asia, Africa, and the islands of the sea. If the student was instructed through the medium of a Western language in which such a literature existed, he seldom had facility in that tongue and had difficulty in passing on to his flock conceptions acquired through it. Divided as they were into many denominations, Protestants did not readily pool their resources in a few first-class institutions. As a result, through most of Asia, Africa, and Latin America in theological education the Protestant missionary enterprise had one of its greatest weaknesses.

Yet by 1962 vigorous measures were being taken to meet the challenge. For example, following World War II the International Missionary Council initiated an extensive survey of Protestant theological education in Africa south of the Sahara.[39] The Nanking Theological Seminary Foundation, with income from a bequest in the United States, first undertook to coördinate and assist Protestant theological education in China and then, especially after the mainland of China was closed to its efforts, broadened its scope to parts of East and South-east Asia.[40] Through the initiative of a general secretary of the International Missionary Council, begun in 1956, the Theological Education Fund came into being and at the meeting of the Assembly of the International Missionary Council over the year end of 1957–1958 it was formally created by that body. It was made possible by a gift of $2,000,000 by John D. Rockefeller, Jr., matched by an equal sum contributed by eight mission boards in the United States. Charles W. Ranson, at whose instance the project had been launched, resigned from the general secretaryship of the International Missionary Council to become the director of the fund. The purpose was to strengthen strategic theological seminaries in Asia, Africa, the islands of the Pacific, Madagascar, and Latin America. Although the total available was much less than that assigned by the Roman Catholics to their seminaries outside Christendom, it was of substantial help in facilitating an advance towards solving one of the central problems of the Protestant enterprise.[41] Moreover, increasingly candidates for the ministry and clergymen already in service came to Europe or North America for further training, most of them aided by mission boards.

In the approach to Christian unity outside "Christendom" the main advances were made by Protestantism—or rather, within Protestantism. The Roman

[39] *Ibid.,* Vol. XXXIX, p. 39 (January, 1950); Vol. XLI, pp. 36, 37 (January, 1952); Vol. XLIII, p. 39 (January, 1954).
[40] From the author's personal knowledge as a former member of the committee.
[41] *The International Review of Missions,* Vol. XLVII, pp. 432–438 (October, 1958); Vol. XLIX, pp. 137–147 (April, 1960).

Catholic Church was already one in structure, dogma, and the Communion. It could make progress towards visible unity only by winning accessions from other branches of the faith. Here and there, as in the Middle East and India, it attracted small splinter groups from the Eastern Churches, but numerically its gains in this fashion were not large. On the other hand, in the 1950's it lost substantial numbers through a Communist-inspired schism in China of which we are to hear more later. Protestantism, already fissiparous, displayed two contrary tendencies, one towards increased division and the other towards co-operation and organic union. In the chapters which follow we are to see instances of both.

So far as they could be traced, the influences exerted by Christianity on the non-Occidental world outside "Christendom" emanated more from Protestantism than from the Roman Catholic Church, partly because of the more varied approaches of Protestant missionaries, a diversity arising from differing conceptions of the purpose of missions. Like the Roman Catholics, the majority of Protestant missionaries were intent on bringing into being churches which would take their full part in the life of their respective nations. But many Protestant missionaries also sought to assist, in the name of Christ, in rendering wholesome every phase of the life of a people, even though that did not lead to conversions or contribute directly to the Church. In many ways—through medical care, hospitals, and dispensaries, through educational institutions of several kinds, through improved methods of agriculture, through social centres which served the poverty-stricken in the great cities, through recreation and athletics, and through a myriad of other channels—Protestant missionaries endeavoured to bring a richer life to peoples among whom they laboured. Some of the institutions which served all mankind, notably the Red Cross and the League of Nations and its successor, the United Nations, were mainly of Protestant origin.

As was true of Roman Catholics, Protestants in the twentieth century paid increasing attention to the scholarly study of missions among non-European peoples. Particularly after the World Missionary Conference, in Edinburgh in 1910, missions were made a subject of teaching and research in universities and theological seminaries. Here and there professorships were created on the Continent of Europe. They multiplied with great rapidity in the United States.[42] The International Missionary Council had a research group, eventually the committee on research. In 1930 the Council inaugurated a department of economic and social research and counsel, and under its director several important and scholarly investigations were undertaken in Asia, Indonesia, Africa, the Carib-

---

[42] See a thorough, comprehensive account in Olav Guttorm Myklebust, *The Study of Missions in Theological Education* (Oslo, Egede Instituttet, 2 vols., 1955, 1957), *passim*.

bean, and Latin America.[43] In addition to these and other projects of the International Missionary Council several bodies engaged in extensive and careful study. As tools of research important libraries were gathered. The two largest were the Day Missions Library in Yale University, begun before World War I but greatly augmented in succeeding decades, and the Missionary Research Library in New York City, inaugurated on the initiative of John R. Mott after 1910. Increasing attention was paid to the theology of missions. The literature on the subject rapidly mounted. Because of the variety of outlook and conviction which was to be expected from the nature of Protestantism, it revealed many different attitudes. Two extremes were represented by the widely read and much discussed opening chapters of *Re-Thinking Missions,* the work of W. E. Hocking in the volume which summarized the recommendations of the Laymen's Foreign Missions Inquiry,[44] and by a book written by Hendrik Kraemer at the instance of the International Missionary Council in preparation for its enlarged meeting in Tambaram in 1938.[45]

SUMMARY

As we move from the "Christendom" of Europe, the Americas, and Australasia to that vast and rapidly growing majority of mankind in the rest of the world, we will observe in region after region and country after country the striking contrast which has confronted us in the other areas and periods of our story. On the one hand, forces were operating which appeared to threaten the existence of such Christian communities as had arisen before the twentieth century. Some of the forces issued from the erstwhile "Christendom" and were phases of the revolution which had its rise in that portion of the human race which had been longest under the least-hampered influence of the faith. Through industrialization, secularism, Communism, and the heightened nationalism which came as an infection from "Christendom," they appeared to be either sapping or openly combatting whatever of Christianity existed. Other antagonistic forces issued from the peoples of these areas. They were in part rebellion against Western colonialism and imperialism and so could be expected to oppose a religion which had come in association with the rejected dominance of the Occident. They were also expressed in the resurgence of ancient religions which were part of the ancestral heritage of the peoples who were through them asserting their independence of the Occident.

[43] John Merle Davis, *An Autobiography* (privately printed in Japan, 1960, pp. 248), pp. 123–243, contains an extended account by the first director.

[44] *Re-Thinking Missions. A Laymen's Inquiry After One Hundred Years* (New York, Harper & Brothers, 1932, pp. xv, 349), pp. 3–59.

[45] Hendrik Kraemer, *The Christian Mission in a Non-Christian World* (New York, Harper & Brothers, 1938, pp. xvi, 455). Almost the entire gamut of Protestant thought on missions at mid-century is in Anderson, *op. cit.*

On the other hand, Christianity continued to spread, for the most part among the underprivileged elements of animistic or near-animistic faiths and primitive or near-primitive cultures. In most of Asia, much of Africa south of the Sahara, and the majority of the islands of the sea only minorities were won, some of them very small and seemingly negligible. Here and there by 1962, especially on the mainland of China, in North Vietnam, and in North Korea, the minorities were dwindling. Yet mostly they were growing. Moreover, partly for the purpose of divorcing themselves from association with Western colonialism but also because of inner vitality, they were becoming more deeply rooted in indigenous leadership and were being received as equals by the larger Christian communities of the West. In the Protestant branch of the faith, many Christians were moving away from the fissiparousness which characterized that tradition. Moreover, Christianity was having an increasing influence outside the churches. It was far from dominant, but it was making itself felt. Both Roman Catholics and Protestants shared in the spread and the deepening rootage of Christianity outside the Occident. In both branches of the faith and in spite of the wars and the domestic revolutions which had racked "Christendom," the numbers of missionaries sent to the non-Occident mounted and indigenous leadership increased. More of the details of this contrast, but still only in summary form, will be seen as we pursue our geographic pilgrimage.

CHAPTER X

Western Asia and North Africa

I N WESTERN ASIA and North Africa were the remnants of the churches which
had existed before the conquests by the Arabs and by the religion, Islam, of
which the Arabs were the bearers. As we saw in earlier volumes,[1] through the
centuries, under the encircling pressure of Islam, the churches had been slowly
dwindling and by 1800 had completely disappeared in North Africa west of
Egypt. Occasionally they were subjected to persecution and always they suffered
from restrictions on the public exercise of their faith and from social discrimination against their members. Their members could defect to Islam, but no converts could be made from that religion: the penalty for apostasy from the
dominant faith was death—or at least social ostracism.

The churches had managed to maintain their existence, but in doing so, to
preserve their heritage they had become extremely conservative. They feared
any variation from their ancestral traditions as a threat to their continuance.
Their services were in the forms inherited from a creative and more prosperous
past. Their liturgies were still in the languages of an earlier day and for the
most part were unintelligible to the rank and file of the worshippers. The
structures inherited from more fortunate pre-Moslem years were preserved. The
parish clergy were married and the bishops were drawn from the monasteries
and were either unmarried or widowers. Monasticism continued, although often
badly decayed. The divisions which had existed before the Arab conquest persisted and a few new ones had been added. The Orthodox perpetuated the
church of the Byzantine Empire and had as their ranking bishop the Ecumenical Patriarch, with his seat in Istanbul (Constantinople). Those who were sometimes labeled Jacobites, but preferred to be known as Syrian Orthodox, refused
to subscribe to the Chalcedonian formula accepted by the Orthodox and the
Roman Catholics. The Armenians (or the Gregorian Church) also dissented
from Chalcedon and were held together partly by the fact that their church
was that of their nation, a bond of their ethnic particularism. Those known as
Nestorians, but who chose to be called the Church of the East or the Assyrian

---

[1] Volume I, pp. 9, 48, 65, 66; Volume III, pp. 384-399.

Church, were the survivors of a communion which had formerly stretched across Asia, although usually embracing only minorities. The Copts were the remnants of what had once been the church of the majority in Egypt. They were in communion with the Church of Ethiopia, an ancient body which conserved its faith in the highlands of that country as yet unengulfed by Islam. In addition were groups which at one time or another had submitted to the Pope, either as Uniates, such as the Maronites in Syria, who preserved their ancient liturgies and ecclesiastical customs, or in full conformity to the Latin rite. All of the churches had a ghetto existence. Through what was known as the millet principle the Turkish regime under which they had lived for centuries treated them as political entities. Their members were Christians by heredity and habit rather than profound religious conviction.

In the nineteenth century both Roman Catholics and Protestants had sought to instill fresh life into these churches. The Roman Catholics had endeavoured to do so by bringing them into communion with the Pope. For the most part Protestants at first attempted to revive them without drawing converts from them. However, the conservatives, alarmed and angered by the innovations advocated by the Protestants, severed fellowship with those persuaded by the missionaries, and distinct churches, usually called Evangelical but in reality Protestant, came into being. They were minorities, most of them very small. Both Roman Catholics and Protestants began and maintained schools and sought through them to leaven both the Eastern Churches and Islam. They also, Protestants especially, tried through hospitals and clinics to serve the public, regardless of religious affiliation.

THE OLDER EASTERN CHURCHES

In general the five decades which followed the outbreak of World War I witnessed the numerical decline of the Eastern Churches. The political vicissitudes of the years wrought a continuation of the shrinkage which had marked the centuries since the initial incursion of Islam.

The greatest numerical losses were in Turkey and resulted from a revolution staged by the "Young Turks" on the eve of and during World War I and its aftermath. Educated in Western Europe, the leaders, quite secularized and infected with a nationalism which had been made more virulent by their residence in the Occident, sought to rid Turkey of what they regarded as the incubus of Islam and the caliphate, to make it a secular republic with nationalism as its major tie, and to rid the land of the religious minorities which, as they saw it, jeopardized political unity. They were the more of this conviction since, under the historic policy of the Turkish sultans, Christians—Greeks, Armenians, Roman Catholics, and Protestants—were recognized as distinct political enclaves. Early in World War I the Turks, aligning themselves with the Central Powers and accusing the Armenians of siding with the Russians, engaged in wholesale massacres of that unfortunate people and deported most of those whom they did not kill or who had not fled. The hatred of the Turks for the Armenians was of long standing, and the war gave the former an occasion for removing once for all what they viewed as a handicap to the state they were attempting to create. Several tens of thousands of Armenians perished or left the country and only small and poverty-stricken remnants survived.[2] The Armenian Uniates and the Armenian Evangelicals also suffered severely. As an outcome of World War I the boundaries of Turkey were considerably reduced and most of the traditional Armenia was not included within them.[3] The majority of the Armenians were now in the U.S.S.R. The Supreme Catholicos acknowledged by most of them had his headquarters at Etchmiadzin. Except for those under the Catholicos of Sis (which included as well those in Cyprus, Syria, and Lebanon) all bishops in whatever part of the world looked to him for consecration. Efforts were made to induce Armenians to rally to the support of their fellow believers in Russia.[4]

Following the defeat of the Central Powers and the collapse of Turkey and its near elimination as a territorial entity, Turkish nationalism again took heart. Under the leadership of Mustafa Kemal a republic was set up, the invading Greeks were driven out, and by the Treaty of Lausanne (1922) through what was euphemistically called an exchange of populations such Greeks as had not already sought refuge in Greece were removed to that country and the Turks in Greek territory, a much smaller number, were domiciled in Turkey. The millet system was abolished.[5] The result was that in Turkey the Orthodox, survivors of the once powerful Byzantine and professedly Christian empire, were reduced to still smaller minorities. The Ecumenical Patriarch continued to reside in Istanbul but with a much diminished constituency—estimated in the 1930's to be about 100,000 but including many wealthy Greek merchants.[6] In September, 1955, a further blow was dealt the Orthodox by anti-Greek riots in Istanbul which destroyed or badly damaged between sixty and eighty

[2] Sarkis Atamian, *The Armenian Community. The Historical Development of a Social and Ideological Conflict* (New York, Philosophical Library, 1955, pp. 475), pp. 185 ff.; William Stearns Davis, *A Short History of the Near East from the Founding of Constantinople (330 A.D. to 1922)* (New York, The Macmillan Co., 1922, pp. xv, 408), p. 383; Bertha S. Papazian, *The Tragedy of Armenia: A Brief Study and Interpretation* (Boston, Pilgrim Press, 1918, pp. xii, 164), pp. 100 ff.

[3] Latourette, *A History of the Expansion of Christianity*, Vol. VII, pp. 266, 267. On the Armenian Uniates—who are said to have suffered the loss of seven bishops, over one hundred priests, and thirty thousand of the laity—see Attwater, *The Christian Churches of the East*, Vol. I, p. 184.

[4] H. Waddams in *World Dominion*, Vol. XXXIV, p. 35 (January, 1956); *Ecumenical Press Service*, April 20, 1956.

[5] Arnold J. Toynbee and Kenneth P. Kirkwood, *Turkey* (London, Ernest Benn, 1926, pp. xiv, 329), pp. 78–113, 208, 209.

[6] Attwater, *The Dissident Eastern Churches*, pp. 46, 47.

churches in that city.[7] The violence appears to have been due to resentment among many of the Turks over the attitude of the Greek majority towards the Turkish minority in Cyprus.

The difficulty in Cyprus did not issue in any reduction of the Christian community in that island and was an example of the role of the Orthodox Church as a political as well as a religious institution. Cyprus was conquered by the Turks in the 1570's. It was occupied by Great Britain in 1878 and formally annexed in 1914. In 1923 Turkey officially recognized this action. Greeks, ostensibly members of the Orthodox Church, constituted about four-fifths of the population and Turks, Moslems by religion, were about a fifth. The Greeks desired annexation by Greece—what was called *enosis*. In the 1950's the cry for that step was echoed in Greece, and in Cyprus it led to violence against the British rule. The leader of the Greeks was Archbishop Makarios, the head of the Orthodox Church of the island. In an attempt to curb the disorder, in 1956 the British authorities deported him.[8] Violence between Greeks and Turks punctuated the struggle. Eventually, in 1959, an agreement was entered into by the British, the Greeks, and the Turks by which the island was to have its independence as a republic with a government in which Greeks and Turks shared and with a provision for the retention of bases by the British. In December, 1959, Makarios was elected president.[9]

In Iraq, a state which emerged from the disintegration of the Ottoman Empire that accompanied and followed World War I, Christians suffered severely. They were in several minority groups—Syrian Orthodox (Jacobites), Church of the East (Nestorians), Syrian Uniates, Chaldeans (Nestorians who had submitted to Rome), and Protestants. At the beginning of World War I Turks and Kurds, on the pretext that the Nestorians were potential allies of Russia, then at war with Turkey, fell on them, especially in the mountains between Mesopotamia and Persia, killed hundreds, and made refugees of many. The slaughter continued after the war, in spite of the efforts of the League of Nations to prevent it. About a third of the Chaldeans are said to have perished. In 1933 conflicts with Iraqi troops brought more suffering to the Church of the East.[10] So long as the British held the mandate to Iraq the Church of the East was protected, but when in 1932 they withdrew, the government of Iraq disarmed its adherents. The latter had hoped to be allowed to form a distinct state, but they were dispersed and numbers were killed.[11] The Church of the East moved its headquarters to the United States. There its Catholicos—who held

[7] *The International Review of Missions*, Vol. XLV, p. 42 (January, 1956).
[8] *The New York Times*, March 15, 1956.
[9] *Britannica Book of the Year, 1960*, p. 193.
[10] Latourette, *op. cit.*, Vol. VII, p. 269; Attwater, *The Christian Churches of the East*, Vol. I, p. 202.
[11] Attwater, *The Dissident Eastern Churches*, pp. 224, 225.

an office which had long come down from uncle to nephew—found haven. Such of the Church of the East who remained in Asia were mostly in Iraq and Syria.[12] A few survived in Iran.

World War I witnessed the massacre in Persia, or Iran as it was soon to be called, of many of the Church of the East, Armenians, and Aissors (Christians who had been affiliated with the Russian Orthodox Church). Early in the war Russian troops who had been defending the Christians were withdrawn, and Kurds and some Moslem Iranians vented their fury on the now defenseless minorities. A few found haven in Protestant and Roman Catholic mission compounds, but Urmia, long the chief Christian centre, was decimated.[13]

The Syrian Orthodox dwindled and numbers of them became Syrian Uniates. For example, in the 1920's several thousand took that step. In the 1930's the total of those who remained with the Syrian Orthodox was said to be about 80,000. Most of them were in Iraq, but some were in Syria and Lebanon and some had come to the United States.[14]

The creation of the independent state of Israel in 1948 and the ensuing fighting between Jews and Arabs resulted in thousands of Arab refugees from Israeli territory. Although the majority were Moslems, a number of Christians were among them and thus a blow was dealt to the Arab Christian minorities in Palestine.

Some Christian refugees of various communions found asylum in the post-World War I states of Lebanon and Syria. For example, following a meeting of its bishops in Rome in 1928 to reorganize their church after the disasters of World War I, the seat of the Patriarch of the Armenian Uniates was moved from Istanbul to Beirut.[15]

The Coptic Orthodox Church did not suffer as acutely in the twentieth century as did most of the other Eastern Churches. In the 1950's it was reported to have 1,186,353,[16] but this figure was not entirely accurate. Pressures from the dominant Islam which had been exerted since the Arab conquest in the seventh century continued but were not in the form of the overt and severe persecutions which had sometimes been seen. It was estimated, also in the 1950's, that each year about 1,000 Copts became Moslems. The defections were largely from the very poor who had hoped by that step to obtain employment. Some later attempted to return to the church of their fathers.[17] Numbers of Copts also became Protestants or Roman Catholics. Whether the Copts were declining in numbers could not be determined. Presumably a high birth rate and, among

12 Waddams, *op. cit.*, p. 37.
13 Latourette, *op. cit.*, Vol. VII, p. 270.
14 Attwater, *The Dissident Eastern Churches*, p. 274.
15 Attwater, *The Christian Churches of the East*, Vol. I, p. 184.
16 *World Christian Handbook, 1957*, p. 162.
17 S. A. Morrison in *World Dominion*, Vol. XXXIII, p. 221 (July-August, 1955).

the more prosperous, a lower death rate kept their numbers about constant. In the 1950's many Copts believed that the Government of Egypt was against them because it was taking divorce cases out of ecclesiastical courts and entrusting them to civil judges and was trying to break up the endowments by which the monasteries and the theological seminary were supported.[18] Yet in 1960 the state, to offset the rising secularist tide, was seeking to promote religious education in its schools in the faith, including either Islam or Christianity, of the parents of the children.[19]

Efforts were being made by many of the Copts to offset the inroads of secularism among the laity. Although the majority of the parish clergy were poorly educated and the preparation of the monks from whom the episcopate was traditionally recruited did not fit them to deal with the problems of the day, numbers of the laity were highly cultured and some were wealthy and prominent in the life of the country. The laity organized many societies to reform their church. Although handicapped by the divisiveness which had long characterized that body, they made improvements in several directions. Quite a number of men with university training entered the monastic life, hoping that some would eventually be made bishops and so could be effective in the central councils of the church. In this purpose they were balked by the conservative majority of the monks. In several parish churches parts of the service—the reading from the Bible, the sermons, and some of the liturgy—were in Arabic, the vernacular of the congregations. In the 1950's 440 reform groups and societies were said to exist. In 1954 the Higher Institute of Coptic Studies was founded in Cairo with three branches—academic, practical, and social—in the hope of raising the cultural level of the Coptic Church. In the 1950's hostels were being built for Coptic university students, summer camps for youth were conducted, counsel on family problems was being provided, and at least one orphanage was maintained. A society known as the Friends of the Bible sought to promote the study of the Scriptures. Sunday Schools flourished. In the 1950's many young people attended services, in contrast with the situation a few years earlier when the congregations were largely of old women. Several professional men, lawyers and physicians among them, became priests and brought a higher degree of competence than in the days when many priests knew only enough Coptic to repeat the ritual. While undenominational, the Society for the Salvation of Souls, akin to the Youth for Christ movement in the United States and elsewhere, was holding open-air meetings and was encouraging converts, including Copts, to align themselves with the church of their choice. In the 1950's the laity forced a weak Patriarch to retire to the desert until he promised reforms. When he assented and, returning to power, rescinded the reforms, the state

[18] Information given the author from confidential sources, July, 1952, and September, 1957.
[19] *Worldmission Fides Service*, April 9, 1960.

stepped in and at its instance a synod (September, 1955) suspended him.[20]

In 1959 a new Patriarch was enthroned as Kyrollas VI. At one time a clerk in a tourist bureau, he had felt constrained to go to the desert as an anchorite. After five years he returned (1936), rented an abandoned mill in Cairo, and began preaching. He attracted hearers, was regarded as a holy man, and was elevated to the highest office in his church. But his election was only after a three-year vacancy of the post due to a violent dispute over electoral procedures in which representatives of the Church of Ethiopia were involved and withdrew, aggrieved.[21]

In the meantime a promising effort was being made to improve the education of the clergy. In 1953 the Coptic Community Council (*Megliss Milli*) purchased a modern building in Cairo for the Coptic Theological College. That institution offered a four-year course for students with a baccalaureate degree, an intermediate course for students with only a pre-secondary school certificate, a department to train choir leaders, and the Higher Institute for Coptic Studies. In 1957 the seminary enrolled about two hundred students.[22]

Other Eastern Churches continued to be represented in Egypt. In the 1950's the Orthodox bodies were said to number 89,062.[23]

In the post-World War II years the Church of Ethiopia recovered from the blows dealt it by the Italian occupation on the eve of that conflict and made progress towards an independent and more vigorous life. The Italian invasion of 1935 for a few years appeared to work marked changes. The Roman Catholic Church, while technically neutral, sought to take advantage of the situation facilitated by its accord with Mussolini (1929) over its status in Italy. It created an apostolic delegation, divided the country into prefectures apostolic and at least one vicariate apostolic, and hoped to bring the Church of Ethiopia into obedience to the Pope. But the Italian Government was more intent on promoting its own interests than those of the Papacy. It endeavoured to separate the Church of Ethiopia from its historic connexion with the Coptic Church and to replace non-Italian with Italian missionaries, whether Roman Catholic or Protestant.[24] The British expulsion of the Italians and the restoration of Emperor Haile Selassie during World War II gave opportunity for changes in the Church of Ethiopia. One development was an alteration in the relations with the Coptic Church. Traditionally the *Abuna*, the ranking official in the Church of Ethiopia, had been a Coptic monk, appointed and consecrated by the Coptic

[20] *World Dominion*, Vol. XXXIII (1955), pp. 221–224; Vol. XXXIV (1956), pp. 36, 223; *Missions*, December, 1958, p. 10; confidential information given to the author from several sources in 1955, 1956, 1959, 1961.
[21] *Time*, March 11, 1959; *The New York Times*, May 11, 1959.
[22] Allen, *A Seminary Survey*, pp. 511, 512.
[23] *World Christian Handbook*, *1957*, p. 162.
[24] Latourette, *op. cit.*, Vol. VII, pp. 260, 261.

Patriarch. This seeming subordination of the Church of Ethiopia to its Egyptian neighbour proved irksome to a rising nationalism, especially since at the mid-twentieth century the Ethiopian Christians were about three times as numerous as the Copts. The Ethiopians might unilaterally have declared their complete independence of the Copts had not Haile Selassie intervened. By a formal agreement entered into in 1959 both churches were affirmed to be of the See of Saint Mark, the reputed founder of the Church in Egypt. "The Pope of Alexandria, Patriarch of the See of Saint Mark, successor of the Evangelist Saint Mark," was recognized as the "highest spiritual father of the Church of Ethiopia." He was required to be an Egyptian Copt of Egyptian parentage and his permanent seat was to be in Alexandria. His name was always to be mentioned in the services of the Church of Ethiopia. Representatives of the Ethiopians, their number determined by the Coptic Patriarch, were to share with Egyptian electors in the choice of a successor of Saint Mark. The metropolitan of the "established Orthodox Church of Ethiopia" was to be raised to the rank of Patriarch. He was to be chosen from among the Ethiopian, not the Coptic, monks, his election was to be confirmed by the Emperor of Ethiopia, and his consecration and investiture were to be by the Coptic Patriarch. The Patriarch of Ethiopia was to consecrate the bishops and archbishops of Ethiopia after the approval of their election by the Emperor of Ethiopia. The Patriarch of Ethiopia was always to rank next after the "Pope of Alexandria." A General Holy Synod called by the Pope of Alexandria, but always with the knowledge of the Patriarch of Ethiopia, could deal with matters, including doctrine, affecting the entire See of Saint Mark. The two churches were to exchange monks and teachers and students in the field of religious education.[25]

Haile Selassie sought to improve the quality of the clergy. He sent young men to study in Greek Orthodox seminaries in Athens and near Istanbul, which, although adherents of Chalcedonian theology which the Ethiopians, with the Copts, rejected, he deemed preferable to Roman Catholic or Protestant theological schools. He also inaugurated two theological schools in Addis Ababa. He hoped through these steps to work substantial improvement in the life of the Church of Ethiopia.

The obstacles to lasting improvement in the Ethiopian Church were formidable. Although priests and monks were numerous and about a third of the land of the country was said to be owned by the Church, the training given in the monasteries was traditional and did not prepare their inmates to deal with the problems of the revolutionary age. The priesthood tended to be hereditary and often quite young boys were ordained. Most of the priests were poorly educated and knew only enough Geez—the ecclesiastical language, now unintelligible to the masses—to repeat the services. Numbers were given to drink and in other

25 The Ecumenical Review, Vol. XII, pp. 82–84 (October, 1959).

ways lived unworthily of their office. Although some movements among the laity were initiated to raise the level of the Church, especially of the youth, few of the clergy had the respect of the laity. Indeed, on the whole the educated despised the clergy and the Church. The pagans in Ethiopia were being converted either to Christianity or to Islam, but in the 1950's, because of a differential in the birth rates, Moslems were increasing more rapidly than Christians. Nasser was sending Moslem missionaries to Ethiopia. Few of the graduates from the seminaries in Addis Ababa were ordained, and still fewer who came from the Greek institutions entered the priesthood. Yet in 1959 the Ethiopian Church was training missionaries for Africa south of the Sahara and Haile Selassie was subsidizing a school in Addis Ababa for that purpose—presumably as a means of extending the influence of Ethiopia in the newly independent nations in that area.[26]

THE RAPIDLY SHIFTING POLITICAL PICTURE AND THE INROADS OF SECULARISM

The shifts in the political situation in the Middle East affected not only the Eastern Churches but also the missions staffed and supported from Western Europe and America. The break-up of the Ottoman Empire which followed World War I profoundly disturbed missions in Turkey. It also was the prelude to drastic political changes elsewhere. By the post-war settlement France was given a mandate to Syria and Lebanon under the League of Nations. Great Britain was entrusted with mandates to Iraq and Palestine, and Egypt was declared to be independent, although with surviving traces of the British protectorate. The rising tides of nationalism, with their attacks on Western imperialism and colonialism, brought the complete independence of several states. Most of Arabia became free not only of Turkish but also of British rule. In 1936 Egypt achieved its full independence. In 1932 the British mandate over Iraq was terminated. As an accompaniment of World War II, in 1941 France permitted Lebanon to declare its independence. Following the war, in 1946 Great Britain surrendered its mandate over Jordan and recognized the independence of that country. The British mandate over Palestine was ended in 1948 and was followed by the proclamation of the state of Israel and the division of the country between Israel and Jordan. Syria became a republic in 1941, was fully independent on January 1, 1944, and saw the last French troops leave in 1946. Egypt led in the formation of the Arab League (1944) and in 1951 abrogated its treaty of 1936 with Great Britain. In 1956 Egypt nationalized the Suez Canal, Israel and Egypt were at war, and late in the year Great Britain and France attempted to occupy the Suez Canal Zone but in December with-

---

[26] Information acquired orally, largely through confidential and authoritative channels, in 1959.

drew in face of aroused world opinion. In 1956 Gamal Abdel Nasser was formally elected president of the republic which had been proclaimed in Egypt in 1953. In 1956 the Sudan, for some years a condominium of Egypt and Great Britain, was recognized by the United Nations as independent. The United Arab Republic was formed in 1958 by Egypt and Syria. In 1958, partly as a result of the tensions and fears aroused by this step, civil strife in Lebanon led to the landing there of armed forces of the United States (temporarily as it proved). British forces were also air-lifted into Jordan. Not far from the same time a violent *coup d'état* changed the government in Iraq. All these developments had repercussions on missions from the Occident, some of which we are to see as our story unfolds.

The impact of the Occident of the revolutionary age also brought intellectual changes. Secularism began to make inroads on Islam. The application of Western scholarship to the Koran and other Moslem literature aroused questioning among some intellectuals. In contrast, as a result of quickened nationalism through conflict with the West, a revival was seen in Islam—not so much from religious conviction as from pride of cultural heritage.

ENLARGED ROMAN CATHOLIC ACTIVITY

In a variety of ways and through several channels the Roman Catholic Church was seeking to enhance its strength in Western Asia and North Africa. Since it regarded the Bishop of Rome as the true head of the entire Church and believed that all Christians should be brought into its communion, that there might be "one fold and one shepherd," from the days of the Epistles of Clement it had expanded its efforts. In the twentieth century it continued them.

One channel through which the Roman Catholic Church sought to win the region was the Uniate Churches. For many centuries the Middle East had had churches in that category. Yet the Franciscans, long the chief Roman Catholic missionaries in the Middle East, tried to assimilate converts to the Latin rite. However, in the second half of the nineteenth century the Popes discouraged that method and encouraged the emergence and growth of the Uniate bodies. In the twentieth century the Holy See stressed and expanded the programme. In 1917 it created the Congregation for Oriental Churches with the purpose of eventually placing under its jurisdiction all in the Middle East, even of the Latin rite, who were supervised by the Propaganda. It would thus add dignity to these churches by withdrawing them from a status which might be interpreted as inferior to the main body of the faithful and putting them on an equal basis with the latter.[27]

In accord with this policy, seminaries in Rome were encouraged to prepare

[27] Latourette, *op. cit.*, Vol. VII, p. 263.

clergy for the Uniates. In the 1950's seven were maintained. Two of them were of sixteenth-century origin, two were begun in the second half of the nineteenth century, and three were founded between World War I and World War II.[28] In addition, in the 1950's there were two others in Rome, one in another part of Italy, and three in the United States.[29] The year 1917 was marked by the creation of the Pontifical Oriental Institute, eventually a section of the Gregorian University in Rome, to study the Oriental Uniates and thus to reduce prejudice against them.

With his far-ranging vision and his desire to increase the world-wide spread of the faith, Pius XI took concrete steps to further Roman Catholic activity in the Middle East. In the encyclical *Rerum Orientalium* (September 8, 1928)[30] he expressed the hope that in every diocese a student would be set aside to specialize in the Middle East and that each seminary would have a member of the faculty with that area as his concern. In 1926 he inaugurated the Mission Aid to the Near and Middle East. In 1931 he transformed the Catholic Near East Welfare Association, begun in the United States to give relief to the sufferers from World War I and its aftermath, into an agency for the collection of funds and the promotion of interest in Roman Catholic programmes in the Middle East. In the 1950's it was the largest source of financial support for the Congregation for Oriental Churches. Pius XI also encouraged Latin orders and congregations to form branches using the Eastern rites. In 1924 he requested that in every Benedictine congregation one abbey should specialize on the Eastern Churches.[31]

In the twentieth century growth was registered in several of the Uniate Churches. Thus in Egypt in 1946, of the 227,000 Roman Catholics slightly over one-half were of the Latin rite and 63,000 were of the Coptic rite. The latter group was growing more rapidly than any of the other Roman Catholic bodies in the country. It counted about 2,000 converts each year. In 1957 it had two major seminaries for the preparation of clergy.[32] However, the rise of nationalist feeling and especially the Suez crisis of 1956 brought about the exodus of thousands of Roman Catholics.[33] In 1957 the Roman Catholics were conducting fourteen major seminaries and scholasticates in Lebanon, Jordan, and Iraq. Nine of them were in Lebanon. The one with the largest enrollment was part of the University of St. Joseph in Beirut, a Jesuit institution, the only pontifical university in the Middle East. It served students of all rites, but each rite maintained its own "college." Since priests for the Maronite rural parishes in Lebanon were

[28] Allen, *op. cit.*, p. 344.
[29] *Ibid.*, p. 345.
[30] *Acta Apostolicae Sedis*, Vol. XX, pp. 277–278.
[31] Allen, *op. cit.*, pp. 343–346.
[32] *Ibid.*, pp. 410, 411.
[33] Etteldorf, *The Catholic Church in the Middle East*, p. 60.

too few to meet the need, married men of proper ability and character were ordained after studying in a special seminary equipped for that purpose.[34] After the massacres and deportations which accompanied and followed World War I the chief centres of the Armenian Uniates were in Lebanon and Syria. Their patriarchate had its headquarters in Beirut from 1928 until it was transferred to Rome. From 1937 to the time these pages were penned the incumbent was Gregory Agagianian. In 1945 Agagianian was created cardinal, on the death of Pius XII he was thought of as one of strong possibilities for the succession, and in 1960 he was appointed the head of the Congregation for the Propagation of the Faith.[35] In the mid-1940's the Chaldeans (Nestorian Uniates), although they had suffered heavily in World War I, totalled over 96,000, living mostly in the great plain of Mesopotamia. Their Patriarch-Catholicos resided in Mosul and their clergy were prepared in several places.[36] In the mid-1940's the Melkites, Uniates gathered from the Greek Orthodox, were said to number about 150,000 in Egypt, Syria, Lebanon, Palestine, and Transjordan. Rivalry with accompanying friction between the Melchites and adherents of the Latin rite was chronic in Syria and some other places. Several thousands of the Melkites migrated to the United States.[37] The Ethiopians, Uniates from the Church of Ethiopia, were not numerous and in the 1940's were mostly in Eritrea, not Ethiopia. They numbered about 28,000.[38] In the 1940's the Maronites were predominantly in Lebanon and were mostly peasants and mountaineers. They were said to have about 300,000 in that country. Thousands had migrated to the United States and lesser numbers to Uruguay, Argentina, Brazil, Australia, and South Africa.[39]

Although the Roman Catholic Church directed most of its effort in the Middle East to the Uniate Churches and to seeking to win what it called the "separated brethren," it did not confine itself solely to that channel of endeavour. From experience it knew that because of Moslem law, social pressure, and centuries-long dislike of Christians few converts could be won from Islam. Yet it persevered. It maintained schools in which both Christians and Moslems were welcomed. The most notable was the St. Joseph's University at Beirut which we have already mentioned. During World War I it was closed and some of its buildings were damaged, but with the coming of peace it was reopened. Soon after World War I the Dominicans inaugurated the Institute for Oriental Studies in Cairo with the purpose of obtaining a better knowledge of Islam through the study of Moslem theological treatises. In this it had the coöperation

---

[34] Allen, *op. cit.*, pp. 428, 429; Etteldorf, *op. cit.*, p. 101.
[35] Attwater, *The Christian Churches of the East*, Vol. I, pp. 184, 185.
[36] *Ibid.*, pp. 202–204.
[37] *Ibid.*, pp. 112, 113.
[38] *Ibid.*, pp. 146–148.
[39] *Ibid.*, pp. 172, 173.

of members of the faculty of the University of al Azhar, the main centre of theological study in the Moslem world.[40] In the 1950's the Franciscans had thirty-eight parishes, forty-two elementary schools, and five secondary schools in Palestine, and in them were enrolled not only Roman Catholics but also "dissident" Christians, Jews, and Moslems.[41] In the same decade Palestine had members of the Little Brothers of Jesus and the Little Sisters of Jesus, congregations following the ideals of Charles de Foucauld. One of the former was a convert from Islam who maintained a kindergarten and a dispensary.[42] In Egypt in the 1950's members of several orders conducted about three hundred schools. In 1932 Jesuits from the United States began a college in Baghdad for both Christians and non-Christians.[43] After World War II Benedictines inaugurated a mission in Morocco.[44]

CONTINUED BUT CHANGING PROTESTANT EFFORT

The twentieth century saw a continuation of Protestant missions in the Middle East, but with striking changes. The outstanding contrast was in Turkey. There the political revolution for a time threatened to end Protestant efforts. They persisted, but under greatly altered conditions. The major Protestant programmes had been directed to the Armenians and the Greeks. For them schools had been founded and maintained, some of them of college grade, and hospitals and clinics had been conducted, and from them Protestant churches had come into being. Robert College in Constantinople had drawn many of its students from Bulgaria. With the near-extinction of the Armenian and the Greek communities the previous constituencies to which Protestant efforts had been directed were all but erased. During the Balkan wars, in which the Turks and Bulgarians were at odds, the student body in Robert College was altered. Moreover, the new Turkish regime forbade any efforts at conversion to the Christian faith. In every place of Christian worship all religious signs, emblems, and pictures had to be removed. Special garb worn by priests and clergymen—as well as by Moslem teachers and officials—was forbidden. In the schools, whether Christian or Moslem, religious services and instruction were banned. Every foreign school was required to have a Turkish co-director. The chief Protestant agency in Turkey was the American Board of Commissioners for Foreign Missions. With the elimination of the Armenians and Greeks and the restrictions placed on evangelism by the government, some missionaries and their support-

---

[40] Allen, *op. cit.*, p. 411.
[41] Etteldorf, *op. cit.*, p. 11.
[42] *Ibid.*, p. 12.
[43] *Ibid.*, pp. 59, 130.
[44] Peter Beach and William Dunphy, *Benedictine and Moor. A Christian Adventure in Moslem Morocco* (New York, Holt, Rinehart and Winston, 1960, pp. x, 214), *passim.*

ers questioned whether the American Board should continue in Turkey. However, the decision was to remain. Some schools and hospitals were maintained and efforts were made to give a Christian witness by example, by friendship with the Moslems, and by serving helpfully in any way that the state would permit. The schools conducted by the missionaries were popular as a source of the kind of education which the new day demanded. Robert College had a full enrollment.[45] Its sister institution, Istanbul (Constantinople) Women's College, survived World War I and made important contributions in preparing the kind of graduates which were of strategic importance in a day when the traditional status of women was changing.[46] In time, restrictions were somewhat relaxed. A law enacted in 1949 restored to the Church the control of churches, schools, and social welfare institutions. Schools of the American Board were crowded and its hospitals and clinics were thronged.[47] Periodicals prepared by the missionaries in an attempt to provide wholesome if not explicitly Christian literature were in wide demand.[48] At the end of the 1950's the American Board's schools continued to be popular, with nine times the numbers of applicants that could be admitted.[49]

Elsewhere in the Middle East political developments brought problems to Protestants as well as Roman Catholic missions. The creation of Israel with the resulting exodus of thousands of Arabs affected both the Christian minority and the Moslem majority. The Suez crisis led to the sequestration by the Government of Egypt of much of the property of the foreigners involved, including that of the missions, and the departure of some of the missionaries. It also resulted in the withdrawal of British missionaries from some other parts of the Middle East. Yet for the most part Protestant schools and hospitals were able either to continue or to resume, often with indigenous staffs.[50] The political divisions stimulated the raising of the Anglican episcopate in Jerusalem to the rank of an archbishopric (1957)—"the Episcopal Church in the Middle East" —with the inclusion under it of existing bishoprics in Egypt, Libya, the Sudan, and Iran, and the erection of a new diocese for Jordan, Syria, and Lebanon.[51]

[45] Latourette, *op. cit.*, Vol. VII, pp. 268, 269. On Robert College after 1914 see Caleb Frank Gates, *Not to Me Only* (Princeton University Press, 1940, pp. x, 340), pp. 207 ff., and Lynn A. Scipio, *My Thirty Years in Turkey* (Rindge, N.H., Richard R. Smith, 1955, pp. 364), pp. 79 ff. For the life of Lyman MacCallum, long a representative of the Bible Lands Agency, North, in which the American Bible Society and the British and Foreign Bible Society coöperated, see Constance E. Padwick, *Call to Istanbul* (London, Longmans, Green and Co., 1958, pp. xii, 209), *passim*. On the Young Men's Christian Association in Istanbul, which was required to drop the designation "Christian" and in 1939 was reopened under the name of Dershane, see Latourette, *World Service*, p. 344.
[46] Mary Mills Patrick, *A Bosporus Adventure: Istanbul (Constantinople) Woman's College, 1871–1924* (Stanford University Press, 1934, pp. ix, 284), pp. 161 ff.
[47] *The International Review of Missions*, Vol. XXXIX, p. 37 (January, 1951).
[48] *Ibid.*, Vol. XLIII, pp. 37, 38 (January, 1954).
[49] *Ibid.*, Vol. XLIX, p. 38 (January, 1960).
[50] *Ibid.* Vol. XLVII, p. 35 (January, 1958); Vol. XLVIII, p. 40 (January, 1959).
[51] *Ibid.*, Vol. XVII, p. 35 (January, 1958).

An Arab was consecrated to the new bishopric.[52] The growing nationalism in Iran which issued in the confiscation of foreign oil properties had as one of its phases the closing of foreign, including mission, schools. An attempt was made to maintain Christian influence in the government schools by building hostels for Christian students.[53]

As may have been inferred from the preceding paragraphs, Protestant missions from the West, like Roman Catholic missions, emphasized schools and philanthropic service and won most of their converts, not from Islam, but from the Eastern Churches. In 1962 the Protestant denomination with the most widely extended activity in the Middle East was the United Presbyterian Church in the United States of America. It had been formed by the union, in 1958, of the Presbyterian Church in the United States of America and the United Presbyterian Church of North America. The resulting body had missionaries in Egypt, Ethiopia, the Sudan, Syria, Lebanon, Iraq, and Iran. As had been true on the eve of World War I, the largest of the Protestant churches in the Middle East was the Evangelical Church in Egypt, Synod of the Nile (also known as the Coptic Evangelical Church), which had been gathered by the United Presbyterian Church of North America, chiefly from the Coptic Church. It seems to have experienced a marked growth in the twentieth century. In 1924 its communicant membership was said to have been 16,011 and its constituency about 40,000.[54] In 1949 the corresponding figures were 25,000 and 78,000, and in 1952, 26,007 and 75,000.[55] In accord with the nationalistic temper of Egypt, in 1926 it became independent of the church which had founded it. In Iran in the nineteenth century Protestants were still drawn partly from the Eastern Churches, but the sharp reduction of the Nestorians and Armenians by the massacres of World War I and its aftermath rendered them a dwindling source of adherents. Efforts were more and more directed towards the Moslems. The Islam of Iran—that of the Shiite wing as contrasted with the Sunni majority in the Arab lands—was only slightly less resistant to Christianity than the other. In the twentieth century some converts were won from it. In the 1950's the large majority of the Christians in Iran were said to be Armenian—about 135,000 —with about 2,000 Russian Orthodox, 3,000 Armenian Uniates, and 10,000 Protestants.[56] Of the Protestants, the greatest number were gathered by American Presbyterians. In 1952 the Evangelical Church of Iran, the outgrowth of their mission, and to a less extent of the Reformed Church of America and the Evangelical and Reformed Church, was said to have 1,984 communicants. The

[52] *Ibid.*, Vol. XLVIII, p. 36 (January, 1959).

[53] *Ibid.*, Vol. XLVII, p. 38 (January, 1958).

[54] Beach and Fahs, *World Missionary Atlas*, p. 108.

[55] *World Christian Handbook, 1952*, p. 178. On the history of that church see Earl E. Elder, *Vindicating a Vision. The Story of the American Mission in Egypt, 1854–1954* (Philadelphia, Board of Foreign Missions of the United Presbyterian Church of North America, 1958, pp. 336), pp. 146 ff.

[56] Etteldorf, *op. cit.*, pp. 123, 124.

Anglicans, through the Church Missionary Society, working largely in the South, were reported to have 236 communicants in that year.[57]

Arabia, the historical source of Islam and the heart of the Arab world, was penetrated very slowly by Christianity. In the twentieth century the major activity was by medical missionaries, schools, and the distribution of the Bible. In the mid-1930's the entire area was said to have only 688 Roman Catholic and 23 Protestant Arabs. The latter figure was 40 in 1950.[58]

Although medical missionaries did much to reduce prejudice against Christianity,[59] outright conversions seldom resulted from their work.

The same was true of the schools, of which there were many.[60] In addition to Robert College and the Istanbul Woman's College, the most widely known were the American University of Beirut and the younger American University at Cairo (founded in 1919). The American University of Beirut had been begun in 1866 as the Syrian Protestant College and changed its name in 1919. To it came students from several countries in the Middle East, most of them non-Christians. Although it held required Christian religious services, it made no attempt to win avowed converts. It was intent, rather, on cultivating in its students what it regarded as worthy character. Some of its graduates became prominent in their respective countries. In the 1930's an arrangement was made by which students from the neighbouring Greek Orthodox seminary could take part of their courses in the university.[61] With the University was affiliated the Near East School of Theology, in the 1950's the only Protestant theological school in Western Asia. Other similar institutions had been discontinued or combined with it and in it the Presbyterians, the Union of Armenian Evangelical Churches, and the Anglicans coöperated. In 1958 these bodies together had a membership of about ten thousand and the School had twelve students.[62] In 1958 the only other Protestant theological seminary in the Middle East was that maintained by the Evangelical Church in Egypt in Cairo; it then had twenty-five students.[63]

One of the major Protestant activities in the Middle East in the decades

[57] *World Christian Handbook, 1952*, p. 154. On the Seventh Day Adventist minority see Michael Simonovitch Beitzakhar, *Light Through the Shadows*, translated by Daniel V. Kubrock (Washington, Review and Herald Publishing Associatfion, pp. 184), *passim*.

[58] W. Harold Storm, *Whither Arabia? A Survey of Missionary Opportunity* (London, World Dominion Press, 1938, pp. xvi, 132), *passim*, especially pp. 62 ff.; *World Christian Handbook, 1952*, p. 138.

[59] Rosalie Slaughter Morton, *A Doctor's Holiday in Iran* (New York, Funk & Wagnalls Co., 1940, pp. xi, 335), pp. 206 ff.

[60] For examples of Protestant schools of various grades and in several countries see James Batal, *Assignment Near East* (New York, Friendship Press, 1950, pp. 119), pp. 39 ff.

[61] Stephen B. L. Penrose, Jr., *That They May Have Life. The Story of the American University of Beirut 1866-1941* (New York, The Trustees of the American University of Beirut, 1941, pp. xv, 347), pp. 147 ff.

[62] Allen, *op. cit.*, pp. 87-92.

[63] *Ibid.*, p. 21.

which followed the outbreak of World War I was the manifold effort to relieve the victims of that war and of World War II and its aftermath, and to alleviate the chronic poverty of the region. In 1915, at the instance of Protestant missionaries from the United States, what was called Near East Relief was organized. It received much of its support from Protestant churches and Sunday Schools. By 1930 it had raised over $91,000,000 from many thousands of individuals and had distributed about $25,000,000 in food and supplies from the United States Government, railroads, and foreign governments. It served the Armenians who fled from Turkey, Russian refugees from the Communists, Greek refugees from Asia Minor, and sufferers in Syria, Persia, and the Caucasus. It rescued, fed, and educated about 132,000 orphaned children who otherwise would have perished or would have become disorderly vagabonds. It introduced new industries, advanced agricultural methods, better seeds, and improved strains of cattle.[64] It was followed by the Near East Foundation. World War II and especially the refugee problem posed by the Arabs dislocated by the formation of Israel and by the Jews who suffered from Arab hostility evoked many relief efforts. Not all were Protestant. The chief burden was carried by the United Nations and the governments of Great Britain and the United States. However, the World Council of Churches, the Friends, and various other Christian agencies, some Protestant, some Roman Catholic, made substantial contributions in money, in kind, and in personnel.[65]

Protestant coöperation in the Middle East and North Africa was achieved mainly through the Near East Christian Council, one of the constituent bodies of the International Missionary Council. In 1924 a conference of missionaries was held by John R. Mott in Jerusalem. Out of it came, in 1927, a Christian Literature Committee for Moslems. In 1929 the Near East Christian Council followed. Its first secretary was Robert P. Wilder, the chief founder more than forty years before of the Student Volunteer Movement for Foreign Missions, who gave the later years of his active life to this pioneer project which called for bringing into association over a hundred missionary societies with many and varying polities and theological convictions and from several countries.[66]

THE MOUNTING CRISIS IN NORTH AFRICA WEST OF EGYPT

The twentieth century witnessed a mounting crisis for Christianity in North Africa west of Egypt. It sprang from the rising tide of nationalism with its

---

[64] James L. Barton, *Story of Near East Relief (1915–1930). An Interpretation* (New York, The Macmillan Co., 1930, pp. xxii, 479), *passim;* Frank A. Ross, C. Luther Fry, and Elbridge Sibley, *The Near East and American Philanthropy. A Survey* (New York, Columbia University Press, 1929, pp. xiii, 308), *passim.*

[65] *International Review of Missions,* Vol. XLVII, p. 36 (January, 1958).

[66] Ruth Wilder Braisted, *In This Generation. The Story of Robert P. Wilder* (New York, Friendship Press, 1941, pp. xiv, 205), pp. 170–193.

revolt against Western European imperialism which was a feature of the post-World War I stage of the revolutionary age.

In the nineteenth-century heyday of Western colonialism, France had extended its rule over a large part of North Africa and the hinterland in the Sahara. In the 1830's and 1840's France had annexed Algeria. In 1881 it had extended its control eastward in the form of a protectorate over Tunisia. In 1912 France and Spain obtained protectorates over their respective zones in Morocco. Colonization from Europe followed. It was mostly from France and chiefly in Algeria, but with substantial elements, both French and Italian, in Tunisia, and with about 500,000 French and Spanish settlers in Morocco. Most of the settlers were at least nominally Roman Catholics, and through dioceses and parishes their church made provision for their pastoral care. A few from Europe were Protestants. It was in North Africa that Lavigerie initiated the White Fathers. The overwhelming majority of the population was Moslem. The Berber element was prominent, but in general the region was part of the Arab-Moslem world—a connexion going back to the Arab conquest in the seventh and eight centuries. In the fore part of the twentieth century the French population, a little over a million strong, was mostly in the fertile and well-watered lands in Algeria on the shores of the Mediterranean. Both its birth rate and its death rate were lower than those of the Moslems.

After World War I, agitation began among the Moslems for equal rights with the Europeans. Following World War II, nationalistic pressures against European rule in North Africa were heightened. In 1956 France and Spain relinquished their protectorates over Morocco. In 1955 France granted internal autonomy to Tunisia and the following year conceded the full independence of the country. In 1947–1948 Moslems in Algeria were declared to be full French citizens and in 1958 all citizens were placed on the electoral lists and Moslem women were accorded civil rights. But these concessions did not satisfy the extreme nationalists. In the 1950's the disaffected in Algeria demanded full independence, fighting broke out, and the French army proved unable to crush the resistance. Arabs to the east, notably Nasser in Egypt, were outspoken in their support of the rebels, and the prolonged war proved a severe drain on French resources in both money and personnel. The struggle was the chief cause of the downfall of the Fourth Republic and the coming to power of De Gaulle and the Fifth Republic. The termination of the prolonged and exhausting hostilities proved the crucial test of the De Gaulle regime.

The churches could not but be affected by the course of events. A major exodus of Europeans from Tunisia accompanied the anti-imperialistic agitation in that country. The Christian population was said to have dwindled from about 280,000 in 1954 to approximately 100,000 in 1960. For a time friendly relations continued between the Archbishop of Carthage and the Tunisian Government.

The Archbishop turned over to the civil authorities church buildings which the departure of the parishioners had left without worshippers, and they were used for schools, government offices, dispensaries, and other public purposes. But friction arose over several issues—especially over the expropriation of some buildings which the Archbishop insisted were still being utilized for worship, over the control of ecclesiastical property, and over a possible voice of the state in the appointment to church posts.[67] In Algeria part of the problem was that in contrast with most of metropolitan France (in Europe) half or more than half of the financial support of the clergy, both Roman Catholic and Protestant, came from the state. Here and there some converts were made from Islam, but many of them went to metropolitan France for their education and did not return to Algeria. In the 1950's the Roman Catholics had several hundred missionaries in North Africa. In Algeria and Tunisia they were all White Fathers, but in Morocco they were of other orders and congregations. Protestants had a few score missionaries, mostly from the United States and Great Britain.[68]

The atrocities which were the accompaniment of the prolonged fighting in Algeria disturbed the consciences of both Roman Catholics and Protestants in France. Public protests were made. Among them were repeated statements by the French Roman Catholic hierarchy condemning acts of terrorism by the French. Similar utterances came from French Protestants. In April, 1959, thirty-five Roman Catholic priests in the army in Algeria spoke out against the use of torture and the summary execution of civilians and military prisoners by the French.[69] The next month Maurice Cardinal Felton for the Roman Catholics and Pastor Marc Boegner, the ranking Protestant clergyman, issued a joint statement saying that the Christian conscience could not remain indifferent to the treatment of Algerians in French re-groupment camps.[70] The following year the plenary assembly of the French Protestant Federation exhorted every member of the Church to pray for peace and authorized the president of the Federation, if possible in coöperation with other religious authorities in the country, to appeal to the head of the state and responsible leaders of the Algerian nationalists to proclaim a truce as soon as possible. About the same time the Roman Catholic hierarchy denounced acts of terrorism.[71]

SUMMARY

As, in 1962, the historian looked back over the nearly five decades in the Middle East and North Africa since the outbreak of World War I, he was

[67] *Worldmission Fides Service*, January 9, 1960.
[68] Information, partly confidential, given to the author in November, 1959.
[69] *The New York Times*, April 13, 1959.
[70] *The Christian Century*, Vol. LXXVI, pp. 1021, 1022 (September 6, 1959).
[71] *Ecumenical Press Service*, November 4, 1960.

impressed with the fact that, both actually and still more in proportion to the growing population, taken as a whole the Christian communities had shrunk. For more than a thousand years Islam had been dominant politically and numerically. When the Koran took shape from the utterances of Mohammed, most of the region west of Mesopotamia had belonged to Christendom. Slowly the Christian churches had declined in membership and morale. World War I and World War II and their aftermath brought about a continuation of that recession. The massacres and the deportations associated with World War I decimated several of the Eastern Churches. The accentuation of Arab nationalism which followed World War II brought about a substantial reduction of the professedly Christian Europeans in Tunisia. Neither Roman nor Protestant missions had been able to stay the decline. Whether in 1962 Christianity was more or less of a force in the region than in 1914 could not be determined. It was certain that through schools, philanthropic institutions, and extensive works of relief missionaries from the West were making more of an impression in the mid-twentieth century than they had fifty years earlier. But whether by the criteria which the historian and the social scientist could use Christianity had become more potent in the lives of individuals and of nations could not be accurately established.

CHAPTER XI

The Record in Changing India

As we pursue our way eastward to the vast sub-continent of India we come to a region where the first half of the twentieth-century stage of the revolutionary age had worked and was working profound changes. Here the impact of the forces which were issuing from the former "Christendom" was drastically altering an area of ancient civilizations where lived between a sixth and a fifth of the human race.

The most obvious change was political—in part the fruitage of what had come from the West. British rule had brought more of India under one government than any other regime had ever done. Through the mechanical features of the revolutionary age—railway, telegraph, telephone, and postal service—it had made possible a geographically more comprehensive administration than earlier ages had known. The infection of nationalism and the revolt against the white man's inperialism had stimulated resistance to the British *raj*. But British tutelage and example had given the country a structure and a training in the kind of institutions which had been developed in the democratic Anglo-Saxon portion of the Occident. The result was political independence from a Britain weakened by two world wars. That independence was finally attained in 1947. It had been foreshadowed late in the nineteenth century and was hastened by the rapid march of events in the fore part of the twentieth century. Yet complete unity was not achieved. The religious differences long basic in Indian life, notably the cleavage between Moslems and Hindus, gave rise to two states—India, a republic, with a Hindu majority, and Pakistan, predominantly Moslem. Indeed, in the 1960's Pakistan was the largest Moslem state in the world and was divided into two sectors about seven hundred miles apart. The Republic of India was the creation of the Congress Party, which had Mohandas K. Gandhi, usually called Mahatma Gandhi or simply the Mahatma, as its head. Jawaharlal Nehru was its leader after Gandhi's death and was the first premier and the dominant figure in the Republic. Pakistan owed its existence immediately to the Moslem League, of which Mohammed Ali Jinnah had been president. Both the Republic of India and Pakistan remained within the British Commonwealth. At the time of separation thousands of Hindus fled from Pakistan and thousands of

Moslems left the Republic of India. The shift was accompanied by much suffering and loss of life and was followed by a serious refugee problem.

The Republic of India absorbed most of the native states which under the British had had a semi-autonomous status. Kashmir remained a bone of contention between the Republic of India and Pakistan. The Republic of India was also able to annex the remnants of the former French possessions. However, in spite of Indian protests, Portugal clung to its footholds, notably Goa, which it had acquired in the fifteenth and sixteenth centuries, until 1961.

Closely allied with the political developments was the exuberant nationalism which had achieved them. It found expression through additional channels, particularly a revival and modification of Hinduism. Many Indians stressed Hinduism as what they insisted was the national religion and their country's unique contribution to the spiritual life of mankind. Under the influence of the revolutionary currents from the West some were reinterpreting Hinduism. For many of its adherents that faith, which had traditionally been flexible, was being transformed. For example, the doctrine of *karma,* which had long been believed to entail an inescapable fatalism and so was held responsible for the passivity associated with much of Indian life, was conceived as not interfering with human freedom and as permitting the reconstruction of the individual and society. *Maya,* formerly interpreted as declaring the world to be an illusion and so as making history meaningless, was now said only to remind man of the transitory nature of this world. Much of earlier Hinduism encouraged withdrawal from the world for meditation. In contrast, Hinduism was now said to enjoin intense activity in the world to right wrongs and renounce selfish desires through working for a better social order. God Himself was declared to be ever seeking to redeem the world and to make it over. In the 1950's, as a concrete example of this change, Vinobha Bhave, a Hindu, travelled about the country persuading owners to donate land to be used by the landless poor. Much of the change could be traced to the impact of Christianity and the effort to incorporate some of its tenets into Hinduism.

The influence of Christianity contributed to at least two other changes—the legal abolition of untouchability and the improved status of women. Under the pressure of various forces issuing from the West, barriers separating castes were being weakened. So far as legislation could accomplish it, the traditional relegation of the depressed classes to permanent inferiority was abolished. Many years would be required to remove all traces of that status, but a beginning had been made. So, too, the historic prejudice against educating women and allowing them to participate in political and economic life and in the professions would not immediately disappear, but it was passing. In both innovations Christian missionaries, notably Protestants, had been among the pioneers.

Phases of the revolutionary age which posed problems to Christianity as well as to India as a whole were the rapid growth of industrialization, with the attendant increase in urban centres; the emphasis on the Western patterns of education to prepare Indians for industries and other aspects of the revolutionary age, which was responsible for the rapid multiplication of those attending schools and the hundreds who sought in the Occident to drink of the sources of the coveted knowledge; and the vast increase in population made possible by the reduction of famines through Western methods and by the drugs and techniques introduced from the West. Communism was a force with which to reckon, notably in the 1950's in the state of Kerala. The Republic of India was endeavouring to maintain neutrality in the struggle between the power blocs led respectively by the United States and the U.S.S.R. but found that difficult, particularly late in the 1950's and early in the 1960's because of the expansionist activities of the People's Republic of China in Tibet and elsewhere on the northern borders of India.

Some intellectuals and men and women who were politically conscious were reluctant to discuss religion. Here was a phase of the secularism prominent in the revolutionary age. It was reinforced by awareness that religion, especially the historic conflict between Hindus and Moslems, was hindering the unity for which the Indian nationalists longed. Those who took this attitude were inclined to say that religion should be a purely private concern and not be obtruded into politics. The currents of the revolutionary age brought much agnosticism and materialism. Earlier forms of a revived Hinduism—the Arya Samaj and the Mahasabha—were waning. Sikhism as a religion was losing ground, but the Sikh community as a self-conscious social entity was strong.[1]

The shifting world scene was reflected in some features of foreign aid to Indian Christianity. During World War I many French Roman Catholic missionaries were called to the colours and German missionaries were interned. Not until 1925 were the latter permitted to return. The stress of the war, moreover, reduced contributions from Europe to Roman Catholic missions.[2] Protestant missions were not so badly disturbed, for a smaller proportion of their personnel came from Europe than to the Roman Catholic staffs. German Protestant missionaries were repatriated, but assistance from the British Isles, North America, and neutral countries kept their enterprises from disintegrating. The reaction from giving to missions which came in the United States soon after the war wrought some curtailment. The world-wide financial depression of the 1930's brought further reductions.[3]

More persistent were the restrictions on the entrance of missionaries which followed independence. Several factors led the Government of the Republic of

[1] Braden, *War, Communism and World Religions,* pp. 137 ff.
[2] Latourette, *A History of the Expansion of Christianity,* Vol. VII, pp. 279, 280.
[3] *Ibid.,* pp. 290, 291.

India to deny entrance visas to many missionaries. Some were prevented from going to the animist tribes on the northern frontiers. Moved by nationalistic motives, the government was determined to incorporate these peoples into a predominantly Hindu state. As they became Christians—and they were moving rapidly into Protestantism—the hill people wished to be autonomous and at times engaged in guerrilla warfare to attain their purpose.[4] Widespread opposition to what was dubbed "proselytizing" contributed to the reluctance to admit missionaries, for that was declared to be their objective. In 1956 wide publicity was given to a report of a committee appointed by the Government of Madhya Pradesh, a state near the centre of the country, to investigate Christian missionary activities in that area. It had high praise for missionaries for establishing schools, hospitals, dispensaries, orphanages, and institutions for the handicapped. It commended them for elevating the neglected classes to a better social position, for improving the status of women, and for stimulating many social and religious reforms in Hindu society. But it objected vigorously to changing the religious orientation of Indians and charged that non-religious inducements were offered to produce conversions, especially among the hill tribes and the depressed classes. It accused missionaries of mixing in politics. It maintained that missionaries were placing obstacles to the creation of the secular welfare state which was the goal of the Republic of India. It recommended, among other measures, that the large influx of foreign missionaries be checked, that missionaries whose primary object was "proselytization" be asked to withdraw, that the Indian Christians establish a united church in India which would be independent of foreign support and control, that the use of medical or other professional services to effect conversions be prohibited by law, that the employment of any means to induce individuals to change their religious faith should be absolutely interdicted, that the circulation of literature for religious propaganda be not permitted unless with government approval, and that no non-official agency be allowed to obtain foreign assistance except through government channels.[5] Although the report was not adopted by the national government, it embodied the convictions of many Hindus, some of them influential. Visas were often granted only for limited periods and not renewed. As a general principle they were not issued unless it could be proved that the missionary was not assigned to a position which could be filled by an Indian. Another reason given, either explicitly or tacitly, for reluctance to grant visas, especially to Americans, was that, in India's determination to remain neutral in the strug-

---

[4] As one example of the tension between the authorities of the Republic of India and one of the hill tribes, the Nagas, see *The New York Times,* December 28, 1960. On the Nagas as they were shortly after World War I see William Carlson Smith, *The Ao Naga Tribe of Assam. A Study in Ethnology and Sociology* (London, Macmillan and Co., 1925, pp. xxvii, 244), *passim.*

[5] *Report of the Christian Missionary Activities Enquiry Committee, Madhya Pradesh, 1956* (Nagpur, Government Printing Office, Madhya Pradesh, 2 vols., 1956).

gle between the power blocs, if entrance was permitted to Americans it must also be granted to Soviet citizens.[6] Reducing the admission of missionaries had the effect of accelerating the rootage of the faith in India and in Indian leadership. The process was already under way, but it was given added impetus.

As we enter upon the record of Christianity in the first half of the twentieth century in the sub-continent which we call India, we cannot hope to give it in detail. The land was too large and the varieties of Christianity were too numerous to permit a complete account in the space which is properly ours. Moreover, while growing in numbers and in their percentage of the total population, even in 1962 those who bore the Christian name were only about two out of a hundred of the population of the Republic of India and Pakistan. We must content ourselves with sketching the outlines of the main developments and pointing out a few striking features, institutions, and personalities. We will begin with the oldest Christian community, that of the Syrian Orthodox, noting some of the divisions and the Mar Thoma Church, which came out of the parent body in the nineteenth century. We will then go on to the Roman Catholic Church as the branch of Christianity which was next in reaching the country. Protestantism will follow, as the latest branch to be represented. Finally we must say something of the effect of the faith upon India as a whole, especially upon the millions who were not counted as Christians.

Mounting Vigour Among the Syrian Christians

The Syrian Christians claimed to owe their beginnings to the Apostle Thomas in the first century. That origin was neither proved nor disproved. Evidence existed of the presence of the community in India for over a thousand years.[7] They were chiefly on the Malabar coast but were also found in some other parts of India. In the twentieth century they constituted about a fourth of the population of the state of Travancore-Cochin. More than half of their number were

---

[6] *National Christian Council Review,* Vol. LXXIX, pp. 65 ff. (February, 1959), gives the government regulations. Before the independence of India, to enter the country new missions had to have the approval of the British Secretary of State for India and he looked to the Archbishop of Westminster for endorsement of Roman Catholic congregations or societies and to the Conference of Missionary Societies of Great Britain and Ireland or to the Foreign Missions Conference of North America for approval of Protestant societies. After independence, the Indian Government asked the sponsorship of the Catholic Bishops' Conference for Roman Catholic applications and the National Christian Council for an opinion on Protestant applications.

In 1955 the Government of India said that visas were to be granted to new missionaries only if the applicant had outstanding qualifications or special experience; that they would normally be given for the return to India of missionaries who had been in the country five years or more; that new missionaries would not be admitted to border or tribal areas; and that to enter new centres missions must have its permission. It later gave the same treatment to applications of missionaries from Commonwealth countries as it did to other citizens of those lands.

[7] Of the large literature one of the best accounts is in Brown, *The Indian Christians of St. Thomas,* pp. 43 ff.

Roman Catholic Uniates with a chequered history which went back to the sixteenth century. The portion which was not in communion with Rome suffered from divisions. Of these the two with the largest number of members were the Orthodox Syrian Church of Malabar, under the Catholicos of the East, with about 450,000 in its fold in the mid-1950's and the Malankara Jacobite Syrian Church, which acknowledged as its head the Patriarch of Antioch of the Syrian Orthodox Church and had about 700,000 on its rolls.[8] Controversy between the two churches had been in progress since at least 1910.

The main strength of the Catholicos was in the central and southern part of Travancore, and the Patriarchate section was chiefly in North Travancore. The issue was not doctrinal but administrative, and it entailed prolonged litigation in the civil courts. Attempts were made to effect reconciliation both from within the Syrian constituencies and by concerned churchmen outside the two bodies but for years were frustrated. However, a court decision in favour of the Catholicate led to the union of the two wings (December, 1958) to form the Syrian Orthodox Church of Malabar.[9]

The division did not prevent a marked advance in the life of the Syrian Christians. Economic prosperity increased. Education was greatly improved. In the 1950's the Syrian community was said to be completely literate—or at least to have between 75 per cent. and 95 per cent. in that category—and many proceeded to higher education. Men and women were active in the professions and in trade not only in many parts of India but also in East Africa, Ceylon, and Malaya. The Union Christian College at Aluva, begun soon after World War I, not only inculcated a spirit of service in its members but also endeavoured to promote the unity of the Syrian Christians.[10] For a time difficulty was encountered in obtaining a sufficient number of educated candidates for the priesthood. The discord within the church led to the closing of several theological seminaries and to a reduction in the quality of the students in the two which survived. In 1957 the two had only twenty-eight students in their higher grades.[11] By 1962 the dearth no longer existed. Increasingly the services were in Malayalam, the vernacular language, instead of Syriac—although in the 1950's some of the older priests clung to the latter.[12]

In spite of the discord, promising efforts were put forth to win non-Christians and in social service. In 1924 the Servants of the Cross Society was founded by Bishop Mar Eustathius, a member of the party of the Catholicos. By 1958 it had twenty-six full-time missionaries and over a hundred centres, mainly among

[8] *The Christian Handbook of India, 1954–1955*, pp. 172, 173.
[9] Brown, *op. cit.*, pp. 132 ff.; Keay, *A History of the Syrian Church in India*, pp. 102–105; Allen, *A Seminary Survey*, pp. 537, 538; K. K. Kuruvilla in *The National Christian Council Review*, Vol. LII, pp. 302–307; *The Ecumenical Review*, Vol. XI, pp. 300–306 (April, 1959).
[10] Brown, *op. cit.*, pp. 159, 160.
[11] Allen, *op. cit.*, pp. 538, 539.
[12] Brown, *op. cit.*, p. 235; *The Ecumenical Review*, Vol. XIII, pp. 285, 286 (April, 1961).

the depressed classes in Travancore-Cochin. By 1961 it was said to have made about 25,000 converts. In 1925 the Evangelistic Association was begun by members of the Patriarchate section, also for the depressed classes. By the mid-1950's it had about fifty centres.[13] The Christu Sishya Ashram, begun in 1925 by (Anglican) Bishop H. Pakenham-Walsh, was the first mission of the Syrian Christians to go to the Tamil-speaking areas. It translated the liturgy and the prayer-book into that language. We also hear of a woman's missionary society and the Mount Tabor Mission, monastic in character.[14]

The Mar Thoma Syrian Church began in the 1880's. Expelled from the older body of reformers who had been in touch with Anglican missionaries, it was a movement similar to those in the Middle East that emerged from the Eastern Churches through contacts with Protestant missionaries. It was much larger than any of the Evangelical bodies in the Middle East. In the mid-1950's it was said to have 257,000 members. Unlike its Middle Eastern parallels, in liturgy and structure it retained many of the features of the church from which it sprang. In the 1950's it had as metropolitan Johanon Mar Thoma, who had had part of his education in Union Theological Seminary in New York City and from 1956 to 1961 was one of the presidium of the World Council of Churches.[15] It was actively missionary, drew converts, largely from the depressed classes, and, standing against caste distinctions, incorporated fully into its fellowship all its members regardless of their social background. The Maramon Convention, begun in 1895, continued to grow until in the 1950's at its annual meetings it gathered between thirty and fifty thousand for religious addresses and the strengthening of the spiritual life.[16]

In 1961 a division occurred in the Mar Thoma Church between the "evangelical" and "orthodox" wings. The "evangelicals" declared that they would be guided only by the Bible. They took the name of the St. Thomas Evangelical Church of India.[17]

In 1921 Union Christian College, in Alwaye, was begun by graduates of the Madras Christian College, who came from more than one branch of the Syrian Church. It sought to inculcate in its students the same high spirit of self-dedication that had inspired the founders and it enjoyed a healthy growth.[18]

The Church of Trichur, or Mellusian Church, was a branch of the Church

---

[13] Brown, *op. cit.*, pp. 160, 161; *New Missionary Review*, Autumn, 1956, p. 8; *The Ecumenical Review*, Vol. XI, pp. 304, 305 (April, 1959); Vol. XIII, pp. 283–286 (April, 1961).

[14] Keay, *op. cit.*, pp. 91–100.

[15] *The Christian Handbook of India, 1954–1955*, p. 173; K. K. Kuruvilla, *A History of the Mar Thoma Church and Its Doctrines* (Madras, Christian Literature Society for India, 1951, pp. 55), pp. 26 ff.

[16] Brown, *op. cit.*, p. 149.

[17] *Ecumenical Press Service*, January 20, 1961; *The Ecumenical Review*, Vol. XIII, p. 283 (April, 1961).

[18] *The Christian College in India*, pp. 298, 299; Neill, *Out of Bondage. Christ and the Indian Village*, p. 12.

of the East (Nestorian), also known as the Chaldean Syrian Church. In the 1950's it counted about 10,000 members, largely engaged in trade and fairly wealthy, with their centre in the northern part of Travancore-Cochin.[19]

In the post-1914 years a Russian Orthodox mission was founded in Malabar by refugee clergy from Russia. Its contacts were primarily with the Syrian Christians,[20] and it remained less than twenty years. In 1954–1955 Nicholas Zernov, a Russian Orthodox scholar from Oxford, gave a year as principal of a newly founded university college of the Catholicate at Kottayam.[21]

THE CONTINUED GROWTH OF THE ROMAN CATHOLIC CHURCH IN NUMBERS AND INDIAN LEADERSHIP

In the twentieth century the Roman Catholics continued the growth in numbers which had marked their history in the preceding century. Evidence of their vigour was shown in the increase in Indian leadership in the hierarchy. The mounting numbers were due partly to the differential between births and deaths in the membership and partly to conversions. In 1912 the total Roman Catholic population, including that in the Portuguese and French possessions, was about 1,750,000.[22] In 1918 it was not far from 2,500,000.[23] In 1936 it was about 3,500,000.[24] In 1959 the corresponding total for India and Pakistan was 4,424,615. These figures were only for regions under the Propaganda and did not embrace the Roman Catholics under bishops in whose appointment Portugal shared and who were supervised by the Congregation for Extraordinary Ecclesiastical Affairs. Nor did they include the Uniates, for they were under the Congregation for the Eastern Church (also known as the Oriental Congregation). When these two groups were added, the total of Roman Catholics in India and Pakistan in 1959 was about 5,744,000. In 1961 the figure had risen to about 6,000,000. Of the 4,424,615 under the Propaganda 4,120,054 were in the Republic of India and 304,561 in Pakistan.[25] These statistics, officially reported by the ecclesiastical authorities, seem to indicate that Roman Catholics had grown more than two and a half times in a little less than a half-century since the eve of World War I. This was a much larger proportional increase than that of the population—about 40 per cent.—in the same period.

Between 1912 and 1959 the increase in priests did not quite equal proportionately that of the total of the faithful. From 2,108 in the former year the number

19 Allen, op. cit., p. 539; The Christian Handbook of India, 1954–1955, p. 173.
20 Keay, op. cit., p. 105.
21 New Missionary Review, Nos. 17–18, 18–19, Autumn, 1956, p. 8; 1960, pp. 12, 13.
22 Streit, Atlas Hierarchus, p. 99.
23 Catholic Directory of India, 1918.
24 Fides News Service, April 18, 1936. The figures there given are for both India and Ceylon.
25 Worldmission Fides Service, August 6, 13, 1960; April 26, 1961; Worldmission, Vol. XI (Fall, 1960), p. 12.

rose to 4,778 at the latter date, or about two and a quarter times. This was about one to every 930 Roman Catholics in 1959—a better ratio than we have seen in some other countries. The number of brothers had more than kept pace with the growth of Roman Catholics—from 430 in 1912 to 1,264 in 1959, or nearly a three-fold increase. Sisters had an even better record—from about 2,600 in 1912 to 13,780 in 1959, which meant a quintuplication in slightly less than fifty years.[26]

Still more impressive was the growth in Indian personnel. In 1901 Indian priests totalled 1,580 and in 1958 they were 4,977, more than 75 per cent. of all the priests. In 1958, similarly, 70 per cent. of the brothers and 88 per cent. of the sisters were Indians.[27] The first Indian bishop of the Latin rite—as contrasted with the Uniates—was consecrated in 1921.[28] In 1958, out of 77 bishops in India (including auxiliary bishops), 37 of the Latin rite and 8 of the Oriental rite were Indians. Earlier Indian priests were mostly from the west coast from families which had been Christians for centuries. Latterly a mounting number were from Chota Nagpur, where a mass movement from the underprivileged had planted the faith as recently as the 1880's. Of the Indian priests in 1959, those in territories under the Propaganda, as distinguished from the total under the Propaganda, in the Portuguese sphere, and under the Oriental Congregation were 3,135, an increase from 2,292 in 1953.[29]

Large provision was made for the education of Indian clergy. In 1959 the sections of India under the Propaganda had 955 students in major seminaries.[30] In 1956 major seminary students, including the latter, those in the Portuguese sphere, and those under the Oriental Congregation, totalled 1,321. In addition 659 were scholastics—that is, studying to be regulars in scholasticates of the several orders and congregations. Of the major seminaries the one with the most students was in Ernakulam in Alwaye; it enrolled men from more than one rite. Poona was the seat of six seminaries and scholasticates and, accordingly, had more men preparing for the priesthood than any other city in India. The institution with the largest number of scholastics was that named for De Nobili, a famous missionary of the seventeenth century, and it was conducted by the Jesuits. Poona was also the seat of the Papal Athenaeum. In 1959 it drew students from India, Ceylon, Indonesia, and Bhutan and from several congrega-

---

[26] The 1912 figures are from Streit, *op. cit.,* p. 90, and the 1959 data from *Worldmission Fides Service,* August 6, 13, 1960.

[27] *Worldmission,* Vol. XI, p. 12 (Fall, 1960). Another set of figures says that in 1957, of the priests in South Asia (India, Pakistan, and Ceylon) 6,570 were native, and of both foreign and native priests 47.5 per cent. were seculars and 52.5 per cent. were regulars.—*Worldmission Fides Service,* April 25, 1959.

[28] *Worldmission,* Vol. X, p. 9 (Spring, 1959); Vol. XI, p. 12 (Fall, 1960). Another account says that the first Asiatic consecrated to the episcopate in territories under the Propaganda was Bishop Roche of Tuticorn, appointed in 1923.—*Worldmission Fides Service,* July 25, 1959.

[29] *Worldmission Fides Service,* August 13, 1960.

[30] *Ibid.*

tions and orders as well as those preparing to be seculars. The Papal Athenaeum was a continuation of the Papal Seminary, founded in Kandy, Ceylon, and transferred to Poona in 1956.

Before the nineteenth century the clergy of the Syro-Malabar rite had inferior preparation, but in the twentieth century they were given a thorough education, in the 1950's in the seminary in Ernakulam, to which students of the Latin rite were also admitted. The Uniates had no dearth of priests. In addition to those educated in India some of the clergy were prepared in Rome.[31]

In general, at the mid-twentieth century the large majority of the Roman Catholics in India were still south of an imaginary line drawn between Goa and Madras. As formerly, they were roughly in three main constituencies: (1) those with Portuguese blood or claiming Portuguese descent, who were not only in Goa and the other former remnants of Portuguese possessions but scattered widely elsewhere in India; (2) the Uniates of the Syro-Malabar rite drawn from the Syrian Christians; and (3) the converts from non-Christian faiths, most of them won in the nineteenth and twentieth centuries. The larger proportion of the Uniates began their connexion with Rome before the twentieth century. But substantial numbers made the transition after 1900. For example, in the 1930's about 18,000 came, led by a metropolitan, Mar Ivanios, a scholar of distinction and the organizer of a congregation of men and one of women. He and those with him were called the Syro-Malankara Church to distinguish them from the older Syro-Malabars. Their numbers continued to grow, partly by accessions from the Syrian Christians, partly by the adherence of Protestants and Mar Thomites, and partly by conversions from depressed classes. Before his death (1953) Ivanios founded a university college. In 1956 the Syro-Malankara Church had more than 90,000 members.[32] The Uniates were under the Oriental Congregation (the Congregation of the Eastern Church).

In the twentieth century friction still arose over Portuguese claims under the Papal grants given in the early days of Portuguese expansion permitting Lisbon to control the Church in India much as Portugal and Spain controlled it in the Americas in colonial days.[33] Since Portugal had never been able to provide enough missionaries to cover that vast area, conflicts had repeatedly arisen over the efforts of Rome to put territorial limits on the right of patronage and to entrust the spread of the faith to the Propaganda.[34] Efforts in the nineteenth century to settle the issue were accompanied by prolonged controversy.[35] In 1928 a fresh settlement was reached in a concordat between the Holy See and Portugal. Lisbon still retained a voice in the filling of bishoprics which had

[31] Allen, *op. cit.*, pp. 363, 432, 433, 436, 437; *Worldmission Fides Service*, July 25, 1959.
[32] *Fides Service*, October 20, 1934; Tisserant, *Eastern Christianity in India*, pp. 158–160.
[33] Latourette, *A History of the Expansion of Christianity*, Vol. III, p. 250.
[34] *Ibid.*, pp. 266–269.
[35] *Ibid.*, Vol. VI, pp. 75, 76.

traditionally been under its jurisdiction, but its powers were substantially curtailed.[36] The bishoprics which were included in the concordat were under the Congregation for Extraordinary Ecclesiastical Affairs, not the Propaganda.

Most of the remarkable numerical growth of the Roman Catholic Church in India in the twentieth century was a result of the excess of births over deaths in its constituency. As one example, in 1876 the Uniates of the Syro-Malabar rite numbered about 200,000, of whom about 180,000 were under the Archbishop of Verapoly and about 20,000 under the Portuguese *padroado*. They then had 420 priests, 215 churches and chapels, and 125 seminarians. In 1931 the totals were 532,351 members, 635 secular priests, and 617 schools with 78,149 pupils. In 1956 the corresponding figures were 1,171,235 members, 892 secular priests, 439 seminarians, and 925 schools with 251,251 pupils. In 1923 as a recognition of the increase and as part of the programme of encouraging the churches of the Oriental rites and an indigenous clergy, Pope Pius XI created the Syro-Malabar ecclesiastical province with Ernakulam as the metropolitan see with three suffragan eparchies (bishoprics). By 1954 two more eparchies were instituted. In 1942 the Syrian Carmelites, completely distinct from their brethren of the Latin rite, had 247 priests, 86 scholastics, and 76 lay brothers, conducted 16 schools, and edited 3 papers.[37]

In proportion to the total of nearly six million Roman Catholics in 1962, the number of accessions from the non-Christians was small. The energies of the priests, whether Indian or foreign, and of the brothers and nuns were devoted chiefly to the faithful. For example, in the mid-1930's only between 35,000 and 40,000 a year were converted from the non-Christians.[38] Most of them, as was true of conversions to Protestantism, came from the depressed classes and the hill tribes of primitive culture. We hear of several examples of what were akin to mass movements from these classes.[39] But in the 1950's the complaint was heard that in the North, where Roman Catholics were relatively few, the number of clergy was quite insufficient, that very few priests were coming from the Roman Catholics of the region, small minorities as they were, and that in many areas catechists, through whom the initial approaches to non-Christians were usually made, were entirely too few and those assigned to go to non-Christians were so lacking that many missionaries who might have used them were unaware of their existence.[40]

[36] *Ibid.*, Vol. VII, pp. 281, 282.

[37] Tisserant, *op. cit.*, pp. 134, 135, 139.

[38] *Zeitschrift für Missionswissenschaft*, Vol. XXVI, p. 203. For a picture of the situation in one of the older missions, that growing out of the Jesuit enterprise in Madura, see Joseph C. Houpert, *A South Indian Mission. The Madura Catholic Mission from 1535 to 1935* (Trichinopoly, St. Joseph's Industrial School Press, new ed., 1937, pp. xii, 344), pp. 80 ff.

[39] *Fides Service*, May 4, 1934; July 28, 1934; October 20, 1934; March 23, 1935; September 28, 1935; December 19, 1935; September 16, 1939.

[40] *Worldmission*, Vol. XI, p. 18 (Fall, 1960).

Roman Catholics did not confine their activities in India to recruiting and training an indigenous clergy and making converts. Through a variety of channels they sought to serve their constituency and helpfully to touch Indian life. They might have adopted the policy, as a small although growing minority, of becoming a ghetto community. That was what the Syrian Christians had done, either consciously or unconsciously, until the twentieth century. Although much of the energy of the hierarchy was devoted to raising the level of the Roman Catholics and giving them pastoral care, and the increase of the faithful was due less to conversions than to the birth rate, the Roman Catholic Church still kept as its objective making Christ King in all India and serving the country in every possible wholesome way.

Much of the Roman Catholic effort was expended through schools. Because of the policy of the British regime, which subsidized education regardless of its religious affiliation if certain professional standards were maintained, the Roman Catholics built up a more extensive system of schools than they possessed in any other country where they were so small a percentage of the population. By 1960 nearly a million and a half students were enrolled, more than half of them Roman Catholics. In 1956 Roman Catholics were maintaining 58 university colleges, 6,176 schools, 145 technical and industrial schools, and a number of teacher training institutions. Out of a teaching staff of about 40,000, approximately 9,400 were priests or nuns. Government aid continued after India became independent.[41]

The number of Roman Catholic hospitals, dispensaries, and homes for the aged mounted after the independence of the country. In 1960, 508 hospitals and dispensaries were said to be widely scattered across the country. A striking example of service to the destitute was given by Agnes Gouxha Bojaxha, a native of Albania. In 1928, when she was eighteen, she joined the Institute of the Blessed Virgin Mary (the Loreto Nuns) and was sent to India where she taught until 1948 in a school in Calcutta. Then, impressed by the needs in the slums of that metropolis, as Mother Teresa she founded the Missionaries of Charity, who, in addition to the customary vows of poverty, chastity, and obedience, added a fourth vow of dedication to work among the poor. By 1960 they were conducting primary day schools for about 3,000 children, two commercial schools to teach girls shorthand and typing, seven clinics, a home for dying destitutes, a children's hospital, a mobile leprosy clinic, and a home for fallen girls.[42] In several other places girls from middle-class families were serving in the slums. In 1934 a league of decency was begun to fight immorality on stage and screen.[43] Catholic Action sought not only to spread the faith, to

[41] *Ibid.*, pp. 13, 15, 16, 76.
[42] *Ibid.*, pp. 79–84.
[43] *Fides Service,* July 21, 1934; May 15, 1937.

promote Roman Catholic education, and to safeguard religious liberty but also to further the spiritual and economic improvement of the underprivileged and to succour the poor and suffering.[44] Periodicals were published, among them at least one daily paper and more than a score of weeklies. One, begun in 1937, was devoted to social justice, and another, started in the preceding decade, dealt with Indian and Christian philosophy.[45]

Various methods were employed to nurture the spiritual and moral life of the faithful: Eucharistic Congresses,[46] pilgrimages to Rome, passion plays, and pilgrimages to Indian shrines.[47] Something of the same end was served by ashrams, the Legion of Mary, the sodalities of the Blessed Virgin Mary, the Xavier associations, boards which sought to bring uniformity of purpose and methods to the management of schools and university colleges, and the Federation of Students.[48]

Roman Catholic laymen organized in defense of what they regarded as their rights. The Catholic Union of India was especially active when in the 1950's Communists came to power in the state of Kerala. The cause of the Communist victory seems to have been a protest against the extreme poverty of many of the population. Kerala had a larger proportion of Christians—Syrian Orthodox, Mar Thoma, Roman Catholic, and Protestant—than any other state in India, but no correlation appears to have existed between religious faith and the voting. The Communist government ordered the Christian schools placed under the state, with the danger of the elimination of Christian teaching and staffing by Communist teachers. The minister of education who led in these measures was a former Roman Catholic who had become a Communist. Roman Catholics, Syrian Orthodox, Mar Thomists, and Protestants united in their opposition and staged a strike by closing their schools (in the spring and summer of 1959) in their insistence on the right to appoint Christian teachers. So serious was their pressure that the central government stepped in (1959), dismissed the Kerala government, and took over the administration. In the election of 1960 the Communists were defeated.[49]

Coördination of the Roman Catholics of India of all ecclesiastical jurisdictions was furthered by the Catholic Bishops' Conference of India, which first met in 1944. The initial Plenary Council of India was held in 1950. It brought together the hierarchy from the North and the South and from the Latin and

---

[44] *Proceedings of the Congress of Catholic Action, held at Karachi, October 18th to 21st, 1931* (pp. 181), *passim.*
[45] Latourette, *op. cit.*, Vol. VII, p. 285.
[46] *The Fifth Eucharistic Congress in India held at Old Goa December 4th, 5th, and 6th, 1931* (Mangalupusha, Alwaye, Jubilee Memorial Press, St. Joseph's Apostolic Seminary, pp. 168), *passim.*
[47] *Fides Service*, August 11, 1834; November 3, 1934; January 26, 1935; May 25, 1935.
[48] *Worldmission*, Vol. XI, pp. 13, 14 (Fall, 1960).
[49] *Ibid.; Worldmission Fides Service*, September 26, 1959; Braden, *War, Communism and World Religions*, p. 143; *International Review of Missions*, Vol. XLIX, p. 19 (January, 1960).

Oriental rites. Its decrees formulated directives for episcopal action. It also gave authority to the Catholic Bishops' Conference to act in its behalf on an all-India scale in such matters as the lay apostolate, the wider extension of the faith, spreading among non-Christians the social doctrines of the Church, safeguarding what were considered fundamental rights in education, and giving to the faithful clear guidance on the programmes of political parties on issues of faith and morals. In the autumn of 1960 all the bishops of India gathered in New Delhi for their quinquennial meeting and had as the presiding officer Cardinal Agagianian, prefect of the Propaganda.[50]

Christianity could not be expected to have a large following in Pakistan, for that country was predominantly Moslem. Yet the Roman Catholic Church was represented there, although not by large numbers. Dominicans from New York came to reinforce Italian Dominicans and Capuchins. The growth was much more rapid proportionately than was that of the population of the country. Between 1953 and 1960 the latter increased from 76,759,690 to 82,010,000, or about 3 per cent., while in the same years the Roman Catholic membership rose from 228,491 to 304,446, or about 31 per cent. Conversions were mostly from the Hindus and animists and from the lowest economic levels. The initial approach to non-Christians was usually through catechists. The government was said to be more cordial than in any other Moslem state. Indeed, in 1960 a Roman Catholic layman was appointed chief justice. But the Roman Catholic authorities realized that if many conversions were made from Islam the friendliness would quickly cool. One method was the gathering of Roman Catholics in agricultural villages on lands owned by the Church and on which the faithful were tenants. As in the Republic of India, much emphasis was placed on hospitals and the care of lepers and especially on schools. Ten periodicals were published, some in English and some in Urdu and Bengali.[51] Since the Roman Catholic Church was relatively weak in Pakistan, an indigenous clergy was slow in being developed there. In 1957, of the 338 priests in that country only 64 were nationals.[52] In the previous year students in the major seminaries and scholasticates totalled 36.[53]

GROWING PROTESTANTISM

Neither on the eve of World War I nor in 1960 were Protestants as numerous in India as were Roman Catholics. Yet in that interval they grew slightly more, both in numbers and proportionately. As we have seen, in 1959 Roman Cath-

[50] *Worldmission*, Vol. XI, pp. 19, 20 (Fall, 1960).

[51] *Ibid.*, Vol. IX, pp. 96–100 (Winter, 1958); Vol. XI, pp. 57–64 (Fall, 1960); *Ecumenical Press Service*, November 11, 1960.

[52] Allen, *op. cit.*, p. 438.

[53] *Ibid.*, p. 439. Another set of statistics, for 1959, gave it as 21; *Worldmission Fides Service*, August 6, 1960.

olics were said to total 5,744,000, and to have about tripled since 1912 and more than doubled since 1918. Figures for Protestants were more difficult to obtain and probably suffered from incompleteness and therefore a higher degree of inaccuracy, especially for purposes of comparison. The census of 1921 showed not far from 1,900,000 Protestants. By 1928 the figure was approximately 2,154,000.[54] In 1949 it was said to be about 3,500,000,[55] and in 1956 the total Protestant community was reported to be about 5,000,000.[56] If these figures are somewhere nearly accurate, they indicate that the Protestants had multiplied about two and a half times between 1921 and 1956, which was more rapidly than the Roman Catholics, and in the latter year were about a sixth less numerous than the latter. We must recall, however, that by the mid-twentieth century Protestants had had missionaries in India only slightly more than 250 years, whereas Roman Catholics had been continuously represented for more than four and a half centuries. We must also remind ourselves that Roman Catholics had brought into communion with the Pope a large proportion of the Syrian Christian community which had been in India for at least a thousand years, and we are not counting in the Protestant total the Mar Thoma Syrian Church, which, while not Protestant, owed its separate existence to the influence of Protestantism. Moreover, we are not including in the Protestant figures the Anglo-Saxons resident in India or the Anglo-Indians, whereas the Roman Catholic totals embraced the several hundred thousand who were either Portuguese or a mixture of Portuguese and Indian blood. The Roman Catholic growth was due far more to an excess of births over deaths in the traditional adherents of that branch of the faith than to conversions from non-Christians, and the Protestant increase was far more from the latter than the former source. In general, Indian Protestants had back of them fewer generations of Christian ancestry than the Roman Catholics and were, therefore, much newer in the faith. Since the overwhelming majority of them were from the depressed classes, the problem of creating an indigenous leadership was more serious than for the Roman Catholics, the Syrian Christians, or the Mar Thoma Syrian Church.

A large proportion of the twentieth-century growth of Protestantism, as in the preceding centuries, was by mass movements from the depressed classes. These classes were closely associated with caste, a social structure which characterized India. There were hundreds of castes, partly but by no means entirely occupational. Castes tended to act as groups. What were called mass movements

[54] *Directory of Christian Missions, 1928–1929*, p. iv.
[55] *The Christian Handbook of India, 1954–1955*, p. 40. The figure of 3,500,000 is arrived at by deducting from the 4,374,847 "non-Roman Christian community" the number of Syrian Christians and Mar Thoma Christians.
[56] *World Christian Handbook, 1957*, pp. 31–38. The 5,000,000 represented the deduction of roughly 1,000,000 Syrian Christians and Mar Thoma Christians from the total given of 5,999,561.

usually began with an individual or a few individuals convinced of the truth of the Christian faith who, often after an initial period of persecution by their caste, carried its members with them. The decision to become Christians was a collective act. Sometimes the movement did not spread to an entire caste but was confined to a single village or adjacent villages. On occasion the movement eventually embraced the entire caste. Mass movements were not confined to Protestantism or to the twentieth century. They had been seen in some of the non-Christian religions—in the adoption of Islam, for example. From the sixteenth century they had been a frequent phenomenon in conversion to the Roman Catholic Church and from the eighteenth century onward to Protestantism.

Early in the 1930's careful studies showed that the overwhelming majority of the Protestants had mass movements back of them. One estimate declared that 70 per cent. of the Protestants were the product of mass movements. Another, more detailed, investigation said that this figure was entirely too low and that in some regions between 85 and 95 per cent. of the Protestants had come through these channels.[57] Following World War I the mass movements were accelerated. Some were in groups heretofore touched little or not at all by Christianity. Others, such as those among the Madigas and Malas, were continuations of what had begun in the nineteenth century. Between 1921 and 1931 Protestants among the hill tribes in Assam increased from 132,106 to 249,246, or 88.7 per cent.[58] Mass movements appeared in the years after 1914 among the Sudras, notably in the Telugu country. The Sudras were the lowest in the traditional Indian social scale—Brahmans, Kshatriyas, Vaisyas, and Sudras—but were definitely above the depressed classes. In the Telugu area, where a large proportion of the Madigas and Malas were becoming Christians, many Sudras were taking that step too. One reason was the impression made on them by the improvement wrought by the faith among neighbours whom they had previously despised. As an evidence of this and of the weakening of caste barriers by Christianity, some of the Sudras received baptism from clergymen who had come from these very groups.[59]

The post-1914 mass movements into Protestantism were not limited to any one area. Their acceleration was attributed partly to the unrest among the depressed groups due to the impact of the revolutionary currents which were entering from "Christendom." Through becoming Christians the underprivileged sought release from their age-long exploitation and greater opportunity for themselves and their children.[60]

A major problem posed by the large influx to the faith from the under-

[57] Pickett, Christian Mass Movements in India, pp. 313, 314.
[58] Ibid., pp. 52, 314. For a bibliography see Latourette, op. cit., Vol. VII, p. 292 nn.
[59] Pickett, op. cit., pp. 294 ff.
[60] Latourette, op. cit., Vol. VII, p. 292, and especially the extensive citation of references in footnote 136 on that page.

privileged was provision of the pastoral care and education which would ensure growth in the faith adopted in such a wholesale manner. Some missionaries advocated early baptism of the enquirers which came from the mass movements, to be followed with careful instruction. Others stood for prolonged instruction with fairly exacting standards of knowledge of the faith and quality of life before baptism. All were agreed that adequate care, instruction, worship, and fellowship should follow baptism. The reduction of funds from the West in the post-World I recession in giving and during the depression years of the 1930's curtailed the budgets for this kind of care. Thus for many the acceptance of Christianity meant little beyond the adoption of the Christian name and, in some instances, baptism. The problem was made more difficult because of the feeling of inferiority which had been bred in the depressed classes by the contempt of the higher castes, the illiteracy, and the vices associated with their lot.[61] Always the danger was faced that the Church itself might take on some features of the caste background—with an unwillingness to admit new members and the coldness and lack of deep religious conviction of the third and fourth generations of those who were Christians by heredity.[62]

Indian Protestantism was chiefly rural, in some degree because of the mass movements among the depressed in the villages but also because India was predominantly a land of villages. Through the currents of the revolutionary age urban populations increased, and, as elsewhere in the world, Protestantism was faced by the problems associated with the growth of cities.

In spite of the difficulties, taken as a whole conversion was followed by distinct improvement among the mass converts. Instruction and worship with the acceptance of God's love did much to remove the sense of helpless degradation. Many gave evidence of the release by engaging in occupations other than those to which custom had confined them. Marked advance was noted in family life and in the neatness of the dwellings of Christians. A large percentage of literacy took the place of almost complete illiteracy. Worship was in physical cleanliness and had the hearty participation of the congregation. Contrary to the tradition which condemned them to a subordinate position, women engaged in church activities. Child marriage became less frequent. Through the education provided by the church, numbers of the men to whom the professions had been closed became lawyers, physicians, teachers, and clergymen, and here and there men who had emerged from the underprivileged masses were appointed to the judiciary. Gambling and the consumption of alcohol and drugs were reduced, the economic level was raised, and, with education, exploitation by the moneylenders who preyed on the ignorant became less common.[63]

As was true in the preceding hundred years, in the twentieth century Protes-

[61] Pickett, *op. cit.*, pp. 128, 129, 227, 236–248.
[62] Confidential information from first-hand observation by a missionary in the 1950's.
[63] Pickett, *op. cit.*, pp. 130–154.

tantism was propagated in India by many societies and denominations. In 1914 Protestant missionaries totalled 5,465 and came from several countries.[64] About nine out of ten were from the British Isles and the United States, those from the latter country being about five-sixths as numerous as those from the British Isles. Some were from other members of the British Commonwealth—Canada chiefly, but also Australia and New Zealand. Of the denominations, the Anglicans covered more of India than any other non-Roman Catholic communion and had an ecclesiastical structure which embraced most of the country. A number of Anglican societies aided in the planting and nurture of what was then called the Church of India, Burma, and Ceylon. The denomination which had the most widely distributed missions of any from the United States was the Methodist Episcopal Church. In 1914 the churches served by the American Baptist Foreign Mission Society, the organ of the Northern Baptists, had more baptized members than any except the Church of India, Burma, and Ceylon and the Methodist Episcopal Church. Lutheranism, indebted to missionaries from several churches in Germany, Sweden, Denmark, and the United States, was strong on the south-east coast but was also vigorous among the animistic peoples in Assam and Chota Nagpur. The Basel Mission, on the south-west coast, had a larger personnel than any other society from the Continent of Europe.

In the half-century which followed 1914 the number of Protestant missionaries fluctuated. In 1924 it was said to be 5,682, a slight advance over a decade earlier.[65] The year 1938 shows a decline, to 5,399,[66] presumably due to the world-wide depression of the 1930's. Twenty years later—that is, after World War II—the total had risen to 5,656, but only for the Republic of India. To permit comparison with the former figures, which had included what later became Pakistan, the total in that country—700—must be added, making 6,356, an increase of 963, or of 17.8 per cent.[67]

Protestant Christianity displayed striking response to the demand for the transfer of authority and control to indigenous leadership and ecclesiastical bodies which was an accompaniment of the surging nationalism, anti-colonialism, and anti-imperialism of the revolutionary age. The transition was made difficult by the nature of the Protestant constituency. Since most of the converts were from the underprivileged on the lowest rung of the social scale, educated clergy and laity did not quickly emerge. The traditional poverty handicapped the development of financial self-support and of competence in self-government

---

[64] Volume III, pp. 407 ff.
[65] Beach and Fahs, *World Missionary Atlas*, p. 76.
[66] *Directory of Christian Missions and Churches in India, Burma, and Ceylon*, 1938–1939 (Nagpur, The National Christian Council, 1938, pp. 513), p. 22.
[67] *World Christian Handbook*, 1957, pp. 38, 57.

and the management of property when transfer was made from foreign owner-ship.

Adequate preparation of the ministry was not easily or quickly achieved.[68] But it was the more imperative because of the rising standard of education in the country as a whole and in much of the Protestant constituency. The oldest Protestant theological college was at Serampore. Founded in 1818 as part of the far-seeing vision of William Carey and his colleagues, at mid-twentieth century it still occupied the dignified building erected by Carey. A charter granted in 1827 by the King of Denmark gave it the authority to confer degrees. The first degrees in theology were not awarded until 1915. Thirty-five years later Serampore College obtained most of its financial support from the (Eng-lish) Baptist Missionary Society (which owed its origin to Carey). Both the Council in London which governed it and the Senate in India (created in 1918) which was responsible for the courses of study and the examinations were interdenominational. All the theological degrees granted in India were through the Serampore institution under its Danish charter. In the late 1950's India had five theological colleges: Serampore; United Theological College of South India and Ceylon, founded in 1910 at Bangalore by five denominations as a union institution; Leonard Theological College, Methodist, growing out of a semi-nary in Bareilly in 1872 and established in Jabalpur as a college in 1923; Bish-op's College, Anglican, in Calcutta, which had its origin in a school founded in 1824 and which became a theological college in 1918; and Gurukul Lutheran Theological College and Research Institute, preceded by several schools and established in Madras in 1953 by twelve Lutheran churches and agencies in India and Europe. Yet in 1956 these five institutions, the only ones of their grade in Protestantism in India, had only 152 theological students and 36 non-theological students. Half of them were in Leonard Theological College in Jabalpur. In addition to the five which were rated as theological colleges, fifteen institutions were affiliated with the Serampore Senate and were classed as theo-logical schools. Together they had 264 theological and 63 non-theological stu-dents. Ten schools not affiliated with Serampore, with 246 theological and 89 non-theological students in 1956, were called seminaries or training colleges, and there was one divinity school and one theological school. Of these twelve the largest had seventy-two students.

The distinguishing characteristics of the three groups of institutions training

[68] See especially C. W. Ranson, *The Christian Minister in India. His Vocation and His Training. A Study Based on a Survey of Theological Education Conducted by the National Christian Council* (Madras, Christian Literature Society for India, 1945, pp. xiv, 289), *passim;* Allen, *op. cit.,* pp. 93–113. On United Theological College see *The South-east Asia Journal of Theology,* April, 1960, pp. 51–53. On the situation in the mid-1950's see M. H. Harrison, *After Ten Years. A Report on Theological Education in India* (Nagpur, The National Christian Council of India, 1957, pp. 71).

for the Protestant ministry had chiefly to do with their academic requirements. The five theological colleges admitted only students with a bachelor of arts degree, used English as a medium of instruction, required that courses in Greek be taken, and awarded their graduates a Serampore bachelor of divinity degree. The fifteen theological schools made the possession of a high school diploma the standard for admission, taught in the vernacular, and conferred (through Serampore) a licentiate in theology on their graduates. Between 1912 and 1956 a total of 532 bachelor of divinity degrees and 485 licentiates in theology were awarded. The annual number increased. From 1914 through 1944 the B.D.'s granted totalled 322, an average of a little over 10 a year. From 1945 through 1956 the corresponding figure was 210, or about 20 a year. The L.Th. totals were 205 from 1914 through 1944, or not quite 7 annually, and 280 from 1945 through 1955, or about 24 annually. The twelve schools unaffiliated with Serampore kept aloof from that connexion, partly to avoid restrictions on their curriculums and partly from fear of what they regarded as the theological liberalism of that institution. Their instruction was in the vernacular. The largest, the Union Theological Seminary at Yeotmal, was maintained by fourteen theologically conservative church groups. Provision was made for specialized study and research. In the 1950's this was seen chiefly in the Henry Martyn School of Islamics in Aligarh and in the Christian Institute for the Study of Religion and Society at Bangalore.

In the main, in the 1940's and the 1950's, preparation for the ordained ministry was one of the weakest points in the Protestant enterprise in India. Many of the institutions were isolated from the general trend of education and were poorly equipped to prepare men for leadership in the revolutionary age. With a few exceptions libraries were inadequate. Students in the colleges which taught through English were usually imperfectly prepared in that language, and in few of the vernaculars did a body of theological literature exist which enabled the students adequately to meet the problems of Indian society. In spite of the fact that more Indians were being placed on them and the administration was being transferred to them, in the 1950's the teaching staffs were predominantly foreign.

Recruitment for the ministry was a chronic problem. Although many Christian students in the colleges maintained by the churches and missions were true to the faith and were little troubled by the intellectual questions raised by the revolutionary age, economic obstacles made difficult their entrance to the ministry. Stipends in that calling were below those in several other occupations and as a rule were insufficient to meet the needs of a well-educated man and of the relatives depending on him. Moreover, the position of a pastor was often not held in high respect by the Indian churches.

However, more and more strong men were coming forward for the ministry and lay leadership and were given places of trust. We can take the space only for the barest mention of a few outstanding individuals. The first Indian bishop of the (Anglican) Church of India, Burma, and Ceylon was Vedanayakam Samuel Azariah (1874–1945).[69] Born of Christian parents, a graduate of Madras Christian College, he was early closely associated with Sherwood Eddy, who had come to India for the Young Men's Christian Association. He was one of the organizers of the Tinnevelly Missionary Society (1903), the first secretary of the National Missionary Society (1905), and a secretary of the Young Men's Christian Association. In 1909 he became a missionary to the depressed classes in Hyderabad, and at the World Missionary Conference in Edinburgh (1910) he made an address which was long remembered. In 1912 he was consecrated Bishop of Dornakal. There he gathered into the Church thousands, at first from the depressed classes and then from the middle and higher castes, as they saw the transformation taking place in groups which they had despised. Not many years after his death the Christian community in his diocese was said to number over 400,000.

Kanakarayan Tiruselvam Paul (1876–1931), also of Christian parentage and in Madras Christian College a classmate of Azariah, was trained in the law but was early caught up in the life of the Young Men's Christian Association. He was one of the founders of the National Missionary Society. In 1913 he joined the staff of the National Council of the Young Men's Christian Association and led in the organization of rural YMCA's and rural credit societies for what he called "rural reconstruction." In 1916 he became general secretary of the National Council of the YMCA, continuing in that post until his conscience took him into the Indian nationalist movement. There he had a mediating role. He participated in the First Round Table Conference, which attempted to find a peaceable solution to the thorny question of Indian self-government. The strain of the ordeal probably hastened his death.[70]

By the 1960's additional Indians had come to positions of leadership in Protestantism. For example, although the majority of the bishops were still English, the Metropolitan of the Anglican Church was A. N. Mukerjee, who was also Bishop of Calcutta.[71] In 1922 a constitution was framed for the Church of the Province of India, Burma, and Ceylon, and in 1930 that body was legally freed from its connexion with the state and so was at liberty to become a truly autonomous Indian church.[72] In the 1950's the president of the Baptist Union of India, Pakistan, Burma and Ceylon was an Indian, and the majority of the

[69] Knud Heiberg, *V. S. Azariah, Biskop of Dornakal* (Copenhagen, Danske Missionsselskab, 1950, pp. 133), *passim;* Eddy, *Eighty Adventurous Years*, pp. 53–57; Latourette, *World Service*, pp. 113, 117.

[70] H. A. Popley, *K. T. Paul, Christian Leader* (Calcutta, Y.M.C.A. Publishing House, 1938), *passim;* Latourette, *World Service*, pp. 123, 124, 128–132, 135–137, 140, 146; Eddy, *op. cit.*, pp. 51, 52.

[71] *The Christian Handbook of India, 1954–1955*, p. 1.

[72] Latourette, *A History of the Expansion of Christianity*, Vol. VII, p. 302; Neill, *Anglicanism*, pp. 328, 329.

regional Baptist associations had Indians as presidents and secretaries.[73] The American Methodists moved in a similar direction. In the 1920's the General Conference of the Methodist Episcopal Church, which met in the United States and heretofore had appointed bishops for India, gave more authority to the Central Conference representing the Indian constituency. One of the results was the election by the Central Conference (1930) of J. R. Chitambar as the first Indian bishop. In subsequent years other Indians were elevated to the episcopacy[74] until, by 1961, no foreigner was left in that position. In 1930 an Indian woman was chosen as principal of Isabella Thoburn College, Methodism's leading educational institution for Indian women. In 1940 Sarah Chakko, also an Indian, succeeded to that post. She later became a president of the World Council of Churches. In 1922 Lucknow Christian College, the corresponding Methodist institution for men, was given its first Indian principal.[75]

Increasingly the "missions" through which the foreign personnel functioned either were merged with the indigenous churches or turned over their property and other responsibilities to them.[76]

Full financial support was not easily or quickly achieved by the indigenous churches. That was to be expected, since the large majority of the membership were from the lowest economic levels of society. Yet progress was made. Many missions encouraged that aspect of independence by progressively decreasing their grants to the churches. In the mid-1930's the Indian churches were supplying a little over one-third of their upkeep and were finding that their spiritual life improved as they assumed more of the financial burden.[77] However, much of the giving was by members connected with institutions which relied on foreign funds for at least part of their budgets, and Christians were not contributing to the churches as large a part of their earnings as was the accepted standard of Moslems—a fortieth of their income to their religion.[78] However, notable instances were seen of complete self-support. In the 1940's two examples were in Chota Nagpur in Bihar. There both the Anglican Church and the Lutheran Church drew their members from the aboriginal tribes and were completely independent of foreign administrative control. The Gossner Evangelical Lutheran Church was the first large ecclesiastical body in India to attain full autonomy. That step was hastened by World War I and the attendant loss

[73] *The Christian Handbook of India, 1954-1955*, pp. 3-5.

[74] Hollister, *The Centenary of the Methodist Church in Southern Asia*, pp. 249-259. See also Marvin Henry Harper, *The Methodist Episcopal Church in India. A Study of Ecclesiastical Organization and Administration* (Lucknow, The Lucknow Publishing House, 1936, pp. vi, 222), pp. 144-181.

[75] Hollister, *op. cit.*, pp. 263-265.

[76] For some instances see *The International Review of Missions*, Vol. L, p. 22 (January, 1961).

[77] J. Merle Davis, *Mission Finance Policies and the Younger Churches* (Bangalore, Scripture Literature Press, 1938, pp. 104), p. 10.

[78] *Ibid.*, p. 24.

of the German personnel through which the church had been brought into existence. The cutting off of funds from Germany which was an incident of the war compelled the church to assume the entire support of its pastors and catechists. Such was the poverty of the members and the pressure of the rising cost of living that many pastors were forced to add to their primary functions secular employment to supplement their salaries. The ordained ministers proved to be too few to give adequate care to the faithful and the quality of Christian instruction declined.[79]

Protestantism expressed itself through a wide variety of channels. As heretofore, a major form of service was in education. Government subsidies encouraged the growth of schools on elementary, secondary, and higher levels. They were continued after India obtained its political independence. Christian schools had an important part in raising the literacy rate of the depressed classes and providing training which enabled many to improve their economic lot. Following a precedent established in the nineteenth century,[80] Protestants maintained a number of colleges. In 1930 thirty-seven were rated as arts colleges, but only twenty-six carried students all the way to the B.A. degree. The others had the first two years towards that goal. Six of the colleges were for women—evidence of the place which Protestantism had in higher education for that sex. A further witness to that pioneering effort was the fact that in all but one of the six the majority of the students were Christians. In the Protestant colleges as a whole, the proportion of Christians was somewhat higher in the South, where the percentage of Christians in the population was greater, than in the North, where numerically Christianity was weak. About half of the teaching staffs were non-Christians and of the Christians approximately 60 per cent. were Indians. More than half of the colleges had their headquarters in Great Britain and slightly more than a fourth in the United States. Several were union institutions, drawing their support from more than one denomination and from British and American sources. About a third were Anglican and approximately a fourth were Presbyterian in their connexions. Not far from a third of the money for current budgets came from abroad and most of the rest was from fees and government grants.[81] In the 1920's Protestant schools were already losing something of their position as pioneers in education of a Western kind. Earlier they had been outstanding in providing under Christian auspices an introduction to the kind of learning needed to prepare India for the revolutionary age. In 1926–1927 they still had roughly a fourth of the college students of the country. But in those years only about five out of a hundred of the primary grades were in Protestant schools, and in 1922–1927 the number of students in

[79] Davis, *New Buildings on Old Foundations*, pp. 163–166.
[80] Latourette, *A History of the Expansion of Christianity*, Vol. VI, pp. 116, 145, 190.
[81] *The Christian College in India*, pp. 12–16.

Protestant schools of all grades was not mounting nearly as rapidly as in government and non-mission schools.[82] By the mid-1950's some Protestant colleges had disappeared or had been merged with others and several new ones had been created. About 40 per cent. of their resident students and about 16 per cent. of their non-resident students were Christian.[83]

Protestants had long been engaged in medical and surgical service. In the mid-1950's they were maintaining 266 hospitals and more than 200 dispensaries. Over two score hospitals were training nurses.[84] In addition Protestants were conducting half a hundred institutions for lepers, thirteen tuberculosis sanatoria, ten institutions for the blind and deaf, many orphanages and homes for women, and numbers of social and welfare centres.[85] In 1918 Ida Scudder founded a medical school for girls. The daughter of missionaries of the Reformed Church in America, she was impressed by the need for women physicians in India and in 1899 began medical practice in that country. Her medical school was in Vellore. Eventually it had the support of forty missions. Although the majority of. its students were women, in the 1950's a substantial minority were men. Connected with it were a hospital and roadside bus clinics. Its staff came from four continents.[86]

From the early days of its missions in India Protestantism had concerned itself with famine relief. The political division between the Republic of India and Pakistan (1947) resulted in a massive and continued refugee problem. The National Christian Council quickly sought to help the sufferers. In 1960 Church World Service, one of the agencies of the National Council of the Churches of Christ in the U.S.A., assigned $1,000,000 for a five-year project for the relief of refugees from East Pakistan in West Bengal and Calcutta.[87]

Much was being done to raise the economic level of the rural population, especially of the depressed classes. Coöperative banks and societies were organized, agricultural settlements were founded, specialists in rural reorganization were maintained, and the remarkable institution developed in Allahabad by Sam Higginbottam for research and training in better agricultural methods was continued.[88]

Protestant missionaries devoted much of their attention to the issuing and distribution of Christian literature in the vernaculars. They stressed the translation and circulation of the Bible. In the 1950's they had scores of presses and

[82] Laymen's Foreign Missions Inquiry. Supplementary Series, Vol. IV, Part Two, pp. 299, 309.
[83] The Christian Handbook of India, 1954-1955, pp. 221-223.
[84] Ibid., pp. 248-255; Laymen's Foreign Missions Inquiry. Supplementary Series, Vol. IV, Part Two, pp. 415 ff.
[85] The Christian Handbook of India, 1954-1955, pp. 255-267.
[86] Time, February 16, 1953, pp. 64, 65; The International Review of Missions, Vol. XXXIV (1945), pp. 315, 321.
[87] The New York Times, February 5, 1960.
[88] Latourette, A History of the Expansion of Christianity, Vol. VII, p. 298.

book stores and carried on correspondence courses on the Bible. By the mid-1950's all or parts of the Bible had been translated into about one hundred of the vernaculars of the country and additional translations were in preparation.[89]

A feature of Protestantism in India was growing coöperation among denominations and organic unions. By the twentieth century coöperation had long been in progress in a variety of ways, including regional conferences of missionaries and decennial all-India missionary conferences. Following the World Missionary Conference of 1910 in Edinburgh John R. Mott as chairman of its continuation committee made a world tour, out of which arose, in 1912, the National Missionary Council of India, Burma, and Ceylon. In 1922, largely through the wise counsel of J. H. Oldham, one of the first secretaries of the International Missionary Council, this body became the National Christian Council of India, Burma, and Ceylon, with the express stipulation that at least half its members must be Indians. In 1948, owing to the political separation of Ceylon from India, it became the National Christian Council of India, Pakistan, and Burma.[90]

An association closer than that of coöperation but not going as far as organic union was found in several denominational families. Representative was the Federation of Evangelical Lutheran Churches in India. It was formed in 1928 and grew out of the India Lutheran Conference, which first met in 1908. In 1952 it had a baptized membership of 557,605. Its largest unit was the Andra Lutheran Evangelical Church, with a baptized membership of 239,887.[91] That church had been organized in 1927 as a union of various Lutheran bodies.[92] In accordance with the widespread trend to place control in Indian hands, by 1962 the one episcopal office in Indian Lutheranism, that in the Tamil Evangelical Lutheran Church, was filled by Rajah Bushanam Manikam (1897——), who had been reared in that body. The post had been created in 1921[93] and its first incumbent was a Swede, but when in the 1950's it became vacant Manikam, who had been an official in the World Council of Churches and the International Missionary Council, was placed in it.

The outstanding example of organic union was the Church of South India.[94] It had as a nucleus the South India United Church, which came into existence in 1908 through the fusion of Congregational and Presbyterian bodies. In that

---

[89] *Christian Handbook of India, 1954–1955*, pp. 41–43, 215–219.

[90] Rouse and Neill, *A History of the Ecumenical Movement, 1517–1948*, pp. 392, 393; *National Christian Council Review*, Vol. LXVIII, pp. 462 ff. (November, 1948).

[91] Snavely, *The Lutheran Enterprise in India*, pp. 242–247.

[92] *Ibid.*, p. 47.

[93] *Ibid.*, p. 137.

[94] Of the vast amount of literature on the Church of South India the most scholarly and comprehensive account is Bengt Sundkler, *Church of South India. The Movement towards Union, 1900–1947* (London, Lutterworth Press, 1954, pp. 457). It contains an excellent bibliography and has extensive footnote references to the sources.

body the Congregationalists were the more numerous. In the initial stages of the conversations concerned with achieving a broader union Azariah and Sherwood Eddy were prominent but not the only figures. The pressures for union arose partly out of Indian nationalism, with the conviction that the Church in India should not be bound by divisions of Western origin, partly from the tide for Christian unity which was running strong in Protestantism throughout most of the world, and, probably chiefly, from the belief that if India was to be won to the Christian faith a united witness was imperative. Anglicans and Methodists engaged in discussions with the South India United Church. Among the issues which proved difficult were the Anglican insistence on the historic episcopate and the conviction of the non-Anglicans that their ministries were valid and must be received in the united church on full equality with those whose ordination had been by bishops in the apostolic succession; the non-Anglican emphasis on the laity and participation of presbyters in ordination; and the variety in the forms of worship and in the views of the sacraments, especially the Communion. Gradually the majority moved towards agreement. By a vote in which the laity were conspicuous for their endorsement, the (Anglican) Church of India, Burma, and Ceylon gave its consent to the separation from its body of the dioceses which were involved and to its bishops to transmit apostolic succession to the bishops of the new church. Assent was also obtained from the other denominations involved. In 1947 the final steps were taken and the Church of South India came into being. It was a union of the South India United Church, the Anglicans, and the Methodists. Of its fifteen initial bishops three were former Congregationalists, three former Methodists, one a former Presbyterian, and eight former Anglicans. One of the Anglicans, the elderly and saintly H. Pakenham-Walsh, who had long been prominent in the negotiations, was elected bishop without a diocese.

At the formal inauguration of the Church of South India the five bishops who had entered from the Church of India, Burma, and Ceylon accepted the constitution of the new body and were commissioned by a South India United Church presbyter and a Methodist presbyter. The other ten were consecrated through the laying on of the hands of three of the former Anglican bishops and three presbyters of the South India United Church and the Methodist Church. Thus both the apostolic succession and the place of the presbyters of the non-Anglicans were assured. The first moderator of the new church was a former Anglican bishop.

The Church of South India was not welcomed by some of the Anglo-Catholics. Although henceforth all ordinations in that body would be by bishops in the historic episcopate, the clergy entering from the non-Anglican bodies were accepted by the new church on a basis of full equality with those having episcopal ordination. Therefore several of the Anglican congregations in South

India did not affiliate themselves with the Church of South India, and none of the Anglican bodies represented in the Lambeth Conferences entered into communion with it. On the whole the Lambeth members were friendly, but some Anglicans, especially in the Church of England, believed that the Church of South India had produced a fresh schism.

The Church of South India grew in corporate life and in numbers.[95] In the 1950's it was the largest of the non-Roman Catholic churches in India, with 343,563 communicants reported and a total community of 1,008,797, as contrasted with the comparable figures five years earlier of 335,492 and 895,168 respectively.[96] Exploratory conversations were held for the adherence of additional bodies in South India—the Mar Thoma Church, some of the Baptists, and the Lutherans—but by 1962 they had not brought the desired consummation.

In the 1950's a similar and denominationally more inclusive union was in progress in another part of India. In 1924 the United Church of Northern India had come into being as a union of Presbyterians and Congregationalists.[97] In the mid-1950's its Christian community numbered 440,415.[98] Negotiations were under way to bring into it the Anglicans, the British and Australian Methodists, the Baptists, and the Disciples. By 1962 the Anglicans and Methodists had given general approval, the Methodist Church in Southern Asia (connected with the Methodist Church in the U.S.A.) had withdrawn its earlier objections, but the issue of believers' baptism was still an obstacle to the Baptists and Disciples.[99]

In a variety of other ways Protestants were unitedly approaching their common problems. Thus in some of the new industrial and mining centres by the 1950's several denominations were together creating congregations of labourers recruited from different language areas.[100]

The temptation is great to enter upon sketches of the more notable missionaries from other lands who served in India in the twentieth century. However, in a comprehensive and necessarily as condensed survey as this we must confine ourselves to a very few. They are not necessarily typical but they will at least give some slight indication of the widely varied character of that goodly company.

Amy Beatrice Carmichael (1868–1951) was born in Northern Ireland into

[95] See reviews of three books treating phases of its first decade in *The International Review of Missions*, Vol. XLVIII, pp. 105–107 (January, 1959). See also Marcus Ward, *The Pilgrim Church. An Account of the First Five Years in the Life of the Church of South India* (London, The Epworth Press, 1953, pp. 216), *passim*.

[96] *World Christian Handbook, 1957*, p. 31.

[97] H. Paul Douglass, *A Decade of Objective Progress in Church Unity, 1927–1936* (New York, Harper & Brothers, 1937, pp. xxii, 140), p. 47.

[98] *World Christian Handbook, 1957*, p. 33.

[99] *The International Review of Missions*, Vol. L, p. 23 (January, 1961).

[100] *Church Labor Letter* (Osaka Christian Center, mimeographed), No. 46, September, 1946.

a family of well-to-do devout Presbyterians. She early came in transforming touch with the kind of Evangelicalism which was nourished by the Keswich movement and gave herself to underprivileged girls in Belfast. In the 1890's she was briefly in Japan but illness brought her back to England. In 1895 she went to Bangalore under the Church of England Zenana Missionary Society. From 1896 onward her home was in the Tinnevelly District in the extreme South. There she made her mission the "unwanted girls" who were prostitutes in the temples. She created the Dohnavur Fellowship, which rescued hundreds from that unhappy lot. Eventually boys were added to the orphanage. With some of her girls she formed the Sisterhood of the Common Life, somewhat after the pattern of the Brethren of the Common Life founded by Gerhard Groote in the fourteenth century, but did not bind them by vows. She fed her soul on the writings of great mystics and introduced them to the Sisterhood. She depended on prayer for the funds to maintain her growing family and to add land and buildings to her physical plant. She refused government aid for fear it would handicap the Christian atmosphere of the Fellowship. In 1925 she became independent of the Church of England Zenana Missionary Society and for legal reasons in 1926 and 1927 had the Dohnavur Fellowship officially registered. Its members were from several countries. A hospital was erected. Some of her charges when grown became nurses and evangelists. For the last twenty years of her life she was an invalid and seldom left her room. An accident had left her a cripple, but in spite of her suffering she wrote books and endless letters and saw streams of visitors and groups of children. Hers was a radiant life which embodied love for Christ and for all whom she touched.[101]

A missionary with a somewhat different contribution, but like Miss Carmichael inspired, radiant, and self-giving from a warm devotion to Christ, was Charles Freer Andrews (1871–1940).[102] "Charlie" Andrews, as he was affectionately known and liked to be called, was a son of a clergyman of the Catholic Apostolic Church.[103] Sensitive, with the soul of a poet, reared in a deeply religious home, when he was nineteen he had an experience of conversion which was marked by an agonizing sense of sin and unworthiness followed by the joy and peace of assured forgiveness. Soon thereafter he went to Cambridge. There he was popular with a wide variety of men, struggled through the intellectual questions familiar to that stage of the revolutionary age, found that he could not honestly remain in his father's church, but never doubted Christ,

---

[101] Frank Houghton, *Amy Carmichael of Dohnavur. The Story of Lover and Her Beloved* (London, S.P.C.K., 1953, pp. xv, 390), *passim*.

[102] Of the several biographies the best is Benarsidas Chaturvedi and Marjorie Sykes, *Charles Freer Andrews. A Narrative* (London, George Allen and Unwin, 1949, pp. xiv, 334), with a foreword by M. K. Gandhi and an appendix containing a full bibliography of the books by Andrews, *passim*. See also the autobiography, C. F. Andrews, *What I Owe to Christ* (London, Hodder and Stoughton, 1932, pp. 321).

[103] Volume II, p. 344.

immortality, or that God is love, and was profoundly influenced by the friendship of Brook Foss Westcott and the writings of Charles Gore.[104] He was ordained in the Church of England, served for a time in the slums of London, returned to Cambridge as a fellow and chaplain in his college, and in 1904 went to India as a member of the Cambridge Brotherhood and served on the staff of St. Stephen's College in Delhi. There he early established intimate friendly relations with Indians, stood out against the exclusive British haughtiness towards Indians, and was pained by the caste structure of Indian society and the lot of the depressed classes. He had a great gift for friendship. He became a warm admirer and intimate of the Hindu poet and educator Rabindranath Tagore, of leaders of the anti-Christian Arya Samaj, and of Lord Hardinge, the viceroy, and Lady Hardinge. The school which Tagore conducted at Santiniketan became for him a kind of home. In 1914 he went to South Africa to labour against the discrimination from which Indians were suffering in that country. There he met Gandhi and began the close friendship which was to be one of the outstanding features of his life. In 1914, back in India, while emphatically remaining a Christian, he felt that he could no longer honestly repeat the words of the creeds and sought to divest himself of his ordination. To that his bishop did not consent but asked him to take more time to consider the step. Later he could again repeat the creeds. The Church of England remained his spiritual home. Espousing the cause of the indentured Indian labourers in Fiji, he strove to have their recruitment terminated, to have higher wages paid those already there, and to obtain improved living conditions for them. He worked for better provision for labourers in the factories which the revolutionary age was spawning in India. Again and again he was in Africa, seeking fairer treatment for the Indians. In India he endeavoured to bring reconciliation between clashing forces and stood for Gandhi's programme for Indian independence, the redemption of the depressed, the brotherhood of Hindus and Moslems, the honouring of women, and freedom from drugs and drink. He and Gandhi did not always agree. For instance, Andrews believed in conversion to Christianity if the motive was not ulterior, and Gandhi opposed it. But the two kept very close to each other. Andrews travelled widely, always with the purpose of bringing peace and justice, and was repeatedly in his native England. He wrote prodigiously. He was the author of innumerable pamphlets, articles, and letters to the press and of more than twenty books.

Still different from Amy Carmichael and Charles Andrews but closely akin to them in spirit, Eli Stanley Jones (1884——) first came to wide public notice as a missionary in India. A native of Baltimore and a graduate of Asbury College, an institution noted for its warm Evangelical atmosphere, in 1907 he went to India as a missionary of the Methodist Episcopal Church. For several years

[104] Volume II, pp. 297, 298, 305, 306.

he was in charge of a school for boys. In 1917 he launched into what was to be his life work, that of an evangelist. For several years he gave himself to the educated Indians. Through ashrams, an Indian device employed, with modifications, by many missionaries, he sought to bring the Christian message to them in language and through channels which would not seem to them alien and European. The book which first gave him a wide hearing, *The Christ of the Indian Road,* grew out of this experience.[105] Translated into many languages, it had a circulation of hundreds of thousands of copies. Elected a bishop of his church (1928), he refused the appointment and continued as an itinerant evangelist in many parts of the world. He returned to India for several months each year and made his headquarters in his ashram at Acharya, where he met selected groups of students, pastors, missionaries, educators, and new converts. He wrote many books and articles, chiefly for the nourishment of the life of the spirit.[106]

To turn from Protestant missionaries to Indian Christians, we are again perplexed by the number and the variety but must confine ourselves to a few individuals. Some we have already noted. One other was so unique and attracted such wide interest both in India and elsewhere that even the brief coverage which is ours must find a place for him. A contemporary of the three missionaries whom we have described, he so impressed one of them, Andrews, that the latter felt constrained to write an account of him.[107] Sundar Singh (1889–1929?) was notable as a mystic and as an example of the fashion in which the Christian faith found expression in a part of the Indian religious tradition. The title "Sadhu," the designation of one kind of Indian holy man, became inseparable from his name. Sundar Singh was the son of a wealthy landowner of the Sikh religion and was reared in that faith and in Hinduism. When he was fifteen he had what he believed was a vision of Christ. From it came his conversion. His family cast him off and one of his relatives attempted to poison him. His deeply religious mother had instilled in him the desire to be a sadhu. Determining to conform to that pattern, but as a Christian, he went about preaching, living in poverty and through prayer. During these years he and Andrews became fast friends. Beginning in 1912 he spent some months each year in Tibet and on its southern borders as a travelling preacher, and the other months on the plains preaching. He also preached in the Himalayas. Christ was the

[105] E. Stanley Jones, *The Christ of the Indian Road* (New York, Abingdon Press, 1928, pp. 223).
[106] Hollister, *op. cit.,* pp. 261, 262. *Who's Who in America,* Vol. XXVI (1950–1951), p. 1415.
[107] C. F. Andrews, *Sadhu Sundar Singh. A Personal Memoir* (London, Hodder & Stoughton, 1934, pp. 255). See also B. H. Streeter and A. J. Appasamy, *The Sadhu. A Study in Mysticism and Practical Religion* (London, Macmillan and Co., 1921, pp. xv, 264); A. J. Appasamy, *Sundar Singh. A Biography* (London, Lutterworth Press, 1958, pp. 248); Friedrich Heiler, *The Gospel of Sadhu Sundar Singh,* abridged translation by Olive Wyon (London, George Allen and Unwin, 1927, pp. 277); Sadhu Sundar Singh, *With and Without Christ. Being Incidents Taken from the Lives of Christians and of Non-Christians which Illustrate the Difference in Lives Lived with Christ and without Christ* (London, Cassel and Co., 1929, pp. xii, 129).

centre of his life and once, in imitation of Him, he sought to fast for forty days. He made a deep impression on both Christians and non-Christians. He visited East Asia, Europe, Great Britain, America, and Australia, speaking often to large audiences. These brief notes, however, give little hint of Sundar Singh's visions and of what he interpreted as miracles. To the matter-of-fact among his hearers his accounts of them appeared to be either deliberate lying or self-delusion. But to him they were real. He wrote extensively and his books were translated into many languages. In 1929 he went on another preaching tour to Tibet and did not reappear. No information of him could be obtained. By what means or when he came to his death was not known.

As with Roman Catholicism, so with Protestantism, the strength in predominantly Moslem Pakistan was numerically and proportionately much less than in the Republic of India. The largest bodies were those connected with two Presbyterian churches in the United States, the Anglicans, the Salvation Army, the Baptists—Australian and English—and the Methodists. In the 1950's, although some churches appear to have lost members, on the whole increase was reported. In 1952 the number of communicants was given as 98,806 and in 1957 as 111,636, and the total Christian community as 254,872 in the former and 272,166 in the latter year.[108] Most of them were in West Pakistan. In the 1950's Protestants had only two theological seminaries, with an enrollment of about thirty-one.[109]

THE GROWING EFFECT OF CHRISTIANITY ON TWENTIETH-CENTURY INDIA

To determine with any degree of accuracy the effect of Christianity upon India in the first half of the twentieth century would be impossible. Influences of Christian origin had been entering for many years and through diverse channels. To the degree that English literature had been shaped by Christianity, its study as an integral part of Indian education was one source. Indians who had been educated in Great Britain and bore the impress of British culture could not but have been moulded to some extent, even if unconsciously, by the faith that was part of the warp and woof of British life. British institutions and British laws long in operation in India and bearing something of the impress of the official religion of Great Britain had left a legacy. The Christian schools had helped to form the ideals and characters of their students, both non-Christian and Christian. Although minorities, the churches inevitably had an effect upon their members. On many it was slight but upon others it was transforming. Moreover, the minorities were growing, both absolutely and in proportion

[108] *World Christian Handbook, 1957*, pp. 55–57. For the autobiography of an Anglican missionary from New Zealand in Pakistan see C. W. Haskell, *A Sinner in Sind* (Wellington, Wright and Carman, 1957, pp. 256).
[109] Allen, *A Seminary Survey*, pp. 102–104.

to the population. Christianity was in part responsible for the improvement in the status of women, for the rising literacy rate, especially among the underprivileged, for the enhanced value placed on the individual, particularly among the depressed groups, and for the weakening of the caste barriers which had condemned millions to hereditary inferiority. Such Hindu movements of the nineteenth century and the early years of the twentieth century as the Brahmo Samaj, the Servants of India Society, and even the vigorously anti-Christian Arya Samaj owed their inception to Christianity. By the mid-twentieth century they were waning, but they had left a continuing deposit in Indian life. For example, Rabindranath Tagore, one of the two most widely influential Indians of the twentieth century, had back of him the heritage of the Brahmo Samaj. Most of the impact of Christianity on India as a whole came through Protestantism. The Syrian Orthodox and the Roman Catholic contributions were limited chiefly to the adherents of those faiths.

Through Protestantism came most of the currents from Christ and the Church which entered profoundly into the life of Mahatma Gandhi and thus into an India which regarded him as the most outstanding of her sons since the Buddha. This is not the place to speak at length of the part which that remarkable man had in shaping the India of the half-century which followed World War I. Here we can only call attention to the fact that Gandhi, although a Hindu by faith and critical of all attempts of Christian missionaries to change the religion of Indians, had a profound admiration for Jesus, meditated deeply on His teachings, life, and death, and included Christian hymns of Protestant authorship among his favourites. In his years in South Africa he was in close contact with devout Protestants of conservative Evangelical views who sought his conversion. In Durban he was almost a member of the family of the head of the South Africa General Mission. The latter never invited him to become a Christian but witnessed to his faith by his daily life. Gandhi trusted C. F. Andrews, at least one other missionary to India, and some Indian Christians.[110] He believed profoundly in God, but he did not regard Christ as the unique incarnation of God. He would probably have found it impossible to say how far he was indebted to Christ, but that Christ, largely as he had met Him through Protestants, had entered into the growth of his religious faith and his motivation was clear.[111] In so far as Gandhi was influenced by Christ, Christ through him had a permeating, even though not a major, effect on the India of the twentieth century.

[110] M. K. Gandhi, *Gandhi's Autobiography. The Story of My Experiments with Truth* (Washington, Public Affairs Press, 1948, pp. xi, 640), pp. 149–156, 169–172, 197–200, 544.

[111] Otto Wolf, *Mahatma und Christus. Eine Charakterstudie Mahatma Gandhis und des modernen Hinduismus* (Berlin, Lettner Verlag, 1955, pp. 275), pp. 35–37, 85–95, 123–137, 141, 142, 253 ff.

SUMMARY

That Christianity was more potent in India in 1962 than it had been in 1914 is clear. That it enrolled only a minority and was not the main force shaping that sub-continent is obvious. It was represented by the ancient Syrian Orthodox Church, by the Roman Catholic Church, and by the chief varieties of Protestantism. In numbers and in proportion to the growing population it was stronger in 1962 than it had been fifty years earlier. Its gains had been chiefly among the depressed classes and the animistic hill tribes, but it had done much to improve the character and to raise the status of elements once held in contempt by the dominant classes. Partly because of the inner vitality of the faith and partly in the effort to respond to the revolt of the non-European peoples against the Western colonialism and imperialism which were a feature of the revolutionary age, the Indian churches were increasingly rooted in Indian life with Indian leadership. This had long been true of the Syrian Orthodox Church. It was rapidly becoming characteristic of the Roman Catholic Church and Protestantism. Indian Protestants were prominent in the Ecumenical Movement and were reaching out to help their fellow Protestants in other parts of Asia.

CHAPTER XII

The Mixed Record in South-East Asia and the Fringing Islands

FROM India we move eastward to South-east Asia and the fringing islands, not only because geographically they follow after the Middle East and India, but also because most of the area was culturally influenced profoundly by one or both of these two regions. Buddhism, the majority religion in Nepal, Ceylon, Burma, Thailand, Cambodia, and Laos, was of Indian origin. In the twentieth century Nepal had a Hindu ruler but most of its population were Buddhists. Indeed, the Buddha had been born in Nepal. At one time Indonesia had been part of the Hindu-Buddhist world, and the island of Bali remained ostensibly Hindu. Hinduism and Buddhism were important in Annam. Islam prevailed in Malaya and was the religion of more than half of the population of Indonesia and of an important minority in the Philippines.

All the area except Thailand had in common the fact of coming to World War I under the sway of the Western imperialism which had reached its climax in the nineteenth century. That century saw Nepal, Ceylon, Burma, and Malaya brought within the British Empire. It also witnessed the completion of the extension of French power, largely in the form of protectorates over native ruling houses, in Cambodia, Laos, and the later Vietnam. Thailand succeeded in maintaining its political independence but began to be penetrated by Western culture. The Dutch expanded their rule over the later Indonesia. The rest of the East Indies was either the remnant of the earlier Portuguese empire in that region, perpetuated in part of the island of Timor, or under the English in the west and north of Borneo. Spain had been displaced in the Philippines by the United States.

The fifty years which followed the outbreak of World War I were marked by the nearly complete disappearance of Western rule in the region. By 1962 all that survived of direct Occidental rule was Portuguese Timor and the British possessions in Borneo. Some countries remained within the Commonwealth which found its tie in the British Crown. Most of the attainment of independence had followed World War II. It was accomplished and accom-

panied by the mounting nationalism which was conspicuous in the revolutionary age. In Ceylon and Burma nationalism found partial expression in a revival
of Buddhism as the faith of the majority and in opposition to Christianity:
Christianity was regarded as a form of Western cultural imperialism. Yet in all
the area the churches tended to be increasingly rooted in their constituencies.
In the Roman Catholic Church this was evidenced through a rapid increase
in an indigenous clergy and hierarchy. In Protestantism it appeared in self-
governing churches, often with steps towards a national church, either by co-
operation in a national Christian council, by organic union, or both.

Following World War II all South-East Asia and the fringing islands were
involved in the power struggle between the Communist bloc and the "free
world." The U.S.S.R. and the People's Republic of China led the one and the
United States of America was the champion of the other. Each sought to penetrate the region and to exclude the other from it.

As in most of the non-Western world, along with the revolt against Western
"colonialism" and "imperialism" went the eager adoption of many features of
the revolutionary age which had their origin and major development in the
Occident: "modern" science, the machines, the industrialization made possible
by the machines, railways, the automobile, the telegraph, the telephone, the
radio, the cinema, television, the medical and surgical skills, and the forms of
education which were essential if these inventions and discoveries were to be
utilized. The adjuncts of civilization which were being imported from Western
"Christendom" were accompanied by such characteristics of the revolutionary
age as urbanization, a rapid growth in population with its threat of heightened
poverty matched by the demand for the masses for a larger share in the material and cultural "good things" of life, and among many, especially the intelligentsia, mounting secularism and religious scepticism.[1]

In this revolutionary setting, for the most part Christianity continued to
spread and to become more deeply rooted. In some areas it suffered reverses—
in Ceylon, Burma, and North Vietnam. On the whole, however, it grew in
numbers and in indigenous leadership.

NEPAL

On the northern, mountainous frontiers of India, with a population (1958)
of about 8,500,000 in picturesque valleys, Nepal was late in being drawn into
the currents of the revolutionary age. However, by 1962 it was beginning to be
affected by them. It became a member of the United Nations. Air service and
motor roads made it accessible to the outer world. Financial aid came from the

[1] For one set of interpretations of these developments from the standpoint of Asian Protestants
see Rajah Bhushanam Manikam, editor, *Christianity and the Asian Revolution* (Madras, Diocesan
Press, 1955, pp. iv, 293).

United States, the U.S.S.R., Communist China, India, and Australia. What professed to be popular government of the Western type was established in 1951. A constitution was proclaimed by the king in February, 1959, with a parliament of two houses and a cabinet. Within a few weeks elections gave the (Socialist) Nepal Congress Party a large majority in parliament.

Under these changing conditions Protestant missionaries gained access to the country. Nepal had long been closed to Christianity. In the eighteenth century Capuchins had placed there some converts who had been expelled from Tibet,[2] but no long-continuing mission was established. In the nineteenth century a few Nepalese on the outer borders were Christians, but there were no churches in Nepal itself.[3] Sundar Singh appealed for missionaries for Nepal. In 1950 several Mar Thoma theological students were able to spend the summer there preaching the Gospel. Mar Thoma Christians followed up the beginnings thus made. In 1954 the National Christian Council of India initiated a united mission to Nepal which was undenominational and specialized in medical service. The National Missionary Society of India coöperated in it. The King of Nepal gave it a five-year permit and it created a favourable impression. Here Indian non-Roman Catholics were giving evidence of vitality by propagating the faith among other peoples. Converts were made and a church was gathered. In addition to the united mission, in 1957 the Nepali Evangelistic Band, the Mar Thoma Evangelistic Association, and the Assemblies of God—all classed as Indian societies—were represented.[4]

CEYLON

Ceylon, with an area less than half that of Nepal and a population (1959) of approximately 9,600,000, by its geographic position was much more exposed to the revolutionary age than was the Himalayan kingdom. Much of it had been ruled by the Portuguese in the heyday of their power, and through missionaries who had come under the aegis of Lisbon a substantial number of converts had been won to the Roman Catholic Church. In the seventeenth century the Dutch displaced the Portuguese and sought to eliminate the Roman Catholic Church and to promote Protestantism. During the Napoleonic Wars the Dutch were expelled and Ceylon became a member of the British Empire. In contrast with the Portuguese and Dutch regimes—which had not brought all Ceylon under their sway—the British sovereignty was extended over the entire

---

[2] Schmidlin, Catholic Mission History, p. 492, n. 32.
[3] Alexander McLeish, The Frontier Peoples of India. A Missionary Survey (London, World Dominion Press, 1931, pp. v, 202), pp. 119–129.
[4] National Christian Council Review, Vol. LXXVII, pp. 22–29 (January, 1957); Vol. LXXVIII, pp. 20–252 (June-July, 1958); World Christian Handbook, 1957, p. 54.

island. During the religiously neutral British administration the Roman Catholic Church revived, most of the artificially nourished Dutch Protestantism disappeared, and British and American Protestantism entered and made progress. In 1911 the civil census gave the Roman Catholic total as 339,300, and the ecclesiastical count put it at 322,163. About two-thirds were Sinhalese on the lowlands, less than a third were Tamils (mostly on the northern peninsula), and a few thousands were Burghers (a mixture of European and non-European stocks) and Sinhalese in the uplands. The increase, of about 90 per cent. since 1873, was due, as in India, mostly to an excess of births over deaths.[5] The major Protestant denominations were the Anglicans, the British and American Congregationalists, the British Methodists, and the British Baptists. In 1901 the Protestant totals were said to be 12,887 communicants and 18,184 non-communicants. The Methodists were the most numerous, with the Anglicans a close second.[6] By 1914 Christians were about one-seventh of the population, a larger proportion than in any country on the mainland of South and East Asia.[7]

Ceylon was more and more swept into the flow of the revolutionary age. As in the nineteenth century, its economy was largely dependent on markets in the industrialized West. In the 1950's its chief export was tea, most of which went to the United Kingdom, other nations in the Commonwealth, and the United States. Next was rubber. Coconuts and coconut products were also important. Another manifestation of the impact of the revolutionary age was a surging nationalism. Through it, in 1948, soon after World War II, when much of Asia and Africa were throwing off the rule of Western peoples, Ceylon became independent but remained within the British Commonwealth.

The tide of nationalism was associated with a revival of Buddhism. This was the kind of Buddhism known as Theravada, "the way of the elders," and was believed by its adherents to be much closer to the teaching of the Buddha and his immediate disciples than was the Mahayana which in one or another form prevailed in Tibet and Mongolia and had been strong in China, Korea, and Japan. Theravada Buddhism was also the dominant religion, as we shall see, in Burma, Thailand, and Cambodia. Associated as it was with Sinhalese nationalism, it became aggressive and intolerant. It sought to restrict all other religions, including Christianity.

Late in the 1950's and early in the 1960's efforts of the Sinhalese to enforce the use of their language as the national vernacular and in other ways to assimilate the non-Sinhalese minorities led to clashes, especially with the largest of the minorities, the Tamils, who had their own tongue and were Hindu by

---

[5] Latourette, *A History of the Expansion of Christianity*, Vol. VI, pp. 215–219.
[6] Beach, *A Geography and Atlas of Protestant Missions*, Vol. II, p. 24.
[7] Latourette, *op. cit.*, Vol. VI, pp. 221–224.

faith—both those who had long resided in the northern peninsula and the later immigrants.

Another concomitant of the revolutionary age which Ceylon shared with several countries was the burst of population and its attendant problem of meeting the rising demands of the masses for more of the good things of life in the face of increasing pressures on the food supply. Ceylon imported much of its rice (the staple diet), but the chronic poverty was an inescapable problem. In 1857 the population was said to be 1,700,000. In 1921 it had mounted to 3,578,333, and in 1959, as we have noted, it was about 9,600,000.

In the first half of the twentieth century the growth in the number of Christians did not keep pace proportionately with that of the population. In 1959 Roman Catholics were said to total 737,259.[8] In 1957 the Protestant community was said to be 97,248.[9] Thus the former had increased about 218 per cent. in forty-eight years and the Protestants 313 per cent. in forty-six years. The Christian total late in the 1950's was only slightly more than double its size shortly before World War I, whereas the population of the country had mounted about 270 per cent. in a shorter period, namely, between 1921 and 1959. In 1959, then, Christians were only about 8.4 per cent. of the population as against at least 13 per cent. in 1921.

Although percentage-wise Roman Catholics were not as prominent in 1962 as on the eve of World War I, they still constituted a larger proportion of the population than in any other country in South and East Asia and the fringing islands except the Philippines and Vietnam. As during the Portuguese era, they were most numerous in the coastal regions. About a third were in urban centres. In some rural areas almost none were found. They had erected many impressive institutions—orphanages, convents, schools, and colleges. Their literacy rate was higher than that of the population as a whole. Even in 1960 the state continued the policy adopted by the British and subsidized the Christian schools, both Roman Catholic and Protestant. Because of their better education in what was demanded in the revolutionary age, many Roman Catholics were in government service and the big business firms. However, with the rise in the educational level of the non-Christian population that advantage was not as marked as it had been earlier in the century. Under pressure of nationalism accompanied by the emphasis on Buddhism as the religion of the country, by 1960 the government refused to recognize any more Christian schools, whether Roman Catholic or Protestant, and pressures were mounting to nationalize the existing ones.[10] Roman Catholics tended to be an ingrown community. In the two years between July 1, 1957, and June 30, 1959, for example, only 3,332

[8] *Worldmission Fides Service*, June 6, 1959.
[9] *World Christian Handbook, 1957*, p. 26.
[10] *Worldmission*, Vol. XI, pp. 65 ff. (Fall, 1960).

baptisms of adults were reported as against 46,046 of children—the latter presumably being the offspring of Christian parents.[11] This characteristic was ascribed to a lack of clergy and to the fact that the priests were too few to do more than give pastoral care to the faithful. Moreover, by 1960 all "proselytism" was being denounced by the fervid nationalists. The presence of Roman Catholic nuns in government hospitals was meeting so much criticism that the systematic withdrawal of the sisters from them was under way. Obstacles were raised to the entry of foreign personnel. Christians were looked upon as second-class citizens and the activity of missionaries was regarded as "cultural imperialism." Now that Sinhalese was being pushed as the national language, the lack of religious literature in that tongue was proving a handicap. Little had been done to adapt the art and liturgy to national traditions. The Roman Catholic schools had neglected instruction in the history, literature, and language of the nation.[12]

Even so, some improvement was seen. The indigenous clergy were increasing. In 1957, 320 native and Indian priests were serving as against 161 foreign missionaries, and the numbers of students preparing for the secular and regular clergy were advancing. In 1960 four of the six bishops, including the head of the hierarchy, the Archbishop of Colombo, had been born on the island.[13]

The rising nationalism confronted Protestants with much the same problems as the Roman Catholics met. Protestants faced the possibilty of the nationalization of their schools, which had been receiving state aid, and, in that event, the problem of providing instruction in the faith and of adequately using the time allotted for religious teaching in the government schools.[14] In the twentieth century the Anglicans outstripped the Methodists in numerical strength, and in the 1950's the two denominations together constituted more than half of the Protestants.[15] The Anglicans were still part of the Church of India, Burma, and Ceylon. Little progress had been made among the Sinhalese, strongly Buddhist as they were. Converts came mostly from the Tamils, Hindus by heredity. As a result Protestants, like Roman Catholics, were challenged with creating a Christian literature in Sinhalese. Much Christian literature existed in Tamil, but little in Sinhalese.[16] In 1944 the British and Foreign Bible Society transferred to the newly organized Bible Society of India and Ceylon responsibility for the production and distribution of the Scriptures in those two countries. Translations of the entire Bible already existed in Sinhalese and Tamil. In 1949

[11] *Worldmission Fides Service,* June 6, 1959.
[12] *Worldmission,* Vol. XI, pp. 67–70 (Fall, 1960).
[13] *Ibid.,* pp. 70, 71.
[14] *The International Review of Missions,* Vol. L, p. 31 (January, 1961).
[15] *World Christian Handbook, 1957,* p. 26. For a history of Anglicanism see F. Lorenz Beven, editor, *A History of the Diocese of Colombo. A Centenary Volume* (Colombo, The Times of Ceylon Co., foreword 1946, pp. xvii, 426), *passim.*
[16] *The International Review of Missions,* Vol. XLVIII, p. 29 (January, 1959).

a large new edition of the Sinhalese version was printed.[17] Native candidates for the ministry went to India for their theological training. Only one theological seminary was maintained in Ceylon. It was Anglican and in 1956 had nine students.[18]

Some progress was being made towards unity among Protestants. The former Congregationalists, mostly on the northern peninsula, were members of the Church of South India. The National Christian Council provided coöperation. In the 1950's conversations were under way for the union of the Anglicans, Methodists, Baptists, Presbyterians, and the Jaffna Diocese of the Church of South India in what was to be called the Church of Lanka, but by 1962 they had not been consummated.[19]

BURMA

Burma presented Christianity with a challenge which resembled that in Ceylon but also differed from it. As in Ceylon, Theravada Buddhism was the religion of the Burmans. The Burmans and their closely allied peoples constituted the large majority of the population and had long been the civilized and ruling race. Their Buddhism incorporated a pre-Buddhist animism, and it was said that the Burmans loved the Buddha but feared the nats (the spirits inherited from animism). Like Ceylon, in the nineteenth century Burma had been part of the British Empire, but it became independent in the 1940's. Like Ceylon, Burma was faced with a "population explosion." In 1911 the officially reported total had been 12,790,754; in 1959 it was estimated at 20,457,000. The rapid increase threatened the nation's livelihood and was compounded with the demand for more of the material goods of life. Like Ceylon, Burma was caught in the currents of the revolutionary age. Intense nationalism, an infection from "Christendom" and a reaction from British domination, was responsible for the political independence. Similarly, to conserve independence and national unity, attempts were made to adopt and adapt political institutions developed in the West. Burmese nationalism and Theravada Buddhism were closely allied. A Buddhist revival was encouraged by the government and in 1954–1956 what was called the Sixth Buddhist World Council was held in Rangoon culminating in the commemoration of the two-thousandth anniversary of the Buddha's entrance into Nirvana. The government used Buddhism to fight Communism.[20] The economy of Burma was enmeshed in the world

---

17 The First Report of the Bible Society of India and Ceylon (Mysore, The Western Press and Publishing House, 1945, pp. 81), p. 5; ibid., 1948, p. 53.

18 Allen, A Seminary Survey, p. 104.

19 The International Review of Missions, Vol. XLII, p. 24 (January, 1953); Vol. L, pp. 30, 31 (January, 1961); Ecumenical Press Service, May 26, 1961.

20 Pacific Affairs, Vol. XXXIII, pp. 290–299 (September, 1960).

commerce. To meet the problems thrust on the country by the revolutionary age efforts were made to create an educational system embodying features developed in the West.

The contrasts with Ceylon were marked. An Indian immigrant element was present, but it was a much smaller minority. The variety of peoples was greater, the most numerous being the Karens. The majority of the non-Burman elements had been or were animists, but on some of them, notably the Shans, Buddhism had made a deep impression. Burma had not been as long ruled by Europeans or as many years part of the British Empire as had Ceylon. The initial annexation was in 1824, the next in 1852, and the final one in 1885–1886, when what was known as Upper Burma was incorporated into the British realm. Ceylon remained in British hands during World War II, but in 1942 the Japanese drove the English out of Burma. Following the Japanese defeat (1945) and after much unrest in the vain British effort to satisfy the Burmese nationalists by gradual steps towards independence, in October, 1947, the United Kingdom agreed to immediate independence, which became effective in January, 1948. Again in contrast with Ceylon, when it became independent Burma chose to remain outside the Commonwealth. Much civil strife followed World War II, notably between the national government and the Karens. Communism posed a greater menace than in Ceylon, partly because it entered into the civil strife and partly because in 1949 and 1950 the mainland of China fell into Communist hands and friction followed on the border between the two countries.

Unlike Ceylon, Christianity was more prominently represented in Burma by Protestants than by Roman Catholics. It had been introduced by the Portuguese in the seventeenth century in its Roman Catholic form. However, by the dawn of the nineteenth century no missionaries were left. The Church did not entirely. disappear, for a few Roman Catholics remained. Roman Catholic missionaries, from the *Société des Missions Étrangères* of Paris and the Milan Society, resumed their labours in the nineteenth century. Protestantism was introduced by English Baptists, who prepared the way for American Baptists. It was chiefly through the latter that Protestantism was propagated. By 1914 they had reached practically all the peoples of Burma. Only a few Burmans were won, staunchly Buddhist as the ruling race was. The gains were mainly among the animistic peoples, mostly Karens. Indeed, the Burmans tended to regard Christianity as the Karen religion. Anglicans, American and English Methodists, and a few other denominations came, but the Baptists were the major Protestant denomination.[21] In 1914 Roman Catholics were said to number about 84,000.[22] In 1902 Protestant communicants and non-communicants

[21] Volume III, pp. 419, 420.
[22] Streit, *Atlas Hierarchicus*, p. 99.

were reported to be 91,111.[23] In the census of 1921 Christians totalled 257,106, or slightly less than 2 per cent. of the population; 207,760 were from indigenous stocks and the remainder were Indians, Europeans, or Anglo-Indians. Of the indigenous Christians 69.3 per cent. were Karens and constituted nearly 15 per cent. of that people. Only 16 per cent. were of the Burmans and the Taliang, the majority group. According to the census of 1921, 170,384 of the Christians were Protestants.[24]

In spite of the political vicissitudes of the half-century which included the two world wars, the Japanese occupation, political independence, civil strife, and the Buddhist revival, Christians continued to multiply, both in numbers and in proportion to the population. In 1959 Roman Catholics totalled 183,713 and had had 5,780 baptisms of adults in the preceding two years.[25] In other words, they had more than doubled since 1914, while the population had less than doubled. Moreover, in contrast with Ceylon, in which, with a much larger body of Roman Catholics, only 3,332 adult baptisms had been recorded in the two-year period, in Burma Roman Catholics were increasing more by fresh conversions than in that country. By the mid-1950's Protestants were said to have 224,878 communicant members and a Christian community of 506,132. More than four-fifths were Baptists.[26] In 1924 the number of communicants was said to have been 84,678[27] and in 1926 the total of Protestants, communicants and non-communicants, was reported by the missions to have been 192,027.[28] These figures indicate that Protestant communicants had more than trebled since the eve of World War I and that the Protestant community had multiplied about as rapidly. By 1960, in contrast with the proportion of slightly less than 2 per cent. in 1921, Christians had now about 3 per cent. of the population. Owing in part to the influence of Christian schools, the Christian community included many teachers, physicians, and other professional people.[29] This was the more remarkable in view of the fact that over half the Christians were Karens and that when missionaries first gained access to them that people were without a written language, were primitive in culture, and were exploited by the Burmans.

As had long been true, in the 1950's Baptists, aided by American Baptists, enrolled a majority of the Protestants. They were in several parts of Burma but were strongest among the Karens. In 1954 their foreign staff out-numbered the total of all the other Protestant missionaries and their indigenous personnel

23 Beach, op. cit., Vol. II, p. 24.
24 McLeish, Christian Progress in Burma, p. 84.
25 Worldmission Fides Service, January 18, 1961.
26 World Christian Handbook, 1957, p. 25.
27 Beach and Fahs, World Missionary Atlas, p. 103.
28 McLeish, Christian Progress in Burma, pp. 83, 89.
29 Review and Expositor, Vol. LVIII, pp. 35–39 (January, 1961).

was six times larger than that of all the non-Baptist Protestants. The Anglicans were next in size, with strong contingents among the Indians. The Methodists were chiefly in Buddhist areas and so had few converts.[30]

As elsewhere in much of the non-Occidental world, the churches in Burma were increasingly under indigenous leadership. Thus in 1959 the Roman Catholics had thirty-two enrolled in major seminaries.[31] Either late in 1959 or early in 1960 an indigenous secular was appointed Archbishop of Mandalay, a step which signalized the transfer of that archdiocese from the *Société des Missions Étrangères* of Paris to the native secular clergy. The appointee was a descendant of Portuguese merchants who had come to Burma in the seventeenth century. In 1960 Bassein had an indigenous bishop.[32]

During the Japanese occupation all the foreign personnel were compelled to leave the country, and foreign subsidies, which had been used chiefly to support schools, to open new churches, and to pay the salaries of missionaries, were stopped. The indigenous Christians were thus forced to assume entire responsibility for the churches. They rose to the challenge and after the invaders were expelled a revival was seen among the Protestants.[33]

Under the pressures of the growing nationalism, Protestant Burmese leadership increased. The Protestant theological institution of the highest academic grade was the Burma Baptist Divinity School at Insein. In 1956 the word "Baptist" was dropped from its title and Methodists and Anglicans were added to its board of trustees. In 1955 about fifty-five students were enrolled and in 1957 the total was sixty-two.[34] In 1960 an extension of the Burma Divinity School in Rangoon began preparing students for the Serampore bachelor of divinity degree.[35] The urgency of indigenous leadership was accentuated by the government opposition to the entrance of missionaries.[36] By 1953 nearly all the Protestant schools were directed by nationals with managing bodies representative of their local communities. The majority of the officers of the Burma Christian Council were nationals.[37] In 1959 several former Buddhist monks were ordained by the Anglicans to become missionaries in pioneer areas.[38] In the 1950's the American Baptists were transferring authority and mission properties to the Burma Baptist Convention.[39]

The rootage of the faith was furthered by the tradition of self-support which

---

[30] Thomas and Manikam, *The Church in Southeast Asia*, p. 81.
[31] *Worldmission Fides Service*, January 18, 1961.
[32] *Ibid.*, February 13, 1960; February 1, 1961.
[33] Thomas and Manikam, *op. cit.*, p. 80.
[34] Allen, *op. cit.*, pp. 115, 116.
[35] *The International Review of Missions*, Vol. L, p. 32 (January, 1961).
[36] *Ibid.*, Vol. XLV, p. 33 (January, 1956).
[37] *Ibid.*, Vol. XLII, p. 27 (January, 1953).
[38] *Ibid.*, Vol. XLIX, p. 30 (January, 1960).
[39] *Ibid.*, p. 29.

was adopted in the nineteenth century among the Baptists. It was especially marked among the Karens. In some areas complete self-support had been the rule from the beginning of the local churches. In others it developed quite early. Even before the Japanese occupation threw the entire burden on the Christians, Karen Baptists were bearing the full cost of erecting and maintaining their church buildings, meeting the current expenses of their congregations, supporting their ministers and lay workers, and building and operating their schools for Christians and to some extent for non-Christians. Only the salaries of the missionaries came from abroad.[40]

The methods of Christian missions in Burma did not differ greatly from those in other countries. Always the effort was made to win converts. A variety of institutions and enterprises were initiated and maintained. Much emphasis was placed on schools. Hospitals, a leper asylum, and a tuberculosis rest home were maintained. Attempts were made to improve the livelihood of the country by introducing better procedures in agriculture and animal husbandry. Education for women helped to raise the status of that sex. In common with the practice in other British colonial possessions, before the Japanese occupation the government subsidized mission schools as it did those of any or no religion if they conformed to official educational standards. Most of the schools under Christian auspices were in Karen villages which were wholly Christian, and often the teacher was also the pastor. After independence the Protestant Judson College was taken over by the state. With the growing emphasis on the welfare state and the multiplication of state schools, the Christian schools were more and more brought within the government's educational system.[41] As in many other countries, much stress was placed by Protestants on the preparation and distribution of literature, and especially on vernacular translations of the Bible.

In common with what was taking place the world around in Protestantism, increased coöperation was developing among non-Roman Catholics. The Christian Council of Burma came into being in the 1920's. In the 1950's the Burmese Christian Youth Council was made up of delegates from several churches and youth organizations. The Burma Christian Youth League was interdenominational and interracial.[42]

In a number of ways Christianity was making an impression on Buddhism. For example, in the 1950's several of the most influential monks had kept in close touch with Moral Rearmament and had been in its Swiss and American headquarters.[43]

---

[40] Davis, *New Buildings on Old Foundations*, pp. 158–163; *Laymen's Foreign Missions Inquiry. Supplementary Series*, Vol. IV, Part Two, pp. 644–666.

[41] Thomas and Manikam, *op. cit.*, pp. 86, 87.

[42] *Ibid.*, p. 85.

[43] Braden, *War, Communism and World Religions*, p. 114.

THAILAND

Thailand, or Siam as it had formerly been called (the change of designation was a symptom of surgent nationalism), had a population only slightly larger than that of Burma. It, too, was experiencing a rapid growth—from an estimated 9,831,000 in 1925–1926 to an approximate 21,474,000 in 1958. About 40 per cent. were Thai, not quite as many were the closely related Laos, about 6 per cent. were Chinese, mostly in Bangkok, about 3 per cent. were Malays, and the rest were of several minority groups.

In the half-century which was ushered in by World War I, Thailand had a less stormy course than its neighbours. It had never been a part of any of the European empires, it was neutral in World War I, and, although overrun during World War II by the Japanese and formally at war with Great Britain and the United States—a status which the latter did not officially reciprocate—it suffered very little. Nor, in the decade and a half which followed that war, did it experience as many internal disturbances as did its neighbours on the east, north, south, and west.

Yet Thailand could not escape repercussions of the revolutionary age. Some changes in the government bore witness to the impact of the forces which were typical of that day. Commerce had its effect. The country remained predominantly rural, but the chief city, Bangkok, shared in the growth of urban centres which was seen in most of the world. Educational programmes were adopted reflecting the demand for adjustment to the age.

Religiously and culturally Thailand was more nearly solidly Buddhist than either Ceylon or Burma. As in these two lands, the Buddhism was of the Theravada school, but perhaps because nationalism, although marked, was not stimulated by the throwing off of alien rule to the fervid temper which it displayed in Ceylon and Burma, the revival of Buddhism was not so striking. Animism prevailed along mountainous borders and in places it diluted Buddhism, but the latter had long been so integral a part of the nation's life and was so little weakened by secularism and so slightly endangered by Communism that it did not react with a self-conscious revival as it did in Ceylon and Burma.

Chiefly because Buddhism was overwhelmingly the religion of the land and the non-Buddhist population was so small, Christianity did not make as large numerical gains as in the two countries we have just examined. Thailand had experienced no period of Portuguese rule which left a large legacy of Roman Catholics, as it had in Ceylon. No extensive Indian element existed such as that from which most of the conversions to Protestantism were made in Ceylon, and animistic peoples were not of the dimensions of the Karens and other non-Burman peoples among whom Christianity had gathered most of its constituency in the neighbour on the west.

Christianity had been introduced by Roman Catholic missionaries in the sixteenth century and since then that branch of the faith had been continuously represented.[44] In 1959, however, Roman Catholics numbered only 109,717, although in the preceding two years 2,176 converts had been baptized. Both figures were smaller than the corresponding ones in Ceylon and Burma, and Thailand had a larger population than either.[45] But the Roman Catholic community in 1959 was over four times the approximately 24,000 of 1912, in spite of the arrest of some missionaries and the pillaging of mission property during the Japanese occupation.[46] Percentage-wise the increase was much larger than that of the population.

Roman Catholic missionaries emphasized schools, and many non-Christians as well as Christians were educated in them. Although religious instruction was not compulsory, a large proportion of the pupils elected it. Schools were considered the chief means of spreading the faith.

A substantial proportion of the Roman Catholics were farmers. With their large families they contributed to the growth of the body of the faithful. Roman Catholics were gathered into rural communities, and as they increased in numbers additional land was obtained, virgin forest was cleared, and more soil was brought under cultivation.[47]

Protestantism did not reach Thailand until the first half of the nineteenth century, when it was introduced by several societies. In time the largest mission was that of the Presbyterian Church in the U.S.A.[48] Its major growth was in the North, centring in Chiangmai, for here Buddhism was not as deeply entrenched as in the South and animism was more prevalent. The Japanese domination in World War II with the accompanying state of war with Great Britain and the United States brought the internment of American and British missionaries and the requisitioning of many Protestant buildings for military purposes. The Japanese opposition to Christianity and the internment of the missionaries compelled the Protestant Thai to depend on their own resources and prepared them for more self-government. The congregations kept in touch with one another through messages and messengers. They increased the number and financial support of Thai evangelists and raised funds to aid Christian schools destroyed by Japanese bombings and to purchase medicines for sick soldiers.[49]

[44] Latourette, A History of the Expansion of Christianity, Vol. III, pp. 295, 296; Vol. VI, pp. 241–243.

[45] Worldmission Fides Service, January 18, 1961; February 1, 1961.

[46] Streit, op. cit., p. 99. On the situation during the Japanese occupation see Thompson and Adloff, Minority Problems in Southeast Asia, pp. 268, 269.

[47] Worldmission, Vol. IX, pp. 86, 87 (Winter, 1958).

[48] George Bradley McFarland, editor, Historical Sketch of Protestant Missions in Siam, 1828–1928 (Bangkok, Bangkok Times Press, 1928, pp. xvii, 386), passim.

[49] The International Review of Missions, Vol. XXXIII, p. 25 (January, 1944); Thomas and Manikam, op. cit., pp. 98, 99.

Protestantism had a fairly steady numerical growth. In 1925 it was said to have 8,344 communicants and a total community of 14,846.[50] In 1957 the corresponding figures were 20,736 and 26,730.[51] Like the Roman Catholics, in communicants this was a more rapid proportionate growth than that of the population.

The methods employed by Protestant missions had much in common with those in use in other countries in Asia and Africa. The winning of converts, gathering them into churches, and training leadership, lay and clerical, had first place. The translation and distribution of the Bible and the preparation and circulation of other Christian literature were stressed. Schools were developed from primary grades to a college. Hospitals, the training of nurses, and care for lepers were prominent.[52]

As in many other lands the growth of unity among Protestants and the transfer of control from foreigners to nationals were marked. In 1930 the National Christian Council of Siam was organized as a result of a visit of John R. Mott, the chairman of the International Missionary Council.[53] Much of its membership was Thai. More and more institutions such as hospitals and schools were transferred from foreign to Thai leadership.[54] In 1934 the Church of Christ in Siam (later Thailand) was organized as an autonomous national body and by 1940 it had only one foreigner on its board of officers and he was in a subordinate position. In 1954 with the approval of the Roman Catholics and the Seventh Day Adventists the government transmitted through the Church of Christ in Thailand the per capita subsidy to Christians which it made to Buddhists and Moslems.[55] In 1930 the first class to complete the full course was graduated from the theological seminary. All the work of its first class had been done in English, but the institution also now gave instruction to students whose only language was Thai.[56] Early in 1947 missionaries whom the Japanese occupation had forced to leave began returning, but their arrival did not jeopardize the Thai control of the Church of Christ. In 1952 the Presbyterian Board in New York announced its determination to transfer to that church all its property in Thailand except the residences of the missionaries.[57] In 1957 the Presbyterian Mission in Thailand as such was dissolved and its members were integrated with the Thai Church. Henceforth the missionaries were under the full control of that church.[58] Some other denominations became members of the Church of Christ in Thailand. Among them were Baptists,

[50] Beach and Fahs, *op. cit.*, p. 77.
[51] *World Christian Handbook, 1957*, p. 64.
[52] Wells, *History of Protestant Work in Thailand, 1828-1958*, pp. 184–189.
[53] *Ibid.*, pp. 142, 143; Fahs and Davis, *Conspectus of Coöperative Missionary Enterprises*, p. 66.
[54] Wells, *op. cit.*, pp. 143 ff.
[55] *Ibid.*, pp. 143, 157, 158; Thomas and Manikam, *op. cit.*, p. 100.
[56] Wells, *op. cit.*, p. 157.
[57] *Ibid.*, pp. 164, 173.
[58] *Ibid.*, pp. 191–194.

the Disciples of Christ (from the United States), and the Marburger Mission (from Germany).[59]

Other Protestant bodies entered Thailand, most of them after World War II. In 1960 the Overseas Missionary Fellowship of the China Inland Mission had more missionaries in the country than any other one body. Most of them had been in China and had left that country when the Communists took over the mainland. They directed their chief efforts to the animistic tribes and to the Moslems.[60] In 1962, however, the overwhelming majority of the Thai Protestants were in the Church of Christ in Thailand.

MALAYA AND SINGAPORE

The portions of the Malay Peninsula and its adjacent islands which in 1914 were included in the British Empire experienced striking political changes in the half-century which followed that year. On the eve of World War I the region had a three-fold division: The Straits Settlements, a crown colony, included Singapore, Malacca, a few islands, among them Penang, and a strip on the mainland. On the Malay Peninsula were the Federated Malay States and the Unfederated Malay States. The region had prospered as a source of tin for the industries of the West and particularly of rubber as automobiles multiplied. The growing prosperity attracted Chinese and Indians. Singapore became predominantly Chinese. In Malaya itself about half the population were Malays, slightly more than a third were Chinese, and a little over a tenth were Indians. Religiously the Malays were almost solidly Moslem, the Chinese tended to be secularized, and the Indians were predominantly Hindus.

Until World War II Malaya and Singapore went on much as they had in the years immediately preceding World War I. During the second war the Japanese made themselves masters of the Malay Peninsula and Singapore. After the defeat of Japan British rule was restored, but only to be followed by Communist guerrilla warfare in the jungles, the independence of Malaya, and the autonomy of Singapore. The Straits Settlements were dissolved in 1945–1946. In 1948 the Confederation of Malaya was formed with a large degree of autonomy. In 1957 Malaya became an independent constitutional monarchy but remained within the British Commonwealth. The following year Singapore was transformed from a crown colony into a self-governing state and, like Malaya, remained in the Commonwealth.[61]

---

[59] *Ibid.*, pp. 197–199, 210.

[60] *Ibid.*, pp. 195–211. On the China Inland Mission see Isobel Kuhn, *Ascent to the Tribes. Pioneering in North Thailand* (Chicago, Moody Press, 1956, pp. 315), *passim*. On the American Baptists, who were chiefly among the Karens, see Fridell, *Baptists in Thailand and the Philippines*, pp. 20 ff.

[61] For an account of a stage in the situation, see J. B. Perry Robinson, *Transformation in Malaya* (London, Secker and Warburg, 1956, pp. 232), *passim*.

The striking political changes, with the growth of nationalism and, in Singapore, the threat of Communism, did not immediately bring revolutionary alterations in the Christianity of the region. Population continued to grow—in Singapore from 425,912 in 1921 to 1,580,000 in 1959, or nearly a four-fold multiplication; in Malaya from about 2,425,000 in 1921 to approximately 6,500,000 in 1957, an increase of between two and three fold.

The Roman Catholic Church had been continuously in the region since the days of Portuguese might. In 1912 its members were said to number 32,500.[62] In 1959 Malaya and Singapore were reported to have 151,565 Roman Catholics and in the preceding two years to have had 2,768 baptisms of adults—presumably conversions—and 3,841 baptisms of infants. This meant that percentage-wise the Roman Catholics had increased much more rapidly than the population. They were served by 177 priests, 216 lay brothers, 529 sisters, and 96 catechists. Nineteen major seminarians were under instruction.[63] Eleven years earlier slightly over half the priests and somewhat less than half the sisters had been nationals.[64]

Protestants in Malaya and Singapore also grew in numbers. Reported figures for 1925 were 10,781 communicants and 6,862 baptized non-communicants, or a Christian community of 17,849;[65] for 1948, 19,775 communicants and a Protestant community of 47,461;[66] for 1957, 23,687 communicants and a total community of 50,112.[67] Here too was an increase; although not as marked as that of the Roman Catholics, it was proportionately slightly more rapid than that of the population as a whole. Numerically the largest denominational bodies, both in 1925 and in 1957, were those connected with the American Methodists, followed at some distance, more marked in 1957 than in 1925, by the Anglicans. In the 1950's many strong Chinese Protestant churches existed, some planted by evangelists from China, which were fundamentalist in doctrine and did not coöperate with other bodies. To Malaya, as to Thailand, the Communist mastery of the mainland of China brought members of the China Inland Mission—now called the Overseas Missionary Fellowship.[68] For both Roman Catholics and Protestants it must be said that, as elsewhere, very few of the conversions were from the Moslems. Converts were mainly among the Chinese and Indians.

A major Protestant approach was through schools. In 1961 American Methodists had a more extensive educational system than in any other country outside the West. Increasing effort was put forth to prepare an indigenous clergy. Some of it was through Bible schools with slight academic requirements. But in

[62] Streit, *op. cit.,* p. 99.
[63] *Worldmission Fides Service,* January 18, 1961.
[64] Chelliah and McLeish, *Malaya and Singapore,* p. 36.
[65] Beach and Fahs, *op. cit.,* p. 101.
[66] Chelliah and McLeish, *op. cit.,* p. 36.
[67] *World Christian Handbook, 1957,* pp. 53, 54.
[68] Amy McIntosh, *Journey into Malaya* (London, China Inland Mission, 1956, pp. 190), *passim.*

Trinity College, in Singapore, higher scholastic standards were maintained. Trinity College was an interdenominational institution which was conceived in a Japanese internment camp during World War II when missionaries of several denominations were there in intimate fellowship. It was opened in 1948. The chief participants were Methodists, Anglicans, and Presbyterians.[69] Not only in theological education did Protestants in Malaya and Singapore co-operate. The Malayan Christian Council aided in other ways. In the 1950's collaboration was undertaken to prepare workers for social service in the "new villages" which had been created by the government in an attempt to combat the Communist menace.[70]

By 1962 evidence was accumulating that the political developments, including the disruption brought by the Japanese occupation during World War II and the unrest and the achievement of independence which followed, had not prevented the continued growth of the Christian churches and their rootage in indigenous leadership.[71] Moreover, the Methodist Church of Malaya sent missionaries to the Dyaks in Sarawak.[72]

CAMBODIA

As we move on into what for several decades before World War II was called French Indo-China we come to Cambodia. In the 1860's, to counter the efforts of Siam to extend its control over his realm, the King of Cambodia had placed Cambodia under the protection of France. Siam accepted the situation and renounced its claim to tribute. In 1884 a treaty with France reduced the power of the king to a shadow, and French advisers and administrators set about developing the country in such fashion that it felt the impact of the revolutionary age. In 1947, following the expulsion of the Japanese, a fresh constitution in theory replaced the absolute monarchy. In 1949, under the pressure of rising nationalism, Cambodia became an associated state within the French Union. In 1953 it declared its independence of France and in 1955 was admitted to the United Nations. But French continued to be widely used. A modified form of Western learning was promoted through several thousand primary schools and institutions of higher learning. Buddhism was still the state religion. The population increased, from about 2,500,000 in 1926 to approximately 5,000,000 in 1957.

[69] Allen, *A Seminary Survey*, pp. 117, 118.
[70] *The International Review of Missions*, Vol. L, p. 16 (January, 1961).
[71] On two developments during the Japanese occupation see a description of the deepened religious life among the British internees in J. N. Lewis Bryan, *The Churches in Captivity in Malaya* (London, Society for Promoting Christian Knowledge, 1946, pp. 71), *passim,* and the autobiography of a Chinese Christian nurse in Janet Lim, *Sold for Silver. An Autobiography* (Cleveland, The World Publishing Co., 1958, pp. 252), *passim.*
[72] Thomas and Manikam, *op. cit.,* p. 59.

Christianity was not strong in Cambodia. Roman Catholics had been present since at least the sixteenth century. Early in the twentieth century they were said to number 66,000 and to be mostly on the rivers and canals.[73] In 1959 the total was reported to be 52,632. This loss of ground was apparently confirmed by the fact that only 314 catechumens were enrolled and that the preceding two years had seen 437 baptisms of adults, but 5,102 of infants—an indication that very few conversions were being made and that the existing Christian community was being perpetuated by births. Moreover, in 1960 fifty-seven priests and two major seminarians were reported, fewer than in any other country in South, South-East, or East Asia in lands that were open to missionaries.[74]

LAOS

Laos, north of Cambodia and less accessible from the outer world, had also been within the French sphere of influence. Racially it was a mixture, with the Laos as the dominant element but with several tribes of primitive culture and some Chinese. In religion it was predominantly Buddhist. Indeed, Buddhism was the state religion and was organized in a hierarchy which paralleled the civil administration. But the country had many animists. Mountainous and much of it heavily forested, not readily united politically, and at times invaded by Siam, partly to obtain defense against the latter in 1893 Laos became a protectorate of France. During World War II the Japanese suppressed the French authority. In 1947, after the defeat of Japan, a constitution was adopted which professed to unite the country. In 1949, like Cambodia, Laos became an independent state within the French Union. In 1955 it was admitted to the United Nations. In the 1950's and the fore part of the 1960's it was caught in the power struggle between the Communists and the "free world." Internally divided and weak, it was a pawn in the contest between the giants. With an estimated population in 1956 of about 3,000,000 it had no large cities. It was imperfectly supplied with roads, and the navigation of its rivers was impeded by falls and rapids.

Under these circumstances Christianity was late in being introduced and made slow progress. The earliest continuing mission was that of the *Société des Missions Étrangères* of Paris, begun in the eighteenth century.[75] After the French connexion was formed, the French administration, then at the height of its anti-clericalism, was unfriendly. The Paris society was supplemented by the Oblates of Mary Immaculate, who opened their first station in 1935 in the northern part of the country.[76] In 1959 Laos was reported as having 23,764

[73] Schmidlin, *Catholic Mission History*, pp. 310, 605.
[74] *Worldmission Fides Service*, January 18, 1961.
[75] Schmidlin, *op. cit.*, pp. 490, 604.
[76] *Worldmission*, Vol. IX, p. 74 (Winter, 1958).

Roman Catholics and 2,565 catechumens and in the preceding two years 774 baptisms of adults and 2,548 baptisms of infants. It then had eighty priests and seven major seminarians, a showing better than in Cambodia but poorer than in any other country in South-East Asia.[77] The civil disturbances late in the 1950's and in the 1960's, with the occupation of some areas by Communists, made the work of missionaries difficult and forced several to leave their flocks.[78]

A striking and heroic life of a Roman Catholic layman unconnected with any ecclesiastical mission was that of Thomas A. Dooley, an American physician. In the 1950's on his own initiative, influenced by the example of Albert Schweitzer, he organized MEDICO (Medical International Coöperation Organization) and with colleagues built and operated a hospital in Laos in a village not far from the China border. His life was cut short by cancer. But by 1961 MEDICO had seventeen projects in twelve countries in South-East Asia, South America, the Caribbean, and Africa.[79]

Protestantism reached Laos late in the nineteenth century through American Presbyterians and by way of Siam. Since many of the Laos were in that country, Chiangmai became a natural centre for the mission to them. Bibles, hymnals, booklets, and a monthly periodical were issued by a press in that city. Medical service allayed suffering and fought disease. Most of the converts were in Thailand, but the state of Laos itself was penetrated.[80]

VIETNAM

What in the 1950's and 1960's was known as Vietnam had long constituted the main portion of French Indo-China. It was made up of the former Tongking, Annam, and Cochin-China. In its southern section, especially in Cochin-China, Indian cultural influence had long been strong, with Hinduism and Buddhism, but on the coast east of the mountain barrier which formed the backbone of the southward-jutting portion of Asia that included part of Burma, Thailand, Malaya, Cambodia, and Laos Chinese civilization, with Confucianism, had been potent and from time to time the region had been incorporated in the Chinese Empire.

French political interest dated from the latter part of the eighteenth century and French rule had been established in the nineteenth century with the protection of French missionaries as the original ostensible purpose. In the 1780's, at the instance of a French missionary bishop, French aid contributed to the

[77] *Worldmission Fides Service,* January 18, 1961.
[78] *Ibid.,* January 5, 12, 1961.
[79] Thomas A. Dooley, *The Night They Burned the Mountain* (New York, Farrar, Straus and Cudahy, 1960, pp. 192), *passim;* *Worldmission Fides Service,* February 8, 1961.
[80] Wells, *op. cit.,* pp. 84–89.

seating of an Emperor of Annam, who also made vassals of Cambodia and Laos. In 1858, to protect French and Spanish missionaries from severe persecutions, the governments of France and Spain sent armed forces to the area. Spain soon withdrew, but France persisted and in 1863 the Annamite emperor was forced to cede to that country part of Cochin-China. In the ensuing five years France further extended its control. Because of the defeat of France in the war with Prussia in 1870, for a time French expansion paused. But in the 1870's and 1880's it was renewed. On the eve of World War I Cochin-China was a French colony and Annam-Tongking was a French protectorate. Between the two wars some advance was made towards increasing the share of the nationals in the administration, and French citizenship was granted to a few of them.

During World War II the Japanese occupied the area. After the Japanese collapse, Vietnamese nationalism mounted. In 1946 Ho Chi Minh set up the Vietnam Republic with a government in which Communists and a number of other elements were represented. The French resisted, and prolonged and exhausting war followed. Aid to Ho Chi Minh came from the Chinese Communists, much of the rest of the world was involved, and in 1954 an armistice was reached which left the country divided between South Vietnam and North Vietnam. Both were independent of France. Ngo Dinh Diem became president of South Vietnam, which, with its capital at Saigon, was known as the Republic of Vietnam. To it came aid from the United States, and some church forces in the United States helped in the relief of refugees. In 1900 South Vietnam's population was estimated as 13,000,000. North Vietnam, with its capital at Hanoi, had the designation of the Democratic Republic of Vietnam. In 1960 its population was said to be about 16,000,000. In area it was slightly smaller than its southern neighbour.

Christianity in Vietnam was represented almost entirely by the Roman Catholic Church. Protestants were a very small minority, mainly the fruit of the Christian and Missionary Alliance, with an estimated community of 45,000 in 1957.[81] The Roman Catholic Church had been continuously in evidence since early in the seventeenth century. Its propagation had been chiefly through the *Société des Missions Étrangères* of Paris and in part through Spanish Dominicans and a few other orders and congregations. The record had been punctuated by severe persecutions, but the growth was phenomenal. In 1914 the Roman Catholic Church was said to have a membership of about 950,000,[82] or about 5 per cent. of the population. This, it will be noted, was more than the total number of Roman Catholics in Ceylon, Burma, Thailand, Malaya, Cambodia, and Laos on the eve of World War I. In 1935 the Vietnam Roman Catholics

[81] *World Christian Handbook, 1957*, p. 29.
[82] Streit, *op. cit.*, p. 99.

were about 1,441,124.[83] Proportionately they had increased slightly more rapidly than the population. The staff had become overwhelmingly indigenous, with about four times as many native as foreign priests and more than fourteen times as many native as foreign sisters.[84] In 1925 an apostolic delegation was created for the better supervision and coördination of the Church.[85] In 1933 an Annamite bishop, the first of his race to be accorded that dignity, was consecrated,[86] and he was followed by another in 1935.[87] With World War II, the subsequent civil strife complicated by the French effort to maintain their rule, and the mastery of the North by the pro-Communist regime, statistics became more difficult to obtain. In 1959 the figures for the Republic of Vietnam, admittedly imperfect, were 1,226,318 Catholics, 97,407 catechumens, 54,770 baptisms of adults, and 128,134 baptisms of infants.[88]

The division of the country by the events of the 1940's and 1950's led to very different developments in its two sections. Thousands of Roman Catholics fled from the Communist Democratic Republic to the Republic of Vietnam. Missionaries were expelled from the North and by the end of 1960 the last of them had left.[89] In the North a state-inspired effort was made to create a church of "Independent Catholics," which would cut its ties with Rome.[90] In the Republic of Vietnam, in striking contrast, the regime was friendly. Ngo Dinh Diem was a devout Roman Catholic, unmarried, and his brother was a bishop.[91] Dalat was made a centre of Roman Catholic education. In 1957 a university was founded there and the following year the Pius X Pontifical Seminary was begun.[92] There also the Redemptorists had a scholasticate.[93] In 1961 most of the high officials in the Republic of Vietnam were Roman Catholics; their church had sent them to France for their education and they were therefore better prepared for the posts than were others.[94] New churches were erected and Christian villages were set up for refugees from the North.

Presumably to meet the situation created by political independence, in 1960

[83] Fides News Service, May 2, 1936. On the attitude of the state before World War II see Philip Grandjean, Le Statut Légal des Missions Catholiques et Protestantes en Indochine Française (Paris, Librairie du Recueil Sirey, 1939, pp. 145), passim. For descriptive sketches by a Dominican see Alejandro Gallego, Almas de Oriente (Madrid, Ediciones Studium de Cultura, 1953, pp. 166), passim.

[84] Testo-Atlante Illustrato delle Missioni, p. 33.

[85] Latourette, A History of the Expansion of Christianity, Vol. VII, p. 326.

[86] Fides Service, March 9, 1935.

[87] Ibid., April 6, 1935.

[88] Worldmission Fides Service, January 18, 1961.

[89] Ibid., March 19, 1960; Ecumenical Press Service, October 21, 1960.

[90] Worldmission Fides Service, March 12, 1959. On a statement of the situation from the side of sympathizers with the (North) Democratic Republic of Vietnam see Was tun die Katholiken Vietnams, by various authors (Berlin, Union Verlag, 1956, pp. 64), passim.

[91] Worldmission Fides Service, January 30, 1960.

[92] Ibid., March 19, 1960.

[93] Allen, op. cit., p. 442.

[94] Information from a first-hand source, 1960.

Pope John XXIII gave Vietnam an episcopal hierarchy in place of the previous organization by vicariates apostolic. Three archiepiscopal sees were erected, each with suffragan dioceses, and three dioceses were added to the existing ones. One of the archdioceses had headquarters at Hanoi, in the North. The others were at Hue, in the centre of the country, and at Saigon, in the South. All but two of the bishops were Vietnamese.[95]

THE EAST INDIES

In what once bore the Western designation of the East Indies, as a result of the revolutionary age and especially World War II and its aftermath the major portions both of the area and of the population were embraced in a new independent state, the Republic of Indonesia. Sections of Borneo remained British enclaves acquired in the nineteenth century, and the eastern part of Timor and some smaller islands continued in Portuguese hands, remnants of the formerly widely extended colonial empire in that region. It is with Indonesia that we have most to do.

Indonesia arose out of a combination of nationalism and of embroilment in World War II which gave incipient nationalism the opportunity to attain its goal. The vast congeries of islands large and small which Europeans called the East Indies had never all been brought under one rule. The Dutch had made the nearest approach to attaining that end, but the larger part, territorially, of their conquests had been in the nineteenth century and too little time had elapsed before World War II to enable them fully to weld together the sprawling archipelago with its many races, languages, and religions. For it they constructed a centralized administration. In response to the rising tide of anti-colonialism, after World War I the Dutch made a beginning of bringing Indonesians into that structure, partly through membership in the *Volksraad,* which after 1927 had legislative powers, and partly by recruiting them for the lower ranks of the civil service. Under Dutch encouragement and in large part with Dutch capital, the Netherlands East Indies supplied a substantial proportion of the demands of the industrialized West for raw materials—especially rubber, petroleum, sugar, tea, quinine, pepper, and kapok fibre.

In 1942 the Japanese occupied all the East Indies except the Portuguese holdings. Following the defeat of Japan (1945) Indonesian nationalists proclaimed the Republic of Indonesia with Achmed Soekarno as president and with its capital at Jakarta, the former Batavia. The Dutch offered to grant freedom in domestic affairs and partnership in the Kingdom of the Netherlands. Soekarno and his colleagues insisted upon full independence. Confused fighting followed, with various attempts, through conferences, at peace. Eventually (1954) the

[95] *Worldmission Fides Service,* December 10, 1960; January 25, 1961.

separation of Indonesia from the Netherlands became complete. Friction continued over the claims of the Republic of Indonesia to the Dutch-held Irian, the western portion of New Guinea. Most of the Dutch left Indonesia and more and more Dutch property was expropriated. Although Indonesia attempted to maintain a neutral position between the two great power blocs represented on the one hand by the United States and on the other by the U.S.S.R. and the People's Republic of China, Communist influence was strong. The scene was further confused by civil war between the central government heading up in Jakarta and peripheral peoples, notably in Sumatra and the eastern islands. The burgeoning population brought, as in much of the rest of the world, chronic and unsolved problems. The totals rose from slightly less than 50,000,000 in 1921 to nearly 90,000,000 in 1959. In both years more than half were on Java and the neighbouring and smaller Madura—which together comprised less than a tenth of the land area of the country. Religiously, at the mid-twentieth century in relative numbers the picture did not differ greatly from that in the nineteenth century. Moslems were in the large majority, with substantial minorities of animists, a small enclave of Hindus, and irregularly scattered Christian groups, recruited chiefly from the animists but with a few thousand from the Moslems.

Between the two world wars Christianity in the Dutch East Indies showed a striking growth in numbers and towards self-government—and in spite of a revival in Islam which in one of its aspects was anti-Christian.[96] The vigorous Bataks, among whom Protestant Christianity had such a phenomenal growth that by 1939 about a third had become Christians,[97] achieved a degree of autonomy for their church. In the 1920's that church had been given a new organization which, while not entirely independent of the missionaries, had more self-government than formerly and was recognized by the state as a legal body.[98] The Batak Church was largely self-supporting, although it obtained some government aid for its schools. It also had a missionary society through which it sought to win the non-Christian Bataks, largely animists.[99] The East Indian Church, in which were enrolled more members, Indonesian and Dutch, than in any other Protestant body in the Dutch East Indies, and which had state financial support, in 1935 became administratively independent of the state and changed its name to the Protestant Church in the Netherlands Indies. It was really a federation of churches, and some of its branches, especially those in Minahassa (the northern peninsula of Celebes) and the Moluccas, assumed a large degree of autonomy.[100] In the 1920's and 1930's several smaller churches

96 Rauws et al., The Netherlands Indies, pp. 91–93, 104–106.
97 Davis, New Buildings on Old Foundations, p. 152.
98 Rauws, op. cit., pp. 121–123.
99 Davis, op. cit., pp. 150–152.
100 Amry Vandenbosch, The Dutch East Indies (Berkeley, University of California Press, 3rd

also obtained autonomy and subsequently showed increased zeal in spreading the faith.[101] The statistics displayed fully as striking a growth in numbers as in autonomy. In 1910 Protestants exclusive of the state church were said to total 403,000.[102] In 1924 the corresponding figure was 751,000.[103] In 1936 the parallel total was 883,000.[104] If the (established) East Indian Church was added, in 1931 the Protestant total of indigenous Christians was 1,610,533 and of Europeans about 115,000.[105]

The Roman Catholic growth was impressive but its totals were not as large as those of the Protestants. Yet proportionately it was more rapid, possibly because of the mounting vigour of the Roman Catholic Church in the Netherlands. In 1913 the Dutch East Indies was reported to have 35,336 European and 46,950 "coloured" Roman Catholics.[106] An official source put the number of Roman Catholics in all the East Indies at 122,143 in 1923, at 237,587 in 1933, and at 493,932 in 1937.[107] The figures in the last sentence seem to have included only non-Europeans. In 1935 European Roman Catholics were reported to total 77,898.[108] More than half the Roman Catholics were in the vicariate apostolic of the Little Sunda Islands, which included Timor with its Portuguese sector and Flores. In 1913 it had been transferred from the Society of Jesus to the Society of the Divine Word. In 1931 it had 169,699 Roman Catholics,[109] and in 1934 about 10,000 adult baptisms were reported in it, or approximately 70 per cent. of the total in the entire East Indies.[110]

Until 1935 the government forbade Protestants and Roman Catholics to have missions in territory where the other branch of the faith was represented. Roman Catholics were restive under this restriction, partly because, regarding theirs as the only true form of the faith, they believed that they should be permitted to go everywhere, and partly because, being late in arriving in the Dutch portions of the islands, they found that Protestants had preëmpted the most promising areas.[111]

---

ed., 1942, pp. viii, 458), pp. 41–44; *The International Review of Missions*, Vol. XXIV (1934), p. 134; H. Kraemer, *De Huidige Stand van het Christendom in Nederlandsch-Indië* (The Hague, 1937, pp. 89), pp. 69 ff.; *World Dominion*, Vol. XXXIV (1956), pp. 271–281.

[101] Latourette, *op. cit.*, Vol. VII, p. 202, with the accompanying footnotes.

[102] Dennis, Beach, and Fahs, *World Atlas of Christian Missions*, p. 88.

[103] Beach and Fahs, *World Missionary Atlas*, p. 101.

[104] Parker, *Interpretative Statistical Survey of the World Mission of the Christian Church*, p. 52. On the degree to which conversion affected the indigenous culture patterns see C. Van Vollenhaven, *Adat-Recht der Christen Inlanders* (Oegsgeest, Zendingsbureau, 1935, pp. 135), *passim*. On another aspect of missions see Joh. Rauws, *Oversicht van het Zendingswerk in Ned. Oost-en West-Indie* (Oegsgeest, Zendingsbureau, ca. 1931, pp. 73), *passim*.

[105] Parker, *op. cit.*, pp. 282–284.

[106] *Zeitschrift für Missionswissenschaft*, Vol. III (1914), p. 315.

[107] *Fides Service*, March 26, 1938.

[108] *Ibid.*, April 6, 1935.

[109] *Testo-Atlante Illustrato delle Missioni*, p. 110.

[110] *Fides Service*, April 6, 1935.

[111] Conversation of the author with a Dutch colonial official, March 29, 1935.

Conversions to Christianity, whether to Protestantism or Roman Catholicism, were predominantly from the animists. Yet a good many were from Islam, for that religion sat somewhat more lightly upon its adherents in the East Indies than it did in most other parts of the world.

World War II and its aftermath brought striking changes to Christianity in Indonesia. The foreign missionary element declined, but the churches grew in numbers and in rootage. The first stages of the war saw the occupation of the Netherlands by the Germans. The Dutch authorities in the East Indies, therefore, interned or expelled the German missionaries. The seizure of the East Indies by the Japanese was accompanied by the death or the internment of the Dutch missionaries. Thus the two main foreign contingents in the missionary forces were eliminated. Although the defeat of the Japanese permitted the resumption of missionary activities, the ensuing conflicts between Indonesian nationalism and the Dutch made the participation of the latter in the life of the churches difficult and at times impossible.

Between the outbreak of World War II and the Japanese occupation, Protestantism faced problems but did not suffer greatly. The absence of the German missionaries and the cutting off of funds from Germany were followed by increased autonomy and self-support in the Batak Church. In 1940 the first three Batak ministers were ordained.[112] The financial difficulties brought by the interruption of contributions from the Netherlands during the German occupation of that country were partly resolved by added government grants to mission schools and by aid from Christians of other lands through the Orphaned Missions Fund of the International Missionary Council.[113]

The Japanese conquest brought striking developments in the Protestant churches. The internment or death of Dutch missionaries deprived the churches of that kind of aid. Following the pattern which they adopted in Japan for more convenient control by the state, the Japanese authorities required all the churches in a particular area to come together and to receive no foreign aid.[114]

Somewhat similar changes were seen in the Roman Catholic Church during World War II. Because of the German occupation of the Netherlands, no funds or personnel could be obtained from the latter. In the Dutch East Indies the laity came to the rescue financially and a central committee was formed to help meet the most urgent needs. A Javanese Jesuit was consecrated bishop and placed in charge of a vicariate apostolic.[115] In 1941 two Indonesians in the missions in charge of the Society of the Divine Word were ordained priests,

112 The International Review of Missions, Vol. XXXI (1942), pp. 322, 328.
113 Ibid., Vol. XXXI, p. 21 (January, 1942); information given the author by a secretary of the International Missionary Council.
114 The International Review of Missions, Vol. XXXII, p. 15 (January, 1943); Vol. XXXIII, p. 26 (January, 1944).
115 Latourette, op. cit., Vol. VII, p. 207.

the first of their race to be so honoured in the area entrusted to that congregation.[116]

After the expulsion of the Japanese and during the painful achievement of independence and the civil strife which marked the next sixteen years, Protestantism made distinct gains. In 1957, according to government figures the Protestant community totalled at least 3,286,265.[117] This was approximately twice that of 1931. The number of communicants was much smaller, for many of the Christians had come through mass movements, and the lack of a sufficient body of clergy to give the instruction required for admission to full church membership led to a marked disparity between the two figures.[118] This rate of growth, it will be seen, was far more rapid than that of the population as a whole. Converts were chiefly from animists, although by the mid-1950's about 85,000 were from the Moslem population in Java and were said to constitute the largest body of accessions from Islam to Protestantism.[119]

As was to be expected because of the Dutch origin and connexion, the Protestants were predominantly of the Reformed wing of that branch of the faith. But the large Batak Church owed its beginning and its nourishment to the Rhenish Missionary Society, in which Lutherans and Reformed joined, and in the post-World War II years it had most of its assistance from abroad through the Lutheran World Federation. Protestants were in several groups. The largest was still the former state church, now called the Protestant Church of Indonesia. Disestablished in 1935 and in 1950 deprived of further financial subsidy to its ministry from the government, it was still a loose federation of regional bodies and included Europeans and Indo-Europeans (a minority) as well as Indonesians (a majority). In the mid-1950's its constituents were the Christian Evangelical Church of Minahassa (in North-East Celebes), the Protestant Church of the Moluccas (also known as the Church of Ambon), the Evangelical Protestant Church of Timor, and the Protestant Church in Western Indonesia. Much larger in aggregate membership, but not as near to forming one body as the Protestant Church of Indonesia, were the churches which arose from the missions of the nineteenth and twentieth centuries. Since the colonial government had assigned them particular areas, they tended to be territorial or folk churches. There were also Chinese churches and churches founded through the missionary activities of Indonesian and Chinese-Indonesian churches. Thus the Bataks sent missionaries to the Dyaks on the Indonesian portion of Borneo (Kalimantan) and Sarawak, and the Protestant Church of the Moluccas had representatives among the aborigines in Irian (West New Guinea). By a comity arrangement with the Dutch, the American Methodists

116 *The International Review of Missions*, Vol. XXXII, p. 15 (January, 1943).
117 Thomas, *Indonesia and the Indonesian Church in Today's World*, p. 3.
118 Thomas and Manikam, *The Church in Southeast Asia*, p. 114.
119 *Ibid.*, p. 108.

had been in parts of Sumatra before World War II. The Seventh Day Adventists had also arrived before that war. After the war several American denominations sent missionaries, but by 1962 they had not gathered large numbers.[120]

Indonesian nationalism contributed to an effort to unite the many Protestant bodies, scattered as they were over most of the vast extent of the country. Preliminary steps were taken in 1945, and in 1950 the National Council of Churches in Indonesia (or the Indonesian Council of Churches) was inaugurated with the avowed purpose of achieving a single Protestant church in the nation.[121] It had thirty-one member churches. The majority of Protestants were embraced in it, but some held aloof. However, most of the Chinese churches entered. A council of Chinese churches brought many of the latter together and the four classes (or presbyteries) of that organization were individually members of the National Council.[122] One of the many services of the Indonesian Council of Churches was to give aid to the peoples of Central Celebes uprooted by recent political disturbances.[123] We must also note that in the contests under the Republic of Indonesia Protestants organized a distinct political party. This competed with Moslem, Communist, and other parties and held seats in the national legislature.

A major problem of Indonesian Protestantism was the recruiting and training of an indigenous clergy. In 1962 the numbers were quite inadequate to give pastoral care to the scattered constituency. The gap had partly been filled by the laity, but they could not completely meet the need. Moreover, after World War II and independence foreign personnel had not returned to their earlier strength. Nationalism, and especially antagonism to the Dutch, made difficult the position of reinforcements from abroad, even when visas could be obtained. Encouraging efforts were put forth to fill the gap. The major ones were located in strategic centres in the widely separated areas in which Christians were found. In Sumatra was the theological faculty of Nommensen University, founded by the Bataks in 1954 and in 1957 having about a hundred students in various grades, but with only approximately twenty-five college graduates. Jakarta Theological College, in the nation's capital, was the only union theological school in the country on a university level. It was under the administrative authority of the National Council of Churches and in 1957 its student body numbered not far from eighty. The Jogjakarta Theological School in Central Java was largely controlled by the theologically conservative Christian Reformed Church. The Union Theological School in Makassar in Celebes was a post-

---

[120] *Ibid.*, pp. 108–116; Hallock, *East from Burma*, p. 64; Freytag, *Kirchen im neuen Asien*, p. 36.
[121] Thomas and Manikam, *op. cit.*, pp. 116, 117.
[122] Hallock, *op. cit.*, p. 60.
[123] *The International Review of Missions*, Vol. XLVII, p. 18 (January, 1958).

World War II merger of fourteen pre-war theological schools in Eastern Indonesia and served about 1,500,000 Protestants in that area. The Ambon Theological School trained clergy for the Moluccas, the earliest centre of Protestant strength.[124]

As in many other countries, Protestantism placed great emphasis on schools and hospitals. In the 1950's more than 1,500 schools were Christian in the sense that they had been founded by the churches and that their teachers were either Christians or were sympathetic to Christianity. They had been subsidized by the colonial government and aid was continued under the republic. So, too, the state had given most of the money for erecting the physical plants of the hospitals and assisted their budgets.[125]

One indication of the vigour of Indonesian Protestantism and of the growing sense of fellowship among the Protestants of South and East Asia was the requests which came to the Indonesian Council of Churches for personnel to serve in the churches in the Philippines, Sarawak, Malaya, and New Caledonia.[126]

Although Roman Catholics were not as numerous as Protestants in Indonesia, in the post-World War II decade and a half they also increased. In 1959 they were said to total 1,176,693, or about double the figure of 1937.[127] While in the two years which ended in June, 1959, they reported 63,701 adult baptisms, these were not as many in proportion to the membership as in Burma, Laos, or South Vietnam during those years; but percentage-wise they were more than in Thailand, Malaya, Cambodia, or the Philippines.[128] In 1958 more than half the Indonesian Roman Catholics were on the island of Flores. Most of the Roman Catholic missionaries were teachers or doctors. On the whole they were said to give better higher education and medical care than the Protestants. In the years which followed World War II Roman Catholic missionaries went to areas where under the Dutch regime they had not been admitted—on the principle of not permitting them in sections where Protestantism was already represented. Among other places they were in Sumatra seeking to win the Bataks and on the island of Bali. Indigenous personnel was slow in emerging and the difficulty of obtaining visas kept down the number of missionaries from abroad. In 1960, except in Flores and Portuguese Timor, the Roman Catholic Church was admittedly still young and weak.[129] In 1953 the Portuguese portion of Timor had 53,725 baptized Roman Catholics in contrast with 270,000 Protes-

---

[124] Allen, *A Seminary Survey*, pp. 121–130. See also on theological education *The South East Asia Journal of Theology*, Vol. II, pp. 43–48 (April, 1960).

[125] Thomas and Manikam, *op. cit.*, p. 113.

[126] *The International Review of Missions*, Vol. L, p. 17 (January, 1961).

[127] *Worldmission Fides Service*, January 18, 1961.

[128] *Ibid.*

[129] *Worldmission*, Vol. IX, pp. 88–95 (Winter, 1958).

tants on the portion which was in the Republic of Indonesia.[130]

In 1961 Pope John XXIII instituted an ecclesiastical hierarchy for Indonesia in place of vicariates apostolic. Six ecclesiastical provinces were created, each with suffragan dioceses. Two of the archbishops were Indonesians, but most of the hierarchy were foreigners. The Indonesian Roman Catholic Church was still suffering from a shortage of indigenous clergy.[131]

The British portions of the East Indies were in North-West Borneo and the adjacent islands. As before World War II, they consisted of Sarawak, a crown colony; Brunei, a protectorate, administratively distinct from Sarawak since 1959 and a source of petroleum and rubber; and North Borneo, a crown colony to which the island of Labuan was added in 1946. The total population in the 1950's was about 1,200,000. Many of the people were Chinese. Protestantism was represented chiefly by the Anglicans and the American Methodists. The latter had come originally to minister to Chinese colonists but had as well reached out to the Dyaks. The Anglicans also had Chinese and Dyaks among their members and indigenous clergy were emerging. The Japanese occupation during World War II was a temporary interruption. In the 1950's Protestant membership grew but it was still less than one in a hundred of the population.[132] Roman Catholics had approximately the same numerical strength.[133] This meant that in 1960 Protestants and Roman Catholics together constituted about one per cent. of the population.

THE STORM-TOSSED AND INDEPENDENT PHILIPPINES

The setting in the Philippines was a combination of mounting nationalism issuing in political autonomy, Japanese conquest followed by the expulsion of the Japanese, the final accomplishment of independence, the Communist threat, and a burgeoning population. In 1935, following favourable action by the Congress of the United States, the Philippines adopted a constitution which gave them commonwealth status with the reservation of some powers to the United States. The Japanese invasion coincided with the attack on Pearl Harbour in December, 1941. After stubborn resistance by Filipinos and Americans, Japan took possession of Manila and of most of the islands. In 1945 the Japanese were expelled, but both the conquest and the expulsion were accompanied by much destruction of property. The following year, carrying out the time schedule which had been set up in 1934, the Philippines became fully independent. The damages inflicted by the war were rapidly repaired. Communism proved a threat

---

[130] *De Katholieke Encyclopaedie*, Vol. XXIII, p. 145.

[131] *Worldmission Fides Service*, January 25, 1961.

[132] Latourette, *op. cit.*, Vol. VII, p. 207; *World Christian Handbook, 1957*, p. 24; World Council of Churches, *Monthly Letter about Evangelism* (Geneva, mimeographed), March, 1960.

[133] *Worldmission Fides Service*, February 10, 1961.

and fed, as elsewhere, on the unrest which accompanied poverty. By 1962 that threat, as an internal one, had largely subsided. Yet the pressure of population which was one of the causes of poverty persisted. In 1903 the population was 7,637,000, in 1918 it was 10,314,000, and in 1959 it was estimated as 24,718,000.

On the eve of 1914 the religious situation in the Philippines differed from that in any other portion of South-East Asia and the fringing islands. Here were more who called themselves Christians than in all the rest of the region —and, indeed, in all East Asia. The large majority of the population were Roman Catholics. That was the result of the Spanish rule, which had been ended in 1898 by annexation to the United States. The Spanish occupation in the sixteenth century had as its primary object not trade but the expansion of the Christian faith. Long before the end of the nineteenth century the bulk of the Filipinos had become Roman Catholics. A few thousand, mostly in the mountains, remained animists. Moslems, usually called Moros, were a strong minority. They were in the South and were the fruits of the spread of Islam which had won most of the Malays and of the peoples of the East Indies to that religion. The Roman Catholic Church was already facing a grave crisis when American rule confronted it with additional problems. It had been slow to develop an indigenous clergy, partly, as in the Americas, out of a belief that neither members of the native stock nor mestizos could safely be raised to the priesthood. They were held to be morally unfit because of the remnants of paganism and the enervating effects of the tropical climate. Some attempts were made to remedy the lack, especially when after the expulsion of Jesuits in the eighteenth century the Archbishop of Manila tried to fill the parishes formerly in their care by recruiting Filipinos. But the quality of the Filipino seculars was so low that they were looked upon with distrust and contempt. In 1870, out of the 792 parishes in the Philippines only 181, and they considered the least desirable, were in the hands of Filipino priests.[134]

On the eve of the American annexation Filipino nationalism gave rise to the *Iglesia Filipina Independiente* (Independent Catholic Church of the Philippines or the Filipino Independent Church). Filipinos had been increasingly restive under the domination of the Spanish regulars. The latter had accomplished the conversion of the islands. They owned a large proportion of the land and filled the high ecclesiastical posts. Growing Filipino nationalism resented their monopoly and asked Rome to appoint Filipinos to the episcopate, but Rome declined. Disappointed, on his return the envoy sent to the Vatican to present the request led in a movement to create a national church. A Filipino priest, Gregorio Aglipay y Labayan, had been appointed by Aguinaldo, who led the movement for political independence, to direct the national church which had sought approval of Rome. Over his protests, Aglipay was elected

[134] *Worldmission*, Vol. X, pp. 100 ff. (Winter, 1959–1960).

head of the schismatic body. He was called archbishop and several Filipino priests were elected bishops. Many Filipino priests and hundreds of thousands of Filipino Roman Catholics went with them. Under the influence of European liberalism a creed was adopted which had kinship with Unitarianism. Understandably, the members of the *Iglesia Filipina Independiente* and their leaders were excommunicated by Rome. The new church permitted the clergy to marry and put the liturgy into the vernacular. It took possession of many of the church buildings on the ground that they rightly belonged to the Filipino people. A decision in the civil courts deprived it of most of the structures to which it laid claim. In 1918, however, it still had about a seventh of the church edifices of the country. But it faced difficulties in recruiting and training a body of clergy. In view of the previous low quality of most of the indigenous priests this was not surprising.[135]

As a fruit of Filipino nationalism, other religious movements arose, at least one of them before the American occupation, which were much farther removed from historic Christianity than was the *Iglesia Filipina Independiente*. They attracted fewer followers than did the latter.[136]

After annexation by the United States the majority of the Spanish regulars died or left the country. In 1903 only 246 remained as compared with more than 1,000 in 1898. Negotiations between the Vatican and the American authorities led to the purchase (1903) by the civil government of over 410,000 acres of lands owned by the regulars, and the settlement gave the orders large funds and diverted from them much of the popular animosity which had been engendered by ecclesiastical landlordism. Rome agreed to replace some of the Spanish bishops with Americans and to prevent the return to the islands of friars who were personally obnoxious to their flocks. American Archbishops of Manila were appointed and several Filipino priests who had not gone with the Aglipayan schism were raised to the episcopate. Numbers of priests came from the United States—although several, discouraged by the difficulties in adjusting to the situation, returned to America. Several non-Spanish orders and congregations sent representatives to the Philippines. Many of the church schools were reorganized to meet the altered conditions and new ones were opened.[137]

Soon after the transfer of the Philippines to the United States, Protestant missionaries from several of the larger American denominations began to arrive. With the exception of the Episcopalians, who did not wish to seek mem-

135 Latourette, *op. cit.,* Vol. V, pp. 267, 268; Thomas and Manikam, *op. cit.,* pp. 33, 34; Pedro De Achutegui and Miguel A. Bernad, *Religious Revolution in the Philippines. Life and Church of Gregorio Aglipay.* Vol. I, *From Aglipay's Birth to His Death* (Manila, Ateneo de Manila, 1960, pp. xvi, 580), *passim.*

136 Latourette, *op. cit.,* Vol. V, pp. 268, 269.

137 *Ibid.,* pp. 272, 273. On the Society of the Divine Word, one of the new congregations to arrive, see Joh. Thauren, *Die Missionen auf den Philippinen in den Prov. Abra, Mindoro und Zumbalez* (Post Kaldenkirchen, Missionsdruckerei, Steyl, 1931, pp. 32), pp. 9 ff.

bers from the Roman Catholic Church on the ground that this would be proselytizing from another Christian church, and who confined their efforts to caring for Americans and to missions among the animistic non-Christian peoples in the mountains, American Protestant missions were directed chiefly to the nominal Roman Catholics. By the year 1914 they had 204 missionaries and 46,444 communicants.[138] The former were almost entirely from the United States.

World War I brought almost no changes in the developments begun in 1898. The Japanese occupation during World War II with its fighting and its destruction of property was an interruption, but recovery was rapid and no basic shifts in emphases by the churches followed.

The Roman Catholic Church continued its adjustment to the conditions brought by the revolutionary age through the American regime and the strong Filipino nationalism which issued in political independence. In 1934 a Filipino was made Archbishop of Manila, the highest ecclesiastical post in the country. By 1936 the majority of the parishes were in the charge of Filipino priests, and of the ten bishops seven were Filipinos, two were Americans, and only one was a Spaniard.[139] In 1957 twenty-four of the fifty-seven bishops and archbishops were Filipinos.[140] In 1960 a Filipino was created cardinal. In 1937 Filipinos were gratified by the choice of Manila for an International Eucharistic Congress.[141] National Eucharistic Congresses followed at intervals and helped to stimulate the devotion of the Roman Catholic constituency. Under the Commonwealth a chronic source of criticism was eased through the purchase by the state of some of the *haciendas,* the great landed estates, which still belonged to the Church.[142]

The Society of Jesus became more and more domesticated. After its dissolution in the eighteenth century and its restoration in the early part of the nineteenth century, an initial contingent arrived in 1859. But, as was natural, it was Spanish. In 1921 the first American Jesuits reached the islands, and in 1927 the Philippine mission was separated from the Spanish province of Aragon and became dependent on the Maryland-New York province. In 1952 the mission became a vice-province and in 1958 a province. In 1958, of the 442 members of the Society in the Philippines, 195 were Americans and Spaniards and 247 were Filipinos.[143]

In 1959 official figures showed that the Philippines had one priest to about every 6,000 Roman Catholics. The priests totalled 3,087—1,553 seculars, mostly

[138] Latourette, *op. cit.,* Vol. V, pp. 269, 270.
[139] Hayden, *The Philippines,* p. 563.
[140] Allen, *op. cit.,* p. 447.
[141] Hayden, *op. cit.,* p. 564.
[142] *Ibid.,* p. 570.
[143] *Worldmission,* Vol. X, pp. 54–61 (Spring, 1959).

Filipinos, and 1,534 regulars, of whom 1,325 were foreign and 209 were Filipinos.[144] Another report put the average in 1954 as one priest to every 8,359 Roman Catholics and said that a third of the priests were in Manila and that many of them taught in the schools rather than served parishes. Partly because of the shortage of priests it was said that many professedly Roman Catholic Filipinos were in church only three times—to be baptized, to be married, and to be buried.[145] In 1960 Filipino priests were still far short of the requirement for adequate care of the faithful. The complaint was heard that vocations to the priesthood were much too few.[146] The rural areas especially were poorly supplied with priests. Some parishes were said to contain 15,000 or 20,000 Roman Catholics, and many rural communities saw a priest only two or three times a year.[147] Part of the difficulty was reputed to be financial—the lack of funds on the part of students and bishops to meet the cost of education.[148] Although they were far less numerous than Roman Catholics, in 1959 Protestants had more ordained Filipino ministers than the Roman Catholics had Filipino priests.[149] But in the school year 1958–1959 Roman Catholic major seminarians numbered 786 and minor seminarians 1,309, so the prospect was for improvement.[150] Another source put the number of major seminaries and scholasticates in 1956 as 18 with 916 students.[151] In the Philippines the year 1959 was officially declared a missionary year and the hierarchy said that in spite of the needs of their country for clergy they were willing to send missionaries to other lands in Asia. They were encouraged by a growing number of vocations.[152] In 1959 the corner-stone was laid in Rome for a college for Filipino clergy.[153]

In June, 1959, in spite of the protests of Protestants, President Carlos P. Garcia reconsecrated the country to the Sacred Heart of Jesus.[154] In 1959 the Roman Catholics had three radio stations in the Philippines. One of them was used by a bishop in Mindanao to reach his flock, for he had only one priest to every 10,000 members in his diocese.[155]

Catholic Action was introduced in 1939, but it failed to make headway and was reorganized soon after the expulsion of the Japanese. It still did not function as well as its advocates wished, and in 1951 the Episcopal Commission of

[144] *Ibid.*, p. 100 (Winter, 1959–1960).
[145] Allen, *op. cit.*, p. 448.
[146] *Worldmission Fides Service*, June 13, 1959.
[147] Confidential information to the author, November, 1960.
[148] Allen, *op. cit.*, p. 448.
[149] *The Christian Century*, Vol. LXXVI, p. 389 (April 1, 1959).
[150] *Worldmission*, Vol. X, p. 100 (Winter, 1959–1960).
[151] Allen, *op. cit.*, p. 447.
[152] *Worldmission Fides Service*, September 26, 1959.
[153] *Ibid.*
[154] *Ecumenical Press Service*, June 19, 1959.
[155] *Worldmission Fides Service*, September 19, 1959.

the Philippines gave it another structure. The lack of success was attributed to the fact that it had been unitary, a national federation of existing parochial and diocesan organizations, and that better results would be obtained if it was more nearly decentralized.[156]

The *Iglesia Filipina Independiente* continued but did not play as large a part in the religious scene as at its outset. In proportion to the population it was said to have declined from about 13.7 per cent. in 1918 to about 9.8 per cent. in 1939.[157] In 1957 its communicant membership was reported as about 1,500,000, or about 6 per cent. of the population, and its constituency as twice that number.[158] As had been true since its inception, it suffered from a lack of well-educated clergy. During the Japanese occupation a number of its clergy lost their lives and no assistance in achieving recovery came from abroad as had come to Roman Catholicism and Protestantism. The *Iglesia Filipina Independiente* was kept alive more from nationalism and inertia than by inner religious vitality.[159] Many of its members—usually from the better-educated elements— became either Protestants or Roman Catholics. In 1948 three of its bishops received consecration through the Protestant Episcopal Church and thus were in the apostolic succession as held by the Anglican Communion and could transmit it to their fellow bishops.[160] That meant accepting the Apostles' and the Nicene Creeds. Since the original position of the church was Unitarian, a split occurred. On the one hand was the wing which was Trinitarian in its convictions. On the other hand were those, led by a well-educated former secretary of Aglipay, who held to Unitarianism. Some of the younger clergy were trained in the Episcopal theological seminary in Manila and so were better prepared than had been most of their predecessors.[161] The able Isabelo de los Reyes, Jr., son of a prominent Filipino lawyer, as *Obispo Maximo* put the church on its feet after World War II.[162]

Protestantism continued to grow rapidly, both in numbers and in proportion to the population. The communicants reported rose from 46,444 in 1914[163] to 334,000 in 1957.[164] If these figures are correct, they indicate that while the population had increased about three fold, Protestants had multiplied between seven and eight fold. The gains were due partly to an excess of births over

[156] Victor J. Sevilla, *A Guide to Catholic Action in the Philippines* (Pasay City, The Pious Society of St. Paul, pp. xv, 182), pp. 80 ff.
[157] Hayden, *op. cit.*, pp. 572, 573.
[158] *World Christian Handbook, 1957*, p. 57.
[159] Hayden, *op. cit.*, p. 573.
[160] Allen, *op. cit.*, p. 135; Neill, *Anglicanism*, p. 374.
[161] Neill, *op. cit.*, p. 356.
[162] *The Christian Century*, Vol. LXXVIII, pp. 550, 551 (May 3, 1961).
[163] Beach and St. John, *World Statistics of Christian Missions*, p. 67.
[164] *World Christian Handbook, 1957*, p. 59.

deaths but chiefly to conversions. Converts were mostly from the nominal Roman Catholics and the Aglipayans, but some were from the animist minorities.[165] Very few were from the Moros.

Owing to the initiative taken within a few months of the American annexation,[166] several of the major denominations of the United States were mainly responsible for the planting and growth of Protestantism in the Philippines. Outstanding were the Congregationalists, the Northern Presbyterians, the Northern Baptists, the Methodists, and the Disciples of Christ. In 1962 the churches which had arisen through their efforts enrolled about two-thirds of the Protestants. Of the Protestant bodies the largest was the United Church of Christ in the Philippines. It sprang from the efforts of the Northern Presbyterians, the Congregational-Christians, the Evangelicals, the United Brethren, about half the Disciples of Christ churches, and the Philippine Independent Methodist churches.[167] In the course of the decades, a number of other American denominations took root; in the 1950's the one with the largest number of communicants was the Seventh Day Adventist Church.

In 1939 the Philippine Federation of Evangelical Churches was formed. It represented the Philippines in the International Missionary Council[168] and eventually embraced the large majority of the Protestants. Much emphasis was placed on recruiting and training an indigenous clergy. In the 1950's more than half the theological students in institutions of high academic standards were in two schools supported by more than one denomination. The larger was the Union Theological Seminary in Manila, in which a number of churches joined. Next was the Silliman University College of Theology, in which the Congregationalists and the (Northern) Presbyterians coöperated.[169] Indigenous leadership was coming to the fore. It included some Methodist bishops. In 1959 the first Filipino suffragan bishop of the Episcopal Church was consecrated.[170]

As may be gathered from the preceding paragraphs, the Protestantism of the Philippines differed markedly from that of Latin America. Both were in predominantly Roman Catholic regions where that faith had been planted in the heyday of Spanish and Portuguese colonialism and by missionaries under the auspices of the government of one or the other of these powers. Yet in contrast with Latin America, in the Philippines the large majority of Protestants were in denominations which might be regarded as the "standard" ones in the United

[165] For missions among the animists see Felix M. Keesing and Marie Keesing, *Taming Philippine Headhunters. A Study of Government and of Cultural Change in Northern Luzon* (London, George Allen and Unwin, 1934, pp. 288), pp. 81, 82, 225–233; *Handbooks on the Missions of the Episcopal Church. No. III. Philippine Islands* (New York, The National Council of the Protestant Episcopal Church, Department of Missions, 1923, pp. 58), pp. 27 ff.
[166] Latourette, *op. cit.,* Vol. V, pp. 270–272.
[167] Thomas and Manikam, *op. cit.,* p. 35.
[168] *Ibid.,* p. 37.
[169] Allen, *op. cit.,* p. 135.
[170] *Ecumenical Press Service,* March 13, 1959.

States—Congregational, Presbyterian, Methodist, Baptist, Disciples of Christ, and Episcopal. Coöperation and participation in the Ecumenical Movement were shown by a larger proportion of the Protestants of the Philippines than of Latin America. With one exception, no movement comparable to the Pentecostals attained such dimensions in the Philippines as in Latin America. That exception was the *Iglesia ni Cristo* (Church of Christ). It was founded in 1914 by Felix Manalo, a Filipino, who had been associated at one time or other with the Disciples of Christ, the Seventh Day Adventists, and the Pentecostals. It received no funds or personnel from abroad. It claimed to be strictly Biblical but was non-Trinitarian. It erected large church structures, had orderly services of worship, and held its members to a strict discipline of contributing to the organization and attending church services. In the 1950's it claimed a membership of 4,000,000, but its critics said that it had only 100,000 adherents. Even the latter figure constituted a substantial proportion of the Protestants of the country. It had doctors, lawyers, teachers, and government servants on its rolls as well as many from the humbler classes.[171]

Another contrast with Latin America was the full religious liberty enjoyed by Protestants in the Philippines. This was the policy of the American regime. The government which followed, the Republic of the Philippines, wrote religious freedom into its constitution. Among the educated there was much anti-clericalism, and Freemasonry was strong. Yet the Roman Catholic Church was gaining in strength and in the 1950's most thoughtful Protestant Filipinos regarded it as a greater threat to their branch of the faith than Communism.[172] Under the Republic Roman Catholics were participating actively in politics. They were endeavouring to control the state schools and to introduce in them required instruction in their faith. Although provision was made for optional religious teaching in school buildings outside school hours on Saturdays and Sundays, and in the 1950's about a third of the pupils in elementary grades were electing it, the Roman Catholic authorities insisted that this was not enough and were seeking to take the direction of public education out of the hands of what they declared to be free-thinking Masons.

The brief, almost statistical summary to which we have been constrained to limit our account gives only a slight hint of the vigour in Filipino Protestantism. Although in 1962 it still received assistance from abroad in personnel and funds, a large proportion of its churches were self-supporting. It was touching the country through a variety of channels—in education, in social service of many kinds, in medical care, in improving family life, in raising the status of women, and in spreading the faith.[173] It was sending missionaries to other countries;

[171] D. A. McGavran to the author, June, 1956; McGavran, *How Churches Grow*, p. 158.
[172] Thomas and Manikam, *op. cit.*, pp. 40, 41.
[173] For a summary of the contribution of one denomination see Lerrigo, *Baptists in Thailand and the Philippines*, pp. 52–72. For efforts to solve the problems posed by industry see *The International Review of Missions*, Vol. L, pp. 165–172 (April, 1961).

The Twentieth Century Outside Europe

in the 1950's Filipino Protestants were going as missionaries to Malaya, Okinawa, Indonesia, Korea, and Hawaii.[174]

The Philippines saw the beginnings of a unique Protestant enterprise which eventually attained world-wide proportions. In 1915 Frank Charles Laubach (1884——) was sent to Mindanao as a Congregational missionary and there became interested in the Moros. But he was transferred to Manila and taught in the Union Theological Seminary. Late in 1929 he returned to Mindanao, made friends among the Moros, and began a programme for teaching them to read. He did it partly by a technique based upon sympathetic understanding and love. He adopted as a slogan "Each one teach one." He trained teachers and prepared and issued simple books and periodicals. So successful and popular was the programme that it was taken up elsewhere in the Philippines and eventually by the government. In the course of the years Laubach travelled through much of the world—in India, Latin America, awakening Africa, and the islands of the Pacific—introducing his method for teaching illiterates. In many places it was adopted by the state, if not in its complete form at least with modifications. Through all the years Laubach made much of prayer. He believed that it was through prayer that the initial vision and resolution had come to him and he depended on prayer for continued guidance and for opening closed doors. Whenever he returned to Mindanao he was enthusiastically received by his first pupils and the Moro community.[175]

PROTESTANTS FORM A COMPREHENSIVE ORGANIZATION IN EAST ASIA

One of the striking developments of the post-World War II years was the formation of the East Asia Christian Conference. Although embracing more than South-East Asia and the fringing islands, it was centred in that region. It was the expression of a purpose of Protestants to come together, not for protection against the alien environment in which they were set, but to act unitedly to bring the Gospel in all its manifold applications to the millions of their neighbours.

A foreshadowing was seen at the Madras meeting of the International Missionary Council in 1938, when the suggestion was made that a Far Eastern office of that body be established. World War II brought postponement, but in 1949, at the instance of the National Christian Councils of India and Japan,

[174] Hogg, One World, One Mission, pp. 147, 148.
[175] Marjorie Medary, Each One Teach One. Frank Laubach, Friend to Millions (London, Longmans, Green and Co., 1954, pp. vii, 227), passim; Frank C. Laubach, Teaching the World to Read. A Handbook for Literacy Campaigns (New York, Friendship Press, 1947, pp. ix, 246), passim; Frank C. Laubach, Thirty Years with the Silent Billion Adventuring in Literacy (New York, Fleming H. Revell Co., 1960, pp. 383), passim.

what was called the Eastern Asia Christian Conference met in Bangkok.[176] Following that gathering Rajah B. Manikam, then a secretary of the National Christian Council of India and later to be the first Indian Lutheran bishop, was appointed jointly by the International Missionary Council and the World Council of Churches as their representative in East Asia. That step helped to pave the way for an inclusive regional organization. In the summer of 1955, aided by a grant from a Chinese business man, a small representative group met in Hong Kong and formed the Asia Council on Ecumenical Mission. In March, 1957, a larger representative gathering convened in Prapat, Indonesia, in the heart of the Batak country. Delegates came from the Protestant churches of India, Pakistan, Ceylon, Burma, Malaya, Singapore, Indonesia, Thailand, the Philippines, Taiwan, and Japan. Churches in South Vietnam and Hong Kong sent observers. A few attended from the West, but only as consultants. In the organization which emerged Australians and New Zealanders were included. The meeting was preceded by a study conference on rapid social change. The theme adopted for the new project was "the common evangelistic task in the churches of East Asia." In May, 1959, a gathering was held in which the East Asia Christian Conference was formally inaugurated and its constitution adopted. It dealt with such topics as the resurgence of non-Christian religions, Christian witness in the midst of social change, and outreach beyond a church's geographic frontiers. Most of the churches involved were small minorities. They might have been content to lead ghetto existences. Instead, in discovering one another they sought to reach out to the hundreds of millions of non-Christians about them. From them were going more and more missionaries, some of whom we have noted. Although funds from the West were still coming to aid the project, the Asian churches were increasing their giving. Significantly, representatives of the newly formed All-Africa Church Conference, of which we are to hear later, were present. The East Asia Christian Conference officially described itself as "an organ of continuing coöperation among the churches and the National Christian Councils in East Asia, within the framework of the wider Ecumenical Movement."[177]

Other phases of the challenge of the revolutionary age were faced by Protestants in special gatherings. Thus in 1958 what was described as the first Asian conference on industrial evangelism met in Manila. It was sponsored by the

[176] *The Christian Prospect in Eastern Asia. Papers and Minutes of the Eastern Asia Christian Conference, Bangkok, December 3–11, 1949* (New York, Friendship Press, 1950, pp. iv, 156), *passim.*

[177] Hogg, *op. cit.*, pp. 139–142; *The Common Evangelistic Task of the Churches in East Asia (Papers and Minutes of the East Asia Christian Conference, Prapat, Indonesia, March 17–26, 1957)* (no place or date, pp. 167), *passim; Report on East Asia Christian Inaugural Conference, Kuala Lumpur, Malaya, May 14–24, 1959* (mimeographed); *The International Review of Missions,* Vol. XLIX, p. 12 (January, 1960).

East Asia Christian Conference in coöperation with the World Council of Churches and the International Missionary Council.[178]

SUMMARY

In spite of involvement in two world wars and in the wave of revolt against Western colonialism and imperialism, in the half-century which was ushered in by the outbreak of the First World War Christianity continued the growth in South-East Asia and the fringing islands which had been marked in the nineteenth century. In most areas its proportionate numerical gains were greater than the increases in the total populations which were a striking feature of the period. This was true of both the Roman Catholic Church and Protestantism. Along with numerical advances went a deeper rootage in the several countries. A mounting proportion of the clergy and of the higher ecclesiastical officials —bishops or their equivalent—were nationals. Progress was made in self-government and in national organizations—for the Roman Catholics through ecclesiastical hierarchies in place of vicars and prefects apostolic; for Protestantism through Christian councils of churches or federations of churches, and, on a more inclusive scale, the East Asia Christian Conference. In a variety of ways Christians were seeking not only to win non-Christians but also to influence wholesomely the cultures about them and to face constructively the changes being wrought by the currents of the revolutionary age.

Sobering facts tempered the optimism which these advances might have created. Christianity was losing in areas which had passed under Communist control—most strikingly in North Vietnam. The Christians were still drawn predominantly from animistic peoples. No great accessions had come from Buddhism and Islam, the chief high religions of the region, and these two faiths, especially Buddhism, were displaying revivals and were associated with the swelling nationalism. Christianity was regarded by millions—when they thought about it at all—as alien and a phase of Western cultural imperialism. Because of the "population explosion," millions more non-Christians were in the area than in 1914. That gains had been made by Christianity must be obvious to all who were acquainted with the over-all picture. But that Christianity was still a movement of minorities, most of them small and not of the dominant elements, is also clear. Particularly disturbing was the spread of Communism and the fate of Christianity in the areas under Communist regimes.

[178] To Understand Christian Responsibility in the Asian Industrial Awakening. Report on the First Asian Conference on Industrial Evangelism. Manila, Philippines, June 2–13, 1958 (no place or date, pp. 29).

CHAPTER XIII

The Course in War-Smitten, Revolutionary China

THE SETTING

IN NO other part of the globe was the revolutionary age marked by more drastic changes than in China. Here was the most numerous segment of mankind. At the outset of the nineteenth century its population was generally given as 400,000,000. By 1962 it was said to be approximately 650,000,000. This was more than its largest Asian neighbour, India, had, even if the Republic of India and Pakistan were taken together. It was also more than were in all the Americas, all Europe, or all Africa. Here had been a high civilization, one of the greatest in its originality and in the richness of its achievements that had been produced by men. Chinese culture had profoundly influenced all East Asia, especially Korea and Japan. Again and again China had been the centre of one of the mightiest empires on the globe. Immediately before and after the beginning of the Christian era it had rivalled the Roman Empire in wealth, geographic extent, and civilization. In the seventh and eighth centuries the only empire which approached it in territorial extent, in brilliance of culture, and in wealth was that of the Arabs. In the eleventh century no other realm was as fertile in creative art and thought, or as wealthy. In the eighteenth century China covered a larger area and had more people than any other empire of the day. Upon this ancient people with its memorable past the revolutionary age thrust itself with shattering force.

The initial impact came in the sixteenth, seventeenth, and eighteenth centuries. The effects then were chiefly in the introduction of new food plants from the Americas, which contributed to the doubling of the population, the reduction of more land to cultivation, and extensive soil exhaustion on the uplands. The more immediately obvious results began to be seen in the nineteenth century and mounted as that century drew to its close. The repeated defeat of China in wars with Western countries, the contribution to the T'ai P'ing movement, which devastated some of the richest provinces, the encroachments on the empire's sovereignty by what her people denounced as the "unequal treaties," the cessions of territory, leaseholds on other portions, spheres of influence which threatened partition, the humiliating defeat by Japan in the 1890's, the reduction of the empire to the status of a foreign-occupied country following the Boxer outbreak, and the war between Russia and Japan fought mostly on Chinese soil while the Chinese stood helplessly by—all these came in such appallingly quick succession that many of the thoughtful were convinced that if the country was not to be permanently reduced to vassalage a radical internal transformation was imperative. In the last third of the nineteenth century the attempt to restore the old with some slight adjustments to revolutionary forces which were impinging on the empire had palpably failed.

On the eve of World War I the fabric of Chinese culture was rapidly crumbling. The traditional civil service examinations and the kind of education which prepared for them were abolished. Western forms of education were introduced to equip the Chinese with the learning of the revolutionary age. Thus the system that had inculcated the ideology called, rather loosely, Confucianism was thrown into the dust bin and with it went the standards by which Chinese civilization had been shaped for two thousand years. In 1911–1912 the Manchus who had ruled China since the middle of the seventeenth century were swept aside. More important, so was the traditional imperial structure, which had been built on indigenous philosophies, chiefly Confucianism and secondarily Legalism, and which had survived the rise and fall of more than twenty dynasties. The country was now called a republic, a Western form of government with which the nation had had no experience.

During the two decades immediately following the outbreak of World War I the Chinese floundered about in bungling attempts to achieve national unity and a set of institutions which would enable them to regain their independence and win the respect of other peoples. Technically they were participants in World War I, but for them the chief immediate results were the menace of Japan, already entrenched in Manchuria and seeking other gains, and, as it later proved, the capture of Russia by the Communists. What was called the New Tide or, by some, the Chinese Renaissance was a confused set of efforts by intellectuals to formulate philosophies as the desperately needed foundations to replace what was disappearing, and to devise a form of the language which would aid in educating the masses. Chinese nationalists pressed for the abolition of extraterritoriality and control over the tariff rates, the relinquishment by foreigners of the "settlements" and "concessions" in the treaty ports, notably in Shanghai, and the removal of foreign post offices. China's participation in World War I, the defeat of the Central Powers, and the collapse of the tsarist regime in Russia brought a breach in the solid wall of foreign privilege, for the post-war treaties with Germany and Austria did not contain extraterritoriality or restore the concessions and leaseholds held by Germany, and Communist Russia renounced extraterritoriality and other special privileges in China—an act which chiefly inconvenienced the anti-Communists who constituted almost all the Russians in that country. Chinese employed boycotts on foreigners and foreign commerce to obtain their desires. By 1930 China had won the removal of foreign post offices, full authority to fix its customs dues, and some of the British "concessions." The reorganization of the educational system to take account of the Western science of the revolutionary age proceeded apace, and thousands of Chinese youths went to Europe, America, and Japan to drink from the springs of the "new learning."

Internally, for more than a decade after the inauguration of the republic the political situation rapidly deteriorated. Numbers of "warlords" made themselves masters of areas large and small and fought one another for the control of the country. By the mid-1920's only the shadow of a central government survived.

Political integration began in 1924. The foreign-educated Sun Yat-sen, who had come to prominence in the revolution which unseated the Manchus, organized the *Kuomintang* (usually translated the Nationalist Party). In this he had the advice of Russian Communists, but he was not a Communist. The *Kuomintang* adopted the programme which Sun Yat-sen had outlined in his book, the *San Min Chu I* (*The Three People's Principles*). Sun died in 1925 and the effective leadership of the *Kuomintang* was taken by his warm admirer, Chiang Kai-shek, a military man who had had part of his education in Japan. Under the command of Chiang Kai-shek, "the Generalissimo," in 1926 the armies of the *Kuomintang* moved north from their headquarters in Canton and by June, 1928, had made themselves masters of much but not all of the country. The capital was established in Nanking. In the course of his northward campaign, Chiang broke with the Communists and they continued in stubborn opposition.

Had the Japanese not interfered, the *Kuomintang,* with Chiang as its dominant figure, might have brought all China together under a government which combined aspects of Western democracy, Sun Yat-sen's Three Principles of the People, and some of the heritage of the older China. Chiang was gradually eliminating or making his peace with the rival warlords. He so vigorously pressed his campaign against the Communists (who had set up a government south of the Yangtze) that they felt it wise to transfer their headquarters to Yenan, a remote town in the North-west, a step which they took by a famous "long march" over a circuitous inland route inaccessible to Chiang's forces. In an effort to unify all China, Chiang and his fellow Nationalists were seeking to extend their control over Manchuria. Since the revolution of 1911–1912 Manchuria had been independent of Peking under a powerful warlord. The latter had been removed by violent death (1926) and had been followed by his son, a much weaker character. Since taking the Russian leaseholds in South Manchuria in 1905 the Japanese had been developing the resources of the region.

When the Nationalists attempted to counter them, in September, 1931, the Japanese suddenly lashed out, quickly seized all Manchuria, and engineered the setting up of a puppet government which they called Manchukuo. In the following years they sought to extend their control over much of the northern part of China.

Resentment in China against Japanese aggression increased. From its capital in Nanking the *Kuomintang* made progress in strengthening its regime. The Communists were still a threat but in face of the common menace of Japan they and the Nationalists reached a truce, temporary as it proved. Anti-Japanese agitation and boycotts mounted. In July, 1937, set off by an armed clash near Peking, the Japanese began a full-scale invasion of China. The Nationalist Government was forced to retreat inland and eventually fixed its capital at Chungking, in the far West. The Japanese set up a rival puppet regime in Nanking, but it evoked little loyalty among the Chinese. The United States opposed the actions of the Japanese as undermining the autonomy and territorial integrity of China to which its Open Door policy had committed it. Step by step it sought to restrain the Japanese by public utterances and by restrictions on the shipping of war materials to them.

In December, 1941, Japan struck in a dramatic attack on the American navy in Pearl Harbour in Hawaii. Within a few hours the United States, Great Britain, and the Netherlands East Indies formally declared war on Japan. Australia quickly followed. For the first few months of 1942 the tide seemed to be running for Japan. Hong Kong fell. British and Dutch power were seemingly erased in South-East Asia and the East Indies. The Philippines were overrun. French Indo-China, Siam, and Burma were in Japanese hands. Some of the Pacific Islands were seized. Australia was threatened. The United States, Great Britain, the U.S.S.R., and their colleagues had their hands too full with curbing the Germans and their associates in Europe to give much aid to the beleaguered Chinese. The Nationalists were approaching exhaustion, and the Communists, carrying on a guerrilla war, could do little more than hold their own in portions of the North-west. Moreover, Nationalists and Communists, while in theory joining forces against the invaders, eyed each other with ill-concealed animosity.

Gradually the Japanese were halted in their wide advance, but aid could be sent to the Chinese only across the difficult terrain of high mountains and deep gorges which separated them from Burma and India. In 1944 the plight of the Nationalists, who bore the main brunt of the Japanese attack, was more desperate than at any time.

The defeat and surrender of Japan in the summer of 1945 owed more to frontal attack from the sea than to the Chinese. The Nationalists were exhausted and, but for the aid of their Western associates, mainly the Americans, would probably have been crushed. As was natural in their position, in spite of some honest and high-minded men, their ranks were honeycombed with corruption. In their attempt to occupy the territory which the Japanese were evacuating they were handicapped by inefficiency and self-seeking. They had never controlled all of China and in their efforts to undertake that task and to repair the damage done by the long years of war they were confronted by the impossible. Popular disgust quickly mounted. Such remnants of confidence as existed were dissipated by run-away inflation which the Nationalists were unable to curb.

The one viable alternative to the discredited Nationalist regime was the Communists. In their haven in the North-west where the Japanese had been unable to reach them, they had developed a disciplined party and army led by men hardened by long adversity, and united in fanatical loyalty to a Communist ideology. Their outstanding leader was Mao Tse-tung, of rural parentage and a revolutionist from boyhood. The Russians, at first distrustful, recognized them as the government of China and cut off diplomatic connexions with the Nationalists. In 1946 the United States through a special envoy, George C. Marshall, attempted to bring the Nationalists and the Communists together in a coalition government, but reciprocal antagonism and conflicting ambitions proved insuperable and a truce quickly broke down. Fighting between the Communists and Nationalists continued. The Communists won most of the battles. On October 1, 1949, they proclaimed a national government, "the People's Republic of China." The next February a thirty-year pact of friendship and mutual aid was negotiated with the U.S.S.R. Both the Chinese and the Russians stressed the friendship between the two regimes. Russian became the second language, supplanting English. Russian technical experts assisted in developing Chinese economy. The Nationalists were defeated and driven southward. Eventually they took refuge in Taiwan (Formosa) and there continued the government which they insisted was the only legitimate one for all China. They were protected by the United States and through that powerful support continued to hold China's seat in the United Nations, both in the Assembly and in the Security Council.

Masters of the mainland, the Communists set about the reorganization of the country after their pattern. They entered upon a programme of "land reform," by which the holdings of the landlords were redistributed among the former tenants. They sought to eliminate the last traces of Confucianism. The Confucian educational system and the Confucian state had previously disappeared. The Confucian family with its loyalties was now held up to scorn. In the process several hundred thousand, probably millions, of those accused of supporting the old order were killed, many of them after public mass trials. The Communists denounced what they dubbed "imperialism" in its political, cultural, and economic forms. To them the United States was the chief enemy and they made as a prerequisite to reconciliation the removal of American assistance to the Nationalists and the "liberation" of Taiwan from Nationalist rule. Internally they gave the mainland of China the strongest government that it had known in centuries, perhaps ever. They stopped inflation, put the railways into working order, constructed new ones, set about industrializing the country, organized rural collective farms and then communes, pushed literacy, stressed the preparation of scientists and technicians, promoted public health through campaigns against flies and rats and the preparation of physicians and nurses, cleaned up the cities physically, endeavoured to eliminate professional beggars and prostitutes, strove to utilize the natural resources of the country, and inaugurated colossal enterprises for flood control, irrigation, and hydro-electric power. The cities saw the erection of apartment houses on a vast scale. These and other changes were carried through by high-powered propaganda utilizing radio, moving pictures, the printing press, systematic indoctrination, and forced labour. The Communist Party enlarged its membership and had the country completely under its control. A disciplined army made impracticable popular uprisings or invasion from Taiwan. Under an ideology first developed in London and Russia, China was being completely reshaped. The old China, already undermined, was wiped out and a new China was emerging. Some basic attitudes survived and were even strengthened—among them the religious scepticism of the educated, which now became a militant atheism, and the long tradition that the state must create a society in which the material goods would be available to all, a this-worldly emphasis—but they were given distinctive forms by what men like Mao Tse-tung believed they had derived through Marx and Lenin.

A conviction prominent in the old China was now cherished in ways which sought expressions compatible with the Mao Tse-tung version of Marxism. It held China to be the centre of true civilization and considered that the privilege and obligation of the Chinese was to propagate it until all mankind conformed. This entailed building an empire which would have the broadest dimensions attained by the most powerful dynasties of earlier centuries. Thus support was given to the attempt to conquer all Korea for Communism, to "liberate" Tibet, to claim territories on Tibet's southern borders which the Indians believed to be theirs, to extend Communism into Vietnam and Laos, to develop the natural resources of Sinkiang, and to send experts and give technical assistance to Outer Mongolia. The Communists were emboldened by the fact that through them in Korea in the 1950's for the first time in history Chinese armies defeated Westerners on a large scale. Communist China also reached out into Latin America and Africa. Late in the 1950's strains developed with the U.S.S.R.

Under the Communists, religion, including Christianity, fared badly. In theory the Communists allowed freedom of religious belief, but in practice they made difficult what they regarded as superstition. Their propaganda denounced it. They took the lands which had served as the endowments for Buddhist temples and compelled the Buddhist and the Taoist monks to engage in what they called useful labour. To win the friendship of Buddhist countries they preserved and even repaired some Buddhist monasteries in Peking, but they gave the *coup de grâce* to a religion which in China had been suffering from mortal sickness for a thousand years. The same was true of Taoism. It had long been all but moribund and was easily given the finishing blows. The more popular polytheism and ways of manipulating the unseen spirit forces were not as quickly eliminated, but they, too, were weakening. Islam proved more resistant and could not be dealt with in such summary fashion. Of Christianity we will speak more in detail.

THE RAPID GROWTH OF CHRISTIANITY FROM 1914 TO 1922

From the outbreak of World War I until about 1922 both the Roman Catholic Church and Protestantism continued the rapid advance in China which they had displayed in the second half of the nineteenth century and especially after 1900. With the disappearance of the Confucian monarchy in 1911–1912 and with the hunger for education in the civilization which had enabled Western powers to reduce China to the status of an occupied country, a degree of open-mindedness towards Christianity as associated with that civilization gave to the Christian faith the greatest opportunity in that realm that it had known. Confucianism was disappearing. In spite of some evidences of revival, Buddhism was weak. Taoism was almost on the verge of dying. The popular polytheism and animism could not hope to flourish in the secular age. Could Christianity fill the religious vacuum?

World War I brought a reduction, only temporary as it proved, in the numbers of Roman Catholic missionaries. In 1914 more than half of the foreign priests were French and about a third of the latter were either summoned home to serve in the armed forces or were assigned to East Asia as reservists.[1] The German contingents were not as badly dislocated, but after the armistice under pressure from the Entente a number of German missionaries, along with their compatriots, were expelled from the country.[2] Financial contributions from Europe fell off during the war, and while an increase from the United States more than made good the loss in the Society for the Propagation of the Faith, the Association of the Holy Childhood suffered a marked decrease in revenue

[1] *Zeitschrift für Missionswissenschaft*, Vol. V, p. 73; Vol. VI, p. 246.
[2] Latourette, *A History of Christian Missions in China*, p. 706.

and the work for children which it supported declined sharply. Several schools in China were closed from lack of funds, and some catechumenates which were a means of winning converts were discontinued.[3] In the domestic unrest following the fall of the Manchus a number of missionaries and Christian communities suffered from banditry. Yet on the whole Roman Catholics mounted in number, from a reported total of 1,615,107 in 1914 to 1,963,639 in 1918.[4] Foreign priests increased slightly and Chinese priests markedly. The preparation of the latter was stressed to make up for the paucity of foreign clergy, but in 1916 Chinese priests were still only about half the number of the Western clergy. In 1918 Chinese lay brothers were fewer than brothers of foreign birth, but of the sisters Chinese were almost twice as many as those from abroad. In spite of the shortage of funds, some additional schools were opened and new Roman Catholic newspapers were begun.[5]

In the years immediately after World War I steps were taken to increase the Chinese clergy and to give the Roman Catholic Church a national organization. In 1918 the Chinese priests totalled 834, or about 35 per cent. of the clerical body. In 1923 they were 1,088, which was 41 per cent. of the whole. The number of seminarians mounted from 1,638 in 1913 to 3,022 in 1923.[6] As part of its imperialist ambitions France had long insisted on a protectorate over Roman Catholic missions in China. An attempt in 1918 to circumvent it by establishing diplomatic relations between Peking and the Holy See had been dropped because of the opposition of the Entente, possibly at the instance of France.[7] In 1922 Rome appointed an apostolic delegate to China and although he was received formally by the president, his functions were religious, not diplomatic. In 1923 Costantini, as the apostolic delegate, presided at seven regional synods, and in 1924 a general synod was convened in Shanghai and the missions in China were consecrated to the Virgin Mary.[8]

In the years 1914–1922, as in the nineteenth century, Protestantism displayed an even more striking growth than the Roman Catholic Church. Near the outbreak of World War I Protestant missionaries numbered 5,978, the largest denominational contingent being Presbyterians, with the China Inland Mission a close second, followed by Methodists and Anglicans. In 1914 Protestant communicants were said to total 253,210, with the Presbyterians again leading, Methodists second, the China Inland Mission third, and the Baptists fourth.[9] The baptized community rose from 330,926 in 1915 to 398,760 in 1917 and to

---

[3] Ibid., pp. 707, 708.
[4] Ibid., pp. 709, 710.
[5] Ibid., pp. 711, 712.
[6] Ibid., pp. 725, 730.
[7] Ibid., p. 713.
[8] Ibid., p. 728.
[9] The China Mission Year Book, 1915, appendix, pp. iv, vii.

451,664 in 1920. In 1920 the communicant membership was reported to be 366,524 and the Christian community, which included all the baptized together with those under Christian instruction, 806,926. These figures indicated a growth of about 40 per cent. in five years. The foreign staff had increased, but per-centage-wise less than a third. In the five years the Chinese staff had more than doubled, from 836 in 1915 to 1,745 in 1920.[10] Since most of the foreign personnel and financial support were from the British Isles and the United States, they did not feel the adverse effects of the war as much as did those of the Roman Catholics, predominantly from the Continent of Europe.

In a wide variety of ways Protestants sought to serve the Chinese when a relative openness existed to what Christians from the West had to offer. In 1917 three-fourths of the Protestants were in the seven coastal provinces, evidence of the close association of the spread of that form of the faith with the invading culture from the West[11]—coming as most of it did by the sea routes. Yet in the two decades which followed 1920, proportionately the spread of Protestantism took place more rapidly in the interior than on the seaboard.[12]

From the phenomenal growth in numbers it may be gathered that a major phase of the Protestant effort was winning non-Christians to the faith. As might have been expected from the rising tide of nationalism, much of this came about through indigenous movements. One of several was the Chinese Home Mis-sionary Society, begun near the end of World War I.[13] The methods which had long been followed by the individual churches and missions were the chief means of evangelism. In a number of provinces and cities united efforts were undertaken by the majority of the Protestant forces.[14] Again and again Sher-wood Eddy held mammoth meetings, largely for the intelligentsia and in the leading cities. In at least one of the earliest John R. Mott was also present. They were mainly under the auspices of the YMCA, but usually other Protestant organizations coöperated. In retrospect Eddy believed that they reached their crest in 1914. Eddy's appeal was directed to those who realized China's weak-ness in the revolutionary world. He insisted that basic to renewal was the moral and spiritual reformation of individuals and he held up the Gospel as the means to that end.[15]

Another channel largely utilized by Protestants for spreading the faith and nourishing it among the believers was literature. Literature had many features and was addressed to the educated as well as to the semi-literate. By 1922 the Bible had been translated in whole or in part not only into the language of the

[10] *The Christian Occupation of China,* pp. xc, xci.
[11] *The China Mission Year Book, 1917,* pp. 53–57.
[12] *The Christian Occupation of China,* p. 34.
[13] *The China Mission Year Book, 1923,* pp. 112–115.
[14] *Ibid.,* pp. 121–145.
[15] Eddy, *Eighty Adventurous Years,* pp. 62–81; Latourette, *World Service,* pp. 259–262.

scholars but also into several vernaculars and utilized both the Chinese characters and phonetically devised systems for readers to whom the characters proved an obstacle. The sale of the Scriptures reached a high-water mark in 1914-1916 and thereafter fell off slightly.[16]

Seeing the hunger of the Chinese for the kind of education which would fit their nation to take its place in the revolutionary age, Protestants gave much attention to developing schools, particularly on the more advanced levels. St. John's University, in Shanghai, began and continued by American Episcopalians, and long a leader in Protestant higher education in that metropolis built on commerce with the West, was enlarged in student body and physical equipment.[17] Thanks in no small degree to the vision and energy of Henry W. Luce, an American (Northern) Presbyterian, Shantung Christian University, under its Chinese name Cheeloo University, brought its three components together on one site in Tsinan, the capital of the province, with the beginnings of an adequate physical plant.[18] Larger and also inclusive denominationally, Yenching University, in Peking, had Luce as the vice-president, who raised much of the money. Its chief creator was John Leighton Stuart, an American (Southern) Presbyterian. In it were united four denominational institutions founded in the preceding century by American Methodists, Congregationalists, and Presbyterians, and by English Congregationalists. In 1919, after prolonged consultations, it came into being with Stuart as its president. Stuart had imagination, devotion, and administrative ability, combined with an unusual gift for friendship and the desire to give precedence to the Chinese. He commanded the respect of thousands of Chinese in both high and low position. Under him, with Luce's loyal coöperation, a campus of unusual beauty arose outside the western walls of Peking, with buildings which utilized Chinese architectural traditions adapted to the type of education demanded by the new China.[19] In 1916 Fukien Christian University opened its doors. It, too, came out of prolonged negotiations and was a coöperative undertaking. It occupied a picturesque site on the Min River a short distance below the provincial capital, Foochow.[20] Before 1914, for the most part only a few years before, other institutions, the majority of them undenominational or supported by more than one denomination, had come into being, chiefly, like the others, at American initiative and with American support: Canton Christian College, later Lingnan University; Soochow University (Southern Methodist); the University of Nanking; Ginling College, for women, in Nanking; several institutions in the

---

[16] *The Christian Occupation of China*, pp. 443-456.
[17] Mary Lamberton, *St. John's University, Shanghai, 1879-1951* (New York, United Board for Christian Colleges in China, 1955, pp. ix, 261), pp. 77-98.
[18] B. A. Garside, *One Increasing Purpose. The Life of Henry W. Luce* (New York, Fleming H. Revell Co., 1948, pp. 271), pp. 106-152.
[19] Stuart, *Fifty Years in China*, pp. 49 ff.; Edwards, *Yenching University, passim*.
[20] Scott, *Fukien Christian University*, pp. 3-30.

centre of the Yangtze Valley, which had as its main cities Wuchang, Hankow, and Hanyang (together known as Wuhan); and West China Union University, in Chengtu, the capital of Szechuan, most populous province in the West.[21] All were attempts to aid China in her difficult and painful adjustment to the revolutionary age and, through surrounding the students, presumably the future leaders of China, with Christian influences, to help to permeate the new China with the faith.

Protestants continued to be pioneers in introducing the medical science of the West—one of the striking developments of the revolutionary age. Even before 1914 they had not only ministered to the sick but had also begun the creation of medical and nursing professions which would bring the best of the skills developed in Western Christendom to prevent or alleviate disease in China.[22] The major event between 1914 and 1922 was the founding of the China Medical Board by the Rockefeller Foundation and its creation of the Peking Union Medical College. Taking over the existing Union Medical College in Peking, an interdenominational Protestant institution, it quickly built what soon became the best medical school in China. It was frankly Christian but was undenominational. The cornerstone of the new group of buildings was laid in 1917. The China Medical Board gave financial aid to other Protestant medical institutions, including the Hunan-Yale (soon to be called Hsiang-ya) Medical School in Changsha, the best in Central China.[23]

Several projects for widespread popular education were inaugurated by Protestants. Thus under the YMCA C. H. Robertson created a lecture department (begun in 1911 but developed more extensively after 1914) to demonstrate various forms of Western science which would help to improve individual and group living. William Wesley Peter lectured widely and vividly on public health, at first also under the YMCA, and from his effort came (1915) the Joint Council on Public Health, later (1920) called the Council on Health Education. A Chinese, Y. C. James Yen, devised a method of teaching illiterates to read and through his programme, at first under the YMCA but later under the independent Mass Education Movement, blazed new trails in raising the level of literacy.[24]

Attempts were made to plan inclusively for all forms of Protestant education in China. To this end various organizations had been developed before 1914. In 1922 the China Educational Commission reported on a comprehensive study made the previous year of Christian—primarily Protestant—education in

---

[21] Latourette, *A History of Christian Missions in China*, pp. 627–634.

[22] *Ibid.*, pp. 222, 268, 269, 452–460, 638, 639. See an account by a pioneer in Central China in Edward H. Hume, *Doctors East, Doctors West. An American Physician's Life in China* (New York, W. W. Norton and Co., 1946, pp. 278), *passim.*

[23] Latourette, *A History of Christian Missions in China*, pp. 745, 755.

[24] Latourette, *World Service*, pp. 258, 259.

China. The Commission was an American project and was headed by Ernest D. Burton of the University of Chicago, but its membership was international—Americans, Chinese, and British. It pointed out that although the Protestant community was only about half the size of the Roman Catholic community and only about one-fourth of one per cent. of the population of China, its schools enrolled a fourth more students than did the Roman Catholic institutions and were providing three and seven-tenths per cent. of all the education given in the country. It made recommendations for the better functioning of the Protestant enterprise.[25]

The year 1922 also saw the creation of the National Christian Council of China. It came from the impulse given by earlier all-China missionary conferences and by the (Edinburgh) World Missionary Conference of 1910. In May, 1922, what was called the National Christian Conference convened in Shanghai.[26] Elaborate preparations had been made, including a huge quarto tome, *The Christian Occupation of China,*[27] which had the most detailed and extensive survey of the existing Protestant enterprise in China that ever had been made for that country—or, indeed, for any country. As in other national Christian councils which were organized in connexion with the International Missionary Council, in the National Christian Council of China nationals had a substantial share in the direction. By the 1930's it included the churches in which were three-fifths of the Protestants of China.

Although the National Christian Conference and the National Christian Council brought increased coöperation and added Chinese participation, a serious rift in the Protestant missionary forces handicapped the effort. It arose as a reflection of the contemporary tensions between "fundamentalists" and "liberals" which were especially marked in the United States. It found expression in the Bible Union of China, which had its beginning in 1920 and held its first national convention in Shanghai immediately after the National Christian Conference. By that time it was said to have about 2,000 members. They were predominantly missionaries—reportedly in seventy of the ninety boards then represented in China.[28] The China Inland Mission, conservative theologically, was a member of the National Christian Council but after a few years withdrew (1926).

[25] *Christian Education in China. A Study by an Educational Commission Representing the Mission Boards and Societies Conducting Work in China* (New York, Committee of Reference and Council of the Foreign Missions Conference of North America, 1922, pp. xv, 430), *passim.*

[26] *The China Mission Year Book, 1923,* pp. 35–65; *The Chinese Church as Revealed in the National Christian Conference Held in Shanghai Tuesday, May 2, to Thursday, May 11, 1922* (Shanghai, 1922, pp. viii, xi, 724), *passim.*

[27] *The Christian Occupation of China,* Milton T. Stauffer, editor (Shanghai, China Continuation Committee, 1922, pp. 468, cxii).

[28] *The China Mission Year Book, 1923,* pp. 95–101.

MOUNTING STRESS WITH CONTINUED BUT RETARDED GROWTH, 1923-1937

In retrospect, the decades from the Boxer year into 1922 were seen to be the period of the most rapid and least hampered growth of Christianity in China— so far as by 1962 the scroll of history had been unrolled. Resistance had not ceased. The political changes and the civil wars had brought perils, but under the pressure of the revolutionary age the structure of the inherited Chinese civilization was crumbling and the Chinese, adrift, were groping for answers to their questions, personal and collective. Since Christianity stemmed from that West whence came the forces that were bringing their ancestral culture to the point of collapse, many Chinese were willing to listen to its message, particularly since its concomitants included education, medicine, and other aspects of the invading revolution from which they were seeking to learn.

In the fifteen years between 1922 and the full-scale invasion by Japan which exploded in the summer of 1937, several currents were running which made increasingly difficult the continued spread of Christianity.

One current was the New Tide or the Chinese Renaissance. It had begun before 1922. Connected with it was a religious scepticism and a secularism reinforced by visits from such American and European thinkers as John Dewey and Bertrand Russell. Some who were influenced by it, including several of the outstanding intellectuals who were in the forefront of the current, maintained that the Chinese would be the first people to outgrow religion.[29]

The New Tide contributed to an anti-Christian movement. The first wave came in 1922. Its immediate occasion was a meeting of the World's Student Christian Federation in Peking in the spring of that year, bringing together students from many lands. To counter it an anti-religious federation was formed. Its leaders declared that science and religion were incompatible and that Christianity was a tool of imperialism and capitalism to oppress weaker nations. The publication of *The Christian Occupation of China,* by its title as well as its dimensions, was used to support the latter accusation.

For a time the anti-Christian movement died down, but it reappeared in 1924, supported by student strikes in Christian institutions. It also brought trouble in 1928 and 1929. Nationalism had mounted to fever pitch. Christian education was denounced as destructive of the national spirit and Chinese civilization. The agitators demanded the "restoration of educational rights," the registration with the government of all foreign schools and colleges, and the exclusion of religious teaching from the curriculum of these schools. In 1928 new educational regulations required all foreign-controlled schools desiring government recognition—which was necessary if their graduates were to be employed by the

[29] Hu Shih, *The Chinese Renaissance* (University of Chicago Press, 1934, pp. xi, 110), pp. 78–93; Latourette, *A History of Christian Missions in China,* pp. 691–694.

state—to have at least two-thirds of their governing bodies Chinese, to have principals and presidents of Chinese nationality, to have no teaching of religion in the elementary grades, to make attendance at religious exercises in middle schools and colleges optional, to display a picture of Sun Yat-sen, a copy of his last will and testament, and a Chinese flag, and to hold weekly assemblies in his honour. A national organization was formed, and periodicals, pamphlets, and books supporting the anti-Christian movement poured from the press. Impetus had come from an incident on May 30, 1925, when several Chinese were shot by the foreign police in the International Settlement in Shanghai in an effort to curb a demonstration in favour of some strikers. Nationalistic, especially student, rage against extraterritoriality and other foreign privileges swept across the country and saw in Christianity and particularly in Christian schools a phase of the hated imperialism. Student strikes in Christian schools were frequent. Violence directed against churches was common.[30]

Further accentuating the anti-Christian, anti-missionary movement was the association of the Communists with the *Kuomintang* armies in their northward march in 1926. Radicals denounced missionaries as "imperialists" and "capitalists" and Chinese Christians as "running dogs of the foreign imperialists." In 1927 looting and the destruction of property were seen in a number of centres. In Nanking an attack on foreigners in March of that year was accompanied by the shooting of the (American) vice-president of the University of Nanking.[31] By the summer of 1927 a large number of missionaries had withdrawn from the interior to the coast.[32] Chiang Kai-shek's break with the Communists and their suppression—incomplete and temporary as it proved—relieved the situation for the time being.

The continued civil strife and especially the mounting menace in the areas controlled by revived Communist power brought obstacles in wide regions. The Communists were first strong in the Central South-east—parts of the provinces of Fukien, Kiangsi, and Hunan—and then, after their "long march" to escape the pressures of Chiang Kai-shek's armies, in the Central North-west.

Added to the domestic difficulties in China were adverse financial conditions in the West. First there was a reaction in the United States from the high-power "drives" for money for the many benevolent enterprises connected with World War I. Then followed the even more drastic decline in giving brought by the world-wide depression in the 1930's.

---

[30] *The China Mission Year Book, 1925,* pp. 51–60; *1926,* pp. 480–483; *1928,* pp. 111–119; Latourette, *A History of Christian Missions in China,* pp. 695–699; Williamson, *British Baptists in China, 1845–1952,* pp. 127, 142, 149.

[31] W. R. Wheeler, *John E. Williams of Nanking* (New York, Fleming H. Revell Co., 1937, pp. 222), pp. 169 ff.

[32] Latourette, *A History of Christian Missions in China,* p. 699.

The Roman Catholic record in the years 1923–1937 showed numerical growth. Percentage-wise it was not as marked as in the preceding quarter-century, but a proportionately larger increase in the foreign staff, rapid indigenization, especially in leadership, and more emphasis on higher education were seen.

The increase in numbers is quickly summarized. In 1924 the total was said to have been 2,208,880;[33] in 1929, 2,486,841;[34] and in 1937, 2,934,175.[35] In other words, while in the decade between 1914 and 1924 the Roman Catholics had added about 40 per cent. to their number, in the fourteen years between 1924 and 1937 the corresponding percentage was only about 18 per cent. In the period between 1901 and 1914 the increase had been more than 100 per cent.[36]

Proportionately the foreign staff mounted more rapidly than the body of the faithful. In 1914, 1,365 foreign priests, 247 foreign brothers, and 743 foreign sisters were serving in China.[37] In 1929 the corresponding figures were 1,975, 314, and 1,327 and in 1939 they were 2,979, 585, and 2,281.[38] This meant that in 1912–1929, an eighteen-year period covering World War I, the number of foreign priests had approximately a 42 per cent. gain, whereas in the decade 1929–1939, two-thirds as long a time, the gain was nearly 50 per cent. Proportionately the increase in lay brothers had not been as marked in either period and that in sisters had been larger, with a similar advance between 1929 and 1939.

Much of the augmentation of the foreign staff was due to the arrival of new orders and congregations. Several came from Europe and Canada.[39] But the Roman Catholics of the United States were beginning to assume more of the burden. Contingents were coming from American provinces of orders and congregations of European origin, and the Maryknollers, of the recently founded Catholic Foreign Mission Society of America, for the time being were concentrating most of their effort on China.[40] The mounting interest of the United States in China was apparent among Protestants as well as Roman Catholics; indeed, it had appeared earlier among the former than the latter.

The indigenization of the Roman Catholic Church proceeded apace, owing partly to the renewed life in its Chinese members, partly to the world-wide policy which was deeply indebted to Pope Pius XI and his great Secretary of the Propaganda, Willem van Rossum, partly to the initiative of some of the foreign priests, and in no small degree to Archbishop Costantini, the apostolic delegate. Between 1912 and 1929 the body of Chinese priests nearly doubled, and the same

---

[33] Planchet, *Les Missions de Chine et du Japon*, 1916, p. 28.
[34] *Fides News Service*, May 18, 1930.
[35] *Ibid.*, April 9, 1938.
[36] Latourette, *A History of the Expansion of Christianity*, Vol. VII, p. 334.
[37] Streit, *Atlas Hierarchicus*, p. 100.
[38] *Fides News Service*, May 18, 1940.
[39] Latourette, *A History of the Expansion of Christianity*, Vol. VII, pp. 338, 339.
[40] *Ibid.*, p. 339.

was true of the lay brothers and the sisters. Between 1929 and 1939 Chinese priests increased about 50 per cent. and Chinese brothers and sisters between 40 and 46 per cent.[41]

Fully as significant was the degree to which administration and pastoral care were being transferred to the Chinese clergy. The Roman Catholic Church was being given a national structure under the direction of the Vatican, approaching the status of the Roman Catholic Church in Europe and the Americas. In 1926 six Chinese priests were consecrated bishops by Pius XI in St. Peter's in Rome, the first to be accorded that dignity since a single precedent in the seventeenth century.[42] This was only the beginning. Additional Chinese were raised to the episcopate. By 1936 the vicariate apostolic which included the national capital, Nanking, had a Chinese as its head.[43] Costantini gave superb leadership. He accelerated the training of Chinese clergy and the transfer of responsibility to them. He encouraged the development of a distinctly Chinese Christian art. He stimulated the founding of a Chinese congregation, the Disciples of the Lord, whose purpose it was to win fellow Chinese to the faith.[44] He encouraged the formation of youth groups in connexion with Catholic Action.[45]

The emphasis on a Chinese clergy and the transfer of administrative authority, including the subordination of Westerners, met with serious and determined opposition among some of the foreign clergy.[46] An especially notable struggle centered around Frédéric Lebbe (1877–1940). From a devout Belgian family, Lebbe went to China under the Lazarists (the Congregation of the Mission). There he sought to identify himself with the Chinese, was intensely critical of the practice in some ecclesiastical quarters of treating Chinese priests as inferior to foreign clergy, lashed out against the French protectorate of Roman Catholic missions as allying Christianity with Western imperialism, and was openly doubtful of the policy of his bishop in employing Boxer indemnity funds to support indigent Chinese in catechumenates and in making final payment of the subsidy to individuals contingent upon the reception of baptism. His superiors punished him by transferring him from Tientsin to a subordinate post in a very different part of the country. Some missionaries who sympathized with him were compelled by the ecclesiastical authorities to leave the country. For a time after World War I Lebbe was in Europe. There he received the emphatic support of van Rossum and Costantini. Returning to China, he prepared the

---

[41] *Ibid.*, p. 335.

[42] Pascal d'Elia, *Catholic Native Episcopacy in China. Being an Outline of the Formation and Growth of the Chinese Catholic Clergy, 1300–1926* (Shanghai, T'usewei Printing Press, 1927, pp. v, 386), pp. 85–88.

[43] *Les Missions de Chine, Quinzième Année, passim,* especially pp. 201, 202.

[44] *Fides News Service,* April, 1939; Planchet, *op. cit.,* 1929, p. 580.

[45] *Priester und Mission. Jahrbuch der Unio Cleri pro Missionibus in den Ländern deutscher Zunge* (Aachen, Unio Cleri pro Missionibus, 1917 ff.), 1929, pp. 25–39.

[46] A Roman Catholic expert on missions to the author, April 21, 1934.

way for raising Chinese to the episcopate, furthered Chinese Catholic Action, stimulated the formation of Chinese religious, and promoted Roman Catholic universities. He helped to found a centre in Louvain for training Chinese clergy which, fittingly, was given his name. He died while aiding the Chinese in their resistance to the Japanese invaders.[47]

Catholic Action was introduced in 1908 to enlist the laity in furthering the faith. By the time of its twenty-fifth anniversary (1933) it had opened about twenty churches and chapels, seventy-one lecture halls, seven schools, five hospitals, nineteen dispensaries, two orphanages, and two homes for the aged. It had brought many applicants for instruction in at least one district where they had been lacking, and had been responsible for the baptism of about a quarter of a million infants. Its first national congress met in 1935.[48]

Conscious of the demand for education, Roman Catholics stressed more than formerly schools on the secondary and higher level. They still did not engage in this kind of education as extensively as Protestants. In addition to the pre-1914 universities in Shanghai and Tientsin, in 1925 *Fu Jen*, a university, was founded in Peking by the Benedictines and in 1933 was transferred to the American province of the Society of the Divine Word.[49] In 1936 the Roman Catholics had 103 colleges and middle schools, of which 15 had been opened the preceding year, with 18,604 enrolled (about two-thirds were not Roman Catholics), and 4,283 primary schools, to which 166 had been added in a recent three months, with 180,704 enrolled.[50] Because of the reluctance to register their schools with the state and to transfer the administration to Chinese, for a time in the early 1930's the enrollment declined, but later, when the adjustment had been made, it again increased.[51]

An interesting development was what amounted to the end of that rites controversy which had troubled the Roman Catholic Church in China in the seventeenth and eighteenth centuries. In seeking to quiet it, the Pope had then said that until it was decided otherwise the rites in honour of Confucius were forbidden to the faithful. In 1935, when the Japanese-controlled state of Manchukuo made the rites in reverence of Confucius obligatory, the bishops in Manchuria asked the Holy See to permit their flocks to participate in them. Rome replied that since they were now clearly only civil and not religious, Christians might take part.[52]

---

[47] Jacques Leclercq, *Vie du Père Lebbe. Le Tonnerre qui Chante au Loin* (Tournai, Casterman, 1955, pp. 453), *passim.*

[48] *Fides News Service,* June 29, 1935; September 7, 1935; September 21, 1935; July 17, 1937; January 8, 1938.

[49] *The International Review of Missions,* Vol. XXIII (1934), pp. 100, 101; Latourette, *A History of Christian Missions in China,* p. 731.

[50] *Fides News Service,* February 20, 1937.

[51] Latourette, *A History of the Expansion of Christianity,* Vol. VII, p. 341.

[52] Delacroix, *Histoire Universelle des Missions Catholiques,* Vol. II, p. 274.

The Protestant story in the years 1923-1937 paralleled that of the Roman Catholic Church. Here, too, were a slowing down of numerical growth and emphasis on indigenization and education. But the total of foreign personnel fluctuated more markedly, and, as had long been true, the methods were much more varied.

The reported Protestants communicant membership grew, but less rapidly than in the preceding two decades. In 1914 it was said to have been 253,210.[53] in 1924, 402,539,[54] an increase of about 70 per cent. in a decade, and in 1936, 567,390.[55] A gain of about 40 per cent. in twelve years. Yet proportionately the latter growth was between three and four times that of the Roman Catholics during the thirteen years 1924-1937. In contrast with many other parts of the world, early in the 1930's men outnumbered women in the Protestant church membership, in a ratio of about six to four.[56]

The Protestant foreign personnel at first continued to be larger than that of the Roman Catholics, but, although growing during the earlier years, it fell sharply in the later years. It rebounded and in 1936 seems to have been slightly larger than in 1914. In 1914 it was reported to be 5,750, of whom 2,862 were from the United States and Canada.[57] In 1924 the total was reported as being 7,663, of whom, 4,492 were from the United States and Canada.[58] The great increase was due chiefly to the mounting interest in China in Protestant circles in those two lands, especially the United States, and reflected the burst of optimism in the missionary forces which followed the prodigious giving to philanthropic objects connected with World War I. By 1928 the total had plummeted to 3,113,[59] a loss assignable partly to the sharp falling off in missionary contributions in the United States brought by the reaction against the zeal of the war years and the trend towards isolationism in the international policies of the American Government. The decline was also due to the questioning of missions which was reflected in the Laymen's Foreign Mission Inquiry and to the exodus from China which accompanied the anti-foreign demonstrations in that country in 1925-1927. In 1936 the total was said to be 6,020, of whom 2,808 were from the United States and Canada.[60] In other words, the fluctuations in numbers of foreign personnel were due more to changes in the

[53] The China Mission Year Book, 1915, appendix, pp. iv, vii.
[54] Beach and Fahs, World Missionary Atlas, p. 99.
[55] Parker, Interpretative Statistical Survey of the World Mission of the Christian Church, p. 50. Another set of figures, gathered by the National Christian Council in 1936, showed a Protestant membership of 536,089 in more than 7,000 organized congregations and 8,000 branch churches and chapels, a Protestant constituency of about 1,000,000, over 14,000 pastors and other full-time church workers, and about 6,000 foreign missionaries.—Price, China. Twilight or dawn? p. 105.
[56] Laymen's Foreign Missions Inquiry. Supplementary Series, Vol. V, Part Two, pp. 243, 244.
[57] Beach and St. John, World Statistics of Christian Missions, p. 63.
[58] Beach and Fahs, op. cit., p. 82.
[59] China Christian Year Book, 1932-1933, pp. 212-221.
[60] Parker, op. cit., p. 20.

support from the United States and Canada, mostly the former, than from Europe. Indeed, in 1936 the figures of the personnel from the British Isles and the Continent were about the same as in 1924 and in the latter year were a little larger than in 1914, in spite of the blows dealt Europe by World War I. In both 1928 and 1936, in contrast with 1924 and still earlier in the twentieth century, the foreign personnel of the Roman Catholics outnumbered that of the Protestants.

The rootage of Protestantism in China more than paralleled the numerical growth of the communicant membership. In terms of ordained Chinese clergy the statistics showed 764 in 1915, 1,305 in 1920,[61] and 2,196 in 1936.[62] These figures indicated that between 1915 and 1920 the ordained men had risen by about 72 per cent., and that between 1920 and 1936, in spite of the anti-Christian movement of these years with its attacks on Chinese Christians, the body of Chinese clergy had grown by about 61 per cent. In other words, it had more than kept pace with the communicant membership.

The rate of increase was not quite that of Chinese Roman Catholic priests. In 1939 the latter's total was slightly more than that of the Protestant ordained clergy in 1936, whereas in 1914 it had been slightly less than that of Protestant ordained men in 1915. The numerical parallel does not take into consideration the differences in the training which led to ordination in the two branches of the Church. Here the contrasts in method were too great to permit dependable judgements. On the average, the Roman Catholic preparation extended over more years, but in Protestantism the educational requirements varied more widely.

The problem of recruiting and training men for the Protestant ministry engaged the attention of some of the most thoughtful Protestants, both Chinese and foreign. In 1935 a careful study was made, more complete even than that included in the findings of the commission headed by Burton (1921).[63] It reported what were in some respects losses and in others gains. A continuing problem was economic—finding sufficient funds, especially from Chinese sources, to support a highly educated parish ministry. The study noted that owing to government regulations which forbade a theological faculty to be a school of a university recognized by the state, only one of the Protestant colleges and universities retained its theological school, and it had not registered. Of the eight Christian universities in existence in 1921, all had theological departments or schools. By 1935 three had closed or given up this department, and four had registered but had not included the theological school in their regis-

---

[61] *The Christian Occupation of China*, p. xc.
[62] Parker, *op. cit.*, pp. 49, 50.
[63] *Education for Service in the Christian Church in China. The Report of a Survey Commission, 1935* (Shanghai, The National Committee for Religious Education in China, 1935, pp. vi, 157), *passim*.

tration. In 1921 twenty-six theological students were full college graduates and seventy had partial college training. In 1934 twenty-six were college graduates and fifteen others had had at least a year of college training. This indicated a loss of 57.3 per cent. in the enrollment of college students in the Protestant seminaries in China—and that in years when the number of college graduates in the country as a whole was rising. However, in 1921–1922, 295 students had been enrolled in eight institutions requiring middle school graduation for entrance, and in 1935 fourteen institutions required a minimum of middle school graduation for entrance and together had 373 students with at least middle school preparation. In the so-called Bible schools the students having the preparation of junior middle school and above had increased from 96 in 1922 to 472 in 1934.

In a wide variety of ways Protestantism registered progress in the stormy years between 1922 and 1937. We have called attention to the growth in numbers. Here we can rapidly note a few of the other aspects of the advance.

Coöperation and unity among Protestants increased, and with an augmentation of Chinese leadership. The National Christian Council proved its worth. It took on many functions. For example, in 1927 it sent a number of Chinese Christians to fill the place of missionaries who had been evacuated from the interior because of radical anti-foreign agitation. Chêng Ching-yi (1881–1940) was appointed general secretary of the Council.[64] A Manchu, the son of a pastor long connected with the London Missionary Society, he had first come to prominence in the (Edinburgh) World Missionary Conference and was a vice-chairman of the International Missionary Council. He had chaired the National Christian Conference in Shanghai in 1922. In 1934 he resigned the secretaryship of the National Christian Council to become the head of the Church of Christ in China.[65] That body held its first General Assembly in Shanghai in 1927. Sixteen denominational groups from the British Isles, Canada, and the United States joined in its formation. About half were Presbyterian and Reformed, but included as well were Congregationalists, United Brethren, English Baptists, the United Church of Canada, and independent Chinese churches. Later at least two churches affiliated with the China Inland Mission joined.[66] Chêng Ching-yi was also prominent in the Chinese Home Missionary Society, a purely indigenous organization.

Several projects and institutions sought to help solve the basic problems of the use of China's land—of first-class importance in a country the large majority of whose population was rural. The College of Agriculture and Forestry of the

---

[64] *The China Christian Year Book, 1928*, pp. 66–72. On an early English secretary see H. G. Wood, *Henry T. Hodgkin. A Memoir* (London, Student Christian Movement Press, 1937, pp. 281), pp. 200–243.

[65] *The International Review of Missions*, Vol. XXX, pp. 513–530 (October, 1941).

[66] *The China Christian Year Book, 1928*, pp. 73–89.

University of Nanking broke the trail. Soon schools of agriculture and forestry were begun by two other Christian universities. By the year 1925 some of the theological seminaries had rural work departments. Other efforts were made to improve rural conditions.[67] In the 1930's at least two-thirds of the Protestants were in rural villages and towns. Some rural churches centered their efforts in their church buildings, but others sought to permeate the entire country-side.[68] In 1930 the Shantung Baptist Union organized a rural education department and in a few months it had 113 centres with 2,115 students and was bringing new life to the country churches.[69]

What seemed to the advantage of Protestantism and of Christianity in general followed the break of Chiang Kai-shek with the Communists (1927). On December 1, 1927, Chiang Kai-shek married Soong Mei-ling, an American-educated daughter of active Methodists. In 1930 he was baptized by a Chinese Methodist pastor.[70] A number of Protestants were prominent in the Chiang Kai-shek regime.

Several other outstanding Chinese of the 1920's were Protestants. The picturesque warlord, Fêng Yü-hsiang, who had his first favourable impression of the faith in seeing a missionary go to her death at the hands of the Boxers, furthered Christian preaching among his troops and sternly curbed their camp vices.[71] In the 1930's he weakened in his Christian profession. Chang Po-ling, nationally prominent as an educator, traced his conversion to contacts with a YMCA secretary soon after 1900. He remained constant in the troubled years of the Japanese invasion.[72] The list could be greatly lengthened.

As the years passed, most of the bishops in the Anglican and Methodist communions were Chinese, and Chinese held the leading posts in denominations which did not have bishops. Increasingly the presidents and principals of Christian universities and schools were Chinese.

Among men and women prominent in the government and in public life the proportion of Protestants was much larger than the size of the Protestant body would have warranted. One reason was that Protestants had had opportunity for the kind of education demanded by the revolutionary age. Another was that they possessed the requisite qualities of character.

Numbers of Chinese churches arose which were independent of foreign initiative, aid, or control. A union hymnal (*Hymns of Universal Praise*) was

[67] Latourette, *A History of Christian Missions in China*, pp. 784, 785.

[68] Frank W. Price, *The Rural Church in China. A Survey* (New York, Agricultural Missions, Inc., 1948, pp. xi, 274), *passim.*

[69] Williamson, *British Baptists in China*, p. 137.

[70] *Ibid.*, pp. 131, 132.

[71] *The China Mission Year Book*, *1919*, pp. 281–286; Marshall Broomhall, *General Feng, a Good Soldier of Jesus Christ* (London, China Inland Mission, 1923, pp. xiii, 80), *passim;* Marcus Ch'eng, *Marshal Feng, the Man and His Work* (Shanghai, Kelly and Walsh, 1926, pp. 107), *passim.*

[72] Latourette, *World Service*, p. 258.

published, with Chinese tunes and words as well as foreign tunes and translations of Western words.[73]

In some of his efforts for the moral improvement of the country which
Chiang Kai-shek undertook, the influence of the Christian faith was apparent.
They were predominantly Confucian but were indebted to Christianity. Among
them were the New Life Movement[74] and the Officers' Moral Endeavour Association, frankly modeled on the YMCA.[75]

The 1920's and the 1930's brought striking changes to the Russian Orthodox
minority in China. The Russian Orthodox community dated from the 1680's.
At that time a small band of prisoners taken in a frontier war between Russia
and China were domiciled in the north-east corner of Peking and had as a
fellow captive a priest. At least some of the descendants of the captives continued in the care of clergy sent them from Russia.[76] In the second half of the
nineteenth century an effort was made to reach non-Christians, but converts
were few.[77] More extensive missions were undertaken after the suppression of
the Boxer outbreak. In 1901 a bishop was appointed. Soon more clergy were
sent and in 1914 thirty-two mission centres existed and a Chinese baptized
membership of 5,035 was claimed.[78] Because of World War I and the revolution
in Russia, most of the missions to the Chinese were discontinued.[79] Then came
hundreds of "White" Russians, refugees from the Communist regime. To them
the Orthodox Church was a symbol and rallying point of resistance to the
"Reds." Most of them were in Manchuria. In 1922 their parishes were organized
into a diocese with its centre in Harbin. The Japanese were not unfriendly
and after their creation of Manchukuo the Orthodox Church was not disturbed,
and a theological seminary and an Orthodox university were conducted. An
archbishop had his seat in Peking and a bishop lived in Shanghai. Some parishes
existed in Sinkiang.[80]

THE TRAGEDY AND HEROISM OF THE EIGHT YEARS OF
FULL-SCALE JAPANESE INVASION, 1937–1945

The eight years of full-scale Japanese invasion which began in July, 1937,
brought tragedy, but tragedy mixed with heroism. Until December, 1941, many
of the missionaries from France, the United States, and the British Common-

---

[73] Price, China. Twilight or Dawn? pp. 128, 129, 135–156.
[74] The Chinese Recorder, Vol. LXVIII, pp. 279–290.
[75] Latourette, World Service, p. 285.
[76] Latourette, A History of Christian Missions in China, pp. 199, 200.
[77] Ibid., pp. 488, 489.
[78] The China Mission Year Book, 1910, pp. 425 ff.; 1915, pp. 583, 584.
[79] Ibid., 1926, pp. 92, 93.
[80] Serge Bolshakoff, The Foreign Missions of the Russian Orthodox Church (London, Society
for Promoting Christian Knowledge, 1943, pp. 120), pp. 68, 69, 81–83.

wealth were able to remain at their posts in the areas occupied by Japan. With the attack of Japan on the latter two powers, missionaries from them who did not escape were interned. Thousands of Christians shared in the migration of millions of Chinese from "occupied" to "unoccupied" territory. On the whole, Christians in "occupied" regions were permitted to continue their services, but with restrictions on their activities imposed by the invaders.

The Roman Catholic Church could not but suffer from the fighting and dislocation of population brought by the eight years of invasion. For a time the rate of increase slowed, but by 1940 it was again mounting and was about 100,000 a year. By 1939 Roman Catholics were said to total 3,182,950, which was about 250,000 more than in 1937. In 1939 catechumens were reported as 654,000. Chinese continued to be trained for the priesthood. In 1939 major seminarians were reported to total 870 and minor seminarians to be 5,114. Roman Catholics provided camps for refugees. In the years 1937–1939 they had cared for about 1,250,000 in this fashion.[81] In 1940 Roman Catholics were said to be 3,262,678, an increase from 2,498,015 since 1930, or a growth of about 30 per cent. Native priests were reported to be 2,091 and foreign clergy 3,064.[82] In 1937, during the Japanese attack on Shanghai, a priest created a neutral zone in which about 250,000 Chinese found shelter.[83] In 1943, during the stress of the war years, in an effort to obtain the support of the Roman Catholic Church in the life-and-death struggle with Japan, the Chinese Government sent an envoy to the Holy See. In 1939 Rome created a new vicariate apostolic in the North. In Manchukuo it had sought to adjust itself to the new political situation by additional vicariates apostolic in 1932, 1937, and 1944.[84] Many Christians, including some of the clergy, lost their lives. By 1941 forty priests, Chinese and foreign, had perished, in one vicariate alone by that time forty-seven Christians had been killed by bombings, and the deaths of 275 could be attributed to the war.[85]

In the years of stress, one of the first objectives of Protestants was to minister to the sufferers from the Japanese attack. In this they were not alone. In addition to the Roman Catholics, the Buddhist Red Swastika and many Chinese and foreign organizations sought to help. The National Christian Council assisted. In the United States the Church Committee for China Relief was organized. Much of the aid was administered by committees made up of Chinese and

---

[81] *The International Review of Missions,* Vol. XXX (1941), pp. 449 ff.; Delacroix, *Histoire Universelle des Missions Catholiques,* Vol. II, p. 274; *The China Christian Year Book, 1938–39,* pp. 270–278.

[82] *Annuaire des Missions Catholiques de Chine, 1941,* p. xv.

[83] Delacroix, *op. cit.,* Vol. II, p. 273. See also, on relief work in the Chusan Archipelago in these years, M. L. H., *Sister Xavier Berkeley (1861–1944), Sister of Charity of St. Vincent de Paul: Fifty-Four Years a Missionary in China* (London, Burns & Oates, 1949, pp. xxi, 257), pp. 211 ff.

[84] Delacroix, *op. cit.,* Vol. II, pp. 275, 285, 286.

[85] *Annuaire des Missions Catholiques de Chine, 1941,* pp. viii, ix.

foreigners, Roman Catholics and Protestants, and was given on the basis of simple need, not of religious affiliation.[86] During the Japanese rape of Nanking a few foreigners, largely Protestant missionaries, at the risk of their lives set up a safety zone to protect civilians and disarmed soldiers.[87] Wounded soldiers in transit were cared for.[88]

As the Japanese armies moved into the interior many missionaries remained at their posts, and mission compounds became havens for the civilian population. Much church property was damaged or destroyed, but here and there foreigners were able to obtain protection for non-combatants. Resistance to the Japanese by the Chinese increased the danger. Guerrilla warfare was waged against the invaders and often the enemy could feel only moderately secure behind the walls of a town and in the daytime. At night the guerrillas would swoop down on scattered Japanese and retake what the latter had held during the day. Numbers of villages and towns were completely deserted and the church members either perished or were scattered. In the insecurity many Christians suffered.[89] Much of the able leadership was drained away by migrations to the "unoccupied" regions. In some areas a marked loss of membership was seen. Yet in several regions within the "occupied" zones the numbers of Protestants increased.[90]

When, after December, 1941, British and American missionaries were interned, the Chinese Christians increasingly suffered. The Japanese authorities attempted to cut off all ties between their churches and the churches in the Occident and at least in Manchukuo tried to force the Protestants into a single body.[91]

As the Nationalist armies were forced westward many Protestant institutions, including schools and colleges, shared in the vast migration to areas unoccupied by the Japanese.[92] More than two-thirds of the universities, colleges, and technical schools moved to areas which it was hoped would be beyond the reach of the Japanese, and nearly a third went to West China. Among the latter was a branch of the Nanking Theological Seminary. There it repeated what it had done near its original site and constructed a rural centre for the training of its students in ministering helpfully to the farming and village folk.[93] Taken the country over, the theological schools showed a decline in ministerial students with a senior middle school preparation. The decrease was 48.5 per cent. from

[86] Ballou, *Dangerous Opportunity*, pp. 139–148; *The China Christian Year Book, 1938–39*, pp. 263–270.

[87] The author's personal knowledge through participants.

[88] *The China Christian Year Book, 1938–39*, pp. 324–329.

[89] Ballou, *op. cit.*, pp. 148–165.

[90] Price, *China. Twilight or Dawn?* pp. 107–109.

[91] *The International Review of Missions*, Vol. XXXII, pp. 10, 11 (January, 1943).

[92] See a list of the schools included in a larger list of government and non-Christian private institutions in *The China Christian Year Book, 1938–39*, pp. 242–262.

[93] Ballou, *op. cit.*, pp. 172, 191.

1933–1934 and 54.4 per cent. from 1921–1922. From 1921 to 1945 the numbers of college graduates in theological schools remained fairly constant. The totals of men declined and of women increased.[94] Protestants joined with other agencies in giving aid to the migrant students through scholarships, food, clothing, shelter, books, and medical care.[95] Christians served in the Chinese Industrial Coöperatives and helped the Friends Ambulance Unit to carry medicines to hospitals and to care for the wounded at the front.[96] Special efforts were put forth to present the Christian message to students, both in "occupied" and in "unoccupied" areas. They were in part a continuation of the Youth and Religion Movement which had been launched in 1934.[97]

In general, between 1937 and 1945, in spite of losses, Protestantism gained in numbers and strength. One estimate by a well-informed missionary said that between 1936 and 1948 Protestant communicants had increased from about 600,000 to approximately 750,000. Mature theological thought was slow in appearing, but in view of the political stresses of the day this was not surprising. In the testing of the years the Christian faith and experience of many Christians were deepened.

BRIEF RECONSTRUCTION AND RENEWAL, 1945–1949

The defeat of the Japanese in the summer of 1945 seemed an opportunity to help reconstruct a country that had been ravaged and exhausted during the long years of war. Into this project the Christian forces entered enthusiastically. Many missionaries who had been interned and then repatriated returned and reinforcements were sent.

The Roman Catholic Church endeavoured to move ahead in what was hopefully believed to be a new day of opportunity. In 1946 Pope Pius XII took a step towards planting the Church more firmly in China by creating a hierarchy and substituting it for the structure of vicariates apostolic. A Chinese, Thomas Tien, was appointed Archbishop of Peking and raised to the cardinalate. An internunciature was placed in Peking. In 1947 the Chinese Government sent an ambassador to the Holy See.[98] The hierarchy embraced twenty archdioceses and seventy-nine dioceses, said to have been the largest number in any one country in the world. In addition an Institute of Apologetic and a Secretariat of Agriculture were planned, enlarged emphasis was contemplated on training religious and lay personnel for hospitals and dispensaries, and the founding of more industrial schools was projected.[99]

[94] *The International Review of Missions*, Vol. XXXIV, pp. 385, 386 (October, 1945).
[95] *The China Christian Year Book, 1938–39*, pp. 306–317.
[96] Price, *China. Twilight or Dawn?* pp. 111, 112.
[97] *The China Christian Year Book, 1938–39*, pp. 153–171.
[98] Delacroix, *op. cit.*, Vol. II, p. 275.
[99] *The International Review of Missions*, Vol. XXXVI, p. 71 (January, 1947).

Ominously, however, in Communist-controlled areas much ecclesiastical property was confiscated and schools and other activities for young people were suppressed.[100] By 1949 reports were beginning to come of extensive persecution in Communist areas, with martyrdoms of Chinese and foreign priests, especially the former.[101]

Protestants entered upon the work of reconstruction and sought to effect fresh advances. Many buildings were repaired or restored. By 1947 over 200 hospitals had been re-opened, and medical staffs, Chinese and foreign, had returned to them.[102] Schools, colleges, and universities once more occupied their pre-war campuses. They and the churches greatly missed the personnel who had perished during the war. Spiralling inflation brought costs to fantastic heights. Yet at its first full meeting after the war the National Christian Council called for a three-year forward movement to "rise out of pessimism and despondency" in opposition "to all corruption, to all types of human bondage, inequality, unrighteousness, and inhumanity, to all lawlessness and Godlessness."[103] Visual aids, public address systems, and the radio were employed to spread the Christian message. A pre-war unique mission to Buddhist priests and devotees, with its distinctive buildings near Hong Kong, resumed its ministry; new printings of the Bible were made and distributed; through the United Christian Publishers, constituted during the war years and reorganized as the Council of Christian Publishers, several Protestant publication societies combined their efforts. By the end of 1947 returning veteran missionaries and new recruits brought the total foreign staff to approximately 3,000, but only about half of the pre-war strength.[104] What looked like the beginning of theological thinking was appearing, true to the historic Christian heritage and in the Chinese philosophical tradition. Among the leaders were T. C. Chao, dean of the School of Religion in Yenching University, and Francis C. M. Wei, president of Hua Chung College.[105]

As the civil war between the Nationalists (*Kuomintang*) and the Communists was resumed with the removal of the Japanese menace, an outstanding Protestant missionary became actively involved. George C. Marshall, sent as a special envoy by the President of the United States to attempt to bring peace between the belligerents, asked J. Leighton Stuart, president of Yenching

---

[100] *Ibid.*

[101] *Ibid.*, Vol. XXXVIII, p. 71 (January, 1949).

[102] Price, *China. Twilight or Dawn?* p. 122. For the story of an American missionary physician who had reached the interior of China during the war, returned to a hospital which had been gutted by fire, and helped to restore it and the medical and nursing schools connected with it, see Edward H. Hume, *Dauntless Adventurer. The Story of Dr. Winston Pettus* (New Haven, the Yale-in-China Association, 1952, pp. 195), *passim*.

[103] Price, *China. Twilight or Dawn?* pp. 123–127.

[104] *Ibid.*, pp. 128–133; *The International Review of Missions*, Vol. XXXVIII, p. 16 (January, 1949).

[105] Price, *China. Twilight or Dawn?* pp. 140, 141.

University, to become American ambassador to China to help in the negotiations. Stuart reluctantly accepted (July, 1946). With his long intmacy with China and many of its leaders and his unfailing courtesy, he was an admirable choice. But the deep-seated reciprocal distrust of the Nationalists and Communists made agreement impossible. Stuart remained in Nanking until after the Communists had taken the city and then left for the United States.[106]

CHRISTIANITY UNDER THE COMMUNISTS

The capture of the mainland of China by the Communists, completed in 1950, brought to Christianity its most serious reverses since the eighteenth century. In theory the Communists, while unabashedly atheists and encouraging anti-religious propaganda, granted freedom of religious belief and worship as long as it did not interfere with their programme. They set up a religious affairs department with headquarters in Peking and offices in the main cities. All religions were under its supervision.

The Communists were convinced that as Christianity existed in China it was closely tied to the Western imperialism and colonialism from which they were determined to free the country. Although in the 1940's the British and American treaties had been revised in such fashion that extraterritoriality and other features which the Chinese declared were "unequal" were expunged, Communists were not loath to remind the country that in the nineteenth and twentieth centuries Christianity had been associated with Western imperialism, that permission for its propagation and protection had been written into treaties wrested from China at the mouths of cannons, and that missionaries, like other foreigners, had enjoyed extraterritorial privileges. Communists insisted that all ties be cut between the churches and the West. With this in mind they either expelled all missionaries from abroad, permitted them to withdraw, or imprisoned and tried them on the charge that they were spies and agents of the enemies of China. Overt persecution on purely religious grounds was not part of their policy. They sought to avoid making religious martyrs. However, Christians experienced much suffering, whether they were Roman Catholics or Protestants, and although fresh conversions were recorded and no accurate figures were available, presumably the Christian communities dwindled in numbers. In areas which were historically part of China, notably Hong Kong and Taiwan (Formosa), the churches continued and had substantial accessions.

Communist animosity to Christianity and especially to any foreign connexions was heightened by the knowledge of the adamant opposition of the Vatican to Communism and by antagonism to the United States. Chinese Communists regarded the United States as their chief enemy and often declared that

---

[106] Stuart, *Fifty Years in China*, pp. 160–260.

Rome supported the United States. Their hostility was aggravated by the latter's defense of the *Kuomintang* regime in Taiwan and the leadership that the American Government took in the United Nations' resistance to the Communist attempt to take over all Korea which in 1950–1953 brought war, with the heavy engagement of Chinese Communist "volunteers."

The Communist policy towards the Roman Catholics had in the main two aspects. One was the attempt to discredit the foreign and Chinese personnel by imprisonment and court proceedings, which often led to death. The other was the effort to induce the Chinese Catholics to set up a church which would be independent of the Holy See.[107]

It was said that from 1944 to 1952 the Communists murdered 105 Chinese priests or liquidated them in prison, that in 1952 over 200 Chinese priests came to their end either in prison or in forced labour camps, and that in 1954 the total was swelled by 400 or 500. The Legion of Mary, with its enrollment of the laity in the spread of the faith, was labelled "reactionary" and "fascist."[108] Many missionaries were arrested and were subjected to prolonged and often continuous questioning in an effort to force them to confess to espionage. Numbers of the laity were hauled before courts, were given long examinations on their faith, including their belief in God, the virgin birth of Christ, the Ten Commandments, and the Church's teaching on divorce and re-marriage, and were hounded from day to day in an attempt to compel them to "confess the errors of their past belief" and to sign a statement renouncing their belief in God and affirming their belief in "our Communist leader, Mao Tse-tung." Schools and charitable institutions were taken over.[109]

The Communists were determined to induce Roman Catholics to set up a

---

[107] See a comprehensive, documented survey of the propaganda of the Chinese Communists against the Roman Catholic Church, compiled by a Roman Catholic scholar, Johannes Schütte, *Die katholische Chinamission im Spiegel der Rotchinesischen Presse. Versuch einer missionarischen Deutung* (Münster i.W., Aschendorffsche Verlagsbuchhandlung, 1957, pp. xli, 394).

[108] *Ibid.*, pp. 58, 276–320.

[109] Palmer, *God's Underground in Asia*, p. 44. Of the vast literature on the trials and other persecutions, see [Renault-Roulier, Gilbert] Rémy, *Pourpre des Martyrs* (Paris, Librairie Arthème Fayard, 1953, pp. 379); Robert W. Greene, *Calvary in China* (New York, G. P. Putnam's Sons, 1953, pp. 244); Thomas J. Bauer, *The Systematic Destruction of the Catholic Church in China* (New York, World Horizon Reports, 1954, pp. 42); Ambros Rust, *Die Rote Nacht. Schweizermissionare erleben den Kommunismus in China* (Munich, Rex-Verlag, 1956, pp. 264); Jean Lefeuvre, *Les Enfants dans le Ville. Chronique de la Vie Chrétienne à Shanghai, 1949–1955* (Tournai, Casterman, 1957, pp. 366); Amelio Crotti, *Piu' Forti della Tormenta. Documenti sulla Persecuzione Religiosa in Cina* (Milan, Pontificio Istituto Missioni Estere, 1957, pp. 191); Bernard T. Smyth, editor, *But Not Conquered* (Dublin, Browne and Nolan, 1958, pp. xv, 216); Jean Monsterleet, *Les Martyrs de Chine Parlent . . . l'Empire de Mao Tsé-toung contre l'Église du Christ* (Paris, Amiot Dumont, 1953, pp. 244), translated by Antonia Pakenham as *Martyrs in China* (Chicago, Henry Regnery Co., pp. 288); Carlo Suigo, *In the Land of Mao Tse-tung*, translated by Murriel Currey and edited by Clifford Witting (London, George Allen and Unwin, 1953, pp. 311); Mary Victoria, *Nun in Red China* (New York, McGraw-Hill Book Co., 1953, pp. vii, 208); Robert Loup, *Martyr in Tibet. The Heroic Life and Death of Father Maurice Tornay, St. Bernard Missionary to Tibet*, translated from the French by Charles Davenport (New York, David McKay Co., 1956, pp. 238); Francis Dufay, *The Star Versus the Cross*, translated by Cassein-Bernard (Hongkong, Nazareth Press, no date, pp. 219); Alain van Gaver, *J'ai eté Condamné à la Liberté* (Paris, Le Centurion,

"Patriotic Catholic Church" or "Catholic Patriotic Association" which would not be controlled by the Holy See. Their attempts met with stubborn resistance by many of the faithful, both clergy and laity. The government took stern measures against some of the most outspoken of the priests.[110] Yet, under pressure, in April, 1958, four Roman Catholic bishops, all of them Chinese, were persuaded to consecrate two priests as bishops for the "Catholic Patriotic Church" in Wuchang and Hankow.[111] Within a few weeks two more bishops were consecrated.[112] By the autumn of 1958 a total of ten bishops had been consecrated and an eleventh had been elected and installed.[113]

The Vatican obviously could not assent to these acts. In 1952 an encyclical deplored the religious persecution; it was followed by another in 1954 which reproved those who were attempting to separate Chinese Catholics from the unity of the Church.[114] On June 29, 1958, in the encyclical *Ad apostolorum principis* Pius XII denounced the Catholic Patriotic Church and the election and consecration of bishops in ways contrary to canon law.[115] By 1960 about thirty Chinese were reported to have been elected and consecrated to the episcopate.[116] Plans were made by the Catholic Patriotic Church for the participation by priests in productive labour and for shortening the time devoted to religious devotions to make possible that participation.[117]

The Communist authorities took steps to suppress the bishops and clergy who remained loyal to Rome. In the autumn of 1958 it was reported that of the 143 ordinaries recognized by the Holy See only 25 remained. They were said to be all Chinese, and eight were in prison, five were free after having served a prison sentence, eleven were free but under surveillance, and the fate of one was not known.[118] In 1960 one was sentenced to life imprisonment for "treason."[119] In 1960 James Edward Walsh, an American Maryknoll bishop, was sentenced to twenty years' imprisonment for "espionage and conspiracy."[120] In October, 1960, two Chinese Jesuits were reported to have been assigned to "re-education

---

1953, pp. 221); Jean Barbier, *Monseigneur Tchou. Colporteur de Chaussettes* (Paris, Le Centurion, 1954, pp. 114); Harold W. Rigney, *Four Years in a Red Hell* (Chicago, Henry Regnery Co., 1956, pp. 222); Raphael Montaigne, *China in Chains* (Chicago, Franciscan Herald Press, 1958, pp. 47); Egidio Maria Foghin, *Le La Crime della Libertà* (Pavia, Commissione Storico Missionaria, 1957, pp. 178); Eugenio Pellegrino, *Mao Cerca un Papa* (Rome, Direz. Naz. Pont. Opere Missionarie, 3rd ed., 1953, pp. 181); Mark Tennien, *No Secret is Safe behind the Iron Curtain* (New York, Farrar, Straus and Young, 1952, pp. 270).

[110] Palmer, *op. cit.*, pp. 138–175.

[111] *China Bulletin*, May 5, 1958.

[112] *Ibid.*, December 1, 1958.

[113] *Ibid.*, October 6, 1958. A slightly later report put the number at fourteen. *Ibid.*, October 20, 1958.

[114] *Acta Apostolicae Sedis*, Vol. XLVII (1955), pp. 5–14.

[115] *Ibid.*, Vol. L (1958), pp. 601–614.

[116] *Worldmission Fides Service*, September 28, 1959.

[117] *China Bulletin*, December 1, 1958.

[118] *Ibid.*, October 20, 1958.

[119] *The New York Times*, March 18, 1960.

[120] *Time*, March 28, 1960.

through labour," a third to have been condemned to seven years' imprisonment, and a Chinese bishop to have been given fifteen years in prison.[121] A little earlier, in January, 1955, 233 Chinese priests, brothers, and sisters, including two bishops, were known to be in prison.[122]

Not all Chinese Roman Catholics submitted tamely to affiliation with the Catholic Patriotic Association. In addition to the resistance we have noted in the preceding paragraph, it was said that wherever the Legion of Mary existed, the "anti-imperialistic patriotic movement" failed to gain a foothold. In 1953 a well-informed Protestant missionary reported that only about one in ten of the Legion of Mary had given up membership.[123] In 1958, presumably for unwillingness to conform, 80 priests, 20 sisters, and 4,000 laymen were reported to have been compelled to spend months under Communist "indoctrination."[124]

The Communists adopted essentially the same policy towards Protestants as towards Catholics. They insisted that they cut off all ties with Protestants in Western countries and support the Communist programme. As with Roman Catholics, this entailed the denunciation of all Western connexions and personnel, the withdrawal or expulsion of missionaries, and the imprisonment and attempt at indoctrination of some of the latter.

Early in the 1950's many Protestants were haled before peoples' courts for trial and punishment. The general charge was that they were reactionaries and agents of Western imperialism. In public meetings Christians denounced one another and individual missionaries, on much the same ground.[125] In the Communist press outstanding missionary leaders such as John R. Mott and prominent missionaries of a slightly earlier generation, notably Timothy Richard, were accused of cultural imperialism. Several missionaries wished to remain but became convinced that to do so, even if it were permitted, would bring additional embarrassment to their Chinese brethren. A few missionaries were placed under house arrest and some were imprisoned. Here and there attempts were made to wring from them confessions of espionage and collaboration with China's enemies.[126] Few Protestant missionaries lost their lives. Nor were as many subjected to the excruciating trials which were the lot of their Roman Catholic counterparts. By the end of 1952 most Protestant missionaries had left the mainland.[127]

[121] *Worldmission Fides Service*, October 29, 1960.
[122] *Mission Bulletin*, Vol. VII, pp. 223, 224 (January, 1956).
[123] *Ibid.*, Vol. VI, pp. 435, 436 (May, 1954); F. W. Price to the author, April, 1953.
[124] *Worldmission Fides Service*, September 26, 1959.
[125] Williamson, *British Baptists in China*, p. 185; the author's personal knowledge.
[126] As two instances see F. Olin Stockwell, *With God in Red China. The Story of Two Years in Chinese Communist Prisons* (New York, Harper & Brothers, 1953, pp. 256); Geoffrey T. Bull, *God Holds the Key (Being the Record of His Meditations and Reflections Centring in the Period of His Imprisonment in China, October, 1950, to December, 1953)* (London, Hodder and Stoughton, 1959, pp. 254).
[127] Williamson, *op. cit.*, p. 185.

Numbers of Chinese Protestants were subjected to pressure and some to imprisonment, either as individuals or in groups. Thus Quentin K. Y. Huang, a bishop of the Chinese branch of the Anglican Communion, was imprisoned, tortured, and indoctrinated in an effort to make him conform to Communist purposes.[128] The Jesus Family was scattered and killed. Although having its origin from contact with a missionary, it was completely independent of foreign leadership or financial aid. It had arisen in Shantung, held its property in common, and won the amazed admiration of many Communists, for its members, honest, thrifty, marked by their love for one another and by unselfish service to others, were practising some of the ideals preached by Communists, but much better than the latter. Yet by 1955 their communities had been liquidated and their members scattered or killed.[129] In May, 1956, Mao Tse-tung proclaimed as a public policy: "Let all flowers bloom and all schools of thought contend." Many, among them some Protestants, responded with outspoken criticisms of the Communist regime. Before long the government took stern measures against them. Numbers of Protestants who had voiced their opinions were silenced, but how many were killed was not known—at least outside of China.[130]

The Communists sought to induce the Protestants to form a national organization which would, like the Catholic Patriotic Association, be fully independent of any foreign connexion and support the Communist programme. In this, as with Roman Catholics, they met with some success. In July, 1950, Chou En-lai, of the People's Republic of China, called together a few Protestant leaders. They drafted what was called "the Christian Manifesto." As eventually revised it was approved by several hundred organizations, including the National Christian Council (at a meeting in December, 1950, which was entirely Chinese in membership), and by November, 1951, approximately 300,000 Protestants had affixed their signatures. The Communist invasion of South Korea began about the time the Manifesto was framed and in the late autumn of 1950 the Chinese Communist "volunteers" had joined in the resistance to the United Nations' counter-attack. The Christian Manifesto said that close relations had existed between foreign imperialism and missionaries, that the Christian churches and institutions would support the common programme framed by the Chinese People's Political Consultative Conference which had been assembled under Communist leadership, that they would oppose "imperialism, feudalism, and bureaucratic capitalism," that Christians must be brought to recognize the crimes which the imperialists had committed against China and the use which had been made of the churches by the imperialists, that they must

[128] Quentin K. Y. Huang, *Now I Can Tell. The Story of a Christian Bishop under Communist Persecution* (New York, Morehouse-Gorham Co., 1954, pp. xviii, 222), *passim.*
[129] D. Vaughan Rees, *The "Jesus Family" in Communist China* (Chicago, Moody Press, 1956, pp. 126), *passim.*
[130] *China Bulletin,* October 20, 1958.

keep on the alert against the imperialists, especially United States imperialist intrigues, and that Christians must support the government's movement for peace and its land reform policy.[131]

In April, 1951, a conference of Christian leaders and associations met in Peking. To it came delegates and invited guests. It appointed a council of twenty-five which had as chairman Wu Yao-tsung (Y. T. Wu). Wu was a Protestant who had had part of his education in the United States, was a secretary of the YMCA in China, and was already noted for his advocacy of social and political reforms. He led in the adoption by the Peking gathering of a statement which declared the "resist-United States and Aid-Korea movement the most important duty and work of the Church" and summoned all the churches of China to support the "Three-Self Movement." That enterprise, following a slogan framed by leaders of Protestant missions early in the nineteenth century as the goal of their efforts, called on the churches to be self-governing, self-supporting, and self-propagating.[132]

Under a government decree of July, 1951, for the control of churches receiving aid from Americans, a number of church organizations applied for registration by the state as independent and members of the Resist-America, Aid-Korea Three-Self-Reform Movement. In accordance with government requirements they held accusation meetings against members who were charged with having aided the imperialists.[133] *T'ien Feng,* a Protestant publication, became the organ of what was often known briefly as the Three-Self Movement.

Here and there were missionaries who actively sympathized with these measures and saw in Communism a great advance for China. Among them were James G. Endicott and his wife. They were Canadians, and Endicott's father had been prominent as a missionary in China.[134]

Opposition to the efforts to bring Protestants to the support of the Communist regime was not lacking. The Little Flock, an indigenous movement akin to the Plymouth Brethren and with hundreds of groups in various parts of China, was largely non-conformist; it was either exterminated or won to concurrence. But it was represented in the second assembly of the Three-Self Patriotic Movement which convened in Peking in March, 1956. Some other preachers widely known among Protestants were outspoken in their resistance.[135] In 1958 several pastors and other Protestant leaders were being denounced by Protestants who

131 Ferris, *The Christian Church in Communist China to 1952,* pp. 1–6; Williamson, *op. cit.,* pp. 183, 184.

132 Ferris, *op. cit.,* pp. 8, 9.

133 *Ibid.,* pp. 10–12.

134 One expression of their convictions was Mary Austin Endicott, *Five Stars Over China* (Toronto, the author, 1953, pp. xvi, 464), *passim.*

135 Leslie T. Lyall, *Come Wind, Come Weather. The Present Experience of the Church in China* (Chicago, Moody Press, 1960, pp. 95), *passim.*

coöperated with the government for opposition to socialism and for criticizing the Communist regime.[136]

The Communists further tightened the cords by which they were seemingly attempting to strangle the Church, both Roman Catholic and Protestant. In 1958 government regulations forbade services, prayers, or Bible reading except in regular church buildings at announced hours with a representative of the state present to report on what was said.[137] That year also saw the closing of all but between 12 and 15 of the 200 church buildings in Shanghai. It was reported that in Peking only 4 of the 65 church buildings remained. With this went the scrapping of the entire denominational structure of Protestantism and its replacement by a (Protestant) Chinese Christian Church whose governing officers on the national, provincial, and local levels were to be the Three-Self Committees. The properties thus vacated were to be turned over to the government, and the staffs connected with them were to be assigned to labour in the farm communes. The consolidation of Protetsant churches was extended to many cities and to at least some areas on the provincial level.[138] Yet conversions and the baptism of adults continued. For example, in the eighteen months between January, 1959, and July, 1960, in a single denomination on the mainland in the South 2,900 adults were said to have been baptized—although this was less than the 7,500 in the same denomination the year before the Communists took over the region.[139]

From time to time visitors from abroad brought news of the status of Protestantism. Thus in 1957 Walter Freytag, a distinguished German Protestant specialist on missions, covered much of the South-east. He reported that on the whole the Protestants with whom he talked spoke favourably of what the Communist regime was doing for the Chinese people, morally as well as materially. He noticed that the church services were well attended. He felt that among some Christians the understanding of the faith was deepening. His impression was that more adults were being baptized than in several churches in India and Indonesia, that in one town with about 50,000 Protestants an increase of about 10 per cent. in membership had been seen in the past year, that a number of student secretaries were at work, that the publication of Christian literature in relation to the numbers of Christians was higher than in Germany, and that he saw some recently built churches and others which had been restored or enlarged.[140] That same year a delegation of Japanese Protestants found

[136] *China Bulletin*, October 6, 1958; January 19, 1959.

[137] *Ibid.*, January 5, 1959.

[138] *Ibid.*, January 19, 1959, and May, 1961; *Ecumenical Press Service*, March 20, 1959.

[139] Confidential information to the author, January, 1961.

[140] Walter Freytag in *The International Review of Missions*, Vol. XLVI, pp. 410–416 (October, 1957). See also Walter Freytag, *Die junge Christanheit im Umbruch des Ostens. Vom Gehorsam des Glaubens unter den Völkern* (Berlin, Furche-Verlag, 1958, pp. 272), pp. 122–133.

about 400 students enrolled in six theological seminaries.[141] In 1960 a Protestant woman visiting China reported old and young people in church services, with men in the majority, 46 students in the theological seminary in Peking, and 100 students, of whom 30 were women, in the theological seminary in Nanking.[142]

The Russian Orthodox Church in China suffered severely from the Communist regime. The Communists wished to expel all the Russians from Manchuria, presumably because they were refugees from the Soviets. In the 1950's the Russian residents and clergy in that region declined sharply. Some Chinese Orthodox remained and in 1950 a Chinese was consecrated bishop in a ceremony in Moscow.[143]

Over fragments of what was historically China—Macao, Hong Kong, and Taiwan—the Communists had not extended their rule when these pages were penned. To them we must turn, although with regrettable but necessary brevity.

MACAO

Macao had been in Portuguese hands since the sixteenth century. A peninsula on an island in the estuary of the West River and close to the major southern port of the mainland, Canton, it had long been a sleepy settlement more famous for opium and gambling than for trade or religion. From the sixteenth to near the middle of the nineteenth century it had been a crack in the coastal wall which China presented to the Western world. Through it Roman Catholic Christianity had had one of its means of entrance to the Middle Kingdom. In the secularism and religious somnolence which characterized Portugal in the nineteenth century, Macao remained ostensibly Roman Catholic, but it had no importance in the spread of the faith in China. It continued to be under the Portuguese padroado and its bishops were appointed from Lisbon. It did not change materially in the five decades which were introduced by the outbreak of World War I. During World War II it was spared occupation by the Japanese and gave haven to several thousand refugees. Long noted for its colourful religious processions, in the 1950's it experienced an upsurge of attendance at religious services.[144] After the occupation of the mainland by the Communists, it was again a refuge and through it many escaped to Hong Kong. Here, in 1952, with the timorous permission of the authorities, the Legion of Mary was organized,[145] proscribed though it was on the mainland. In 1958 the single major

---

[141] Report of the Japanese Christian Delegation to China (West Haven, Conn., Promoting Enduring Peace, no date, pp. 16), p. 3.

[142] Church News of the Northern Countries (Sigtuna, Sweden, mimeographed), December 20, 1960.

[143] New Missionary Review, Spring, 1952, and Spring, 1956.

[144] Mission Bulletin, Vol. VI (1954), pp. 582, 895, 919 ff., 953–955, 987.

[145] Ibid., Vol. VII (1955), p. 82.

seminary, founded in the first half of the eighteenth century, had twenty-eight students.[146] Yet, in spite of the long presence of the Church, in 1949 only about 6 per cent. of its population were Roman Catholics.[147]

HONG KONG

Hong Kong had a quite different story. First ceded to Great Britain in 1842, it was made up of several islands, on one of which was the chief city, Victoria; a portion of the adjacent mainland, Kowloon, acquired in 1860; and a slightly larger area, the New Territories, held on a lease due to expire in 1997. A British crown colony, the large majority of its population were Chinese. It became a major port and after its occupation by the Japanese from December, 1941, to 1945, it again came under British rule. Following the Communist occupation of the mainland, its population was swelled to slightly over three millions in 1962 by hundreds of thousands of refugees. They constituted a major problem in subsistence and housing, but by a combination of private philanthropy, largely by churches, the energy of the colonial administration, private capital in trade and manufactures, and the industry, resourcefulness, and adaptability of the Chinese, by 1962 some of the must acute features had been ameliorated. From the beginning of British ownership Christianity had been represented by missions, both Roman Catholic and Protestant.

Down to the Japanese occupation the course of Christianity in the twentieth century was much as it had been to the eve of World War I. The Communist triumph on the mainland brought rapid developments. Numbers of missionaries, both Roman Catholic and Protestant, came to the colony to continue their efforts for the Chinese. Many Chinese Christians also found homes there.

By July, 1959, Roman Catholics were said to total 146,464. During the preceding two years they reported 26,335 baptisms of adults and 8,632 of children. These numbers indicated a very rapid growth by conversion as against that by births.[148] Of the priests only about a fourth were Chinese.[149] Yet, because of the political conditions on the continent, Hong Kong was becoming a major centre of theological education. To care for refugees, the Jesuits expanded a seminary founded in the 1920's, and between 1950 and 1956 its major seminarians more than tripled. On graduation they served in various places in South-east Asia. In 1954 the Dominicans transferred from North Vietnam to Hong Kong a regional seminary which they had begun in 1930. The Salesians of Don Bosco and the Milan Missionaries had scholasticates. The Dominicans maintained a priory. In 1948 the Franciscans transferred to Hong Kong an institution begun

---

[146] Allen, *A Seminary Survey*, pp. 452, 454.
[147] *Enciclopedia Cattolica*, Vol. VII, p. 1949.
[148] *Worldmission Fides Service*, January 18, 1961.
[149] *Ibid.*, March 12, 1959.

in Peking in 1945 for the translation of the Bible into Chinese and the preparation of theological treatises in easy Latin for use in scholasticates and theological seminaries.[150]

Protestants were of several denominations. In the mid-1950's eighteen societies were represented—most of them American but some British and Continental. In 1957 they were reported as having 184 places of worship, a staff of 345, and 55,237 adult members. The largest staff and the most members were in the interdenominational and non-denominational churches. Of the denominations the Anglicans had the largest membership followed in descending order by the Baptists, the Church of Christ in China, the Pentecostal Holiness Church, the Lutherans, and those connected with the Rhenish Mission.[151] For Protestants as for Roman Catholics, Hong Kong became a centre of preparation for the ministry not only for the colony but also for Chinese in some other parts of East Asia. In 1948 the Lutheran Theological Seminary moved from Hankow to Hong Kong. Three years later the Southern Baptists placed there a seminary which they had formerly maintained in Shanghai. In the 1950's the smallest of the three institutions for training Protestant clergy was the Union Theological Seminary, a joint enterprise of the Anglicans, the Church of Christ in China, the London Missionary Society, the American Methodists, and the YMCA.[152]

All this meant that in 1962 about one in twelve of the population of Hong Kong were regarded as Christians. Roman Catholics were about twice as numerous as Protestants.

TAIWAN

Taiwan entered the twentieth century in the possession of Japan. It had been ceded by China as the price of defeat in the war of 1894–1895 with her island neighbour. It remained in Japanese hands until 1945 when, as a result of World War II, it was returned to China. After their defeat on the mainland the Nationalists retired to Taiwan. There, protected by the Formosa Strait and the navy of the United States, they continued the Republic of China, maintaining that it was the only legitimate government for the entire country.

Under the Japanese the population of Taiwan was predominantly of Chinese ancestry, chiefly from the coastal provinces of the mainland. In the mountains were a few thousand aborigines of primitive culture. After the expulsion of the Japanese, the population was augmented by about two million mainlanders—Chinese, but speaking the kuo yü, usually called Mandarin, the national language of China, different from the Chinese spoken by the native Taiwanese.

Between 1914 and 1945 Christianity was represented by both Protestantism

---

[150] Allen, op. cit., pp. 454, 455; Mission Bulletin, Vol. VI (1954), p. 986.
[151] World Christian Handbook, 1957, p. 30.
[152] Allen, op. cit., pp. 170, 171.

and the Roman Catholic Church. The former had been introduced by the English and Canadian Presbyterians—the English in the South and the Canadians in the North. The Roman Catholic Church was dependent on the Dominicans. In 1929, of a population of about four millions, slightly less than one per cent. were said to be Christians, three-fourths of them Protestants and a fourth Roman Catholics.[153] By 1945 Protestants were said to number about 30,000 and Roman Catholics about 8,000.[154]

The Nationalist immigration brought marked changes. Many missionaries, both Protestant and Roman Catholic, followed the Nationalists, numbers of whom were Christians, from the mainland. Other missionaries entered, for here was the largest accessible body of Chinese. Christianity spread rapidly, notably among the aborigines. It was estimated that in 1959 between 60 and 80 per cent. of the 150,000 tribesmen in the eastern part of the island professed to be Christians. Both Protestant and Roman Catholic missionaries were responsible.[155]

After 1949 Protestantism was represented by many different denominations and missions. In 1957 the Presbyterians who had come from the missions of the English and Canadian churches united to form the Presbyterian Church in Taiwan. In that year they had about a third of the Protestant membership and four-fifths of the estimated Protestant community. The Little Flock, the indigenous movement which we noted on the mainland, was next in the reported membership. It was closely followed by the Church of Christ in China and the (indigenous) True Jesus Church. These three were chiefly among the mainlanders. In addition many Continental European societies, British societies, and especially American societies were present. Most of the newly arrived Protestant societies did not coöperate with the International Missionary Council.[156] Estimates varied widely as to the number of Protestants. A study made in 1957, confessedly incomplete, reported the total in the Protestant community as 155,-294.[157] Another, completed in 1959, put it at 230,000.[158] Protestants were endeavouring to recruit and train an indigenous body of clergy. In 1960 the strongest academically of the theological seminaries was the one founded in 1876 in Tainan by the English Presbyterians. In the 1950's it coöperated with Tunghai University, a Protestant institution founded in that decade. Late in the 1950's three other theological seminaries were operating and a number of Bible schools had been begun, chiefly·by theologically ultra-conservative groups.[159]

In the 1950's several societies, orders, and congregations added personnel to the Roman Catholic Church. Many of the new arrivals were from the main-

[153] *Testo-Atlante Illustrate delle Missioni*, p. 116.
[154] *The New York Times*, December 19, 1959.
[155] *Ibid.*
[156] *World Christian Handbook, 1957*, pp. 62, 63.
[157] *Ibid.*
[158] *The New York Times*, December 19, 1959.
[159] Allen, *op. cit.*, pp. 166–169.

land. In 1952 Taiwan was given a hierarchy, with a Chinese as the first arch-bishop.[160] Foreign priests mounted from 120 in 1952 to 310 in 1956, and Chinese priests from 44 in 1952 to 95 in 1956. Adult baptisms were 2,067 in 1953 and rose quickly to 22,261 in 1956. In the same years infant baptisms were 1,545 and 7,895 respectively. The Roman Catholic body was said to be 20,112 in 1952 and 80,661 in 1956.[161] In 1959 the total was reported to be 163,814.[162] That is close to another estimate, of 170,000, made in 1959.[163]

In 1959, then, roughly about one in twenty-five of the population of Taiwan was counted as a Christian. Approximately three-fifths were Protestants and two-fifth Roman Catholics. A fifth were aborigines. Mainlanders were a larger percentage than Taiwanese. The influx of aborigines corresponded with what we have found elsewhere—the more rapid spread of the faith among peoples of primitive cultures and animistic religions than among the more traditionally civilized and adherents of the "higher" religions. The growth among the main-landers may have been due to the fact that they were uprooted from their ac-customed environment and thus were relatively open to the Christian message.

SUMMARY

From 1914 to the Communist occupation of the mainland, the Christians in China increased in numbers. The growth was most marked before 1922, pre-sumably because so much of the traditional culture was disintegrating under the impact of the revolutionary age. The resistance of the older cultural patterns was weakening. Many were searching for secure foundations for their individ-ual lives or were hoping that the remedy for China's obvious weakness was in the religion that seemed to be an integral part of the civilization invading China; perhaps it was the source of the vigour which enabled that civilization to overcome China's resistance.

Beginning in 1922 a series of movements and events retarded but did not fully check the growth of Christianity. Anti-Christian agitation led the way. It arose partly from the influx of the religious scepticism which was a phase of the revolutionary age in the erstwhile Christendom, partly from nationalistic agitation against a missionary enterprise associated with Western imperialism, and partly from Communism. The Japanese invasion which began in 1931 and reached full-scale dimensions in 1937 added obstacles.

As in the nineteenth century, the growth of Protestantism was relatively more rapid than that of the Roman Catholic Church. Yet the latter continued to have more adherents than did the former. But Protestantism, especially that

[160] *Mission Bulletin*, Vol. VI (1954), pp. 116–120.
[161] *Ibid.*, Vol. IX (1957), p. 153.
[162] *Worldmission Fides Service*, January 15, 1961.
[163] *The New York Times*, December 19, 1959.

propagated by British and American organizations, touched Chinese life from a much greater variety of angles than did Roman Catholicism. As in other parts of the world, both branches of the faith placed a mounting emphasis upon giving the faith a rootage in Chinese leadership and initiative.

After the brief breathing space which followed the expulsion of the Japanese came the Communist domination of the mainland. Communist rule, while not eliminating Christianity or completely halting conversions, reduced the number of professing Christians and insisted upon the severance of ties with the churches of the West and coöperation with the People's Republic of China. In the process many Christians were liquidated, along with much larger numbers of non-Christians who were labeled as reactionary and opposed to Communism, and all missionaries left or were expelled—except a few who were imprisoned on the charge of being spies for China's enemies.

Inevitably reasons were sought for this reverse. Here was the major recession in the tide of Christian advance among non-European peoples which had made the nineteenth century and the first half of the twentieth century the greatest period from the standpoint of geographic dimensions in the expansion of Christianity—or of any other religion. Why this major defeat? Many were the explanations among Protestants and Roman Catholics and in non-Christian and religiously neutral circles.

Here also was defeat for the liberal forces in the West, notably in the United States, which had striven to encourage the emergence of a Chinese government and society which would incorporate democratic ideals as the Western world and especially the United States understood them. It was chiefly with this dream—although reinforced by the hope of profiting by the China market—that the United States had stood for the "Open Door" and the independence and territorial integrity of China as against Japanese and European ambitions, which would have parceled out the country or have dominated it completely. The dream had caused Americans to welcome the thousands of Chinese students who flocked to colleges and universities in the United States. The dream was responsible for the American effort to check Japan in her adventures in China, and it brought on Pearl Harbour and the entrance of the United States into World War II by way of the Pacific. The dream led to the inclusion of China, then ostensibly under the *Kuomintang,* as a major power in the United Nations and with a permanent seat in the Security Council. Here was the purpose which motivated the United States in its massive assistance to that government and which sent General Marshall on his foredoomed effort to effect a reconciliation of Nationalists and Communists. The dream was important in American support of the Republic of China in its bastion on Taiwan and in resisting the admission of the People's Republic of China to the United Nations.

An obvious source of the Christian reverse was the close association of

Christian missions with Western imperialism. The pressure of that imperialism with its economic ambitions was responsible for the treaties which made possible the entrance of missionaries and the acceptance of the faith by Chinese. Communists and ardent nationalists rang the changes on the theme.

Another factor was the numerical weakness of Christianity. Never at any one time did foreign missionary personnel, even if all branches of the faith be included, reach fifteen thousand. It was usually far below ten thousand. Nor did Christians ever constitute as much as one per cent. of the population. The influence of Christianity was proportionately much greater than its numerical strength would have led the neutral observer to expect. It was especially noteworthy in the variety of channels in which Protestants sought to help the Chinese. Yet, even when this influence was fully taken into account, Christianity was clearly very much a minority movement.

An important reason for the triumph of Communism on the mainland was the indigenous character of its leadership. In the mid-1920's an impetus and some direction came from Russians. However, they were discredited by the break with Chiang Kai-shek and the disintegration of the first attempt at a Communist regime. The later Communist leadership, both south of the Yangtze and then in Yenan, was entirely Chinese. Communist ideology was taken over from the West, chiefly through Russia, but during the Yenan period Moscow appears to have been cool to the Chinese Communists. In contrast with Christianity, in which constant contact was maintained with the churches of the Occident and extensive financial support and much of the personnel were from the "older churches" of the West, when Communism captured the mainland its leadership was entirely indigenous and only in the later stages was help given by the U.S.S.R. Many Chinese looked to Mao Tse-tung rather than to Khrushchev as the true dogmatician of Marxism. Technical advisers came from Russia, but only on Chinese invitation. Russia also gave help in finances and physical equipment, but at Chinese initiative and invariably for a price. The Communists appealed to the nationalistic fervour which demanded emancipation from foreign imperialism.

The Communists used physical force and wholesale indoctrination made possible by the application of physical force. They put to death millions of opponents. If they were true to their ideals, Christians could not employ any of these methods. In several centuries and countries formal adherence to Christianity had been obtained by similar measures, but some of the more sensitive Christians deplored them and in the Christian missions of the nineteenth and twentieth centuries, except as missionaries took advantage of treaties wrested by force from economic and political motives, the earlier methods were never openly and very seldom indirectly employed.

Still another factor was the fashion in which Communism perpetuated much of the historic cultural ideology of China and so was not as alien as was Christianity. It is true that the Communists sought to uproot much of the inherited culture and most of the historic institutions. They set up what they called a republic and not an empire. They endeavoured to eliminate the Confucian family and the loyalties and customs connected with it. Their education ignored Confucianism except to brand it as a feature of the "feudalism" which they were determined to erase. Yet Communism had much in common with the Confucianism and Legalism under which the Chinese state and society had been shaped. It and they were centred on improving the physical and moral conditions of the masses. Communists, like Confucianists and Legalists, insisted that the officials seek the welfare of the governed, and interpreted that welfare in materialistic this-worldly terms. Although Confucianists and Legalists were not overtly atheistic as was Communism, much in their philosophy, especially in Confucianism, was religiously agnostic. The Communists decried much of Confucian morality, but they had their conceptions of morality and endeavoured to inculcate them. Confucius had made much of moral self-examination. The Communists went him one better and emphasized self-examination and confession to the group with rectification by the group. The Chinese had traditionally called their realm the Middle Kingdom, regarded their culture as the only true civilization, and been glad when the "barbarians" adopted it. In accordance with that tradition the Communists esteemed their form of Marxism the best ideology for all men and strove to spread it.

More important than any of the factors we have mentioned as responsible for the reverse suffered by Christianity in Communist China was the contrast to which we have repeatedly called attention between the secularizing movements issuing from alleged Christendom in the revolutionary age and the essence of the Christian Gospel as seen in the apparent weakness of the incarnation and the cross. In the revolutionary age the secularizing forces, always present, attained their most gigantic and mostly widely spread dimensions, and a Christianity which more nearly embodied the weakness and the power of the Gospel than it had since its earliest centuries permeated more of mankind than ever before.

In the mid-twentieth century human prophecy could not wisely predict the immediate future either in China or elsewhere. The historian could simply note that in the former Christendom Christianity was showing fresh vigour, although often in creative minorities, and that outside Christendom it was continuing to spread and bear fruit, albeit also in minorities which only imperfectly embodied the genius of the Gospel. Whether Christianity as such would survive in China no one could know, but that in the 1950's thousands of Chinese Christians were seeking to hold true to the Gospel as they understood it, and often at great price, was indisputable.

CHAPTER XIV

The Record in Tragic Korea

THE half-century introduced by the outbreak of World War I brought almost unrelieved tragedy to Korea. That country, by its geographic location a pawn in the game of empire-building of ambitious neighbours much larger in area and population, suffered again and again in the power struggle of the closing decades of the nineteenth and the first six decades of the twentieth century. Late in the nineteenth century China and Japan fought over it with Russia an interested spectator (1894–1895). Japan won and compelled China to recognize the independence of Korea—a step which Japan had taken some years earlier. Russia opposed Japan in Korea, and to protect her interests Japan fought and defeated Russia (1904–1905). After a brief attempt to govern the country through its ruling house, in 1910 Japan formally annexed the country. The Japanese administration was resented by Korean patriots, stimulated as they were by the rising tide of nationalism which was one of the features of the revolutionary age. They were heartened by the stress placed on self-determination by Woodrow Wilson in his stirring appeals during World War I. Japan countered by a combination of police repression and efforts to improve the economy and the education of the Koreans. In the 1930's, as a phase of their expansionist programme on the Continent, the Japanese strove to assimilate the Koreans, especially by requiring participation in the rites of the state Shinto employed to inculcate loyalty to the emperor. These measures were heightened when, during World War II, Japan endeavoured to give reality to her dream of hegemony in Greater East Asia. With the defeat of Japan and the expulsion of the Japanese from Korea, the latter tried to form an independent government. But Russia and the United States had set up zones of occupation divided by the 38th parallel of latitude. North of that parallel the Russians stimulated the formation of the North Korean People's Government, a Communist regime, which in 1948 became the Democratic People's Republic of Korea. In the South, with the encouragement and aid of the United States, the Republic of Korea came into being and in 1948 was recognized by the United Nations as the sole legitimate government of the country. In June, 1950, equipped with Russian arms, tanks, and planes, the North Koreans surged across the 38th parallel and quickly overran most of the South. Under American initiative, the Security Council of the United Nations sent forces to Korea, chiefly those of the United States, and drove back the North Koreans. Chinese Communist "volunteer" armies came to the rescue. The battle line swayed back and forth. After months of fighting, in July 1953, an armistice was signed which was in effect an uneasy truce with the armed forces of the rivals watching each other warily across a no mans' land which roughly corresponded to the 38th parallel. In the summer of 1953 the United States and the Republic of Korea signed a mutual security treaty. In the summer of 1961 similar treaties were signed by the North Koreans and the U.S.S.R. and the People's Republic of China.

The devastation wrought by the aftermath of World War II brought untold distress to millions of Koreans in both North and South. It was aggravated by the striking increase of population—from about 15,500,000 in 1914 to about 22,800,000 in 1938 and to an estimated 32,970,000 in 1959, of which 22,973,000 were in the Republic of Korea. The latter figure had been swelled by refugees from the North. Also contributory to the suffering was the unnatural division between the predominantly agricultural South and the potentially industrial North with its resources of minerals and forests. Massive aid from the United States only partially alleviated the distress.

THE PRE-1914 COURSE OF CHRISTIANITY

As we have seen, the continuing history of Christianity in Korea began late in the eighteenth century.[1] The Roman Catholic branch of the faith was introduced in the 1780's through Korean contacts with missionaries in China. It was accepted by small minorities but was checked by recurring persecutions, one of the most severe of which came in the 1860's. With the establishment of treaty relations in the 1880's between Korea and Western powers, the government-inspired persecutions ceased. The Roman Catholic missions were resumed and reinforced and Protestantism was introduced, mainly from the United States and chiefly through Presbyterians and Methodists, with the former the more prominent. By 1912 Roman Catholics were said to number 78,950[2] and in 1914 baptized Protestants were reported to total about 96,000.[3] The Presbyterians especially encouraged self-support and self-propagation and the Korean Presbyterians were vigorous in spreading the faith. With Protestantism came education of a Western kind, including that on the college level, and Western medicine.

[1] Volume III, pp. 446–449.
[2] Delacroix, *Histoire Universelle des Missions Catholiques*, Vol. III, p. 282.
[3] Beach and St. John, *World Statistics of Christian Missions*, p. 62.

THE 1914-1937 YEARS

The course of Christianity in Korea was mingled inextricably with political developments. This was true of both branches of the faith but was less marked among Roman Catholics than Protestants.

The number of Christians continued to mount, and more rapidly proportionately than the population. In 1934 Roman Catholics were said to total 147,476,[4] and in 1936 baptized Protestants were reported as 168,477.[5] Christians were more numerous in the North than in the South, possibly because in the North society was somewhat more fluid.

The rate of Protestant growth fluctuated markedly and seemed to have been affected by political developments and the temper of the Koreans. Between 1911 and 1919 it was slow. Although the number of missionaries and of Koreans giving full time to the Church increased, the annual total of baptisms declined and the membership fell off. This sobering situation was ascribed in part to police measures introduced because possible centres of nationalistic unrest were seen in Protestant churches, connected as they were with American missionaries who tended to be critical of the annexation by Japan. It appears to have arisen, too, from a feeling of hopelessness among patriots who had looked to the churches as potential agencies for achieving political independence.[6] Then came five years of rapid growth (1920-1925), said to be due in part to the confidence aroused in World War I by the idealistic pronouncements of Woodrow Wilson and the belief that independence was near at hand. Indeed, while the peace conference was meeting in Paris to effect the post-war settlement, thirty-three Koreans, among them fifteen Christians, signed a declaration of independence. Moved by the world-wide trend towards democracy for which the victors had ostensibly fought the war, the Japanese adopted a conciliatory policy. In the desire to capitalize on the war idealism to spread the faith to "make the world safe for democracy," for a time additional help in money and personnel came from the United States.[7] Reaction followed. The anti-Christian movements in China and Russia had repercussions. Funds from the United States decreased. Economic conditions in the country as a whole were bad. Many were disillusioned. In some churches the numbers of Christians declined.[8] The financial contributions of Korean Protestants fell off sharply.[9] The reasons for the defection of so many Christians were not entirely clear. They may have been disappointed in the failure of the faith to meet expectations, or discouraged by the stern discipline demanded by churches of their members, or both. The

[4] *Fides Service*, January 19, 1935.
[5] Parker, *Interpretative Statistical Survey of the World Mission of the Christian Church*, p. 18.
[6] Wasson, *Church Growth in Korea*, pp. 78-97.
[7] *Ibid.*, pp. 98-124; Soltau, *Korea. The Hermit Nation and Its Response to Christianity*, p. 59.
[8] Wasson, *op. cit.*, pp. 125 ff.; Soltau, *op. cit.*, p. 59.
[9] Soltau, *op. cit.*, pp. 1, 103.

migration to the cities and to Japan and Manchuria, and the extreme poverty may have been factors.[10] But, as the statistics we have cited show, in spite of many who had fallen away, in 1936 the Protestants were 75 per cent. more numerous than in 1914. In 1924, in consonance with a general trend in Protestantism the world around, the Korean National Christian Council was organized. It took over many of the functions of the earlier Federal Council of Protestant Evangelical Missions in Korea.[11] Korean Protestants were active in spreading the faith, not only in Korea, but also abroad. Korean Presbyterians sent missionaries to the province of Shantung, China.[12]

Success in self-support was seen in the fact that in 1937 about two-thirds of the Presbyterians fully supported their pastors and other phases of their programmes.[13] Increasingly Protestantism was rooted in Korea. In addition to the independent church which embraced most of the Presbyterians and which was organized before 1914, in 1930 the autonomous Methodist Church came into being and elected a Korean as its bishop.[14]

The years 1914–1937 saw the arrival of additional Roman Catholic missionaries, among them the Maryknollers. They also witnessed the transfer to Korean clergy of a prefecture apostolic, an indication of the increasing rootage of the Roman Catholic Church.[15] Yet in 1931 foreign priests and brothers—from the three orders and societies represented—outnumbered the Koreans in those categories.[16]

Distress Is Brought by Japan's East Asian Ambitions (1937–1945)

The efforts of the Japanese to dominate East Asia brought problems and

[10] James D. Van Buskirk, *Korea. Land of the Dawn* (New York, Missionary Education Movement, 1931, pp. xii, 200), pp. 51–53.

[11] Soltau, *op. cit.*, pp. 58–60. Some indication of the growth was seen in four historical volumes: J. S. Ryang, editor, *Southern Methodism in Korea. Thirteenth Anniversary* (Seoul, Board of Missions, Korea Annual Conference, Methodist Episcopal Church, South, introduction 1929, pp. 186, 299); Harry A. Rhodes, editor, *History of the Korea Mission, Presbyterian Church, U.S.A., 1884–1934* (Seoul, Chosen Mission Presbyterian Church, U.S.A., preface 1934, pp. 672, x); Charles Allen Clark, compiler, *Digest of the Presbyterian Church in Chosen, 1934* (Seoul, Presbyterian Publication Fund, preface 1934, pp. 195, vi); Harry A. Rhodes, editor, *The Fiftieth Anniversary Celebration of the Korea Mission of the Presbyterian Church in the U.SA., June 30–July 3, 1934* (Seoul, Post Chapel, John D. Wells School, no date, pp. 236). See also *The Korea Mission Year Book, Issued under the Direction of the Federal Council of Missions in Korea* (Seoul. The Christian Literature Society of Korea, 1928, pp. 238), *passim*.

[12] Charles Allen Clark, *The Korean Church and the Nevius Methods* (New York, Fleming H. Revell Co., 1930, pp. 278), p. 162.

[13] J. Merle Davis, *Mission Finance Problems and the Younger Churches* (Bangalore, Scripture Literature Press, 1938, pp. 104), pp. 59, 60; Herbert E. Blair, *Christian Stewardship in Korea* (New York, International Missionary Council, 1938, p. 36), *passim*.

[14] Wasson, *op. cit.*, p. 4; *The Christian Century*, Vol. XLVII, p. 1629.

[15] Delacroix, *op. cit.*, Vol. III, p. 282; Schmidlin, *Catholic Mission History*, p. 626. On the situation early in the 1930's see *The Catholic Church in Korea* (Hong-Kong, Imprimerie de la Société des Missions-Étrangères, 1924, pp. 108), pp. 78 ff.

[16] Soltau, *op. cit.*, p. 110.

increasing distress to Christians in Korea, both foreigners and nationals. They began with the Mukden episode in September, 1931, but did not become acute until Japan's full-scale invasion of China in 1937. They mounted steadily as Japan stepped up her war measures and after the United States and the British Empire became active belligerents (December, 1941).

Most of the Protestant missionaries were from the United States, and the Japanese were vividly aware of the criticisms of their policies in China by both the government and the public opinion of that country. Therefore Korean Protestantism, associated as it was with Americans and long the seed bed of anti-Japanese movements, was especially under suspicion. The police closely eyed Korean Christians who had studied in the United States and kept some of them under what amounted to house arrest. The government insisted (1937) that Christian schools comply with the rule applied to other schools and have their students participate in ceremonies at Shinto shrines as a symbol of their loyalty. Rather than comply, the Southern Presbyterians closed their schools, but the Methodists conformed, on the plea that the rites were civil and not religious.[17] In 1938 the Japanese went further and ordered some of the churches to require their members before coming to the Christian services to present themselves before a shrine of the Sun Goddess, the putative ancestress of the imperial house, and in villages where a Shinto shrine did not exist to erect one on the church premises. The issue divided the Christians. Some obeyed, on the assurance of the government that the rites were patriotic and not religious. Others refused, insisting that to accede would be tantamount to idolatry.[18] That same year the government closed the offices of the National Christian Council and several other organizations and urged that connexions be established with the corresponding bodies in Japan.[19] By the close of 1941 the government had ordered all the Korean Protestant churches to affiliate themselves with the Church of Christ in Japan, which was being organized under pressure from the state to bring together all the Protestants in that country.[20] Meantime most of the missionaries had left the country, partly to relieve the Korean Christians of the embarrassment of the presence of citizens of countries with which tensions were mounting and partly out of unhappiness over the fashion, as they thought, in which some Christians were compromising their faith.[21] If any remained in Korea, they were interned and later repatriated after the United States and members of the British Commonwealth had been drawn into the war with Japan.[22] Yet it was said that only to Christians was the right of assembly given.

[17] *The International Review of Missions*, Vol. XXVII, pp. 11, 12 (January, 1938).
[18] *Ibid.*, Vol. XXVIII, p. 10 (January, 1939).
[19] *Ibid.*, p. 11.
[20] *Ibid.*, Vol. XXXI p. 11 (January, 1942).
[21] *The Japan Christian Quarterly*, Vol. XVI (1941), pp. 40–44.
[22] *The International Review of Missions*, Vol. XXXII, p. 7 (January, 1943).

The departure of the missionaries was reported to have lessened the suspicion of foreign intrigue entertained by the government.[23]

As the tide of war began to run against Japan, by government orders public worship was greatly restricted, the use of the Old Testament was forbidden, and that of the New Testament was heavily censored. Many buildings of churches and Christian schools were commandeered for war purposes. Increasing pressure was applied to ensure participation in Shinto observances and, so it was said, to receive Shinto baptism. Many of the older clergy were forced to resign and numbers of the younger clergy were conscripted for labour in industries connected with the war. Much church life was forced underground or found expression in family and private worship.[24]

Since most of the Roman Catholic missionaries were from France and Germany, they and their church were not as badly disturbed by the political situation in the 1930's and during World War II as were the Protestants. Beginning in December, 1941, those who were citizens of countries at war with Japan were interned and eventually repatriated.[25]

THE TROUBLED POST-WAR YEARS, 1945——

The defeat of Japan and the evacuation of the Japanese from Korea seemed to bring fresh opportunity to Christianity. The Republic of Korea, the government set up in the South (1948), had as president Syngman Rhee, a Methodist, who had headed what was called the government-in-exile. Some missionaries returned and new ones were sent. But the internal troubles, especially the division between the North and the South, the Communist invasion of the South, the counter-attack by the United Nations, the uneasy armistice, and the continued Communist domination of the North brought untold suffering to Christians as well as to non-Christians. For the Protestants the situation was made more difficult by divisions within their body which were the aftermath of the controversy over the attitude towards the Shinto shrines. With the defeat of Japan the latter had disappeared, but memories were long and those who had complied with the Japanese in observing the rites of state Shinto were looked upon by those who had not done so as having both collaborated with the hated alien rulers and compromised the faith.

In the South, where the American military government was in control, Protestant missionaries quickly returned and were welcomed by the Korean Christians. The demand for Bibles and other Christian literature was great. Steps were taken to repair the many church buildings which had fallen into decay and to rebuild those that had been destroyed. Yet in the Russian zone no

[23] *Ibid.*, Vol. XXXIII, p. 16 (January, 1944).
[24] *Ibid.*, Vol. XXXV, pp. 15, 16 (January, 1946).
[25] *Ibid.*, Vol. XXXII, p. 7 (June, 1943).

missionaries were permitted and the restrictions on Christian activity, partly through the destruction of church property during the war, were said to be great.[26]

Even before the Communist invasion of the South, in the three years after the Japanese defeat about five million refugees were said to have flooded the South. Some were repatriates from China and Japan. Others were returning workers from the battalions of forced labour recruited by the Japanese. Even more were fugitives from the Communist terror in the North. Among them were pastors, teachers, and lay leaders. Numbers showed marked initiative in organizing congregations and erecting church buildings. Many families gave shelter to relatives and friends from the North. The churches undertook to aid the thousands of orphans, to provide schools, employment, and guidance to youth, and to assist others who were in dire distress. At the outset, missionaries were mostly returning veterans, but new recruits began arriving.[27]

By 1950 substantial progress had been made. More missionaries had come. In the North the churches were attracting many by their consistent Christian living. In the South the National Christian Council launched a "save the country evangelistic campaign," a Christian broadcasting station was erected in Seoul, the distribution of Bibles and other Christian literature was increasing, the scope of Christian education was broadened, and steps were taken to train Christian physicians abroad to help meet the clamant need for medical care.[28]

Then came the Communist invasion of the South, the counter-attack by the forces of the United Nations with its surge beyond the 38th parallel, the coming of Chinese Communist "volunteers," and the retreat of the United Nations' armies to what became the line fixed by the armistice. The fighting entailed an enormous destruction of property and life in which Christians and church property were heavily involved. Thousands of children were orphaned, millions were forced below the poverty line—a condition aggravated by the mounting population—and public and individual morality declined. Prostitution, corruption in government circles, and bands of lawless youth appeared. During the Communist occupation of the South thousands were accused of coöperating with the Republic of Korea and were tortured or killed. Among them were many Christians.[29] The refugee program was aggravated by hordes who fled

[26] *Ibid.*, Vol. XXXVI, p. 9 (January, 1947). On the experiences of one of the returning missionaries see Mary L. Dodson, *Half a Lifetime in Korea* (San Antonio, The Naylor Co., 1952, pp. xv, 197), pp. 124 ff.

[27] *The International Review of Missions,* Vol. XXXVIII, pp. 8–10 (January, 1949). On the situation in the North see Bob Pierce, *The Untold Korean Story* (Grand Rapids, Zondervan Publishing House, 1951, pp. 89), pp. 46, 47.

[28] *The International Review of Missions,* Vol. XXXIX, pp. 8, 9 (January, 1950).

[29] For some examples see John W. Riley, Jr., and Wilbur Schramm, editors, *The Reds Take a City. The Communist Occupatoin of Seoul, with Eyewitness Accounts* (New Brunswick, N.J., Rutgers University Press, 1951, pp. xiv, 210), pp. 188–192; Arch Campbell, *The Christ of the Korean Heart* (Columbus, Ohio, Falco Publishers, 1954, pp. 144), pp. 107 ff.

from the North and, with those from the South, moved again to escape the advancing Communist forces.[30] For a few months most of the missionaries were evacuated, chiefly to Japan, but they soon began returning. At least one theological seminary and Ewha University reopened in Pusan, for a time the only major city not in Communist hands.[31]

When the division of the country was stabilized at the armistice line, the Protestant forces, Korean and foreign, put forth valiant efforts to rebuild churches and educational and medical plants and to erect new ones. Relief poured in from abroad.[32] Yet as late as 1960 the World Council of Churches reported that, although 1,600,000 refugees had been settled on their own land and 400,000 on government land, about 3,000,000 or 4,000,000 were still unassimilated—homeless, hungry, and in need of help.[33] Evangelistic campaigns were undertaken. Theological seminaries grew in enrollment. In 1957 Protestants had nine such institutions with a total of 1,346 students.[34] Yonsei University was begun as a union of Chosen Christian University and the Severance Union Medical School, both interdenominational. It put up new buildings, largely with foreign money, and in 1958 had an enrollment of about 3,900.[35] Much stress was placed on Christian education in the local congregations, partly to raise the level of Christian faith and living of the members and partly as a means of spreading the faith. Chapels were constructed for factories and special efforts were made to reach non-Christian students. The circulation of the Bible mounted; in 1958 it was said that half as many copies were distributed as in Japan, with about four times as large a population, and about two-thirds as many as in India, which had twenty times the population.[36] Late in the 1950's Protestantism was reported to have 1,234,-258 adherents. Presbyterians led, with Methodists second, and the churches connected with the Oriental Missionary Society, a Holiness movement, third. Although the cities had many Protestants, that branch of the faith was predominantly rural.[37] Another statistical summary gave the Protestant communicants in 1952 as 219,745 and in 1957 as 293,806, and the total Christian community as 744,031 in 1952 and as 844,377 in 1957.[38] All sets of figures showed

---

[30] Donald Owens, *Challenge in Korea* (Kansas City, Mo., Beacon Hill Press, 2nd printing, 1957, pp. 95), pp. 67 ff.

[31] *The International Review of Missions*, Vol. XLI, p. 8 (January, 1952).

[32] *Ibid.*, Vol. XLII, pp. 6, 7 (January, 1953); Richard Gehman, *Let My Heart Be Broken . . . with the Things that Break the Heart of God* (New York, McGraw-Hill Book Co., 1960, pp. x, 245), ppp. 27–85.

[33] *The International Review of Missions*, Vol. L, p. 8 (January, 1961).

[34] Allen, *A Seminary Survey*, p. 159.

[35] *The International Review of Missions*, Vol. XLVIII, p. 9 (January, 1959).

[36] *Ibid.*, Vol. L, pp. 8, 9 (January, 1961).

[37] *Ibid.*, Vol. XLVIII, p. 8 (January, 1959).

[38] *World Christian Handbook, 1957*, p. 52. Allen, *op. cit.*, p. 158, gives the total of adherents, reported by the National Christian Council, as 1,324,000.

the Presbyterians as leading, but the second set placed the Oriental Missionary Society ahead of the Methodists in membership. It also showed a much more rapid growth of the Oriental Missionary Society, both in membership and in its total Christian community. A number of other denominations were represented, but none approached these three in size. In 1957 the Southern Baptists and the Seventh Day Adventists were next, but together they were only about a tenth as numerous as the Presbyterians. Obviously none of the sets of figures was more than approximately accurate and neither included the North. Indeed, when these lines were penned no dependable information was obtainable of the status, or even the existence, of Christianity in the part of Korea that was under Communist control. Clearly such Christians as remained would be even more suspect as possible collaborators with the enemies of the regime than were those on the mainland of China.

In spite of its rapid growth, and in part because of it, Korean Protestantism faced many difficult problems. It was badly divided, not only between denominations but within them. The Presbyterians, for the most part conservative theologically, were deeply troubled. The causes were partly controversy between degrees of theological conservatism, partly sectional differences between Christians from the North and those of the South, partly the degree of former resistance to the Japanese requirement of participation in Shinto rites, and partly the historical origins of the constituent bodies.[39] In 1957 three distinct Presbyterian bodies were reported, which together had more than half of the Protestant communicants and adherents in that year.[40] The Presbyterians were divided to some degree because a conservative minority opposed any association with the Ecumenical Movement.[41] Late in 1960, out of the controversy over that issue, the general secretary and the entire office staff of the National Christian Council resigned.[42] The fact that Syngman Rhee was a Methodist complicated the situation when in 1960 a popular movement, headed by students, drove him out of office and into exile.

Yet in the same breath it must be said that Korea had more Protestant theological students than any other country in Africa, Asia, or Latin America, that in 1957 the theological seminary of the largest of the three Presbyterian bodies had more enrolled than any other Presbyterian seminary in the world, and that the graduates of all three Presbyterian institutions were insufficient to staff the growing number of churches. It was affirmed that each of two of the cities in the Republic of Korea had more Presbyterian churches than any other city in

[39] First-hand information from a number of sources; *The International Bureau of Missions,* Vol. XLIX, p. 8 (January, 1960).

[40] Allen, *op. cit.,* pp. 158, 160.

[41] *The Christian Century,* Vol. LXXVI, pp. 1462, 1463 (December 16, 1959); *Ecumenical Press Service,* December 11, 1959.

[42] *The New York Times,* January 23, 1961.

the world.[43] In the new government which succeeded that headed by Rhee, the president was a Presbyterian elder, his wife was a theological seminary graduate, the premier was a Roman Catholic, and the speaker of the upper house of councillors was a Presbyterian.[44] As typical of what was happening in several denominations, in 1960 Bishop Chong Pil Kim of the Korean Methodist Church reported that the full members of his church had increased about 17 per cent. in the past five years, that the Methodists were maintaining 32 orphanages, 23 centres for widows, 3 social centres, 3 hospitals, and Ewha University with over 6,000 girls enrolled, that of 996 churches 826 were entirely self-supporting, that 95 per cent. of the salaries of pastors and Bible women was from Korean sources, and that in addition the families of Methodist chaplains in the armed forces were cared for.[45]

The Roman Catholic Church, while growing in numbers, by 1962 had attained not more than a third of the numerical dimensions of the Protestants. In 1959 those in the Republic of Korea were said to total 413,485.[46] In 1960 the Roman Catholics were served by the Columban Fathers, the *Société des Missions Étrangères* of Paris, Benedictines, Maryknollers, Salesians, Franciscans, and Jesuits, in addition to at least two congregations of women. The Columban Fathers had more than half the foreign priests.[47] In 1959 the increase of Roman Catholics was 34,729, as compared with 69,000 and 62,000 in the two preceding years. The decline was said to have been due to the political situation. The complaint was also made that Syngman Rhee, a Protestant, had discriminated against Roman Catholics.[48] The Roman Catholic authorities complained of the paucity of foreign clergy. In 1960 they had 243 Korean and 198 foreign priests. Reinforcements to the latter were insufficient to fill the gaps made by the departures due to health and normal furloughs. Moreover, many of the Korean priests were engaged in advanced studies or were assigned to teaching or chancery work. The clergy were in insufficient numbers to give adequate pastoral care to the mounting numbers of the faithful and to have time for evangelism.[49] In 1958 the only major seminary was in Seoul under the administration of seculars and enrolled 243 students. It had been begun in 1908 by the (Bavarian)

[43] Allen, *op. cit.*, p. 161.

[44] *The Christian Century*, Vol. LXXVII, p. 1228 (October 19, 1960).

[45] Chong Pil Kim, *The Korean Methodist Church. Report to the Council of Bishops, Denver, Colorado, 1960* (Seoul, Korea Methodist News Service, 3rd printing, June, 1960, pp. 10), *passim*.

[46] *Worldmission Fides Service*, January 18, 1961. Another set of figures, those of the National Christian Council of Korea, said that in 1958 Roman Catholics numbered 242,034 as against 1,323,091 Protestants and 200 Orthodox.—*The Christian Century*, Vol. LXXV, p. 1294 (November 12, 1958). All these figures were for the Republic of Korea. None were obtainable for the North. Another Roman Catholic source said that in 1956 there were 214,496 baptized and 27,382 catechumens, making a membership of 241,830.—*Mission Bulletin*, Vol. IX, p. 60 (January, 1957).

[47] *Worldmission Fides Service*, January 5, 1961.

[48] *Ibid.*, September 17, 1960.

[49] *Ibid.*

Missionary Benedictines of St. Ottilien, but the activities of that order in the North had been terminated by the Communists and the buildings of the Seoul institution had been destroyed by the fighting which followed the Communist invasion of the South. In 1959 plans for an additional seminary were announced for the South-west.[50] In 1956, of the five vicariates apostolic and prefectures apostolic in the South, three were administered by Korean clergy.[51] By the 1960's the Roman Catholic Church in the North had been completely disorganized. Some of its members, including Bishop Patrick James Byrne (1888–1950), a Maryknoller, had been martyred.[52]

Roman Catholics were engaged in the activities which were also features of their missions in other countries. Always there was the effort to win converts and to give pastoral care to the faithful. Education was stressed. For example, in 1957 Jesuits from the United States, who had begun their mission in Korea only about 1954, purchased a site for a university.[53] The National Catholic Welfare Conference in Korea and the Catholic Relief Services helped to find homes in the United States for Korean orphans.[54] Maryknoll Sisters conducted a clinic for thousands of the more extreme cases of poverty and disease and built and equipped a hospital in Pusan.[55] At the instance of Cardinal Spellman a village was constructed for blind veterans of the Korean army and their families to help them regain normal living.[56]

SUMMARY

The remarkable advances made by Christianity in Korea in the last quarter of the nineteenth century continued in the next sixty years in spite of political vicissitudes connected with World War II—first Japanese measures in the 1930's and the fore part of the 1940's, then the Communist occupation of the North followed by the Communist attempt to take over the entire country, and the ensuing fighting and destruction of life and property during the years 1950–1953. Although by the mid-1950's the faith appeared to be stamped out or driven underground in the North, it flourished in the South, in no small degree because of the thousands of Christians who migrated to the South. By 1958 about a sixth of the population of South Korea (the Republic of Korea)

[50] Allen, *op. cit.*, pp. 454, 455.

[51] *Mission Bulletin*, Vol. IX, p. 60 (January, 1957).

[52] Raymond A. Lane, *Ambassador in Chains. The Life of Bishop Patrick James Byrne (1888–1950). Apostolic Delegate to the Republic of Korea* (New York, P. J. Kenedy and Sons, 1955, pp. 249), pp. 218–249.

[53] *Mission Bulletin*, Vol. IX (1957), p. 208.

[54] *Ibid.*

[55] *Ibid.*, pp. 413, 414.

[56] *Ibid.*, p. 562.

was said to be professedly Christian, with 1,323,091 Protestants, 242,034 Roman Catholics, and 200 Russian Orthodox.[57]

Protestantism arose largely through the efforts of missionaries from the United States, with Presbyterians in the majority. From its inception it was predominantly self-supporting, self-propagating, and self-governing. It tended to be theologically conservative. The Roman Catholic Church, although represented more than twice as long as Protestantism and growing rapidly, had many fewer adherents than Protestantism. The Orthodox were only a few hundred. The Church was doing much to assist the Koreans to adjust to the revolutionary age. Through relief agencies it was helping to alleviate the intense suffering brought by war. Its schools were aiding Koreans to take advantage of the knowledge and the techniques developed in the West. Through the medicine and surgery which were achievements of the revolutionary age disease and the high death rate were being fought.

The reasons for the rapid growth of Christianity were often discussed and were in part conjectural. The fact that religiously Korea presented a partial vacuum was important. None of the other high religions had much hold. Buddhism, once strong, had been declining for centuries and was all but moribund. Confucianism had influenced the elite but had not gripped the masses. As in China, it was suffering from the impact of the revolutionary age. Among the majority, religion was a form of shamanism, not very far removed from animism; as was true of animism elsewhere, it could offer slight resistance to the sophistication which came with the revolutionary age. In the new and fluid society Christianity had an opportunity such as offered itself in peoples of primitive or near-primitive cultures. In the uncertainties of the day many Koreans welcomed it with the sense of security which it gave in a world where the inherited structures were crumbling and the hereditary beliefs about the universe were undermined.

[57] *The Christian Century*, Vol. LXXV, p. 1294 (November 12, 1958).

CHAPTER XV

The Striking Change in Japan

IN THE five decades introduced by World War I Japan passed through at least four stages which were phases of its reaction to the revolutionary age. By 1914 it seemed to have made an unusually successful adjustment to the irruption of the revolutionary forces brought by the aggressive West. It had never been subject politically to the colonialism and imperialism which Occidental powers had imposed on much of Asia and Africa. For a few decades its full autonomy had been compromised by extraterritoriality and the control of its customs duties by treaties, but not to the extent that was seen in China. Before 1914 it had freed itself from these restrictions. It had adopted some features of Western representative institutions and cabinet government, but in such fashion that its national solidarity appeared to have been enhanced around its ancient imperial house. It had so effectively adopted and adapted the educational system of the revolutionary West that the vast majority of its people were literate, and in its universities and technical schools it had appropriated the science of the day, both theoretical and applied. It had become highly industrialized and was active in the world's shipping and commerce. Yet many of its historic customs had been preserved. Its family structure was but little altered. Its military tradition was reinforced by what was seen in the West and expressed itself through an organization and weapons which were modeled on Occidental precedents. The reverence for the emperor was enhanced. Shinto was continued and was utilized to augment the heightened nationalism that was a feature of the revolutionary age. Buddhism was revived. Confucian ideals were inculcated through the schools.

The first stage in the post-1914 reaction to the revolutionary age was a swing towards political liberalism. This stemmed partly from the contagion of the widespread idealism following the defeat of the Central Powers and the appeal of the slogan "Make the world safe for democracy" which contributed to that defeat. Most of the statesmen who had engineered the changes of the second half of the nineteenth century had died. New, complex, and confused currents were making themselves felt. Christianity, although professed by less than one per cent. of the population, had its adherents mainly among intellectuals and the professional classes and exerted a disproportionate influence on the country as a whole. The result was a movement towards liberalism in politics and other aspects of the nation's life.

Then came, as a second stage, a swing towards ultra-nationalism and militarism, which culminated in the full-scale invasion of China, the attempt to dominate all East Asia, and dramatic defeat, near exhaustion, and the occupation of the country by the late enemies—a completely new experience for the Japanese. This stage was ushered in by the Mukden incident in September, 1931, but did not reach its height until the total invasion of China in 1937. It ended with Japan's surrender in August, 1945.

The third stage was the occupation by the victors, in which the Americans, led by Douglas MacArthur as the Supreme Commander of the Allied Powers, were dominant. The occupation forces set about a drastic reconstruction of Japan. They preserved the imperial house but insisted that the emperor renounce his traditional claim to divinity and that the connexion between the state and Shinto, an instrument of the hyper-nationalists, be abolished. Under the occupation Japan was given a new constitution, framed more nearly on Western democratic patterns than the old, which demilitarized the country so far as law could do it. The occupation reorganized the educational system and brought about a redistribution of the land, taking it from the landlords and giving it to the farmers who tilled the soil. In April, 1952, the occupation was terminated.

Now followed the fourth stage, one which had not ended when these lines were written. American troops were still in Japan, largely to protect the country against the Communist menace in the cold war. Relieved of the crushing burden of financing a huge army and navy and aided financially by the United States, through their ability and industry the Japanese made an amazing economic recovery. They rebuilt the cities devastated by enemy bombings. They created a new industrial complex, taking advantage of the destruction of the old to adopt the latest improvements in machines. By drastic birth-control measures they reduced the growth of the population—although in 1961 it passed the ninety million mark. They regained much of their pre-war share in the world's commerce. The cities grew, until Tokyo became the largest urban centre in the world. In 1962 many of the reforms introduced by the occupation remained.

A striking feature of the post-World War II Japan was the sharp contrast between generations. Youth, especially in the cities and in student circles, was sharply critical of the pre-war generation and of militarism and was receptive to the currents of the contemporary phase of the revolutionary age. Many were impressed by Communism. It was said that about three-fourths of the students had no interest in religion and that most of the remaining fourth were not committed to any religious faith but were seeking and were at least open-minded. Only a small minority were Buddhists, Christians, or adherents of one of the new syncretistic cults.

Although official state Shinto was outlawed, some of its shrines were maintained by private initiative because of their historic and patriotic associations. Sect Shinto was waning. New syncretistic cults were flourishing, compounded of appropriations from Buddhism, Shinto, Christianity, and other faiths. They were popular in rural areas and among the urban proletariat. Their attraction was the sense of security, physical healing, and material prosperity which they promised in an uncertain world and the peace of mind which they engendered. As such they had kinship with some of the contemporary expressions of Protestantism in the United States and Latin America and, more remotely, with the Spiritism widespread in Latin America.

As we have seen,[1] Christianity entered the post-1914 decades as the faith of small minorities. It was represented by Protestantism, the Roman Catholic Church, and the Orthodox Church. Protestantism in its several denominations had more adherents than the other two branches of the faith taken together. It owed its introduction chiefly to Americans. In 1914 Protestant churches were said to have 103,119 members. They were mostly in the cities and were mainly women and professional and business men who had been much influenced by Western culture. The denominations with the largest numbers were first the Presbyterians, next the Congregationalists, then the Anglicans, the Methodists, the Baptists, and the Disciples of Christ. These denominations had become firmly rooted, with Japanese lay and clerical leadership, and were largely self-supporting and self-governing. Much emphasis was placed on schools, especially those on secondary and higher levels. Although the Roman Catholics included about ten thousand descendants of those who had secretly preserved their faith during the centuries of proscription and who, brought to light in the 1860's, had renewed their connexion with Rome, they did not multiply as rapidly as the Protestants. Their total in 1912 was said to be 66,134. They were served chiefly by missionaries from Europe and had only begun to create a body of Japanese clergy.[2] The Orthodox, fruits of the one extensive mission of the Russian Church among non-Christians outside the tsar's domains, in 1912 were about 32,000, mostly from the humbler elements of society. In 1914 the only foreign clergyman was a bishop, a Russian. The other priests were Japanese.[3]

GROWTH IN THE LIBERAL PERIOD, 1914–1930

In the sixteen or seventeen years which followed the outbreak of World War I Christianity grew in adherents and in its rootage in the life of Japan. In 1911 the government gave it formal recognition by inviting representatives of the

[1] Volume III, pp. 450–457.
[2] Streit, *Atlas Hierarchicus*, p. 100; Laures, *The Catholic Church in Japan*, p. 242.
[3] *The Christian Movement in Japan, 1911*, pp. 289–292; *1913*, pp. 417, 418; *1914*, p. 22 and the statistical table.

Protestant, Roman Catholic, and Orthodox Churches to share with representatives of Shinto and Buddhism in what was called the Three Religions Conference. Spokesmen for the state urged the religions to help in the moral guidance of the nation. Similar conferences were subsequently convened, the third in 1924.[4]

Protestants continued to be more numerous than Roman Catholics and Orthodox combined. In 1939 they were said to total 210,384, of whom all but 1,422 were communicants.[5] This was slightly more than double the number in 1914 and was a more rapid percentage growth than in the discouraging 1890's, but not as rapid as between 1900 and 1914. Variations in the size of the missionary body reflected the economic situation in the United States, from which most of the personnel came. In 1914 the figure was 1,123,[6] about half again as large as that in 1900. In 1925 it was 1,253,[7] and in 1936 it had shrunk to 829,[8] largely because of the depression of that decade.

As part of their programme in the hopeful 1920's, in 1928 Protestants undertook what they called the Kingdom of God Movement in an effort to reach the entire nation with the Gospel. At least two-thirds of the Protestant churches joined in it. It sought to make contact with the classes which had heretofore been untouched, especially the farmers, the factory labourers, the fisher folk, the miners, and the transport workers. It stressed the application of the Gospel to the social problems of the country. About 2,000 decisions a month were counted. Yet the totals of baptisms and church members did not notably rise, and in 1934 the movement was allowed to end without a public report.[9]

The Kingdom of God Movement had as its chief evangelist one of the most remarkable Christians whom Japan had seen, Toyohiko Kagawa (1888–1960). Kagawa was the son of a well-to-do father by a concubine.[10] He was formally given legitimacy, but the early death of his parents left him in the ancestral home where he was not wanted and where, a sensitive child, he was desperately unhappy. While attending school he came in touch with an American missionary, found in him the affection for which he was hungry, and became a Christian.

[4] Iglehart, *A Century of Protestant Christianity in Japan*, pp. 139, 185, 186.
[5] Parker, *Interpretative Statistical Survey of the World Mission of the Christian Church*, p. 18.
[6] Beach and St. John, *World Statistics of Christian Missions*, p. 62.
[7] Beach and Fahs, *World Missionary Atlas*, p. 82.
[8] Parker, *op. cit.*, p. 84.
[9] Iglehart, *op. cit.*, pp. 197–199.
[10] Of the large literature by and about Kagawa the following are especially useful: William Axling, *Kagawa* (New York, Harper & Brothers, rev. ed., 1946, pp. ix, 195), by an intimate friend with the coöperation of Kagawa and his wife; Toyohiko Kagawa, *Before the Dawn*, translated from the Japanese by I. Fukumoto and T. Satchell (New York, George H. Doran Co., 1924, pp. 398), a novel which was in part autobiographical; Toyohiko Kagawa, *Meditations on the Cross*, translated by Helen F. Topping and Marion R. Draper (Chicago, Willett, Clark and Co., 1935, pp. ix, 211); Toyohiko Kagawa, *Love, the Law of Life* (Philadelphia, The John C. Winston Co., 1929, pp. vii, 313); T. Wemyss Reid, *Kagawa, Mystic and Man of Action* (London, Independent Press, 1937, pp. 72); Cyril J. Davey, *Kagawa of Japan* (Nashville, Abingdon Press, 1960, pp. 150).

He went to a Presbyterian college and then to a theological seminary. There he showed the zest for books and learning, the eagerness to write, the sacrificial care for the unfortunate, whether animals or human beings, and the passion for social reform which were to characterize all his future years. Frail physically, he contracted tuberculosis but recovered sufficiently to continue his education. While still a student in the theological seminary in Kobe he took up his residence in the slums, seeking to serve the disease-ridden and the extremely poor. He shared his humble lodgings with some of the most unfortunate and from one of them contracted the trachoma which left him with permanently impaired eyesight. In an area marked by murder and rampant vice he preached, followed the way of non-violence and love, and won some to a better life. He wrote novels, several of which had a wide circulation, and from them came fame and an income. He had over two years of study in the United States. Book after book poured from his facile pen, some of it fiction, some poetry, some meditations, and some on social problems. He became convinced that the poverty which he saw about him was largely a concomitant of the industrial revolution which was then flooding Japan. He endeavoured to remove poverty by attacking it at its source, the kind of urban society which, as in the Occident, was a product of the machine age. He became a Christian socialist and helped to form a labour union. A strike ensued which, in spite of his efforts to induce it to follow the way of non-violence, brought police action and his imprisonment. Attacking the problem of poverty in the rural population he initiated a peasants' union. In other ways he sought to remove the social ills which either were the product of the revolutionary age or were intensified by it. He organized coöperatives. He opposed Communism with its materialistic philosophy and was attacked by Communists as an ally of the capitalists. In the mid-1920's the government undertook measures to wipe out the slums in the six largest cities and also permitted labourers to organize. Kagawa was credited with having contributed to both developments. He founded and supported social settlements in Kobe, Osaka, and Tokyo. When the depression of the 1930's struck Japan, bringing with it intense and widespread suffering, at the request of the mayor of Tokyo he became chief adviser of that city's welfare bureau. He started several new social centres and inaugurated a programme of unemployment insurance. He was an indefatigable evangelist, addressing audiences large and small. He became known and honoured in Protestant circles the world around, travelling and lecturing widely.

Kagawa was not the only Protestant Japanese to undertake new measures. For example, after World War I Protestants had missions to Japanese in Formosa, Manchuria, and Brazil. They endeavoured to establish friendly contacts with Chinese Christians.[11] In the post-1918 years Kanzo Uchimura began the lectures

[11] Iglehart, *op. cit.*, pp. 144, 145.

and the periodical leading to the birth of the *Mukyokai* ("no church church") movement, which was greatly to expand among intellectuals in the succeeding years.[12] Uchimura died in 1930, but his influence and the methods of study which he inaugurated continued to spread. The *Mukyokai* was an indigenous expression of the Christian faith which regarded the churches as foreign importations and sought to avoid denominationalism with its divisions. Uchimura and some Japanese evangelists of the day stressed the early second coming of Christ.[13] An influential Presbyterian pastor, Masahisa Uemura, from his church in Tokyo ministered to individuals of many kinds—from students to cabinet ministers—but did not address himself to social or political issues.[14]

In accordance with what was happening in several other countries as an expression of the Ecumenical Movement, in 1922 the National Christian Council was organized. Its initial achievement was serving as a centre for coöperative Christian efforts to relieve the distress created by the devastating earthquake which in 1923 all but destroyed Yokohama and did immense damage in Tokyo.[15]

In view of the high literacy rate in Japan and the eagerness of the reading public, it is not strange that great quantities of Christian literature were issued. In the 1920's the circulation of the Bible, as a whole or in portions, was over a million copies a year. Christian periodicals numbered nearly two hundred. About two hundred new titles and many translations of foreign books appeared annually. Most of them were published without subsidy.[16] In 1926 the Christian Literature Society of Japan was formed through the union of two earlier bodies. In its direction it was primarily foreign. A predominantly Japanese committee called the Library of Christian Thought also came into being.[17]

Protestants were pioneers in the higher education of women. This fact was additionally apparent when, in 1918, several missions joined in creating the Tokyo Women's Christian College.[18] Through the YMCA Protestants did much to further athletics and physical education, introducing indoor swimming, basketball, and volleyball. Through the YMCA the Japanese participated in the Far Eastern Games in 1913 and subsequent years.[19]

In the years 1914-1930 Roman Catholics continued to grow, although not as rapidly as Protestants, either in numbers or proportionately. In 1912 they were said to total 66,134, with 152 foreign and 33 Japanese priests.[20] In 1936 their

---

[12] Volume III, pp. 456, 457; Iglehart, *op. cit.*, p. 154; Raymond P. Jennings, *Jesus, Japan, and Kanzo Uchimura* (Tokyo, Christian Literature Society, 1958, pp. viii, 160), pp. 35-38.

[13] Iglehart, *op. cit.*, p. 181.

[14] *Ibid.*, p. 155.

[15] *Ibid.*, p. 183.

[16] *Ibid.*, p. 207.

[17] *Laymen's Foreign Missions Inquiry. Supplementary Series*, Vol. VIII, pp. 8, 9.

[18] Iglehart, *op. cit.*, p. 161.

[19] Latourette, *World Service*, pp. 174, 439.

[20] Streit, *op. cit.*, p. 100.

total was reported to be 108,934.[21] This was an increase of about two-thirds in the quarter-century, in contrast with the slightly more than doubling of the Protestant body in approximately the same period. Several additional orders and congregations sent missionaries, most of them from the Continent of Eurpoe.[22] Like the Protestants, Roman Catholics conducted schools. In 1928 an institution which the Jesuits had opened in Tokyo in 1913 became a full-fledged university, Sophia, which in 1938 had over a thousand students.[23] Roman Catholics produced an extensive literature—in 1937 over four hundred books on the Roman Catholic faith.[24] Unlike the Protestants, who were mostly in the professional and business middle classes, the majority of the Roman Catholics were from the humbler walks of life. But they too were predominantly in the cities.[25] Exceptions were seen, of course. A daughter of the Fujiwara, an ancient and highly aristocratic family, joined the Carmelites in their house in Tokyo which had been founded in 1930. In the 1930's the daughter of a former premier was converted.[26]

The Roman Catholic Church rapidly developed a national organization and took steps to transfer local administration to Japanese. For example, in 1919 an apostolic delegation was created for the Japanese Empire.[27] In 1927, in accord with the procedure adopted for China, the Pope himself consecrated a Japanese to head the diocese of Nagasaki, where, because of the sixteenth-century mission, were more than half of the Roman Catholics in the country.[28] In 1937 a Japanese was appointed Archbishop of Tokyo.[29] Even before 1940 when the government brought pressure on the churches to become independent of foreign financial aid and to transfer all administration to Japanese, the Roman Catholic Church had taken steps in that direction. It was the first Christian body to obtain official recognition under the religious bodies law of 1939.[30]

The Orthodox Church continued, but lacked the rapid growth of its earlier years. The founder of the Japanese mission, Nicolai, died in 1912. Before that date the Russo-Japanese War, with the attendant hostility to Russia, retarded accessions and in 1912 the membership was said to be about 32,000.[31] The revolution and the coming to power of the Communists in Rusisa cut off the financial

[21] *Fides News Service*, January 30, 1937.
[22] Latourette, *A History of the Expansion of Christianity*, Vol. VII, p. 381.
[23] *Fides News Service*, December 3, 1938.
[24] *Ibid.*, February 27, 1937.
[25] *Missiones Catholicae Cura S. Congregationis de Propaganda Fide*, 1927 (Rome, Typis Polyglotis Vaticanis, 1930, pp. xiv, 534), pp. 184, 185.
[26] *Fides News Service*, May 26, 1934; June 19, 1937.
[27] Paul Lesourd, editor, *L'Année Missionnaire 1931* (Paris, Desclée de Brouwer et Cie, pp. 667), p. 146.
[28] *Fides News Service*, December 26, 1936.
[29] *Ibid.*, December 11, 1937.
[30] John J. Considine, *Across a World* (New York, Longmans, Green and Co., 1942, pp. xvi, 400), pp. 202, 203.
[31] *The Christian Movement in Japan, 1914*, statistical table.

assistance from that country on which the Japanese Church had depended, and the Japanese staff was reduced. However, since emphasis had long been on planting the Church in Japan and almost all the clergy were Japanese, some financial support came from the faithful and in 1937 the membership was said to be slightly over 40,000, although less than half were considered active.[32]

THE ADVERSE WAR YEARS, 1931–1945

The Mukden incident of September, 1931, introduced a decade and a half of growing adverse pressures on Christianity in Japan. Through the ultra-militarists and hyper-patriots, Japan's overseas adventures were parelleled by demands that all, including the Christians, conform to state Shinto and its rites as evidence of loyalty. In 1937 the government had another meeting of the Buddhists, Shintoists, and Christians, and many religious people called the conflict in China a holy war.[33] When the Western powers were drawn into belligerency with Japan, strictures on the churches became increasingly severe. Christians were urged to coöperate in building Japan's "Greater East Asia." As the life-and-death struggle became more intense, pastors as well as others were required to join in the war effort, whether in the armed services or in industries ancillary to the war. As the agony approached its climax, ecclesiastical structures shared in the destruction wrought by enemy bombings. Since the Church was mostly urban and the bombings were concentrated on the cities, a larger percentage of its buildings were involved than if the Christians had been distributed evenly throughout the nation. The severe rationing bore heavily on the Christians as it did on others of the non-belligerents.

Protestantism was affected in a wide variety of ways. At first its leaders endeavoured to press forward in evangelism as in earlier days. In 1939, as a result of plans made in November, 1938, at the All-Japan Christian Conference, the United Evangelistic Campaign was launched, with Kagawa as the outstanding speaker and the entire country as its objective. It continued through 1940.[34] The shrine issue brought a division of opinion. With some exceptions Japanese Protestants took the government at its word and conformed to the ceremonies with the understanding that they were simply expressions of patriotic loyalty and were not religious.[35] Yet when in 1940 the Home Ministry ordered that shrine tablets be installed in every home the National Christian Council resisted

---

[32] *The Japan Christian Year Book, 1938*, p. 167; Bolshakoff, *The Foreign Missions of the Russian Orthodox Church*, p. 78.

[33] Iglehart, *op. cit.*, p. 217.

[34] *The National Christian Council Bulletin* (Tokyo, The Chrisian Council of Japan), February, March, May, 1939; December, 1940; January, 1941. On developments in one church, Presbyterian, see James A. Cogswell, *Until the Dawn* (no place, Board of World Missions, Presbyterian Church U.S., 1957, pp. 226), pp. 139–173.

[35] Iglehart, *op. cit.*, p. 173.

and for this or other reasons the order was not enforced.[36] That body had also criticized the circulation by the Osaka police of a document demanding of all pastors categorical answers to such questions as their attitude towards the emperor, the worship of the national gods, and whether imperial rescripts took precedent over the Bible.[37] Missionaries were even less compliant.[38] However, in July, 1937, the month in which full-scale war broke out in China, the National Christian Council voted to support the government in the crisis. In September of that year it declared its loyalty to the imperial aims to accomplish "the unity and peace of the Far East." It pledged its member churches to aid in the Spiritual Mobilization Movement and the Movement for Spiritual Awakening. In 1937 and 1938 several denominations adopted similar resolutions.[39]

In 1941 in the months before Pearl Harbour all but about a hundred Protestant missionaries left Japan. The Protestant missionary body, American and British, had been increasingly critical of Japan's programme, especially the invasion of China. As tensions mounted between the United States and Japan, missionaries were more and more under police surveillance. Most of them were either withdrawn by their boards or felt that they could not remain without embarrassing their Japanese colleagues. By June, 1941, the vast majority had sailed for home.[40]

Before the mass evacuation of the foreign personnel an important development had occurred through Japanese initiative that gave a structure to the Protestantism in the country which, with important modifications, was still in existence when these lines were written. That was the formation of the Church of Christ in Japan (*Nihon Kirisito Kyodan*), usually known briefly as the *Kyodan*. For many years numbers of Protestants, both Japanese and foreign, had dreamed of a united church embracing all Protestants. Now they were told by some of their friends in official circles that if they did not come together voluntarily the government would require this step as an administrative measure in order to have a responsible organization through which it could channel its directives. Moreover, the government wished to terminate all possible control of the churches and other institutions from abroad—either through financial assistance or in the administration of schools, hospitals, or congregations. In October, 1940, the decision to create the new body was formally made, and in June, 1941, the initial meeting of the General Assembly was held. In the pre-

---

[36] *Ibid.,* p. 220.

[37] *Ibid.,* p. 219.

[38] See a thoughtful, outright presentation of the conviction that state Shinto was in fact a religion in Daniel Clarence Holtom, *Modern Japan and Shinto Nationalism. A Study of Present Day Trends in Japanese Religion* (University of Chicago Press, 1943, pp. ix, 178). It was based on a doctoral dissertation. A revision appeared in 1947 under the same title (University of Chicago Press, pp. ix, 226).

[39] Iglehart, *op. cit.,* p. 221.

[40] *Ibid.,* p. 236.

ceding weeks a deputation was sent to America to explain to the churches which had supported Protestant missions the reasons for the step and, if possible, to avert the war which seemed to be impending. They met with a representative group of Americans in the Mission Inn in Riverside, California, and there a fellowship of prayer came into being which outlasted the war.[41]

Pearl Harbour was followed by further developments. It brought the internment of such missionaries of the enemy countries as remained in Japan. Almost all were later repatriated. In the *Kyodan* the original organization had been by blocs representing the several member bodies—in a kind of federation. In November, 1942, at the command of the government, the blocs were in theory discontinued and a monolithic Protestantism was substituted. Actually much informal autonomy persisted. Everything outside the country was placed under the Greater East Asia Bureau. The several religions, including Christianity, were included in the Great Japan Wartime Religious Patriotic Association, with the Japan Christian Patriotic Association as one of its branches. The Director of the *Kyodan* obeyed all government directives. Spiritual Mobilization was furthered. In connexion with the Patriotic Airplane Fund-Raising the churches collected enough money for six planes. Through the Greater East Asia Bureau Protestants endeavoured to cultivate fellowship with the churches within the Japanese conquests and to encourage their coöperation with the Japanese authorities. Regular Sunday services became all but impossible, but many pastors were able to maintain a fixed period for public worship. Prayers for victory were offered. Hymn-books were revised to eliminate references to peace and to God as Creator, Judge, and Arbiter of human destiny. The government provided pastors with themes for their sermons and the police knew whether they were used. In the *Kyodan* the Bureau of Education was superseded by the Bureau of Indoctrination. Pastors were required to receive instruction in the purposes of the war. An effort was made to stress the distinctive quality of Japanese Christianity. Yet the *Kyodan* resisted government pressure to formulate a creed which would eliminate such distinctive Christian convictions as "God the Father Almighty, Maker of Heaven and Earth." Kagawa was twice arrested for his peace sentiments. The Seventh Day Adventists were dissolved and their properties were confiscated. About 250 ministers of the Holiness churches were arrested. The issue in both cases was the teaching of the approaching end of the world and the Divine judgement on the emperor. Many of the buildings of Christian schools were commandeered for war industries, and the teachers and students were assigned to work in factories and on farms.[42]

The Roman Catholic Church was inextricably involved in the storm of the

---

[41] *Ibid.*, pp. 229–238. The author was a member of the Riverside group.
[42] *Ibid.*, pp. 239–258.

war years. A few paragraphs above we noted that in 1937 a Japanese was appointed Archbishop of Tokyo. This was in pursuance of a general policy which the Roman Catholic Church was adopting in several other countries as part of its programme of giving rootage to the faith in indigenous leadership. Tatso Doi, the Archbishop of Tokyo, was named the *Torisha,* or head of the Roman Catholic Church in Japan, with whom the government was to deal.[43] In 1936 Rome formally permitted the faithful to be present at ceremonies which had only a purely patriotic character, such as those paying respect to the imperial family and the benefactors of the country.[44] In 1937 the Roman Catholics organized the National Committee of Catholics for Foreign Propaganda "for enlightening Catholics in other countries in regard to the nation's true aims and motives." It sent priests to Manchuria and China. Additional missionaries came, partly from the United States but chiefly from Germany and Italy.[45] In September, 1940, the decision was reached to replace foreign with Japanese principals of Roman Catholic schools.[46] Roman Catholics were permitted to be present at funerals, weddings, and other private ceremonies which had features of pagan origin on the ground that they merely had the significance of "urbanity and reciprocal benevolence."[47] On the anniversary of the founding of the empire, prayers were said in the churches for the imperial family and the prosperity of the realm.[48] In 1940 and 1941, in addition to the two Japanese already with dioceses, since the foreign ordinaries had resigned on the hint that if they did not the government would require them to, Japanese were named apostolic administrators of all the other ecclesiastical territorial divisions of the country.[49] When the atomic bomb fell on Nagasaki, about 7,000 Roman Catholics perished.[50]

The Orthodox encountered great difficulties. In 1939, although the numbers of adherents were said to be slightly over 41,000, the actual membership was estimated as between 13,000 and 14,000.[51] Candidates for the priesthood were so few that in spite of efforts in 1939 to revive the theological seminary no applicants for admission came forward.[52] Yet, because of the attitude of the government towards foreign heads of churches, in 1940 the Russian Archbishop of Tokyo, Sergius, resigned his see and transferred the property of the mission to

[43] *The National Christian Council Bulletin* (Japan), May, 1941.
[44] *Fides News Service,* February 22, 1936, and July 4, 1936.
[45] Iglehart, *op. cit.,* p. 218.
[46] *The Japan Christian Quarterly,* Vol. XV, p. 404.
[47] *Fides News Service,* July 4, 1936.
[48] *Ibid.,* April 6, 1935.
[49] Delacroix, *Histoire Universelle des Missions Catholiques,* Vol. III, p. 295.
[50] *Ibid.* Another report gave 8,500 as the figure and said that the Roman Catholic community which survived the persecutions of the seventeenth and eighteenth centuries was almost completely wiped out.—Laures, *The Catholic Church in Japan,* p. 244.
[51] *The Japan Christian Year Book, 1940,* p. 180.
[52] *Ibid., 1940,* p. 188.

the Japanese church. In 1941 an elderly Japanese was consecrated in Harbin to succeed him.[53]

REVIVAL UNDER THE FOREIGN OCCUPATION, 1945–1952

Following defeat came occupation by the victors, predominantly, as we have said, by Americans. Under the occupation not only were drastic changes made in several aspects of the life and structure of the country, but the amazing economic recovery was also seen which continued after the occupation ended. As we have suggested, the recovery was due primarily to the resourcefulness and industry of the Japanese, but it was facilitated by massive aid from the United States. How far the motives of the Americans were of Christian origin would be impossible to ascertain. They were undoubtedly a mixture of self-interest and altruism. That the altruism had back of it much from the Christian heritage was certain, but to what extent that heritage was determinative was not clear.

Protestantism was revived and strengthened. The first purely civilian delegation allowed entrance to Japan was of American representatives of the Riverside fellowship as a return visit of the Japanese spokesman of the *Kyodan* who had come to the United States in the spring of 1941.[54] The premier called Kagawa to assist him in guiding the nation to a new spiritual course and at the latter's suggestion September, 1945, was proclaimed a month of penitence.[55] Extensive contributions came from Protestants in other countries, especially the United States, in money, food, clothing, and medicine to aid in the relief of the Japanese population. The chief channel was Church World Service, a co-operative agency of American Protestants. The Church of the Brethren, the American Friends Service Committee, the Mennonites, the Lutherans, and the Roman Catholics were also represented. Coördination was through LARA (Licensed Agencies for Relief in Asia). Among the personnel of the occupation forces, both military and civilian, were Christians, some of them former missionaries, who beyond their official duties did what they could to help the Japanese. Some chaplains in the armed forces were of assistance.[56] Large shipments of Bibles in Japanese were sent by the American Bible Society to meet an urgent demand. Japanese hymnals were reprinted. SCAP, as the occupation administration was known, insisted that with these exceptions no special favours be shown to Christians. Gradually missionaries were permitted to enter, at first only those with previous experience in the country.[57]

---

[53] Bolshakoff, *op. cit.*, p. 80.
[54] The author's personal knowledge; Iglehart, *op. cit.*, pp. 270, 271.
[55] Iglehart, *op. cit.*, p. 269.
[56] *Ibid.*, pp. 271–274, 283.
[57] *Ibid.*, pp. 282, 283.

The *Kyodan* held its first post-war assembly in June, 1946. Several bodies which had been constrained by government pressure to enter it eventually withdrew, but those that remained included the majority of the Protestants of the country. Freed from control by the state, the *Kyodan* faced problems of organization and creedal agreement. However, it reached solutions. The numerically largest denominations which were integrated into the structure were the Congregationalists, the Presbyterians, and the Methodists. A coöperating committee of the mission boards of the mother denominations in America (the Interboard Committee for Work in Japan) was set up in New York and all foreign personnel sent through it were assigned to the *Kyodan* for its direction.[58]

Protestant secondary and higher education was revived and strengthened. The post-war demand for education filled the Christian schools to overflowing, as it did state and other institutions. In addition to the repair and enlargement of the physical plants, the International Christian University arose. A Christian university of the highest academic grade and a coöperative enterprise of the Protestant forces had long been a cherished dream. Now, chiefly through the imagination and initiative of Ralph E. Diffendorfer (1879–1951), a Methodist long prominent in the missions of his church and in the Ecumenical Movement, it became a reality. Diffendorfer brought together in Japan a board of Japanese Protestants and organized in New York the Japan International Christian University Foundation, which drew its financial support from mission boards, foundations, and individuals. The Japanese raised from the general public what in the poverty of the first post-war years was a very substantial sum. A campus was obtained on the outskirts of Tokyo. Hachiro Yuasa, an eminent Japanese Christian scholar who had suffered at the hands of the military authorities because of his faith, was appointed president. The name chosen was an indication of the purpose. Here was to be a university of the highest scholarly quality, emphatically Christian, and, while predominantly Japanese in control, student body, and faculty, was to attract students from other countries, both in Asia and the Occident, and was to have on its teaching staff citizens of several countries, including Japanese, Chinese, Americans, Europeans, and, hopefully, Koreans. In contrast with most Japanese universities it had a high ratio of faculty to a carefully selected student body and was increasingly residential. Its graduates immediately gained unusual recognition in the intense competition for employment, and pressure for admission mounted.[59]

Many church structures destroyed during the war were rebuilt and new ones were added. Funds came from abroad, but the *Kyodan* ruled that no one congregation could accept more than $3,000 from that source and that each

[58] *Ibid.*, pp. 284, 286, 291–294.
[59] The author succeeded Diffendorfer as president of the Foundation (1951).

must meet at least one-tenth of the cost. Pastors' salaries, pitifully small, were gradually improved, and pastors' libraries, many of which had been lost, were replenished.[60]

Personnel from abroad came in increasing numbers, some of them through organizations which had been in the country in the pre-war years, but more and more from societies which were now for the first time represented in Japan. Most of them were from the United States. Prominent were bodies which were ultra-conservative theologically—among them Pentecostals and fundamentalists —and which would not coöperate with many of the pre-war groups. With the formation of the *Kyodan* the National Christian Council had been dissolved as no longer needed. In the post-war withdrawal of some denominations from the *Kyodan* it again filled a useful function and in 1948 it was reconstituted. But several agencies, including most of those newly arrived, would not join in it. Some of them found fellowship in the Evangelical Alliance Mission (TEAM).[61]

The years which immediately followed Japan's surrender appeared unusually propitious for acquainting the Japanese with the Christian message. Thousands were adrift emotionally and were searching for an answer to life's deepest questions. The foundations on which the super-nationalists had based their adventures in East Asia and which had depended on high-powered propaganda had crumbled. What spiritual resources had enabled the Americans to overpower Japan? That was what many were asking. Chronic unemployment gave leisure for attendance at public meetings. Evangelistic campaigns were launched to seize the opportunity. Kagawa was prominent in them and foreign preachers engaged in them. E. Stanley Jones was repeatedly in the country. The Swiss theologian Emil Brunner spent some years in Japan, mainly on the faculty of the International Christian University, lectured in theological seminaries, had contacts with the intellectuals, and conceived a high regard for the *Mukyokai*.[62] Several of the imperial family were deeply interested. In 1947 a Protestant, Tetsu Katayama, prominent in the Presbyterian church of which Uemura had been pastor, became premier and during his year in office engineered the enactment of some of the most progressive legislation of the period.[63] Soichi Saito, the leading YMCA secretary, directed the repatriation of overseas Japanese.

The Roman Catholic Church undertook to meet the opportunity afforded by the foreign occupation and the relative open-mindedness of the Japanese. The country was given a fully native hierarchy as a *de jure* act, in succession to the *de facto* indigenous hierarchy which had served during the war. Rome encouraged orders and congregations, some of them not hitherto represented, to send personnel. To meet the clamant needs for relief the Catholic Rehabilita-

---

[60] Iglehart, *op. cit.*, pp. 299, 300.
[61] *Ibid.*, pp. 295, 296.
[62] *Ibid.*, pp. 301, 302; the author's personal knowledge.
[63] *Ibid.*, p. 289.

tion Committee was formed of influential clergy and naval and military men. *Caritas Japan* became a member of *International Caritas,* which had its headquarters in Rome. Roman Catholic chaplains in the occupation forces extended their activities to the Japanese. Many converts came, some of them from despair of finding meaning in life and from near-suicide. The majority of them were women.[64] The total of Roman Catholics mounted. In 1941 it had been 121,128. In spite of the losses during the war, especially from the atomic bomb in Nagasaki, by 1948 approximately the same goal had been reached. In 1952 the number were said to be 171,875.[65]

THE POST-OCCUPATION YEARS, 1952——

In the decade which followed the termination of the occupation, a revival of religion was seen. Although state Shinto had been abolished, many of the shrines connected with it were restored by voluntary effort. Isé, the historic central shrine, was thronged with worshippers. The Shrine Headquarters Association aided the folk shrines to resume their place in rural life. A Buddhist renewal ensued. Popular cults proliferated, some Buddhist and others syncretistic.[66] Yet, as we have said, much of youth, especially students, remained untouched.

Under these circumstances, Protestantism had a fairly steady but unspectacular growth. Of the thousands who signed cards at public evangelistic meetings expressing their interest, many went on to church membership, but more either did not affiliate with a church or, if they did, drifted away. Several foreigners conducted evangelistic campaigns. In 1960 a notable city-wide effort in Osaka organized by World Vision centred in meetings in the largest auditorium in the city. In 1961 a similar project was undertaken in Tokyo. Protestant totals increased from 233,000 in 1941 to 348,000 in 1958. Of the latter, about half were in the *Kyodan. Mukyokai,* although it gathered no statistics, was estimated to have grown in the same period from about 50,000 to about 70,000.[67] Although fully half the Protestants were from among the urban intelligentsia, efforts were made to reach the rural population.[68] Mediums of mass communication were employed, among them several broadcasting stations, and Bibles and other Christian literature were distributed. In as avid a reading public as Japan, large use was made of literature.[69]

[64] Tibesar, *The Catholic Position in Post-War Japan,* pp. 4–10.
[65] Laures, *op. cit.,* pp. 146, 147.
[66] Iglehart, *op. cit.,* pp. 315–318.
[67] *Ibid.,* p. 337. In 1959 the number of Protestants was given as 376,267.—*Ecumenical Press Service,* January 29, 1960.
[68] *The Japan Christian Year Book, 1954,* pp. 82–84.
[69] *Ibid., 1959,* pp. 56–66. For one audio-visual programme, SAVE (*Shinseika Audio-Visual*

Many forms of social service were undertaken. One was a post-war movement called *Aino-Kai* ("Love of Agriculture"), begun by a farmer's son who was converted in his teens. Distinctively Protestant, it centred around an academy which endeavoured to teach better agricultural techniques to young men and to prepare girls for marriage; daily Bible study was a part of every course.[70]

Specialized evangelistic methods were devised. In the 1950's, for example, the *Kyodan* sent young men into rural villages to begin churches which were to be self-supporting in five years. At least a third of the funds to inaugurate each project was to come from Japan and no more than two-thirds from abroad. Success was had in about two-thirds of the efforts.[71] Protestants also sought to reach the labourers in the rapidly mounting industries of Japan. Among other measures, through Labour Gospel Schools in local churches the workers were helped to see the bearing of their faith on their daily tasks and also to witness to their fellows.[72]

By 1961 the overwhelming majority of the foreign Protestant personnel in Japan were post-World War II arrivals. Only a very small percentage were veterans. They came from about 125 different organizations, a very large proportion of which had begun operations in Japan after 1945.[73] In addition several scores of missionaries were independent of any board or society.

In view of the fact that Protestantism was so heavily represented in the urban intelligentsia and of the emphasis on self-supporting and self-governing churches, it is not surprising that much attention was given to theological education. In 1956 twelve theological schools were maintained with an enrollment of 590. More than two-fifths of the students were in two institutions, the larger of which was the Tokyo Union Theological Seminary and the other, only slightly smaller, the Doshisha University School of Theology, a department of the oldest Christian university in the country. Both were affiliated with the *Kyodan*.[74] Theologically much variety existed, but in the main the stress was upon neo-orthodoxy of various stripes, with Barth very influential. In general the philosophical approach was ruled out and the emphasis was upon the self-revelation of God.[75]

Considering the pre-war experience with shrine Shinto, it is no wonder that

Education), see Dorothy A. Stevens, editor, *Voices Speak* (Philadelphia, Judson Press, 1957, pp. 93), pp. 54–56.

[70] *A Monthly Letter about Evangelism* (Geneva, The World Council of Churches, mimeographed), December, 1959.

[71] Charles W. Forman to the author, November 18, 1959.

[72] *A Monthly Letter about Evangelism*, November 8, 1958.

[73] See a list in *The Japan Christian Year Book, 1954*. On the situation of the Church Missionary Society in the early 1950's see reports of a visitor in H. A. Wittenbach, *Western Horizons* (London, The Highway Press, 1954, pp. xiii, 98), pp. 1–40.

[74] Allen, *A Seminary Survey*, pp. 148–154.

[75] Carl Michalson, *Japanese Contributions to Christian Theology* (Philadelphia, The Westminster Press, 1959, pp. 192), *passim*.

some Protestant circles felt alarm at its revival, even though that was by voluntary organizations. In 1955 the National Christian Council formally protested against the homage paid by government officials at the shrines and emphatically stood for religious freedom as guaranteed by the constitution. Other Protestant bodies also spoke out.[76]

The Roman Catholic Church continued to grow. In 1959 it reported 266,262 members. In the preceding two years it had had 19,939 baptisms of adults, nearly a sixth of which were in Tokyo, a city where it had been very weak before World War I. About the same number were in Osaka, a major industrial centre, and about a tenth were in Kyoto, long at the heart of Japanese conservatism. Between a third and a fourth of the Roman Catholics were in the diocese of Nagasaki, and that in spite of the losses through the atomic bomb which had been dropped on that city. Here, too, as might have been expected, were a third of the infant baptisms in the entire country.[77] The country-wide growth, it will be seen, had been 56 per cent. since the close of the occupation, as compared with about a 52 per cent. increase in the number of Protestants in the same years.

The Roman Catholic Church was also making a striking advance in its rootage in Japanese leadership. In 1959 Japanese priests numbered 392—more than double the 181 in 1949. Japanese bishops had increased from six in 1949 to nine a decade later, and in 1959 instead of one archbishop there were two. In 1959 students in major seminaries totalled 237 and scholasticates 118. All the dioceses and archdioceses were headed by Japanese, but the three prefectures apostolic were directed by foreigners. In 1960 a Japanese was raised to the cardinalate. Yet in 1959 more than three-fourths of the priests were still foreigners, evidence of the personnel which the Roman Catholic Church was pouring into Japan.[78] However, the large majority of the sisters were Japanese—in 1960, 3,559 out of 4,349.[79] But it was noted that by 1960 the number of adult baptisms had fallen off.[80]

The Roman Catholic Church carried on its mission in Japan through a variety of channels. Obviously it sought to win converts and to that end, as elsewhere, had many catechists as well as priests, lay brothers, and sisters. It maintained a large number of schools, from kindergartens to Sophia University, and in 1955 was said to have 102,000 students enrolled in 409 institutions. The Jocists, men and women (*Jeunesse Ouvrière Chrétienne* and *Jeunesse Ouvrière Chrétienne Féminine*), were introduced for Catholic young workers. The National Catholic

[76] John M. L. Young, *The Two Empires in Japan* (Philadelphia, The Presbyterian and Reformed Publishing Co., 1959, pp. xvi, 234), pp. 183–196.
[77] *Worldmission Fides Service*, April 2, 1960.
[78] *Ibid.*
[79] *Worldmission Fides Service*, April 2, 1960; October 22, 1960.
[80] *Ibid.*, October 22, 1960.

Committee of Japan had a social action group. Catholic students to the number of about 3,000 were organized, but in the mid-1950's youth work was reported to be weak.[81]

The Orthodox made a partial but not complete recovery. In 1959 they were said to number 35,295.[82] Many of their churches, schools, and houses were destroyed by the enemy bombings in World War II and the fires which followed. With the coming of peace a marked shortage of priests, liturgical books, and Bibles hampered a revival. The Orthodox wished to restore their relations with the Russian Orthodox Church, but because of the cold war the occupation authorities objected and at their suggestion Benjamin Basaluiga, an American-born prelate, was elected bishop (1947). The Japanese archbishop, Ono, would not conform. After seven years in office, Basaluiga was succeeded by Irinei Bekish, and reconciliation with Ono followed. A theological seminary was revived, a new building was erected, and by 1960 seventeen had been graduated, of whom some went to St. Vladimir's Seminary in New York City for further training. In 1959 the Tokyo seminary had nineteen students. American Orthodox serving in the armed forces, some of them as chaplains, gave aid. In 1958 three new churches were constructed and 317 joined the church, the majority of them in their teens.[83]

SUMMARY

In 1959 Christians celebrated the centenary of the re-introduction of Roman Catholic missions and the beginning of Protestant missions in Japan. In numbers the results of the hundred years of missions were not particularly impressive. By that year all the churches contained less than one per cent. of the population. Yet percentage-wise since 1914 they had grown far more rapidly than the population, and that in spite of the adverse fourteen years of war and the explosion in population which after 1945 had only begun to subside. In 1962 more than half of the Christians were Protestants. They were the result mainly of missions from the United States. But their churches had early become self-governing and self-supporting. They were chiefly urban and from the intelligentsia. With the large influx of new societies after 1945, many of them ultra-conservative theologically and appealing to lower income and educational strata, the pre-war character of Protestantism was somewhat altered, but not in a major fashion. Efforts, too, were being made to reach the rural populations. The latter, conservative and not as affected by the revolutionary age as were the city-dwellers, had only begun to respond when these lines were written. In

---

[81] Tibesar, *op. cit.*, pp. 14, 17, 25.
[82] *Ecumenical Press Service*, January 29, 1960.
[83] *New Missionary Review*, No. 1 (2) (Spring, 1952); No. 5 (Spring, 1954); No. 7 (Spring, 1955); Nos. 11–12, 12–13 (1957); Nos. 14–15, 15–16 (1959); Nos. 17–18, 18–19 (1960).

1962 about half the Protestants were in the *Kyodan,* a Japanese-inspired-and-led union of several denominations. Missionaries sent by the coöperating denominations in North America were assigned to it and appointed by it to their work.

Out of Protestantism a unique Japanese movement had arisen—*Mukyokai,* the "churchless church." Appealing predominantly to the intelligentsia, it was purely indigenous, eschewing imported, Western forms of the faith. It differed strikingly from the indigenous movements which sprang from Protestantism elsewhere—as in Latin America, among the New Zealand Maoris, in the Philippines, and in Africa—in stemming from the highly educated and not from the humbler ranks of society.

Roman Catholics at first drew mainly from the communities which had gone underground because of seventeenth- and eighteenth-century persecutions. In 1960 their chief numerical strength was in and around Nagasaki, where those communities had centred. However, after World War II they grew rapidly and, in conformity with Roman Catholic policy elsewhere, were increasingly served by Japanese clergy and governed by Japanese bishops.

The Orthodox, begun by Russians, persisted but were a minority.

In spite of the seemingly slight minority of its avowed adherents, Christianity exerted an increasing influence on the life of Japan.[84] On a superficial level, Christmas became a festival which competed with and even surpassed the traditional New Year's celebration.[85] In 1960 Japan ranked next to the United States in the number of Scriptures distributed and sold.[86] Many individuals who were not church members read the Bible and prayed. Intellectuals held that the Bible was part of Western civilization and that to be educated they must at least own a copy.[87] In 1960 the assertion was made that the Christian community was the most creative element in the moral life of the country.[88]

---

[84] For some of the ways between the two wars see Soichi Saito, *A Study of the Influence of Christianity upon Japanese Culture* (Tokyo, no publisher, 1931, pp. 72), *passim.*
[85] *Worldmission Fides Service,* October 24, 1959.
[86] *The Christian Century,* Vol. LXXVII, pp. 1448–1450 (December 7, 1960).
[87] W. T. Thomas to the author, October 29, 1960.
[88] *The Christian Century,* Vol. LXXVII, pp. 1448–1450 (December 7, 1960).

CHAPTER XVI

The Changing Islands of the Pacific

W E MUST now turn to the numerous but widely separated islands and island groups which dot the Pacific Ocean from a few degrees north of the equator to a few degrees south of that line. They vary in size from small coral atolls to Papua (also called New Guinea), an eastward extension of the East Indies. We have earlier seen something of their general features and the initial impact on them of the revolutionary age.[1] We noted that in the main the collective names given by Westerners to the chief divisions are Polynesia, Melanesia, Micronesia, and Papua and that by a rough generalization this designation is racial as well as geographic. We called attention to the fact that at the advent of the Westerner late in the eighteenth century the cultures were "primitive," with Stone Age implements and weapons and varieties of animism. We summarized the contrast, familiar to us in other regions, in the impact of the revolutionary age. It was felt first through explorers, then through traders and missionaries, and eventually through governments. The traders had material gain as their objective and with them came such distintegrating features of the revolutionary age as alcohol, slavery, and, unintentionally but no less disastrously, diseases to which the islanders could not offer the resistance which had been developed by Europeans through long contact. Missionaries endeavoured to offset the exploitation by their fellow countrymen, to win the islanders to the Christian faith, and to help them reorganize their individual and collective lives in such fashion that the coming of the Westerner would be a blessing and not a curse. The majority of the missionaries were Protestants, mostly from the British Isles and the United States, but many came from New Zealand, Australia, and Germany. Indeed, some of the Australian churches regarded the islands of the South Pacific as their peculiar obligation. A minority of the missionaries were Roman Catholics, for the most part from France. As a result of the efforts of the missionaries the majority of the Polynesians and Micronesians, a large minority of the Melanesians, and some of the Papuans accepted the Christian faith and were aided in re-ordering their patterns of living on Christian principles and acquiring the kind of education demanded by the revolution-

[1] Volume III, pp. 458–462.

ary age into which they were being hurried. In the latter half of the nineteenth century Western governments annexed the islands. The larger proportion came under the British flag, and the French, Americans, and Germans extended their authority over others. The Dutch took the western part of Papua and held it under the designation of Irian. On several islands the Protestant churches became self-governing and self-supporting and sent missionaries to non-Christian peoples in other islands.

The post-1914 decades brought changes. World War I with its defeat of Germany transferred the islands and areas held by that power to the victors, but as mandates under the League of Nations rather than as outright possessions. In that fashion Japan acquired most of Micronesia, and Australia held part of Papua and adjacent islands. World War II transformed the mandates into trusteeships under the United Nations, transferred the Japanese holdings to the United States as trustee, and brought New Zealand into the picture as trustee for several of the islands. During World War II hostilities between the major belligerents engulfed some of the islands and brought to them the armed personnel of the combatants. Because of the large immigration of non-Polynesian elements of many races and incorporation in the United States, first as a territory (1900) and then (1959) as a state, Hawaii ceased to function with the Pacific Islands in their kind of life.

Because of the small population involved, between two and three millions in the 1950's, in the global dimensions of our story we must content ourselves with mention of a few developments, especially in the Christianity of the Pacific islands, and with statistical summaries for the decades introduced by World War I.

One feature of the years, especially during and after World War II, was the growing involvement of the islands in the world scene and the impinging of the revolutionary age on peoples previously entirely or only slightly affected. That was notably the case in Papua. Papua was mountainous and heavily wooded and even in the mid-twentieth century some of its peoples were scarcely aware of the white man. During the war the hostilities penetrated beyond the previous outposts of Western culture. After the war additional exploration and the extension of the white man's government were undertaken. Missionaries, both Protestant and Roman Catholic, established themselves farther inland. In many instances missionaries were pioneers. Their task was complicated by the multiplicity of languages. In 1960 Roman Catholics of several orders and congregations from France, the Netherlands, the United States, Australia, and Germany were represented.[2] Among other achievements was the publication, in 1959, of a Roman Catholic hymnal with Papuan melodies.[3] In 1957 Protestants

[2] *Worldmission*, Vol. XI, p. 56 (Winter, 1960–1961).
[3] *Worldmission Fides Service*, July 25, 1959.

from fifteen different organization from Australia, New Zealand, Great Britain, Germany, and the United States were at work.[4]

In World War I the islands were not as deeply involved as in World War II. But the global epidemic of influenza which accompanied it decimated some of them.[5] World War II brought many of the Allied forces to the islands. Numbers among the troops were much impressed by what they saw of the effects of Christianity on the natives.[6] In some places the coming of the Japanese worked hardships for missionaries.[7]

Statistics can be only approximate. But in 1930 what were called "wholly evangelized areas" (exclusive of Hawaii), with a population of 170,000 were reported to have about 35,000 communicant Protestants and a Protestant community of about 96,000. "Partly evangelized" islands were said to have a population of around 2,000,000, with about 71,000 Protestant communicants and a Protestant community of approximately 261,000. At the same time Roman Catholics were reported as totalling about 41,000 in the "wholly evangelized areas" and about 138,000 in the "partly evangelized" islands.[8] This appears to indicate that by that year practically the entire population of the Society, Cook, Tonga, Samoan, Gilbert, Ellice, and Tokelau Islands thought of themselves as Christians, and that nearly a fifth of the population of the others regarded themselves as in that category. In 1930 in all the Pacific islands exclusive of Hawaii Protestants, communicants and non-communicants, were about 463,000 and Roman Catholics were approximately 179,000. In 1957 Protestants were said to be 906,000, of whom 312,000 were communicants,[9] and in 1960 Roman Catholics estimated their numbers to be 510,300.[10] If these figures approach accuracy, they indicate that in twenty-five or thirty years professing Christians had not quite trebled in numbers and late in the 1950's were at least three-fifths of the total population as against one-fourth in 1930. Here was a kind of mass conversion. Proportionately the Roman Catholic increase had been more than that of the Protestants, although at the mid-twentieth century Protestants were still nearly twice as numerous as Roman Catholics.

The preparation of indigenous clergy for the Pacific islands faced many difficulties. Among them were the vast distances, the multiplicity of languages, and the small size of such theological seminaries and Bible schools as could be

---

[4] *World Christian Handbook, 1957*, pp. 154, 155. The introduction of a new enterprise in the 1940's, that of the Missouri Lutherans, is given in Willard Bruce, *Our New Guinea Mission During Its First Seven Years* (no place or publisher, 1955, pp. 40, mimeographed), *passim*.

[5] Goodall, *A History of the London Missionary Society, 1895–1945*, pp. 361, 362.

[6] Henry P. Van Dusen, *They Found the Church There. The Armed Forces Discover Christian Missions* (New York, Charles Scribner's Sons, 1945, pp. xi, 148), *passim*.

[7] James Benson, *Prisoner's Base and Home Again. The Story of a Missionary P.O.W.* (London, Robert Hale, 1957, pp. 192), *passim*.

[8] Burton, *Missionary Survey of the Pacific Islands*, pp. 87–90.

[9] *World Christian Handbook, 1957*, pp. 154–161.

[10] *Worldmission*, Vol. XI, pp. 21, 22 (Winter, 1960–1961).

maintained. In 1957 Protestants had nine theological schools with an enrollment of 154. In addition, some of the more gifted students were sent to Australia and New Zealand for training.[11] In 1962 a project was under way for a central institution which would be of a higher grade scholastically than any in the islands and which would have English as the medium of instruction. Roman Catholics attempted to solve the problem of an indigenous clergy by sending promising young men to Australia and New Zealand and, later, to Manila and Madagascar. The results were disappointing. In the 1950's they had two major seminaries in the islands, but by 1948 only 27 ordained priests had come from them.[12] For other than the priestly office Roman Catholics had recruited and trained a number of natives. In 1960 the roll of the sisters had on it 785 foreigners and 625 natives and of the brothers 236 were foreigners and 95 were natives.[13] In recruiting indigenous leadership Protestants did much better than Roman Catholics. In 1957 the staffs which were reported showed 1,394 native and 222 foreign ordained men, 5,214 native and 222 foreign laymen, and 663 native and 444 foreign women.[14]

The growth in numbers, especially in islands where the large majority of the population were professedly Christian, was accompanied by serious problems. Protestants noted that in several areas, of which Samoa was an instance, tribalism had absorbed Christianity rather than the reverse. This brought with it the need for the nurture of the Christian communities in a deeper understanding of the Christian faith, a less compromised and more intelligent commitment to it, and the creation of a genuinely Christian culture. Self-support, while having made progress and not difficult in a region where nature was lavish in providing means for simple living, was not always achieved. Self-government, although general and growing, was not everywhere complete.[15]

Areas which were described as only partially evangelized presented a challenge. In Papua, for example, although the faith was spreading rapidly, thousands had as yet been scarcely touched. New cults were emerging from paganism, with some ideas of Christian origin. After World War II, in Papua, New Britain, and the Solomon Islands, what were called cargo cults sprang up. Seeing the fashion in which supplies were brought by ship and air to the armed white forces, the islanders constructed installations on the shore similar to those

[11] Allen, *A Seminary Survey*, pp. 130, 131.

[12] *Ibid.*, pp. 441, 442.

[13] *Worldmission*, Vol. XI, p. 22 (Winter, 1960–1961).

[14] *World Christian Handbook, 1957*, pp. 154–161.

[15] *Ibid., 1952*, pp. 15, 16. On the mixture of Christian and pre-Christian beliefs in Samoa see Felix M. Keesing, *Modern Samoa. Its Government and Changing Life* (London, George Allen and Unwin, 1934, pp. 506), pp. 409–413. On the situation in Rarotonga and Aitutaki see Ernest Beaglehole, *Social Change in the South Pacific, Rarotonga and Aitutaki* (London, George Allen and Unwin, 1957, pp. 268), pp. 194 ff. On attained self-support see Burton *op. cit.*, p. 16; Goodall, *op. cit.*, pp. 372, 373. See also C. E. Fox, *Lord of the Southern Isles. Being the Story of the Anglican Mission in Melanesia, 1849–1949* (London, A. R. Mowbray and Co., 1958, pp. xv, 272).

erected by the foreigners with the expectation that in some miraculous fashion food, clothing, and other material features of the white man's civilization would come to them.[16] Then, too, many of the Indians who had been brought to the Fiji Islands by plantation owners as indentured labourers remained and multiplied and by their industry escaped from the abject poverty and servitude which had been a major concern of Charles F. Andrews. By 1952 less than one out of a hundred had become Christians. Conversion was made the more difficult by the fact that the Indians looked with disdain on the Fijians, and the latter were Christians.[17]

As we look back over the nearly five decades between the outbreak of World War I and the year when these lines were written, we note striking progress in the formal conversion to Christianity of the population in the islands of the Pacific. The peoples were still under the rule of Occidental powers—Western European, Australasian, and North American. That rule had been varied by the global political changes of the period. Germany had been eliminated. For a time between the two wars the Japanese had replaced Germany north of the equator, but they had been supplanted in World War II, chiefly by Americans. Western Papua (Irian) was claimed by the Republic of Indonesia, but in 1962 the Dutch still held it. In contrast with Asia and Africa, no successful revolt had been staged by the natives against colonialism. Under the aegis of the governing peoples the revolutionary age was further penetrating the area—even the mountain fastnesses of Papua (New Guinea).

So far as statistics could show, by 1960 about three-fifths of the population called themselves Christians. As heretofore, Protestants were more numerous than Roman Catholics. Advance was made in self-support and in self-government with increasing independence of aid from foreigners. In 1960 the first Anglican indigenous bishop in the Pacific islands was consecrated. He was a Papuan.[18] The quality of the Christians was varied, but the fruits of their faith deeply impressed numbers of the foreign troops who were in the islands during World War II. As previously, much attention was paid to education and to preparing the Christians for the kind of world into which they were being hurtled by the revolutionary age.

---

[16] *Worldmission,* Vol. XI, p. 24 (Winter, 1960–1961); *The International Review of Missions,* Vol. XXXVII, p. 59 (January, 1949); G. H. Cranswick and I. W. A. Shevill, *A New Deal for Papua* (Melbourne, F. W. Cheshire, 1949, pp. xiii, 159), pp. 86–93.

[17] *World Christian Handbook, 1952,* p. 16; Burton, *op. cit.,* p. 64; J. W. Burton and Wallace Dean, *A Hundred Years in Fiji* (London, The Epworth Press, 1936, pp. 144), pp. 106, 141.

[18] *Ecumenical Press Service,* November 11, 1960.

CHAPTER XVII

Christianity in Rapidly Changing Africa South of the Sahara; Madagascar

Nor until after World War I did the impact of the revolutionary age begin to have marked effect upon Africa south of the Sahara. It then gathered momentum and following World War II brought fully as striking changes as anywhere else on the globe. By the 1960's what in the second half of the nineteenth century had been called "the dark continent" was experiencing as basic alterations in its inherited social and political patterns as any other large region on the earth's surface. Of the major masses of population only the Chinese showed as sweeping a disruption of the old order. Madagascar, which we are including in this chapter, was less altered. Ethnically it was different. But geographic propinquity, the "primitive" nature of the cultures of many of its peoples, and parallels in its political history place it more nearly with the adjacent continent than with any other segment of the globe with which we have dealt.

Until the second half of the nineteenth century the penetration of the interior of Africa south of the Sahara by Europeans had only barely begun. Since the sixteenth century white men had possessed footholds on the coast. At the outset and until the nineteenth century these enclaves had served as ports for the slave trade. Only in South Africa had that not been their chief purpose. There it had been to provide Dutch ships with food and water on their long voyages to South and East Asia and the East Indies. There white settlements had been begun which were to expand to major dimensions in the nineteenth and twentieth centuries. In the nineteenth century the suppression of most of the slave trade and the abolition of Negro slavery in the Americas altered the purpose of the white man in Africa. Trade in other commodities developed and the surge of life in Protestantism and the Roman Catholic Church sent missionary pioneers to some of the coastal regions.

Then came the explorations which revealed the interior of the continent to the astonished eyes of Western Europe and America. The most notable were by a Protestant missionary, David Livingstone, and Henry M. Stanley. The latter's introduction to Africa was his assignment by a New York newspaper to find Livingstone, who in his lonely attempts to discover the head waters of the Nile had been lost to sight to the Western world. In the 1880's Western European governments, in the heyday of their imperialistic and colonial adventures, divided among themselves most of the continent that had thus been disclosed. By that partition the majority of the political entities and their boundaries were created which, with modifications, were to persist into the twentieth century and were to form the basis of the states which then achieved their independence.

Christian missionaries, both Protestant and Roman Catholic, saw in the "opening of Africa" a challenge and penetrated most of the area. In the second half of the nineteenth century there were more Protestant than Roman Catholic missionaries and they were more likely to come from the Continent of Europe and the British Isles than from North America. Both branches of the faith were represented in all the main political units. The trend was for Protestants to be more numerous in the possessions of governments traditionally of that allegiance and for Roman Catholics to be stronger in the areas ruled by peoples in which they were in the majority. That meant, in general, that Protestantism was more extensive in the British colonies and the Roman Catholic Church grew more rapidly in Portuguese, French, Belgian, and Spanish territories. In the German possessions, as was to be expected from the relative strength of the two branches of the faith in that country, Protestants and Roman Catholics were about equal in number.[1] In Madagascar, which did not become a French possession until 1895, for years Protestants outnumbered Roman Catholics.

Beginning with World War I the rate of change in Africa south of the Sahara quickened. Improved transportation, in part by the railway and automobile and latterly by the airplane, furthered travel. The need for labour in the white man's mines attracted thousands of Africans who were thus brought into centres of the revolutionary age. In connexion with the mining and commerce of the white man's world cities grew, chiefly by the influx of Africans. Thousands of Africans were deracinated and de-tribalized and the traditional patterns of their lives were weakened or completely shattered. Many Africans had been recruited in the armies of the Allies, had served outside Africa, and, returning, had brought experience with the revolutionary age which hastened the disintegration of their home constituencies. Education on the white man's pattern reached tens of thousands, mainly through schools operated by missionaries, although often subsidized by colonial governments.

World War II was accompanied and followed by accelerated disintegration of the inherited culture and by a strident nationalism and racialism which led to the political independence of much of the area and to repeated and chronic

---

[1] Volume III, pp. 463–480. For more extended but still condensed treatments, see Latourette, *A History of the Expansion of Christianity*, Vol. III, pp. 240–246; Vol. V, pp. 301–464.

friction and at times violence in the effort of the white minorities to retain their privileged positions and of the non-whites to achieve equality with the whites or to throw them out of the continent. Such political independence as had been attained when these pages were written came in the 1950's and 1960's. By 1962 the extensive French possessions either had been granted independence and remained within the French Community or had chosen and been conceded complete independence. Several of the British colonies on the west and east coasts had become independent but had elected to remain within the Commonwealth which had its tie in the British Crown. The Union of South Africa became a republic and cut its ties with the Commonwealth.

In the decades which followed the outbreak of World War I the course of Christianity south of the Sahara was in general characterized by nine developments. (1) The number of Christians continued to mount. The growth varied from area to area. In some political divisions by 1962 nearly half the population called themselves Christians. In others they constituted small minorities. Everywhere growth was seen, although at varying rates. A kind of mass conversion was in progress. Yet taking the region as a whole, Christians were still a minority. (2) The growth was chiefly through Protestantism and the Roman Catholic Church. The Orthodox were represented, but only by a few hundred. (3) In the over-all statistics, the increase of Roman Catholics was greater than that of Protestants, but this was not uniformly the case. It was partly but not entirely because of the very rapid growth of Roman Catholics in the Belgian Congo and the Belgian trust territory of Ruanda-Urundi. (4) Islam was advancing in the West, as it had been for centuries, and was especially strong on the southern borders of the Sahara. One reason for the growth seems to have been that the impact of the revolutionary age was weakening the traditional religious beliefs and patterns of life and that Islam was moving into the vacuum. Certainly it was growing in a broad belt stretching westward from the Sudan. It was making gains, but not as marked, on the east coast. (5) Among both Roman Catholics and Protestants rapid progress was achieved in raising up an indigenous leadership and in transferring administration to it—partly because of the general policy which we have seen elsewhere and partly from the pressure, as in other regions, from the non-whites as a result of nationalism and the revolt against white supremacy. (6) Most of the education of the modern kind was still, as it had been earlier, carried on through Christian schools. However, more and more it was passing into the hands of governments. The teaching and the pastoral functions, formerly combined, were increasingly separated. Since teachers were paid larger salaries and had social prestige and the ministry was less well paid and was not regarded highly by Africans, the churches faced a problem in recruiting able men for the pastorate. (7) Because Christian schools had long been the chief and in large areas the only places where the education essential in the revolutionary age could be obtained, a large proportion of the men who led in forming the new governments had come from them. Many were professedly Christian, but for the majority the Christian connexion became only formal. (8) With exuberant nationalism and political independence a recrudescence of pagan cults and practices was seen. The charge was made that Christianity was alien to the African way of life and was an importation of the white man from whose rule the Africans were seeking emancipation. (9) In some areas, notably in South Africa, indigenous cults were arising which claimed to be Christian. As we proceed with our story we will see many concrete examples of these developments. Some were more prominent than others and their proportions varied from area to area.

Our procedure will be to group our narrative by political divisions. In the limited space at our disposal we will not be able to cover all of them. We will confine ourselves chiefly to the larger ones and will not go into detail in any of them. We will conclude with a brief description of some of the major issues which confronted Christians in the area as a whole.

South Africa Presents Christianity with Acute and Urgent Problems

In no other part of the world was Christianity faced with such a complexity of racial problems combined with economic and social factors, largely of the revolutionary age, as in South Africa. In 1959 the population was estimated to be 14,673,000. Of these 3,067,000 were of European ancestry. The latter were divided between the Boers, or Afrikaners, chiefly of Dutch origin, the majority of whose forefathers had arrived before the nineteenth century, and whites from a background of the British Isles, most of whom dated from a nineteenth- and twentieth-century immigration. They were separated religiously and linguistically and by the unhappy heritage of a war. Almost to a man the Afrikaners were adherents of one or another of the Dutch Reformed Churches and had Afrikaans as their language. They were prevailingly rural—although in the twentieth century their urbanization was advancing. The Europeans with a parentage stemming from the British Isles were either Roman Catholic, if from Ireland, or affiliated, if they had any religion, with the Church of England, the Church of Scotland, or another of the denominations of British origin. They were predominantly but not exclusively urban. The South African war (1899–1902) between Afrikaners and the British whites had contributed to a bitterness which chronic political and economic tensions had perpetuated.

The non-white majority were also of varied stocks. Bushmen and Hottentots had been in the region when the first Dutch came. Bantu of several tribes had begun to move in from the North about the time that the Dutch arrived. In the twentieth century they constituted a large majority. The Coloured, a substantial minority, were descendants of individuals brought in by the Dutch from other parts of Africa, Asia, and the East Indies and of unions between whites and non-whites. Indians constituted a minority in defense of whom Gandhi had first worked out his policy of non-violent resistance. The multiform racial tensions were aggravated by the city-ward movement of the non-Europeans, mainly Bantu, as labourers, notably in the mines on which Johannesburg built its wealth. They inhabited de-tribalized festering slums, and such of the youth as made their way back to their villages after a period of work in the mines contributed to the disintegration of hereditary customs. With the growth of the rural non-white population and wasteful methods of farming, much of the agricultural soil was exhausted and eroded and its cultivators were impoverished.[2] In 1962 the region was not fully under one government. Southwest Africa was held as a trust of the United Nations, a condition to which the Union of South Africa refused to accede. Within the geographic boundaries of the Union were Basutoland, Bechuanaland, and Swaziland, still part of the British Empire, the first a reservation in which whites were not allowed to own land and which in 1959 was accorded partial self-government, and the other two protectorates.

In an inflammable situation such as that presented by unhealthy racial and economic conditions, the whites endeavoured to maintain supremacy by monopolizing the more profitable occupations and the positions which carried prestige and power. A majority of the Afrikaners, by controlling the government, sought to carry through a policy called *apartheid*. By this they meant keeping separate the two largest racial elements, the whites with their European culture and the Africans, whom they professed to wish to encourage in their own cultural development. To achieve this end they imposed various restrictions on the non-Europeans. They were adamantly opposed to integration in any form, whether in education, worship, or social intercourse.[3] They argued that otherwise the European minority would be swamped and its civilization would disappear. They insisted that in South Africa the Bantu had greater opportunities for livelihood and education than in the regions to the north, and

[2] For a vivid picture of some of the problems, no less accurate for being fiction, see Alan Paton, *Cry the Beloved Country. A Story of Comfort and Desolation* (New York, Charles Scribner's Sons, 1948, pp. ix, 278). See also Leopold Marquard, *Peoples and Policies in South Africa* (New York, Oxford University Press, 1952, pp. 258). On the situation in Johannesburg see Ray E. Phillips, *The Bantu Are Coming. Phases of South Africa's Race Problem* (New York, Richard R. Smith, 1930, pp. 238), and Ray E. Phillips, *The Bantu in the City. A Study of Cultural Adjustments in the Witwatersrand* (Lovedale, South Africa, Lovedale Press, no date, pp. xxix, 452).

[3] See a factual description in Eugene P. Dvorin, *Racial Separation in South Africa. An Analysis of Apartheid Theory* (University of Chicago Press, 1952, pp. xii, 256). See an earlier statement before the issue had become so acute in Edgar H. Brookes, *The Colour Problems of South Africa* (Lovedale, South Africa, Lovedale Press, 1933, pp. viii, 237). Also see, for a conference of Dutch Reformed leaders, *Christian Principles in Multi-Racial South Africa. A Report on the Dutch Reformed Conference of Church Leaders, Pretoria, 17–19 November, 1953* (Johannesburg, no publisher, 1954, pp. 185).

held that if not restrained the Bantu would pour in and take over the country. The *apartheid* policy created tension between and within the churches. Roman Catholic authorities denounced it as far as segregated worship and unequal employment were involved. In 1960, for example, they ordained three African priests.[4] In 1959 Archbishop Denis Hurley of Durban publicly declared that *apartheid* was impossible and that the only solution of the racial problem was integration.[5] The following year Archbishop Owen McCann of Capetown emphatically took a similar position.[6] Anglican spokesmen were particularly out-spoken in their criticism. For example, Joost de Blank, Archbishop of Capetown, said that unless the Dutch Reformed Church repudiated *apartheid* it was doomed to extermination. To this the synod of the Dutch Reformed Church of the Cape Province took exception.[7] In 1960 the government ordered Bishop Ambrose Reeves of Johannesburg to be deported. Among other acts to which the South African authorities objected was his protest against the shooting of African demonstrators by the police and his appeal for aid to the sufferers and for consultation between the government and responsible leaders of the African people.[8] As if to counter the government, which was a trustee of the area and sought to annex it outright, in 1960 an African was elected moderator of the Evangelical Lutheran Ovambokavango Church in South-west Africa. That church had emerged from a mission of the Finnish Lutherans and in 1956 had become autonomous.[9]

Within the Dutch Reformed Churches the support of *apartheid* was not unanimous. In 1960 several of their prominent pastors and theologians came out publicly against the policy.[10] Late in 1960 a consultation was held in Johannesburg between representatives of the World Council of Churches and the three Dutch Reformed churches of South Africa. It was interracial. It adopted a statement from which the only dissident was the Hervormde Kerk, the smallest of the Afrikaner churches. Among other affirmations, the lengthy document declared that "all racial groups who permanently inhabit our country . . . have an equal right to make their contributions towards the enrichment of life of their country and to share in the ensuing responsibilities, rewards and privileges," that "no one who believed in Jesus Christ may be excluded from any church on the grounds of his colour or race," that "a more effective consultation between the government and leaders accepted by the non-white people of

[4] *Worldmission Fides Service*, August 6, 1960.

[5] *Ibid.*, September 12, 1959.

[6] *Ecumenical Press Service*, January 6, 1961.

[7] *The New York Times*, April 14, 1960; *Ecumenical Press Service*, September 23, 1960. On another Anglican, Michael Scott, and his protests, see Freda Troup, *In the Face of Fear. Michael Scott's Challenge to South Africa* (London, Faber and Faber, 1950, pp. 227), *passim*.

[8] *Ecumenical Press Service*, April 8, 1960, and September 23, 1960.

[9] *The New York Times*, January 1, 1961.

[10] *Christianity and Crisis*, Vol. XXI, p. 22 (March 16, 1961); *Ecumenical Press Service*, December 2, 1960.

South Africa should be devised," that "there are no Scriptural grounds for the prohibition of mixed marriages," that "the wages received by the vast majority of the non-white people oblige them to exist below the generally accepted standard for healthy living," that "the present system of job reservation must give way to a more equitable system of labour," that "opportunities must be provided for the inhabitants of the Bantu areas to live in conformity with human dignity," that "non-whites should be permitted to collaborate in the government of the country," and that in the "foreseeable future" the Coloured should be represented in Parliament. It regretted the circumstance that large numbers had been detained for months without being brought to trial. It stood for a greater security of tenure of homes by non-whites, for a normal family life for Africans in white areas, and for better "pastoral care for non-white people living on their employer's premises." Yet in 1961, in protest against this statement, the Dutch Reformed Church of the Transvaal withdrew from the World Council of Churches.[11]

The churches were not alone in these attitudes. About the same time a citizens' group of Afrikaners and of British ancestry and made up of both laymen and clergy passed a somewhat similar declaration. A movement was also on foot for better agricultural training for labourers on farms.[12]

Ten years earlier, in 1950, a church congress on which the Gereformeerde and Hervormde Churches were represented stood for separate churches and schools for Europeans and non-Europeans but was emphatic that *apartheid* did not mean that "the native should continue to live in a primitive state" but that "in his own sphere he should have every possible facility for development so that there may be created a healthy synthesis of the worthwhile elements of his old Bantu culture and the sound and essential elements of Western culture, resulting in a new social order."[13]

Many attempts were made to aid in the solution of the problems posed by the impact of the revolutionary age on the African. Some were private and others were initiated by the government or with government assistance. Most of the education of the Africans had long been carried by Christian missions. Financial support was increasingly given by the state. In 1904, 93,000 Bantu children were in school and mission institutions numbered 1,265. In 1949 the number of Bantu children enrolled had risen to 758,811 in 4,612 primary and 74 secondary schools.[14] In 1916 the South Africa Native College at Fort Hare

[11] *The Ecumenical Review*, Vol. XIII, pp. 244–250 (January, 1961); *Ecumenical Press Service*, December 23, 1960, and April 14, 1961; *The New York Times*, December 8, 1960.

[12] *The New York Times*, December 27, 1960.

[13] *Statement for General Information Issued by the Church Congress of the Dutch Reformed Federated and Mission Churches on which the Hervormde and Gereformeerde Churches were Represented in Connection with the Native Question, held in Bloemfontein on April 4–6, 1950* (no place given, pp. 4).

[14] Gerdener, *Recent Developments in the South African Mission Field*, p. 242.

opened its doors. Built on foundations laid by the United Free Church of Scotland, it was on the university level and from the beginning attracted students from all the provinces of the Union and Basutoland. Methodists, Anglicans, and Presbyterians erected hostels.[15] In 1953 the Bantu Education Act authorized the transfer of primary and secondary schools to local and regional authorities and training institutions to the Union Department of Native Affairs. This entailed the withdrawal of government subsidies to mission schools, formerly about three-fourths of the total funds. The implementation of the act brought crises to many mission institutions, but by 1958 about 1,250,000 Bantu children were in government schools. In the latter year approximately half the Bantu children of school-going age were enrolled.[16] A project which attracted much attention was the Jan H. Hofmeyr School of Social Work founded in 1940 in Johannesburg by the South African National Council of the YMCA. Here, in the city where the urbanization of the African brought problems on a huge and tragic scale, American Congregationalists, on the precedent set by F. B. Bridgman and under the leadership of Ray E. Phillips, trained social workers who served in many parts of South Africa as probation officers, directors of recreation and youth organizations, secretaries of social and community centres, instructors in physical education, principals and matrons of homes for delinquent boys and girls, and in various other capacities.[17] We must also note that much was done by white missionaries to meet the medical needs of the Bantu. The government more and more undertook to provide hospitals and other medical care and with its larger funds was eventually to do more than could be accomplished by private agencies. In the meantime missionaries helped to fill the gap.[18]

Christianity continued to hold the professed allegiance of the overwhelming majority of the white population of South Africa. In 1959 the membership statistics of the larger bodies were as follows: Nederduits Gereformeerde Kerk, 1,107,482; Nederduits Hervormde Kerk, 182,198; Gereformeerde Kerk, 112,235; Anglicans, 416,472; Methodists, 219,021; Roman Catholics, 141,330; Presbyterians, 100,739; Baptists, 26,717; Lutherans, 26,262; Apostolic Faith (Pentecostal), 50,765; and Congregationalists, 13,915. These figures indicated that as compared with 1911 the Dutch Reformed were almost the same percentage as in the earlier year, that Anglicans had declined from 20 to 16 per cent., that Methodists had risen from about 6.3 per cent. to about 8 per cent. and that Roman Catholics were about 5.8 per cent. of the population.[19] In 1958 most of

---

[15] *Ibid.*, p. 243; Robert H. W. Shepherd, *Lovedale, South Africa, the Story of a Century, 1841–1941* (Lovedale, South Africa, Lovedale Press, 1941, pp. xiv, 531), *passim.*

[16] Gerdener, *op. cit.*, pp. 242, 247. On the hardships, direct information to the author from various sources. See also *World Dominion*, Vol. XXXIII, pp. 273–275 (September-October, 1955).

[17] Gerdener, *op. cit.*, pp. 252, 253.

[18] As one example see Anthony Barker, *The Man Next to Me. An Adventure in African Medical Practice* (New York, Harper & Brothers, 1959, pp. 175), *passim.*

[19] Latourette, *op. cit.*, Vol. VII, p. 225; *The Statesman's Year Book, 1960*, p. 253.

the British and Continental European churches and missionary bodies were members of the South African Christian Council. The Afrikaners' churches were not affiliated with it. Yet two of the Afrikaners' churches were members of the World Council of Churches.[20]

By their history the Dutch Reformed churches and the Afrikaners were all but inseparable. Much as Irish and French Canadian nationalisms were closely associated with the Roman Catholic Church, so Afrikaner particularism and the Dutch Reformed Churches were intimately connected and strengthened each other. The theological conservatism of the major Dutch Reformed Churches was reinforced by the rural character of much of the Afrikaner community, resistant to the currents of the revolutionary age which were beating on the land. In these churches was a strong, warm Evangelical tradition which had had a prominent representative in the younger Andrew Murray (1828–1917).[21] It found partial expression in extensive missions, but, characteristically, with one exception they were entirely in South Africa and the territories immediately to the north, and the exception was in the Sudan, still in Africa.[22]

The next largest body of Protestant whites, the Anglicans, had a high-church tradition and were largely served by bishops, clergy, and sisterhoods of those convictions. Some of the laity, especially if they were farmers, were critical of clergy who made fraternal contacts with Bantu, but, as we have said, the attitude of the episcopate tended to be adverse to *apartheid* and policies associated with it.[23]

Among the non-whites the numbers of those who called themselves Christians grew, both in totals and in proportion to the non-white population. In 1911 about a third of the non-whites claimed the Christian name.[24] In 1946 about 60 per cent. were in that category.[25] Of the churches or groups to which they belonged, it was said that some were indigenous, several were only semi-Christian, and others were more or less replicas of a Birtish, Continental European, or American denomination.[26]

To go more into detail on the denominational alignment of the non-white Christians: In 1946 in the Union of South Africa the largest number, about a fifth of the whole, were Methodists, about a seventh were Anglicans, approximately a twelfth were Lutherans (the fruits of Continental European missions), less than a twentieth were Congregationalists, and still fewer were Presbyterians.[27] Although their congregations were not integrated, the Dutch

[20] Ben J. Marais in *Christianity Today*, December 22, 1958, p. 9.
[21] Volume III, p. 469.
[22] *The Christian Handbook of South Africa*, pp. 28–36.
[23] See the life of a Bishop of Pretoria (1920–1933) in F. H. Brabant, *Neville Stuart Talbot, 1879–1943. A Memoir* (London, SCM Press, 1949, pp. 160), pp. 77–116.
[24] *The Statesman's Year Book, 1919*, p. 210.
[25] *Ibid., 1960*, p. 253; Marais, *op. cit.*, p. 8.
[26] Marais, *op. cit.*, p. 8.
[27] *The Statesman's Year Book, 1960*, p. 253.

Reformed bodies had about a ninth of the non-white Protestants as members.[28] Another set of figures showed about one in twenty-four of the non-white church members in Dutch Reformed churches, but if the adherents were added the proportion was second only to the Methodists, or about a fifth of the non-white Christian constituency. In 1959 non-white full members and adherents of the Dutch Reformed churches were increasing, the former at the annual rate of about 3 per cent. and the latter of about 4 per cent.[29] The 1950's showed a rapid growth in the missionary personnel of the Dutch Reformed bodies, especially the largest, who served among the non-whites. They worked in close co-operation with the government. The emphasis was upon evangelism, hospitals, and literature. Among the missionaries were some of the ablest of the younger clergy.[30] In 1942 the Federal Missionary Council was formed. In it the Dutch Reformed Churches coöperated and the Bantu and Coloured churches of Dutch Reformed origin were represented.[31] The non-white Dutch Reformed were organized into nine autonomous Mission Churches, seven of which, embracing about 60 per cent. of the membership, had been founded after 1914.[32] Anglican missionaries were largely in the communities of men and women and were therefore Anglo-Catholics.[33]

A striking feature of South African Christianity was the multiplication of Bantu sects.[34] They were of Protestant background and began not far from the year 1900. They increased rapidly, especially during and immediately after each of the two world wars. Many were ephemeral, and fully dependable statistics were not available. The census of 1946 gave their number as about 13,000 and their followers as 1,089,479. A somewhat later census estimated the bodies at 2,000 and their adherents as 1,509,295. They arose from a wide variety of causes, not all of them operating in any one body: rebellion against white control, desire to create a distinctive African expression of Christianity, impatience with im-ported forms of worship, personal ambitions of individual leaders, appeal to the emotions, and confidence in faith healing. Some of the sects had seceded from historic denominations. Others were fresh creations. The government hesi-tated to give them official recognition with authority to their clergy to celebrate marriages and to engage in other professional functions. Only a few were thus registered. Most of their leaders had little or no formal education. They had

---

[28] *Ibid.*

[29] *Ecumenical Press Service,* February 12, 1960.

[30] Marais, *op. cit.,* p. 10.

[31] Gerdener, *op. cit.,* pp. 36, 37.

[32] Allen, *A Seminary Survey,* pp. 66, 67.

[33] See a biography of a member of the Community of Resurrection in Doris Thompson, *Priest and Pioneer. A Memoir of Father Osmund Victor, C.R., of South Africa* (Westminster, Md., The Faith Press, 1958, pp. 134). See also Gerdener, *op. cit.,* pp. 67–73.

[34] Gerdener, *op. cit.,* pp. 188–206; Bengt Gustaf Malcolm Sundkler, *Bantu Prophets in South Africa* (London, Lutterworth Press, 1948, pp. 344), especially pp. 317–337 with a list of the sects; Davis, *Modern Industry and the African,* pp. 408–414; *Occasional Papers of the International Missionary Council* (London, mimeographed), No. 4 (January, 1960).

kinship to similar movements elsewhere in Africa and among lower income strata in several other parts of the world, whether in Europe, the Americas, or Asia. Attempts to bring them into coöperation, either with one another or with the standard denominations, did not succeed. They were more numerous and proliferated more rapidly in South Africa than in any other part of the world.

Preparation for the ministry of the Protestant churches varied from denomination to denomination and often within denominations. In general, that for the white churches was not unlike what was offered in Europe, North America, Australia, and New Zealand.[35] That for the non-white churches showed greater contrasts. The standard denominations endeavoured to make it as nearly as possible comparable in quality with that of the white clergy.[36] Between 1925 and 1958 the proportion of ordained men, white and non-white, for the Bantu population, Christian and non-Christian, rose from one for every 3,676 to one for every 2,075. Percentage-wise the non-white ordained clergy increased more rapidly than the white. In 1925 the ordained whites totalled 839 and in 1952 they were 2,460. In the former year the ordained non-whites were 537 and in the latter year they were 1,878.[37] A careful comprehensive survey made in 1953 said that while the grade of theological education of non-whites in South Africa was on the average higher than that in areas to the north, it was not keeping pace with the rise in education of the Bantu whom the clergy served, that salaries of the clergy were not equalling those of teachers, that the economic condition of the churches together with the supply of candidates ruled out the possibility of a full-time paid and ordained ministry, and that far too many of the institutions giving theological training were badly understaffed.[38] Because of the *apartheid* policy of the government and the legislation of the 1950's the situation in 1962 was fluid and uncertain.[39]

In the decades introduced by World War I the Roman Catholic Church poured more and more personnel and funds into South Africa. Between 1911 and 1951 the number of Protestant missionaries in the region was said to have multiplied about two and a half times, while that of the Roman Catholics had a nearly fourteen-fold increase. Moreover, the latter were reported to be far better prepared in the languages of the peoples to whom they were sent than were the former. In at least one area, Basutoland, where French Protestants had been at work for over a century and in the 1950's Protestants still slightly outnumbered Roman Catholics, the latter bade fair soon to be in the majority.[40] The great period of expansion began soon after 1918. Late in 1922 the Apostolic

[35] Allen, *op. cit.*, pp. 68–79.
[36] *Ibid.*
[37] Gerdener, *op. cit.*, p. 18.
[38] International Missionary Council, *Survey of the Training of the Ministry in Africa*, Part III, pp. 10, 60, 61.
[39] Sundkler, *The Christian Ministry in Africa*, pp. 39, 40, 262, 263.
[40] Marais, *op. cit.*, p. 9. On the history of the French mission after 1914 see V. Ellenberger, *Un*

Delegation for Southern Africa was created. New ecclesiastical territories were set up and additional personnel sent. In 1921 the priests numbered just over 300. By 1936 over 700 were at work. In the same period religious brothers and sisters mounted from about 2,000 to approximately 4,000. In 1925 and 1926 two Irish of South African birth were raised to the episcopate. Soon after the close of World War II a new archbishop was consecrated to succeed one who had served for twenty-five years. Under him the administrative coördination of the Roman Catholic Church in South Africa continued, many new ecclesiastical territories were established, and a national seminary was erected (but only for white students). Other theological seminaries were already in existence. Schools were provided for non-whites, several of them for Indians. Most of the efforts of the Roman Catholic Church for non-whites were by orders and congregations. Around their monasteries and convents Christian communities arose, some of them with as many as 10,000 members. Among the Bantu religious societies developed and priests were trained.[41]

In 1924 the Oblates of Mary Immaculate established a seminary at Roma, in Basutoland. Since Basutoland was not part of the Union of South Africa, the race laws of the Union did not extend to it. Moreover, the immigration of white settlers and the acquistion of land by them was restricted. These conditions and the rapid growth of Bantu Roman Catholics furthered the growth of the seminary. Between 1924 and 1949 twenty-one of its non-white graduates became priests. In 1945 the Pius XII University for non-white students was founded at Roma with a staff of Canadian Oblates. The Trappists had founded Mariannhill in 1882, but their manner of life made the winning of converts difficult. They were, accordingly, authorized to drop their connexion with that order and in 1914 they organized themselves into a new community, the Religious Missionaries of Mariannhill. In 1925 they established a major seminary. In 1951 it became a regional seminary, said to have been the first in Africa. But its student body remained small.[42]

With all their growth, in 1960 Roman Catholics in South Africa were a small minority. Although in Basutoland they were 41 per cent. of the population, in the Union of South Africa, when both white and non-white members were included, the Roman Catholic Church had only 5.8 per cent.[43] In conformity with its world-wide policy, the Roman Catholic Church took steps to

Siècle de Mission au Lessouto (1833–1933) (Paris, Société des Missions Évangéliques, 1933, pp. 447), pp. 371–432.

[41] *The Catholic Church and Southern Africa. A Series of Essays* (Capetown, The Catholic Archdiocese of Capetown, 1951, pp. xxii, 180), pp. 120, 121, 127, 128, 154–162; Beckmann, *Die katholische Kirche im neuen Afrika*, pp. 83–85.

[42] Allen *op. cit.*, pp. 423, 424.

[43] *Worldmission Fides Service*, March 18, 1961. In 1959 the Union of South Africa was reported to have 850,230 Roman Catholics, with 25,227 adult baptisms between June, 1957, and July, 1959.—*Ibid.*, July 9, 1960.

plant the faith ever more firmly in indigenous leadership with the hope of further expansion. In 1961 the new archiepiscopal see of Maseru was created and centred in Basutoland. At its head was placed a non-white African, a member of the Missionary Oblates of Mary Immaculate.[44]

The Changing Scene in the Federation of Rhodesia and Nyasaland

Immediately north of the Union of South Africa were Southern Rhodesia, Northern Rhodesia, and Nyasaland. In 1953 they were brought together as the Federation of Rhodesia and Nyasaland. Southern Rhodesia was self-governing. The other two were British protectorates. Southern Rhodesia had a fairly substantial white element, in 1960 about 223,000 in a population of approximately 3,070,000. Northern Rhodesia, much larger, in 1960 had about 76,000 whites in a population estimated at 2,430,000. In the same year the population of Nyasaland was reported to be 2,770,000, of whom 9,300 were whites. The formation of the Federation was in theory preliminary to granting full autonomy within the Commonwealth. Tensions arose over the degree of participation of the non-whites in the government. They were an accompaniment of the continent-wide rising tide of nationalism and came to a climax late in 1950's and early in the 1960's. The non-whites were vociferous and disorder ensued, notably in Nyasaland. Many of the whites feared non-white domination and resented the efforts of the imperial government to hasten the participation of the non-whites and full independence.

The way for the penetration of the white men with their civilization, bringing with it the revolutionary age, had been prepared by Livingstone. In the twentieth century the population of both whites and non-whites soared. The whites engaged in cattle-raising, farming, and mining. Southern Rhodesia became an important gold-producing country. A notable development was seen in Northern Rhodesia, where beginning between the two world wars extensive deposits of copper were exploited by white companies employing non-white labour. The copper mines extended into Katanga in the Belgian Congo.

Christianity was introduced to the area by Roman Catholics in the seventeenth century, but by the nineteenth century all traces had disappeared. Christianity next came through Protestants in the 1850's, initially through Robert Moffat of the London Missionary Society. By 1914, mostly in the 1890's and thereafter, other Protestants of several denominations had come and Roman Catholics had gained a foothold. Owing chiefly to Livingstone, the 1870's and 1880's were marked by the arrival in Nyasaland of Anglicans of the Universities Mission to Central Africa, Presbyterians from the Church of Scotland and the Free Church of Scotland, and the Dutch Reformed from South Africa. Roman

[44] *Ibid.*, January 25, 1961.

Catholics of the White Fathers did not effect a permanent mission until 1901.[45] In the year 1914, then, Christianity as a continuing religion was young and was represented chiefly by British Protestants, with a few American and Afrikaner Protestant missionaries.

In the decades which followed 1914 Christianity displayed a marked growth in the Rhodesias. In 1924 the baptized Protestants in the two regions numbered about 30,000.[46] In 1936 they had increased to approximately 130,000.[47] The 1957 totals were 207,206 full members and 677,901 in the Protestant community.[48] In 1957 Southern Rhodesia had more than twice as many Protestant full members as Northern Rhodesia but only about three-fifths as many in the Protestant community.[49] In 1931 Roman Catholics in the Rhodesias were said to be about 89,000,[50] and in 1957 to total about 487,000.[51] A quite different set of figures put the total in 1959 at about 784,000.[52] If the latter statistics are accurate, in 1959 about 19 per cent. of the population of Northern Rhodesia were Roman Catholics. At nearly the same time about 15 per cent. were Protestants.[53] These figures seem to indicate that late in the 1950's about a third of the Africans of Northern Rhodesia thought of themselves as Christians. In Southern Rhodesia the proportion appears to have been less, about 7.8 per cent. Roman Catholic and about 8 per cent. Protestant, or together slightly less than a sixth of the Africans.[54] Yet in both Rhodesias the rapid spread of the faith in the post-1914 years was approaching a mass movement. In Nyasaland the story was similar. In 1924 baptized Protestants were reported to be about 66,000[55] and in 1936 to be approximately 174,000.[56] In 1957 the totals given were 213,942 full members of Protestant churches and a Protestant constituency of 557,338.[57] This indicates that in 1957 about a fifth of the population thought of themselves as Protestants. In 1959 approximately 16 per cent. were counted as Roman Catholics.[58] The latter had about doubled since the slightly over 100,000 given in

[45] Latourette, *op. cit.*, Vol. V, pp. 381–397.
[46] Beach and Fahs, *World Missionary Atlas*, p. 77.
[47] Parker, *Interpretative Statistical Survey of the World Mission of the Christian Church*, p. 71. For a picture of one of the Protestant missions, see E. M. Jakeman, *Pioneering in Northern Rhodesia* (London, Morgan and Scott, no date, pp. 63).
[48] *World Christian Handbook, 1957*, pp. 90, 98–100.
[49] *Ibid.*
[50] *Testo-Atlante Illustrato delle Missioni*, p. 122.
[51] *World Christian Handbook, 1957*, p. 166.
[52] *Worldmission Fides Service*, March 10, 1961.
[53] *World Christian Handbook, 1957*, p. 90.
[54] *Ibid.*, p. 100; *World Mission Fides Service*, March 10, 1961.
[55] Beach and Fahs, *op, cit.*, p. 77. For a general survey of Protestant missions in Nyasaland in the mid-1920's see Wm. J. W. Roome, *A Great Emancipation. A Missionary Survey of Nyasaland, Central Africa* (London, World Dominion Press, 1926, pp. 64), *passim*. For one of the missions see Alexander Hetherwick, *The Romance of Blantyre. How Livingstone's Dream Came True* (London, James Clarke and Co., ca. 1927, pp, 260), *passim*.
[56] Parker, *op. cit.*, p. 19
[57] *World Christian Handbook, 1957*, p. 91.
[58] *Worldmission Fides Service*, March 16, 1961.

1936.[59] Late in the 1950's, then, nearly a third of the peoples of Nyasaland were in some sense Christian, with Protestants in the slight majority.

Several societies, Protestant and Roman Catholic, were represented in the Federation of Rhodesia and Nyasaland. In 1914 the General Missionary Conference of Northern Rhodesia held its first meeting. It included all the societies, among them the Jesuits and White Fathers. A similar conference existed in Southern Rhodesia.[60]

Much of the conversion was through mission schools, for in the two Rhodesias and in Nyasaland the British administration, as elsewhere in its colonies, depended on them for education of the white man's kind to prepare the non-whites to take their place in the revolutionary age and subsidized them financially. From the mission schools came the clerks and interpreters in government offices and others of what might be called the emerging intellectuals.[61]

The development of the copper mines in Northern Rhodesia by the white man's capital posed, as did that of the mines in the Union of South Africa, serious problems for Africans and Christian missions. Africans were employed as labourers. Their young men came from miles around and their absence from their villages weakened the latter. In the neighbourhood of the mines prostitution flourished. Among the labourers were Christians. Some yielded to the temptations around them. Others withstood them and their characters were strengthened.[62]

To meet the challenge some of the Protestants joined in coöperative efforts to reach the labourers. At the outset this was at the initiative of African Christians. Coming from varying denominational backgrounds, they organized a united, self-supporting church and undertook vigorous evangelism. Missionaries from several denominations collaborated in the United Missions of the Copperbelt to meet the religious needs of the labourers. In general the companies provided excellent housing and had at heart the moral and material welfare of their employees. Some erected chapels for the use of the Christians. Since the mineral deposits spanned the boundary between Northern Rhodesia and the Belgian Congo, the Christian programmes were found on both sides of the line.[63]

[59] Parker, *op. cit.*, p. 33.
[60] Edwin W. Smith, *The Way of the White Fields. A Survey of Christian Enterprise in Northern and Southern Rhodesia* (London, World Dominion Press, 1928, pp. viii, 172), *passim*, especially pp. 71, 72, 97, 98. On American Methodist missions see Henry I. James. *Missions in Rhodesia under the Methodist Episcopal Church, 1898–1934* (Old Umtali, The Rhodesia Mission Press, 1935, pp. 138), *passim*. For another mission see *A Dominican Sister. In God's White-Robed Army. The Chronicle of the Dominican Sisters in Rhodesia, 1890–1934* (Cape Town, Maskew Miller, no date, pp. x, 276), *passim*.
[61] Davis, *op. cit.*, pp. 346 ff.; *Worldmission Fides Service*, March 22, 1961.
[62] Davis, *op. cit.*, pp. 279 ff.
[63] *Ibid.*, pp. 292–303; Groves, *The Planting of Christianity in Africa*, Vol. IV, p. 229; Taylor and Lehmann, *Christians in the Copper Belt*, pp. 37–50.

The preparation of clerical leadership for the Protestants and Roman Catholics in the Federation of Rhodesia and Nyasaland was handicapped by the relatively recent penetration of the region by the revolutionary age, the immaturity of the churches, and the low level of education on the European pattern. Although in the 1950's several hundred thousand were in schools of primary grade, in 1950–1951 secondary schools had only 436 enrolled. Not until 1957 was instruction on a university level begun in the government-financed University College of Rhodesia and Nyasaland at Salisbury in Southern Rhodesia.[64] As a result the institutions for preparing for the Protestant ministry had small teaching staffs, usually only one full-time man, a white, with possibly two or three part-time members of the faculty, white and non-white. Enrollments were small. Although admission required preliminary education and the courses were three or four years long, few could be adequately trained to guide their flocks in the inevitably difficult adjustment to the change forced on them by the inflooding currents of a revolutionary world. In the 1920's three bodies in Nyasaland, two of them Scottish and one Dutch Reformed, joined in forming the Church of Central Africa (Presbyterian), but in the 1950's there were only 91 ordained African ministers for a community of about 386,000.[65] A step towards autonomy was taken by the Anglicans in 1955 with the creation of the Province of Central Africa, which included the diocese of Nyasaland, Northern Rhodesia, Matabeleland, and Mashonaland,[66] but this did not evoke immediately any great increase in African clergy. The Roman Catholics were doing very little if any better. In 1956 they had two theological seminaries in the area, one in Southern Rhodesia and the other in Nyasaland, with a total enrollment of eighty-three major seminaries.[67] Presumably their course was longer than that of the Protestants. By 1961 they had consecrated an African bishop in the region. He was in Nyasaland.[68]

Cults arose containing elements derived from Christianity. Two attained major dimensions. One was the Watch Tower Movement and the other the Alice Movement. The Watch Tower Movement, sprung from Jehovah's Witnesses, became prominent in the 1930's. It seems to have entered from South Africa, to have been under indigenous leaders, and to have been entirely self-supporting. Its propagators, forceful and with oratorial gifts, appealed to the slumbering resentment against white domination. They taught that the second coming would sit in judgement on their former rulers and oppressors. They

[64] Allen, *op. cit.*, p. 62.

[65] International Missionary Council, *Survey of the Training of the Ministers in Africa*, Part III, pp. 22–29.

[66] *The International Review of Missions*, Vol. XLV, p. 51 (January, 1956).

[67] Allen, *op. cit.*, p. 424.

[68] *Worldmission Fides Service*, February 1, 1961.

encouraged "speaking with tongues" and belief in the avenging power of the ancestors. They denounced governments, both white and black, and missions, whether Protestant or Roman Catholic. The Movement provoked riots, and chiefs and the colonial governments sought to suppress it.[69] The Alice Movement, issuing in the Lumpa Church, arose in the 1950's in a strong Church of Scotland centre in Northern Rhodesia and attracted many both from Protestantism and from the adjoining Roman Catholic mission. Its leader was Alice Lenshina Mulenga, who believed that she had died four times, had risen again, and had been called by Jesus to "meet Him at the river." There He had commissioned her to attack witch-craft. She went about preaching, was believed to be spoken to again and again by Jesus, and taught her followers simple songs of her composing. Thousands were attracted, gave up their fetishes, and were baptized by her. She and her preachers spoke out against polygamy as well as sorcery. Her followers were drawn partly from the churches and erected little chapels in their villages.[70]

PROGRESS IN PORTUGUESE AFRICA

On either side of the Federation of Rhodesia and Nyasaland were the Portuguese possessions—Portuguese West Africa (Angola) and Portuguese East Africa (Mozambique). Angola was the larger and in 1959 had an estimated population of 4,550,000, of whom about 120,000 were Europeans. Mozambique, only about two-thirds the size of Angola, in 1958 had a population of about 6,234,000. In theory Angola and Mozambique were not colonies but were overseas provinces of Portugal. They were late in feeling the full impact of the revolutionary age. Yet by 1962 that impact was strengthening. Although only a small minority of the population were in schools, the government was providing scholarships in them and in universities in Portugal. Unrest, reflecting that in the Republic of Congo, was appearing with a demand for independence, and cities were growing, with an accompanying disintegration of the old patterns of life. As the twentieth century progressed the government attempted to assimilate the Africans to Portuguese culture, but with the realization that the full attainment of that goal would be very slow.[71]

Roman Catholic missions were carried on under agreement with the Portuguese Government. The latter continued to control them through the *padroado* granted by the Pope in the early days of Portuguese exploration and empire-

[69] *The International Review of Missions*, Vol. XXIX (1927), pp. 216, 226; Davis, *op. cit.*, p. 241; Taylor and Lehmann, *op. cit.*, pp. 112, 113, 227–247.

[70] International Missionary Council, *Occasional Papers Issued by the Department of Missionary Studies* (London, August, 1958, pp. 9, mimeographed), *passim;* Taylor and Lehmann, *op. cit.*, pp. 165, 248–268.

[71] Duffy, *Portuguese Africa*, pp. 189 ff.

building. The civil strife in Portugal in the nineteenth century with the rampant anti-clericalism which isued in the suppression of orders and congregations was followed in 1911 by the separation of Church and state and the severing of diplomatic relations with the Vatican (1913).[72] This meant that in Portuguese Africa Roman Catholic missions, which had already suffered from the scepticism of the eighteenth century, all but lapsed. A few seculars served Portuguese in the coastal cities and African minorities.[73] In the twentieth century conditions improved, but only slowly. From 1911 to 1919 the Lisbon government forbade Roman Catholic missions in the colonies, but in the latter year it permitted them to revive.[74] The use of Portuguese was required in all schools, and even in religious instruction the vernacular was forbidden. In 1921 that prohibition was removed, but with the reservation that in the public teaching of the catechism, the Bible, and prayer books only Portuguese was to be employed. Restrictions on missions were progressively relaxed by decrees of 1926 and 1933. In the concordat of 1940 between the Holy See and Lisbon and the accompanying Missionary Agreement all legal obstacles to missions were removed. The government promised financial support for schools, hospitals, missionary travel, and the salaries of bishops and missionaries, and specified that religious instruction should be in the vernaculars and in accord with the basic convictions of the Church. As had been true in earlier days, the state was to name the bishops.[75]

Under the improved relations with the government the progress of the Roman Catholic Church was impressive, especially in Angola. In 1931 after a vacancy of thirteen years the See of Luanda was again filled. In 1941 Luanda was made an archbishopric, and two newly created dioceses, later four, were placed under it. By 1939 Angola had over a half-million Roman Catholics. Growth was especially marked in the valley of the Cubanga. There the number of the faithful mounted from 8,240 in 1908 to 284,561 in 1939. In 1933 a major seminary was opened in Nova Lisboa in that area for the preparation of secular clergy.[76] In 1952 Roman Catholics in Angola were said to total about 800,000 served by 250 foreign and African priests. The same totals were repeated in 1957.[77] In 1956 the seminary at Novo Lisboa was reported to have eighty-four major seminarians and the archdiocesan seminary at Luanda to have twenty-two. Both institutions were under the Holy Ghost Fathers.[78]

Protestantism made substantial progress in Angola in spite of the coolness of

---

[72] Volume I, pp. 424, 425.
[73] Beckmann, *op. cit.*, p. 68.
[74] Duffy, *op. cit.*, p. 114.
[75] Beckmann, *op. cit.*, p. 69.
[76] *Ibid.*, pp. 70, 71; *The Statesman's Year Book, 1960*, p. 1339.
[77] *World Christian Handbook, 1952*, p. 265; *1957*, p. 166.
[78] Allen, *op. cit.*, p. 422.

the government to it, an attitude based on the fact that the missionaries were non-Portuguese and at times were critical of the forced labour of which they accused the regime.[79] Protestants were chiefly represented by the American Board of Commissioners for Foreign Missions, in 1957 with twice the number of communicants and Christian community of any other, by the United Church of Canada, by the (American) Methodists, and by the (English) Baptist Missionary Society, each of the three with about the same number of communicants, totalling together approximately that of the American Board. In the 1950's all four were growing.[80] The census of 1950 said that Protestants numbered 286,000 as against 712,000 Roman Catholics. If these totals approximate accuracy, they indicate that at the mid-twentieth century those associated with the churches were between a fifth and a fourth of the population—a striking advance. The Protestants were chiefly among the Ovimbundu people, and mainly in the area where the Roman Catholics were strongest.[81] In the 1950's the Ovimbundu numbered about 1,500,000 and so constituted about a third of the population of Angola. Much of the growth of the faith was by spontaneous propagation by the Africans.[82] Preparation for the ministry was mainly through a theological seminary at Dondi, in the heart of the Ovimbundu country, in which, beginning in 1957, Methodists joined with the American Board and the United Church of Canada. It trained ministers for the Kimbundu (about 1,000,000 strong) as well as the Ovimbundo.[83]

In 1961 revolt broke out in Angola, chiefly in the North, and the Portuguese authorities sent troops to quell it. The Portuguese press accused Protestants of being responsible for the outbreak. In the fighting, many Protestant schools, chapels, and churches were damaged or destroyed, and scores of African pastors were killed or imprisoned.[84]

In Mozambique the advance of Christianity was much less marked than in Angola, both in actual numbers and in proportion to the population. In the nineteenth century the Roman Catholic Church suffered, as in Angola, from an unfriendly government and the low ebb of its life and of missionary zeal in

---

[79] *The International Review of Missions*, Vol. XXXI, p. 58 (January, 1942).

[80] *World Christian Handbook, 1957*, p. 67.

[81] *The International Review of Missions*, Vol. XXXIII, pp. 55, 56 (January, 1944). See also John T. Tucker, *Old Ways and New Days in Angola, Africa* (Toronto, Committee on Young People's Missionary Education, ca. 1936, pp. 112), *passim;* John T. Tucker, *Drums in the Darkness* (New York, George H. Doran Co., 1927, pp. 202), *passim.* For the story of an American Negro long a Protestant missionary in Angola under the American Board, a pioneer in agricultural education, see Samuel B. Coles, *Preacher with a Plow* (Boston, Houghton Mifflin Co., 1957, pp. xi, 241), *passim.*

[82] John T. Tucker, *Angola, the Land of the Blacksmith Prince* (London, World Dominion Press, 1933, pp. viii, 180), pp. 76–81, 133.

[83] Allen, *op. cit.,* pp. 49, 50.

[84] *Ecumenical Press Service,* April 28, 1961; *The Christian Century,* Vol. LXXVIII, p. 645 (May 24, 1961).

Portugal. In 1881 Jesuits sought to renew the lapsed missions of earlier days. They suffered heavily from tropical diseases—thirty-seven deaths by 1902. When the anti-clerical government which came to power in 1910 expelled them, their places were taken by the (German) Society of the Divine Word. Several other orders and congregations came before World War I. But the entrance of Portugal into that war (1916) led to the internment and then the expulsion of the members of the Society of the Divine Word and not until 1941 were the Jesuits re-admitted. Between the two world wars additional congregations came —Italian, French, and Dutch as well as Portuguese.[85] Lourenço Marques was raised to archiepiscopal status in the same year (1940) that a similar step was taken for Luanda, and like the latter was in time given four suffragan sees.[86] In the mid-1940's the total Roman Catholic population, including the Portuguese, was said to be 85,000.[87] An estimate in 1957 put the figure at 200,000, with 213 native and foreign clergy.[88] In the mid-1950's the only Roman Catholic theological seminary was at Lourenço Marques with thirteen students of major rank.[89]

In Mozambique Protestantism was represented by more different organizations than in Angola, but in 1957 its communicants were estimated to be only 39,843. Although that was an increase of nearly 7,000 in five years, the total was less than half that in Angola and the increase was proportionately slightly less than in the latter. In point of numbers of communicants the major bodies were the Anglicans, followed by the Mission Suisse dans l'Afrique du Sud and the American Methodists. To the latter must be added the Free Methodists of North America.[90] The Methodists maintained what Portuguese administrators said was the best village and agricultural school in the country. They and other Protestants also conducted several hospitals and dispensaries which provided an important part of the woefully inadequate medical care of the country.[91] For preparation for the ministry, in 1958 the Mission Suisse dans l'Afrique du Sud and the Methodists, who by that time had joined in creating the Church of Christ in Mozambique, opened a union theological seminary a few miles north of Lourenço Marques. At least three other bodies coöperated.[92]

[85] Duffy, *op. cit.*, p. 113; Beckmann, *op. cit.*, p. 71.
[86] *Statesman's Year Book, 1960*, p. 1339.
[87] Beckmann, *op. cit.*, p. 72.
[88] *World Christian Handbook, 1957*, p. 166.
[89] Allen, *op. cit.*, p. 422.
[90] *World Christian Handbook, 1957*, pp. 86, 87. For letters from a Methodist missionary in the 1950's see Clara Evans Keys, *We Pioneered in Portuguese East Africa. A Methodist Missionary's Memoirs of Planting Christian Civilization in Mozambique* (New York, Exposition Press, 1959, pp. 89).
[91] Duffy, *op. cit.*, pp. 128, 129.
[92] Allen, *op. cit.*, p. 50; International Missionary Council, *Survey of the Training of the Ministry in Africa*, Part II, p. 86.

Rapid Growth in Changing Tanganyika

Tanganyika, lying directly north of Mozambique, was less than half the size of Portuguese Africa (Angola and Mozambique) and in 1959 had a population, largely Bantu, of about 9,076,000, or approximately nine-tenths that of the two Portuguese possessions. In the mid-1950's it contained a Protestant community estimated at 575,158, of whom 263,702 were communicants, which was more than twice that in Angola and Mozambique,[93] and a Roman Catholic community which in 1959 was said to be 1,331,708,[94] about a third more than that in the Portuguese territories. This meant that early in the 1960's those who were regarded as Christians were a little over a fourth of the population. Yet Islam had long been in the country and in the twentieth century continued to spread.

On the eve of World War I Tanganyika was known as German East Africa. It had been acquired by Germany in the 1880's, when most of Africa south of the Sahara was being partitioned by earth-hungry Europeans. Germans settled in the highlands. They also entered upon the exploitation of the rich economic resources and with German thoroughness developed a colonial·administration. During World War I the region saw much fighting and was badly ravaged. The peace settlement gave it to Great Britain as a mandate under the League of Nations, except for a portion, Ruanda-Urundi, which went to Belgium under a similar provision. Reconstruction was difficult and prolonged. With the formation of the United Nations the mandate was transformed into a trusteeship under that body. In the 1950's Tanganyika moved rapidly towards independence. On May 1, 1961, it began to govern its own internal affairs and late that year it became fully independent.

The history of Christianity in Tanganyika reflected the political changes through which the country had passed. Before the German annexation both Protestants and Roman Catholics had begun missions. Protestantism had been brought by British societies—the London Missionary Society, the Church Missionary Society, and the Universities' Mission to Central Africa (an Anglo-Catholic organization which arose from an appeal by Livingstone).[95] The Roman Catholic pioneers were Holy Ghost Fathers. For both Protestants and Roman Catholics an early coign of vantage was the adjacent Zanzibar, a solidly Moslem island whose sultan was willing to admit Christian missionaries. Following the German annexation additional missionaries came. They were from both Protestant and Roman Catholic organizations and were predominantly from the Continent of Europe, largely from Germany. World War I brought the repatriation of the German missionaries. Some help in maintaining what they had begun was given by non-German missions, but not until 1923 were the

[93] *World Christian Handbook, 1957*, pp. 106, 166.
[94] *Worldmission Fides Service*, April 2, 1960.
[95] Latourette, *A History of the Expansion of Christianity*, Vol. V, pp. 403, 404.

Germans permitted to return. Then the financial situation in Germany was a serious handicap.[96] World War II also caused the partial interruption of German missions, but thanks to aid from the Orphaned Missions Fund of the International Missionary Council and especially from the Swedes, operations were maintained, even though on a reduced scale. But the German missionaries were either interned or repatriated.[97] As a result of the war the German missions were transferred to Swedish and American Lutherans.[98] Eventually the Germans resumed work. The Lutheran World Federation was of help and encouraged the training of an African ministry.[99] In the 1950's the largest body of Protestants was Lutheran, the fruits of several missions, Continental European and American.

A remarkable Lutheran pioneer was Bruno Gutmann, of the Leipzig society. He formulated principles for utilizing Bantu tribal traditions and customs in building an African church.[100] An African Lutheran church arose which held its first synod in 1930.[101] In 1937 the *Ostafrikanische Missionskirchbund* (East African Church Federation) was formed on Lutheran principles and brought together bodies founded by eight missions. It flourished and in time was followed by the Haya Synod. The Africans displayed marked zeal in spreading the faith.[102] To provide clergy for the Federation a theological seminary was organized in 1947 which became one of the strongest in East Africa.[103] In 1959 the Evangelical Lutheran Church of North Tanganyika elected an African as its president—the first time that had been done.[104]

Next to the Lutherans in numerical strength were the Anglicans, the product of the missions of several societies, chiefly the Church Missionary Society and the Universities' Mission to Central Africa.[105] Among several distinctive features was an adaptation of the tribal initiatory rites in an attempt to conserve the social values of the old order until Christian standards could be effective.[106]

To further the Roman Catholic Church, in 1930 an apostolic delegation was created for East Africa which included Tanganyika and had as its first in-

[96] Richter, *Tanganyika and Its Future*, p. 30.

[97] *The International Review of Missions*, Vol. XXXIII, p. 58 (January, 1944); Vol. XXXIV, p. 51 (January, 1945); Groves, *The Planting of Christianity in Africa*, Vol. IV, pp. 241, 242.

[98] *World Christian Handbook, 1952*, p. 209.

[99] Groves, *op. cit.*, Vol. IV, p. 242 n.; confidential information to the author.

[100] Richter, *op. cit.*, p. 21; Bruno Gutmann, *Gemeinde Aufbau aus dem Evangelium Grundsätzliches für Mission und Heimatkirche* (Leipzig, Evang. luth. Mission, no date, pp. 214), *passim*.

[101] Richter, *op. cit.*, p. 21. On Lutheran enterprises see Frits Larsen, *Mødet med Tanganyika* (Copenhagen, Luthersk Missionsforenings Forlag, 1955, pp. 231), *passim*.

[102] Groves, *op. cit.*, Vol. IV, p. 233; *The International Review of Missions*, Vol. XXXIX, pp. 270–276 (July, 1950).

[103] Allen, *op. cit.*, p. 27.

[104] *The International Review of Missions*, Vol. XLIX, pp. 46, 47 (January, 1960).

[105] *World Christian Handbook, 1957*, pp. 104, 105.

[106] Groves, *op. cit.*, Vol. IV, p. 216; *The International Review of Missions*, Vol. XXXIV, pp. 389–396 (October, 1945).

cumbent Archbishop Hinsley, later to be the Cardinal Archbishop of West-minister.[107] By 1961 Tanganyika had six African archbishops and bishops, two of whom were auxiliary, but four of whom, including one archbishop, were in full charge of their respective sees. This was more than in any other of the countries in Africa south of the Sahara.[108]

When in 1961 Tanganyika obtained its independence, its first prime minister was Julius K. Nyerere, the leader of the Tanganyika African National Union. A man of strong Christian convictions, he had taught in a Roman Catholic secondary school. Several other Roman Catholics held government posts.[109]

UGANDA: A MATURING CHRISTIANITY

Uganda, a British protectorate lying north of Tanganyika and on the equator, was only 93,981 square miles in extent. Yet in 1959, with an area about a fourth of its southern neighbour, it had a population estimated at 6,517,000, or two-thirds that of the latter. Uganda was remarkable for the near approach to civilization developed by the Baganda, a Bantu people with a dynasty which had some Hamitic blood and which was said to have ruled from at least the beginning of the fifteenth century. The dynasty governed in Buganda, which included between a fourth and a third of Uganda. In the 1950's Uganda was on the road to self-government and independence and in 1960 the impatient Baganda voted to attain that status at once.

Uganda was noted for the rapidity with which Christianity had won a large proportion of the population, especially among the Baganda.[110] It entered on the initiative of Henry M. Stanley, who in 1874 taught the King of the Baganda the principles of Christianity and reported to Europe that that monarch desired missionaries. In response the Church Missionary Society and the White Fathers sent pioneer staffs. The former arrived in 1877, the latter in 1879. After many difficulties, including persecutions, both branches of Christianity made rapid gains, notably among the Baganda. In 1894 Uganda was declared a British protectorate. Under the domestic peace which followed, the baptized Anglicans increased from a few score to 62,000 in 1911 and to 98,477 in 1914. The Bible was translated, schools were begun, and the congregations erected their own churches and supported the African staff. Through Baganda missionaries the faith spread to neighbouring tribes.[111] The White Fathers were supplemented by the

---

[107] Beckmann, *op. cit.*, p. 82.

[108] *Worldmission Fides Service*, March 19, 1960, and February 1, 1961.

[109] *The Christian Century*, Vol. LXXVII, pp. 189, 190 (February 17, 1960); *The New York Times*, March 30, 1960; *Worldmission Fides Service*, December 3, 1960.

[110] Volume III, pp. 476, 477; Latourette, *op. cit.*, Vol. V, pp. 412–419.

[111] On one of the converts who became a missionary to the pygmies see Margaret Sinker, *Into the Great Forest. The Story of Apolo of Central Africa* (London, Wyman and Sons, 1950, pp. 92), *passim.*

Mill Hill Fathers. On the eve of World War I the White Fathers had 113,811 Christians in their charge, and that in spite of a protracted four-year cate-chumenate, and the Mill Hill Fathers had 22,393 of the faithful in their vi-cariate. Education was promoted, but in 1914 there were only about a third as many students as in the Anglican schools.[112]

Between World War I and the early 1960's the numerical growth of both Protestants and Roman Catholics continued. A few other Protestant societies were represented, but in 1957 Anglicans affiliated with the Church Missionary Society constituted about five-sixths of the estimated 443,735 Protestant com-munity of that year.[113] Numerically the Roman Catholics outstripped the Protestants. They were reported to total 985,633 in 1949, to have risen to 1,553,504 in 1957, and in 1959 to be 1,701,348.[114] If these figures are to be trusted, by 1960 those bearing the Christian name constituted about a third of the population. Among the Baganda the proportion was still higher. In the 1950's 41 per cent. of the population were Roman Catholics, 24 per cent. were Anglicans, 27 per cent. held to the old religions, 7.5 per cent. were Moslems, and 0.1 per cent. were Christians other than in the two major groups.[115]

Various causes were ascribed for the rapid spread of the faith. One was emancipation from the fear of the Arabs brought by the advent of Christianity and the British protectorate. Another was the desire to acquire the culture of the Europeans. Among the non-Baganda was the wish to emulate the Baganda, who were rapidly adopting the faith.[116]

Increasingly both Anglicans and Roman Catholics were raising up an African clergy. By the 1960's the Anglican African clergy were almost entirely responsi-ble for the pastoral care of the Christians and the further spread of the faith. They provided much of the personnel for the Diocese of the Upper Nile when it came into existence.[117] Yet they were far too few for their task. In the 1940's each clergyman had about five thousand Christians under his care. Moreover, because of the multiplicity of tribes, inter-tribal tensions, and resentment against the aggressive Baganda, true unity was difficult. Criticisms were heard, too, of the preparation of teachers and clergy in the same institution—although the statement was made that since the ordinands were usually older, their presence in the student body was wholesome and made for less immorality than in

---

[112] For a White Father pioneer who lived beyond World War I see J. Cussac, *Evêque et Pionnier, Monseigneur Streicher* (Paris, Éditions de la Savane, 1955, pp. 277). On the Mill Hill Fathers to 1914 see H. P. Gale, *Uganda and the Mill Hill Fathers* (London, Macmillan and Co., 1959, pp. ix, 334), *passim*.

[113] *World Christian Handbook, 1957*, p. 108.

[114] *Worldmission Fides Service*, February 8, 1961.

[115] Taylor, *The Growth of the Church in Buganda*, p. 124.

[116] Oliver, *The Missionary Factor in East Africa*, pp. 176–207.

[117] A. L. Kitching, *From Darkness to Light. A Study of Pioneer Missionary Work in the Diocese of the Upper Nile* (London, Society for Promoting Christian Knowledge, 1935, pp. 64), pp. 34–42.

institutions where only teachers were trained.[118] In 1961 the Anglicans in Uganda and Ruanda-Urundi were made an ecclesiastical province independent of Canterbury.[119]

Roman Catholics had a high ratio of adult baptisms to the number of priests. In 1960 it averaged seventy-five per priest, a record surpassed in only four other political divisions in Africa south of the Sahara.[120] For years the Roman Catholics had African priests serve as assistants to European clergy, but in 1921 an entire mission station was entrusted to four of the native clergy.[121] In 1939 an African, Joseph Kiwanuka, was consecrated bishop and was given charge of a new vicariate apostolic which was to be entirely staffed by African secular clergy. He was the first African bishop since the sixteenth century.[122] By 1961 Kiwanuka was still the only African in the Ugandan episcopate, but he was in charge of an archdiocese.[123]

Out of the Christianity of Uganda at least one movement arose which claimed a Biblical basis but was far from historic Christianity. In 1913 what were known as the Malakites—"the Church of the One Almighty God"—sprang up and drew heavily from both Anglicans and Roman Catholics. They forbade recourse to physicians or medicine and rejected monogamy on the ground that it was not commanded by the Bible—this last with its appeal to African customs which found Christian sex ethics rigid. Eventually the government took action against them because of their menace to public health, especially in their resistance to vaccination for smallpox, and they died out.[124]

More serious than the rise of African religious movements with a smattering of Christianity was the deterioration of the faith of the third or fourth generation of Protestants, a phenomenon not limited to Uganda or even to Africa. The first generation of Baganda Anglicans included some chiefs and others with gifts of leadership who became zealous missionaries. Not far from the year 1900 a decline set in. It was due to a number of causes. The possession of a Christian name and baptism were regarded as indications of being "civilized"— of conforming to the modern age. Other factors were the irruption of secularism through more intimate contact with non-missionary Europeans, disease, especially sleeping sickness, the reduction of the European staff, very marked as contrasted with the growth in the Roman Catholic foreign personnel, the

[118] International Missionary Council, *Survey of the Training of the Ministry in Africa*, Part I, pp. 36, 37.

[119] *Ecumenical Press Service*, April 14, 1961.

[120] *Worldmission Fides Service*, March 16, 1961.

[121] Beckman, *op. cit.*, p. 320.

[122] *Fides News Service*, June 3, 1939; *Worldmission Fides Service*, March 8, 1961.

[123] *Worldmission Fides Service*, February 1, 1961, and March 8, 1961. In 1961 another Roman Catholic, Benedikto Kiwanuka, became Uganda's first prime minister.—*Ibid.*, April 8, 1961.

[124] Groves, *op. cit.*, Vol. IV, pp. 125, 126; Taylor, *op. cit.*, pp. 97, 125.

promotion of the abler clergy to higher posts in administration with the care of the parishes left to the less competent, the decline in the number of catechists, the lack of adequate pastoral care, a recession of zeal on the part of some Africans, and the tendency of the faith to become cold and conventional in those who were church members by heredity. Sexual looseness, plurality of wives, the use of spirit mediums, and drunkenness were common.[125]

Countering the decline, revivals were seen. A notable movement began in the 1930's. At the outset it was sparked by the son of a sub-chief who was converted in 1922. Impressed by the low spiritual and moral level of many of the clergy and catechists, he gave up a political career to preach the urgency of conforming to higher standards. Missionaries who had been touched by the Oxford Groups (associated with Frank Buchman) and the Keswick Conventions contributed to the awakening. The revival was marked by mutual confession of sin, a more sincere fellowship, and what was called "walking in the light." Huge conventions were held. African features developed. An element of nationalism and resentment of control by the missionaries was present. Much stress was placed on lay initiative. A tendency was seen for those committed to the movement to display spiritual pride and form exclusive groups. But on the whole the movement remained within the Anglican Church.[126]

A different development in the Christianity of Uganda was a movement which found fellowship with the Orthodox. It is said to have begun in 1932 when by his study of church history a Baganda Protestant became convinced that the Orthodox Church was the only true continuation of the early Church. He gathered a congregation. Prelates from the Orthodox Patriarchate of Alexandria visited Uganda and received the congregation into its jurisdiction. Students were sent to the seminary in Cairo and the University of Athens. In 1954 the Orthodox were said to number about 10,000 in Uganda, Tanganyika, and Kenya, and were mostly humble folk.[127] In December, 1958, an archbishop was consecrated in Alexandria for a new archiepiscopal see for East and Central Africa. A few congregations of Greeks were in the Congo, and in 1959 the African Orthodox were said to number 15,000, mostly in Uganda. A committee was formed in Athens to aid the Orthodox missions, and students were sent to Greece to prepare as nurses and priests.[128]

---

[125] Groves, *op. cit.,* Vol. IV, pp. 221, 222; Taylor, *op. cit.,* pp. 76–105; John V. Taylor, *Processes of Growth in an African Church* (London, SCM Press, 1958, pp. 30), *passim.*

[126] Taylor, *The Growth of the Church in Buganda,* pp. 99–104; Groves, *op. cit.,* pp. 223–235; *Awake! An African Calling. The Story of Blasio Kigozi and His Vision of a Revival* (London, Church Missionary Society, 1937, pp. 56), *passim.*

[127] *New Missionary Review,* No. 7 (Spring, 1955); Nos. 11–12 (12–13) (1957).

[128] *Ibid.,* Nos. 14, 15, 15–16 (1959), and Nos. 17–18, 18–19 (1960). On the completion of two church buildings in Uganda see *Ecumenical Press Service,* November 18, 1960.

THE COMPLEX PATTERN IN KENYA

Kenya, formerly known as British East Africa, directly to the east of Uganda and like it spanning the equator, in the first half of the twentieth century was included in the British Empire. In 1959 its estimated population was 6,450,000, of whom about 66,400 were Europeans, 169,900 were Indians, Pakistanis, and Goans, and about 37,000 were Arabs. The coastal strip, with some islands, was leased from the Sultan of Zanzibar, and the remainder was a British colony. Several African tribes made up the bulk of the population. The largest was the Kikuyu, embracing about a fifth of the population, but four others had between a tenth and a seventh of the whole. The British East Africa Company, chartered in 1888, was an opening wedge for British rule. One of its objects was the suppression of slavery and the improvement of the lot of the Africans, with the prohibition of the liquor traffic, the building of roads, and the starting of industrial missions. In 1895 the British Government bought the company's interests and assumed direct responsibility for the administration. A railway was constructed into the interior, some of the tribes were pacified, and the discovery was made that the thinly peopled high plateau was suited to European residence. Europeans came, some of them Afrikaners and British whites from South Africa, and others directly from Europe. They took up lands, engaged in agriculture and stock-raising, and employed African labour. After World War I a few hundred British veterans were given homes. Compulsory labour was forbidden. Much of the policy to protect the African arose from pressure from Protestant missionaries, especially J. H. Oldham of the International Missionary Council, on the London authorities. To the same influence was largely due the policy of the British Government of subsidizing education through mission schools, not only in Kenya, but also elsewhere in Africa.[129] Reserves were set up for the Africans. In 1920 the change was made from a protectorate to a crown colony. In 1923 the British Government declared that the interests of the Africans must be paramount and steps were taken progressively to prepare the Africans for self-government. The situation was complicated by the demand of the Europeans for a share in the government. The Indians, who had been introduced as labourers to help build the railway and whose numbers had been augmented by others who had come as traders and who soon outnumbered the Europeans, also insisted on a voice in the government.

In the 1950's the Mau Mau movement broke out. Its members were Africans, largely Kikuyu, who bound themselves by oaths, increasingly violent and ruthless. They sought to exterminate all foreigners, to dominate the Kikuyu tribe, to rule all Kenya, and to restore African society as it was before the advent of the Europeans and the Indians. It was sparked by fierce resentment against the occupation of land by the foreigners and the threat to the traditional African

---

[129] Oliver, op. cit., pp. 247–288.

way of life. To achieve their purpose the Mau Mau employed terror and murder, not only against foreigners but also against Africans who would not go along with them. The uprising attracted world-wide attention. Drastic measures were employed to suppress it and it came to an end early in 1960. The British authorities adopted a programme for the participation of Africans, Europeans, Asians, and Arabs in the government of the region with the prospect of eventual independence.[130]

With the exception of possible early contacts through Nestorians, Syrian Orthodox, and Roman Catholics, Christianity was first brought to what was later known as Kenya through Protestants in the 1840's. In the 1860's a continuing enterprise was begun by the (English) United Free Methodists. Before the outbreak of World War I several societies, mostly British, had gained footholds. Roman Catholics were slightly later in arriving: before 1914 at least three congregations were represented, chief among them the Mill Hill Fathers.[131]

Although the population of Kenya more than doubled between 1914 and 1959, proportionately the number of Christians mounted more steeply. In 1962 Christians were still a minority, but, as in most areas south of the Sahara, a rapidly growing minority. Baptized Protestants were said to number 47,078 in 1924.[132] In 1957 Protestant full members were reported as 291,118 and the Protestant community as 610,561. In the latter year more than a third in both categories were Anglicans, with Christians arising from a remarkable mission of American Friends (Quakers) second, followed closely by the Salvation Army, the Seventh Day Adventists, and the Church of God. But all the latter three taken together did not equal the Anglicans.[133] Roman Catholics were said to number 8,556 in 1921 and to have increased to 324,744 in 1949 and to 764,238 in 1959.[134]

The Mau Mau brought a crisis to the African Christians, for the rebels looked upon them as allied with the hated Europeans. Under pressure many denied their faith. However, numbers held true and some paid for their loyalty with their lives.[135] Much of the persistent adherence to the faith stemmed from the awakening which we noted in Uganda. It spread to Kenya, arriving in 1937, and led to reconciliation between members of rival tribes and between Euro-

---

[130] Of the large literature on the subject, see Groves, *op. cit.*, Vol. IV, pp. 266, 267; *Britannica Book of the Year, 1959*, p. 385; *1960*, pp. 379, 383; *1961*, p. 386.

[131] Latourette, *op. cit.*, Vol. V, pp. 409–412.

[132] Beach and Fahs, *World Missionary Atlas*, p. 77.

[133] *World Christian Handbook, 1957*, pp. 82, 83. On the Friends mission see Irene E. Hoskins, *Friends in Africa* (Richmond, Ind., American Friends Board of Missions, no date, pp. 66), *passim*. For the reminiscences of an Anglican missionary in Kenya from soon after World War I into the 1930's, see William Joseph Wright, *Their Excellencies* (Leicester, Edgar Backus, no date, pp. ix, 106), pp. 24–84.

[134] *Fides News Service*, July 31, 1937; *Worldmission Fides Service*, February 8, 1961.

[135] H. Virginia Blakeslee, *Beyond the Kikuyu Curtain* (Chicago, Moody Press, 1956, pp. 267), pp. 174–193; *Mau Mau and the Church* (Edinburgh, The Church of Scotland Missionary Committee, 1953, pp. 11), *passim*; T. F. C. Hewes, *Kikuyu Conflict. Mau Mau and the Christian Witness* (London, The Highway Press, 1953, pp. 76), pp. 44–75.

peans and Africans.[136] When the uprising was suppressed and many of its leaders were put in prison or detention camps, the rebels were visited by Christians and some of them were won to the faith.[137]

The Mau Mau storm did not seriously halt the spread of Christianity and may have hastened the development of African leadership. As we have seen, between 1952, on the eve of the outbreak, and 1957, when the height had passed, Protestant full members and communicants were reported to have increased from 134,037 to 291,118 and the Protestant Community from 330,666 to 610,-561.[138] Roman Catholic totals were similarly said to have risen from 411,510 in 1953 to 606,242 in 1957, and to 764,258 in 1959.[139]

For their ministry Protestants depended chiefly on a number of Bible schools. In the 1950's the beginnings of a theological institution of higher academic standard were seen near Nairobi, where Anglicans, Presbyterians, and Methodists coöperated. Here as elsewhere a major problem was one of language, partly because of the absence of suitable literature in the vernaculars. Some advocated the use of Swahili, a *lingua franca* in East Africa, but others felt that it was a dying tongue.[140] Inspiration was given to the Anglicans in East Africa when, in 1955, the Archbishop of Canterbury consecrated in Uganda four bishops from territories in and adjoining that country—one for Tanganyika, one for the Sudan, and two for Mombasa, in Kenya.[141] In 1960 the (Anglican) Province of East Africa was created and became independent of Canterbury. In 1961 Uganda and the regions of the Upper Nile also were given full autonomy. By that act the ecclesiastical authority of the Archbishop of Canterbury entirely disappeared from Africa—evidence that the Anglican Communion in Africa had come of age.[142]

The Roman Catholics were also training priests, but in the mid-1950's had far fewer major seminarians than in Uganda or Tanganyika. However, late in the 1950's plans were announced for creating a regional seminary in Nairobi through the investment of $700,000. In 1957 the first Roman Catholic African bishop for Kenya was consecrated.[143]

Protestants moved towards coöperation and unity. Preliminary steps had been taken shortly before World War I, one of which, at Kikuyu in 1913, led to

[136] *The International Review of Missions*, Vol. XLIII, pp. 77–81 (January, 1954); *A Monthly Letter About Evangelism* (Geneva, February, 1960, mimeographed).

[137] K. N. Phillips, *From Mau Mau to Christ* (London, Stirling Tract Enterprise, Africa Inland Mission, 1958, pp. 91), *passim*.

[138] *World Christian Handbook, 1957*, pp. 82, 83.

[139] *Worldmission Fides Service*, February 8, 1961.

[140] International Missionary Council, *Survey of the Training of the Ministry in Africa*, Part I, pp. 34, 35; Sundkler, *The Christian Ministry in Africa*, pp. 240, 241, 259; *The International Review of Missions*, Vol. XLV, p. 51 (January, 1956).

[141] *The International Review of Missions*, Vol. XLV, p. 51 (January, 1956).

[142] *The Christian Century*, Vol. LXXVII, p. 1128 (September 8, 1960).

[143] Allen, *A Seminary Survey*, pp. 414, 415; *Britannica Book of the Year, 1958*, p. 380.

controversy in Anglican circles in England and elsewhere because of a Communion service of Anglicans and non-Anglicans. In 1918 a further conference was held from which emerged the Alliance of Missionary Societies in British East Africa. Out of it came, in 1924, the United Missionary Council to handle questions of the relation of missions to government.[144]

RAPID GROWTH IN RUANDA-URUNDI

We must take time in passing to mention Ruanda-Urundi, not because of its area, for it was one of the smallest of the African political units—only 20,540 square miles—or because of the size of its population, for in 1959, at an estimated 4,630,000, it was less than that of its immediate neighbours, though denser. But here Christianity, especially in its Roman Catholic form, made phenomenally rapid gains after 1914.

Ruanda-Urundi, it will be recalled, had been a part of German East Africa. Following World War I it had been transferred as a mandate to Belgium under the League of Nations. Administratively it was divided between Ruanda and Urundi and on the formation of the United Nations it was held, still by Belgium, under a trusteeship of that body. Most of it was in the highlands. The majority of the population were Bantu, but the ruling race was akin to the Baganda in Uganda. Early in the 1960's a movement towards independence was seen.

Both Protestants and Roman Catholics were represented. Christianity had been introduced before World War I. Its spectacular gains were in the decades which followed the transfer to Belgium. As a result of the war the responsibility for the former German Protestant missions was assumed by the Belgian Protestants and the Friends' Africa Gospel Mission. Following the war, in 1921 Anglicans entered as the Ruanda Mission of the Church Missionary Society. By the mid-1930's the Seventh Day Adventists, the Danish Baptists, and the Swedish Free Mission were also represented. The Belgian Protestants as citizens of Belgium received financial subsidies from the government for their educational work. By 1936 Protestant church members were reported to be 1,842 and the Protestant community was said to be 17,648.[145]

The Roman Catholic Church was planted and nourished by the White Fathers. In 1936 they were caring for about 283,000 Catholics and approximately 314,000 catechumens. They early began training indigenous personnel and in the mid-1930's were reported to have 28 African priests, 28 African brothers,

[144] Latourette, *op. cit.*, Vol. V, pp. 411, 412; Groves, *op. cit.*, Vol. IV, p. 131.

[145] Stonelake, *Congo, Past and Present*, pp. 53, 54, 104, 158. For the Swedish Baptists see Henry Gjerrild, *25 Ar i Urundi, Belgisk Kongo, Afrika. De Danske Baptisters Hedninge-Mission* (Copen- · hagen, De Danske Baptisters Hedningemissionsselskab, 1954, pp. 120), *passim*.

and 48 African sisters.[146] Although Protestant totals continued to mount, Roman Catholics far outstripped them. In 1949 they were said to number 956,313 and by 1959 to have increased to 1,959,461,[147] in spite of the long catechumenate required by the White Fathers as a general policy. This meant that in 1959 about 45 per cent. of the population of Ruanda-Urundi were professedly Christian, the overwhelming majority of them Roman Catholics. The White Fathers paid special attention to the sons of chiefs who would eventually succeed to their fathers' position. As a result, one who became head of a tribe which in the 1950's totalled 2,000,000 was reported to have consecrated his realm and his subjects to Christ the King (1946). In Urundi, in 1933, 21 of the 36 great chiefs had been baptized. By 1957 all but one of the great chiefs were Roman Catholics and of the 600 sub-chiefs 95 per cent. had been baptized.[148] It was reported that the Pope instructed the missionaries in Urundi, where Roman Catholics were 49 per cent. of the population, to go more slowly in administering baptism until a sufficient number of priests could be provided to give the converts adequate care.[149] Vigorous effort was put forth to supply the need for clergy. In 1956 the two major seminaries maintained by the White Fathers had 137 major seminarians enrolled as against 349 major seminarians in all the Belgian Congo.[150] The better to nurture their flocks and to give material aid and direct the ethical and religious lives of their charges, the White Fathers in Ruanda had a system by which heads of Catholic families chose a president, or *mukuru*, to be responsible for his relatives. In the 1940's the *mukuru* were said to number about 8,000. Missionaries brought them together monthly, by groups, for reports, counsel, and instruction.[151] For the firmer planting of the Church, Africans were raised to the episcopate. By 1961 three were in charge of dioceses.[152]

THE BELGIAN CONGO AND ITS STORMY TRANSITION TO THE REPUBLIC OF CONGO

Ruanda-Urundi was on the eastern border of what on the eve of World War I was known as the Belgian Congo. On June 30, 1960, this latter was declared to be independent as the Republic of Congo. It had an estimated area of about 900,000 square miles and in 1958 was said to have a native population of 13,540,-182 and a foreign population of 112,182, of whom slightly over three-fourths were Belgians. The natives were Bantu, Sudanese, Nilotics, pygmies, and Hamites and were divided into many tribes. In area the Republic of Congo was

---

[146] Stonelake, *op. cit.,* Appendix VII (b).

[147] *Worldmission Fides Service,* February 8, 1961. See Alexandre Arnoux, *Les Pères Blancs aux Sources du Nil* (Paris, Librairie Missionnaire, 1953, pp. 197).

[148] *Worldmission,* Vol. VIII, p. 57 (Fall, 1957).

[149] Allen, *op. cit.,* pp. 431, 432.

[150] *Ibid.,* p. 420.

[151] Beckmann, *op. cit.,* pp. 294, 295.

[152] *Worldmission Fides Service,* January 28, 1961, and February 1, 1961.

larger than any other of the political divisions of Africa south of the Sahara and had more people than any except the Union of South Africa and Nigeria. In the partition of Africa by the European powers in the 1880's it had been allotted to Leopold II, King of the Belgians, as the Congo Free State. In 1907-1908 it was formally annexed by Belgium. Its large natural resources were rapidly exploited by Europeans, especially and in mounting fashion after World War I. With that exploitation as well as through Christian missions the country was increasingly penetrated by the revolutionary age. Urbanization, notably in the spectacular growth of the capital, Leopoldville, proceeded apace. Disintegration of the traditional culture followed, but unequally. In 1962 millions were still slightly or entirely unaffected. Under the Belgians internal order was achieved and education of the kind demanded by the revolutionary age spread rapidly, mainly through Christian missions with government subsidies, but predominantly on the elementary level. Few Congolese had received secondary and still fewer higher education.

The coming of political independence was promptly followed by extensive disorder. Many Congolese took the occasion to vent on Europeans their smouldering resentment. Outrages were perpetrated and most of the Europeans left the country. Civil war broke out—inter-tribal, inter-factional, and inter-regional. Several foreign governments, some African and some Communist, sought to take advantage of the situation to promote their ambitions. The United Nations endeavoured to enable the Congolese to achieve internal peace and unity and to prevent any one power, whether Western, African, or Communist, from furthering its particular interests.

In the twentieth century Christianity had a phenomenal numerical growth and in many ways affected the transition of the Congolese to the world of the revolutionary age. Missions, both Protestant and Roman Catholic, were the medium through which that growth took place. Since Belgium was overwhelmingly Roman Catholic, on the whole its government tended to favour Roman Catholic misisons, especially since the large majority of the personnel were Belgians. From 1923 to 1948, for example, by an arrangement with the Vatican Roman Catholic missions were given a monopoly of official education. Not until 1948 did Protestant schools become eligible for subsidies.[153] Beginning in 1955 the government began promoting state secular schools.

Protestant missions early came to the Congo. The international agreement through which the Congo Free State was set up promised religious liberty. Since in Belgium Protestants were a small minority, most Protestant missionaries were non-Belgians. They came from the British Isles, the United States, and the Continent of Europe, their pioneers arriving late in the 1870's. Among the societies represented some were of the standard denominations. Several were

[153] *Christianity and Crisis*, Vol. XX, p. 130 (September 19, 1960).

undenominational and conservative in theology.[154] Before World War I Protestants had achieved coöperation through missionary conferences, and in 1911 the Congo Continuation Committee of the Edinburgh Missionary Conference was organized. After World War I that committee was succeeded by the Congo Protestant Council (*Conseil Protestant du Congo*), which became a member of the International Missionary Council. It sought to build up one "Church of Christ in Congo."[155] By 1925 Protestants were reported to have 653 missionaries in the Belgian Congo, a Congolese staff of 4,528 (but of whom only 5 were ordained), 9,259 communicants, and a Christian community of 108,190.[156] By 1937 the foreign staff was said to be 500, the Congolese staff about 11,000, the full church members nearly 200,000, and the Protestant community approximately 503,000.[157] In 1952 the figures, which included Ruanda-Urundi, were 504,226 communicants or full members and a total Protestant community of 1,166,559. Five years later the corresponding totals were 654,728 and 1,179,589. In 1957 the Baptists had the most members of any denomination, followed in descending order by the Disciples of Christ, the Presbyterians, and the Seventh Day Adventists.[158] Protestants engaged heavily in education, even before they were aided by government grants. In the mid-1950's they had 9,400 schools as against 14,500 maintained by the Roman Catholics.[159] They maintained hospitals and dispensaries. Since the deposits of copper which were worked by foreign companies spanned the border between Northern Rhodesia and the Belgian Congo, the coöperative but not all-inclusive Protestant efforts to serve the labourers which crossed denominational lines that we have noted in the former were also found in the latter. Yet in Katanga, on the Belgian side of the line, the *Union Minière* refused to allow Protestant agents on its properties and entrusted all religious training and social welfare to Roman Catholics.[160] Protestants were backward in recruiting and educating an African ministry. In 1956 they were reported to have only four theological seminaries, all of them weak.[161]

Roman Catholic missionaries began coming to the Congo in the 1880's, nearly a decade after the Protestant pioneers. Leopold II early asked the Congregation of the Immaculate Heart of Mary, of Belgian origin, and Belgian Jesuits to send representatives. The former undertook the responsibility in 1888 and the latter early in the 1890's. Other orders and congregations quickly followed, and by 1914 more orders and congregations were engaged in the Belgian Congo than in any other political entity south of the Sahara. Most of the missionaries were

[154] Latourette, *op. cit.*, Vol. V, pp. 422–427.
[155] Stonelake, *op. cit.*, pp. 59–62.
[156] Beach and Fahs, *op. cit.*, pp. 76, 77.
[157] Stonelake, *op. cit.*, p. 158.
[158] *World Christian Handbook*, 1957, pp. 68–70.
[159] Allen, *op. cit.*, p. 45.
[160] Davis, *Modern Industry and the African*, pp. 300–303; Groves, *op. cit.*, Vol. IV, p. 229.
[161] Allen, *op. cit.*, p. 46.

Belgians. That was to be expected, for *Congo Belge* was Belgium's only colonial possession and, as we have more than once seen, in the nineteenth and twentieth centuries the Roman Catholic Church was very vigorous in Belgium. The Belgian Government tended to favour Roman Catholic as against Protestant missions, particularly since most of the latter's personnel were non-Belgians. This support was most marked when an administration friendly to the Roman Catholic Church was in power.[162] At the outbreak of World War I Roman Catholics in *Congo Belge* were said to number more than 100,000.[163]

After World War I Roman Catholic personnel continued to mount and the Roman Catholic community grew even more rapidly. Congolese on the Roman Catholic staffs multiplied and increasingly were assigned responsibilities. In 1912 the priests were 242, the lay brothers 129, and the sisters 149. None was a Congolese.[164] In 1931 priests totalled 691, of whom 24 were Congolese, lay brothers were 556, of whom 71 were Congolese, and sisters were 642, of whom at least 28 were Congolese.[165] Eleven years later priests numbered 1,361, of whom Congolese were 123, foreign brothers 586, and sisters 1,767, including 263 Congolese.[166] In 1959 Congolese priests totalled more than 400.[167] Two years later two dioceses had Congolese bishops at their head and two other dioceses and an archdiocese had auxiliary Congolese bishops.[168] To prepare Congolese clergy, in 1956 the White Fathers, the Jesuits, the Dominicans, and the Congregation of the Immaculate Heart of Mary maintained 5 major seminaries with 349 major seminarians and scholasticates. The largest, with more than a third of the total, was that of the White Fathers. The major seminarians were carefully screened to make sure of their vocation and their fitness. Of the students in the minor seminaries less than half were graduated.[169] According to the official statistics of the Roman Catholic Church, the number of the faithful in the Belgian Congo increased from 2,554, 712 in 1949 to 4,865, 813 in 1959.[170] This meant that in 1959 about 36 per cent. of the Congolese were Roman Catholics. If Protestant figures are added, in that year about 45 per cent., or nearly half of the Congolese, were counted as Christians.

Aided by government funds, Roman Catholics gave much attention to education. The major emphasis was on the primary grades, but they also had middle and professional schools and eventually they began Lovanium University, on the

---

[162] Latourette, *op. cit.*, Vol. V, pp. 421, 422; Vol. VII, pp. 240, 241.

[163] Streit, *Atlas Hierarchicus*, p. 101.

[164] *Ibid.*, p. 101. The statistics included Ruanda-Urundi.

[165] *Testo-Atlante Illustrato delle Missioni*, p. 121.

[166] Delegato Apostolia in Congo Belgico et Ruanda Urundi, *Résumé des Statistiques des Missions du Congo Belge et du Ruanda-Urundi, au 30 Juin, 1942.*

[167] *Worldmission*, Vol. X, p. 73 (Summer, 1959).

[168] *Worldmission Fides Service*, February 1, 1961.

[169] Allen, *op. cit.*, p. 420. Another figure, for 1959, gave the total of major seminarians as 260.— *Worldmission Fides Service*, April 16, 1960.

[170] *Worldmission Fides Service*, February 8, 1961.

outskirts of Leopoldville. At the outset Lovanium stressed medicine; later it introduced technical courses, and in 1957 a few of its students were in theology.[171] It was affiliated with the University of Louvain.

In view of the rapid spread of the faith and of experiences in other countries, it need be no cause for surprise that indigenous religious movements sprang up in the Belgian Congo which contained elements of Christian origin. Thus in 1921 what was called the "prophet movement" arose. It began with Simon Kibangu, a Baptist, who believed that he had a Divine commission to undertake a ministry of healing. Thousands, both Roman Catholics and Protestants, brought their sick to be touched by him. Fetishes and charms were discarded and the polygamous put away all their wives but one. Soon other leaders appeared who made similar claims. Although the movement seems to have had no politically subversive aspects, the colonial authorities were alarmed and imprisoned or deported some of the leaders. They condemned Kibangu to death, but on petition by missionaries he was reprieved by King Albert.[172]

In 1959 Kibanguism revived. Its leaders held Simon Kibangu to be the Messiah of the Negroes, as Christ, so they said, was the Saviour of the whites. They insisted that the teachings of Kibangu were essentially those of Christ, but adapted to the needs of the Africans. They sought to make their movement the only true national church.[173]

The disorder which followed immediately upon the granting of political independence bore heavily upon the Christianity of the Congo. Many missionaries were roughly handled, sometimes by Congolese troops which got out of hand and sometimes by other Congolese. Roman Catholic missionaries especially suffered because they were either Belgians or in the popular mind were identified with the Belgians. Several nuns were raped. Many priests and brothers were robbed and beaten and some were killed.[174] A large exodus of missionaries, both Protestant and Roman Catholic, followed. Yet many remained and within a few months numbers returned.[175] Aid came from Church organizations in several countries to relieve the famine from which thousands of Congolese were suffering as a result of the internal disorder and the disruption of the normal economy.[176] Many Congolese came out for law and order.[177] In October, 1960, Lovanium opened its doors for a new academic year. With the

---

[171] Allen, *op. cit.*, p. 421; Delacroix, *Histoire Universelle des Missions Catholiques*, Vol. III, p. 321.

[172] Groves, *op. cit.*, Vol. IV, p. 127.

[173] *Worldmission Fides Service*, December 7, 1959.

[174] *Worldmission Fides Service*, February 22, 1961; March 4, 1961; May 31, 1961; *Christianity and Crisis*, Vol. XX, p. 131 (September 19, 1960); *The New York Times*, March 13, 1961.

[175] *The New York Times*, October 16, 1960.

[176] *Ecumenical Press Service*, January 20, 1961; *Church News from the Northern Countries* (Sigtuna, mimeographed), No. 64, January 17, 1961; *The Christian Century*, Vol. LXXVIII, pp. 250, 251 (February 22, 1961).

[177] *Worldmission Fides Service*, August 20, 1960.

coming of political independence its administrative council was transferred from Belgium to the Congo.[178]

THE CONGO REPUBLIC

The Congo Republic, before 1958 a portion of French Equatorial Africa, proclaimed its independence in that year but remained within the French Community. Although separated from the Republic of Congo for a long distance only by the Congo River, it did not suffer from the throes of domestic war as did the other. It was much smaller than its neighbour and in 1959 had a population of about 764,000. In 1959 approximately a third of the population were Roman Catholics, roughly a 50 per cent. increase in the preceding ten years.[179] The first president of the Congo Republic was Fulbert Youlou, a Roman Catholic priest, and although his church no longer permitted him to function in a clerical capacity, in 1960 he was still garbed as an ecclesiastic.[180]

Protestants were not as numerous as Roman Catholics. In 1957 all French Equatorial Africa was reported to have only 88,030 full members of Protestant churches and a Protestant community of 187,075. Yet proportionately they were increasing more rapidly than Roman Catholics, for in both categories their growth was said to have been between 30 and 40 per cent. since 1952. The largest number of Protestants were the result of the missions of the *Svenska Missionsforbundet* and the *Société des Missions Évangéliques* of Paris.[181]

The mission in the Congo Republic which in the first half of the twentieth century most had the attention of the world was that of Albert Schweitzer. The son of an Alsatian pastor, Schweitzer (1875——) first won wide notice by his bold study, *The Quest of the Historical Jesus*.[182] From his boyhood he had been moved by stories of French Protestant missionaries in Africa. He was already noted as a scholar in the New Testament and philosophy and as a skilled organist and specialist on Bach when, in 1905, he entered upon a medical course to prepare himself for Africa. He defrayed his expenses by giving organ concerts. By the same means he raised funds to equip his African venture. In 1913 he went to Lambaréné, not far from the coast of what was then French Equatorial Africa. In World War I he was deported (1917) as a prisoner of war, but he returned to Lambaréné in 1924, where he built a hospital and gave himself unstintedly to the Africans. From that perspective he meditated on the New Testament, the state of European civilization, the thought of India, Goethe, mysticism, the issues of war and peace, and the threat of war to mankind. From

[178] *Ibid.*, November 12, 1960; *The New York Times*, October 31, 1960.
[179] *Worldmission Fides Service*, February 8, 1961.
[180] *The New York Times*, October 4, 1960.
[181] *World Christian Handbook, 1957*, pp. 74, 75.
[182] Volume II, p. 53.

time to time books on these subjects issued from his pen which were widely read in thoughtful circles in Europe and the Americas. Presumably he had few converts among the Africans, nor was he interested in laying foundations for a continuing Christian community. But his example, his writings, and above all his character influenced thousands around the world.[183]

CAMEROONS AND CAMEROUN

We must not dwell long on Cameroons and Cameroun, north of the Congo Republic—not because they are unimportant, but because in our necessarily condensed survey we cannot spare much space for them. As Kameroun they had once been a German possession. Following World War I Kameroun was divided into mandates under the League of Nations and continued as trusteeships under the United Nations, the one bordering on Nigeria, as Cameroons, to Great Britain, and the other, as Cameroun, to France. World War I saw fighting in Kameroun and in World War II both parts of the country were involved, although not with much fighting. Both wars, especially the first, brought dislocations of missions and other hardships.[184] On January 1, 1960, Cameroun became an independent republic within the French Community. In 1959 the population of Cameroun was reported to be about 3,240,000. In 1960 Cameroons, with a population of approximately 1,650,000, was undecided whether it would join the Federation of Nigeria or the Republic of Cameroun. During the agitation for independence in Cameroun tribal wars and clashes between the underground movement and the government brought much disorder.[185] It was said that in a single district about one out of a hundred of the population were killed, also that three-fourths of the Protestant churches, schools, and manses were destroyed.[186] In 1957 Protestants in British Cameroons numbered about 5 per cent. of the population, chiefly the fruits of the Basel Mission.[187] At the same

---

[183] Of the many books and articles by and about Schweitzer the following give some idea of the man, his thought, and his work: Albert Schweitzer, *Aus meinem Leben und Denken* (Leipzig, F. Meiner, 1933, pp. 211); Albert Schweitzer, *Civilization and Ethics,* translated by John Naish (London, A. and C. Black, 1923, pp. xxvi, 298); Albert Schweitzer, *The Forest Hospital at Lambaréné* (New York, Henry Holt & Co., 1931, pp. 191); Albert Schweitzer, *On the Edge of the Primeval Forest,* translated by C. T. Campion (London, A. and C. Black, 1928, pp. 180); Albert Schweitzer, *The Mysticism of Paul the Apostle,* translated by William Montgomery (London, A. and C. Black, 1931, pp. xvi, 193); Henri Babe, *La Pensée d'Albert Schweitzer. Sa Signification pour la Théologie et la Philosophie Contemporaines* (Neûchatel, Messeiller [1956], pp. 239); Oskar Kraus, *Albert Schweitzer. His Work and His Philosophy* (London, A. and C. Black, 1944, pp. x, 75); Norman Cousins, *Dr. Schweitzer of Lambaréné* (New York, Harper & Brothers, 1960, pp. 254); George Seaver, *Albert Schweizer, The Man and His Mind* (New York, Harper & Brothers, 1947, pp. viii, 346).

[184] Groves, *op. cit.,* Vol. IV, pp. 12, 20, 21, 65, 66, 243, 244, 253.

[185] *The International Review of Missions,* Vol. L, p. 42 (January, 1961).

[186] *The Christian Century,* Vol. LXXVIII, pp. 250, 251 (February 22, 1961).

[187] *World Christian Handbook, 1957,* p. 70. On the Basel Mission see J. Wilbois, *Le Cameroun. Les Indigènes, les Colons, les Missions, l'Administration Française* (Paris, Payot, 1938, pp. 256); Fritz Raalaub, *Die Schulen der Basler Mission in Kamerun, ihre Geschichte und Gegenswartssauf-*

time Protestants in what was then French Cameroun were approximately 10 per cent. of the population, and were mainly in churches founded by the *Société des Missions Évangéliques* of Paris and the Presbyterian Church in the U.S.A.[188] In 1959 Roman Catholics in Cameroun constituted about 22 per cent. of the population.[189] Percentage-wise Roman Catholics were increasing more rapidly than Protestants, but both were mounting. Enrollments in Roman Catholic primary schools shared in the increase. In 1959 and 1960 they grew by about 22 per cent., or at approximately five times the rate of that of Roman Catholic membership as a whole.[190] Roman Catholic conversions were largely by families as natural social groups.[191] In the preparation of the clergy, in the 1950's Roman Catholics were said to be far ahead of the Protestants. They did much more, too, in providing staffs, buildings, and spiritual discipline. Yet it was reported that neither the Protestant nor the Roman Catholic theological students were being prepared in an understanding or even an awareness of the problems of the revolutionary age in which they were engulfed.[192] In both branches of the Church the trend was towards a deeper planting of the faith through African hands. Late in the 1950's and early in the 1960's the churches which arose from the Basel and American Presbyterian missions moved towards autonomy, discussed the possibility of union, and undertook measures to strengthen theological education.[193] By 1961 the Roman Catholics had placed an African bishop at the head of one diocese and another as coadjutor to an archbishop.[194]

Growing Pains in Nigeria

Nigeria, larger than Cameroons and Cameroun but not as large as the Republic of Congo, with a population estimated in 1959 to be 35,000,000, had more people than any other country in Africa south of the Sahara. In the nineteenth century and especially after the partition of Africa among Western European countries in the 1880's and in the fifteen years before the outbreak of World War I, it was gradually brought within the British Empire. Much of the administration was in the form of protectorates over the several areas and native states which comprised the region. Under British rule communications and transportation were greatly improved, a more comprehensive administration

---

gabe (Basel, Basel Missionsbuchhandlung, 1948, pp. 198); Emanuel Kellerhals, *Das Volk hintern Berg. Land, Leute und Missionsarbeit* (Stuttgart, Missionsverlag, 1955, pp. 186).

[188] *World Christian Handbook, 1957*, pp. 77, 78.

[189] *Worldmission Fides Service*, February 8, 1961, and March 18, 1961. On the first quarter-century of one of the congregations see Hermann Skolaster, *Die Pallottiner in Kameroun. 25 Jahre Missionsarbeit* (Limburg/Lahn, Verlag der Kongregation der Pallottiner, 1925, pp. 327), *passim*.

[190] *Worldmission Fides Service*, February 25, 1961.

[191] Beckmann, *op. cit.*, p. 157.

[192] Allen, *op. cit.*, pp. 43, 44, 496.

[193] *The International Review of Missions*, Vol. XLIX, p. 42 (January, 1960).

[194] *Worldmission Fides Service*, February 1, 1961.

was developed, and steps were taken, partly through education on levels beyond that of primary schools, towards political independence. Independence was achieved in 1960. The new Federation of Nigeria was made up of three regions—Western, with its capital at Ibadan and with a population estimated to be about 6,000,000 in 1960; Eastern, with its capital at Enugu with a population estimated at 8,224,000 in 1960; and Northern, its capital at Kaduna and with about 18,000,000 inhabitants in 1959. The Federation remained within the British Commonwealth. The United Kingdom continued to be its best customer, and major exports were oil, palm products, peanuts, and especially cocoa. Soon after independence a government commission recommended an extension of education, with a large increase in enrollment, particularly in secondary schools.

Religiously Nigeria was divided between Islam, animism, and Christianity. In the latter part of the nineteenth century and the first half of the twentieth Islam spread rapidly in Northern Nigeria, notably among the Hausa (who numbered about 5,500,000 in the 1950's). Its progress was facilitated by the growing trade with Moslem North Africa across the Sahara and by the progressive disintegration of African tribal life and social customs due to the impact of the revolutionary age. The advance of Islam in Nigeria was part of what was happening in a broad belt from the Sudan in the east to the extreme west coast of the continent. It was carried largely by traders, although latterly, in Southern Nigeria, by professional missionaries. It was identified with Arab civilization, and Christianity was regarded as closely associated wth European culture. Islam, therefore, was prominent on the borders of the Sahara, in the direction from which the Arab commerce came, and Christianity was strongest in the coastal regions, for that was the region on which European commerce impinged.[195]

Christianity first came in force to Nigeria late in the first half of the nineteenth century. At the outset and for many years Protestants were more active than Roman Catholics. The Church Missionary Society led the way, chiefly through freed slaves who had been in contact with the Society in Sierra Leone and who, returning to their homes in the Western Region, were followed by missionaries. This was in the 1840's. A steamer, *The Dayspring,* was placed on the Niger River. In 1864 an African, Samuel Adjai Crowther, who in his boyhood had been rescued from a slave ship by a British cruiser and had been educated in Sierra Leone and England, was consecrated in Canterbury Cathedral as Bishop of the Niger Territories. In 1900, when Northern Nigeria was made a British protectorate, the Church Missionary Society extended its operations to that vast area. In 1914 it counted 51,570 baptized in all Nigeria, the majority of them in its oldest fields. English Wesleyans came almost as soon as

[195] J. Spencer Trimingham, *The Christian Church and Islam in West Africa* (London, SCM Press, 1955, pp. 56), *passim.*

the Anglicans, also through freedmen with whom they had been in contact in Sierra Leone. Their chief pioneer was Thomas Birch Freeman (1809–1890), born in England, the son of a Negro father and a white mother. During his long life Freeman was a missionary in both Nigeria and the Gold Coast. In 1846 the United Presbyterians of Scotland began a mission east of the Niger River. Some of the early missionaries had seen service in Jamaica and were assisted by Negroes from that island. In 1850 the first representative of the Southern Baptists reached Nigeria and began a mission which survived the Civil War in the United States and a devastating war in Yorubaland and in 1914 counted 31 churches with 2,880 members. In the 1880's a small independent mission (Qua Iboe) gained a foothold. In 1893 the Free Methodists came. That final decade of the century saw the Sudan Interior Mission penetrate the North. Between 1899 and 1914 the Sudan United Mission, the Mennonites, and the Seventh Day Adventists reinforced the Protestant ranks. Roman Catholics were slightly later than Protestants in adding Nigeria to their fields. The Society of African Missions placed its first contingent at Lagos in 1868 and by 1913 had about 10,000 Christians in its charge. In 1913 the Holy Ghost Fathers had a flock which was said to number 4,789.[196]

Between the outbreak of World War I and the date of the latest statistics available when these lines were penned, Christianty had a remarkable numerical growth and also became more deeply rooted in African leadership. In 1957 Protestantism was represented strikingly by the Anglicans, now in the Province of West Africa independent of Canterbury, with their greatest strength in the Western Region and with assistance from the Church Missionary Society. They had a Christian community of at least 1,000,000 and a communicant membership of over 100,000. That might have been expected because they were first in the country. It is not surprising that with one exception the next in full members were the Southern Baptists, the English Methodists, and the Qua Iboe Mission, in that order. The exception was the Apostolic Church Missionary Movement, which had recently entered and had grown until its membership outdistanced that of all the others but the Anglicans. At least seventeen other missions were at work. The total of communicant or full members was said to be 287,026 and of the Protestant community 1,370,000.[197] Roman Catholics reported their total to be 656,399 in 1949 and 1,676,374 in 1959.[198]

Both Protestants and Roman Catholics recruited and trained an African clergy. Protestant theological education was given in several institutions. The

---

[196] Latourette, *op. cit.*, Vol. V, pp. 436–443.

[197] *World Christian Handbook, 1957*, pp. 88, 89. On a member of the Sudan Interior Mission see Josephine C. Bulifant, *40 Years in the African Bush* (Grand Rapids, Mich., Zondervan Publishing House, 1950, pp. 185), *passim*.

[198] *Worldmission Fides Service*, February 8, 1961. On a Roman Catholic pioneer see John P. Jordan, *Bishop Shanahan of Southern Nigeria* (Dublin, Clonmore and Reynolds, 1949, pp. xiv, 264), *passim*.

largest was that of the Southern Baptists, in 1958 with a full-time faculty of fourteen, ten of whom concentrated on training students for the ministry. It had about a hundred enrolled in that course. In 1939 Anglicans, Presbyterians, and English Methodists joined in a school in Eastern Nigeria which in 1958 had thirty-five students. That year the same number were in a college in Ibadan maintained by Anglicans and English Methodists. The neighbouring University College had a department of religious studies through which, by authorization given in 1958, a B.D. degree could be awarded. In the North a theological college was opened in 1959 by the Sudan United Mission.[199] On the eve of Nigerian independence the Scottish Presbyterians transferred their main responsibilities to the Eastern Nigerian Synod of the Presbyterian Church.[200] Roman Catholics did not make quite as much progress in obtaining an African clergy as they did in East Africa. In 1959 they had 133 major seminarians in two institutions. One was at Enuji, a regional institution for Nigeria and British Cameroon. Maintained by the Holy Ghost Fathers, in the 1950's it had ninety major seminarians, more than in any other Roman Catholic theological seminary in all Africa south of the Sahara except the one at Baudoinville in the Republic of Congo under the White Fathers. Yet this was in contrast with Tanganyika where for a smaller body of Roman Catholics 176 major seminarians were enrolled.[201] But in 1960 Nigeria was second only to Kenya in the number of adult baptisms per priest,[202] and in that year it had four African bishops, three of them auxiliary, surpassed only by the Republic of Congo. In 1950 Nigeria, along with the other British territories in West Africa, was given a hierarchy.[203]

As was true in most of Africa south of the Sahara, in Nigeria missions, both Protestant and Roman Catholic, long provided nearly all the education in the adjustment to the revolutionary age. In this they were subsidized by the government.[204] Following World War I, partly on the initiative of the missionary societies of the United States and of J. H. Oldham, of the International Missionary Council, studies were made which had marked effects on both missions and governments, particularly on the village school level. In the 1920's the Government of Nigeria took steps to improve and expand the elementary schools. It continued financial assistance, provided for better supervision, and placed religious instruction, which might be given voluntarily by missionaries, on the same level as other subjects. Since the country suffered from a lack of

199 International Missionary Council, *Survey of the Training of the Ministry in Africa*, Part I, pp. 4–50; Allen, *op. cit.*, pp. 31–35; *The International Review of Missions*, Vol. XLIX, p. 41 (January, 1960); Vol. L, p. 46 (January, 1961).

200 *The Christian Century*, Vol. LXXVII, p. 1128 (September, 1960).

201 Allen, *op. cit.*, pp. 414–416; *Worldmission Fides Service*, February 25, 1961.

202 *Worldmission Fides Service*, March 18, 1961.

203 *Ibid.*, February 1, 1961; Guilcher, *La Société des Missions Africaines*, p. 76.

204 J. H. Oldham and B. D. Gibson, *The Remaking of Man in Africa* (New York, Oxford University Press, 1931, pp. 185), pp. 155–158.

qualified teachers, missions sought to produce them.[205] Roman Catholics as well as Protestants were active. In 1961 the large majority of the children receiving elementary education were in schools maintained by either churches or missions, most of them in the Western and Eastern Regions. Only a small minority were in the Northern Region, where Islam had its main strength. Even here most of the pupils were in mission schools. Almost all who went on to secondary and university education were from Christian schools, and about four-fifths were Christians. A majority of the schools were in Protestant hands.[206]

In 1957 Roman Catholics in the Eastern Region won in an effort to maintain denominational schools with government subsidy. In 1956 the government proposed to substitute state schools for church schools and while continuing to pay teachers' salaries in the latter to limit enrollment in them and to grant no funds for new buildings for them. Roman Catholic schools numbered about 2,500 with 464,800 pupils—about half the school-going population. The new policy was a stage in providing universal primary education. While favouring that goal, Roman Catholics protested against the limitation on church schools and won the determinative election. Of the ensuing cabinet, six of the fourteen members were Roman Catholics and one was nominally so. In the new Assembly a motion to nationalize all schools was lost.

Throughout the Federation Roman Catholics undertook the building and staffing of more colleges than did Protestants. A Roman Catholic-educated elite was emerging. But Protestants were still more prominent than Roman Catholics,[207] as was seen in the fact that the first governor of Eastern Nigeria was an Anglican, Sir Francis Ibiam (1906——), a physician who with his wife had so devoted himself to his own rural people that he was known as the "black Schweitzer." He presided at the first All Africa Church Conference at Ibadan and had been chairman of the Christian Council of Nigeria.[208]

In Nigeria, as elsewhere, the 1960's saw a strong movement towards church union among Protestants. Discussions were under way among Anglicans, Methodists, and Presbyterians looking towards a united church on much the same basis as that being formulated in Ceylon. In them both Africans and missionaries were active. Together the three denominations had more than half the Protestant communicants and two-thirds of the Protestant constituency in the country.[209]

As in several other countries, indigenous religious movements arose in Nigeria. Here too they emerged through contacts with Protestants or from Protestantism. Thus during World War I on the Lower Niger an Anglican evangelist proclaimed himself Elijah II. He had dreams and visions of future

[205] Groves, *op. cit.*, Vol. IV, pp. 107–116.
[206] Information given to the author directly, May, 1961.
[207] *Worldmission*, Vol. VIII, pp. 18–26 (Fall, 1957).
[208] *Frontier*, Vol. IV, pp. 27, 28 (Spring, 1961).
[209] Information given directly to the author, May, 1961.

happenings which it was said were confirmed by the event. He was reported to have healed numbers of sick folk by his prayers. He attracted many, both Christians and non-Christians, and demanded of his followers that no medical help be sought of either African or European physicians and no alcoholic beverages be used. He denounced idol worship. The civil authorities imprisoned him on the charge that he was obtaining money under false pretences and his movement waned.[210]

The Gold Coast Becomes Ghana

Moving westward from Nigeria and omitting Dahomey and Togo, we come to what was once the Gold Coast but in 1957 as Ghana became independent within the (British) Commonwealth and then in 1960 was proclaimed a republic, still a member of the Commonwealth. With an area of 9,843 square miles, it was one of the smallest of the former British possessions in Africa, but in 1960 the government estimated its population to be 6,690,732, which was triple that of 1921. Historically and to some degree ethnically and culturally it was composed of the Gold Coast, a region in which the English gained a foothold in the seventeenth century, where, on the Gulf of Guinea, was its capital, Accra; Ashanti, annexed by the English in the first half of the nineteenth century; and the Northern Territories, acquired in the 1880's and 1890's during the era of expanding and competitive European imperialism. With Ghana was included a western strip of Togo, German from the 1880's to World War I, thereafter a British mandate under the League of Nations, and then a British trust territory under the United Nations. Rich in minerals, forests, and its chief export, cocoa, Ghana had a higher per capita income than most African states.

Christianity was introduced by the Portuguese in the sixteenth century but with only fleeting effects. In the eighteenth century it was renewed by Protestants—Moravians, Anglicans, and Dutch. Its continuing strength came chiefly through the Basel Mission, the English Wesleyans, the (Roman Catholic) Lyons Missionaries, and later, in the North, the White Fathers.[211]

As a result of World War I the Basel Mission (which had stressed gathering its converts into Christian villages to keep them from contamination by their pagan neighbours and so to help them lead a better Christian community life) was replaced by representatives of the United Free Church of Scotland. It then had 24,000 communicants, with 55 missionaries and 21 African pastors. By 1931, out of the Basel and Scottish missions the self-governing, self-supporting

[210] Groves, *op. cit.*, Vol. IV, p. 126.
[211] Latourette, *op. cit.*, Vol. V, pp. 446–448; Schmidlin, *Catholic Mission History*, p. 652.

Presbyterian Church of the Gold Coast had arisen.[212] By 1957 it was said to have a membership of 36,249 and a Christian community of 110,251. The Basel Mission had long resumed its help.[213] The Scottish Presbyterians also continued to coöperate. The largest Protestant body sprang from the mission of the English Wesleyans. In 1912 it had 16,300 Christians and 27 African pastors. By 1929 these totals had swelled to 110,811 and 44 respectively. The growth was to a large extent in Ashanti and from a mass movement in the 1920's begun by the preaching of a fiery African prophet, Samson Opon.[214] Methodist growth was also in part the fruit of the preaching of an African, William Wadé Harris. A native of Liberia, Harris had come to a Christian faith largely through the Protestant Episcopal mission in that country. About the year 1913 he began preaching, entirely on his own initiative, without foreign support or sanction. He believed himself called of God, went about clothed in a white robe and a stole, and carried a cross and a bowl of water from which to baptize converts. He taught belief in one God, the observance of Sunday, the destruction of all symbols of paganism, and abstention from adultery. Thousands in the Ivory Coast complied. He also preached on the Gold Coast. Other "prophets," inspired by his example, won followers.[215] In 1957 the Methodists were reported to have 57,142 communicants and a Christian community of 149,627.[216] By the year 1961 the British Methodists had granted full independence to the Methodist Church in Ghana.[217] Other denominations had a share in planting Protestantism. We must not take time even to mention them all. But prominent among them were the Ewe Presbyterian Church, which arose from a German society, after World War I was aided by the United Free Church of Scotland and later by the Evangelical and Reformed Church of the United States, and in 1952 had 16,412 communicants;[218] the Seventh Day Adventists; and the Society for the Propagation of the Gospel in Foreign Parts, which after World War I saw its mission grow from a struggling, depressed body to one with 300 churches, hundreds of village schools, secondary schools, a training college, and a theological college.[219] Provision was made for recruiting and training an African Protestant clergy. With the independence of Ghana and the substitution of Africans for Englishmen in goverment and industry,

---

[212] Cooksey and McLeish, *Religion and Civilization in West Africa,* pp. 137, 138.
[213] *World Christian Handbook, 1957,* pp. 80, 81.
[214] Cooksey and McLeish, *op. cit.,* pp. 138, 141.
[215] *Ibid.,* pp. 61, 62; W. J. Platt, *An African Prophet* (London, Student Christian Movement Press, 1934, pp. 157), *passim;* W. J. Platt, *From Fetish to Faith* (London, Edinburgh House Press, 1935, pp. 159), *passim.*
[216] *World Christian Handbook, 1957,* p. 81.
[217] *The Christian Century,* Vol. LXXVII, p. 1129 (September 28, 1960).
[218] Cooksey and McLeish, *op. cit.,* pp. 152, 153; *World Christian Handbook, 1957,* pp. 80, 81.
[219] Thompson, *Into All Lands,* p. 586.

many of the abler Ghanaians were attracted to these posts rather than to the ministry.[220]

Education in the European sense was provided mostly through missions, Protestant and Roman Catholic, subsidized by the government. As the crown of the educational system, in 1924 a university college was founded at Achimoto, not far from Accra. Its first principal was a Protestant missionary, A. G. Fraser, and its first vice-principal was a remarkable African, J. E. K. Aggrey (1875–1927). The son of a prominent Fanti, Aggrey had been educated in Methodist schools and the United States. A radiant, unselfish spirit, with abounding energy, he brought a great lift to education in his native land and his death left an aching void.[221] The college had among its departments one of divinity through which a bachelor of divinity degree could be obtained.

Roman Catholics slightly outnumbered Protestants. In 1957 the latter were reported to have a community of 433,610, although the figures were palpably incomplete.[222] In 1959 Roman Catholics were reported as 562,912, a total which was nearly double that of a decade earlier.[223] They, too, developed an African clergy. In 1961 there were three Africans in the episcopate, one of them an archbishop and all of them in full charge of their respective dioceses.[224] In February, 1951, much impetus was given to the Roman Catholic Church in Ghana by a Eucharistic Congress in Kumasi.[225]

Although Christianity had a phenomenal growth in Ghana, its adherents constituted a smaller proportion of the population than in any of the other countries south of the Sahara which we have thus far covered. It was strongest on the coast, but inland paganism and Islam remained entrenched. The latter was especially vigorous and was growing.

Under its republican regime Ghana gave evidence that Christians were still a minority. Although its president, Kwame Nkrumah (1909——), had been educated in Roman Catholic schools in Ghana, and in the United States had studied in universities of Protestant origin, he publicly attended Christian, pagan, and Moslem rites and services. Strains developed between his government and the churches, especially the Protestant authorities. The latter felt it their duty to protest against some of the government's measures, including the arrest and imprisonment without trial of opponents of Nkrumah. Many Christians were also unhappy because Nkrumah seemed to be seeking to create a political religion with himself as *Osageyfo* (Saviour), and the pedestal of his

[220] Allen, *op. cit.*, pp. 35–39.

[221] Edwin W. Smith, *Aggrey of Africa. A Study in Black and White* (New York, Richard R. Smith, 1930, pp. xii, 292), *passim;* William M. Macartney, *Dr. Aggrey. Ambassador for Africa* (London, SCM Press, 1949, pp. 106), *passim.*

[222] *World Christian Handbook, 1957,* pp. 80, 81.

[223] *Worldmission Fides Service,* February 8, 1961.

[224] *Ibid.,* February 1, 1961.

[225] Bane, *Catholic Pioneers in West Africa,* pp. 194 ff.

statue in Accra bore the words: "Seek ye first the political kingdom and all else will be added." Yet in 1961 every member of the cabinet regularly attended Christian services, either Protestant or Roman Catholic, and many meetings of the dominant party were opened with prayer and were begun and ended with the singing of a Protestant hymn.[226]

THE LESSER BUT GROWING PLACE OF CHRISTIANITY IN OTHER REGIONS IN WEST AFRICA

In the condensed survey which is inescapably ours we must not devote space individually to the countries in Africa west of Ghana. They included some which until late in the 1950's were part of the French colonial empire but which then became independent, either completely separated from France or as members of the French Community. The others were Portuguese Guinea; Spanish Sahara; Gambia, a British colony and protectorate; Liberia, independent from its founding in the fore part of the nineteenth century; and Sierra Leone, formerly British and given its independence in 1961. They varied greatly in area, population, and the degree to which they had been penetrated by the revolutionary age. In all of them Christians increased in number. In 1961 in the Republic of Togo they constituted about a fourth of the population, with the Roman Catholics a large majority. In the Dahomey Republic they were about a sixth, again with Roman Catholics for outnumbering Protestants. In the Ivory Coast Republic they were about one in eleven, with Roman Catholics more than five times as numerous as Protestants. In none of the others did Christians constitute as much as 5 per cent. of the population. In some the Roman Catholics were making progress in creating an African clergy and in 1961 they had an African bishop in each of three countries and two in the Ivory Coast Republic. Protestants were a high percentage in the colony of Sierra Leone but were relatively few on the mainland which, as a protectorate, was by far the largest part of the territory to become independent, and Roman Catholics were still fewer. In Liberia the Afro-Americans descended from the early settlers were predominantly Protestant, although for many the connexion was little more than nominal, and on the tribes in the interior Christianity had made an impression only among a small minority.[227]

[226] *Christianity and Crisis,* Vol. XXI, p. 72 (May 15, 1961); information given directly to the author, 1961.
[227] *Worldmission Fides Service,* February 1, 1961; February 8, 1961; March 18, 1961; *World Christian Handbook, 1957,* pp. 77–80, 84, 92. For comprehensive accounts of Roman Catholic missions in the region see Bane, *op. cit., passim.* For the history of the Roman Catholic Church in Liberia see Martin J. Bane, *The Catholic Story of Liberia* (New York, The Declan X. McMullen Co., 1950, pp. 163), *passim.* For the Lutheran mission in the interior of Liberia, see Harold Vink Whetstone, *Lutheran Mission in Liberia* (no place given, Board of Foreign Missions of the United Lutheran Church in America, 1955, pp. vii, 255), *passim.* In 1955 French Africa was given a hierarchy.—Guilcher, *op. cit.,* p. 76.

THE GROWING COMPREHENSIVE PROTESTANT APPROACH TO AFRICA

A feature of the twentieth century and especially of the post-World War II years was increasing effort among Protestants to approach Africa south of the Sahara as a whole. Surveys of the educational needs were made by the Phelps-Stokes Fund of New York with the coöperation of the American mission boards, aided especially by J. H. Oldham of the International Missionary Council, and led to increasing comprehensive assistance from the British Government to African education through mission schools;[228] various conferences on Africa were held in Europe and America; and a study of theological education in Africa was made under the International Missionary Council in the 1950's. More and more the emphasis was upon comprehensive action in Africa with African leadership. Some was undertaken by denominations. Thus in 1955 an All-Africa Lutheran Conference convened with 100 African and 50 European leaders.[229] Even more significant was the All Africa Church Conference held in Ibadan, Nigeria, in January, 1958. It was composed of representatives of regional Christian councils. Twenty territories sent 150 delegates, 90 of whom were Africans. Fifty guests were present from seventeen countries in Asia, Europe, and America. Interestingly, and possibly significantly, the conference ante-dated by several months the Independent African States' Conference and the All-Africa People's Conference. Under the general theme of "the Church in changing Africa" it dealt with a wide variety of aspects of African life from the Christian standpoint— youth, family, economics, politics, evangelism, the ministry, stewardship, unity, and Church and mission relations. A committee was appointed to ensure continuing consultation and collaboration.[230]

CHANGING MADAGASCAR

The island of Madagascar, which had been occupied by the French since 1895, in 1958 became the Malagasy Republic and, although fully autonomous, in 1960 elected to remain within the French Community. In 1960 its estimated population was 5,290,769. As in many other parts of the world, population was rapidly mounting. The racial composition was varied. The Hòva were dominant. Akin to the Malays, they were of lighter complexion than the other tribes, energetic, keen intellectually, and excellent traders. They were mostly in Imerina, the central plateau, about 4,000 to 6,000 feet above sea level. The non-Hòva were of Indonesian and Melanesian origin. Before the coming of Christianity the large majority were animists,[231] with a Moslem minority.

---

[228] Groves, *op. cit.*, Vol. IV, pp. 107–114; Sundkler, *The Christian Ministry in Africa*, p. 93.

[229] Groves, *op. cit.*, Vol. IV, p. 307.

[230] *The International Review of Missions*, Vol. XLVII, pp. 257–264 (July, 1958); *Christianity and Crisis*, Vol. XXI, p. 41 (March 20, 1961).

[231] On Malagasy paganism see Jorgen Ruud, *Guder og Fedre. Religionshistorisk Stoff fra Madagascar* (Oslo, H. Aschehoug & Co., 1947, pp. 178).

Christianity was first brought to the island by Roman Catholics in the sixteenth and seventeenth centuries, but without giving rise to continuing communities. Its effective introduction was in the first quarter of the nineteenth century through the London Missionary Society. It then took root among the Hòva. Between 1836 and 1861 Christians were persecuted, but the death in the latter year of the queen who had been their relentless enemy was followed by a less unfavourable regime. In the 1860's the new queen and her consort were baptized, and in the following years a large proportion of the Hòva followed their example. During the years of persecution Roman Catholics gained a foothold and by the time of the French annexation Jesuits, the Brothers of Christian Schools, and the Sisters of St. Joseph were well established. The Anglicans came, represented eventually only by the Society for the Propagation of the Gospel in Foreign Parts. By the year 1895 English Quakers and Lutherans were active, the latter from Norway and the United States. Some, notably the Lutherans, found their fields among other tribes than the Hòva. The Bible was translated, education was given through schools connected with the churches, and medical service of a European kind was maintained. The London Missionary Society, as the pioneer, led in the number of churches and Christians. When France obtained control of the island, her officials looked with disfavour on British missions. Accordingly the *Société des Missions Évangéliques* of Paris sent missionaries who worked closely with the London Missionary Society and the English Quakers and by 1908 had a larger staff than any of the British societies. More Roman Catholic orders and congregations came, mostly from France. In 1908 Protestant church members were said to total 66,264 and Protestant adherents to be 218,188. In 1918 the corresponding figures were 74,817 and 449,126. In 1911 Roman Catholics were reported as totalling 210,-000.[232]

The post-World War II decades witnessed a striking growth in the numbers of Christians, both Protestant and Roman Catholic. In 1957 the former were said to have 194,615 communicant members and a community of 641,376. Approximately half were in the churches affiliated with the London Missionary Society and the *Société des Missions Évangéliques* of Paris, and about 45 per cent. of the communicants and nearly a fourth of the Protestant community were connected with the Malagasy Lutheran Church (organized in 1950).[233] Another set of figures for 1956 gave Protestant membership as 350,000 and adherents as 1,046,000.[234] In 1959 Roman Catholics were reported as totalling 1,091,244, an increase from 698,975 ten years earlier.[235] In 1959 they were said to

---

[232] Latourette, *op. cit.*, Vol. V, pp. 302–312.
[233] *World Christian Handbook, 1957*, p. 85. On the French Protestant mission see G. Mondain, *Un Siècle de Mission à Madagascar* (Paris, Société des Missions Évangeliques, pp. 241), pp. 199–240.
[234] Allen, *op. cit.*, p. 51.
[235] *Worldmission Fides Service*, February 8, 1961.

be about a fifth of the population.[236] If these figures are correct, late in the 1950's about two-fifths of the Malagasy regarded themselves as Christians. The chief strength of the Church was on the central plateau, among the Hòva. On the lowlands and among the other tribes the proportion of Christians was lower. The Hòva were active in spreading the faith.

In 1947 a political revolt broke out, directed primarily against French rule and with the purpose of creating an independent republic. It was crushed, but although it was not primarily anti-Christian, in its course many church buildings, Protestant and Roman Catholic, were burned as expressions of a "foreign religion" and numbers of pastors and some missionaries were killed.[237]

In Madagascar, as in many other countries, indigenous religious movements with more or less of historic Christian content were seen, largely from Protestant sources. In 1922 religious awakenings swept through much of the island.[238] The Farihimena revival began in 1947 in the South, where Lutheranism was strong. It spread through the entire island and tended to break with the existing churches.[239]

More than in many countries, but in accordance with a widespread movement elsewhere, Protestants of several denominations closely coöperated. In 1913 the Intermissionary Conference was organized to avoid duplication of effort in any one area. This was followed by the Intermissionary Committee, in which all but the Anglicans joined and which adopted intercommunion and pulpit exchange.[240] In 1937 agreement was reached by all but the Anglicans that the designation "the United Protestant Church of Madagascar" be adopted, with each denominational branch preserving its identity and form of ecclesiastical government.[241] In 1958 the Council of Churches was formed, replacing the Intermissionary Committee.[242]

Striking features of the Protestant churches, especially in Imerina, were the achievement of financial self-support and active missionary zeal. The worldwide financial depression of the 1930's made necessary the curtailment of giving and the dropping of some well-trained men from the pastorate, but recovery came. A missionary society was founded in the 1870's. Although much was due to foreign incentive, under French rule open-air meetings were forbidden, and

---

[236] *Ibid.*, March 18, 1961.

[237] Hardyman, *Madagascar on the Move*, pp. 98, 99, 164–167. On the visit of leading French Protestants during the revolt see, André Roux, *Dans la Grand Ile et au Bord du Zambèze* (Paris, Société des Missions Évangéliques, 1948, pp. 154), pp. 9–98.

[238] *The International Review of Missions*, Vol. XXI, p. 243 (July, 1931).

[239] International Missionary Council, *Survey of the Training of the Ministry in Madagascar, . . . 1956*, by C. W. Ranson and others (London and New York, International Missionary Council, 1957, pp. 51), p. 13.

[240] *Ibid.*, p. 12; Hardyman, *op. cit.*, pp. 201–204.

[241] Harold L. Ridgwell, *The Great Island. Madagascar: Past and Present* (London, The Livingstone Press, 1937, pp. 110), pp. 63, 64.

[242] *The International Review of Missions*, Vol. XLVIII, p. 59 (January, 1959).

the prestige which had formerly accrued to the Hòva as the dominant tribe waned and with it the attention given to their missionaries, something of the missionary spirit persisted.[243]

A Christianity which had spread as rapidly as that in Madagascar, especially in view of the impinging currents of the revolutionary age, could not escape threats of deterioration. Young men who had gone to France for education imbibed much of the scepticism and secularism which flourished in that country. The two world wars had repercussions. Communism infiltrated some circles. Revived nationalism brought recrudescence of pagan customs associated with the Malagasy past.[244] In the 1950's a renewal was seen among Christians of traditional ancestral rites, including the "bone-turning," or re-interment of the deceased members of the family.[245]

Among both Protestants and Roman Catholics advances were registered in the recruitment and preparation of an indigenous ministry and the assumption of more responsibility by the Malagasy Christians. Much of the pastoral function in both branches of the Church, except the administration of the sacraments, was by catechists. The catechists were trained—by Protestants in Bible schools. Among Protestants many laymen shared in preaching, visitation, and care of souls in collaboration with paid church-workers. In the early days of Christianity on Madagascar, numbers of pastors came from the higher social ranks. Under the French, many with such social background went into government service and pastors were recruited from more humble families. However, in the 1950's the average pastor was better trained than his predecessors and was held in respect by his congregation. The time had passed when Europeans were in charge of congregations. Many of the Malagasy were in ecclesiastical administrative posts. In the 1950's theological education for prospective pastors was given in several institutions and entailed a course of four years. Six such institutions existed, of which the strongest was maintained by the Lutherans.[246] In the twentieth century advance into new areas depended largely on foreign initiative. In a society where family and tribal loyalties were marked, the local church tended to be "a family club founded for religious purposes" and scandalous quarrels developed. But in spite of these weaknesses, Protestantism continued to grow.[247]

In the 1950's the Roman Catholic Church suffered from a shortage of Malagasy priests. In 1957 the priests, European and Malagasy, totalled 565, an increase from 400 in 1949, but the growth was due chiefly to an influx of foreign

[243] Goodall, *A History of the London Missionary Society, 1895-1945*, pp. 339, 351.

[244] Hardyman, *op. cit.*, pp. 119-131.

[245] Direct information to the author, 1959.

[246] International Missionary Council, *Survey of the Training of the Ministry in Madagascar*, pp. 14-39.

[247] Goodall, *op. cit.*, pp. 346-350.

priests, largely from China, fleeing from the mainland of that country now dominated by the Communists. In 1959 only fifty-five Malagasy were major seminarians. In 1955 the Holy See created a hierarchy for Madagascar, as it did for all French Africa.[248] In 1961 Madagascar had three Malagasy bishops, one of them in charge of the leading archbishopric and another a coadjutor to an archbishop.[249] In that year 24 per cent. of all the priests in the island were Malagasy, a higher ratio of natives than in any African country south of the Sahara except Uganda, Dahomey, and Ruanda-Urundi.[250] Yet in 1960 the average number of adult baptisms per priest in Madagascar, fourteen, was lower than the record of twenty-three countries in Africa and had only nine countries below it.[251]

SUMMARY

After the generalizations made in the introduction to this chapter, no extensive summary is required. In the nearly five decades which were inaugurated by the fateful summer of 1914 the penetration of Africa south of the Sahara by the currents of the revolutionary age was accompanied by startling changes which seemed only at their inception when these lines were penned. Urbanization and an even more extensive de-tribalization and disintegration of ancestral mores were mounting. Among the intelligentsia who were being shaped by the revolutionary age nationalism was fervent and even feverish. By 1962 most of the former European colonial possessions had attained political independence.

In parallel fashion Christianity was spreading rapidly. At the outbreak of World War I in most regions Christians were small minorities. In the ensuing half-century in almost all the countries south of the Sahara the faith was spreading by the near equivalent of mass movements. With the possible exception of the Union of South Africa, where reliable statistics were not available, Christians were still minorities. But, save for a few political entities, mostly on the west coast, those counted in the Christian communities were from a fifth to nearly half of the population. If the rate of growth seen since 1914 was continued, within the next fifty years in several countries those professing to be Christians would be a clear majority. The spread was through Protestants and Roman Catholics. In the first half of the twentieth century in most of the area the latter had multiplied more rapidly than the former. The Orthodox were represented and by 1962 numbered a few hundred, most of them in Uganda.

In both the Protestant and the Roman Catholic communities the faith was

[248] *Worldmission Fides Service,* May 2, 1959.
[249] *Ibid.,* February 1, 1961.
[250] *Ibid.,* March 22, 1961.
[251] *Ibid.,* March 18, 1961.

being rooted in indigenous leadership. From Protestantism several movements had emerged or were emerging which departed, some but not all of them widely, from historic Christianity. Many of them were ephemeral. Others, in the nature of awakenings of nominal Christians, were bringing a deepening of life in the historic communions. In both Protestantism and the Roman Catholic Church able, devoted African leadership was appearing and was being accorded increased responsibility. African clergy were being trained in both branches of the Church. In 1961 only a minority of the Roman Catholic priests were Africans, but from them a mounting number were being advanced to the episcopate and one had been elevated to the cardinalate. In the 1950's on the eve of political independence the French and British possessions had been given hierarchies in place of the former organization by vicariates and prefectures apostolic. Able Protestant clergy ·and laity were rapidly appearing and were assuming administrative responsibilities. Several of the Protestant churches were becoming fully autonomous instead of being controlled, as formerly, by European missions and missionaries.

The rapid spread of the faith was attended by many problems. Always the danger was acute of a superficial Christianity, with the persistence or recrudescence of pre-Christian superstitions and pagan practices, sex irregularities, and polygamy, especially among the third and fourth generations of Christians. Since much of the conversion had come about through mission schools subsidized by the governments, as education became secularized—the direction that it was taking—numerical advance through those channels would be slowed. Many of the Christians who obtained secondary and higher education would not find congenial the fellowship of congregations most of whose members had only an elementary or no formal education and a poorly trained ministry. Numbers of the more competent Christian youth who, under former conditions, would have become teachers or pastors were being attracted to posts in the governments of the newly independent states, carrying as they did higher salaries and more prestige and power. In some areas, mostly on the southern borders of the Sahara, Islam was spreading apace among animists, whose traditional culture was disappearing. Secularism, religious scepticism, and Communism, which were phases of the revolutionary age into which Africa was being hurtled, were proving contagious, especially among youth who had been educated on European patterns or who had studied in Europe or America.

In spite of these very real perils, in 1962 Christianity was continuing to advance. The churches were growing and were more and more rooted in indigenous leadership, some of it extremely able. A large proportion of the schools were still under Christian direction. Much of the kind of medical service using techniques developed in the erstwhile Christendom continued to be given under Christian auspices. African art forms were being employed to depict Christian themes. Although no adequate devices existed for an accurate measurement of the progress or decline of distinctively Christian character among those bearing the Christian name, competent observers believed that across the years it was becoming more widespread. To judge by what had been seen in the years since 1914, the prospect for the ensuing decades was for an increasing influence of Christianity on the emerging Africa.

Madagascar, much smaller than Africa but adjacent to it, had a somewhat similar record. It, too, was hurried into the revolutionary age with marked cultural changes. It also became independent of its nineteenth-century colonial status. In it Christianity grew rapidly in the twentieth century, in both Protestant and Roman Catholic forms, and with increasing rootage in indigenous leadership.

CHAPTER XVIII

The Youthful and Growing Ecumenical Movement

A STRIKING feature of the twentieth-century course of Christianity was the Ecumenical Movement. "Ecumenical" was from the Greek οἰκουμένη which meant the inhabited world, or the entire human race. It had long been a technical term in Christian circles to designate councils which in theory embraced the entire Church. As employed in "the Ecumenical Movement" it embodied the hope that all Christians the world over might be brought into the unity of love which had been the dream from the begninning of the faith and that into it all mankind would ultimately be drawn.

The revolutionary age presented both a challenge and an opportunity for the realization of the dream. Through the mechanical inventions associated with that age the globe was shrinking. The steamship, the electric telegraph, the telephone, and, latterly, the radio and airplane were annihilating the time-distances which had formerly kept most nations and races out of close touch with one another. All mankind was becoming a neighbourhood. But, tragically, it was a quarrelsome neighbourhood, in which two world holocausts had already wrought more extensive damage than ever mankind as a whole had known from war and which in the early 1960's was threatened with atomic death. Due to the forces released by the revolutionary age, mankind was increasing in volume, and in some nations the resulting pressure on earth's physical resources was nullifying the efforts to raise the physical standard of living. The breath-taking vision of what Christians believed to be embodied in the command of their risen Lord would transform these threats into a new kind of society embracing all men everywhere. It was nothing less than making disciples of all the nations, incorporating them through baptism into the Church, and teaching them to observe all that in the days of His flesh He had taught the intimate group which He had gathered about Him—the seemingly impossible ideals succinctly stated in the Sermon on the Mount and culminating in being perfect as the Heavenly Father is perfect. With the command was the assurance that as Christians sought to obey, the risen Christ to whom "all power" had been "given in heaven and on earth" would be with them to the end of the age. Could that command be obeyed, all men would be knit together in the kind of love which God had shown in the incarnation and which Christ had displayed in allowing His enemies to crucify Him. Were this to come to pass, wars and the threat of wars would vanish. All men would work together to harness the resources of the earth to meet their physical needs and to create a civilization in which their spiritual potential would be fully realized. The resulting knowledge and beauty would be crowned by the adoration of God Who had made Himself known as self-giving love in His incarnate Son and Who was continuing to live with men through His Holy Spirit, which had come in added measure through the life, death, and resurrection of Jesus.

As we have repeatedly reminded ourselves, the revolutionary age which had brought this challenge with its threat and opportunity had issued from Western Christendom. Here the Gospel with its vision and its command had more nearly enjoyed free course over a longer period of time than anywhere else on the planet. When the revolutionary age had begun—some time in the fifteenth or sixteenth century—Western Christendom had been confined to the extreme end of that peninsula of the Euro-asiatic continent which lay between the Mediterranean Sea and the Atlantic and Arctic Oceans. It then embraced only a small fragment of the earth's surface and a mere fraction, and by no means the largest fraction, of mankind. By the mid-twentieth century Western European peoples had become the large majority in the Americas, Australia, and New Zealand, many features of the culture which they had developed were being eagerly adopted by the rest of the world, and the revolution which had originated among them was transforming all aspects of the culture of all peoples. In some places the Christian dream was contributing to movements, notably Communism, which perverted it, often denied its central affirmations, and so distorted it that they became its most aggressive enemies.

Yet many Christians continued to be inspired by the dream. Because of it, in the century and a half which these volumes have covered, Christian communities had been planted in almost every people and country. Indeed, at the time these words were written a least one organized church was found in every country but one which claimed political independence. That exception, Outer Mongolia, was not fully independent. In many countries the faith had been brought chiefly by the immigration of traditionally Christian peoples. In others it had come by conversions from historically non-Christian peoples. In many lands those bearing the Christian name were minorities—in Asia, the continent with the majority of mankind, very small minorities. Taken the world over, in 1962 those classed as Christians were still a minority. Because of the population explosion, never had the world contained as many non-Christians. Yet with the exception of a few countries, among them China, Christian communities were growing. In some places, notably the United States, Sumatra, Africa south of the Sahara, and Madagascar, between 1914 and 1962 the percentage of the population having church membership had rapidly increased.

During the latter part of the nineteenth and the first half of the twentieth century the effort to bring to realization the dream of a world-encompassing Church mounted. In the 1960's the Roman Catholic Church had adherents in all but a few lands. Through an indigenous clergy and episcopate it was becoming rooted in non-European as well as European countries and was knit together by Communion, common statements of faith, and an authoritative organization headed by the Pope. But, with the rapid growth of Protestantism, in 1962 it enrolled a smaller proportion of those who bore the Christian name than it had at the beginning of the nineteenth century and even at the outset of the twentieth. Nor, in 1962, could any indication be seen that more than small minorities of Protestants or members of the Eastern Churches would be drawn into it. The main growth of an inclusive Christian fellowship was coming through Protestanitsm and in the mid-twentieth century seemed to be only starting. By 1962 what was called the Ecumenical Movement embraced the large majority of the Protestants, the Anglicans who wished to be called Catholic rather than Protestant, and the majority of the members of the Eastern Churches.

That the Ecumenical Movement sprang from Protestantism was at first sight surprising. Here, by its very genius, was the seemingly most fissiparous branch of Christianity. Divisions—confessional and denominational—among Protestants had been present from the very first and in the nineteenth and twentieth centuries continued to proliferate. Yet by the mid-twentieth century the Ecumenical Movement brought together a greater variety of Christians than had any other movement in the nearly two thousand years of Christian history.

The Ecumenical Movement had many aspects and found expression through a large number of organizations. In 1962 the most nearly inclusive of these organizations was the World Council of Churches. But even that body—or "fellowship" as it officially described itself—was far from including all the manifestations of the Movement. The strongest motive in bringing into being the Ecumenical Movement was giving effect to the vision of winning all men to Christian discipleship. Along with that motive was the longing for the unity of love among all Christians, which was of the essence of the faith and which Christ was remembered as having given as a commandment during His inauguration of the Eucharist and in His prayer on the eve of His betrayal and crucifixion.

Simply to enumerate a few of the organizations will give some indication of the variety. Most of them arose in the nineteenth and twentieth centuries and their number mounted as the years passed. In several the membership was made up of individuals and not ecclesiastical bodies. Such were the Young Men's and Young Women's Christian Associations. Of Protestant origin, as they grew they attracted youth from many communions—Protestant, Roman Catholic, and Orthodox. In some areas, as in Latin America and the Philippines, a large proportion of both the membership and the leaders were Roman Catholics. In Greece they were predominantly Orthodox. The purpose of the YMCA was officially expressed in the Paris Basis, adopted in 1855 at the time of the formation of the World's Alliance and reaffirmed at the jubilee meeting of the Alliance in 1905: "The Young Men's Christian Associations seek to unite those young men who, regarding Jesus Christ as their God and Saviour, according to the Holy Scriptures, desire to be His disciples in their doctrine and in their life, and to associate their efforts for the extension of His Kingdom among young men."[1]

In the nineteenth century many voluntary student Christian groups sprang up in Protestant circles in the British Isles, the Continent of Europe, and North America.[2] They found a global focus in the World's Student Christian Federation, organized in Sweden in 1895. The World's Student Christian Federation was deeply indebted to the Young Men's Christian Association and to Dwight L. Moody. Through the YMCA the first Protestant student conference was called. It met in Mt. Hermon, Massachusetts, in 1886, under the leadership of Moody. There the Student Volunteer Movement for Foreign Missions came into being with Robert P. Wilder as its central figure. Its watchword was "The evangelization of the world in this generation." John R. Mott, then a student in Cornell University, was at Mt. Hermon and became the first chairman of the executive committee of the Student Volunteer Movement. Wilder carried the vision to the British Isles and the Continent of Europe, and a similar movement arose in the British Isles, which became the heart of the Student Christian Movement of Great Britain and Ireland.[3] Mott became an evangelist to students in many countries. Largely under his leadership the World's Student Christian Federation was brought into being. As its first general secretary Mott travelled around the world organizing national units of the Federation. Students and professors joined the local units as individuals. They came from many denominations. Conferences and meetings of the Committee of the Federation were held in places which were deemed strategic in accomplishing the Federation's purpose of winning the students of the world and through them all

---

[1] Clarence Prouty Shedd and others, *History of the World's Alliance of Young Men's Christian Associations* (London, S.P.C.K., 1955, pp. xvii, 746), pp. 132, 133, 421.

[2] On the history of the ones in the United States see Clarence P. Shedd, *Two Centuries of Student Christian Movements. Their Origin and Intercollegiate Life* (New York, Association Press, 1934, pp. xxii, 466), *passim*.

[3] Robert P. Wilder, *The Great Commission. The Missionary Response of the Student Volunteer Movements in North America and Europe: Some Personal Reminiscences* (London, Oliphant, 1936, pp. 115), *passim*; *Addresses and Papers of John R. Mott.* Vol. I, *The Student Volunteer Movement for Foreign Missions, passim.*

peoples to the Christian faith. For example, noteworthy conferences were convened in Constantinople in 1911 and in Peking in 1922. Orthodox as well as Protestants were drawn into membership of the national units which comprised the Federation.[4] It was significant that Mott became chairman of the World Missionary Conference in Edinburgh in 1910, the first chairman of the International Missionary Council,[5] and the first honorary president of the World Council of Churches. Many of the early staff of the World Council of Churches, including the first general secretary of that body, had gained vision and experience through leadership in the Federation.

Out of the World Missionary Conference held in Edinburgh came the International Missionary Council. Its members were national and regional bodies, some called councils and some conferences,[6] such as the Foreign Missions Conference of North America (later the Division of Foreign Missions of the National Council of the Churches of Christ in the U.S.A.), and the Conference of Missionary Societies in Great Britain and Ireland. By the year 1961 thirty-eight such bodies were members. Sixteen similar regional and national councils and federations existed which were not members of the International Missionary Council.[7]

After 1914 two bodies came into being, the World Conference on Faith and Order and the Universal Christian Council for Life and Work. These were the initial constituents of the World Council of Churches. The movement which issued in the World Conference on Faith and Order was given a decisive impulse through the World Missionary Conference of Edinburgh, but it had antecedents in the nineteenth century and earlier—indeed, almost since the beginnings of Protestantism.[8] Owing largely to Tissington Tatlow, the secretary of the Student Christian Movement of Great Britain and Ireland, the Anglicans were officially represented at Edinburgh. Edinburgh's nineteenth-century predecessors had been composed entirely of Evangelicals and Pietists. Several Anglican bishops and a delegation from the Society for the Propagation of the Gospel in Foreign Parts came to Edinburgh. Among the Anglicans was Charles Henry Brent, bishop in the Philippines. In October, 1910, a few weeks after Edinburgh, partly at the suggestion of Brent, the General Convention of the Protestant Episcopal Church directed that a commission be appointed "to bring

---

[4] Ruth Rouse, *The World's Student Christian Federation, A History of the First Thirty Years* (London, S. C. M. Press, 1948, pp. 332), *passim; Addresses and Papers of John R. Mott.* Vol. II, *The World's Student Christian Federation, passim.*

[5] On Mott's share in the International Missionary Council see *Addresses and Papers of John R. Mott.* Vol. V, *The International Missionary Council, passim.*

[6] Hogg, *Ecumenical Foundations, passim.*

[7] For the list of members in 1961 see *The International Review of Missions,* Vol. L, pp. 124, 125 (January, 1961).

[8] On many of these antecedents see Rouse and Neill, *A History of the Ecumenical Movement, 1517–1948,* pp. 27–349. See also Volume II, pp. 349, 350, and Volume III, pp. 96–100.

about a conference for the consideration of questions touching Faith and Order, and that all Christian Communions throughout the world which confess Our Lord Jesus Christ as God and Saviour be asked to unite ... in arranging for and conducting such a conference." In the same month the Disciples of Christ and the National Council of the Congregational Churches in the United States took similar action. By April, 1911, eighteen American Protestant churches had appointed commissions. Approaches were made to the Anglican Churches in the British Isles and were favourably received. By the close of 1911 the proposal for a world conference had been laid before leaders of churches of every type throughout the world, including all the bishops and cardinals of the Roman Catholic Church.[9]

World War I interrupted the preparations, but in 1919 they were renewed. In 1927 the First World Conference on Faith and Order assembled in Lausanne. A little over 400 were present, the majority of them officially appointed by their churches. Several had previously had experience in the student Christian movements with fellowship across denominational lines. The churches represented numbered 108—Lutheran, Reformed, Old Catholic, Orthodox, Anglican, Methodist, Congregational, Baptist, and Disciples of Christ. The Roman Catholic Church had been invited, but the Pope, while expressing himself as personally cordial, frankly said that because of the well-known conviction of the Catholic Church that the unity of the visible Church of Christ could come only through submitting to the See of Peter, the Holy See could not take part in the gathering. The Lausanne Conference prepared and accepted without dissenting voice statements on the Church's message to the world—the Gospel, the nature of the Church, the Church's common confession of faith, the ministry of the Church, and the sacraments—and appointed a continuation committee.[10]

The Second World Conference on Faith and Order convened in Edinburgh in August, 1937; under the chairmanship of William Temple, then Archbishop of York. It proved to be a genuine conference, one marked by friendly and frank interchange of thought on the central issues. It appointed a committee to consult with a similar committee of the Universal Christian Conference for Life and Work to consider closer coöperation.[11]

The Universal Christian Council for Life and Work, like the World Conference on Faith and Order, had nineteenth-century predecessors. Movements had sprung up in Protestantism in more than one country trying to make the faith effective in the social issues presented by the revolutionary age. On the

[9] Rouse and Neill, *op. cit.*, pp. 405–415.

[10] *Ibid.*, pp. 415, 425; *Faith and Order. Proceedings of the World Conference, Lausanne, August 3–21*, edtied by N. H. Bate (New York, George H. Doran Co., 1927, pp. xxiii, 534), *passim*.

[11] Rouse and Neill, *op. cit.*, pp. 431–437; *The Second World Conference on Faith and Order, Held at Edinburgh August 3–18, 1937*, edited by Leonard Hodgson (New York, The Macmillan Co., 1938, pp. ix, 386), *passim*.

eve of World War I various efforts were exerted by Protestants to resolve the international tensions and promote peace. Such, for example, was the World Peace Union, endowed by Andrew Carnegie. A conference for that purpose met in Constance in the summer of 1914 and was dissolved by the outbreak of war. Yet out of it came the World Alliance for the Promotion of International Friendship through the Churches.[12]

The chief creator of the Universal Christian Council for Life and Work was Nathan Söderblom, whom we have met as scholar, teacher, and Archbishop of Uppsala. As we have seen, in his student days he had been exposed to the student Christian movement through the YMCA in North America with its vision of a fellowship transcending denominational and confessional barriers in an effort to bring the Gospel to all aspects of the life of mankind.[13] During World War I he laboured for peace and in December, 1917, convened a conference in Stockholm of about thirty-five from five neutral European countries. In October, 1919, a meeting was held at Oud Wassenaar, near the Hague, of members of the international committee of the World Alliance for the Promotion of International Friendship through the Churches and of various national committees, with delegates from fourteen countries, including France, Germany, Great Britain, and the United States. At Oud Wassenaar Söderblom presented an invitation in the name of himself and the other heads of the Scandinavian Lutheran churches to convene an international conference on the attitude of the Church on social and international questions. After carfeul preparation that conference convened in Stockholm in 1925. The majority of the members were official delegates of their respective churches. Most of Protestantism and some of the Eastern Churches were represented. As was true of Faith and Order, the Roman Catholic Church was invited but did not participate. Questions of faith and order were carefully avoided but the conference covered the entire range of Christian social concern. Out of it came a continuing body, the Universal Christian Council for Life and Work.[14]

Söderblom died in 1931, but the Universal Christian Council for Life and Work grew. Stockholm had appointed a continuation committee. Research was conducted on pertinent subjects. In 1937 a second world conference was convened at Oxford on the theme of "Church, Community and State." Its chief architect was J. H. Oldham, who had come up through the Student Christian Movement of Great Britain and Ireland, had been secretary for the World Missionary Conference of 1910, and was one of the first two secretaries of the International Missionary Council. It met shortly before the Edinburgh conference on Faith and Order, with 425 regular members including 300 delegates

[12] Rouse and Neill, *op. cit.*, pp. 510–513; Volume II, pp. 122–126, 370–375, and Volume III, pp. 223–233.
[13] Volume II, pp. 179–181.
[14] Rouse and Neill, *op. cit.*, pp. 523–553.

representing 120 communions in 40 countries. In preparation for it a notable series of studies had been prepared. Out of it came a phrase: "Let the Church be the Church," which won wide currency. The Oxford Conference held that the "primary duty of the Church to the state is to be the Church, namely, to witness to God, to preach His Word, to confess the faith before men, to teach both young and old to observe the divine commandments, and to serve the nation and the state by proclaiming the Will of God as the supreme standard to which all human wills must be subject and all human conduct must conform." Coming as it did during the Nazi regime in Germany and on the eve of World War II, the Oxford gathering was a courageous voice against the totalitarian state, which was seemingly becoming the standard form of government as a phase of the revolutionary age.[15] It appointed a committee to meet with the committee of Faith and Order to consider the merging of the two bodies.

The meetings of Life and Work and Faith and Order (as the two movements were briefly called) in the summer of 1937 in Great Britain gave an impetus to the achievement of a world organization of churches which had been in the minds of many, especially since World War I. In 1935 William Temple suggested it in an informal consultation during a visit to the United States. In 1936 J. H. Oldham made concrete proposals which led to the formation of the Ecumenical Consultative Group representing Life and Work, Faith and Order, the International Missionary Council, and the World Alliance for the Promotion of International Friendship through the Churches. The Ecumenical Consultative Group appointed a committee of thirty-five which met in London shortly before the Oxford Conference. It quickly agreed upon a project for uniting Life and Work and Faith and Order under a body representative of the churches and with the designation "the World Council of Churches"—a suggestion of Samuel McCrea Cavert, the general secretary of the Federal Council of the Churches of Christ in America.

The joint committee (the Committee of Fourteen) of Faith and Order and Life and Work called a meeting representing the churches which had sent delegates to the Oxford and Edinburgh conferences to draft a constitution for the proposed World Council of Churches. It convened at Utrecht in May, 1938, with William Temple presiding. The provisional constitution framed by the gathering described "the World Council of Churches as a fellowship of churches which accept Our Lord Jesus Christ as God and Saviour." The new body was to be a "fellowship" and not a "super-church." It was to have no authority over its member churches. It could not act as an ecclesiastical court and was to leave to each church the decision as to whether it could coöperate

---

[15] *Ibid.*, pp. 575–592; J. H. Oldham, *The Oxford Conference (Official Report)* (Chicago, Willett, Clark and Co., 1937, pp. xvi, 290). The preliminary studies were in *Church, Community, and State* (London, George Allen and Unwin, 7 vols., 1937, 1938).

on the Council's basis. The Utrecht gathering appointed a provisional committee to function until the first General Assembly could gather and formally inaugurate the proposed body.[16]

The outbreak of World War II postponed the meeting of the first General Assembly of the World Council of Churches. In the meantime its secretariat, led by W. A. Visser 't Hooft, was extremely active, partly as a channel for the administration of relief to the sufferers from the war and partly as a means of communication between churches in the opposing camps. It was described as "the World Council of Churches in Process of Formation." From its headquarters in Geneva it stimulated a sense of fellowship among churchmen who were standing out against pagan or semi-pagan distortions of Christianity. Its study department aided discussions about the post-war international order. The Ecumenical Institute at Bossey, near Geneva, was founded and increasingly was a centre for conferences and study across national and confessional lines.

During the war several deaths seemed to weaken the World Council of Churches and the entire Ecumenical Movement—of William Temple, recently enthroned as Archbishop of Canterbury; of William Paton, who had come up through the British Student Christian Movement and as a secretary of the International Missionary Council was prominent in keeping it and the incipient World Council of Churches in close collaboration; and of V. S. Azariah, Bishop of Dornakal, outstanding in what were called the "younger churches."[17]

As soon as could wisely be done after the coming of peace, in Amsterdam in the summer of 1948 the postponed General Assembly convened and formally constituted the World Council of Churches. The theme of the Assembly, "Man's Disorder and God's Design," was especially pertinent to the holocaust through which mankind had recently passed and to the troubled peace which followed. The 351 official delegates were from 147 churches in 44 countries. The basis of membership formulated at Utrecht was confirmed. A close tie between the World Council of Churches and the International Missionary Council was forged by the formal declaration that each was "in association" with the other and the setting up of a Joint Committee through which that association could be made effective.[18] In 1949 the two bodies set up a joint secretariat for East Asia. The first incumbent was Rajah B. Manikam of India, later to be a Lutheran bishop in his native land.

Under the impulse given by Amsterdam the World Council of Churches extended both its membership and its operations. Several of the "younger churches" in Asia and Africa applied and were admitted to membership. The programmes of both Faith and Order and Life and Work were continued. In

---

[16] Rouse and Neill, *op. cit.*, pp. 697–705. The author was a delegate to Utrecht.

[17] *Ibid.*, pp. 708–714.

[18] *Ibid.*, pp. 719–724; *Man's Disorder and God's Design. The Amsterdam Assembly Series* (London, S.C.M. Press, 5 vols., 1948, 1949). Vol. 5 was the official Assembly report.

August, 1952, the Third World Conference on Faith and Order was held in Lund.[19] The Commission of the Churches on International Affairs, a joint undertaking of the World Council of Churches and the International Missionary Council, with the able services of O. Frederick Nolde, its director, became important, especially in obtaining the adoption by the United Nations of the draft covenant on human rights, carrying further the Declaration of Human Rights by that body, which provided for freedom of religion, including the right to change one's religion. Nolde also visited trouble spots in the world scene—for example, Korea and Cyprus—to suggest means of resolving the tensions.[20] Through Inter-Church Aid financial assistance was given to hardpressed churches. Much was accomplished toward relieving the millions of refugees from adverse political conditions—both through direct grants and through stimulating other agencies, especially the United Nations.

The Second Assembly of the World Council of Churches met in Evanston, Illinois, in the summer of 1954. The choice of the place was evidence of the growing importance of North America in the Ecumenical Movement and the entire Christian scene. The theme—"Christ, the Hope of the World"—gave rise to theological discussions as to what could be expected in history.[21] The voices of Asia and Africa were more in evidence than at Amsterdam. The Central Committee, the ad interim body which convened annually, had already held a meeting in Lucknow, thus recognizing the importance of the churches in Asia.[22]

We must not take the space even to enumerate all the developments in the World Council of Churches associated with the eight years which followed the Second Assembly. A few, however, cannot be omitted. One was the increasing participation of the Eastern and especially the Orthodox Churches, symbolized by the meeting of the Central Committee on the island of Rhodes in the summer of 1959. In 1961 the Russian Orthodox Church applied for membership. In the autumn of 1961 the Third Assembly convened in New Delhi, thus giving additional evidence of the inclusive sweep of the World Council of Churches. The theme—"Jesus Christ, the Light of the World"—spoke to a generation in which the international tensions and economic and social problems of the revolutionary age were causing many to take a sombre view of the future. By 1961 the membership had risen to 172 churches. At the meeting in New Delhi the integration of the International Missionary Council, long under discussion, was accomplished, as the Commission on World Mission and Evangelism, with accompanying changes in the structure of the World Council of Churches. Thus the dream of winning all men to discipleship and teaching them to obey

---

[19] James William Kennedy, *He That Gathereth. A First Hand Account of the Third World Conference on Faith and Order, Held in Lund, Sweden, August 15–28, 1952* (New York, World Council of Churches, 1952, pp. 112), *passim.*

[20] *Information Service*, November 10, 1956.

[21] James Hastings Nichols. *Evanston. An Interpretation* (New York, Harper & Brothers, 1954, pp. 155), *passim; The Christian Century*, Vol. LXXI, pp. 1125–1167 (September 22, 1954).

[22] *The Ecumenical Review*, Vol. V, p. 203 (January, 1953).

Christ's commands was brought into the very heart of the Ecumenical Movement.

Although when these lines were written the World Council of Churches was very young, already it had brought into fellowship more churches representing a greater variety of the expressions of Christianity than had been seen in all the preceding history of the faith. Into it had been drawn the churches in which were enrolled the overwhelming majority of the Protestants, a large majority of the Orthodox, and a substantial proportion of the other Eastern Christians. In a day when the world was racked by tensions and most of mankind was aligned in two armed camps engaged in a "cold war," Christians were coming together in a fresh and unprecedented fashion in a fellowship through a common loyalty to Christ which reached across the barriers separating the rivals. The Roman Catholic Church, which still had a majority of those who claimed the Christian name, officially held aloof, but increasingly bridges of sympathetic understanding were spanning a chasm marked by an enmity which denied that love enjoined by Christ on His disciples. Many Roman Catholics were watching the Ecumenical Movement closely and not unsympathetically.[23] Numbers of small informal groups of Roman Catholics and Protestants were meeting in an effort to find points of agreement and to understand basic differences. In more spectacular fashion, in 1961 the Archbishop of Canterbury, after visiting some of the Eastern churchmen in Jerusalem and the Ecumenical Patriach in Istanbul, paid an official call on the Pope and was received with marked courtesy.

As we have suggested, the World Council of Churches did not embrace all phases of the Ecumenical Movement. In the Americas were numerous coöperative bodies of Protestants, some of them including Orthodox churches, which, while friendly, were not structurally associated with it. Such were the many city and state councils of churches in the United States, the National Council of the Churches of Christ in the U.S.A., and the Canadian Council of Churches, most of them of twentieth-century origin. In a similar category were the British Council of Churches, constituted in 1942, the Australian Council for the World Council of Churches, begun in 1946, the National Council of Churches in New Zealand, formed in 1941, the Ecumenical Council of Churches in the Netherlands, inaugurated in 1935, the Federation of Protestant Churches in Switzerland, founded in 1920, a federation of churches in Germany, including both the *Landeskirchen* and the Free Churches, created in 1948 and enlarging a predecessor of 1922, the Protestant Federation of France, dating from 1905, and several similar bodies in Italy, Hungary, and Scandinavia.[24]

In January, 1959, for the first time in history, representatives of the majority

---

[23] See, for example, Bernard Leeming, *The Churches and the Church. A Study in Ecumenism* (London, Darton, Longman and Todd, 1960, pp. x, 340), an irenic study by a Jesuit.

[24] Rouse and Neill, *op. cit.*, pp. 620–630.

of the Protestant and Orthodox Churches of Europe, coming from twenty-two countries, met in Denmark and appointed a provisional committee to plan for continuing study and action.[25]

We must also note the several denominational and confessional alliances, all of them having their origin in the latter part of the nineteenth or in the twentieth century. Among them were the Lambeth Conferences, the Alliance of Reformed Churches throughout the world holding the Presbyterian System, the Methodist Council (formerly the Ecumenical Methodist Council), the Union of Utrecht (of the Old Catholic Churches), the International Congregational Council, and the Baptist World Alliance, all of them begun within the fifty years which preceded World War I. Added to them were the Lutheran World Federation, formed in 1947 and succeeding the Lutheran World Convention (which was organized in 1927), the World Convention of the Disciples of Christ, which first met in 1930, the Friends' World Committee for Consultation, which dated from 1920, and the International Association for Liberal Christianity and Religious Freedom, founded in 1930 to give continuity to international congresses of "liberal" churches, the first of which convened in 1900.[26] Some but not all of these organizations collaborated more or less formally with the World Council of Churches.

In addition to the close coöperation with the World Council of Churches of the World's Alliance of YMCA's, the World's YWCA, and the World's Student Christian Federation, all with headquarters in Geneva, an additional affiliated body was what had been the World's Sunday School Association, organized in 1907, and which became the World Council of Christian Education.[27]

In several places in this volume we have noted the emergence of unions of existing ecclesiastical bodies in England, Scotland, Canada, the United States, India, Ceylon, Thailand, the Philippines, China, and Japan.

We must also call attention to some of the many other ways in which Protestants overpassed denominational lines. Among them was the Young People's Society of Christian Endeavour, with a world organization. Although by 1962 it had been largely replaced in the United States, the land of its origin, by denominational youth bodies, in several countries it was more flourishing than ever. We must note that in hundreds of collections, some published under denominational auspices and others with undenominational editorship, hymns by authors of many denominations and confessions were included—not only Protestants but Roman Catholics and Orthodox as well. Indeed, the official hymnals of some churches which refused to coöperate with other churches were in this category. In many cities in the United States community churches were

[25] *Ecumenical Press Service*, January 16, 1959.
[26] Rouse and Neill, *op. cit.*, pp. 613–620.
[27] *Ibid.*, pp. 599–612.

found which either under that designation or with denominational ties were organized on a geographical basis and drew members from two or more denominational backgrounds. They were also seen in lands outside the United States and were called American Churches. Their common tie was the use of English and they attracted not only travellers and residents from the United States but others whose mother tongue was English or who had English as their second language. In such widely different environments as steamers, refugee camps, and prisons, services were held in broadly undenominational patterns, or, if denominational, were open to all who wished to attend. Days and weeks of prayer were encouraged with objects and manuals of prayer which enlisted thousands regardless of their denomination or confession. Much of the material used in Sunday Schools was undenominational. We have repeatedly seen the fashion in which Protestants coöperated across denominational lines in schools, hospitals, literature, and radio and television, especially in Asia and Africa.

The Ecumenical Movement did not enlist the support of all Protestants. In the United States several churches, some very large, would not coöperate with the World Council of Churches or national or regional councils of churches. As we saw earlier in this volume, many Protestants, notably in the Americas but also elsewhere, either kept apart completely from other Protestants or joined in organizations, national and international, which sought to parallel bodies that enlisted the majority of Protestants.

Nor by 1962 had the Ecumenical Movement reached the stage where all who held the Christian name could come together at the Lord's Table, whether that was called the Communion or the Eucharist and was observed at an altar or a table. Here and there gatherings of youth were impatient with the failure to attain this goal. At the assemblies of Faith and Order, Life and Work, and the World Council of Churches it was customary to have a Communion service according to the liturgy of the majority denomination in the city in which the meeting was held, and with an invitation to all to be present and take the Communion, but in none of the larger and in few of the smaller gatherings did all in attendance go to the Communion rail. In the central act of Christian worship Christians were still divided—not only between Roman Catholics, the Eastern Churches, and Protestants, but within Protestantism as well. From the early Christian centuries participation in the Communion had been a symbol of unity, and excommunication or the breaking of fellowship in the Communion had been a method of passing judgement on those who laid claim to the Christian name as being unworthy of fellowship. In some Protestant churches the invitation to share in the Communion was given "to all who have professed themselves or by this act would profess themselves followers of Our Lord Jesus Christ," or "to all who have found in Christ their Saviour," or "to all who love Our Lord Jesus Christ," leaving to the individual the decision of whether to share in the Communion. Some admitted to the Communion all baptized Christians who did not have an opportunity otherwise to partake. Yet on the whole what many Christians sorrowfully regarded as the scandal of the division in the Church, "the body of Christ," continued to be most vividly displayed in the unwillingness of millions who regarded themselves as disciples of Christ to share together in what the majority considered a sacrament, believing that in some way their Lord was peculiarly present, and in what all agreed their Lord had commanded in memory of Him and of His supreme sacrifice for the salvation of men.

CHAPTER XIX

An Attempt to Discern the Meaning of the Story

W E HAVE come to the end of our narrative, but the story does not end here. We must pause at a semi-colon. We have carried our account to the time when these pages must go to the publisher. To go further would be to engage in prophecy. Upon that, if he is wise, the historian must not embark, for in his study of the records of the past he has seen many unfulfilled forecasts by men wiser than himself. Moreover, as a Christian, he was painfully conscious of St. Paul's words: "Whether there be prophecies, they shall fail." When these lines were penned it was obvious that the revolutionary age which has been our theme was not at an end, but how long it would continue and precisely what forms it would take in the future could not be accurately foreseen.

To one who has meditated on the scroll of history so far as it has been unrolled, the questions insistently recur as to whether the story which he endeavoured to recount has meaning and, if so, what that meaning may be. In seeking answers to these questions, as we now essay to do, we must take account of facts. But, as every historian who is honest and informed knows, even in the selection of facts the judgement of which are important cannot be avoided and depends largely on the observer's convictions. For the Christian this means that his faith is involved. It is his faith which enters into his appraisal of what is pertinent. Yet if that appraisal is to approximate the truth the Christian must be aware of observable facts and dodge none of them, including those which challenge his conclusions. He must be willing to modify or even to reject his appraisal if it is not in accord with the facts.

As the historian who is a Christian attempts to ascertain whether the human story has meaning and, if so, what the meaning is, he is confronted with two considerations. One is the difficulty of discerning the fashion in which God works. The ancient prophet recognized it when he declared that God said: "My thoughts are not your thoughts, neither are your ways my ways . . . for as the heavens are higher than the earth, so are my ways higher than your ways, and my thoughts than your thoughts." In viewing the past the historian may miss what from God's standpoint is most significant. A second is the lack of agreement among Christians as to whether "world history" is "salvation history." Many thoughtful Germans have said that *"Weltgeschichte ist nicht Heils-geschichte."* The two difficulties are closely related, for it may be that world history as far as men can perceive it is men's thoughts and ways and that "salvation history"—God's thought and ways—cannot be apprehended by men.

Yet Christians have long affirmed that they "believe in God the Father Almighty, Maker of heaven and earth" and have rejected the ancient heresy of Marcion with its effort to divorce world history from the action of God. All history, could we but see it as God sees it, must be "salvation history"—the record of the fashion in which God has worked and continues to work "for us men and for our salvation." Could the historian perceive the manner in which God seeks to achieve His purpose, the seeming dichotomy between "world history" and "salvation history" would disappear. But the Christian historian is painfully aware of the many attempts to resolve the dichotomy—among them Augustine's *City of God*—and must be modest and cautious as he ventures on another effort.

As we seek to discover whether the record of Christianity in the nineteenth and twentieth centuries has meaning and, if the answer is affirmative, what that meaning is, we must remind ourselves of the momentary character of what we have surveyed and realize that even the total course of Christianity down to the day in which we seek to understand it was very short. When contrasted with the hundreds of thousands of years in which *Homo sapiens* has been on this planet Christianity is a recent phenomenon. It is seen to be still more recent if we contrast its history with the millions of years in which life of some kind has been on the earth and yet more so if we place it in the setting of the universe, in which our sun with its satellites is only one of millions of suns in the galaxy of the Milky Way and the galaxy itself is only one of millions and perhaps billions of other galaxies. Even when compared with the time span of human civilization, which seems to have been at the most only fifteen to twenty thousand years, Christianity is a recent development. It is either in its early youth or a transient experience in the life of mankind. From this perspective the 150 years which have been the subject of these volumes have been only a few seconds of sidereal and even earthly and human time. But, as the public career of Him from Whom Christianity emerged was only a few years and perhaps merely a few months and yet has had a greater effect on mankind as a whole than any other event in the life of humanity and, far from waning, continues to mount, so the century and a half to which our story has been devoted may afford some clue to the record of the human race and to the nature of the universe in which it is placed.

First we must seek further perspective in the record of the faith in the eighteen centuries which preceded these fifteen decades. In our initial volume we summarized it at some length. Here we must repeat it but in much briefer compass. At its inception Christianity faced what appeared to be a most unpromising future. Not only was the life of its central figure brief, but it seemed to offer no hope of being long remembered. Jesus wrote no book. So far as we know, He gave little attention to creating an organization which would perpetuate His teaching. He gathered around him a company of twelve intimates from uninfluential and varied backgrounds. One of them betrayed Him. Another, in a time of supreme testing, denied acquaintanec with Him. He came to His death on a Roman cross, derisively labeled as the King of the Jews, apparently a frustrated visionary. The little company in Jerusalem which perpetuated His memory and declared that He had risen from the dead, a seemingly preposterous assertion, must to the casual observer have appeared to be the smallest of several Jewish sects. As the faith spread and became rooted in the cities of the Roman Empire it still was one of many religions competing for the allegiance of the Mediterranean Basin. Within five centuries it had become the professed faith of the majority in that area, but for most of that majority allegiance was superficial and had slight effect upon their manner of life. True, Christianity displayed vigour in a civilization that had ceased to produce much that was new, created an ecclesiastical structure which embraced the entire Roman realm, and stimulated the minds of a few to produce strikingly original theologies. In the lives of some it had transforming power. Through monasticism it gave rise to extensive efforts to conform fully to the standards of Christ.

But the Roman Empire occupied only a small segment of the earth's surface and did not embrace the majority of even civilized mankind, let alone the tribes which inhabited most of the globe. To the east were great centres of civilization—Persia, India, and China—which had as notable cultural achievements to their credit as had Rome. In only two of them—Persia and India—did Christianity win adherents in its first five centuries and they were very small minorities. China was not even touched until the seventh century and then fleetingly.

Nor did Christianity save the Roman world. By the time the majority in the empire had assumed the Christian name, inner decay had been obvious for some time. Then and in later centuries caustic critics attributed that decay to the contemporaneous spread of the faith. To internal weakness were added invasions. From the North a series of inroads continued intermittently for hundreds of years. Eventually all the Northerners who established permanent homes adopted the Christian faith, but even formal conversion required hundreds of years and at the outset much of it was to a variant, Arianism, and not to that of the Roman citizens, called Catholic. From the South-east came a more formidable invasion, that of the Arabs, propagating a new religion, Islam. Moslem Arabs overran approximately half of what was then Christendom and, except in the Iberian Peninsula and Sicily, under their rule the churches slowly withered, a process which in the twentieth century was still in process. Never down to the time that our story must pause was Christianity again to suffer proportionately to its geographic extent and numerical strength such heavy losses as those inflicted by the Moslem Arabs.

Christianity survived the prolonged adversities and by the end of the thirteenth century was propagated over a wider area than it had been before the rise of Islam. Yet that spread was almost entirely in the Continent of Eurasia and except in the peninsula which we call Europe was confined to small minorities. Moreover, in the eastern continuation of the Roman Empire centring in Constantinople it was hampered by a tradition inherited from the pre-Christian years of that realm which subordinated religion to the state. The Church acquired more liberty than religion had enjoyed before Constantine, but even after the emperors became in theory its loyal sons, to a large degree it was dominated by them. That tradition persisted in lands to which Byzantine Christianity was carried—notably Russia and the Balkans.

In Western Europe Christianity had a nearer approach to freedom than anywhere else until the nineteenth and twentieth centuries. There the Roman rule was followed by disorder, barbarism, and a proliferation of states, largely tribal, with fluctuating boundaries. In time the faith embodied in the Catholic Church became the accepted religion of the peoples of the region. In the absence of strong, continuing governments, the Catholic Church became the tutor of its children, not only in religion and morals, but also in educational institutions, in the service of the ill and the aged, in giving sanctity to marriage and the family, in curbing lawlessness, and in permeating every phase of life with ideals derived from the faith. All aspects of the civilization of what we call medieval Europe were in part shaped by Christianity, especially but not exclusively within the former boundaries of the Roman Empire. Here most of the monastic orders of the Catholic Church had their rise and their richest development. Here most of the theology was shaped which gave intellectual formulation to the faith. From here came the majority of the missionaries who spread the faith in other lands. In Western Europe the Catholic Church became the Roman Catholic Church, perpetuating much of the organization, the law, and the temper of *Romanitas*.

However, to call Western Europe Christian was to be guilty of a deceptive ambiguity. Officially Christian it undoubtedly was. Openly to dissent from the faith was to be visited with drastic ecclesiastical and civil penalties. All except Jews were baptized with Christian names. The Church sought to nurture its children in the teachings of Christ and His Apostles. Yet much in the collective and individual life of Western Europe, even in many whom the Church denominated saints and held up to all Christians as exemplars of the Christian ideal, was far from conforming fully to the standards of Christ. For the rank and file of the high and the lowly, whether in office in church and state or in other occupations, much was palpably counter to the manner of life enjoined in the New Testament. Warfare was chronic and often was waged in the name of the cross with the Church's blessing. Religion still contained gross superstition. Unchastity was common, among both clergy and laity. Although the Popes styled themselves "servants of the servants of God" and annually they and some monarchs ceremonially washed the feet of selected groups of the poor, pride of office and power was so usual as to be censured only by a relatively few tender consciences. Here were the contrasts to which we have repeatedly called attention in our description of the nineteenth and twentieth centuries. On the one hand, lives, movements, and institutions bore indelibly the impress of the Christian Gospel and owed to it their inspiration. On the other hand, contradictions of the Gospel were glaring—all the more flagrant because of their rebellion against the demands of the professed faith.

In its inception and its early stages the revolutionary age which has been our theme ante-dated the nineteenth and twentieth centuries. Some would trace its beginnings to the Renaissance. Clearly the Renaissance had its roots in the Western Europe of the Middle Ages fertilized by contributions from Constantinople and the pre-Christian Mediterranean world. It was also in large part sprung from Christianity, but, like the Middle Ages, it presented a striking contradiction between pagan, un-Christian aspects under a veneer of outward conformity to the Church and high, unselfish commitment to Christ and His Gospel.

Near the heyday of the Renaissance came the outburst of vigour in the Christianity of Western Europe which found expression in the Catholic Reformation and the Protestant Reformation. The former began nearly a generation earlier than the latter but soon was stimulated and partly given direction by it. The Catholic Reformation brought fresh life to some of the old orders, gave rise to the Society of Jesus and new congregations, and raised the moral and spiritual level of the Papacy and the clergy. It was most effective in Latin Europe, the region with which the Roman Catholic Church was closely associated. The Protestant Reformation arose in that portion of Western Europe which either had been on the outer fringes of the Roman Empire or had never been within its borders. It took a variety of forms and was due partly to a profound, fresh experience of the Gospel and partly to political and social factors. The Catholic and Protestant Reformations brought a deepening of the religious life of many and at the same time contributed to devastating wars.

Out of the Catholic and Protestant Reformations came a fresh geographic expansion of Christianity which carried the faith over a wider portion of the globe than it or any other religion had yet reached. The chief agent was the

Roman Catholic Church, reinvigorated by its phase of the Reformation. The expansion was chiefly in connexion with the commerce and colonial enterprises of Spain and Portugal. The initial wave of Spanish and Portuguese conquest was marked by cruelty and the callous enslavement of the peoples with whom the adventurers came in contact. Although Prince Henry the Navigator, who directed the early Portuguese voyages along the west coast of Africa, was Grand Master of the Order of Christ and made efforts to prohibit it, the African slave trade sprang from them and was ultimately the largest-scale exploitation of one race by another that history has seen. Similarly, in his famous voyage Columbus appears to have been sustained by his faith, but the early years of the Spanish occupation of the lands that he disclosed were marked by high-handed barbarity in the treatment of the natives. Yet within a few years the impetus given by the Catholic Reformation inspired men, such as Francis Xavier in the East and Bartolomé de Las Casas in the Americas, to counter the cruelties of Portuguese and Spaniards and to win thousands to the Christian faith. The end of the African slave trade was to wait until the Protestant Evangelical awakening brought about its abolition. Yet through the devotion inspired by the Catholic Reformation, not only were some of the abuses which attended the commercial and political enterprises of Portugal and Spain ameliorated and millions within the overseas domains of these powers won to a formal acceptance of Christianity, but the faith was carried as well beyond these possessions into Japan, China, and India. However, the notable missionary achievements were usually made under the direction and often at the expense of the state and were a phase, although a benevolent one, of European imperialism.

The Protestant Reformation did not immediately give rise to as marked a geographic extension of Christianity as did the Catholic Reformation. Yet by the end of the eighteenth century emigration, the Pietist and Evangelical awakenings, and currents within Puritanism and Anglicanism had reached out to non-Europeans beyond the frontiers of European settlement. Those awakenings, moreover, were deepening the faith among growing minorities in Protestant peoples.

On the eve of the nineteenth century the revolution was mounting which in that century and its successor was to attain global dimensions. Most of its main aspects had their inception in officially Protestant lands. The political phase which issued in democracy appeared first in England as an outgrowth of Puritanism. The Industrial Revolution began in Protestant Great Britain. The intellectual currents which in Deism constituted a major challenge to Christianity had their rise in Protestant England. The *Aufklärung* first found its most notable expressions in the Protestant states of Germany. Rapidly, however, the revolution spread to Roman Catholic countries and was reinforced by indigenous leadership and manifestations. France, euphemistically "the oldest daughter" of the Roman Catholic Church, became the radiating centre of the political and much of the intellectual forces which shook Europe at the end of the eighteenth and the beginning of the nineteenth century.

In the nineteenth and twentieth centuries the revolution swelled and proliferated first in Western Europe and in the lands peopled by Western Europeans, notably the United States. From Western Europe and the larger Western Europe of the Americas and Australasia it spread throughout the world and worked drastic changes in all facets of life. Cultural and political revolutions were not new. They had occurred again and again. But previously they had been limited to segments of mankind. Now all mankind was involved. The Industrial Revolution mounted and with the associated knowledge acquired through natural science brought a fabulous increase in material wealth. To the more favoured, totalling millions—mostly Western Europeans and their descendants—it gave hitherto unimagined physical comforts. From it huge cities arose, at first in England, where it began, but later in most of the earth until in the twentieth century Tokyo, in congested Japan, became the largest metropolis. Industrialization and urbanization worked basic changes in the social structure of every land in which they appeared. With the improved medical care which was a feature of the revolution, populations multiplied until in many countries they constituted a major threat to livelihood and peace. New methods of transportation and communication, at first seen only among Western European peoples but rapidly adopted by others, drew mankind together into a contracting and intimate neighbourhood. But with the emergence of that neighbourhood came acute frictions and world wars. The wars were fought by destructive weapons and forms of organization first created by Western Europeans. In country after country Western forms of government were adopted and adapted, with at least lip service to democracy. Communism, based on an ideology formulated in London, captured a large proportion of the world, almost entirely outside the West. Forms of education developed in the West became, with modifications, standard throughout most of the earth. The sciences first created in the West, through which man's physical environment was explored, both on the earth and outside it, became universal property. Nationalism, which initially had its distinctive expressions in Western Europe, spread rapidly. In other words, a world-wide culture was emerging from what had been begun by Western European peoples. Under its impact inherited institutions were crumbling or at least were being basically changed, not only in Western Europe and the nations that had arisen by migrations from it, but also, and often more spectacularly, in other parts of the globe.

We have spoken of the revolutionary age as having its origin in Western Europe and as being accelerated by movements and forces which continued to issue from it and from peoples whose ancestral home was Western Europe. Of major significance was the fact that here was the heart of the historic Christendom. Here Christianity had had over more centuries a nearer approach to free course in shaping individuals and civilization than in any other region. Was this more than a coincidence? Could a causal connexion be established? For some aspects of the revolution no conclusive proof was possible. For others, notably the emergence of what the West called democracy, it was fairly clear. Democracy had been first formulated by men sprung from Puritanism, notably John Locke. Most of those responsible for the beginnings of science either were devout Christians or had been reared in a Christian atmosphere but had reacted against the faith. The latter was also true of Communism.

Here was a crucial problem. Had Christianity given rise to—or at least contributed to—forces which were threatening the existence of Christianity and, indeed, of all religion? A phase of the revolutionary age which has loomed large in our pages, and rightly so, was the blow dealt to religion by the revolution wherever it appeared. Under its impact some religions either vanished or nearly vanished. The various forms of animism were peculiarly vulnerable. But even so advanced a system as Confucianism, usually classed with religion, was swept aside on the mainland of China and was weakened among Chinese who were not under Communist rule. In some places and countries non-Christian religions showed revivals. However, the revivals were usually associated with nationalism, itself first developed in Western Christendom. Here and there, as in twentieth-century Turkey, nationalism led to the decay of religion. In other countries, as in several of the Arab lands, Ceylon, Burma, and in some elements in India, revivals of the hereditary religions were largely due to an assertion of independence against Western imperialism or to efforts of a majority threatened by a minority which proved difficult of assimilation. Now and again, as in Japan following World War II, synthetic religions became popular in a hunger for certainty left unsatisfied by the decay of the traditional religions. Some twentieth-century movements which arose first in the West had many of the features of religion. Such were National Socialism and Fascism, transient phenomena. Communism, more widespread and persistent and officially antireligious, displayed some of the characteristics associated with religion. Observing these mounting movements, many were declaring that religion as mankind had known it was a passing phenomenon and was to be displaced by secularism or by nationalism or Communism.

Presumably the threat to religion, arising as it did from forces emerging in Western Christendom, would be most destructive to Christianity. If the revolution stemmed in any degree from Christianity, that religion could be said to be digging its own grave. Many features of the nineteenth and twentieth centuries appeared to confirm this diagnosis. Western Europe, especially in lands where the Roman Catholic Church had been the prevailing religious institution, displayed a rabid anti-clericalism. Anti-clericalism was more marked in the nineteenth than in the twentieth century, but by the twentieth century a widespread indifference to Christianity could be interpreted as meaning that that faith was so palpably waning that it did not arouse as much antagonism as when it was stronger. In Western Europe in the mid-twentieth century baptism into the Roman Catholic Church or into one or another Protestant church was still almost universal. But for the majority it was primarily a social convention. In all but a few countries the churches had been disestablished. Church attendance, once nearly universal, at least on the high days of the Christian year, and still marked in the nineteenth century, was dwindling. The decline was especially noticeable in urban areas and in industrial and in mining towns and cities, centres where the revolutionary impact was most potent, but it was also seen in many rural districts. Thousands among the intellectuals held that Christianity was no longer tenable by informed and honest minds. More thousands regarded the faith as irrelevant and at best only a pleasant and interesting fringe interest. In Central and Eastern Europe, on the edge of Western Christendom, Communism was dominant and was seeking to bring the Church to heel. Two world wars had centred in Christendom and had been fought with weapons and machines invented and manufactured in Christendom. The early 1960's saw the world divided into two hostile camps. Although Europe, the Americas, and Australasia were more prosperous than ever, a Damoclean sword which they had forged hung precariously over their heads. A third world war fought with atomic weapons might end all civilization as men had known it. In view of this situation had not Christianity failed, and was not the world entering the post-Christian era? So many were saying.

At the beginning of the nineteenth-century stage of the revolutionary age the prospect for Christianity appeared sufficiently sombre to warrant this grim prognosis. Christianity, whether Roman Catholic, Protestant, or Eastern, was in a parlous condition. The vast majority of Christians were in churches which were tied hand and foot to the state and to a political structure much of which was to be swept aside in the ensuing decades. In France, Spain, and Portugal Church and Crown seemed inseparable. The crown named the bishops. The bishops were from the aristocracy and between them and the lower clergy a vast gulf yawned—in income and in social status. Except in the Papal States the Pope had little effective authority, and in the Papal States misgovernment was a chronic scandal. The wearers of the tiara were men of good character, but few of them were forceful and most of them were accused of nepotism. In the Rhine Valley the archbishops were secular princes and were encouraged by Febronianism to regard themselves as independent of the See of Peter except in doctrine and Communion. Throughout Europe Deism and the Enlightenment were eroding the faith of the intelligentsia, of whatever communion. In the

Protestant parts of Germany with its many states, large and small, the rulers controlled the churches. In Scotland the landlords named the clergy of the established church. In the Church of England pluralism abounded and the bishops spent much of the year in London rather than in their dioceses. Scandinavia was in the midst of the brandy age, with some of its clergy alcoholics. In Russia Peter the Great had replaced the patriarchate with the Holy Synod, subject to the tsar's control. In the Turkish realms, which still embraced the Balkans and Greece as well as Western Asia and most of North Africa, the Moslem rulers controlled the churches; in effect the chief ecclesiastic, the Ecumenical Patriarch, bought his office from them.

In that contradictory world other facts showed that Christianity, far from being moribund, was very much alive. If the entire globe is taken into consideration, never had Christianity been as potent in the life of mankind as a whole as it was when these lines were written. As we have again and again reminded ourselves, from its outset Christianity had a dream and a purpose which embraced all men. In the revolutionary age for the first time in history it had the opportunity to make that dream and purpose effective. The entire world was now a neighbourhood, become so through movements which issued from the region where Christianity had longest had opportunity to shape human society. By the mid-twentieth century the influence of the faith had reached greater proportions than ever before and it was mounting. Christianity was still a minority movement. Those who professed to be its adherents were a mere fraction of mankind and of that fraction only a smaller minority took the faith seriously enough to be fully committed to it. Because of the rapid increase of population, in 1962 the world had more non-Christians than at any previous time. Yet never had Christianity or any other religion been as widely represented as in that year nor had it or any other faith done as much to shape the race as a whole.

The impact of the faith was seen in what had formerly been called Christendom. A large proportion of the population of that area had drifted away from all but a very nominal connexion and could be described as de-Christianized, but never had Christendom been really Christian. Earlier the formal profession had been there and state and Church combined to enforce outward conformity. All aspects of Western civilization bore the impress of Christianity. But, as we have suggested, even in the so-called "ages of faith" no aspect, including the Church itself, fully conformed to the ideals set forth by Christ and His Apostles, and much was in stark contrast to the Gospel—even when under the Christian name. In the nineteenth and especially the twentieth century in a variety of ways Christianity was having a striking and in some features of the life of the quondam Christendom a growing effect.

Much of this we have seen as we pursued our narrative. Here we can only remind ourselves of a few examples. In the nineteenth century the Christian conscience brought an end to Negro slavery, which early accompanied the European expansion beginning in the fifteenth century. In the British Empire and the United States emancipation was brought about largely through those impelled by Evangelical Protestantism. In Latin America it stemmed from a humanitarianism which was not professedly Christian but was indebted to the influence of Christianity. To counter the suffering brought by war, in the second half of the nineteenth century the Red Cross arose from the determination of a young Genevan who was the spiritual son of the Protestant *Réveil* in his native city. In the twentieth century the League of Nations and the United Nations were the creation primarily of men who derived their purpose from the Christian faith, mostly through Protestantism, and were sustained by it. The Red Cross, the League of Nations, and the United Nations enlisted many who had slight or no connexion with Christianity, but in their inception they were the fruits of the Gospel.

In Western Europe many movements, some of them of twentieth-century origin, were deepening the faith of millions. In the Roman Catholic Church were seen, among others, the Liturgical Movement, Eucharistic Congresses, Catholic Action, increased devotion to Mary, and Christian Democratic Parties. So actively did they enlist the laity that the twentieth century was called the century of the laity, and "the priesthood of the laity" was a current phrase. The nineteenth century was marked by the creation of more new congregations than in any other hundred years in history. Although few new ones appeared in the twentieth century, in its first five decades existing orders and congregations were strengthened. From the Roman Catholics of Europe a mounting number of missionaries spread the faith outside the Occident. In the nineteenth century more Roman Catholic missionaries went from France than from all the rest of the world, and the twentieth century saw more Roman Catholic missionaries from France than from any other one country. This was the more significant in view of the active anti-clericalism in nineteenth-century France and the progressive de-Christianization of large elements of the population. The nineteenth and twentieth centuries witnessed a striking increase in the authority of the Papacy. Never had the Popes been able to control and direct the Roman Catholic Church as effectively as in those years. The See of Peter had a succession of able and deeply religious Pontiffs. Here was a church under centralized leadership which enlisted the growing intelligent adherence of millions of the faithful set against the de-Christianizing forces of the age.

In Western Europe Protestantism was making somewhat similar gains. In the nineteenth century it was being reinvigorated by several movements. On the Continent Pietist awakenings stirred the Lutheran and Reformed Churches and a revived confessionalism in Lutheran and Reformed circles offset some of the debilitating effects of the *Aufklärung*. In the British Isles Evangelicalism brought fresh life to the nonconforming and the established churches, and the Oxford Movement, paralleling the renewed confessionalism on the Continent, worked a deeper devotion and a greater emphasis on worship. Both the Continent and the British Isles saw notable efforts towards fresh thinking in theology and the study of the Bible to take account of the intellectual currents of the day. Extensive attempts were made—for example, by the Inner Mission in Germany and Christian Socialism and the Salvation Army in England—to bring the Christian faith to bear upon the social problems which accompanied the revolutionary age. To a much greater degree than formerly Protestants sought to spread the Gospel throughout the world. As Western Europe moved into the twentieth century several of the nineteenth-century movements continued. After World War II had dealt additional blows to the fabric of society and among millions the secularism born of the age of revolution was making inroads, numbers of new movements were seen, some of them only among minorities, others affecting larger numbers, and all of them indications that Protestantism, far from dying, was putting forth fresh shoots: the Evangelical Academies and the *Kirchentag* in Germany, *Kerk en Wereld* in the Netherlands, Sigtuna in Sweden, the Iona Community and the "Tell Scotland" movement, and the industrial chaplaincies in England.

In Eastern Europe where at the outset of the nineteenth century the Church seemed somnolent and corrupt, the Russian Orthodox Church experienced a fresh surge of piety and the churches of Greece and the Balkans, freed from the Moslem Turkish yoke, showed improvement in the quality of their life. The triumph of Communism, in Russia after World War I and in the Balkans after World War II, at first seemed to have doomed Christianity to extinction. But by the 1960's the Russian Orthodox Church had staged a remarkable recovery, Russian Protestantsism was flourishing, and in the Balkans the churches, while beleaguered, were very much alive.

In the world outside Europe, where dwelt the large majority of mankind, Christianity was increasingly a force with which to reckon, in at least five ways. (1) Christianity was continuing to spread and was more widely represented than it or any other religion had ever been. (2) By 1962 that spread was achieved less through government support and direction than at any time since the conversion of Constantine early in the fourth century. (3) Christianity was becoming more deeply rooted among more peoples than at any previous time. (4) Christianity was having a wider effect on mankind outside Europe than it or any other religion had ever exerted. (5) Christians were coming together in a global fellowship embracing both Europeans and non-Europeans as they had not previously done. By 1962 in none of these five ways had a consummation been reached. The world contained more non-Christians than at any earlier time and some of the non-Christian religions were showing fresh vigour and were being propagated among European peoples. As earlier, Christianity had its chief strength in Europe and among peoples of European ancestry. Prestige continued to accrue to Christianity because of its association with Western culture. Christianity was far from moulding the life of all mankind. Christians were still divided: the movement towards unity was only in its infancy. Some of the chronic ills from which mankind suffered had never reached such colossal dimensions: indeed, much of their growth was through forces issuing from the traditional Christendom. We must now go into these generalizations somewhat more extensively but still, necessarily, in a highly summary fashion. Many of the details have been seen in earlier pages.

Christianity was continuing to spread and was more widely represented than it or any other religion had ever been. Much of that spread had come about by the migration of European peoples to the Americas, Australia, New Zealand, and South Africa. However, that did not mean that the migrants automatically held to the Christian faith of their ancestors. As the years passed, the churches had less and less of the support of the state which they had possessed in Europe. In Latin America the Church-state tie proved a handicap and gave rise to serious conflicts which helped to drive many from the official religion. In several countries, notably the United States, at the beginning of the nineteenth century only a small minority of the population were members of churches. In the United States, by mid-twentieth century the most populous and strongest of the countries which had arisen by migration from Europe, with the exception of two decades (those of the Civil War and of World War I) the proportion of church membership in the population had continued to mount. That increase owed very little to help from Europe and was due largely to indigenous leadership. We must also note the spread of Christianity among the Negroes and the Indians in the United States, the former mostly through Protestants and the latter through both Protestants and Roman Catholics. During the nineteenth century Christianity was a waning force in Latin America. After World War I, however, it displayed a marked revival, largely through Protestantism but also through circles in the Roman Catholic Church.

Christianity spread outside Europe by conversions from non-European peoples, mostly in Asia, Africa, the islands of the Pacific, off the south and south-east coasts of Asia, and in Madagascar. Of the missions responsible, both Roman Catholic and Protestant, the former came mostly from Europe and the latter increasingly from North America, mainly the United States. Very few Moslems were converted. In India the proportion of Christians mounted, particularly in the twentieth century, and chiefly from the depressed groups and the hill tribes. In Burma the spread was predominantly among animistic peoples, mainly the Karens. It was slight in Thailand, Cambodia, and Laos but, in the

Roman Catholic form, was marked in Vietnam. Christians, mostly Protestant, multiplied in Indonesia, strikingly among the Bataks but also among animistic folk in the eastern part of the archipelago. Protestantism flourished in the Philippines, but mainly by conversions from the Roman Catholic Church. In the second half of the nineteenth century and until the Communist domination of the mainland (in 1949-1950) the proportion of Christians in China increased, both Protestant and Roman Catholic, but was never more than one per cent. of the population. After 1950 Christianity lost numbers in mainland China but persisted, and conversions were still recorded. In Korea the growth began in the 1880's, after a century of persecution, and thereafter was notable, chiefly of Protestants, but also of Roman Catholics. In 1960 about a sixth of the population of the Republic of Korea bore the Christian name. In Japan in the nineteenth and twentieth centuries never more than one in a hundred called themselves Christians. The majority of the Christians were Protestants, a substantial minority were Roman Catholics, and a small minority were Orthodox. During the nineteenth century Christianity, mostly Protestantism, spread rapidly in the islands of the Pacific, phenomenally among Polynesians and Micronesians, but also to a certain extent among Melanesians. In the twentieth century it advanced more slowly, and chiefly in mountainous and densely forested New Guinea (Papua). In the nineteenth century it began to make gains in Africa south of the Sahara. In the twentieth century its spread was very rapid, until by the 1960's in some areas between a fourth and a third of the population were baptized. Latterly the expansion was more pronounced through the Roman Catholic Church than through Protestantism. Concurrently the Christians multiplied in Madagascar, but more through Protestantism than the Roman Catholic Church: late in the 1950's about a third of the Malagasy were among the baptized. Although in many countries outside the Occident, among them the most populous, at the middle of the twentieth century Christians were small minorities, in others, especially among animistic peoples, their rate of growth was rising. In 1962 only one country which claimed political independence was without an organized church.

The numerical growth of Christianity took place more and more without government support; by 1962 there was less government support than at any time since early in the fourth century. With a few exceptions, in countries peopled by Europeans and their descendants the separation of Church and state was accomplished before the end of the nineteenth century. Christianity spread and the churches were maintained by the voluntary efforts of their members. In Asia, Africa, and the islands of the sea, in the nineteenth century some help was accorded by the colonial governments, mainly through subsidies to education under Christian auspices. But this was usually not because the schools were Christian but because they introduced their pupils to Western forms of learning which would enable their graduates to fit into the revolutionary age. After World War I and especially after World War II, with the rising wave of revolt against Western imperialism and colonialism, the connexion of Christianity with European culture was often more a handicap than an asset. In some quarters a degree of prestige attached to Christianity because of its association with the civilization from which millions desired to learn. But thousands of those impressed by that civilization were intent on acquiring the mechanical appliances of the Western world—to their mind responsible for its power and wealth—and spurned the religion which paralleled them. As a reaction against colonialism and imperialism, because of pride in their historic culture and irritation at the white man's attitude of superiority, many clung to their historic faiths.

By the mid-twentieth century Christianity was more firmly rooted among more peoples than it or any other religion had ever been. Long before World War I the Protestant churches of the United States and Canada had ceased to depend on Europe for clergy or financial support. In Australia and New Zealand the trend was in a similar direction. Although in the 1960's the Roman Catholic Church in the United States continued to obtain many of its priests from Ireland, it was sending more missionaries abroad than it was receiving. In Latin America the Roman Catholic Church was still dependent on other lands for many of its clergy, at first Europe and latterly the United States as well. But in the twentieth century the Roman Catholic episcopate was indigenous and the rapidly growing Protestantism was increasingly so. In Asia, Africa, and the islands of the sea both the Roman Catholic Church and Protestantism were more and more staffed by nationals. In some lands where political exigencies compelled all white missionaries to withdraw, the faith continued to spread. For example, when during World War II the Japanese occupation deprived the Bataks and the Karens of Western missionaries, the numbers of Christians among them continued to mount. The Communists compelled the severing of ties between the Christians on the mainland of China and the outer world, but Christianity, although crippled, persisted.

In the nineteenth and especially the twentieth century Christianity was having deeper and wider effects upon mankind as a whole than ever before. They usually defied accurate measurement. Frequently the very presence of a contribution was debatable. For example, following World War II the government of the United States through the Marshall Plan substantially aided in the economic recovery of much of Western Europe. It also assisted the rehabilitation of its late enemy, Japan. To what extent, if any, these measures sprang from the Christian faith of their initiators and how far from national self-interest would be impossible to ascertain. In some movements a motivation of Christian origin was clear, but even in them other factors were present. The abolition of the international African slave trade was deeply indebted to English Evangelicals, notably to Wilberforce, but the adherence of governments was often due to selfish interest. Lord Shaftesbury's labours for social reform were closely related to his Evangelical faith, but not all who voted for the legislation which he sponsored had that as their dominant impulse. For Livingstone the entrance of the Gospel and the end of the Arab-Portuguese slave trade were major objectives sprung from his Christian faith, but even he would probably have been unable to say to what extent they were compounded by a love of adventure and the spirit of the explorer. In the United States numbers of educational projects were initiated and carried through by men and women impelled by their Christian faith, but many of their supporters were motivated by a combination of selfishness and altruism. Abraham Lincoln was not a member of a church, but in some of his utterances, notably his second inaugural address, his Christian faith was conspicuous. Yet he was also an astute politician, and in his aspiration for public office personal ambition played a part. Woodrow Wilson, the chief creator of the League of Nations, and John Foster Dulles, to whom the United Nations owed much, were devout Christians, but many who laboured for both institutions would have hesitated to confess a Christian purpose.

In Asia and Africa, where Christians were minorities, though growing minorities, the influence of Christ was present and although far from dominant was much more marked in the first half of the twentieth century than in the nineteenth century and more a force in the nineteenth century than in earlier years. We can pause simply for a few examples. Christian missionaries were the pioneers of modern medicine in China, Africa, and much of India and the Middle East. Through schools they helped prepare the peoples of those lands to adjust to the revolutionary age into which they were being hurried. Again and again they opened doors of opportunity to underprivileged segments of the population and to women. Rabindranath Tagore would not have called himself a Christian, but he sprang from the Brahmo Samaj, and the Brahmo Samaj owed much to the contacts of its founders with the Christian faith. His poetry and his school had a profound effect on thousands. Gandhi refused to be called a Christian, but he was glad to confess himself indebted to the teachings and example of Christ and through him all India felt the impact of Christ. When Gandhi succumbed to an assassin, thousands of Indians said that he died a Christ-like death. In that they were tacitly accepting Christ as the standard by which to measure their national hero and were catching a glimpse of the vicarious suffering which is at the heart of the Gospel.

Sometimes the contributions of Christianity were so badly garbled that they became the enemy of the faith. The most notable instance was Communism. Marx, its chief formulator, was of Jewish parentage but had been reared a Christian. Engels, his collaborator, was of Christian ancestry and in his youth had been a member of warm Pietist circles. In its dogmatic proclamation of the goal of social evolution as a classless society and its confidence that the course of history led towards this goal, Communism had much which was so akin to Christian eschatology and apocalypticism that some called it a Christian heresy. Yet in its atheism, its nurture of hatred, and its endorsement of war to achieve its purpose it set itself against basic Christian convictions.

Of the fashion in which Christians were coming together, we must not take the space to enlarge on what was said in the last chapter. Clearly here was something new in history, a reversal, as yet far from complete, of the age-long fissiparousness which from its beginning had been a feature of Christianity.

What if anything is the meaning of the story we have endeavoured to narrate and in this chapter to summarize? May we say at once that much seems strangely to fit into what Christians have believed about the universe, mankind, God, and the fashion in which God works?

Christians believe that God created the universe in which man finds himself. Although men stand confounded by what seems to them the unimaginable vastness and age of the universe, and although much in it appears to men to be evil, Christians insist that the universe is the work of God and that God continues in it and yet is not identical with it. They believe that God is love, that He so loved the world that He gave of His very Self to suffer and die for the world. They hold that in the beginning was the *Logos,* the Word, through Whom God expresses Himself, that the *Logos* was with God and was God. They maintain that once in history the Logos became flesh, that Jesus of Nazareth was fully man and fully God, and that the Incarnate *Logos* dwelt among men full of grace and truth. By grace they mean the love which men can never deserve or earn and of which by the heritage of their long past and their individual thoughts and acts they are completely unworthy. By truth they mean that in the Incarnate Word they are permitted to see into the very heart of the Great Reality, God, and so to gain insight into the significance of the universe and of their individual lives and the history of mankind. They note that the Incarnate Word came in what appeared to men weakness, born to a humble Galilean mother, "a little baby thing" for Whom there was no room in the inn. They remember that most of His life was passed in obscurity, in a small hill town and not in Jerusalem, the centre of His people's history and worship. They recall that after a few months in the public eye He died on a Roman cross, seemingly a pitiable failure.

But in that death Paul, in one of his most famous passages, saw the power of God and the wisdom of God.[1] He recognized that the Jew who expected the fulfilment of his national hope by physical force regarded the cross as weakness,

[1] I Cor. 1:18–25.

and that to the Greek, trained by philosophy in a particular use of reason, the cross seemed not to make sense and was folly. From the standpoint of human wisdom the road which Jesus followed could only end in the complete failure of what He was presumably seeking to accomplish. Yet Paul saw in the cross both the power of God and the wisdom of God.

The course of history has confirmed that insight. As Christians see it, in the long process by which He brought human beings into existence on this planet—from the standpoint of His vast universe merely a small speck rotating around one of the hundreds of millions of stars—God sought to create sons and not robots and gave them a degree of free will. Otherwise they would not be like Him. That freedom was conditioned both by heredity and environment (here is one of the moot issues with which through the ages thoughtful men have wrestled in their philosophies and their religions and which continues to perplex Christians). Christians have maintained that God, too great to be fully comprehended by man's understanding and powerful enough to bring into existence and to govern this vast universe, has at His very heart love. By "love" they understand the self-giving love seen in God's incarnation in Jesus of Nazareth. By its very nature that love could express itself in no other way than by coming in seeming weakness and would anticipate that some men, moved by self-concern, would endeavour to rid themselves of that expression and others, the friends of Jesus, not understanding, would stand helplessly by while self-concern worked its will.

But to the great surprise of the disciples the cross was not the end. The inner group soon had experiences which convinced them—against their initial despair—that the tomb in which His body had been laid was left empty by His resurrection, that Jesus continued to exist, and that He was more radiant and powerful than He had ever been in His flesh. They saw in the cross not defeat but triumph. From what they found growing in themselves and what they observed in others they were sure that God was working through the Holy Spirit, Who is also God, Who had been sent by Jesus, Who in some sense which they could not fully explain is one with Jesus and with Him Whom Jesus called Father.

From their own lives and the lives of others the disciples realized that, as they said (trying to put into words what broke through language and escaped), to those who received Him the Incarnate Son gave power to become, like Himself, sons of God. Again—and only figurative language could be employed, imperfectly, to describe a great fact—here was a new birth. The life to which that new birth introduced them was to go on forever. It was marked by what Paul called the "fruits of the Spirit": "love" (of the kind which God showed in Jesus), "joy" (a wondering joy that the kind of life which they saw in others and found developing in themselves was real), "peace" (peace in their own inner struggles and their struggles with their environment), "patience, kindness, goodness, faithfulness, gentleness, self-control." Those fruits did not immediately appear in their perfection, but in those who yielded themselves to the Spirit they continued to increase.

Early Christians whom later centuries adjudged to be nearest "the mind of Christ" did not blind their eyes to the existence of suffering and evil. They saw about them nature, red in tooth and claw, in travail like a woman in childbirth. They looked upon it as the creation of God. One of them said that God had subjected it to futility, but in hope, and that in His own good time it would be set free from its bondage to decay and "obtain the glorious liberty of the children of God." By "liberty" was meant freedom from the bondage to sin, suffering, and evil. They were convinced that "the God and Father of our Lord Jesus Christ" in "the fullness of time" would "gather in one all things in Christ, both which are in heaven and which are on earth." They insisted that Jesus had assured them that against His Church the gates of hell would not prevail. The imagery was that of evil as a beleaguered city which ultimately would succumb to the insistent siege of the Church founded on Christ and in some sense His body.

The story which we have attempted to narrate fits into this pattern. As the incarnation provoked men to their greatest crime, the crucifixion of the Son of God, so through the peoples among whom the Gospel has longest had its nearest approach to free course several of the chronic evils of mankind have had their largest development. Such have been African slavery, war, the kind of tyranny and atheism embodied in Communism, the practical denial of God embodied in secularism, the exploitation of labour in the early and some of the later stages of the Industrial Revolution, and the application of atomic energy to wasteful and destructive uses rather than to human welfare. This misuse of God's good gifts, some of which came through confidence in Him and in faith derived from Him to explore and utilize His universe, was to be expected from the measure of free will which God has given to man in His desire to beget sons and not to create robots.

On the other hand, from among the peoples through whom the chronic evils have had their most colossal dimensions have issued the most extensive efforts to curb and eliminate these evils that men have ever known. Many of the efforts have clearly been from motives derived from Christ. Others are traceable to a culture which had been permeated with ideals exemplified in Christ.

The continued geographic spread of Christianity and its increasing rootage in other peoples than Europeans in an age when forces issuing from the perversion of the faith in the former Christendom have been mounting are evidence of vigour and universality. The ecclesiastical bodies through which the faith has spread have never been pure embodiments of the faith. In them, as in individual Christians, have existed contradictions between aspiration and attainment. Yet in them the fruits of the Spirit have been present. Frequently the fruits have been most marked among humble folk and in lowly circles which escape the historian. That, too, was to be anticipated from the nature of the Gospel and the manner in which it came to men.

What does the future hold in store? That the historian as historian cannot wisely say. He realizes that from the long perspective of history the course of Christianity thus far has been very brief and that the century and a half to which his five volumes have been devoted cover only a moment. He perceives as he looks back across the years that, measured by the criteria of area covered, inner vigour, and the effect on mankind as a whole, Christianity, beginning in a very unpromising fashion, has gone forward by a series of pulsations of advance, retreat, and advance. Each advance has carried the Christian tide farther than its predecessor, and each major recession has been shorter and less marked than the one before it. He recognizes that in the mid-twentieth century, if mankind is viewed as a whole, Christianity is more a force in the human scene than it or any other religion has ever been. He is aware that these generalizations are cold comfort to those who think, as did Jesus, of individuals, for their lives are too brief to wait for the triumphal consummation which this perspective appears to forecast—when all men will be brought to discipleship, incorporated in the Church, and taught to conform to the high standards which Jesus set for His disciples. He remembers a parable of Jesus which speaks of the wheat and the weeds as *growing* together in the same field. As a historian he believes he has discerned that this is what has happened and is happening—that the chronic ills and evils of mankind are increasing and that the forces issuing from the love of God in Christ are also mounting. Yet as a Christian he recalls that God sent His Son into the world not to condemn the world, but that the world through Him might be saved. He reminds himself that the ancient prophet represents God as saying: "My word . . . shall not return to me void but shall accomplish what I please and shall prosper in the thing whereto I sent it." As a historian he cannot be confident of the outcome. As a Christian he is sustained by the realization that history does not disclose all and that life does not stop with physical death. Believing as he does in personal immortality, not as a mere continuation of existence but as eternal fellowship with the risen and triumphant Christ and with those who had entered upon the life with Christ in a growing knowledge and love of God, he trusts that in ways which he cannot distinguish the seemingly impossible hope will be realized and that God, Who revealed His love in Christ and is ever seeking the wanderers, will triumph not only among human spirits but also in the entire universe, both—to men this side of death—seen and unseen. He sees much in history which puzzles him but nothing that clearly makes this hope illusory.

BIBLIOGRAPHY

As in the preceding volumes, the bibliography includes only those titles which have been cited more than once in the footnotes. For the other works, fully and perhaps twice or three times as numerous, to which only one reference was made, the appropriate bibliographic data are given in the footnote where the citation occurs.

Abrams, Ray H., *Preachers Present Arms* (New York, Round Table Press, 1933, pp. xix, 297). An expanded doctoral dissertation.

Acta Apostolicae Sedis. Commentarium Officiale (Rome, Typis Polyglottis Vaticanis, 1909 ff.).

Alameda, Julian, *Argentina Católica* (Buenos Aires, PP. Benedictinos, 1935, pp. 1031). Largely historical, by a Benedictine.

Allen, Yorke, *A Seminary Survey* (New York, Harper & Brothers, 1960, pp. xxvi, 640). A remarkably comprehensive detailed survey of Protestant, Roman Catholic, and Orthodox theological seminaries in Africa, Asia, and Latin America.

Aloysius, Brother, *The De La Salle Brothers in Australia, 1906–1956* (Sydney, Halstead Press, 1956, pp. xv, 160). By a member of the congregation.

Anderson, Gerald H., editor, *The Theology of the Christian Mission* (New York, McGraw-Hill Book Co., 1961, pp. xvii, 341). A series of studies, mostly by contemporary Protestants, on various aspects of the subject.

Annuaire des Missions Catholiques de Chine, 1941 (Shanghai, Bureau Sinologique de Zi-ka-wei, 1941, pp. xvi, 88).

Arcila Robledo, Gregorio, *La Orden Franciscana en la America Meridional* (Rome, Pontificio Ateneo Antoniano, 1948, pp. xviii, 416). Detailed history and contemporary situation.

Attwater, Donald, *The Christian Churches of the East* (Milwaukee, The Bruce Publishing Co., 2 vols., rev. ed., 1947). Scholarly, by a Roman Catholic.

Attwater, Donald, *The Dissident Eastern Churches* (Milwaukee, The Bruce Publishing Co., 1937, pp. xviii, 349). Scholarly and objective, by a Roman Catholic.

Australia and Reunion. Being the Official Report of Proceedings of the Reunion Conference between Representatives of the Anglican, Presbyterian, Methodist and Congregational Churches in Australia, Holden at the Chapter House, St. Andrew's Cathedral, Sydney, on March 28, 29, 1922 (Sydney, Angus and Robertson, 1922, pp. 144).

The Australian Encyclopaedia (East Lansing, Michigan State University Press, 1958, 10 vols.).

Azevedo, Thales de, *O Catolicismo no Brasil um Campo para a Pesquisa Social* (no city, Ministério da Educaçao e Cutura, no date, but clearly in the 1950's, pp. 70). Mainly factual. Well documented.

Báez Camargo, G., and Grubb, Kenneth G., *Religion in the Republic of Mexico* (London, World Dominion Press, 1935, pp. 166). By Protestant experts.

Ballou, Earle H., *Dangerous Opportunity. The Christian Mission in China Today*

(New York, Friendship Press, 1940, pp. xi, 211). Carefully done by a Protestant missionary with long experience in China.

Bane, Martin J., *Catholic Pioneers in West Africa* (Dublin, Clonmore and Reynolds, 1956, pp. 220). A useful, sympathetic sketch, bringing the story into the 1950's.

Barnes, William Wright, *The Southern Baptist Convention, 1845–1953* (Nashville, Broadman Press, 1954, pp. x, 330). An official history.

Barry, Colman J., *Worship and Work* (Collegeville, Minn., St. John's Abbey, 1956, pp. 447). An official history of the Benedictine abbey and university at Collegeville, Minn.

Bates, M. Searle, *Religious Liberty. An Inquiry* (New York, Harper & Brothers, 1945, pp. xviii, 604). An authoritative factual survey.

Bates, Margaret, editor, *The Lay Apostolate in Latin America Today. Proceedings of the 1959 Symposium Held under the Auspices of the Institute of Ibero American Studies of the Catholic University of America,* (Washington, The Catholic University of America Press, 1960, pp. iv, 66).

Beach, Harlan P., *A Geography and Atlas of Protestant Missions* (New York, Student Volunteer Movement for Foreign Missions, 2 vols., 1903).

Beach, Harlan P., and Fahs, Charles H., *World Missionary Atlas* (New York, Institute of Social and Religious Research, 1925, pp. 178). Authoritative for Protestant missions.

Beach, Harlan P., and St. John, Burton, editors, *World Statistics of Christian Missions* (New York, The Committee of Reference and Counsel of the Foreign Missions Conference of North America, 1916, pp. 148). Authoritative.

Beckmann, Johannes, *Die katholische Kirche im neuen Afrika* (Einsiedeln, Verlagsanstalt Benzier & Co., 1947, pp. 372). A comprehensive history and account of current conditions.

Bögler, Theodor, editor, *Liturgische Erneuerung in aller Welt* (Maria Lach, Verlag Ars Liturgica, 1950, pp. 174). A useful country-by-country survey.

Bolshakoff, Serge, *The Foreign Missions of the Russian Orthodox Church* (London, Society for Promoting Christian Knowledge, 1943, pp. 120). A good summary, something of an *apologia*.

Braden, Charles Samuel, *War, Communism and World Religions* (New York, Harper & Brothers, 1953, pp. 281). Observations from a journey in Asia in 1952 by an expert on religion.

Braga, Erasmus, and Grubb, Kenneth G., *The Republic of Brazil. A Survey of the Religious Situation* (London, World Dominion Press, 1932, pp. 184). Competent, by Protestants, mainly on Protestantism.

Brauer, Jerald C., *Protestantism in America. A Narrative History* (Philadelphia, The Westminster Press, 1953, pp. 307). A useful survey, chiefly on the pre-twentieth-century years.

Britannica Book of the Year (Chicago, Encyclopaedia Britannica, 1938 ff.).

Brown, Arthur Judson, *One Hundred Years. A History of the Foreign Missionary Work of the Presbyterian Church in the U.S.A., with Some Account of Countries, Peoples, and the Policies and Problems of Modern Missions* (New York, Fleming

H. Revell Co., ca. 1936, pp. 1140). By a secretary emeritus of the Board of Foreign Missions of the Presbyterian Church in the U.S.A.

Brown, L. W., *The Indian Christians of St. Thomas. An Account of the Ancient Syrian Church of Malabar* (Cambridge University Press, 1956, pp. xii, 315). Careful and scholarly, by an Anglican bishop with intimate knowledge.

Brown, William Adams, May, Mark, and Shuttleworth, Frank K., *The Education of American Ministers* (New York, Institute of Social and Religious Research, 4 vols., 1934). Based on prolonged study and research.

Browning, Webster E., *The River Plate Republics. A Survey of the Religious, Economic and Social Conditions in Argentina, Paraguay and Uruguay* (London, World Dominion Press, 1928, pp. 139). By a Protestant expert.

Browning, Webster E., Ritchie, John, and Grubb, Kenneth G., *The West Coast Republics of South America. Chile, Peru and Bolivia* (London, World Dominion Press, 1930, pp. 183). By Protestant experts.

Brunner, Edmund de S., *Immigrant Farmers and Their Children* (Garden City, N.Y., Doubleday, Doran and Co., 1929, pp. xvii, 277). Based upon careful study, especially of four immigrant communities.

Burma, John H., *Spanish-Speaking Groups in the United States* (Durham, N.C., Duke University Press, 1954, pp. ix, 209). Carefully done.

Burton, J. W., *Missionary Survey of the Pacific Islands* (London, World Dominion Press, 1930, pp. 124). By a Protestant expert.

Callcott, Wilfrid Hardy, *Liberalism in Mexico 1857–1929* (Stanford University Press, 1931, pp. xiii, 410). Based on extensive research.

Camargo, G. Báez, and Grubb, Kenneth G., *Religion in the Republic of Mexico* (London, World Dominion Press, 1935, pp. 166). By Protestant experts.

Carter, Paul A., *The Decline and Revival of the Social Gospel: Social and Political Liberalism in American Protestant Churches, 1920–1940* (Ithaca, N.Y., Cornell University Press, 1954, pp. x, 265). Based on a Columbia University doctoral dissertation.

Catholic Directory of India, 1918. 68th Annual Issue of the Madras Catholic Directory and Annual General Register (Madras, The Madras Catholic Supply Co., pp. 554).

The Catholic Historical Review (Washington, The Catholic University of America, 1915 ff.).

Chelliah, V. A., and McLeish, Alexander, *Malaya and Singapore. Survey Directory of Churches and Missions in the Federation and Colony* (London, World Dominion Press, 1948, pp. 36). Carefully done under expert direction.

China Bulletin (New York, The Far Eastern Office of the Division of Foreign Missions, NCCC/USA, 1951 ff.). An official Protestant publication, specializing in news of Protestantism in China, especially Communist China, but also with information on the general situation.

China Bulletin (Hong Kong). See *China Missionary Bulletin.*

The China Christian Year Book. The title adopted in 1926 for *The China Mission Year Book.*

The China Mission Year Book (beginning in 1926 *The China Christian Year Book*)

(Shanghai, The Christian Literature Society for China, 1911–1937, with some interruptions). A standard annual Protestant publication.

China Missionary Bulletin (Hong Kong, 1948 ff.). A Roman Catholic periodical under various titles—*China Missionary, China Bulletin, Mission Bulletin.* The later volumes are not confined to China.

The Chinese Recorder (published in Foochow, 1867, as the *Missionary Recorder,* at Foochow, 1868–1872, as *The Chinese Recorder and Missionary Journal,* and at Shanghai, 1874–1941. Beginning about 1911 the title was shortened to *The Chinese Recorder*). The standard interdenominational Protestant missionary journal for China.

The Christian Century: An Undenominational Journal of Religion (Chicago, 1884 ff.). Begun as *The Christian Oracle* and from 1901 with the title given above.

The Christian College in India. The Report of the Commission on Christian Higher Education in India (New York, Oxford University Press, 1931, pp. xiii, 388). A standard survey.

The Christian Handbook of India, 1954–1955 (London, World Dominion Press, 1955, pp. xv, 360). Begun in 1902 as *Directory of Christian Missions.* Published biennially. In 1932 it became *Directory of Churches and Missions* and had various titles. By the collaboration of the National Christian Council and the World Dominion Press.

The Christian Handbook of South Africa. Die Suid-Afraanse Kristen-Handboek (Lovedale, South Africa. The Lovedale Press, 1938, pp. viii, 289).

The Christian Movement in Japan. Under various titles—*The Japan Mission Year Book, The Christian Movement in the Japanese Empire, The Christian Movement in Japan, Korea, and Formosa, The Japan Christian Year Book* (Yokohama and Tokyo, 1903–1941, 1950 ff.).

The Christian Occupation of China. Edited by Milton C. Stauffer (Shanghai, China Continuation Committee, 1922, pp. 468, cxii). An elaborate Protestant study and survey.

The Christian Scholar (continuing *Christian Education*) (New York, Commission on Christian Higher Education, National Council of the Churches of Christ in the U.S.A., 1917 ff.). A quarterly journal.

Christianity and Crisis. A Christian Journal of Opinion (New York, 1941 ff.). Published in association with Union Theological Seminary.

Christianity Today (Washington, 1957 ff.). A conservative Protestant fortnightly periodical.

Church History (Berne, Ind., 1932 ff.). The official organ of the American Society of Church History.

Cole, Stewart G., *The History of Fundamentalism* (New York, Richard R. Smith, 1931, pp. xiv, 360). Based on the sources.

Coleman, William J., *Latin-American Catholicism. A Self-Evaluation* (Maryknoll, N.Y., Maryknoll Publications, 1958, pp. v, 105). By a Roman Catholic expert.

Considine, John J., *Call for Forty Thousand* (New York, Longmans, Green and Co., 1946, pp. 319). Report of an extensive journey in Latin America by a Maryknoll priest describing the condition of the Roman Catholic Church.

Considine, J. J., *The Catholic Church in Today's Latin America* (typescript of lecture in the Yale University Divinity School, December 9, 1959).

Considine, John J., *New Horizons in Latin America* (New York, Dodd, Mead and Co., 1958, pp. xvi, 379). A semi-popular survey by an expert.

Cooksey, J. J., and McLeish, Alexander, *Religion and Civilization in West Africa. A Missionary Survey of French, British, Spanish and Portuguese West Africa, with Liberia* (London, World Dominion Press, 1931, pp. 277). By experts, on Protestant missions.

Crabtree, A. R., *Baptists in Brazil* (Rio de Janeiro, The Baptist Publishing House of Brazil, 1953, pp. 236). A competent record by a Southern Baptist missionary.

Crawford, William Rex, *A Century of Latin-American Thought* (Cambridge, Mass., Harvard University Press, 1944, pp. 320). Competent.

Cuevas, Mariano, *Historia de la Iglesia en México* (El Paso, Tex., Editorial "Revista Catolica," 5 vols., 1928). By a Jesuit.

Cuninggim, Merrimon, *The College Seeks Religion* (New Haven, Conn., Yale University Press, 1947, pp. x, 319). Based on a doctoral dissertation, by a Protestant.

Dabbs, Norman H., *Dawn Over the Bolivian Hills* (Toronto, Canadian Baptist Foreign Mission Board, 1952, pp. 276). A history of the Canadian Baptist Mission in Bolivia.

Davis, J. Merle, *The Church in the New Jamaica. A Study of the Economic and Social Basis of the Evangelical Church in Jamaica* (New York, International Missionary Council, 1942, pp. x, 100). Careful, competent.

Davis, J. Merle, *The Church in Puerto Rico's Dilemma* (New York, International Missionary Council, 1942, pp. viii, 80). Based on a careful, first-hand study.

Davis, J. Merle, *The Cuban Church in a Sugar Economy* (New York, International Missionary Council, 1942, pp. 109). An authoritative survey.

Davis, J. Merle, *The Economic Basis of the Evangelical Church in Mexico* (London, International Missionary Council, 1940, pp. 133). Based on a careful first-hand study.

Davis, J. Merle, *The Evangelical Church in the River Plate Republics (Argentina and Uruguay). A Study of the Economic and Social Basis of the Evangelical Church in Argentina and Uruguay* (New York, International Missionary Council, 1943, pp. 119). Based on a first-hand study by an expert.

Davis, J. Merle, *How the Church Grows in Brazil. A Study of the Economic and Social Basis of the Evangelical Church in Brazil* (New York, International Missionary Council, 1943, pp. 167). A first-hand study by an expert.

Davis, J. Merle, *Modern Industry and the African. An Enquiry into the Effect of the Copper Mines of Central Africa upon Native Society and the Work of Christian Missions Made under the Auspices of the Department of Social and Industrial Research of the International Missionary Council* (London, Macmillan and Co., 1933, pp. xviii, 425). Important.

Davis, J. Merle, *New Buildings on Old Foundations. A Handbook on Stabilizing the Younger Churches in Their Environment* (London, International Missionary Council, 1945, pp. xiv, 320). Based on highly competent research.

Delacroix, Simon, editor, *Histoire Universelle des Missions Catholiques* (Paris, Grund, 4 vols., 1956–1959). A semi-popular, semi-official survey, by several authors.

Dennis, James S., Beach, Harlan P., and Fahs, Charles H., *World Atlas of Christian Missions* (New York, Student Volunteer Movement for Foreign Missions, 1911, pp. 172). A standard work.

Directory of Christian Missions in India, Burma, and Ceylon (Poona, The Scottish Mission Industries Co., 16th ed., 1929, pp. xxxiv, 399). A biennial survey under various titles.

Dominic of Saint-Denis, *The Catholic Church in Canada. Historical and Statistical Summary* (Montreal, Les Éditions Thau. Convent des Capucins. La Réparation. 6th ed., 1956, pp. xiv, 269). In both French and English. A standard reference work.

Drummond, Andrew Landale, *Story of American Protestantism* (Edinburgh, Oliver and Boyd, 1949, pp. xii, 418). A useful survey, chiefly on the pre-Civil War periods.

Duffy, James, *Portuguese Africa* (Cambridge, Mass., Harvard Universtity Press, 1959, pp. vi, 389). Comprehensive, scholarly.

Du Plessis, David J., editor, *A Brief History of the Pentecostal Assemblies* (manuscript, 1957, by several authors). Kindness of the author.

Eckardt, A. Roy, *The Surge of Piety in America. An Appraisal* (New York, Association Press, 1958, pp. 192). Stimulating.

Ecumenical Press Service (Geneva, The World Council of Churches, 1935 ff.). Issued by the World Council of Churches.

The Ecumenical Review (Geneva, 1948 ff.). An organ of the World Council of Churches.

Eddy, Sherwood, *Eighty Adventurous Years. An Autobiography* (New York, Harper & Brothers, 1955, pp. 255).

Edwards, Dwight W., *Yenching University* (New York, United Board for Christian Higher Education in Asia, 1959, pp. xii, 468). Carefully done by one long associated with the university.

Elder, John Rawson, *The History of the Presbyterian Church of New Zealand, 1840–1940* (Christchurch, Presbyterian Book Room, preface 1940, pp. xv, 464). Based on extensive research.

Ellis, John Tracy, *American Catholicism* (University of Chicago Press, 1956, pp. xiii, 206). A brief history by a distinguished Roman Catholic historian. Contains an excellent bibliography.

Ellis, John Tracy, *American Catholics and the Intellectual Life* (Chicago, The Heritage Foundation, 1956, pp. 63).

Ellis, John Tracy, editor, *Documents of American Catholic History* (Milwaukee, The Bruce Publishing Co., 1956, pp. xxiv, 677). A very useful compilation, especially valuable for the introductory note to each document.

Ellis, John Tracy, *A Select Bibliography of the History of the Catholic Church in the United States* (New York, The Declan X. McMullen Co., 1947, pp. 96). Carefully chosen and well annotated.

The Encyclopedia Americana (New York, Americana Corporation, 30 vols., 1955).

Encyclopedia Canadiana (Ottawa, The Canadiana Company, 10 vols., 1957, 1958).

Etteldorf, Raymond, *The Catholic Church in the Middle East* (New York, The Macmillan Co., 1959, pp. 184). A sympathetic popular account by a Roman Catholic based on an extensive journey, with some useful statistics.

The Evangelical Handbook of Latin America, 1939 (New York, Committee on Coöperation in Latin America, no date, pp. 122). An official Protestant publication.

Fahs, Charles H., and Davis, Helen E., *Conspectus of Coöperative Missionary Enterprises* (New York, International Missionary Council, 1935, pp. 252). Factual.

Ferm, Vergilius, editor, *Contemporary American Theology. Theological Autobiographies* (New York, Round Table Press, 2 vols., 1932–1933). Autobiographical sketches.

Ferris, Helen, chief contributor. *The Christian Church in Communist China to 1952* (Lackland Air Force Base, Tex., Air Force Personnel and Training Research Center, 1956, pp. xi, 76). Based on careful research.

Fichter, Joseph H., *Social Relations in the Urban Parish* (University of Chicago Press, 1954, pp. vii, 264). A scholarly study by a Jesuit.

Fides News Service (Rome, 1926 ff.). Sometimes *Fides Service* or *Worldmission Fides Service*. Mimeographed.

Fleming, Daniel Johnson, *Each with His Own Brush; Contemporary Christian Art in Asia and Africa* (New York, Friendship Press, 1938, pp. 85). Made up chiefly of pictures.

Fosdick, Harry Emerson, *The Living of These Days. An Autobiography* (New York, Harper & Brothers, 1956, pp. ix, 324). By one of the greatest preachers of the twentieth century.

Fosdick, Raymond B., *John D. Rockefeller, Jr.: A Portrait* (New York, Harper & Brothers, 1956, pp. ix, 477). By a close friend, sympathetic but objective; based upon extended research in files of correspondence.

Freytag, Walter, *Kirchen im Neuen Asien, Eindrücke einer Studienreise* (Stuttgart, Evang. Missionsverlag, 1958, pp. 63). A thoughtful report by an outstanding German authority on missions.

Fridell, Elmer A., *Baptists in Thailand and the Philippines* (Philadelphia, Judson Press, 1956, pp. 80). By a secretary of the American Baptist Foreign Mission Society.

Frontier (London, 1957 ff.). A quarterly incorporating *Christian News-Letter* and *World Dominion*.

Fry, L. Luther, *The U.S. Looks at Its Churches* (New York, Institute of Social and Religious Research, 1930, pp. xiv, 183). A careful statistical survey of both Protestants and Roman Catholics.

Furniss, Norman F., *The Fundamentalist Controversy, 1918–1931* (New Haven, Conn., Yale University Press, 1954, pp. viii, 199). Based on a Yale doctoral dissertation.

Gerdener, G. B. A., *Recent Developments in the South African Mission Field* (London, Marshall, Morgan & Scott, 1958, pp. 286). By a Protestant specialist.

Gibbons, William J., editor, *Basic Ecclesiastical Statistics for Latin America, 1954*

(Maryknoll, N.Y., World Horizon Reports, 1955, pp. 54). Done at Loyola College, Baltimore.

Gibbons, William J., compiler, *Basic Ecclesisatical Statistics for Latin America, 1956* (Maryknoll, N.Y., World Horizon Reports, no date, pp. 62, mimeographed). Some categories are admittedly incomplete and inaccurate.

Gillard, John T., *The Catholic Church and the American Negro* (Baltimore, St. Joseph's Society Press, 1929, pp. xv, 324). A careful study by a Josephite.

Gillard, John T., *Colored Catholics in the Unted States* (Baltimore, The Josephite Press, 1941, pp. x, 298). A careful study by a Josephite.

Goodall, Norman, *A History of the London Missionary Society, 1895-1945* (New York, Oxford University Press, 1954, pp. xv, 640). Scholarly, sympathetic, based on extensive research.

Groves, C. P., *The Planting of Christianity in Africa* (London, Lutterworth Press, 4 vols., 1948-1958). Carefully done. Covers all Africa from the early Christian centuries, with primary emphasis on Protestant missions.

Grubb, K. G., *The Lowland Indians of Amazonia. A Survey of the Location and Religious Condition of the Indians of Colombia, Venezuela, the Guianas, Ecuador, Peru, Brazil, and Bolivia* (London, World Dominion Press, 1927, pp. 159). By an expert, partly from information acquired through first-hand investigation.

Grubb, Kenneth G., *The Northern Republics of South America: Ecuador, Colombia, and Venezuela* (London, World Dominion Press, 1931, pp. vi, 151). From a personal survey by an expert.

Grubb, Kenneth G., *Religion in Central America* (London, World Dominion Press, 1937, pp. 147). Carefully done, by a distinguished Protestant expert.

Gruening, Ernest, *Mexico and Its Heritage* (New York, The Century Co., 1928, pp. xix, 728). Very critical of the Roman Catholic Church. Based on first-hand investigation in the 1920's.

Guilcher, René, *La Société des Missions Africaines. Ses Origines, sa Nature, sa Vie, ses Oeuvres* (Lyon, Procure des Missions Africaines, 2nd ed., 1956, pp. 175). Favourable.

Hallock, Constance M., *East from Burma* (New York, Friendship Press, 1956, pp. 120). A semi-popular account of Protestant Christianity in South-east Asia and its adjacent islands.

Hardyman, J. T., *Madagascar on the Move* (Westminster, Livingstone Press, 1950, pp. 224). By a representative of the London Missionary Society.

Hayden, Joseph Ralston, *The Philippines. A Study in National Development* (New York, The Macmillan Co., 1942, pp. xxvi, 984). By a former American official in the country.

Herberg, Will, *Protestant-Catholic-Jew. An Essay in American Religious Sociology* (Garden City, N.Y., Doubleday and Co., 1956, pp. 320). Objective, by a scholarly Jew.

Herring, Hubert, *A History of Latin America from the Beginnings to the Present* (New York, Alfred A. Knopf, 1956, pp. xx, 796, xxv). An admirable survey.

Hogg, William Richey, *Ecumenical Foundations. A History of the International Mis-

sionary Council and Its Nineteenth-Century Background (New York, Harper & Brothers, 1952, pp. xi, 466). The definitive account.

Hogg, William Richey, *One World, One Mission* (New York, Friendship Press, 1960, pp. ix, 164). A stimulating, comprehensive study, packed with valuable information.

Holleran, Mary P., *Church and State in Guatemala* (New York, Columbia University Press, 1949, pp. 359). Based on a doctoral dissertation by a Roman Catholic.

Hollister, John N., *The Centenary of the Methodist Church in Southern Asia* (Lucknow, The Lucknow Publishing House of the Methodist Church in Southern Asia, 1956, pp. xxxi, 414). A useful official record.

Holmes, John Haynes, *I Speak for Myself. The Autobiography of John Haynes Holmes* (New York, Harper & Brothers, 1959, pp. vii, 308). By a liberal Protestant clergyman.

Hopkins, C. Howard, *History of the Y.M.C.A. in North America* (New York, Association Press, 1951, pp. xii, 818). An official history based upon extensive research in the original documents.

Houtart, François, *Aspects Sociologiques du Catholicisme Américain. Vie Urbane et Institutions Religieuses* (Paris, Les Éditions Ouvrières d'Économie et d'Humanisme, 1957, pp. 340). A careful study based on extensive statistics. By a Roman Catholic priest.

Iglehart, Charles W., *A Century of Protestant Christianity in Japan* (Rutland, Vt., Charles E. Tuttle Co., 1959). By a distinguished missionary and scholar.

Information Service (New York, Central Department of Research and Survey of the National Council of the Churches of Christ in the U.S.A., 1922 ff.).

Inman, Samuel Guy, *Christian Coöperation in Latin America* (New York, Committee on Coöperation in Latin America, 1917, pp. 186). Report of a trip in 1917 by the secretary of the Committee on Coöperation in Latin America.

The Interchurch News (New York, The National Council of the Churches of Christ in the U.S.A., 1959 ff.). A monthly publication.

International Missionary Council, *Survey of the Training of the Ministry in Africa* (London, International Missionary Council, Parts, I, II, III, 1950, 1954). By several experts.

International Missionary Council, *Survey of the Training of the Ministry in Africa* (London, International Missionary Council, 1957, pp. 49).

The International Review of Missions (London, 1912 ff.). The official organ of the International Missionary Council.

The Japan Christian Quarterly (Tokyo, The Federation of Christian Missions, later The Christian Literature Society of Japan, 1926–1941, 1951 ff.).

The Japan Christian Year Book. See *The Christian Movement in Japan.*

Johnston, Ruby F., *The Development of Negro Religion* (New York, Philosophical Library, 1954, pp. xxi, 201). Based on careful, objective research.

Johnston, Ruby Funchess, *The Religion of Negro Protestants. Changing Religious Attitudes and Practices* (New York, Philosophical Library, 1956, pp. xxvi, 224). Based on careful, detailed investigation.

De Katholieke Encyclopaedie (Amsterdam, Joost van den Vondel, 25 vols., 1949–1955).

Keay, F. E., *A History of the Syrian Church in India* (London, Society for Promoting Christian Knowledge, 1938, pp. 124). A careful and inclusive survey.

Kegley, Charles W., and Brettall, Robert W., editors, *The Theology of Paul Tillich* (New York, The Macmillan Co., 1959, pp. xiv, 370). By various authors.

Kennedy, John J., *Catholicism, Nationalism, and Democracy in Argentina* (University of Notre Dame Press, 1958, pp. xii, 218). An historical sketch by a Roman Catholic scholar.

Latourette, Kenneth Scott, *A History of Christian Missions in China* (New York, The Macmillan Co., 1929, pp. xii, 930). Covers all branches of Christianity from its first introduction to 1929.

Latourette, Kenneth Scott, *A History of the Expansion of Christianity*. Vol. VII, *Advance Through Storm. A.D. 1914 and After, with Concluding Generalizations* (New York, Harper & Brothers, 1945, pp. xiii, 542).

Latourette, Kenneth Scott, *World Service. A History of the Foreign Work and World Service of the Young Men's Christian Associations of the United States and Canada* (New York, Association Press, 1957, pp. xiv, 489). An official history, based upon the original sources.

Laures, Johannes, *The Catholic Church in Japan. A Short History* (Rutland, Vt., Charles E. Tuttle Co., 1954, pp. xii, 252). Semi-popular, by a Jesuit.

Laymen's Foreign Missions Inquiry. Supplementary Series, Orville A. Petty, editor (New York, Harper & Brothers, 7 vols., 1933). Containing the reports of the Fact-Finders and the Commission on Appraisal.

Ledit, Joseph, *Rise of the Downtrodden,* translated by Joseph Ledit and Anthony Santacruz (New York, Society of St. Paul, 1959, pp. 260). A Jesuit account of movements in Mexico.

Lindquist, G. E. E., *Indians in Transition. A Study of Protestant Missions to Indians in the United States* (New York, Division of Home Missions, National Council of Churches of Christ in the U.S.A., 1951, pp. 117). By an expert.

Littell, Franklin H., and Walz, Hans Hermann, editors, *Weltkirchen Lexikon. Handbuch der Ökumene* (Stuttgart, Kreuz Verlag, 1960, pp. 1755). An extremely useful work of reference.

McConnell, Francis J., *By the Way. An Autobiography* (New York, Abingdon-Cokesbury Press, 1952, pp. 286). By a distinguished Methodist bishop.

MacFarland, Charles S., *Chaos in Mexico. The Conflict of Church and State* (New York, Harper & Brothers, 1935, pp. 284). By a distinguished Protestant churchman from the United States, based upon a visit to Mexico.

McGavran, Donald Anderson, *How Churches Grow. The New Frontiers in Missions* (London, World Dominion Press, 1959, pp. vii, 186). A stimulating study based upon extensive travel and long missionary experience.

McLeish, Alexander, *Christian Progress in Burma* (London, World Dominion Press, 1929, pp. 100). A careful survey of Protestant effort.

Maddry, Charles E., *An Autobiography* (Nashville, Broadman Press, 1955, pp. xiii, 141). By a distinguished Southern Baptist.

Mann, W. E., *Sect, Cult, and Church in Alberta* (University of Toronto Press, 1955, pp. xiii, 166). A careful study by an official of the Church of England in Canada, sponsored by the Canadian Social Science Research Council.

Maria del Rey, Sister, of Maryknoll, *In and Out of the Andes. Mission Trails from Yucatan to Chile* (New York, Charles Scribner's Sons, 1955, pp. vi, 281). A survey by travel of Maryknoll operations, chiefly in Bolivia.

Marty, Martin E., *The New Shape of American Religion* (New York, Harper & Brothers, 1959, pp. x, 180). Critical, and highly stimulating.

Masse, Benjamin L., editor, *The Catholic Mind through Fifty Years, 1903–1953* (New York, The America Press, 1952, pp. xxii, 681). Statements by Roman Catholics, mostly American, on various topics.

Mathews, Basil, *John R. Mott, World Citizen* (New York, Harper & Brothers, 1934, pp. xiii, 469). From material supplied by Mott and written at Mott's request and under his supervision.

Mays, Benjamin Elijah, and Nicholson, Joseph William, *The Negro's Church* (New York, Institute of Social and Religious Research, 1933, pp. xiii, 321). Carefully done.

Mecham, J. Lloyd, *Church and State in Latin America. A History of Politico-Ecclesiastical Relations* (Chapel Hill, University of North Carolina Press, 1934, pp. viii, 550). Competent, comprehensive.

Miller, Robert Moats, *American Protestantism and Social Issues, 1919–1939* (Chapel Hill, University of North Carolina Press, 1958, pp. xiv, 385). Based upon extensive research; sympathetic with the social action of Protestant bodies.

Mission Bulletin. See *China Missionary Bulletin.*

Missionary Research Library, Occasional Bulletin. See *Occasional Bulletin from the Missionary Research Library.*

Missions (Boston, followed by New York, 1910 ff.). Formed by the union of various Baptist missionary journals.

Les Missions de Chine. A continuation of Planchet, *Les Missions de Chine et du Japon* (Peking, Lazaristes du Peit'ang, and Shanghai, 1935–1940).

Morant, Adelrich, *Die philosophisch-theologische Bildung in den Priesterseminarien Schwarz-Afrikas. Aktuelle Fragen der Priesterbildung mit besonderen Berücksichtigung Kameruns* (Schöneck-Beckenried, Switzerland, Administration der Neuen Zeitschrift für Missionswissenschaft, 1959, pp. xxi, 263). Based on careful research.

Mott, John R., *Addresses and Papers of John R. Mott* (New York, Association Press, 6 vols., 1947). An important collection of documents, prepared and edited under Mott's direction.

Murtagh, James G., *Australia: The Catholic Chapter* (New York, Sheed and Ward, 1946, pp. xviii, 261). Stressing the Roman Catholic opposition to liberalism and Marxism and the positive efforts for social justice.

The National Catholic Almanac (Paterson, N.J., St. Anthony's Guild, 1904 ff.).

National Council Outlook (New York, January, 1951–June, 1959). Superseded *The Federal Council Bulletin*. Published by the National Council of the Churches of Christ in the U.S.A.

The National Council Review (formerly The Harvest Field). The organ of the National Christian Council of India, Burma, and Ceylon; later (beginning in 1952) of the National Christian Council of India (Mysore—earlier Bangalore—Wesleyan Publishing House, 1862 ff.).

Neill, Stephen, *Anglicanism* (Harmondsworth, Middlesex, Penguin Books, 1958, pp. 346). By a bishop of the Anglican Communion.

Neill, Stephen, *Out of Bondage: Christ and the Indian Village* (London, Edinburgh House Press, 1930, pp. 143). From first-hand experience, chiefly in South India.

Nelson, E. Clifford, *The Lutheran Church among Norwegian Americans*. Vol. II, *1890–1959* (Minneapolis, Augsburg Publishing House, 1960, pp. xvii, 371). Based on competent scholarship.

New Missionary Review (Oxford, 1952 ff.). A mimeographed periodical, issued at irregular intervals by S. Bolshakoff. Covers Orthodox missions.

Niebuhr, H. Richard, Williams, Daniel Day, and Gustafson, James M., *The Advancement of Theological Education* (New York, Harper & Brothers, 1957, pp. xii, 239). A definitive study of the contemporary Protestant theological education in the United States.

Occasional Bulletin from the Missionary Research Library (New York, The Missionary Research Library, 1951 ff.). Mimeographed.

O'Dea, Thomas F., *American Catholic Dilemma. An Inquiry into the Intellectual Life* (New York, Sheed and Ward, 1958, pp. xv, 173). A thoughtful appraisal by a Roman Catholic sociologist.

The Official Catholic Directory (New York, P. J. Kenedy & Sons). An annual publication beginning in 1817.

Oliver, Roland, *The Missionary Factor in East Africa* (London, Longmans, Green and Co., 1952, pp. xviii, 302). A doctoral dissertation by an Anglican covering both Protestants and Roman Catholics.

O'Neill, M. Ancilla, *Tristão de Athayde and the Catholic Social Movement in Brazil* (Washington, The Catholic University of America, 1939, pp. x, 156). A doctoral dissertation.

Oregon Council of Churches, *Church Membership and Population in Oregon, 1926–1952*. A Report of the Department of Research and Survey. Barbara Johnson, Research Associate, John W. Berry, Director. Done by students at Pacific University under the direction of the professor of sociology. May, 1953. Mimeographed.

Osborn, Ronald E., *The Spirit of American Christianity* (New York, Harper & Brothers, 1958, pp. xii, 241). A suggestive study.

Pacific Affairs (Richmond, Va., Institute of Pacific Relations, 1927 ff.). The quarterly journal of the Institute of Pacific Relations.

Palmer, Gretta, *God's Underground in Asia* (New York, Appleton-Century-Crofts, 1953, pp. vii, 376). A sympathetic account of the resistance of Chinese Roman Catholics to Communism.

Parker, Joseph I., *Directory of World Missions. Missionary Boards, Societies, Colleges, Coöperative Councils, and Other Agencies Related to the Protestant Churches of the World* (New York, International Missionary Council, 1938, pp. xi, 255). Authoritative.

Parker, Joseph I., editor, *Interpretative Statistical Survey of the World Mission of the Christian Church* (New York, International Missionary Council, 1928, pp. 323). Standard.

Parsons, Wilfrid, *Mexican Martyrdom* (New York, The Macmillan Co., 1936, pp. vi, 304). An account by a Jesuit of the persecution of Roman Catholics in the 1920's and 1930's.

Pattee, Richard, *El Catolicismo Contemporaneo en Hispanoamérica* (Buenos Aires, Editorial Fides, 1951, pp. 481).

Petty, Orville A., editor, *Laymen's Foreign Missions Inquiry. Supplementary Series* (New York, Harper & Brothers, 7 vols., 1933). The reports of the Fact-Finders and the Commission on Appraisal. Based on first-hand investigation.

Pickett, J. Waskom, *Christian Mass Movements in India* (Cincinnati, Abingdon Press, 1933, pp. 382). Carefully done, by a Methodist missionary.

Planchet, J. M., *Les Missions de Chine et du Japon* (Peking, Imprimerie des Lazaristes, 15 vols., 1916–1940). An annual. Beginning in 1935 not under Planchet's name but still a Lazarist publication. Later issued from Shanghai.

Power, Edward J., *A History of Catholic Higher Education in the United States* (Milwaukee, The Bruce Publishing Co., 1958, pp. xiii, 383). Based on extensive research.

Presbyterian Life (Dayton, Ohio, 1948 ff.).

Price, Frank Wilson, *China. Twilight or Dawn?* (New York, Friendship Press, 1948, pp. vi, 184). By an extremely well-informed Protestant missionary to China.

Ramos, Samuel, *Historia de la Filosofia en Mexico* (Mexico, Imprenta Universitaria, 1943, pp. viii, 187). Comprehensive, from the colonial period into the twentieth century.

Rauws, Joh., Kraemer, H., Van Hasset, F. J. F., and Slotemaker de Brüine, N. A. C., *The Netherlands Indies* (London, World Dominion Press, 1935, pp. 186). An authoritative survey of missions by Dutch experts.

Religion in Life (New York, 1931 ff.). A quarterly journal.

Reulet, Aníbal Sánchez, *Contemporary Latin-American Philosophy*. Translated from the Spanish and Portuguese by Willard R. Trask (Albuquerque, N.M., University of New Mexico Press, 1954, pp. xx, 285). Centers on individual philosophers in several countries, with extensive excerpts from their writing.

Review and Expositor. A Baptist Theological Quarterly (Louisville, Ky., Southern Baptist Theological Seminary, 1903 ff.).

Richardson, Harry V., *Dark Glory. A Picture of the Church among Negroes in the Rural South* (New York, Friendship Press, 1947, pp. xiv, 209). An able survey.

Richter, Julius, *Die evangelische Mission in Niederländisch-Indien* (Gütersloh, C. Bertelsmann, 1931, pp. 165). Only a brief section is on the post-1914 years.

Richter, Julius, *Tanganyika and Its Future* (London, World Dominion Press, 1934, pp. 112). A survey by an eminent German specialist on missions.

Robertson, Archie, *That Old-Time Religion* (Boston, Houghton Mifflin Co., 1950, pp. 282). Popularly written by the son of a distinguished Southern Baptist New Testament scholar. Largely an account of personal observation.

Robledo, Gregorio Arcila, *La Orden Franciscana en la America Meridional* (Rome, Pontificio Ateneo Antoniano, 1948, pp. xviii, 416). An official, largely historical publication.

Roemer, Theodore, *The Catholic Church in the United States* (St. Louis, B. Herder Book Co., 1950, pp. viii, 444). A useful historical survey by a Capuchin.

Romanell, Patrick, *Making of the Mexican Mind. A Study of Recent Mexican Thought* (Lincoln, University of Nebraska Press, 1952, pp. ix, 213). Competent.

Rouse, Ruth, and Neill, Stephen Charles, editors, *A History of the Ecumenical Movement, 1517–1948* (London, S.P.C.K., 1954, pp. xx, 822). The standard work.

Rowland, Stanley J., Jr., *Land in Search of God* (New York, Random House, 1958, pp. 242). A useful survey of contemporary religion in the United States by a Protestant specialist in news and publicity.

Roy, Ralph Lord, *Apostles of Discord. A Study of Organized Bigotry and Disruption on the Fringes of Protestantism* (Boston, Beacon Press, 1953, pp. xii, 437). A vigorous attack on the extreme militant fundamentalists, with much useful factual data.

Rycroft, W. Stanley, editor, *Indians of the High Andes: Report of the Commission Appointed by the Committee on Coöperation in Latin America to Study the Indians of the Andean Highland, with a View to Establishing a Coöperative Christian Enterprise* (New York, Committee on Coöperation in Latin America, 1946, pp. xiii, 330).

St. Vladimir's Seminary Quarterly (New York, St. Vladimir's Orthodox Theological Seminary, 1939? ff.).

Sánchez Reulet, Aníbal, *Contemporary Latin-American Philosophy. A Selection with an Introduction and Notes.* Translated from the Spanish and Portuguese by Willard R. Trask (Albuquerque, University of New Mexico Press, 1954, pp. xx, 285). An anthology.

The Saturday Evening Post (Philadelphia, 1821 ff.). Various titles and sub-titles.

Schmidlin, Joseph, *Catholic Mission History* (Techny, Ill., Mission Press, S.V.D., 1933, pp. xiv, 862). Translated and edited, with additional notes and material, by Matthias Braun. A standard work.

Schneider, Herbert Wallace, *Religion in 20th Century America* (Cambridge, Mass., Harvard University Press, 1952, pp. x, 244). A careful, comprehensive study.

Scott, Roderick, *Fukien Christian University, A Historical Sketch* (New York, United Board for Christian Colleges in China, 1954, pp. 138). By a long-time member of the faculty.

Serle, Percival, *Dictionary of Australian Biography* (Sydney, Angus and Robertson, 2 vols., 1949). Based on years of research.

Shaw, J. G., *Edwin Vincent O'Hara, American Prelate* (New York, Farrar, Straus and Co., 1957, pp. xiii, 274). Sympathetic, based on original sources.

Shedd, Clarence P., *The Church Follows Its Students* (New Haven, Conn., Yale University Press, 1938, pp. xvii, 327). Based on careful research, by a Protestant.

Shedd, Clarence P., *Two Centuries of Student Christian Movements. Their Origin and Intercollegiate Life* (New York, Association Press, 1934, pp. xxii, 466). Chiefly Protestant and on the United States. Comprehensive and breaking new ground in careful research.

Silcox, Claris Edwin, *Church Union in Canada. Its Causes and Consequences* (New York, Institute of Social and Religious Research, 1933, pp. xvii, 493). Careful and thorough.

Snavely, C. H., editor, *The Lutheran Enterprise in India* (Madras, Federation of Evangelical Lutheran Churches in India, 1952, pp. viii, 252). Largely historical. By various authors.

Snavely, Guy E., *The Church and the Four-Year College* (New York, Harper & Brothers, 1955, pp. viii, 216). By the executive director emeritus of the Association of American Colleges.

Soltau, T. Stanley, *Korea. The Hermit Nation and Its Response to Christianity* (London, World Dominion Press, 1932, pp. 123). A careful survey.

Soper, David Wesley, *Major Voices in American Theology. Six Contemporary Leaders* (Philadelphia, The Westminster Press, 1953, pp. 217). A semi-popular survey.

The South East Asia Journal of Theology (Singapore, 1959 ff.). The organ of the Association of Theological Schools in South East Asia.

The Statesman's Year Book (London, Macmillan and Co., 1854 ff.).

Stokes, Anson Phelps, *Church and State in the United States* (New York, Harper & Brothers, 3 vols., 1950). A standard work, based on extensive research.

Stonelake, Alfred R., *Congo, Past and Present* (London, World Dominion Movement, 1937, pp. 202). A careful survey, chiefly of Protestant missions.

Streit, Carolus, *Atlas Hierarchicus* (Paderborn, Typographia Bonifaciana, 1913, pp. 128, 37, 35). A standard work of reference.

Stuart, John Leighton, *Fifty Years in China. The Memoirs of John Leighton Stuart, Missionary and Ambassador* (New York, Random House, 1954, pp. xx, 346). An autobiography.

The Student World (Geneva, Switzerland, 1907 ff.). The quarterly journal of the World's Student Christian Federation.

Sugrue, Thomas, *A Catholic Speaks His Mind on America's Religious Conflict* (New York, Harper & Brothers, 1951, pp. 64). Critical of the Roman Catholic Church in the United States, by one of its lay practising members.

Sumrall, Lester F., *Through Blood and Fire in Latin America* (Grand Rapids, Mich., Zondervan Publishing House, 1946, pp. 246). Sympathetic sketches of Latin American Protestants.

Sundkler, Bengt, *The Christian Ministry in Africa* (London, SCM Press, 1960, pp. 346). A standard work based on personal observation and extensive research.

Sweet, William Warren, *The Story of Religion in America* (New York, Harper & Brothers, 2nd rev. ed., 1950, pp. ix, 492). By an outstanding specialist.

Taylor, J. V., *Christianity and Politics in Africa* (London, Penguin Books, 1957, pp. 127). By a former missionary to Africa of the Church Missionary Society.

Taylor, John V., *The Growth of the Church in Buganda. An Attempt at Understanding* (London, SCM Press, 1958, pp. 228). A careful, frank appraisal based on detailed study by a sympathetic, experienced observer.

Taylor, J. V., and Lehmann, Dorothea, *Christians in the Copper Belt. The Growth of the Church in Northern Rhodesia* (London, SCM Press, 1961, pp. x, 308). Based on a careful survey in 1958 of a few selected areas.

Testo-Atlante Illustrato delle Missioni. Compilato a Cura dell' Agenzia Internazionale "Fides" con i Dati Cartografici e Statistici dell' Archivo della S. Congregazione di Propaganda Fides (Novara, Instituto Geografico de Agostini, 1932, pp. xiii, 53, 60, 160). An official publication.

Theology Today (Princeton, N.J., 1944 ff.).

Thomas, John L., *The American Catholic Family* (Englewood Cliffs, N.J., Prentice-Hall, 1956, pp. xii, 471). A careful study by a Jesuit.

Thomas, Winburn T., *Indonesia and the Indonesian Church in Today's World* (New York, Missionary Research Library, *Occasional Bulletin,* Vol. XX, No. 2, February 10, 1958, pp. 15).

Thomas, Winburn T., and Manikam, Rajah B., *The Church in Southeast Asia* (New York, Friendship Press, 1956, pp. xvi, 171). Semi-popular, by two experts.

Thompson, H. P., *Into All Lands. The History of the Society for the Propagation of the Gospel in Foreign Parts, 1701–1950* (London, S.P.C.K., 1951, pp. xv, 760). An official history, based on the Society's records and published material.

Thompson, Virginia, and Adloff, Richard, *Minority Problems in Southeast Asia* (Stanford University Press, 1955, pp. viii, 295). Carefully done.

Tibesar, Leopold H., *The Catholic Position in Post-War Japan* (Maryknoll, N.Y., World Horizon Reports, 1956, pp. 33). By a Maryknoller in Japan.

Time (New York, 1923 ff.). A weekly news-magazine.

Tisserant, Eugene, *Eastern Christianity in India. A History of the Syro-Malabar Church from the Earliest Times to the Present Day,* translated from the French by E. R. Hambye (Calcutta, Orient Longmans, 1957, pp. xviii, 266). Scholarly, by a Roman Catholic cardinal.

Törnberg, Allen, *Fran Amazonas till La Plata. Med Svenska Pingstmissionärer i Sydamerica* (Stockholm, Förlaget Filadelfia, 1956, pp. 135). An account of the travels of a Swedish Pentecostal in South America.

Torbet, Robert G., *A History of the Baptists* (Philadelphia, Judson Press, 1950, pp. 538). A highly competent, comprehensive, condensed account.

Torbet, Robert G., *Venture of Faith. The Story of the American Baptist Foreign Mission Society and the Woman's American Baptist Foreign Mission Society 1814–1954* (Philadelphia, Judson Press, 1955, pp. xiv, 634). An official history, based upon first-hand sources.

Underwood, Kenneth Wilson, *Protestant and Catholic. Religion and Social Interaction in an Industrial Community* (Boston, Beacon Press, 1957, pp. xxi, 484). A careful, objective sociological study by a Protestant.

United States Department of Commerce, Bureau of the Census, *Religious Bodies: 1926* (Washington, Government Printing Office, 2 vols., 1929, 1930).

United States Department of Commerce, Bureau of the Census, *Religious Bodies, 1936* (Washington, Government Printing Office, 2 vols., 1941).

Vollmar, Edward R., *The Catholic Church in America. An Historical Bibliography* (New Brunswick, N.J., Scarecrow Press, 1956, pp. xxvii, 354). Extensive, without critical descriptive comments.

Walsh, H. H., *The Christian Church in Canada* (Toronto, Ryerson Press, 1956, pp. ix, 355). A competent, inclusive, historical survey.

Ward, Leo R., *Catholic Life, U.S.A. Contemporary Lay Movements* (St. Louis, B. Herder Book Co., 1959, pp. 263). A popular competent account.

Wasson, Alfred W., *Church Growth in Korea* (New York, International Missionary Council, 1934, pp. xii, 175). Careful, scholarly, by a Methodist missionary; chiefly concerned with Southern Methodist missions.

Watters, Mary, *A History of the Church in Venezuela, 1810–1930* (Chapel Hill, University of North Carolina Press, 1933, pp. ix, 260). Based on careful research.

Wells, Kenneth E., *History of Protestant Work in Thailand, 1828–1958* (Bangkok, Church of Christ in Thailand, 1958, pp. viii, 213). Incorporating much detail and many biographical sketches.

Wentz, Abdel Ross, *A Basic History of Lutheranism in America* (Philadelphia, Muhlenberg Press, 1955, pp. viii, 430). A standard survey by an expert.

Wheeler, W. Reginald, and Browning, Webster E., *Modern Missions on the Spanish Main. Impressions of Protestant Work in Colombia and Venezuela* (Philadelphia, The Westminster Press, 1925, pp. xii, 334). From sympathetic first-hand observation.

Wheeler, W. Reginald, Day, Dwight H., and Rodgers, James B., *Modern Missions in Mexico* (Philadelphia, The Westminster Press, 1925, pp. xi, 288). An account of Protestant missions based on a visit to the country in 1922.

Who Was Who (London, A. and C. Black, various successive editions).

Who's Who in America (Chicago, The A. N. Marquis Co., 1899 ff.).

Wilgus, A. Curtis, editor, *The Caribbean Area* (Washington, The George Washington University Press, 1934, pp. vii, 604). By various authors.

Wilgus, A. Curtis, editor, *Modern Hispanic America* (Washington, The George Washington University Press, 1933, pp. ix, 630). By various authors.

Williams, Daniel Day, *What Present-Day Theologians Are Thinking* (New York, Harper & Brothers, 1952, pp. 158). By a competent theologian.

Williamson, H. R., *British Baptists in China, 1845–1952* (London, The Carey Kingsgate Press, 1957, pp. viii, 382). Excellent.

Work, Monroe N., editor, *Negro Year Book. An Annual Encyclopedia of the Negro, 1931–1932* (Tuskegee Institute, Ala., Negro Year Book Publishing Co., 1931, pp. xiv, 544).

World Christian Handbook, 1957. Edited by E. J. Bingle and Kenneth Grubb (London, World Dominion Press, 1957, pp. xii, 312). Primarily on Protestant missions but with other coverage although brief. Authoritative.

World Dominion. An International Review of Christian Progress (London, 1923–1957).

Worldmission (New York, 1950 ff.). The quarterly review by the National Office of the Society for the Propagation of the Faith.

Worldmission Fides Service (edited by Agenzia Internationale Fides and issued by the Society for the Propagation of the Faith, New York). A mimeographed sheet on Roman Catholic missions issued periodically. Also quoted at times as *Fides Service* or *Fides News Service*.

Yearbook of American Churches (New York, National Council of the Churches of Christ in the U.S.A., formerly the Federal Council of the Churches of Christ, 1916 ff.).

Zeitschrift für Missionswissenschaft (Münster i.W., 1911 ff.). A standard Roman Catholic periodical.

Zuretti, Juan Carlos, *Historia Eclesiastica Argentina* (Buenos Aires, Editorial "Huarpes," 1945, pp. 340). Sympathetic with the Roman Catholic Church.

Index